THE INDIAN LAW

Dynamic Dimensions of The Abstract

First Edition	2009
Reprint	2012
Reprint	**2016**

THE INDIAN LAW

Dynamic Dimensions of The Abstract

Justice V. R. Krishna Iyer
Former Judge, Supreme Court of India

Universal Law Publishing
an imprint of LexisNexis

This book is a publication of **LexisNexis®**
(A Division of Reed Elsevier India (Pvt) Ltd)
14th floor, Building No 10, Tower–B, DLF Cyber City, Phase-II,
Gurgaon–122002, Haryana, India.
Tel : + 91 124 4774444 Fax: + 91 124 4774100
Website : www.lexisnexis.co.in / E-mail : help.in@lexisnexis.com

Justice V.R. Krishna Iyer : The Indian Law - Dynamic Dimensions of The Abstract, First Edition, Reprint 2016

ISBN: 978-81-7534-802-8

Printed by: Mudrak, Delhi

Printed and bound in India.

CONTENTS

EVOLUTION FROM MATTER TO MIND AND BEYOND

Introductory

India, in its undivided status, is an unhappy memory and sanguinary history. The tragic chapter about the political operators and terrorist architects of this religious-communal carnage and beyond reversal, emergence of Pakistan is an international reality of military tension. Our national imperative is to recapture our cultural heritage, our human solidarity amidst the diversity of religions and faiths cemented by social justice and human rights. Our ancient ideals have been inalienable humanism and harmonious brotherhood, transcending all fissiparous frictions and feuds and upholding the currently imperiled values of our *secular, socialist, democratic* Republic. The British quit India in 1947 but its colonial hold continued as a cultural addiction. The commercial tycoons and the feudal barons and other native richer brackets became devotees of the Raeganomic adharma, using the cult of globalisation, liberalization and privatization and, America Incorporated being the master-operator in the unipolar world. John Pilger, in his superbly critical work Hidden Agendas, observes:

> *"One of the most eloquent dissenters is the Indian social scientist Vandana Shiva, who has long attacked a Western-imposed 'monoculture of the mind" and called for an 'insurrection of subjugated knowledge' against the 'dominant knowledge' of capitalism. 'This (dominant knowledge) leaves out a plurality of paths to knowing nature and the universe,' she wrote. 'Ninety per cent of it could be stopped without any risk of human deprivation.'"*
>
> (P-534)

Patriotism is incompatible with economic dependencia syndrome and in our current social milieu, must receive a wider meaning for the message of India, with ages of wisdom and discovery of spiritual and temporal values, encompasses universality. We are the heirs of a cosmic philosophy with our cultural doors hospitably kept ajar without fanatical godist terrorism or hide-bound casteist bigotry. Even today, Sri Aurobindo and Swami Vivekananda, Vedic sages, profound Christian thinkers and broad-minded Islamic scholars spreading the high morality of global brotherhood, make India the halcyon home and centre of gravity of cultural humanity.

In this perspectival philosophy of mine I receive complementary copies of books from enlightened authors who seek my response. I am humble and unlearned. Yet, with bibliophilic curiosity, I ponder over the pages and communicate my thoughts occasionally by reviews in the most esteemed daily The Hindu. Alas, today, we are victims of a world order of vulgar commercialism condemning nations, West and East, to the gluttony of materialism. If Gandhiji is truly the Father of the Nation, read Paul Harrison (Third World Tomorrow)

> *The Gandhian concept of development rejected the idea that it should aim primarily at the creation of material wealth or the satisfaction of insatiable, endlessly multiplied needs. In so far as we have made the modern materialistic craze our goal, he wrote, 'so far are we going downhill in the path of progress.'* (p. 19)

But the savagery of hedonism is a kind of die-hard drug addiction. Even judges and administrative and legislature echelons surrender to these temptations. This can be controlled and conquered through bibliophilic therapy. The pity of it is that the meretricious, 'Westoxicated' mantra is biblio-phobia or allergy to serious books and seduction by corrupt sex and profit-racket labelled by Stiglitz as "briberisation". This menace is the affliction of 'affluenza', a colonial cultural curse. Back to the habit of reading good books is the therapeutic solution to the loony malady of violence and vice, infantile adventurism and bedlam nationalism. Read old Bacon:

> *"Reading maketh a full man; conference a ready man; and writing an exact man."* (OQ P:27:20)

> *"Some books are to be tasted, others to be swallowed, and some few to be chewed and digested; that is, some books are to be read only in parts; others to be read but not curiously; and some few to be read wholly, and with diligence and attention. Some books also may be read by deputy, and extracts made of them by others."* (OQ P:27:19)

Recently I received a complementary copy of Aura of Light authored by G.C. Agarwal. Here are seminal thoughts springing from my reading of this collection of essays. Today's world order is a jungle of power-crazy, profligacy-hungry wild, wealthy animals who are the real adversaries of progressive humanity's aspirations for development of the vast masses kept illiterate by high-priced commercialized educational market, *now* with judicial pro-proprietariat prolixity in our Social Democratic Republic. From Darkness to Light—not for *money* but *man*—is the march to reach Enlightenment Destination which is our tryst with destiny.

If we desiderate intellectual, moral advance, we need, as guide, radiant, lofty literature, lest we stumble increase materialism and miss the swaraj of the Soul.

Life is a sacred trust with a deep obligation to do one's best in this world to elevate the lot of our brethren and their moral and material status. The journey of life is not a mechanical flow of time. It is a dynamic march towards a nobler incarnation, transforming the current chaos into a sublime cosmos. Rightly, the first introductory chapter of the book begins with spiritualism dislanguished from religiosity. We speak of the evolution of Life in Matter, the evolution of Mind in Matter and the evolution of the 'supramental' rising above the mind, the ego or self ultimately merging in the Universal Self. The Vedantic view validates the thesis that *development*, even in its higher dimensions, is already involved in Matter. Evolution is the manifestation in a life of involution. This takes us to the fundamental conclusion that 'consciousness' as the basic structure of creation. Progressive incarnations unfold what is embryonically latent.

The author moves on to Freedom and Democracy which are the sine qua non of sound politics if civilized life is integral to social existence. Education is the nidus of Growth with Equity. Today's commercially motivated education must undergo moral metamorphosis, recognize and implement these great truths if the materialist world is to transcend qualitatively, to arise at a meaningful confluence of human ascent and divine descent. It is often said that authentic service of God is true service of man, that selflessness in action and fearlessness in performance of duty are too high to be negotiable for opportunist considerations. A brief quote from Edgar Mitchell:

> *"'Who am I?' the saints and sages have asked throughout history. What is the nature of self, that it can be aware of being aware?"*
>
> (Psychic Exploration, p. 681)

The book I read has with luminous insight, has covered this truth. Currently, the world has lost its purity and ethic resulting in the gluttony of the rich who are victims of the "syndrome of affluenza". Imagine even judges of India who lived an austere life, banging over to five-star life-style at State expense. The storm of sorrow and the tsunami of misery strike at the dignity of life of the vast masses of the world, creating a resolution of the conflict of ethos of the lavishly- living minority and the gloom and tears of the lowliest, the lost and the last, a necessity for peace in society. This contradiction must be dissolved by a new material-spiritual formula of Life Force. The bombast of globalisation, liberalization and privatization is baloney and fraud on semantics. I fully agree that the inner teaching of this book is contained in the following passage:

> *"Teach yourself, teach everyone his real nature, call upon the sleeping soul and see how it awakes. Power will come, glory will come, goodness will come, purity will come and every thing that is excellent will come when the sleeping soul is roused to self-conscious activity."*

The last word with which I conclude is a quote from Karl Marx:

> "The philosophers have only interpreted the world in various ways, the point is to change it."

OMEGA

I wind up, for the nonce, with reference to the economic coup operated in 1991 by the scholarly politician Sri Narasimha Rao who has his stature, another philosophical dimension. He walked into the trap, so I conceive, into the grand project of the World Bank-IMF-cum-giant corporate power of the U.S. to undo our Constitutional Preamble which speaks of the People's resolve of a *Socialist Secular Democratic* Republic. The Rao regime reversed Nehru's dream of Avadi Socialism, virtually undid the Indira Gandhi vision of a Public Sector, Nationalisation of vital enterprises, non-alignment of nations, self-reliance in economy, social justice, policy of 'Gareebi Hatao' and independence from the economic and military domination which the Mighty Global Power imposed on Third World Countries. With pretence of helplessness Mr. Rao accepted, ably advised by then Finance Minister. Mr. Stiglitz, one time leading insider, of the World Bank and later on dismissal from that role, won the Nobel Prize and called this dangerous process of the Bank-Fund duo as "briberisation" because, in his view, the victim countries' 'National Leaders' got 10% commission paid to Swiss Bank Account for undervaluing the sale price of National Assets. Indeed, the peril to the public sector is a deliberate project of our post-1991 Governments and our rupee, what with obliging import duties from abroad has sunk to a new low. What is a wonder to me is that the independent judiciary, which innovated the novel doctrine of the Basic Structure of the Constitution, did not defend its people-oriented, socialistic spirit, but acquiesced in the yen of the Executive in its obliteration of Swaraj and its paramountly Leftist humanism.

LAW IN INDIA: A SILVER JUBILEE CRITIQUE OF A STORY WITHOUT A PLOT

In the Constituent Assembly, Dr. Ambedkar had warned that British authority having ended in India, we could no longer plead the alibi of foreign rule for future failures. This new opportunity and the responsibility of freedom should have turned us towards self-reliance, forsaking the burden of foreign borrowings, especially Anglo-American, in the social sciences and humanities, including law. By swadeshi, I mean not an obscurantist clinging to obsolete jurisprudence but a rejection of the subjection to the colonial 'carry forward' in our *corpus juris* and the substitution of an eclectic brew of the good in British justice and the great in our early legal heritage, a cross-fertilization with modern juristic thought, planned and processed to produce an Indian synthesis. Gandhiji wrote in 1909: 'India's salvation consists in unlearning what she has learnt during the last fifty years... European civilization is, no doubt, suited for the Europeans, but it will mean ruin for India, if we endeavour to copy it' he again exhorted, 'I want the cultures of all the lands to be blown about my house, as freely as possible, but I refuse to be blown off my feet by any. A policy on law of catholicity but not conditioning, of a blend of modern needs and thought with ancient strands—this is the desideratum'. In this sense, have we Indianized our legal culture, with twenty-five years on our own legs? Do we still keep law and life distant neighbours?

Dedicated as the country is to building a modern society informed by humanism, the mutation of socio-cultural values and economic structures assumes supreme importance. While political decisions, economic capabilities and technological know-how dictate the direction and pace of the new order, the actual change-over can be effectively achieved only through the legal process so long as we are constitutionally wedded to the rule of law. The long legal haul from Raj to Republic to which we are committed involved perspective planning with periodical reviewing, and programmes of action from social science research to justice administration, from college campuses, through secretariat cells and *sansad* chambers, to halls of court. The strategy of change through law is the only, democratic road to progress.

For, 'Where law rules tranquility dwells'. No law, no order, is obvious enough, and the art of the law is to preserve order amid change and change amid order, which is still a little obscure for sections of the elite.

It is useful to clarify at the outset that law does not possess the initiative of social change although the interaction is intimate. There can be, and is, social transformation and technological revolution without legislation and vice-versa, but legal engineering is the most legitimate means of responding to the urges and norms of the new order. Dynamic law is the only reply of society to the forces of anarchic terror, violent unrest and economic tyranny.

Legal justice in independent India keeps hobbling a zigzag pace, although the resistance of bureaucratism and the elephantine sloth of the legislative process are, in part, the hidden causes, and the court often but an alibi. A self-critical essay in drawing up a law progress report, if written with critical detachment is a useful jubilee exercise, keeping in mind that time is a political trust and unattended injustice ultimately explodes the existing fabric. People take the law into their own hands if the law fails to take the people into its hands.

To begin with, the basic error is the failure, at the national level, to realize that in this day and age if law fails the wave of change, lawlessness waives allegiance to order—as is currently the case with students, workers, peasants and even teachers. If law is to run conterminous with life, the legal system must develop *pari passu*. And if law turns away from life, a breakdown of the constitutional order is inevitable with wickedness and violence undoing progress and plan, and tensions upsetting the pace. Somehow our planners have not recognized the urgency of a national policy on law reform and comprehensive planning, to steer the revolution through law, lest five-year plans perish at the altar of unconstitutionality or wither for want of regulations and sanctions or succumb to anti-legal forces. Failure to associate lawmen with economic, social and technological changes, on a policy basis, is evidence of a certain myopia. Law, now, is outside the plan and the plan is often outside the law, which is bad for both. There is a great need for attuning legal perspective and social objectives within the plan. Financial, administrative and technological attention will then turn to all stages of the legal complex, and progressive planning and implementation of legislation to sustain the national plan will integrate the two. Legislative programming to channelize increasing grievances into legitimate people's activity may obviate many later evils and be the beginning of law as a social sword of proselytization to the new order. One cannot alter social values or re-structure society radically, even for something as small as implementing a building code or famine code merely through cabinet decisions or parliamentary assurances or scientists' conventions. Law's presence is needed in all the processes.

Sociologists and technologists brief political men, whereupon legislators, essentially political men, begin to act; courts then step in to interpret and enforce the new legislation. This strategic significance of law for the nation insists that the judicial infrastructure, drafting and legislative cadres, the legal profession and the socio-legal academics and experts be informed by the spirit of social justice, and that activists in other disciplines gain an insight into law. 'Garibi hatao', without the edge of law, will not sell as a slogan for long. So it is that perspective plans, periodical performance appraisals, approach document debates and five-year plans for law-in-formation and law-in-action are imperatives. Exercises motivated to implement plan projects and to effect law reform must now be undertaken not as *ad hoc* responses to socio-economic agitations or to legislative proposals but as part of the national plan. As a basis for these moves, the national think-tank—Yojana Bhavan—must organize a summit meet of the Apex Court, the Justice Minister, the Planning Minister and the Law Commission Chairman, to evolve the country's policy and plan on tomorrow's law and the strategy for its effective implementation. Such a far-sighted legal project may prevent the defection of the people from the law and *vice versa*. Law with a mission is a big undertaking and must be directed according to plan. The input will be repaid by social gain. Moreover, justice cannot remain a story without a plot in a developing country.

The awareness of the top echelons in administration, of the role of law in development being assumed, let us break down the components of the law complex, make brief quality studies and seek recipes. It is right to begin with the Indian Council of Social Science Research (ICSSR), a national organization which recognized the importance of socio-legal investigations as an inter-disciplinary exercise, started a wing on law and social change and included projects thereon in its five-year plan. The ICSSR gives publication grants, sanctions research projects and encourages social scientists, including lawmen, to work on socio-legal problems.[1] The Advisory Committee of the ICSSR on Law and Social Change proposes to promote purposeful research with the right motivation and correct identification of strategic areas. The Council—it is a good augury for the plan—seeks to stimulate coordinated research and hopes to maintain fruitful contact with the Law Commission. It is appropriate to mention in this context that the Law Commission has agreed to associate itself with the Council in sponsoring a National Seminar on Law and Social Change. Committed as it is by the broad terms of its reference to clothe the bones of Part IV of the Constitution with flesh, and to streamline the legal system, and headed as is it by one of the country's ablest judicial statemen, the Law Commission may give new impetus to its work. Auxiliary research forces can be set to work under its inspiration or suggestion. In this sense, the Commission under the leadership of Dr. Gajendragadkar, may play a notable role in systematizing and coordinating socio-legal research, in tune with a perspective plan which it may prepare

1. The SSRC its British counterpart, organizes research on topics of law and contemporary society, including the social effects of new legislation.

regarding future legislative projects. The agenda of research centres and units will then have a touch of realism. It is useful to have feed-back devices working in the field, the researchers themselves being rewarded by early consideration of their reports. In short, the Law Commission may appropriately and in due course, become the fountain-head in the mechanism of law-in-formation. After all, legal seminars, workshops and conferences, whether of social welfare bodies, universities or law institutes and societies, can ordinarily be translated into legislation only after processing by the Law Commission and so, all such meetings, if they have legislative objectives, must involve the members of the Commission.[1] Considerable fieldwork, research, specialized study and investigation are necessary if the projects undertaken by the Commission are to be executed with scientific thoroughness. Law centres and institutes as well as official field organizations and research bureaus may supply much matter to the Commission, thus investing currently scattered research activities with cohesion and practicality.

The current Commission's labours also disclose a wide variety of original work which involves the community, the legislators, field institutions of social welfare and the like in the pre-legislative process.[2] The omens are good for democracy since the success of legislation means pre-legislative mobilization of public opinion. Justice Hartt, Chairman of the Law Reform Commission of Canada, hit the nail on the head when he recently observed: 'I want to stop turning people against the law, I want to turn them for it.' Mr. Justice Hartt who has gone on record as saying: 'What I would like to develop in public participation at all levels from all branches of society. I would like to involve students in high schools, in universities and in law schools in discussion of the law. I would like to encourage labour unions and the home and business community into active participation. I would like this Commission to take the law to the people for a thorough airing'.

In the context of a national plan for law in the larger sense, all the cells which work at the level of law-in-formation, must have a challenging agenda of items to be taken up, on the strength of whose work the Law Commission may act. For instance, current tension-social, political and religious, deserve objective study with scientifically tested tools. In this wider area, not merely

1. If, for example, the Indian Council of Arbitration holds a seminar with a view to churning up concrete proposals for change in the law, or if the Central Bureau of Correctional Services runs a national probation conference to pool together all the points which need legislative attention, or the Association for Social and Moral Hygiene collects, at a workshop, experience in the field about the failure of the Suppression of Immoral Traffic Act to press a case for amendments, or the Central Bureau of Investigation, by studies and experiments, makes out a convincing case for modifying the penal law or Evidence Act, the right thing to do is to involve the Law Commission and make it take a lively interest in the subject. It pays both.

2. For instance, the Gajendragadkar Commission heard Members of Parliament and consumer organisations, alongwith others, while formulating its Report on Socio-Economic offences. A Road Safety Organisation and a Pensioner's Association ignited action which resulted in two reports by the law Commission.

regular researchers, but police bureaus, bar associations, social welfare workers and other like cadres may pool their efforts to enrich the research output. Indeed, our constitutional and political developments over the last two decades must be subjected to socio-legal investigation so as to generate a process of change—*ad hoc* responses to occasional untoward rulings of court are insufficient. Centralized planning may help eliminate overlapping and wasteful research on idle subjects because the country cannot afford the luxury of a jungle of legal research units nurtured by the public exchequer to foliate. The ultimate endeavour must be to produce a functional jurisprudence and activated institutions which will make our embryonic economic democracy viable and our social revolution legally tenable. The huminist jurist of India must challenge the sneer of Ivor Jennings who thinks little of the ambitious declarations in Part IV of the Constitution which appear to him as the ghosts of the Webbs. Of course, on a study of Parts III and IV of the Constitution, our courts have assigned to the Directive Principles a somewhat inferior status, sought to be set right by the 25th Constitutional Amendment. If a planned check is made upon the performance of the Constitution as the judges interpret it, the 25th amendment asserting the, primacy of the social conscience declared as fundamental to the governance of the state would have been wrought into that 'social document' two decades earlier.

Had we a plan for law reform, a few other shortcomings and desirable changes in our system would have been taken care of. The legacy of early Indian law we are heir to has a sustaining role to play in the planning of the law of tomorrow. The Hindu system and the Muslim contribution are, of course, a mixed bag. Personal law apart, the jurisprudence and legal institutions of both, properly screened, may well nourish the present legal system and impart to it an Indian personality. Several jurists have praised our ancient system and Mr. Justice Dhavan has opened a new vista for study and research.[1] Dr. Duncan M. Derret of the School of Oriental and African Studies takes the view that our indigenous civilization 'can still be used to revitalize Indian law'.

The ancient roots of gram swaraj, if transformed in modern terms and written into the law of local (including judicial) self-Government and the concept of community ownership of all lands on the Gandhian basis, if legislated into land reforms, will change our power structure and invigorate democracy at the grass roots. Hindu legal thought was familiar with the welfare state, responsible Government and the seeds of socialist ideas, all of which could strengthen the social philosophy articulated in Part IV of the Constitution. The British period superciliously dismissed our past as 'dotages of Brahmanical superstition' and thus conditioned, present

1. *Vide* his lectures at the National Academy of Administration on 'Indian Jurisprudence and Theory of the State in Ancient India'.

academics look askance at native legal lore. Instead, they journey to English speaking campuses abroad with an exotic shopping list or do second-hand research at home. I plead not for the resurrection of primitive law nor a rejection of eclectic borrowing but for a better regard for our own legal ancestry, taking care that the voice of the dead does not enslave the living as now in the field of personal law.

The variegated Indian past has, even in the area of law, much to enrich our system. Pondicherry has kept alive the French law and if judiciously borrowed from, it may leaven our legal system,[1] Goa, under the Portuguese, had a common civil code, a different trial system and grammar for interpreting statutes, all of which, if properly processed, may strengthen the national mainstream. Eventually, the French and Portuguese systems must be replaced by a common Indian system. Currently, it is all an undirected drift.

If politics is prompted by economics, both together inseminate the legal order, law being a response to and instrument of social policy. Social revolution sans legal revolution is moonshine and so a study of the legal experiments of countries which have successfully worked out social justice is rewarding. Our societal pattern is tending towards the socialistic and so socialist states may have legal lessons for us. The Soviet State, fifty years old and the younger systems in Eastern Europe, have a personality all their own in the matter of jurisprudence, court structure, judicial recruitment and role, professional organization and social concern. Their legal regulation of the public sector, the nature and operation of their fundamental rights, the functions of their legislative commission and other lines of legal development are a new juridical phenomenon, deserving of understanding in depth.

In our laws and court judgments social change is gradually gaining currency under atmospheric pressure. The historic 25th Amendment of the Constitution has expressed preference for a humane economic order, in extreme cases even at the expense of individual fundamental rights. The ideological watershed having been reached, the current of law has to be channelled actively along a fresh course. Nevertheless, our legal pundits cling to a curious juridical iron curtain, a sceptical 'have they a law at all?' attitude, political, cultural and other interchanges with the Soviets notwithstanding. Barring A.S.R. Chari's popular but preliminary book, no noted Indian jurist has thought fit to work seriously on the constitutions and legal systems of the socialist countries or critically evaluated the justice of their law. Such researchers may help innovate the new legal order, as in the case of the German Democratic Republic's family law, penal code, court and procedural systems, or the Soviet law of torts and property, their trial-and-

1. A recent article in *the Journal of the Indian Law Institute* entitled 'Justice Delayed—Not under French Law' illustrates my point.

error experiences in capital sentence, their procurator-general institution and the organization of the *inter se* relations of the Soviets and the judiciary. Basic social differences may make adaptation undesirable or prove our system better for our conditions. But the sub-colonial shadows on our legal system are so dark that modernization must be activated by socialist studies in law. Gur planners at the top must be alive to this aspect of Indo-Soviet friendship.

Although our law men look to the West they do not often absorb the best. Intellectual upsurge and social drive which motivate the new legal trends across the Atlantic are stimulating. The remarkable experiments in judicial methodology, sentencing procedures, court-restructuring, 'student judge' programmes, law reform and lawyers' involvement in judicare and other service projects, have relevance for us. Under their impact, a swell of change, technological renovation of the weary instrument and dynamic Indian projects on law and society should have followed. Instead, with us the tired, traditional world persists, indifferent to an impatient generation.

A national policy on legal education and research would have made our teaching houses of legal knowledge, laboratories of serious investigations which could serve as feed-back devices and fault detectors of the system. Today legal education is untouched by Indian innovation and dwells largely in a colonial twilight, and research here is but 're-search' of things done elsewhere. The syllabi approved by a few law faculties of which I was a member showed how the past holds our campuses prisoner. But in fairness, it must be said, that some light now glimmers on the horizon. Delhi University and some others for instance, have proposed or brought about changes in teaching techniques, examination methods and evaluation processes. The Delhi Law Faculty is becoming conscious of Soviet jurisprudence, and Kerala does not treat socialist constitutions as untouchable for students of comparative constitutional law. As in American universities, the Delhi Law School is coming to grips with community good. Legal aid offers a viable and practical programme both for pre-professional training and for national service and social responsiveness. There is wider awakening in this area. Indian law teachers' have been demanding the participation of law schools in national legal aid programmes. Suggestions have been made before the Joint Select Committee, for the Advocates Amendment Bill, to make statutory provision for associating students with the legal aid proposed under the Bill. The Bar Council of India has recently requested law schools to reorganize LL.B. courses to more practical and court-oriented schemes. Against this background, Delhi courses like Law and Poverty, Law and Development and the running of legal aid clinics as components of education itself, are a pioneering enterprise that hold promise. In the years ahead, this salutary trend may spread and a bridge built between the student, society and the bar via legal aid bureaus and socially meaningful law courses.

It is interesting, in retrospect to observe that Mr. Justice Muthusami Iyer, as far back as 1885, had suggested that our law education should equip students to practise the profession as an art. The Law Commission, in its fourteenth Report, underlined the importance of the study of law as a branch of learning and as a science. The Bombay Legal Education Committee, 1949, had stressed the duty of the profession to contribute to wide social adjustments. 'We feel that lawyers cannot remain aloof from these processes of evolution and legal education cannot wait until all other problems of the nation are solved.' The dynamism of law must begin with the student and it is heartening that twenty-five years of freedom has seen a slow awareness in this direction. If the legal foundation at college level fails, the super-structure of the justice administration must also fail.

In a developing country like ours, an enormous amount of legislation has to be processed rapidly covering the entire spectrum of socio-economic development. Inevitably, the legislators have to master the art if they are to be effective. Indira Gandhi rightly insisted, 'For the serious-minded, any career is exacting. This is all the more so for the earnest legislator, who is at the centre of political developments...'. If the rule of law through socially sound law is to succeed, members of the House must have basic grounding in the Constitution, the Parliamentary system, the legislative processes and statutory interpretation, apart from briefings on important legislation as and when it comes up for consideration. Otherwise, the Parliamentary manpower, largely drawn from the legally illiterate laity (taxing the Central and State Legislatures together), may contribute, when bills are discussed, sound and fury signifying nothing rather than constructive criticism amendatory improvement of the clauses. This problem of legislative literacy has led the Institute of Constitutional and Parliamentary Studies to organize courses for legislators. It is significant that the Institute has, since 1968, started a programme of orientation seminars for legislators so as to bring together members from different states under a common forum and to discuss the problems of law-making and allied matters. Legislative business being very technical and the subjects complex, frequent seminars and workshops all over the country will strengthen the operational efficiency of members who come in fresh, periodically. It is heartening that the Union Government and the States and high dignitaries like ministers and governors, have been associated with this work of the Institute. However, the response, so far as I am able togather, has not been too good and one may only hope that an over dose of politics does not leave too little time for legislators to learn the art of law-making which is one or their primary functions. Maharashtra and Kerala have apparently been carrying out some experiments in training their legislators. *Focus,* a fortnightly digest prepared by the Legislature Secretariat meant to be read by the Members of the Kerala Legislative Assembly seeks to educate them in legislative and para-legislative affairs. But we have made only small beginnings and what is needed is a comprehensive, compulsory institutionalised programme of legislative training for those connected with making our laws. Popular votes are an enticement to sit and debate but training is the credential for creative participation. Moreover, the technical demands made on the legislator are growing. Subordinate legislation is so important these days that legislative, committees need expertise to carry out watch-and-ward work. A grasp of the grammar of legal interpretation is also a must. A group of parliamentarians, speakers and secretaries of the House, past and present, may be able to streamline and simplify the knotty, three-stage legislative process we have borrowed. A research team of parliamentarians and a selection of experts from other disciplines may discover areas of darkness where legislation may light up social life. A planned approach to a burning problem of legislative gaps is overdue, without denying the great deal done.

It is an important step at the administrative level, now for India, that the Minister for Law has been put in charge of a really integrated, but till now separately held, portfolio of justice. The same close companionship between law and justice must be manifest in court also, which implies, in the current context, radicalization of the judicial instrument and the organized bar. Although imperial traditions are still with us, not merely in the haberdashery and vocabulary but in the very forensic texture, there are tendencies to put them out of court. There were reports in the papers that the Chief Justice of India proposed to moot the idea of dropping 'My Lording' in court, at a conference of Chief Justices of the High Courts. A recent resolution of the Supreme Court Bar Association enunciated it in the same strain. The revolt against the robes, starting even in Great Britain, is symbolic for us being incongruous with our Constitution and climate. Turning to the substance of change, there is a case for a renovation of the system which has an obsolete and obese structure at once expensive and dilatory, exotic and complicated factors which extenuate Nehru's admonition to judges to come out of the ivory towers. Of course, there are darker towers and more dismal tombs in the secretariats where administration drags on, untouched by humanitarianism. But that is no excuse for the halls of justice to speak from the grave. We want a living law?

The colonial content of our legal culture and literature, still looking for light from courts in Westminister and Washington, calls for considerable change by new legislative measures. The power to make laws resting primarily with the legislators and marginally with others, a large part of the blame for the laws' ills must be borne by the inaction of the House. And if judges were activist, not traditionalist, if precedents did not freeze and legalism did not stultify the judicial process, the court could have introduced interstitial legislation and transformed the legal ethos and become the *avant garde*, not the laggard among national institutions. What mutations in the law can be achieved by a socially sensitive, creative judge, while interpreting the laws, is obvious to those who read legal history. The ordinary run of judicial personnel, however, is professionally conditioned to conservatism and hardly given any orientation course or special training in judge-craft, or refresher exercises in areas where laws have outstripped their equipment. Judges are not born but made. Society is so complex and changes so rapid that lawyers and judges have to keep abreast of the expanding frontiers of law since all of life unravels in court in knotty tangles. Instead of leaving the law functionaries to cope with the inevitable gap between their mental kit and the new knowledge and technology, and to avoid the social and economic costs of professional ignorance, an American writer has argued the case for judicial education. His plea for imparting working know-how to the judiciary through seminars, collegiate courses, workshops and other programmes applies to our country as well. Justice Tom C. Clark put the point neatly, 'Ascendancy to the bench is the beginning not the end, of one's professional striving... On donning the robes, one must continue to be a student.'

The 'student judge ' familiar in the U.S.A. and looked after by the Institute of Judicial Administration of New York and the National College of State Trial Judges, among other specialized institutions, has found its echo in India where the Institute for the Training of Judicial Officers, in Nagpur, recently started, is meant to serve a similar purpose. The Chief Justice of Bombay proposed a scheme for the training of judicial officers in the state and the Chief Minister fell in with his proposal.[1]

In the socialist and civil law countries also, law graduates who opt for a judicial career undergo a specialized training in that behalf. It must be emphasized that education at that level implies also a social orientation so

1. Excerpts from the letter of the Chief Justice are revealing and form the beginning of a new line of judicial education. He wrote: '...the mere selection of a suitable person by the Public Service Commission does not complete the process of inducting into our service the competent Judicial Officer that is needed. The law graduate, notwithstanding his experience of a few years at the Bar, will still require a course of training before he can be entrusted with the work of a Judicial Officer. It is one thing to argue a case well looking to only one side of the case and quite another thing to take a balanced view of both sides of a case which it is necessary for a Judge to do. A senior lawyer in appellate practice is able to develop judicial faculties because he reads the judgments of the Courts below and learns to weigh evidence and appreciate both sides of a case, but these new recruits have little or no experience of appellate work and whatever little experience they have is in conducting original matters in the mofussil. Thus, they have little or no opportunity to read judgments already delivered and appreciate the pros and cons of a case.

   The importance of training seems to be even greater today than it was thirty years ago. Not only has the volume and variety of the work increased but the pace at which a Civil Judge (Junior Division) and Judicial Magistrate, First Class, has to perform his duties has quickened. He has moreover to run his Court efficiently and smoothly and without friction with the Bar, the litigants, the witnesses and others who appear before him and give satisfaction to all these that justice is not only being done but appears to be done. Unless a young officer is given the proper training, he is likely to acquire by reason of his inexperience, unbusiness-like habits which he may find it difficult to shed later on and which may prevent him from becoming an efficient Judge. A certain amount of training in the administrative work of a Court is also essential to a fresh entrant into the service from the Bar, if he is not to be at the mercy of his office clerks.

that social justice may not encounter psychological resistance from the otherwise tradition-bound men of the robes. We must build up a radical judicial cadre, warmly responding to the humanism of our Constitution Directive Principles of State Policy. When I was sworn in as Judge of Kerala High Court, I said, 'The social goals enshrined in the Preamble to our Constitution, the Fundamental Rights Chapter and the Directive Principles of State Policy broadly and vaguely project our current legal philosophy...I shall endeavour, in a humble measure, to be a judicial activist and treat my career ahead as a fresh call to service in the cause of the rule of law...'

In this context, one may recall with profit President Theodore Roosevelt's controversial statement, approvingly quoted by Justice Cardozo: 'The decisions of the courts on economic and social questions depend upon their economic and social philosophy; and for the peaceful progress of our people during the twentieth century we shall owe most to those judges who hold to a twentieth century economic and social philosophy, which was itself the product of primitive economic conditions.'

It is interesting that in the United Kingdom, to which we frequently look for direction, judicial education is becoming acceptable. A demand was made by a Member in the House of Commons a few months ago for the establishment of a judicial staff college. The Lord Chief Justice holds sentencing conferences and other courses for judges. In India, the Tata Institute of Social Sciences organized a course for the criminal judiciary some time ago. In-service training is not *infra dig,* and like administrative staff colleges, judicial staff colleges must be run to set their sights and incline their perspective correctly.

The importance of education for the criminal wing is all the greater when we read the Indian Chief Justice's recent address inaugurating the Probation Year. He said, 'But is it enough to pass a law and say that probation is a good thing? Not only should the serious student and Probation Officers be convinced of its advantages, but the Judiciary and the Bar must also become its votaries. Unfortunately at present, very little serious attention is paid to this aspect by the Judiciary and the Bar. As a matter of fact I was shocked to see that in a number of cases which came to the Supreme Court recently, even the existence of the local Probation of Offenders Act was not known, or easily ascertainable. No reference to the relevant Probation Act was made in the court below but the point was for the first time taken on the grounds for special leave to appeal to the Supreme Court.'

It is important that the judiciary must share the passion for social revolution and make available its experience and counsel on public issues of a legal and/or para-legal significance. The annual report on judicial administration presented by the High Courts is usually a colourless document, whereas it could contain an incisive analysis of social and economic trends and directions, replete with facts and charged with suggestive realism, so that the community may benefit. In Kerala, for the last few years the annual reports are preceded by a socially relevant questionnaire to the subordinate judiciary, so as to bring out the human aspects of litigative dockets and other community oriented matters. It is a new sign that the Allahabad High Court directed the districts to hold legal seminars to mark the silver jubilee of our independence. The court's commitment to the country and humanity, far from being undesirable, is compulsory, for accountability goes with autonomy. A forward-looking judiciary may in some circumstances, lead the country ahead of the political arm, as happened in America in the Warren era. How angry the reactionary politician in authority could be *vis-a-vis* the judicial statesman is best brought out by one of William F. Buckley Jr's witty statements. 'In those days American conservatives, dreaming of the glorious possibility of a Goldwater victory, envisioned the scene on the Capitol steps during the Inauguration ceremony. "Do you", says Supreme Court Justice Earl Warren, addressing President-elect Barry Goldwater, "solemnly swear to defend the Constitution of the United States?" Answers President Goldwater: "I do. You are under arrest, Warren."

Another facet of the judicial question in India is the propriety of the public expression of views by judges: A former Chief Justice of the Supreme Court once made critical reference to a pending Constitution Amendment Bill and another Judge of the same Court expressed himself similarly when he found ground to do so on administrative inaction. I see no particular reason for the total inhibition of judicial expression of views in public, particularly when it will have an advisory effect and when it relates to legal change. The law lords in England have not kept themselves aloof and Lord Denning for instance, in his Riddell Lecture to the Institution of Legal Executives in Lincoln's Inn, criticised the then pending Criminal Justice Bill. Of course, American judges, with their political past, have gone much further and have criticised on administrative policies openly. Mr. Justice Douglas of the U.S. Supreme Court, in a recent C.B.S. interview, discussed the constitutionality of the Vietnam war and called the U.S. action that of 'the new Genghis Khan'. A circuit judge, highly critical of the Vietnam war on the platform, went on to assert in a judicial order, 'I do not believe that a Judge has a duty of loyalty to political administration with respect to any particular policy of that administration—international or domestic. Nor do I believe that he must attempt to believe that all policies or even all laws are wise and just. But I do believe that he must read, interpret and apply laws as written without regard to whether he would like to see them changed. "Without copying Anglo-American volubility, we may as well have a national debate on judicial commitment and standards of judicial behaviour, particularly now that judges are themselves being judged outside the court and must speak in self-defence. Silence is not always golden and the mute are not necessarily saints".

Notwithstanding the lip service paid to the majesty of the law and the great role of the judiciary, courts and judicial personnel are neglected and even humiliated is the way they are dealt with for official ranking and denied primary facilities. The courts are pitiful pictures of physical and other inadequacies. It is to be hoped that the Ministry of Justice will raise the image of the court and its officers in the eyes of the people. Character assassination of the judicial institution may prove a mortal wound, self-inflicted by the nation and, in the long run, an invitation for violent unrest and government by executive fiat! Indeed, the first right step is to listen to judicial observations about executive actions with respect and, to give effect to them in an appropriate manner. And the second is to assign a status to the court and not regard it as an inevitable constitutional evil.

It is commonplace to criticize the explosion of litigation, arrears in courts and other exasperating aspects of the Justice department, and government have been calling for reports, appointing new committees and commissions and reviewing reports, but there is little implementation or even daring official thinking. What we need is not tinkering with, but redesigning the entire judicial process. The court structure from top to bottom and its business methods need radicalizing. Otherwise people will begin to ask with Saint Joan, 'How long, O Lord, how long? In our static system, even the unanimous decisions affecting courts and litigation reached at a Law Minister's Conference back in 1957 sleep in the Central Secretariat.

Any planning of the judicial system must take note of Article 40 which obligates the state to organize self-governing units at village level. Justice at the rural level can be cheap, quick, local and popular provided a dash of democracy at judicial grass roots were injected with faith and hope. Elected judges are neither unknown nor too risky if we cast our eyes across to the West or the socialist areas. Here, in India, it is curious to notice the higher echelons in politics and other departments cock a snook at village level incompetence and factions. Panchayati Adalat, with petty jurisdictions and shadow powers, is not what we want. Healtheir experiments with larger civil, criminal and quasi-judicial planning, elected elements with a dose of judicial training and professional men to guide and to proceed may work well eventually even, if perversions dishearten us initially. We may write, into the law ample safeguards with, regard to educational and other requirements but we need not be wary of making, the trial, in the spirit of the British days when, many foreigners scared us into believing that Indians are unfit, for self-government. Speaking philosophically. Thomas Jefferson's statement applied to non-political area also. He said; 'I know no safe depositing of the ultimate power of society but the people themselves; and if we think them not enlightened enough to exercise their control with wholesome discretion, the remedy is not to take it from them, but to inform their discretion, by education.' To a lesser extent, with little risk and great benefit, we may involve popular elements, in the administration of justice.

The mainspring of the legal system is the lawyer, and so the social concern and group responsibility of the profession become important. The American Bar has interested itself in law reform, and promotion, of social change through the legal process. Many idealistic young lawyers, and students and some of the finest U.S. legal talent have enlisted in the service in the nation's poorest citizens and in support of civic liberties. A brief idea of the American work by enlightened lawyers is obtained from a paragraph in Earl Johnson's article in the American Review:

> ...legal service lawyers, were admonished to utilize their knowledge and skills as conscious instruments of peaceful, orderly, social change. This idea, in time, captured the imagination of a new wave of idealistic young lawyers and law students. Within months, some of the, finest legal talent in the United States enlisted in the service of the nation's poorest citizens.
>
> The influx of lawyers committed to reform had an almost immediate effect. Hundreds of court challenges were launched against landlord-tenant laws, consumer credit practices, welfare procedures, along with other statutes; common law principles, and administration regulations perceived as harmful to the low income citizen.
>
> A sampling of some of the more significant of these so-called "test cases" may suggest how effectively lawyers transformed the courts into instrumentalities of significant social reform. ...In one early case, slum landlords in the nation's capital were told they no longer can evict tenants in retaliation, when the latter report unhealthy and unlawful conditions in their apartments. ...In a series of Supreme Court cases, statutes and regulations barring several hundred thousand people from receiving welfare assistance if they moved from one state to another or if an unmarried mother took up with a paramour, were held to be invalid. ...In another Supreme Court case, creditors were, deprived of their power to attach an alleged debtor's earnings prior to a hearing on the validity of the debt. ...In two California cases, thousands of citizens of Mexican origin who were literate in Spanish but not in English were enfranchised when a state-wide English literary test was held to violate the federal constitution.

Why should we not organizationally react to our social conditions with suitable judicare? The case-load burden in our courts and the long shadows of law's delays reflect poorly on the legal profession, even as mounting litigation costs do. Our adversary system and some sacred cows of the criminal law make justice the martyr. The profession must crusade for overhaul and updating of the machinery and its mechanics. The present public image of the profession, particularly the upper bracket, as a legal wing of the proprietariat, must be substituted by a more attractive social picture. At this stage, it may be mentioned that the Bar Council of India has agreed to co-sponsor the National Seminar on Law and Social Change together with the Law Commission and the Indian Council of Social Science Research.

A question of the policy of the State in helping to bring to the fore lawyers with the social perspective arises in this context. Governments, central and state, and the proliferating public-sector institutions made large drafts on the legal profession. Ordinarily, they engage senior lawyers who have established their importance by caring for the wealthy sections of the community. Talent, which coexists with a desire for a legal revolution in the system has to be nurtured by the public sector, by-passing the established champions in court of the private sector. If such a conscious policy were adapted by the State, a new professional leadership will arise, eventually making its impact on the home Bar in India. The Indian advocate, unlike his Soviet counterpart, is non-political and individual-oriented. His professional life-style has to change and he must make an impact on society through social service rendered in speeding-up the socio-economic re-ordering. The 'aware' lawyer is a social asset and it is creditable that the Bar Council of India is thinking on these new terms by obligating every member of the Bar to render legal aid to the poor by an express rule, and some associations, like the Supreme Court Bar Association, have voluntary legal aid wings. After all, when only the rich can enjoy the law, and the poor cannot have it, the threat to the continued existence of democracy is very real as Justice Brennan of the U.S. Supreme Court, said. An unthinking but dangerous tendency into which the State is tempted must be countered by the lawyer through educating the legislator—I mean the flight from the court into the arms of administrative tribunary. Legislation often tends to by-pass courts in order to entrust the legal process to obedient, untrained hands. While court orientation and method must change, tribunals, from the citizen's point of view, will be a case of 'from the frying pan into the fire'; in these political days particularly. The straight thing to do is to correct the court system so as not to create law charlatans. Of course, such adjudicative agencies are good where policy issues come in and along with the conflict of interests there is something which makes a purely judicial solution of the conflict with its usual court-room tools, unsatisfactory. On this and other issues of social relevance, the lawyer must speak. His new frontiers go far beyond law practice.

Apart from the lesions in the instrumentalities of legal justice mentioned above, the shortfalls in the State's obligations in the matter of law-in-action need brief notice. For instance, ignorance of law is no excuse, runs the maxim. While it is a rule of convenience for law enforcement, it is a gross anomaly where the bulk of the community is backward and the stream of law flows in undefined channels through several higher courts in a confused course and through frequent legislation and sub-legislation from many unrelated agencies. Democratic discipline consists in conformity to legal norms, but how are they to be observed if they are beyond the ken of the common man? Awareness being antecedent to observance, it follows that the observance of the legal maxim imposes a duty on the State to keep the affected areas of society intelligently informed about the laws made for their benefit or behavioural compliance. Land legislation, debt relief measures, labour welfare statutes, laws for protection of consumers and other weaker sections, fail if concerned human categories are not educated on the subject. A law of which the beneficiary is ignorant does not exist for him. Even the small schemes of legal aid to the poor failed for want or knowledge on the part of the indigent. So it is that the theme of law and communication acquires democratic importance. The 'logistics' and 'acoustics' of welfare and penal legislation must be ensured by field agencies created by the State. For meeting this need, the State may well utilize the legal manpower of the bar, draw up a special service educating and advising the handicapped areas of the community on the laws which concern them and plough back into the system, at law-making level, the experiences of operational shortcomings, for future improvement[1].

Regrettably, this line of development has not attracted attention or action anywhere in India afterwards—or before. The bar should organize community cells to campaign in relevant areas through informative lectures, write-ups, assistance at local level through law clinics and by negotiating disputes when the law is blurred or has lacunas. Reporting back to state agencies where the law, as applied by courts needs repair is also its social duty. Law in the book may be dead Letter if the beneficiaries are distant from it, and comes to life when the lawyer, with skill and compassion, alters, enlightens and helps in its social metabolism. The State must take the statutory initiative for this current to flow. Many issues, which embarrass officials, confuse citizens and puzzle courts, arise in a legal order where *ad hoc* administrative action hides the need for correct legislative solution. If

---

1. To mark a statutory beginning in this direction, the Kerala Legislature adopted two provisions in the late fifties, which may be excerpted"

"THE KERALA CIVIL COURTS ACT, 1957

20B. Constitution and functions of Committees.—(1) The High Court may constitute a committee for each civil court subordinate to it or for two or more of such courts.

(2) The functions of the Committee may include, among other things:—

(i) the dissemination of means of publicity, advice and instruction of legal knowledge to the general public.

(ii) the making of recommendations to the High Court or to the Government, regarding the improvements to be made to court buildings, amenities to be provided for the litigant public and lawyers and other matters of a similar nature.

(iii) the bringing to the notice of the High Court the activities of the staff of the court in the discharge of their duties with a view to stamp out corruption and reporting to the Government specific cases of corruption, if any, for appropriate action, and

(iv) the provision of facilities for the closer association between the members of the Bar and the Bench in considering matters of common concern.

(3) The Committee shall discharge such other functions as are assigned to it from time to time by the High court."

narrow legal rights must yield to broad considerations of mass action, and if law must tranquillize popular upsurges, the flaws and gaps in our individual-oriented legal system must be made up by socially concerned, fresh legislation. Now, the administration often temporizes or plays hide-and-seek with the law instead of re-writing it with insight into public peace and social good. We have hardly made any special law to take 'emergency' charge of popular upheavals and agitations, leaving it to teargas shells and lethal bullets, the ordinary law being unequal to meet extraordinary situations. Where social injury must be inhibited legal regulation must step in, not as mere law and order but in the dynamic spirit of new law for new situations[1].

There is a, quasi-judicial segment where practice defeats the public purpose the statute is calculated to serve. The indiscriminate use of judges and retired judges for extra-judicial work has come in for criticism, and unless wisely restrained, may injure judicial credibility. Public enquiries, hundreds of them, ranging from a college girl's death to the corruption among high dignitaries, have been directed by governments. State and Central, even though, judicial skills may be unwanted or inadequate for the job. The expense involved is immense and the delay considerable, the methodology is ineffective and rigid, the probative value of the end-product or report to punish delinquents is nil and the administrative respect shown dubious. The ultimate public good is illusory even as the frequency of use blunts the instrument. They may degenerate into political devices to ward off mounting public disquiet or administrative embarrassment and, occasionally savour of patronage which taints an independent institution. We are not alone in this exploitative use of judicial reputation. The English experience may be gleaned from the following comment by Professors Abel-Smith and Stevens:

> Among the middle classes—the English Judges are held in awe not only as the embodiment of 'all that is good and excellent', but also as the epitôme of impartiality and objectivity. Politicians are not reticent about making use of this reputation. Embarrassing political situations may be resolved by setting up a tribunal chaired by a judge (for example, the Lynskey Tribunal or the Bank Rate Tribunal). The

1. Examples are legion, as I learnt while a Home Minister for a brief While in Kerala. Students, for legitimate or other reasons, resort to violence inside the campus. Workers, genuinely aggrieved or otherwise, commit acts which violate the present penal law. Government employees, and other groups organized on other bases, fight for certain claims, fancied or real, in ways familiar now but on the wrong side of the extant law. Processions and bundhs, satyagrahas and gheraos are other instances. Governments, being ultimately political, are usually indifferent to the 'illegality' element in these group exercises and is worried only of political repercussions. But policemen and other agencies obliged to enforce the law as it is have to take a not-so-political look at it. Courts mandate them to intervene and the administration ambivalently, blinks, cautions or forbids. This dilemma weakens the peace-keeping efficiency of the force which, untempered by legal constraints, 'may break out into organized violence.

> indiscretions of Cabinet Ministers can be made to appear as individual failings rather than those of the political party concerned. The Profumo affair ended, for example, with the Denning Report; Mr. Wilson's mishandling of the D-notice crisis in 1967 was covered up by the appointment of the Radcliffe Committee; and Lord Radcliffe himself has been involved on many occasions with investigating lapses in British security. By importing a judge to head some Commission or Committee, the most embarrassing political matter can suddenly be taken out of politics. Judges can be used to help pacify dissatisfied colonial subjects (for example, the Radcliffe Constitution for Cyprus), to arbitrate national frontiers or to report 'impartially' on wage-structure disputes (Danckwerts on doctors, Pearson on seamen).

An American comment by Professor Terrance Sandalow of the University of Michigan Law School confirms these fears.

> Ultimately, the issue is whether the prestige of the judiciary shall be put at the service of the government for purposes other than the performance of the judiciary's constitutional responsibilities. On the other hand, we must recognize that prestige is not a commodity in limitless supply. A decision that the participation of a prestigious judge will help to create public confidence in the outcome presupposes that the matter is controversial. That controversy is not likely to be entirely stilled as the report of the Warren Commission demonstrates, however, impeccable the credentials of the participants. The risk, which we have no way of measuring in advance, is that judiciary will not emerge unscathed from the controversy thereby impairing its ability to perform its primary role.

Research into the performance of the Public Enquiries Commission statutes in India may reveal the importance and extravagance and poor returns of this pseudo-judicial process and the harm it does by allowing a live issue to be forgotten and public pressure to be stilled, with nothing happening at the end or every action being postponed indefinitely.

The national leadership is not, sufficiently alive to another facet of the democratic perspective of the legal process. The popular involvement at the pre-legislative stage makes for the clan of the law, particularly for social legislation. Popular and quasi-official bodies must ask for law, suggest amendments when found necessary, and vigilantly help in enforcement. A mass movement to support welfare legislation ensures its success while enforcing the suppression of the Immoral Traffic Act. A consumers' movement help price control regulation. An active council of social welfare takes care of legislation for vice eradication. The auxiliary force for the automobile accidents law is popular national safety organization. Anti-corruption law cannot work without the backing of Non-Gazetted Officers Organizations, land legislation without peasant support or labour law without a responsible working class movement. Lawlessness and oblique conduct at official levels can be checked only if a militant popular vigilance body feeds parliamentarians with strategic information and so on. In short, law is not merely the concern of legislator, lawyer and judge but of the community, nor is the policeman its sole selling agent: a watchful people are. Activist people's listening posts must be recognized by the law if the statute book is to serve its mission.

The basic thesis is that the nation's tryst with destiny must be redeemed through law according to plan. Consumer behaviour towards legal justice is going awry because the system is sinking under its own weight. Therefore, we need an architect's blueprint for the nation's law for the next decade.

LAW INDIA—
INDO-ANGLIAN SEMI-CENTENNIAL

Law India still survives as a static, primitive, Victorian heritage with native executives notwithstanding a semi-centennial struggle to build Law, Justice and Development for Bharat Swaraj. A Raj judicature profile, a borrowed judicial apparel, molar Macaulay jurisprudence and molecular Mahatma humanism, a bizarre value vision—this is Law India 2006. Our legal system is administered by a West-visionary forensics and Westminster—imitation judicature. The tryst with destiny spelt out sublimely by the grand rhetoric of Nehru on the historic August 15 and the ideologically fine-tuned Preamble to the Constitution which binds our governance are eclipsed by the Republic's distorted dimensions of Law and Justice, as interpreted by the precedent governed brethren on the bench. The Indian 'lordships', with writ process and arcane case-law, gave rulings which were binding because of their robes. If the rule of law must run close to the rule of life, a transformation of the system is a desideratum. Most crucial for justice, social, economic and political, for happiness, health and humanism of the billions of people and their peaceful progress is the Judicary. We need a dynamic people-oriented legally literate progressive, imaginative, judicature with a swaraj vision. Otherwise, chaos will corrupt, confuse and terrorise the Indian cosmos.

The need to tell the community the truth about the judges is not commission of contempt but democratic duty and probity. Pannick quoted Jerome Frank:

> *Some politicians, and a few jurists, urge that it is unwise or even dangerous to tell the truth about the judiciary. Judge Jerome Frank of the US Court of Appeals sensibly explained that he had little patience with, or respect for, that suggestion. I am unable to conceive ... that, in a democracy, it can ever be unwise to acquaint the public with the truth about the workings of any branch of government. It is wholly undemocratic to treat the public as children who are unable to accept the inescapable shortcomings of man-made institutions... The best way to bring about the elimination of those shortcomings of our judicial system which are capable of being eliminated is to have all our citizens informed as to how that system now functions it is a mistake, therefore, to try to establish and maintain, through ignorance, public esteem for our courts.* (Judges Page-205)

I write this article having been an advocate, minister and judge of the highest court. So I assert, agreeing with Pannick QC:

> *We need judges who are trained for the job, whose conduct can be freely criticized and is subject to investigation by a Judicial Performance Commission; judges who abandon wigs, gowns, and unnecessary linguistic legalisms; judges who welcome rather than shun publicity for their activities.* (Judges P-205)

The way which "Judge and Co." is run is of great concern for the freedom, progress and human rights of We, the People of India.

I proceed to look critically, without fear or favour, at judges, many of them mediocrities and several others savants of learning and justice. The great Holmes (U.S. Supreme Court) wrote:

> *I trust that no one will understand me to be speaking with disrespect of the law, because I criticize it so freely. I venerate the law, and especially our system of law, as one of the vastest products of the human mind. But one may criticize even what one reveres.* (Vol.I Quote It P-340)

Can the Indian legal system be saved? asks F.S. Nariman, a jurisprudent par excellence, in a recent book published by Penguin? You cannot, without a radical vision of progressive transformation integral to Indian realities and cultural roots save the legal pharmacopoeia. Why not jettison alien and arcane jetsam? The citation of exotic precedents, British and American, the superogatory project of appeals upon appeals from deck to deck making finality of fate and verdict an expensive illusion. The Bench-Bar complex so extravagantly exasperating, making the curial pyramid a terrorist trauma and bankrupt victimology for both sides as well as an exposure of forensic gambling and goofiness. These and other pathological features make the legal system 'untouchable' and unapproachable for the common Indian who seeks justice in court and alternatively in the streets. Alas! there is little native flavour in the legal praxis except the costly curial chaos, and adversary logomachy. Even the appointment of judges is a disappointment. The selection process is a dubious secrecy confined to a few Supreme Court judges, keeping the People, the Bar, the academia and the Cabinet without a voice in the choice of those whose pronouncements bind every person. There is an old Roman adage: "Whatever touches us all should be decided by all". In America, the selection of judges is not a closed-door intrigue nor arbitrary majority view of accidentally top three judges. The people have a voice through the Senate Judicial Sub-committee. Even in England, mystery and obscurity is no longer a holy policy. The Lord Chancellor is helped in his selection of candidates by an Appointment Committee. (vide David Pannick):

> *Judges have considerable power to make and apply the law. They are not elected to office by the people whom they govern in these* respects.

The reasons why one candidate, rather than another, has been recommended to the Queen remain hidden in the files of the Lord Chancellor's Department or concealed within the breasts of those senior judges amongst whom'soundings' have been taken. All of this serves to deter public discussion of the criteria of good judges and to perpetuate gossip (most of it untrue) about the reasons for the rejection of certain candidates and the success of others.

The Appointment Committee could comprise representatives of the Law Society, the Bar Academic Lawyers, the Judiciary and perhaps some lay members, for example highly trained and experienced personnel and officers skilled in selection procedures. The Committee is open to the people and would introduce a much-needed public eye into an otherwise private process. Unfortunately, in India the Executive at the highest level was the authority vested with the power of judicial appointment. The Chief Justice was consulted but his concurrence was not a *sine qua non*. In the Constituent Assembly Dr. Ambedkar categorically dismissed the demand that the Chief Justice or the other judges be given the appointment power. Nevertheless, half a century after the Constitution was enacted, with poor reasons but authoritarian ipse dixits which never convinced me, the Supreme Court, by a majority, arrived at a self-serving ruling being accountable to none, that a few judges would decide on who should sit on the Bench, High court or Supreme Court. This intriguing edict has no parallel elsewhere in the English-speaking world. Even if I disagree with the personal dicta of the judges concerned, their decision governs as the law of the land (Art. 141). The delays in choosing judges are by the seniormost few on the Supreme Court appalling; the criteria for choice are almost personal, uncontrolled by socially accountable canons and compromises among the thesis. The candidates once selected or rejected are jettisoned or again midwifed for unknown grounds. The Bar and the public are in the dark. Judges, transferred for suspect behaviour emerge as Chief Justices of a High Courts or even members of the Supreme Court. One High Court judge who rarely attended court or wrote a judgement was made Chief Justice in Kerala by the bizarre wisdom of the feudal few of the apex court accidentally at the top. To be brief, in the art of choice the process is a riddle wrapped in a mystery, inside an enigma. Management of the Judiciary needs vigilance, research, social perspective and national commitment, people's concern and socialist, secular convictions. The Executive is weak and has not brought a constitutional amendment to restore Dr. Ambedkar's view accepted in the Constituent Assembly. A weak Centre, wobbly and cowardly, a Parliament lost in loquacity and "walk-out" strategy and a mute public and local bodies and legislative assemblies with 'sound and fury, signifying nothing' do not care or dare to amend the constitution to keep the high bench truly high. For the sake of justice the judicial management at the top must insist on practicing Parkinson's Law and Peter Principle.

INDIAN SAGA UNDER BRITISH RAJ IN THE THIRTIES—A REPORT BY A BRITISH DELEGATION

When Indian history of the first half of our century comes to be written – fairly it will be acknowledged to be the most stupid, brutal and treacherous in the story of the now dead British Empire. And Krishna Menon will be recognized the most outstanding Indian who battled against Britain from within Britain. The importance of Krishna's single-handed campaign standing on English soil is uniquely patriotic, progressive and instructive for the present and future generations. In T.S. Eliot's lines:

Time present and time past
Are both perhaps present in time future,
And time future contained in time past.

The struggle for freedom was waged in India by Mahatma Gandhi, despite British repression. Simultaneously, a battle was being fought by a man – a phenomenon – called Krishna Menon with the India League as his militant instrumentality. Imperial Britain had to be liberated from its brutal policy by sensitising public opinion in the Island whose people were insulated from information about the malignant viceregal misrule. Wrote Bertrand Russel, Chairman of the India League: "There has been no lack of interest in the misdeeds of the Nazis in Germany; they have been fully reported in the Press, and have been commented on with self-righteous indignation. Few people in England realise that misdeeds quite as serious are being perpetrated by the British in India. Large numbers of men and women, including many of the highest idealism, have been imprisoned under horrible conditions, often without any charge having been made against them and without any hope of being brought to trial.

The elementary liberties that make life tolerable have been taken away from the inhabitants of India, for the crime of desiring self-government. The censorship, combined with British apathy, has made it very difficult for the facts to become known. If they could be widely known, there is, I am convinced, enough decent feeling in the country to compel the Government to mend its way."

Statesmanship is dead; he complained, and demanded a change in the savage strategy of the Raj through dissemination of the harsh facts among the British people. This desideratum was the driving force which made restless Krishna Menon undertake the formidable fight to free India from the Empire by spending every hour to win the cause – Independent India's tryst with destiny. The eloquent locomotion of Menon all over England achieved much and awakened many. The India League, under his tireless leadership, organised meetings, involved great public figures, published pamphlets, books and bulletins and sustained active contact with around 2000 organisations. Menon's marathon operation combated the official information campaign and as integral to this massive efforts he organised a delegation of liberal British notables to India for an on-the-spot investigation which toured our country and produced a magnificent report titled *Condition of India*. Madan Mohan Malaviya, a renowned leader of nation, extended financial help. The task of taking a delegation thro' hostile Viceregal India was tough and Menon was the member Secretary.

The Report made a powerful impact in Britain. Ordinance Raj, in its monstrous dimensions, came to light in London. Subash Chakravarty, a great historian, noble Indian and sensitive humanist, has, in his Introduction, summed up the essence thus: "The report emphasized that these ordinances and methods were directed against unarmed and non-violent people irrespective of age or gender. The Redshorts in the NWFP, the one time proud warriors of the frontier, were then the non-violent patriots with close relations with the Congress. Thousands of them were in prison and their leader had been deported. They had been mercilessly assailed and surprisingly enough they did not retaliate even once. British rule had ruined the prosperous rural civilization of India; racist rule decried the bright men and women of that nation as niggers' agriculture had been neglected willfully; brutality of the police was inhuman; traditional handicrafts had been virtually wiped out; torture was endemic; racial hatred was intense; unemployment was proverbial; 20,000 leaders were imprisoned; Gandhi was revered everywhere by everybody including the simple villagers and the untouchables; the Indians knew that the RTC was dead before Gandhi reached London; the release of Gandhi was the condition of peace; India must achieve her own step to self-government without interference from England. Life in India was being lived in an eternal background; this gave the people poise and dignity; India had not made a god of Henry Ford but she knew the magnificent possibilities of the human spirit. It was in fact legalized State terror and the report wondered how long this reign would continue in the name of the British people. It was going to be a lasting shame in British history and it would certainly sow the seeds of bitterness and resentment among a people otherwise friendly and peace loving. There was optimism that India would win her freedom. The report was, however, despondent about the impact of the rule of the ordinances. It would foster, it claimed, a heritage of ill-will and even racial hatred for which future generations would condemn the British nation."

A barrage of questions in Parliament followed the publication of the Report to chivvy the ministers and exposed the truth of British lies about the *Raj* policy. Subash winds up his Introductory with these powerful words: "The report proved that the Indian National Congress was the only credible political force in the country and it attracted popular sympathy, confidence and obedience despite active official oppression. It established beyond doubt that the national movement had moved into rural India, that nationalism in India was no longer inspired by the urban middle classes but that it was sustained by various strata of peasantry and that women in India had been awakened to the realities of life and they constituted one of the foundations of India's resurgence and democratic movement. The report underlined that Gandhi was the uncrowned ruler of India. Although he was a sensitive soul full of compassion and spirit of conciliation, yet that man of peace was steeped in an uncompromising national pride. For the historians of 1930s the volume would remain an inestimable source of information, analysis and perspective. It is a *locus classicus* of India's struggle for freedom.

Condition of India, a product of the on-the-spot study by the high-minded members from England is an instructive, illuminating and even potentially explosive book, which laid bare the imperialist British hypocrisy. The several chapters that follow deal with the diabolic dual Raj policy, the India League Delegation, the Ordinance era, the calm of Irwin-Gandhi pact and the storm of the next Viceregal misrule and a study of the Ordinances and their legality. The Civil Disobedience Movement, its great leadership and discipline and the most repressive span finds description in the book.

Suppression of Opposition is a universal feature of despotic and authoritarian governance. Severe measures of Raj inhumanity and harsh experiments with official atrocity were let loose. The indomitable will of Gandhi, the national courage of the people and the police atrocities are brought out in the succeeding chapters.

The police and the law is a chapter that the reader should never miss because that brings out the grim, gruesome methodology of police Raj in action, what with lathi charges, firing on crowds, attacks on women and children, cruelty in lock-ups, raids and searches and other forms of police excess and victimisation of the public. Has that cruel culture quiet India with the British? Do ponder.

The Report deals with political prisoners and jails, prison labour, punishment within jails and the lot of detenues in confinement. To deny democracy, the press is gagged. The British in India practised this malefic art with fascist success. The Indian villages also received the attention of the Delegation. Rural suffering, peasant destitution and punitive infliction are portrayed in the book luridly likewise Labour also had its share of police torture. The price of militant demand for freedom is brutal behaviourism of authoritarian echelons in power.

Several important political issues, boycott and picketing, the impact of Gandhi, the problem of Untouchables, Unity Efforts et al find a place in the Report. A convincing collection of vital facts and useful interviews enrich the pages and words of wisdom leading to constitutional advance and prospects ahead add value to the great Report. The members of the delegation commanded respect and their Report helped mobilize public opinion in favour of India. Appendices, which are informatary, make the report complete.

Condition of India is a great work and any patriotic or objective historian of British Rule in India must page through it as it treasures precious material and poignant events. The delegates were Monica Whately, Ellen Wilkinson, Leonard W. Matters and V.K. Krishna Menon. The superlatively dynamic secretary was Krishna Menon. The present Indian reader must realise that the British Raj is not dead and that many undemocratic things that now happen are a *deja vu* of the thirties when the Report was made. The present rulers of India are Indian and brown. But does British heritage still survive after death? Dear reader, do answer to yourself.

LAW INDIA: SOME CONTEMPORARY CHALLENGES

A hapless law-man from Delhi stands before you, the ostensible reason being to deliver the inaugural of the *Justice Bhawani Shankar Niyogi Lecture Series.* Shri Niyogi was a *rara avis,* flying over a sky of many colours and the Lecture Series, in his honour, should have been ignited by someone great in his own right. My sad puzzle, therefore, is how I, with the little glow gone out when the light of my life, my wife, left for the astral, should have been picked and pressured to fulfil an assignment beyond my competence.

A man without the mood of crusade for temporal causes or the know-how needed for execution of learned projects is a wrong choice. I have yielded, aware of my inadequacy, and you will forgive the flaws and the failings in me and my talk. In this world of respectable superstition, wearing the judicial robes, like swearing-in as Minister, supposedly invests the incumbent with wisdom and versatile talents, because he does and is expected to handle affairs till then outside his ken.

I must, on this occasion, express, *in limine,* what ALEXANDER POPE warned against: 'A little learning is a dangerous thing'. I have little more than little learning and I think it better to be honest than to beguile the grateful gathering.

Our ancient country has preserved its great names by legend and memory and its learning and culture have cascaded from generation to generation through soulful, vibrant, chant rather than through mute, petrified pages. Our saints survive through the sheer power of the spirit, not the indelible ink of the printing press. But our own unfree chapter of British Indian history has injected a strange perversity and made us forget the Indian Great of modern times. There is one exception, though. Those who are dressed in temporal and sacerdotal authority have commemorative homages while alive, but the torch-bearers of culture and the silent builders of values, like freedom fighters, great educationists and judicial statesmen, do not adequately receive honour or homage while alive or after death. In this sense, we have a welcome exception in SHRI BHAWANI SHANKAR who is held in high esteem for his felicitous blend of virtues and abilities, and, by God's grace, is happily with us.

BHAWANI SHANKAR NIYOGI belongs to the inner republic of the Bench and the Bar but he was bigger than his office, larger than his profession, greater than many learned men. For his life reflected his faith — rare then and now — and his faith was social justice and liberty for man, a dangerous vocabulary for his time. This little Telugu youth learnt law, married a child widow, became a scholar in Indian philosophy, opposed casteism and gave up in the country's cause, his legal practice in response to GANDHIJI's call for Non-Co-operation with imperial injustice. The nation's conscience was his inspiration, the nation's freedom his passion. Public life, in diverse capacities, consumed his energies and public duty elevated him to the High Court. He thereby elevated the office itself. *Some are elevated to office, some elevate the office and many limp along in the limbo of office.*

The testimony of his vistaramic capacities is found in the fact that he was Vice-Chancellor of the Nagpur University, Chairman of the Municipal Council of that City, radical humanist who presided over the massive function organised by Dr. Ambedkar for mass conversion of *harijans* to Buddhism. Silver hair is no sure index of sage wisdom, but Niyogi at ninety, living with saintly simplicity, giving away his all to a University, is one who never ages and, indeed, such *yogis* eventually belong to the ages.

His long career is a lodestar for us, lesser men, to look at and learn from, at a time when power has become suspect in public office, idealism has been abandoned to opportunism and judges, with but blurred vision of a *brave new world* and dubious mission to do broader justice beyond the letter of the law, are not uncommon. *Law, remember, is for life, and Judge, mark you, is executor, not executioner of Justice.* This noble trust and behest compel the Bench and the Bar to break the fetters of tradition and spell the text of a new gospel. Humanity bleeds and seeks justice and our juridical pharmacopoeia shall, informed by prophetic sights and deep insights, strive to heal through the rule of law the wounds of social injustice. Otherwise, judges will be judged and the law will be outlawed. We must avert that tragic chapter.

A great judge is best remembered by dwelling on the chastened obligations of his office — Human Justice. And no contemporary subject is so charged with power to move into action millions, billions, as Justice — social, economic and political. *Kannagi* demanded Justice of the Pandya ruler, with fire in her eyes; Jesus claimed justice from the Roman governor with love for all; Gandhi asked for justice for enslaved India on the rule of *ahimsa;* and Fidel Castro accused tyrant Batista of gross injustice to Cubans. Justice to the coloureds has been the tumult of American life. History is the story of the battle of right *against* might, of human justice *against* hostile law. The divine, dramatized demand of *Krishna* to *Duryodhana* for a modicum of justice to the exiled *Pandavas* is no longer legend but a universal urge articulated as a human right in the Universal Charter. It is the gravestone of the Old Order and the cornerstone of the New Order. Law by the State has *raison d'etre* only if it organises Justice for Society. That is why the 20-point programme of the Prime Minister, approved by Parliament, has a power far beyond a White Paper, its inner strength being not official authority but extermination of group injustice and inauguration of people-based justice. That is why SHRI GAJENDRAGADKAR, with septuagenarian sageness, in his *G.B. Pant Memorial Lecture,* carried ominous import when he quoted some burning lines from *Pavar,* a Dalit *Panther* poet:

"These clenched fists won't loosen now

The coming revolution won't wait for you

We've endured enough: no more endurance now...."

The Blacks of America are asking, in militant tongue, for living justice, not the tuneful chant of egalitarian legalism. The issues of social justice are diverse, the fighting faith is cosmic. Legal culture must rise to resolve contemporary stresses and most a just jural order.

Let us parachute to Indian social earth. The Constitution of India has added a dynamic status to this age-old quest of man by inscribing in its Preamble words which, if fulfilled, will be the solace of the suppressed and the suffering and the ideology for the development of a fifth of mankind. India is great in her human resources and Indian law must be at the service of its people; and freeing itself from the bonds of little legalistics and obsolescent outfit, build,' with creative skill, a socially conscious jurisprudence to match the current challenges and crises. For this reason, I have chosen to address you on LAW INDIA: SOME CONTEMPORARY CHALLENGES. Shri NIYOGI, I fancy, may be bemused by my critical thoughts and suggested constructs, but judicial statesmen with large heart, ripe experience and commitment to country must discard without tears dead legal wood and direct our juridical future. *We suffer from an overdose of lawyers' law and judicialised justice;* we have to plan and programme a reformative rule of law through original experiments in legal techniques and rural *judicare* — all of them with a fresh focus on the People. In short, *we must humanise the legal system,* radicalise the legislative, as much as, the judicative methodology and man-power and restructure the many institutions of law and administration to suit the imperatives of our country's crying needs. Indeed, Law, in its multiplex sweep, including court rooms, lawyers' chambers, law schools and institutes of socio-legal research, has to change its profile, its process, its heart, head and gaze. Social relevance, setting and delivery are the signature of the People upon the Law — not the static parchment which hardly keeps pace with our urges.

A British politician described once the House of Lords as proof of survival after death. We need not be surprised if a similar compliment were paid by unreverential social scientists to the Indian Legal System whose colonial roots, the no-changers hold, are still our forensic pride! Change leaves law no choice! For, millions of Indians, governed even now by old English common laws thoughtways, will echo the title of an article in the

Modern Law Review (1967) by Prof. H.R. HAHLO: "Here Lies the Common Law; Rest in Peace"! In this context a few observations of the Supreme Court recently made in *Ratanlal*[1] are poignant and apt:

> "Unfortunately, even after liberation, many former colonies, including India, did not shake off this neo-colonial jurisprudence (*See:* AIR 1950 Bom 123). This is the genesis of the idea that Indian 'good conscience' is English Common Law during the reign of Empress Victoria. The imperatives of independence and the jural postulates based on the new value system of a developing country must break off from the borrowed law of England received sweetly as 'justice, equity and good conscience'. We have to part company with the precedents of the British-Indian period tying our non-statutory area of law to vintage English law christening it 'justice, equity and good conscience'. After all, conscience is the finer texture of norms woven from the ethos and life-style of a community and since British and Indian ways of life vary so much the validity of an anglophilic bias in Bharat's justice, equity and good conscience is questionable today. The great values that bind law to life spell out the text of justice, equity and good conscience and CARDOZO has crystallised the concept thus:
>
> 'Life casts the mould of conduct which will someday become fixed as law.'
>
> 'Free India has to find its conscience in our rugged realities and no more in alien legal thought. In a larger sense, the insignia of creativity in law, as in life, is freedom from subtle alien bondage, not a silent spring nor hot-house flower.'

The soul of democratic legality is its social dimension best expressed in the words of JULIUS STONE as Human Law and Human Justice. The expression of the goals of legal justice adopted by a community, based on its historical, social, economic and cultural conditions, and the strategies whereby its value judgments are accomplished, constitute its jural postulates and processes. Law is a normative and regulatory system and mechanism as a means towards social justice. Law ways must lead to orderly progress of the nation if functional justification and social validation must be found for their observance. In sum, Law India fulfils itself only when the spirit of change and the spirit of conservation march in step. *Aware* Law-men are architects, engineers, statesmen and synthesists, not prisoners of *stare decisis*, not robed men who go-it-alone, not trained machinists in litigative techniques or text book teaching. They are the *avant garde* giving pragmatic shape to 'the felt necessities of the time, the prevalent moral and political theories and intuitions of public policy'. They draft, interpret and implement statutes in such manner that rapid evolution keeping pace with the *mores* of the community is organised through socially purposeful normative

1. Civil Appeal No. 1297 of 1975 decided on 9-12-1975.

prescriptions. Lawyers and legislators will do well to realise that our ethos is a precious testament of the past but our nation will break to pieces if we do not break with the unjust part of the past. Mere change without conservation may lose our identifiable entity and end up as a disastrous carbon copy of foreign systems. Mere conservation without change cannot conserve, since the flux of the world around and massive hunger for the good life compel radical readjustment as the price of peaceful continuance. My thesis is that if Law is to be *living,* creative innovations and dynamic synthesis are essential to the rule of law and constitutional order. This is not jural rhetoric nor legal romantics but simple realism and communal sensitivity. The call to lawyers — an expression which must include law-makers and implementors, not merely the Bench and the Bar — must necessarily be to modernise legal technology fertilised by ongoing social interaction, to work out original legal models and to produce viable principles which will clothe with flesh and blood, Article 38 of the Constitution which reads:

> 'The State shall strive to promote the welfare of the people by securing and protecting as effectively as it may a social order in which justice, social, economic and political, shall inform all the institutions of the national life."

Pertinent to the same subject of social transformation are a couple of allied Articles which deserve notice. Article 39 contains a mixed mandate of humanist economics and Article 40 is a Gandhian imperative of decentralization. They read:

> "39. The State shall, in particular, direct its policy towards securing—
>
> "(a) that the citizens, men and women equally, have the right to an adequate means of livelihood;
>
> (b) that the ownership and control of the material resources of the community are so distributed as best to subserve the common good;
>
> (c) that the operation of the economic system does not result in the concentration of wealth and means of production to the common detriment;"
>
> "40. The State shall take steps to organise village panchayats and endow them with such powers and authority as may be necessary to enable them to function as units of self-government."

The Preamble, which is the spiritual key to the New Order, highlights the dignity and worth of the human person and equal justice to every citizen.

Such are the political perspectives, the social problems and legal prospectus which must excite us into action, bearing true faith and allegiance to the founding essence of our free democracy. If we bury our legal heads in the sands of abstract jurisprudence and profusion of precedents, lawyers will be left behind and the nation may go haywire. Anyway, whatever we do about our system is our responsibility since we are a free people. Dr. Ambedkar observed in the Constituent Assembly:

> "By independence we have lost the excuse of blaming the British for anything going wrong. If hereafter things go wrong, we will have nobody to blame except ourselves."

We are living during a creative period of Indian history even as the young Niyogi was fighting during critical days of British subjection. The battle for freedom when we are unfree demands great sacrifice; the battle to build a free nation committed to equal justice under the law is a zig-zag story of daring, disciplined, democratic adventure. The subject I have chosen has a topical appeal and casts collective responsibility on lawyers. For, we are all actors on the stage of Indian legal history-in-the-making. It is a human weakness to dramatize one's day, hyperbolize one's era and aggrandize one's profession — a form of pathetic fallacy whereby one's role becomes important because a crisis threatens law and society. The last two nouns are interwoven conceptually; for, no law, no society; no society, no law. Absent binding legal norms it is chaos, not community. Absent dynamic *dharmik* consciousness, law will rob justice or never take off. Once we grasp the theorem that Power and People go together, the central role of the justice system in the scheme of social change is easy to accept. Democracy, by definition, is power to the people, while the rule of law means nothing less than law for the people, by the people. India is a Republic where 'We, the People' are sovereign. The truth that many in high places miss, stricken by myopic *maya* or illusion of power, is that India means our vast, wailing humanity, and social salvation comes through this immense 'society unlimited' awakening to its destiny. The law of laws, the power behind power, therefore, is *that* people's jurisprudence which engineers our stagnant society into a dynamic escalation of all-round development. The activist sociology of law must elevate our legal system by a militant awareness of social justice, a desideratum of developing countries, sloughing off, changing the metaphor, if I may, individualistic justice of a bygone century and way of life. DEAN POUND, in his *Mahlon Powell Lectures* explained:

> "As the saying is, we all want the earth. We all have a multiplicity of desires and demands which we seek to satisfy. There are very many of us but there is only one earth. The desires of each continually conflict with or overlap those of his neighbours. So there is, as one might say, a great task of social engineering. There is a task of making the goods in existence, the means of satisfying the demands and desires of men living together in a politically organised society, if they cannot satisfy all the claims that men make upon them, at least go round as far as possible. This is what we mean when we say that the end of law is justice. We do not mean justice as the ideal relation

among men. We mean a regime. We mean such an adjustment of relations and ordering of conduct as will make the goods of existence, the means of satisfying human claims to have things and do things, go round as far as possible without the least friction and waste."

Plainly, Austinianism, Kelsenism or Hartism is far from a beautiful totality of jurisprudence but part insularity and part truth. You just can't cripple *dharma* and call one of its components law. This is a Western error. Indian *dharma* insists on recognition of the divine potentiality of each and full material opportunity for the manifestation of the perfection already in man. This is economics, politics, religion, culture rolled up in sublime legality under a spiritual compulsion. That is our synthetic approach. To argue that law is the statute book, court hall, prison house and police billy and little else, is to miss the goal of justice. We may not accept a cloistered theory of law in order 'to avoid a syncretism of methods which obfuscate the essence of legal science and blur the confines which are drawn for it through the nature of its object' (STONE, p. 102). Let us look at men as a whole, not as litigant, husband, heir or criminal. A flower is more than chemistry or collection of petals or little worms inside, but a sweet synthesis for the artist beyond the chemist or the analyst. To dissect is to murder and that is how law has lawfully murdered social justice over the ages and unsuccessfully evolved jurisprudence divorced from jurisconscience. *Dharma* is the *sangham* or confluence of norms of right conduct or code of behaviour sanctioned from within one's being, supported by community consensus and enjoined by the sovereign on his subjects as the trustee of People's Power. Law is for Man and not society for jurisprudence. Change your laws, a Malayalam revolutionary poet sings, or else the People shall push your laws aside!

JOHN BATT, indignantly critical of academic wranglings over 'schools' and theories mindless of *man*, wrote about the cerebrations of famous jurists thus:

> "....Their hollow concepts, tea-cup debates, and impotent ideas debase modern jurisprudence. Their obsessions are unworthy and intellectually subversive — especially so in an age when man's annihilation is a possibility, the individual's alienation is a fact, and world political revolution is in process. In a time of Hamlet's choice, of being or not being, can one rationally choose to watch these Jurisprudes calk up the fissures in their logical castles of absurdity, rumble about non-ideological principles of law, aero-arc through logico-lingnistic feats of verbomania, distinguish "is" from "ought", lust after the "pure law", or dispense sweet allegories about the Light of the Law that failed the Virgin Lady of the Lake? No, for their causes are all shadow causes, fit only for the haunting of some philosophical boneyard. Their grand illusions have nothing to do with life. Such shadow causes, being spiritually dead, can teach nothing about living, a matter of ageless importance. I offer then a return to the basic

question of philosophy (and of jurisprudence). That question is Existence, and its subject matter is the living."

Therefore, our search as jurists is for Indian Man and Woman — those thinly fleshed skeletons, tired pavement progeny and below-the-poverty-line 'masters' of national resources! NIETZSCHE once said. 'The great problems are in the streets', and so our concern is the village street and slum heap. The thrust of my thesis is that the humanist jurist — legislator and lawyer — must make of our Freedom a legal order which will be guarantor of a good society.

Many political and legal people suffer from awesome fear of freedom and creativity and hunt for scapegoats and transplants and, in the bargain, cavil at each other. It is easy to blame it on others, for, hard are the solutions to stupendous problems like slums *versus* sky-scrapers, rural squalor *versus* urban glitter, socialistic promises *versus* capitalistic performances, produce more *versus* distribute less, democratic discipline *versus* anarchic obstruction and decentralised power *versus* centralised exercise, not to speak of the population explosions and waster of human resources. Let us begin to build, not to blame.

Jural infrastructures, constitutional checks and balances, flexible legal control systems, efficient statutory models, court processes which practise the fine art of promoting fluent driving without the complex of constant foot on the brakes, and like projects are based on the inarticulate major premise, not fully remembered by lawyers, planners and governors, that a participatory system of democracy implies a citizenry, civil service, legal and political cadres disciplined to participate, sensible to be responsive and subject to the rule of law as a pervasive principle.

JAWAHARLAL NEHRU once wrote:

> "A Government is apt to go wrong, because it is over-burdened with pressing problems and has little time to think in a co-ordinated and integrated way. It tries to, of course. But, generally, every department of the Government is over-burdened and that again is a difficulty common to all Governments the wide world over. We are facing crisis after crisis — domestic and international — and just cannot think calmly of the future. Therefore, it is quite necessary that there should be people who are not over-burdened by problems of the day and who can think in an integrated way of the steps that should be taken."

Is it not the national duty of jurists who share the goals to help Governments by constructive, not captious, contributions as the 'brains trust' in the organisation of law? Self-preservation and accountability to a changing society leave no option to law-men in this matter. A learned and cautious English Judge like Sir LESLIE SCARMAN has developed the new dimension of English Law, distinguishing change which develops and strengthens the system from change which destroys it. This pregnant presage is a *caveat* for us too:

> "I shall endeavour to show that there are in the contemporary world challenges, social, political and economic, which, if the system cannot meet them, will destroy it. These challenges are not created by lawyers; they certainly cannot be suppressed by lawyers: they have to be met either by discarding or by adjusting the legal system. Which is to be?"[1]

He illustrates the silent, yet significant, changes wrought by responsive court law and legislative law in England:

> "For instance, the common law was exceedingly taciturn for centuries on the subject of the duty of care and the tort of negligence. Pressurised by the developing industrialisation and urbanisation of society in the nineteenth century, the judges, using as a precedent the ancient action on the case, developed the substantive law of negligence, thereby without the intervention of the Parliamentary legislative process providing a legal right to compensation for personal injuries caused by the fault of another. An older and more famous illustration of the same process is the history of equity — developed by the judges as a graft upon the property law, who thus adapted the law to the needs of the time without the necessity of destroying it."[2]
>
> "A law of torts, a land law, and a family law, conceived on common law principles, however, admirable in substance, cannot effectively protect the general public or the weak, the poor, the aged and the sick. To satisfy the conscience of the nation the state has had to move into the empty spaces of the law, the deserts and hill country left uncultivated by distributive justice, and there to make provision for society as a whole, and for those not strong enough to provide for themselves. Thus the welfare state is challenging the relevance, or at least the adequacy, of the common law's concepts and classifications. Fault, trespass, property, even marriage, are now seen to be an insecure base for the development of a law suited to the needs of our society. Family life has been freed from the tyranny of the husband and its obligations buttressed by the state: social security is available on the basis of need and as of right: the use of land, sea and air are controlled in the interests not of property but of society anxious to protect its environment:................"[3]

---

1. English Law — The New Dimension — The Hamlyn Lectures by Sir Leslie Scarman, 1974 — Stevens — p. 1.
2. English Law — The New Dimension — The Hamlyn Lectures by Sir Leslie Scarman, 1974 — Stevens — p. 2.
3. English Law — The New Dimension — The Hamlyn Lectures by Sir Leslie Scarman, 1974 — Stevens — pp. 70-71.

Shall we not conceive of Operation Legal Transformation in the same spirit, facing as we do worse perils? The chaos and confusion in our country could be more dangerous — luckily the situation is not so disenchanting and is really ameliorating in some respects — if unjust, arrogant law or absence of Poverty Law, if unchecked executive arbitrariness or political system operating through a mindless legislative majority, if unanswerable courts sitting as 'Third Chambers' with social unconcern, combine to puzzle and paralyze a penurious, impatient, slogan-fed but slowly awakening people.

Jittery jurisprudes and philosophers of the Establishment will please see the lawless writing on the political wall and be reconciled to the hope of survival of orderly society through the strategy of socio-economic amendments to the Constitution, nationalisation laws, industrial regulations and land reform measures, apart from the nascent complex of economic programmes with Welfare-States bias and benignant mutation of litigative lawyer's law and overly judicialised justice. Indeed, the big triune task of streamlining and simplifying the whole apparatus and mechanics of Law and Justice, re-writing of Poverty Law and legislative landscaping of economic equality, is an enormous undertaking awaiting execution. Challenges to which the law has been unresponsive are, according to Lord Justice Scarman, capable of 'destroying' the legal system. Let us — lawyers and legislators — learn to avoid the Tower of London and the Tower of Babel.

The apotheosised image of the rule of law and the arcane and archaic court process, at a majestic distance from the ragtag, serves the professional aura of the Bench and the Bar but the realities of legal justice project a picture of alienation from the people with a growing tendency for the masses and the classes to ignore or oppose the system itself. Law *versus* Society is destructive of peace and tranquillity, if not arrested before the forces of disorder get out of hand. Speaking without reference to the current Emergency which certainly has produced a qualitative change, leaving aside political quidnuncs to query *'Quo vadis* India?' Society bears testimony to rashes of violence, violations of moral norms, deviance from democratic rules and widespread apathy towards Law, Courts and even Legislatures. The Legal Establishment, under assail from social discontent, is wilting and creaking and even the intellectuals are filled with frustration not only against the policies of administrative power but with what they regard as juristic junk fobbed off by robed erudites whom Shakespeare lampooned as 'in fair round belly, with good capon lined'. The old order changeth yielding place to new, and Law fulfils itself in many ways. *Quo modo?* By the multidisciplinary job of transforming the socio-legal junk pile into progressive architecture! Vision and action are the desiderata.

These are the basic politico-economic lesions which make up the pathology of Law *versus* Justice, and economists, statesmen and social scientists, including lawyers, must be gravely concerned about such an ominous syndrome. It spills over the scope of my lecture to unravel the why of our nation's political ambivalence and the whence of our economic hide-and-seek game, but positing full faith and credit in our basic constitutional mandate of triplex justice and seeing the appalling misery of the people, a reordering of our economy is inescapable. If so, there is a good case for us to develop legal instrumentation to energise the slogan of *garibi hatao* and fulfil the plans that make the 20-point or like programmes. Therefore, lawyers, judges and jurists have a professional obligation to organise Law and Justice in such manner that through service systems and social sanction the broad community becomes friendly consumer of, and even active participant in, the legal order. The psychosis of the parliamentary process in its mid-Victorian style and indolence to respond promptly to set right errors found out in courts and the drafting decrepitude that preserves the mystiques of *legalese* make legislation so archaic, slow-moving, cacophonous and obscure that little gets done, and *that* so ill-done, that litigation becomes an abundant by-product, especially as the judicature interprets it with precedent-bound techniques. The old English jingle will tickle because it is true:

> "I'm the parliamentary draftsman
> I compose the country's laws
> And of half the litigation
> I'm undoubtedly the cause."

The importance of the drafting art to suit Indian conditions and to reduce litigative situations has been highlighted in *Vaswani*[1] where a provision in the Suppression of Immoral Traffic Act, which is calculated to protect the weaker sex, came up for judicial consideration:

> "Had the drafting been more careful and lucid, the argument would have been obviated. This Court has, more than once, pointed out that lack of legislative simplicity has led to interpretative complexity. The home truth that legislation is *for the people* and must, therefore, be plain enough has hardly been realised by our law-makers. Judges, looking at statutes, are forced to play a linguistic game guessing at the general legislative purpose and straining at semantics. In the present case we have had to reach the conclusion against the appellants by broadening the dimensions of *Heydon's case* (1584 3 Co Rep 7a: 76 ER 637), importing a 'context-purpose' teleological approach."

Our Supreme Court deplored recently in *Rajappa*[2]:

> "One should have thought that an activist Parliament by taking quick policy decisions and by resorting to amendatory processes

1. (1975) 2 SCC 829 (832).
2. Civil Appeals 753 & 754 of 1975 decided on 21-1-1976.

> would have simplified, clarified and de-limited the definition of "industry", and, if we may add "workman". Had this been done with aware and alert speed by the legislature, litigation which is the besetting sin of industrial life, could well have been avoided to a considerable degree. That consummation may perhaps happen on a distant day, but this Court has to decide from day to day disputes involving this branch of industrial law and give guidance by declaring what is an industry, through the process of interpretation and re-interpretation, with a murky accumulation of case law."

This testifies to my criticism of parliamentary insouciance even where the working class or weaker sex is involved.

There is need to Indianise, modernise, simplify and radicalise and speed up legislative technology and canons of statutory construction instead of clinging to a colonial carbon copy, as we now do. No more of the dated 'Whereas men' will do, nor the three readings of bills culminating in the 'ayes' and 'nays' dependent on the three-line whip rather than expert study of the true import and impact on social progress or the performance-sheet in court. Today there is a powerful trend against complex, detailed, codification methodology and judicial dictionary-hunting, baffling rules and interpretative intricacies, motivated by a democratic concern to ensure certainty, clarity and accessibility of law to the layman. Men are dismayed by the arcanus of law and the indifference of the legislature to lay down sensible rules of construction of statutes through a socially meaningful, plain and purpose-oriented enactment on the subject of statutory interpretation, removing many dated presumptions and the superstition that legislative debates shall not be a source of help to know the mind of the maker and the meaning of the enactment. It may not be out of context to suggest that a beam of light on statutory construction was thrown in a recent decision of the Supreme Court relating to a land reform measure[1]:

> "The key thought that pervades our approach is that if the constitutionally envisioned socio-economic revolution is not to be a paper tiger, agrarian laws have to be meaningfully enacted, interpreted and executed and the court is not the anti-hero in the drama of limping land reform. Much to the same effect this Court observed in *Amar Singh's case*, 1974 (2) SCC 70:
>
> 'We have to bear in mind the activist, though inarticulate major premise of statutory construction that the rule of law must run close to the rule of life and the court must read into an enactment, language permitting, that meaning which promotes the benignant intent of the legislation in preference to the one which perverts the scheme of the statute on imputed legislative presumptions and assumed social values valid in a prior era. An aware court, informed of this

1. *State of Haryana* v. *Sampuran Singh*, (1975) 2 SCC 810 (814).

adaptation in the rules of forensic interpretation, hesitates to nullify the plain object of a land reforms law unless compelled by its language, and the crux of this case is just that accent when double possibilities in the chemistry of construction crop up while dealing with a somewhat analogous set of provisions under the same Act."

Law-making and pre-legislative preparations are dilatory and disappointing—even unscientific, being innocent of prior empirical research and based on impressionistic kinks. Even if constitutional changes are called for in this behalf we must undertake them to make codification a quick-acting, intelligent, reformative response to the rule of law *vis-a-vis* social justice.

But, in this lecture, my thesis is that currently, for diverse reasons, the judicial and legislative instrumentalities as well as substantive and processual laws operate so quizzically, tardily, expensively and traditionally that the hiatus between lawyer's law-cum-judicialised justice on the one hand and prompt, inexpensive obtainment of remedies in keeping with the rising aspirations of a free, but poor, people for a just society on the other, is widening. The legal fraternity has no long *alibi* for showing unconcern since insularised law courts are on trial and the law-maker's *bona fides* and competence are suspect. Jerome Frank once wrote: 'In a democracy the courts belong not to the lawyers and judges but to the 'citizen'. I intend mainly to turn the lens on the limited landscape of processual justice to the people, understood in its widest connotation, with some emanations into allied substantive fields, and throw light on how to resurrect our jural system, in so far as law men have a commission to help the nation's mission of moving the masses out of the Erebus of legal injustice into the sun-glow of social justice. I wind up this statement of the case for a programschrift of law and social change by two quotes from Friedmann:

> "It would be tragic if the law were so petrified as to be unable to respond to the unending challenge of evolutionary or revolutionary changes in society."

The main assumptions which Friedmann makes are:

> "First, the law is, in Holmes' phrase, not a 'brooding omnipotence in the sky", but a flexible instrument of social order, dependent on the political values of the society which it purports to regulate..........."

Relevant to this theme I had occasion to outline the linkage of the processes of law with changing social values[1]:

> "The assembly line operations may be somewhat like this. The Cabinet and Planning Commission draw up a rough plan for the five-year period ahead. The Law Commission and other bodies engaged in

1. Foreword to Monograph on 'Socio-Legal Research in India': A Programschrift by Prof. Upendra Baxi, published by the Indian Council of Social Science Research, New Delhi, 1975.

pre-legislative studies draw up their five-year plan of work based on and in response to the National Five-Year Plan. The research institutes and University Grants Commission and the research wings of Law Schools get to work selecting, in a co-ordinated way and avoiding duplication, areas for socio-legal research out of this national agenda. May be, post-audit on social legislation also may be undertaken. Sometimes crash research projects may have to be taken up when, for example, the 20-point programme is to be implemented. This framework is not rigid and mobility and flexibility must necessarily be there."

A project for the present and the future needs an understanding of our pre-Independence days of law-in-action. We have inherited, as a hangover of British rule, the theory and practice of the English speaking legal system. Certainly, any legal structure springs from and is shaped by the social and economic order, and Imperial goals and feudal hierarchy were thus the parents of an elitist, alien-tongued system of justice which could afford sophisticated procedures, class conscious Bar ideals and Bench traditions, and gloried in the greatness of an imported jurisprudence. The 'God save the Queen' model suited the Raj and the then upper classes and though, with the declaration of Independence, the Republic was geared to dynamic social justice, the die-hard legal ghosts of a by-gone era haunted the new law-system as voices from the tomb. The shopping list of the new Law was the revolutionary ideals of Part IV of the Constitution but the nation of shop-keepers had left behind them stock-in-trade in the shape of an old model judicature, legal profession and law schools, which did not sufficiently shift their social orientation, equitantly respect Freedom's about-face or prepare a companion legal plan for the national development plan. Thus arose a built-in conflict between the *old law* and the *new justice,* between taught law and human justice, and even occasional flashes of confrontation, between the legislative and judicial branches. People's Justice screamed in the pathetic streets and streamed in the election manifestoes, but the Houses of the Legislature lagged in action, though liberal in promises, the Executive was hesitant or hostile in implementation, and the, sound-proof court houses interpreted laws in the smog of grammatical construction and administered justice as found in the musty and misty statute book. The jurisprudential statesmanship of harmonising the frustrated hopes of the millions, the perfunctory legislative performance, the hide-bound lawyer's law and over-judicialised justice and the arbitrariness and incompetence of administrative bodies, went by default and still remains the difficult but lofty task of *activists* in the field of sociological law and social sciences. 'Reorganise or perish' is the sloganised version of our juridical crisis. Socialise the province and function of law so that Indian jurisprudence may demonstrate in action the soul force of our Republic — such is the broader, deeper, legal philosophy our jurists, including lawyers and judges have to evolve and evangelise. After all, as Julius Stone has reminded[1], 'every change in man and his environment calls for a re-examination of existing values in their application to the new situation, a call more than ever insistent in our mobile democratic type of societies'. This is a polished re-statement by a Western jurist of what NEHRU had urged the legal establishment to ponder and, indeed, what socialist jurisprudence has, in some measure, achieved. Therefore, let us revamp the inherited juristic estate of long-ago values systematically to fit into the current plan of human rights and social discipline summed up in the magnetic phrase, the dynamic 'rule of law'. And, in this jural art of 'weeding out the over-privileged and effectively lifting up the under-privileged' a New Deal in Law is now needed. NEHRU, in his *Autobiography*, articulated this legal dilemma[2]:

> "Even more important are the economic changes that are rapidly taking place the world over. We must realise that the nineteenth century system has passed away, and has no application to present-day needs. The lawyer's view, so prevalent in India, of proceeding from precedent to precedent is of little use when there are no precedents. We cannot put a bullock-cart on rails and call it a railway-train. It has to give way and be scrapped as obsolescent material."

Two basic questions arise: (i) How best should the present justice-system be galvanized and transfigured to subserve our poverty realities? (ii) How can Law be used to promote and discipline National Development? I mean to initiate a discussion, not with infallibility but as an essay in socialistic jurisprudence, jettisoning a legal cargo unsuited to the facts of life. May be, this is the beginning of a programme of socio-legal experimental exercise and scientific investigation, the problem and perspective being all that I propose to outline. One thing is sure. We, lawyers, live on the human level and our art has to have a vital nexus with Developing Country and Developmental-Distributive Justice.

Before I speak on the judicial process and its institutional responsibilities and transformation, a brief reference to the importance of socio-legal research geared to the new goals may be a perspective-setter. I quote Prof. BAXI[3]:

> "The common law culture, which we continue to share, is highly court-centred. Judges, lawyers, law teachers and students are, by and large, accustomed to be indifferent to the state of law in legislative gestation and to its career outside the courtroom. The tradition of taught law (Roscoe Pound rightly used to say that 'taught law is tough law') and of the Bar and the Bench which regards, again by and large, all other aspects save the doctrines of the law as 'given', is principally

1. Human Law and Human Justice, p. 3.
2. Allied Publishers Private Limited, 1962, p. 586.
3. Programschrift by Baxi, supra.

responsible for the excessive preoccupation with the court system. Concern of law men with justice has also been mostly a history of concern with justice under the law."

Lawyer's law is not good enough. I entreat the academics to spread the canvas wider and paint not mere profiles of court-hearings and judgments but use the brush to beckon lawmen to the new lines in the horizon. I again quote Prof. BAXI:

> "Be that as it may, the specialized misidentification of 'law' with the court-system in its normative productivity cannot be wished away. But it could be slowly transformed by a strategy of sponsored social scientific research to a concern with these aspects of the court-system which could make the preoccupation with the normative system itself sociologically more meaningful. In the process, the field of law can also be transformed, slowly but surely, into a multi-disciplinary domain. It is with this objective that we give so much importance to the court-system in our proposals for sociological research in law."[1]

Law and Society can make headway only if socio-legal research stimulates and feeds change. The Indian Council of Social Science Research's paper highlights this aspect. I am party to it and quote, with your pardon, from my foreword[2]:

> "Most of us are painfully aware that the entire legal system, as it now obtains, has several limitations and, consequently, it has to develop its capabilities and overcome limitations before it could play its rightful role in the transformation of our society in the desired direction and pace. Thus I envisage legal research as falling into two distinct categories—first, the entire legal system (pre-legislative, legislative and post-legislative processes, and the institutions of Law-Law Schools, Legislative Committees, Law Commissions, Bench and Bar), and the body of substantive and procedural law; second, making law and its institutions positive instruments for effectuating social policy. This task demands the support of social scientists, for it is equally their social and professional responsibility to study law as a social institution and legal system as an essential sub-system of the social system."

It is good to round off by a reference to like research *vis-a-vis* our developmental plans by quoting again from my foreword to the same brochure[3]:

> "But mere plans and projects prepared with the correct perspective will not work on the ground unless there is law to back it.

1. Programschrift by Baxi, p. 28.
2. Programschrift by Baxi, p. (viii) of the foreword.
3. Programschrift by Baxi, *supra*.

Nationalisation, price control, setting up of public sector corporations, inhibition of private monopolies and restrictive trade practices, proscription of bonded labour and untouchability, fair deal measures for *adivasis,* agrarian reform — why, any serious step towards social amelioration and economic progress will involve legislation. Law being an indispensable component or keystone of the developmental arch, we are compelled to consider the organisation of socio-legal research on a massive scale, to feed the pre-legislative institutions and sister commissions in the field. Legislation should not be *ad hoc* but well thought out and based on objective studies by researchers. The Law Commission and the legislative wing of the Law Ministry should not act on impressionistic ideas but on empirical research data. Likewise, legislations may misfire in actual working, the executive or judicial infra-structure may not be operating on the wave-length of the authors of statutes and defects and deformities and lacunae and gaps may be noticed in the working of socio-economic laws. Only by a post-audit can these be detected and researchers must focus on law reform where socio-economic goals are not attained as intended. All these add upto new vistas for socio-legal research on an inter-disciplinary basis."

A renaissance in law-ways is nationally necessitous. This divagation into an invitation for research gains better relevance when we peep into our judicial anthropology.

India's experience with law-in-action has had a colonial origin. The *adalats* were established by a trading company under royal charter, the profession was organised on British lines and litigation was the pre-occupation of the legal fraternity. Even here, the lawyer has been almost entirely concerned with the conduct of litigation the portrait being British, the goals imperial, although in the post-Constitution era, the State has also contributed considerably, not always virtuously, to cases in court. However, the wider range of activities, particularly non-litigative and developmental, which characterize the practices of legal men in other countries has gone by default. This over-emphasis on litigative dependence for dispute processing makes the legal entre-preneurship narrow and conservative, aggravated by Anglo-Saxon jurisprudence and vintage precedents, too holy to be departed from, as the primary source. The immense potentialities of the profession in non-litigative contributions to welfare and watchdog services like land reforms, environmental control, developmental projects, social benefit schemes, arbitral solutions and legal checks and regulations over the public services and holding within the leading strings of the rule of law public and private sector enterprises, currently fall outside its self-circumscribed orbit. Even such activities as promotion of legal research, of law reform in the fields of adjudicatory structuring and institutional facilities for litigation for the poor, not to speak of pre-litigative legal advice, have not interested the practising lawyer. The erection of institutions and methods like conciliation boards, negotiating bodies, mobile courts, commercial or village tribunals, administrative justice organs, family courts outside the normal civil and criminal court system in dispute settlement, the re-designing of the architecture and management of courts so as to make the delivery system of justice speedy, rational, modern, informal and cheap — these are all regarded as eccentric or impious. The organisation of specialised courses so as to up-grade the efficiency of the lawyer and judge in the social sciences and the creation of socially sensitized agencies for distributive justice, laying down of new legal norms of ceiling on wealth and concentration of means of production contrary to orthodox juristic notions of unlimited property, fundamental freedom to grab and untouchable vested interests — these aspects which are, in a sense, catalysts vital for social progress and lawyer's contribution in that behalf, do not seem adequately to attract his public commitment. A college for judges to give them social orientation, plan awareness and technical proficiency has been a heresy until recently. In short, the nation's call to lawyer-power to play a strategic role in its progress according to the dynamic rule of law goes unheeded, thanks to the traditional non-response of the profession to these extra-litigational summonses. And the politician's opportunity to denigrate the law agencies, hiding his own skeletons in the cupboard, is being partly supplied by an unwitting deal-mute disposition of the law. In one sense this is a Mendelian misfortune, a genetic malformation of British Indian Days.

Out of the plural range of jural concerns I have sketched, I mean to confine myself to glance at the great potential of Law and Development and move to a critical look at the shortcomings in our justice system at the processual level and to suggest recipes which fulfil the constitutional desiderata, my purpose being epitomised and Processual Justice to the People and Law as the Companion of the Plan. The major inarticulate premise of freedom is the right to happiness and in a developing economy on a democratic keel, social justice is its juristic expression. Thus every legal system has the twin goals of development and distributive fairness. *Sans* law, justice goes haywire. Law either saves or sinks society. Which means that there can be no mute jurisprudence; it has to be set to the human tune. All this adds up to the primary question: What is the condition of Indian society and what developmental aims do you set up for the nation, what social and physical targets coupled with periodisation and plan strategies, legal and other, do you programme? Whom do you propose to benefit and what socio-economic priorities and institutionalised models and priorities appeal to you? Secondly, what pattern of judicature, processual systems and rules of evidence flexibly fit the over-all project of National Development and People's Justice? Can the answer to these queries fall from the peaks of high-powered politicians or lawmen? BERNARD SHAW who shocked his readers by ridicule, remarked in one of his well-known plays:

> "He knows nothing; and he thinks he knows everything, That points clearly to a political career."[1]

A political cynic surely may, looking at the anglophonic circus of law courts pronouncing upon highly technical laws demanding specialised knowledge and insight into social segments within the statutory ken, with naive lexicographic learning and pontifical assuredness untouched by sociology, decoding truth from heaps of lying testimony, disputed writing and psychic-social situations with non-chalant certitude, innocent of data-processing methods, and sentencing convicts with severe saws and without any education in correctional strategies and social defence techniques, turn the tables to say '*that* points clearly to a legal career'. Be that as it may, it contains an oyster's pearl of painful truth about both. What I mean to convey is that 'taught law' and court-centred practice can be no substitute for the multiplex of talent and technique the legal and political arts modern social engineers need. Planning a nation's march from frightful and ubiquitous backwardness to *sarvodaya* and socialistic justice calls for multi-disciplinary skills and scholarship. The lawyer must be a planner to organise legal programming and control systems in keeping the national projects within the leading strings of natural justice and equal law and promoting, through flexible administrative law, the objects of socio-economic progress.' Law and Social Change cannot be a vogue phrase or vague clap-trap but careful socio-jural calculus—*Indian Law with a New Dimension.*

The cosmos of law has expanded to comprehend many disciplines and technologies, and so, lawmen, must, in turn, acquire new visions, new competence and new perception of frontiers, lest they should be pushed aside as irrelevant or obstructive to progress. The first requisite of a legal career is the consciousness of this diffusion of sympathies and skills.

The problems of India are not merely poverty which, undoubtedly, is appalling, but human degradation, as Gunnar Myrdal has mentioned in his *Asian Drama.* The subjection of centuries, the colonial exploitation by a foreign power and the implantation of an exotic, sophisticated, legal apparatus with limited objectives, have inflicted irreparable trauma on the creative abilities of the Indian Spirit. We have not recovered from the shock fully and, therefore, our Jurisprudence, like our Science and Public Administration, has not managed to grapple with the great and massive problems that face the country on the social economic and political planes. However, we have the tremendous advantage, with the inauguration of the Republic of a magnificient constitutional perspective which marks a big break from the Raj and its suppressive rule of law sprinkled with some good principles which have the potential for a better jural order. Thus, for us of this generation, the social mission of law is to *preserve* the best that the British

1. Bernard Shaw in 'Major Barbara'.

have left behind as jurisprudential bequest, to *reject* the imperial strands of law which served their interests and blighted the indigenous masses and, more than all, to *construct* a creatively fashioned *swadeshi* legal system which will direct the course of the nation towards a social order, egalitarian in ethos, production-cum-distribution-oriented in economy and democratic in political process — a cross between Westernisation and Sanskritization and Dravidisation! The know-how of law and social change has to be worked out in these culturological terms by imaginative and trained humanist jurists and social scientists backed by empirical researches, not impressionistic conclusions. A perspective judi-plan, with periodic law plans, so as to solve our national reconstruction problems and serve the masses of consumers of justice is thus a necessity if freedom through law is to possess its full meaning for the people as a whole. In the nation's Planning Mansion there must be many houses—a spacious and central one for law.

These generalities illumine, but we have to be far more concrete if justice is to be done to the subject under discussion. Let us define the ends and chalk out the means, so that law and social transformation may be a twin scientific project. Law cannot be clear-cut if your social goals are confused, contradictory and pleasing to the Patricians and tearful for the Plebians. That is also an added complication in our malady. What are the economic and social problems and what is the planning process and apparatus whereby we hope to solve them? How do we involve the Indian in the drama of Development? Illustratively, are we going to have an expansive public-sector or the co-existence of public and private-sectors? Do we intend the public-sector to be a model employer? Are we going to compel the private enterprises to be socially conscious and, if so, in what direction? What should be the place of the co-operative movement and the forms in which this movement should manifest itself? What recognition do we, as a nation, assign to Labour and do we seriously mean to involve the working class in management? Do we intend to bury feudalism through land reforms? What urgency. and methodology do we pack into population control, social hygiene and public health and housing and food for the destitutes? A host of subsidiary questions crop up immediately even on the economic plane. Likewise, an immense variety of legal techniques, problems and experiments will assail the jurists and sociologists as we painfully realise that nearly 30 years after Freedom at Midnight we have not moved into noonday and abolished sex inequalities, communalism, casteism, rural and harijan primitivism or population control and assurance to all at least basic creature comforts. And the British-Indian Secretariate System, de-humanised and delinked with life's realities, has survived so grotesquely in anachronistic style that a whole new edifice of law governing administrative processes, responsibilities and commitments, together with rights and liabilities of the public services, has to be constructed in the Indian Foundry. The legal community must proceed on the fundamental social thesis that Part IV of the

Constitution shall be the national direction. Even Part III has to woo Part IV, as the Supreme Court recently expounded in *Thomas*[1]:

> "The unanimous ruling there (Keshavananda Bharati) is that the Court must wisely read the collective Directive Principles of Part IV into the individual fundamental rights of Part III, neither Part being superior to the other. Since the days of *Dorairajan* judicial opinion has hesitatingly tilted in favour of Part III but in Keshavananda Bharati the supplementary theory, treating both Parts as fundamental, gained supremacy."

The Bench and the Bar, I entreat, must stick to these social principles although I feel hesitant to be sure of politicians, customary cant notwithstanding. I make this fervent appeal because among the judiciary we do have some who stay, delay, distort and act anticlockwise, providing material to the opponents ammunition to shoot.

We may now proceed to spell out my broad thesis with some specificity. The direction of social change must be settled by Party leaders, by Parliament and, in the last resort, by the political nation. If you want a political order with egalitarian values and freedoms, your legal processes will have to be structured and your jurisprudence home-spun accordingly. England, America, Soviet Land are obvious examples. The legal army follows the political flag. So our Constitution has mandated republicanism, secularism and social justice. These are the founding faiths for the jurist to make the nation's legal outfit. Politics, again, shades off into economics and both are conditioned by geography, cultural legacy, history and the impact of the technology and life-style of the One World we inhabit. All these interact and condition the legal system. Our curious secularism and freedom for religious autonomy is an Indian response to Godly pluralism. Our 'reservations' for government jobs, aimed at advancement of backward classes, have echoes in the U.S.A. and its provision for the coloureds. The socialist compulsions are writ large in Soviet Law and may be guidebook for a socialistic pattern of law. In this sense, legal mansions are built to accommodate the orderly change of nations.

The core question then arises: What is India's social mission? What is its cultural legacy, community ethos, constitutional goal and methodology of change? The nation's individuality cannot be alienated from its jural order. Legal tailoring or, more elegantly, juridical engineering, must meet the great expectations and assuage the deep frustrations of our times. I have irritatingly repeated this question because no national consensus for the political, economic, social, parliamentary or judicial values and work plans emerges. We can't wobble longer lest we skid off the road to progress. Are we now hopefully gathering a united will and wisdom, after all?

---

1. C A. No. 1160 of 1974 decided on 19-9-1975, *State of Kerala* v. *N.M. Thomas*.

Formulation of our National Legal Plans must not be mere British-Indian drifts or mindless borrowed models from abroad, but reflect clear perspectives, choice of priorities, practical programmes and legally disciplined exercise of power to attain nationally defined ends. Law, let us realise, is a social science with sister know-hows, its options, problems and flexible projects being closely adapted to achieve the social, economic and political tasks prescribed by our national leadership and necessitated by control of extravagant power. We (lawmen) are all members of a family of committed disciplines — science and technology, politics and economics, medicine and law and other branches of knowledge — committed to Indian humanity in the raw. Our spiritual ground is that all are equally divine — and cannot be legally devalued. In the language of democratic constitutionalism, man — the dignity and worth of the human personality — is the centre of legal planning for social change. Given a culture, great and ancient, the country — populous and ex-colonial like ours, — given a social structure, hierarchical and stagnant and a civil service enjoying power without accountability, given a political machine deadlocked sometimes in dog-fights and suspected often of making hay when the sun shines, given a legal process too exotic, expensive, malformed, and imperfectly serviced to be a competent justice-management system, the dynamics of Plan and Law directed to Social Change has to be developed on a multi-dimensional basis. *Carew and Co.*[1] is a capital instance of law overflowing into economics. I had occasion to focus on this failing:

> "Here we come upon one of the basic deficiencies of our law studies which do not yet take within their sweep, apart from jurisprudence, economics, politics and sociology. These are distinct enough at the core but shade off into each other. As Roscoe Pound observed: 'All the social sciences must be co-workers, and emphatically all must be co-workers with jurisprudence'. Georges Gurvitch supplemented the statement by observing: 'A little law leads away from sociology but much law leads back to it'. The desiderata are neither novel nor detractory but a recognition of the new status of law *vis-a-vis* development in the context of the court's high function of keeping the Executive and allied instrumentalities wisely within the leading strings and formidable grip of the law. Anthony Dickey, in a *University of London Public Lecture in Laws,* advocates the need for making judicial review of administrative action more of a reality than it is at present and adverts to the court having to possess 'adequate background training' and 'first class research assistance'. In another article (33 Mod Law Rev. 497) the same author explains the permissibility in English courts of the practice of seeking assessor-assistance where specialist knowledge and expert advice are called for in complex case situations."

1. (1975) 2 SCC 791 (805).

Garibi Hatao is a political-economic statement — or the 20-Point Economic Programme, for that matter — but it has to be clothed with flesh and blood and here law cannot lag behind. Article 38 takes us towards this objective by pinning us down to a socialistic pattern and the conscience of Part-IV expresses itself in terms of concern for workers, women and children, health of the community, inhibition of concentration of wealth and means of production in private hands, boost for the co-operative movement, diffusion of power and grass-roots government through *gram-swaraj*. This panorama of goals and methods leaves little doubt that loyalty to the Constitution ordains us to adopt developmental strategies broadly along socialist lines. This sense and sincerity of direction must be reflected in the top leadership of the ruling political and judicial complex of forces, for they are provisionally the 'trustees of the faith of the suffering millions' bound to act with collective or coordinated will. What is urgent is the minimum needs of our people; what is important is that we should not drift or dawdle in acting; what is inescapably implicit is that all the steps proposed must be processed legislatively lest administrative action should fail for want of legal backing or otherwise degenerate into arbitrary or oblique exercise.

This broad framework being accepted, a brief economic silhoutte is desirable. Law is the means, but socio-economic techniques canalise the ends. Dr. MINHAS states[1]:

> "The main attraction of the *Garibi Hatao* programme was that it reflected the felt needs of our people. It is probably needless to stress that poverty cannot be banished from our midst without basic changes in the structure of our society. However, what really needs to be stressed is this: For a relevant model of social and economic change, we do not have to run for alien prescriptions. The home-spun insights of Gandhiji can provide all the basic building blocks for the relevant model. My emphasis on the urgent need for a shift from the metropolitan, heavy-industry, and centralised production model to integrated rural development, minimum needs and employment-oriented, decentralised production is rooted in the Gandhian concept of development 'not only for the masses but also by the masses'."

Dr. OOMMEN debunks the GNP idol and underscores the human values of Development[2]:

> "In fine, the rate of growth in GNP cannot be accepted as a reliable measure or the sole desirable objective of development. It never tells us anything about the quality and life of the people for whom all growth is meant. It tells us very little about the social cost with which growth is achieved. An Indian Taj or an Egyptian Pyramid may be

1. Wither Indian Planning? The Indian Renaissance Institute, Dehradun, p. 26.
2. Development: Perspectives and Problems, Edited by M.A. Oommen, Published for Ecumenical Christian Centre, Whitefield, Bangalore, 1973, pp. 3 & 5.

singled out as one of the wonders of the world. Very often the slave labour that built it is forgotten. Rapid economic growth may be achieved with the help of slave labour or at the cost of leisure and aesthetic pursuits for a large number of people, or by polluting the earth's atmosphere. It may be pointed out here that we do not imply that GNP is the villain of the peace and that things would change once this accent is changed. Reduction in inequalities – social as well as economic – and reduction in unemployment and mass poverty depend to a large extent on the existing property relations, the social philosophy of the government, the success of the fiscal measures, investment patterns and a host of other factors. What we have been trying to indicate is that the increased accent on GNP has led to the neglect of several important social goals. Of course, we do not question the fact that such objectives as social justice, economic indepedence etc., which are necessary to ensure the dignity of man, are possible only with economic growth."

* * *

"The purpose of development is admittedly to make people more human, by lifting them out of the dehumanising conditions of poverty, unemployment, ill-health, ignorance and thc like. As the essence of the human is threatend by under development, we may define development as humanisation. Denis Goulet argues that the concept of development is best expressed in the phrase 'the human ascent', the ascent of all men in their quintessence of humanity, including the economic, biological, psychological, social, cultural, spiritual and transcendental dimensions."

Another question of fundamental import is as to whether we opt for mammoth enterprises with sophisticated technology and a few hands or for a whole rural spread-out of small scale industries with its social regeneration potential, distributive justice and involvement of villagers in productive occupations? This debate turns on whether we deny Gandhi in action and worship him during *jayantis*. Wreaths are not tribute enough.

The West has begun to realise that man is the master, not the machine. E.F. SCHUMACHER, with felicity, describes the presiding idea 'Small is Beautiful' and writes on intermediate technology[1]:

"Is there an alternative? That the developing countries cannot do without a modern sector, particularly where they are in direct contact with the rich countries, is hardly open to doubt. What needs to be questioned is the implicit assumption that the modern sector can be expanded to absorb virtually the entire population and that this can be done fairly quickly. The ruling philosophy of development over the

1. 'Small is Beautiful' — Economics as if People Mattered by E.F. Schumacher, Harper Colophon Books, New York, 1975, pp. 158-160.

last twenty years has been: 'What is best for the rich must be best for the poor'. This belief has been carried to truly astonishing lengths.

The starting point of all our considerations is poverty, or rather, a degree of poverty which means misery, degrades and stultifies the human person; and our first task is to recognise and understand the boundaries and limitations which this degree of poverty imposes. Again, our crudely materialistic philosophy makes us liable to see only 'the material opportunities' (to use the words of the White Paper which I have already quoted) and to overlook the immaterial factors. Among the causes of poverty, I am sure, the material factors are entirely secondary — such things as a lack of natural wealth, or a lack of capital, or an insufficiency of infrastructure. The primary causes of extreme poverty are immaterial, they lie in certain deficiencies in education, organisation and discipline.

Development does not start with goods: it starts with people, and their education, organisation and discipline. Without these three, all resources remain latent, untapped, potential........"

"It is necessary, therefore, that at least an important part of the development effort should by-pass the big cities and be directly concerned with the creation of an 'agro-industrial structure' in the rural and small town areas."

The economic *swaraj* of Gandhian India finds its echo in SCHUMACHER:

"The new thinking that is required for aid and development will be different from the old because it will take poverty seriously. It will not go on mechanically, saying: 'What is good for the rich must also be good for the poor'. It will care for people — from a severely practical point of view. Why care for people? Because people are the primary and ultimate source of any wealth whatsoever. If they are left out, if they are pushed around by self-styled experts and high-handed planners, then nothing can ever yield real fruit."

The Gandhian ideology of 'socialism' placed great emphasis on the rural masses and the lovely simplicity of village uplift. For him democracy was:

"The art and science of mobilising the entire physical, economic and spiritual resources of all the various sections of the people in the service of the common good of all."[1]

Gram Swaraj was crucial because 'India lives not in a handful of her big cities but in 7,00,000 villages'. G.D.H. Cole[2] commented on Gandhian economic humanism:

---

1. Gandhi — Democracy, Real and Deceptive — Navjivan Publishing House, Ahmedabad.
2. G.D.H. Cole, quoted by Jawaharlal Nehru in The Discovery of India, Meridian Books Ltd., London, 1956, p. 431.

> "Gandhi's campaign for the development of the home made cloth industry — *khaddar* — is no mere fad of a romantic eager to revive the past, but a practical attempt to relieve the poverty and uplift the standard of the Indian villager."

The Gandhian idea meant that the *'Panchayat* will be the legislature, judiciary and executive.........' — village republics knit into a nation, akin, in many respects, to Lenin's *Soviets,* who gave the call 'All powers to the *Soviets'* and involved the common people in administrative, legislative and judicial functions. The Gandhian conviction is Power to the *Panchayats,* for India means *Rural India.* Under *Swaraj,* wrote GANDHI[1]:

> "I am afraid that for years to come India would be engaged in passing legislation in order to raise the downtrodden, the fallen, from the mire into which they have been sunk by the capitalists, the landlords, by the so-called higher classes, and then, subsequently and scientifically, by the British Rulers. If we are to lift these people from the mire, then it would be the bounden duty of the National Government of India, in order to set its house in order continually to give preference to these people and even free them from the burdens under which they are being crushed....
>
> Look at the condition, if you will, of the untouchables, if the law comes to their assistance and sets apart miles of territory. At the present moment, they hold no land; they are absolutely living at the mercy of the so-called higher castes, and also, let me say, at the mercy of the State. They can be removed from one quarter to another without complaint and without being able to seek the assistance of law. Well, the first act of the Legislature will then be to see that, in order somewhat to equalize conditions these people are given grants freely.
>
> From whose pockets are those grants to come? Not from the pockets of Heaven. Heaven is not going to drop money for the sake of the State. They will naturally come from the moneyed classes, including the Europeans.
>
> It will be, therefore, a battle of the 'haves' and 'have nots'; and if that is what is feared, I am afraid that National Government will not be able to come into being if all the classes hold the pistol at the head of the dumb millions and say: 'You shall not have a Government of your own unless you guarantee our possessions and our rights'."

The Planning Commission, in response to the Gandhian focus on the village humane, has spoken of decentralised industries, village panchayats, block development centres, small scale units and land reforms. After all, the quality of our planning will be judged by the manner and degree to which we employ our vast manpower and womanpower.

---

1. Nation's Voice, p. 71 — Socialism of My Conception, pp. 225-226.

The First Five Year Plan states[1]:

> "The question of land ownership is perhaps the most fundamental issue today in national development. It is clear that the manner of its solution will profoundly influence the pattern of economic and social organisation.......... From the social aspect, which is no less important, it should reduce disparities in wealth and income, eliminate exploitation, provide security for tenants and workers and finally, promise equality of status and opportunity........"

I may enter a caveat here. Do our Governments sometimes speak in two voices? Are all the doings of the Administration and the laws of our Legislatures helpful to the weaker or bonus to the big? Only the future sociologist and legal historian can tell.

I should have elaborated on the social and economic perspectives and procedures and the corresponding legal programmes to effectuate the plan but that will outrun my limited subject into territory where I may be a trespasser without title. Even so, the syncromesh system can be illustrated to prove the relevance of my submission. If you want the public sector to occupy commanding heights in the economic area, a crop of legal issues arises. Do you want government to undertake directly or through companies, statutory corporations or boards? Do you desire Parliament to discuss their working and be accountable through Ministers? Should Ministers be allowed to interfere with the operations of these enterprises and, if so, to what extent? Do the employees enjoy the rights of government servants or of commercial undertakings? Are they to be governed by industrial law or of the civil services? Should the institutions be socially enlightened, politically oriented and lay out funds to and promote welfare schemes and goodwill projects, not strictly blinkered by profit motive? What should be the recruitment policy at various levels, autonomy, workers' role and litigative policies? Should they function like public servants with notorious red-tapes? Should they be held liable for negligence by tort law or criminal law with a new code of discipline — and not behave like tiny economic *maharajas?* What legislative models should be constructed for different kinds of agricultural and industrial activity? At present, we are blundering along, not merely in drafting laws but in interpreting and implementing them.

Let us take another slogan so popular at the moment — 'workers' participation in the management of enterprises'. Norway, Sweeden and Switzerland are considering legislative proposals to give effect to this leading idea. Workers' representation is no longer stranger to Continental law, although the various models and the constant changes at which participation affects economic activity are divergent. While some statutes restrict

1. First Five Year Plan. A Draft Outline. The Publications Division, Government of India, 1953, p. 88.

participation to the plant, others extend it to the enterprise or even include national economic policies. The socialist countries have dealt with trade-union representation more effectively, but workers' participation affected collective bargaining and clothed them with voice in the management. The pattern of participation is a matter of public policy decision and then comes the statutory model tailored to the need. In a recent article by Professor S. SIMITTS published in the *Modern Law Review* (January 1975, p. 21) the learned Lecturer sums up[1]:

> "A growing number of laws consider workers' representation as one of the outstanding points of legal reform. Nevertheless terms like 'participation', 'co-determination' and 'workers' representation' are used for concepts which lastly have nothing more in common than the wording. Furthermore in spite of the wide-spread claim for co-determination, no law has upto now clearly defined its aims and consequences. On the contrary, in order to facilitate compromise, preference is given to a sometimes hopeless ambiguity of expression ingeniously concealing the real implications. In fact workers' representation reflects the wish for co-determination in the true sense of the word. Hence, no law introducing participation will ultimately avoid replacing its company law by an enterprise regulation dominated by radically changed decision-making procedures. Co-determination is, however, by no means only a problem of re-organising enterprises. It also affects collective bargaining and strikes. Whoever supports the claim for participation should therefore openly state whether he is willing to accept these consequences and to what extent."

The thrust of my argument is that workers' participation in the management cannot be achieved by political assertions or executive instructions, but regulations, extensive legislative reform, covering even company law. The perspective is political, the process is legal.

Take examples from the social sector. Population control needs a lot of law and not wall posters only. We have some legislation, but need more. Another item from the 20-Point Economic Programme may be apposite. How do you execute a policy of ending bonded labour enslaving tribals? Mere slogans won't do. Mere legislative declarations won't work. Special presumptions, rules of interpretation of documents, mobile machinery for adjudication and even an educative movement to create awareness among the *adivasis* and administration by agencies sensitive to the mission of the legislation *plus* activist legal aid and advice and early finality for disputes may all have to be thought out as legal engineering if the project is not to be an addition to statutory futility and judicial illusion. Our Anti-dowry Law

1. The Third Chorley Lecture, delivered at the London School of Economics on June 26, 1974, on Workers' Participation in the Enterprise — Transcending Company Law.

and Suppression of Immoral Traffic Act are proof of the law failing society, for lack of will and ability.

The pertinence of this divagation in a legal lecture is that our jural order cannot be cocooned and must respond to socio-economic perspectives and solutions in the shape of mini-or-maxi models, public, joint or private sectors, choice between profits and persons — all guided by the conscience of the Constitution. The over-all system of legal control, the role of the judicial process, the local authorities, their autonomy and powers, the overseeing and servicing agencies of enterprises giving up a top-heavy, inhibitive, hierarchical bureaucracy and their functional relevance and kindred problems like judicial review of legislative acts and administrative processes may have to be discussed by sociologists, economists, politicians and jurists. For instance, the co-operative movement, its contributions and socio-economic limitations as well as the fields of operation and need for regulation may demand a total rewritting of the law of co-operation, if the growth of these institutions in plural manifestations, their autonomy, flexibility, initiative and social attitude are to answer modern Indian socialistic expectations. The virtue of juridical control cannot be denigrated as experience has shown. What a scandalous perversion of the co-operative label to promote upper middle class ends goes on today is painfully brought out by some top-dog housing co-operatives and co-operative farm rackets! The law is an abettor! Again, what a hierarchy of officials, choking paper work and baffling regulations and politically motivated super sessions have to be suffered for a co-operative or local body to work — and then the litigative travails! A dynamic new co-operative law or local self-government statute with power and purity, without being cipherised by Government or irritatingly interfered with or paralysed by courts and capable of canalising socio-economic progress is needed, if we mean business. On co-operatives, Nehru gave the call:

> "My outlook is to convulse India with the co-operative movement; or, rather, with co-operation; to make it, broadly speaking, the basic activity in every village as well as elsewhere and finally, indeed, to make the co-operative approach the common thinking of India."

Long ago, as Municipal Chairman, NEHRU resigned from his office, finding the impotence of these institutions! Are there more powers for local bodies now? The lawyer can respond by making legal models with autonomy, flexibility, vigour, wider range of powers, broad built-in control mechanisms and litigative immunity. When the European Economic Community was decided upon, jurists over the continent and the British Isles became busy getting ready to tackle novel problems! We, in India, have more demanding juristic tasks if developmental law is to rise to the requirements of the nation. We cannot tarry.

It is time we harken to LINCOLN: "The dogmas of the quiet past are no longer adequate to the stormy present." Liberty has many dimensions as the tell-tale title of SCOTT NEARING'S book reminds us: *"Freedom: A Promise or Menance?"*

I often wonder whether lawmen — and other professional men—have to read into the lines of the *Gitanjali* a sad introspection:

> "The song that I came to sing remains unsung to this day.
>
> I have spent my days in stringing and in unstringing my instrument.
>
> The time has not come true, the words have not been rightly set; only there is the agony of wishing in my heart."

I have rambled yesterday only to give a sketchy idea of the plenitude of legal jobs aside from litigation, the targets and methods of law even in the fields of politics and economics. These operations and missions cannot be immutable but changing to meet fresh societal challenges. The age of the atom and of outer space has to face problems unknown to *homo sapiens* a century ago. So the continual process of reassessment and up-dating goes on. The law must, accordingly, keep moving, experimenting, adventuring, revising its processes — the whole focus being on society and justice. While the judiciary has a regulatory and beneficial role in programmes of development, both because the immense resources available to the State when distributed as largesse or channelled for production should not degenerate into invidious discrimination or political, corruption and should not be infected with executive arbitrariness or power absolutism, care should be taken to ensure that judicial despotism, out of fondness for dying values, does not inhibit rapid developmental programmes by interference, in season and out of season, ignorantly or unwittingly, in the clumsy name of legalism or as guardian of great rights. It is regrettable, but true, that a few judges, innocent of the social costs and unconscious of the public mischief involved, paralyse public administration and even criminal investigation by odd exercise of judicial power presumably to protect private rights and thereby help bruiting politicians blaspheme the whole judicature. Judicial power is a public trust and perversion by some is ammunition in hostile hands to blast the bastion of human rights. Judges are not above the law and cannot play the blind Goddess and get away with it. Let not some judicial scapegraces make the entire judicature the scapegoat. Never have so few shaken the faith of so many in national justice by random misuse! The episode of F.D. ROOSEVELT and 'the nine old men' comes to mind. In this connection it serves the Judges to remind themselves of the cautionary note struck by the Supreme Court recently in *Krishna Goud*[1]:

> "No power in a republic is irresponsible or irresponsive, the people in the last resort being the repositories and beneficiaries of public power. But two limitations exist in our Constitutional system. The

1. (1976) 1 SCC 157 (160).

Court cannot intervene everywhere as an omniscient, omnipotent or omnipresent being. And when the Constitution, as here, has empowered the nation's highest Executive, excluding, by implication, judicial review, it is officious encroachment, at once procedurally *ultra vires* and upsetting comity of high instrumentalities, for this Court to be a superpower unlimited."

If the social good of 600 millions who have nothing to lose except their tears is the presiding idea of the nation's Constitution, judicial power must be canalised and cannot be injuriously expansionery — *an imperium in imperio,* omnipotent. Nor I venture to suggest, can the slogan of parliamentary supremacy arrogate to itself the throne which belongs to the political nation — the People. Parliament is not the People and even in England, Sir LESLIE SCARMAN and others have pleaded for a bill of rights to protect the People from transient Parliaments. There is a fine distinction between, *pro tempore* authority and eternal verity. Subject to these paramount limitations, Constitutional mutations so as to redeem the tryst made at the Historic Midnight Hour must be undertaken, even if judicial authority, parliamentary processes and the top Executive have to be disciplined into democratic accountability. Power is not monopoly nor popularity but revolutionary responsibility speaking through law-in-action and tested by the good of the mammoth miserables. In this setting, the fundamental rights of a few may be the martyr for the sorrows of the many. We are all aware that Legislatures and Governments have done things for which the rich will be grateful, and the poor feel orphaned. But all institutions of national life are crusaders and the clauses of the Constitution are not stone flowers but an organic cybernetic system of legal directorate of the 60 crore-member Co-operative.

Speaking as a citizen I feel firmly that our Constitution stands in need of re-shaping to serve the nation better, without flirting potentially with its vital flame or beautiful balance. Constitutional provisions such as we have in Articles 31B and 31C are socially justified by national good even though it may imply interdict on judicial interdict. It is jurisprudential 'boloney' that law becomes legitimate only if it is justiciable by the higher courts.

What is the goal of development? I have endeavoured to make out that man is the centre of the Plan and so the good of the People is the object of Justice. Processual Justice becomes the key-stone in the arch of social justice and some thoughts on this topics may be worthwhile. Legal order is but a part of the wider aims of our Constitutional system. It is heartening to listen to the words of SETON POLLOCK[1] in this larger conspectus and the place of law in the humanist process:

---

1. Seton Pollock in his Preface to 'The English Legal Aid System': Its History and Principles — Orient Longmans Ltd., Madras, 1973.

> "The law itself, though of crucial social importance, is only one element in the total human task. That task is to meet and master those frustrations that diminish man in his humanity and obstruct the realisation of his freedom and fulfilment within the human society. Those frustrations stem from ignorance, poverty, pain, disease and conflicts of interest both within the person (the field of psychological medicine) and between persons (the territory of the law). These manifold and interacting frustrations cannot be met by any one discipline but only by a co-ordinated attack upon the problem through enlightened political and administrative initiatives and by educational, medical, psychological and legal remedies."

The learned writer dwells on what I have often described as the integral *Yoga* of Law and Progress. He says:

> "Our concern is with the human condition and the imperative need to improve it through such resources as we can develop. We are beginning to see more clearly the need for a unitary view which is, in essence, spiritual in its character, reaching down to the realities that underlie our fragmented disciplines. The lawyers, the educationalists, the economists, the medical profession, the politicians, and the administrators cannot in isolation from one another resolve the problem we face in our growingly complex world. Yet each is needed. Frustrations do not fall neatly into any one category and present us with problems which can often not be solved by any one of these several disciplines.
>
> The burning issue of our times is how our resources can be developed and combined to achieve the fulfilment of the human task and the improvement of the human condition."

Fundamental goals demand fundamental systemic alterations and the system of justice is no exception.

Reform of the administration of justice is a giant and multiform undertaking especially for a nation whose indigenous justice system and jurisprudence from Kautilya and Manu was noble and community-conscious but was supplanted by exotic elitism and whose people were benignly neglected by the sophisticated fair procedures, codified but cute rules of evidence, multi-decked appeals upon appeals and unlimited jurisdiction of a court system started by an English Trading Company. At its best, the whole legal system was based on individualistic liberalism and freedom for industrial and peasant exploitation, while the Indian genius and golden geo-historical ancestry had a society — oriented system of law and justice. The consequences of the 'inestimable benefits' of Empire mandates dies hard and we passionately cling to them in many departments. Sir HENRY MAINE and JOHN MACAULAY are fresh even today. MAINE observed:

"The higher courts, while they openly borrowed the English rules from the recognised English authorities, constantly used language which implied that they believed themselves to be taking them from some abstract body of legal principle which lay behind all law and the inferior judges, when they were applying some half-remembered legal rule learnt in boyhood or culling a proposition of law from a half-understood English textbook, no doubt honestly thought in many cases that they were following the rule prescribed for them, to decide 'by equity and good conscience' wherever no native law or usage was discoverable."

MACAULAY noted:

"What is administered is not law but a kind of rule and capricious equity. I asked an able and excellent judge lately returned from India how one of our *zilla* courts would decide several legal questions of great importance — questions not involving consideration of religion or caste — mere questions of commercial law. He told me that it was a mere lottery."

In *Ratan Lal*[1] the Supreme Court has referred to the persistence of this weakness in our system:

"In India and in other colonies during the Imperial era a tacit assumption had persuaded the courts to embrace English Law (the civilizing mission of the masters) as justice, equity and good conscience. Throughout the Empire, in Asia and Africa, there was an inarticulate premise that English Law was a blessing for the subject peoples."

Cannot Free India's jurists boldly commission themselves for 'Operation Juridical Revision' by socio-legal evolution of new norms of administrative law and organs of justice?

The Little Rustic and the Legal Process:

In practice, there is unequal justice under the law, perplexing, protracted legalistics and fear of pyramidical court-justice and, worse, of administrative tribunals and their anfractuosities. Litigation is, by itself, a high-priced, disenchanting spiral. The courts are located in towns and cities while the disputants live in villages. Law and the People are distant neighbours. When the history of Free India comes to be written, the judicial system can claim some place only if we agree to re-write rural justice, simple law and speedy *finis* to the *lis* and popular involvement in the whole process. The small man is not worried about the complex probative rules, nice procedural wrangles and the finer nuances of law, but plain, commonsense justice fairly and promptly given. And, when caught in the spider's web of the law, the poor man should, sounding an Indian Gideon's trumpet, be eligible for free legal

1. *Rattan Lal* v. *Vardesh Chander* (C.A. 1297/75) decided on 9-12-1975.

aid and advice. Thus, in terms of priorities, we must have a re-orientation and re-structuring of the whole legal system and useful techniques and new training — with accent both on Law and Development and Law and Poverty, the humanist-jurist being the organiser and 'We, the People' the beneficiary. Such is the first lesson in the grammar of social justice through the judicial process. Is not the time set true for Indian Law to ask itself, with spiritual concern, self-search for identity and some regret: 'Who am I?' and re-write the legal scriptures, re-design the judicial engine and re-devise jural mechanics which will endow it with the *yuga dharma* of the new equity? We need creative *maharishis* of jurisprudence, not Harvard-Yale-Oxford-Cambridge Holinesses and Templars, to feel and fashion the forward course. The core issue is: Do we accept this Project Law India? If we do, as surely we must, a non-aligned system, not loaded with imported legal wares from the two blocs, has to be inaugurated. In the report on Legal Aid earlier mentioned by me, the Committee cautioned:

> "The lawlessness of the old law, judged by the new *dharma*, can be corrected either by radical reform or by surrender to direct action. The choice is obvious and the hour is late."

Shri Justice Bhagwati referred, in a recent speech, to the barefooted lawyer. The Prime Minister told a Scientists' Meet that technology must travel to rural areas and the Central Committee on Legal Aid, ratiocinated about Law and the Weaker sections of the Community:

> "India lives in her villages which are notoriously underdeveloped. Laws for the uplift of the villagers, protection got from the courts and competent legal advice which gives confidence, wither away in the rural soil. Feudal victimisation, social abuses and denial of the legal process through local tyranny are realities, of the country-side. Even as there are rural extension centres for agriculture, education, etc., block level legal extension services may carry the hope and light of the rule of law to our mofussil areas. Problems of illiterate women will be taken to the legal extension officer by *gram sevikas,* land disputes between adjacent ryots by agricultural extension officers, caste factions, family quarrels and public legal issues by block development officers, or panchayat members. Legal advice by disinterested lawyers employed by Legal Aid Centres may prevent litigation, local fights, family discords and worse evils. Legal guidance will help poor villagers who cannot go to towns and buy legal opinion at high cost. Where drafting has to be done or forms have to be filled in with legal skill, before proceedings can be started or administrative benefits, secured, the centre can be of service."

We must spread out legal service into blocks of villages, reach them and redress wrongs. The Government Gazette which publishes the laws or the journals which report cases and the urban and metropolitan court-bar complex just won't do. The journey of legal justice to the gram panchayats is a must if the rule of law is to communicate with the people. Thousands of lawyers, with a bias for the poor, must be organised to form mobile units, hold village-level meetings, explain welfare legislation, offer on the spot service, settle simple disputes and infuse a new faith in the political rustic.

I pick out land law for special mention because it is the most noisy and critical item on the political agenda and the most significant means to economic and social revolution for India and yet the Achilles' heel of the Executive. The Supreme Court had occasion to observe recently about its poor enforcement in our country in *Sampuran Singh*[1]:

> "A semi-medieval set-up where considerable estates are cornered by a landed gentry, will naturally resist re-distributive reform measures and try ingenious methodology to defeat the law. But the Legislature has to be astute enough to outwit such devious devices and subtle subterfuges. With this end in view, the Act has been amended to block all escape routes unearthed by the law-makers as often as the High Court has upheld certain patterns of alienations and oblique dealings by interpretative process. A study of the history of the Act and the provocation for and frequency of amendments thereto, suggests an unspoken criticism about judicial approach which we will refer to later. Suffice it to say that the law we are construing is a radical agrarian measure: its basic goals are to cut down large holdings and distribute lands to various landless people according to a design and to foster, according to legislative policy, an agrarian community of peasant proprietors."

Earlier, in *Amar Singh*[2] the Court said:

> "It was stated at the Bar that a score of years notwithstanding, the processes of fixing reserved areas and surplus areas on the strength of which alone conferment of proprietory right on tenants and re-settlement of ejected tenants could proceed, are still lingering. If this is true, Government has much to answer for and litigation abounds where delays in executive enforcement occur. We except that this land reform measure will not be a slow motion picture but a strict and swift procedure so that parties affected may know where they stand. There is an 'executive' dimension to law's delays which defeats the rule of law. It must be remembered that the third reading of a bill and the last appeal in Court are not the final scene in the drama of law and society. A post-audit on the enforcement of social legislation, all social scientists will agree, is a material aspect of law-inaction, *inter alia* to avoid the administrative cutting edge of the law becoming blunt."

---

1. (1975) 2 SCC 810 (812).
2. (1974) 2 SCC 70 (93).

The land reform law gets reformed in the process of implementation and rural lawyer-crusaders become law-reform lobbyists with local experience, seeing vividly the contradiction between law in the book and law in action — and, sometimes, seeing through the radical-tongued politician who 'casts stones' at the judiciary which is these days more sinned against than sinning. We need developmental dialectic and a new channelling of professional energies along rural regeneration programmes, with legal caretakers. The money spent on the land reform lawyers will be well-spent — a revolutionary use of the Indian rupee for the Indian village. Its effects are social, economic and developmental — a movement of the villagers out of medieval miasma. Flores wrote about Bolivia[1]:

> "My idea of land reform is that it is deep surgery. I don't mean the bloodshed or violence, but I mean that you are going to shift the whole basis of society, and this is a painful, overwhelming operation."

What I have said about land reform law is illustrative. The working class, especially the unorganised sector and, among them, women, live not by law but by luck, for, statutory promises notwithstanding, they have no rights, no remedies, no lawyer, no court! They have to be imparted militant legal literacy. The *harijan,* one-fifth of Indian humanity, is in an equally hapless plight. Platitudinous legal sympathy has reached a point of no return. To wipe every tear from every eye, the law must go to the eye and not compel the weeper to reach the urban-based lawyer and judge. The simple issue is, 'how does the villager know what and where the law is and the wherewithal to enjoy it?' It is unpleasant to remind ourselves about what an English judge is said to have remarked, *viz.*—

> "......everybody is presumed to know the law except His Majesty's Judges who have a Court of Appeal set over them to put them right."

JACKSON, in his *'Machinery of Justice in England"* wrote:

> "Many appeals are due to uncertainty in the law. The settling of some rules of common law, and the interpretation of some statutes, has cost litigants vast fortunes. Whenever a new trial or an appeal is due to error of judge or uncertainty in the law, the litigant who suffers should not have to bear the cost."

And, I am sure, no Indian lawyer agrees with the barbed words of Lord MANSFIELD:

> "It would be very hard upon the profession if the law was so certain that everybody knew it."

My plea is that justice must become a consumer's market and lawyers have a special responsibility, on a paid, professional, but public obligation basis, to educate, advise, aid, mediate, settle and, if need be, litigate in court

1. Flores et al, Land Reform in Bolivia — The Process of Lan Reform in Bolivia — Wisconsin Land Tenure Center Discussion Paper, No. 2, 1963 — 1965, 50 Iowa LR 530-531.

and, with inventive imagination, propose changes to the system. The inventory of reform is long, but a few may be itemised. Village-level justice and small claims tribunals; welfare programmes, and legal campaigns to popularise, implement and audit their performance; the involvement of the people in the judicial process socio-legal research and data-processing and feed back; instrumentalities which will mediate between the court and the legislature for law reforms and effectiveness. Many more come to the mind but to be exhaustive is to attempt the impossible.

I will discuss some of these ideas haphazardly, leaving it to later occasions and better men to do the job with thoroughness and freshness.

My first emphasis is on settlement of disputes and involvement of villagers in the legal process. Here we may remember Lenin, Lincoln and Gandhiji. Abraham Lincoln advised lawyers:

> "Discourage litigation, persuade your neighbours to compromise whenever you can, point out to them how the nominal winner is often the real loser — in fees, expense and waste of time."

GANDHIJI writes in his *Autobiography:*

> "I realised that the true function of a lawyer was to unite parties driven asunder. The lesson was so indelibly burnt into me that a large part of my time during the twenty years of my practice as a lawyer was occupied in bringing about private compromises of hundreds of cases. I lost nothing, thereby — not even money, certainly not my soul."

In the *Harijan,* he wrote a little before his end:

> "It is the function of the *Panchayats* to teach the villagers to avoid disputes, if they have to settle them. That would ensure speedy justice without any expenditure."

The role of the rural lawyer is interwoven with the judicial process, reconsidered in the light of the functional school of law. After all, the purchasing power of law over community loyalty varies in proportion to its social justice content. Classically, Justice is invariably portrayed as a blind Goddess, but in the dispute-settlement function courts should not be passive, but creative. This takes us on to institutional changes affecting the capabilities and *modus operandi* of courts and lawyers in the delivery system of justice. Obviously, a subject of such wide range cannot be dealt with more than sketchily in the tapering part of a lecture.

India is poor and leaving aside for the moment big litigation where big interests are involved, the crowd of dockets concerns small claims and the humble rustics, the weaker sections and socio-economic legislation affecting their welfare. Professor BAXI writes[1]:

---

1. ICSSR programscrift by Prof. Upendra Baxi, referred to in Part I of Lecture.

> "Who makes what claims? It should be recalled here that the Fourteenth Report of the Law Commission (1954: 17) estimated that nearly 80% of civil suits instituted in 1954 involved claims of Rs. 500 or less. The corresponding 1964 position is that such suits represent nearly 73% of the workload of civil court system. Obviously, studies of recourse pattern, and workload, of small causes courts are of as much importance as those of the Supreme Court of India."

Many civil and criminal actions and reliefs under other laws or against administrative actions never surface up, snowed down by chill penury.

The compulsion of these circumstances is that a radically different non-judicialised forum for conciliation and adjudication, involving little cost and delay should be devised with procedures informal, natural justice broadly complied with and pre-trial settlement given predominance. Indeed, the *Bhagwati Report* on Legal Aid in Gujarat has this pertinent observation to make:

> "The poor who constitute the vast majority of the people of India are concerned in cases of litigation primarily and almost exclusively with the lower courts. They cannot dream of going to the higher courts because of the nature of their claims or disputes as also because of forbidding cost of appeal. Their contact is, in the circumstances, limited only to the lower courts even on those rare occasions on which they can gather sufficient means and courage to engage in litigation or they are compulsorily brought before the courts by their opponents. If, therefore, we really want to help the poor, it is time we cure ourselves of the occupational diseases and devote more thought and attention to the lower courts and bring their organisation and working under rational and scientific analysis. It is in this context that the question of setting up of *Nyaya Panchayats* as the lowest courts easily accessible to the rural population and providing cheap and expeditious justice to them in small cases arising out of their daily lives, requires to be seriously considered."

The then Central Law Minister, Shri ASOKE SEN, stated in Parliament in 1959:

> "There is no doubt that the system of justice which obtains today is too expensive for the common man. The small disputes must necessarily be left to be decided by a system of *Panchayat justice* — call it the people's court, call it the popular court, call it anything — but it would certainly be subject to such safeguards as we may devise — the only means by which for ordinary disputes in the village level the common man can be assured of a system of judicial administration which would not be too expensive for him and which would not be too dilatory for him."

The Study Team appointed by the Central Government to consider *Panchayati* justice observed:

> "The process of democratic decentralisation envisaged by Article 40 of the Constitution and already ushered in, to some extent, has resulted in the general awakening of the people in the village.........*Nyaya Panchayats,* wherever, they are in existence, are serving a real felt need of the village by disposing of cases more expeditiously and with minimum of incovenience and expense to parties........To avoid the baneful effluse of factions, unhealthy rivalries, a *Nyaya Panchayat* may be set up for a group of villages and the grouping may be made having regard to factors like area, population, contiguity, compactness, means of communication, etc."

Of course, complaints about factions in villages are snobbishly exaggerated against *Panchayat Adalats* being given larger powers, an argument which can be used with greater force against party governments and the top executives being given the *de facto* power to appoint the top echelons of the judiciary. We cannot be scared away from the faith in the people by the bogey of local factionalism. On the other hand, true democracy, Gandhian style puts trust in the villagers and insists on decentralisation of powers, including the judicial. We may round off this part of the discussion with the words of LENIN:

> "Every representative of the masses, every citizen, must be placed in conditions which would enable him to participate in the discussion of the State laws, in the election of his representatives and in putting the State laws into practice.
>
> The court is an instrumentality to attract every individual member of the poorest classes to State administration."*

To sum up, let us skim off little litigation, civil and criminal, from urban professional courts and vest *wide powers* in rural tribunals over civil, revenue, land reform and criminal litigation. If need, be and itinerant legal adviser (like the Judge-Advocate for Military courts) plus para-legal training for village cadres will tone up their efficiency. Most minor statutes can be enforced through these local *adalats* and larger jurisdiction vested. Whatever initial shortcomings may be noticed, the pathology can be cured by therapeutic measures and safeguards. We should not cipherise these mini-judges by providing a hierarchical machinery of judicial review. The elective principle, at that level, is nothing strange to Americans or the Soviets and justices of the peace are lay judges, after all. It is a sobering thought that the Supreme Court is, final not because it is infallible. It is infallible because it is final — and occasionally reverses itself here as in America.

Those who point out that even now people's *adalats* exist must realise that wider powers and range of jurisdiction including the power to execute

---

* Quoted by the Study Team on *Panchayat Justice.*

the orders and decrees and convictions must vest in them, with the necessary infra-structure. The over-all social gains will be great, if *Nyaya Panchayats* become popular.

A welfare State which turns out a stream of beneficient statutes, blessing them with measures too baffling for the lay poor and too rarely implemented by government officials, makes rural lawyers' services indispensable. In this setting, we may highlight the importance of taking legal literacy to the village and the slum, to the factory and the indebted peasantry, to the agricultural worker and the bonded labourer — crucial items on the 20-point economic agenda currently kindling the hopes of the nation's weaker sections. Most of the points so put in sharp focus by the Central leadership need supportive law and lawyer mechanism for better translation in action.

Agricultural labour, mostly *harijan,* is untouched by law, whatever the legislatures may claim. A leading daily in an editorial, wrote around three years ago:

> "Unlike their better organised and more articulate counter-parts in industry and white-collar occupations, sharecroppers and landless labourers are for the most part unprotected by laws relating to conditions of work and wages. In addition the weight of tradition and custom is enormous in the country-side and it is always operates to the advantage of the rich and more influential who, in addition, have access to superior legal resources. Most of the contractual relations are broken with impunity by the landlords and employers of agricultural labour. Recourse to litigation is not only limited for the poor because of its expense but also because of the labyrinthine pocedures that daunt most of them. If any amongst them is foolhardy enough to get entangled in them, he emerges from it, if at all, a much battered man."

It is common knowledge that industrial law, apart from its other defects, takes so long for finality in adjudication that even the patience of a saint will be exhausted:

> "The conciliation procedures, the labour courts, and the industrial tribunals require overhaul and renovation as recommended by the National Commission on Labour. Labour laws, imperfections apart, are dubious boons today at the level of implementation because of long, unequal and exhausting litigation, biased jurisprudence, erroneous judicial orientation and the gamble of legal justice. Disenchanted unions prefer struggle tactics to laws' distant benefits. Prevention of litigation and promotion of settlements or rapid resolution of disputes, are part of a fair-legal deal to workers. Irresponsible expenditure by managements in labour litigation has to be inhibited; unions, like employers, must have the use of the industry's resources in industrial litigation when litigation is unavoidable. Legal assistance at State expense for workers and

> dependents in proceedings under other labour welfare statutes is a 'must'".

Says the Central Committee on Legal Aid. It is a pity that the public sector set up with hopes of being a model employer, often plays the reverse role in its relations with workers and in litigation. Judicial experience prompts harsher expression, but moderation has more effect.

I have already adverted to the horrendous conditions of the untouchables and unapproachables to whom the judicial and, even administrative, institutions still remain untouchable and unapproachable. The 18th Report of the Commissioner of Scheduled Castes and Scheduled Tribes contains a mournful observation:

> ".........The mere act of granting constitutional relief to the land-hungry and deprived people is not enough. What is more important is education and organisation of the peasantry in their rights and duties and *assistance to them to assert their rights by constitutional means........*"

I have no doubt that there must also be a radical re-orientation of the legal personnel if success is to attend the legislative programmes calculated to benefit the backward and the poor. The 20-point economic programme, item by item, can be demonstrated to be in compulsory need of companion law which moves into the grievance area. The lawyer-judge personnel must have in-service training and sympathy with the statutory ethos, apart from activism in economic uplift. Orientation and specialisation for the officers, judicial and other, are necessary, if their mentality is to be aligned with the legislation they seek to enforce. I have had occasion to be critical about our complicated procedures. Could we not simplify them at least regarding poverty law and give them an informal touch, consistent with natural justice? Could we not change our Evidence Act considerably, so that formalised witness-examinations and waste of judicial time without adequate reward in the discovery of truth can be avoided and inexpensive, natural and commonsense substitutes found? I do not see any serious objection for mobile or circuit courts, at least for trying smaller cases, civil and criminal, in the locale. The Evening Courts in the American cities and the peripatetic courts even in some of our cities, for SPCA offences, traffic offences, railway cases and the like are small beginnings. Eve-teasing offences and street brawls in cities may be checked if there are quick procedures, informal evidence, ambulatory courts and instant decisions.

Indeed, in our poor country summary trials will go a long way in reducing delay and expense, provided the judge is careful to do justice. Conciliation procedures and pre-trial settlements have been neglected in our country. Many categories of litigation, especially family disputes, lend themselves to mediation, reconciliation and *in camera* trials. The Law Commission has hopefully recommended moderate changes in this behalf.

What is important to know is that all over the world a new awareness about institutionalising settlement procedures, popular, involvement and informal adjudications is manifest. I am excerpting from an article in the *'Judicature'* bearing on Conciliation and Arbitration in the native village and the urban ghetto in Alaska and Philadelphia. Not that what is good for them is good for us, but the justice system has faced logistical challenges out there and village councils have successfully experimented with processes of conciliation outside the State court system:

> "In 1970, spurred by the vigorous advocacy of reforms in rural justice by the late Chief Justice GEORGE BONEY, academicians, legal professions, and native representatives met in the State's First Conference addressed to the problem of bush justice. The conference resolved that 'the locale of decision making in the administration of justice in village Alaska must move closer to the village. To achieve this result there must be greater native participation at all levels in the administration of justice', and, further, that there must be greater access to legal services and the process of justice in Village Alaska".

In Philadelphia, a modified version of village conciliators and arbitrators has been tried for local law enforcement. The essence of the matter is how could the legal system broaden its access to local residents and allow the locus of decision-making in the administration of justice to be retained in the village. Efficient service to the people where they reside is the touchstone of any administration, including the administration of justice. Tested by this standard, developmental law, family law, essential commodities law, land reform law, *adivasi* rehabilitation law, elimination of local tensions and avoidance of the breakdown of the justice-system, consumerism etc., point in the one direction — decentralised justice and people's participation. Man is an ingenious; social animal. The Indian man must experiment with radical revision of traditional lawyer's law and judicialised justice.

The procedural codes we have are good, but of ancient vintage. The Supreme Court has drawn the country's attention to the case for a revision of processual provisions to rise to current Indian requirements, which I will refer to little later.

It is no slur on our legal system to call for re-appraisal of its efficiency and malformation. It is no reflection on the judges to investigate the performance of the whole process, adopting new parameters of social justice, judicial logistics and participatory element for the people at some levels. Surely, the Central Law Commission softly spoke in its 58th Report on the Structure and Jurisdiction of the Higher Judiciary when it observed:

> "...........all sensitive Judges and lawyers have been feeling an increasing concern about the problem of growing arrears in the administration of justice. Delay made in the decision of cases at all stages inevitably leads to accumulation of arrears and these arrears

have now assumed a somewhat alarming dimension. In fact, the problem of growing arrears has received the attention of several committees appointed from time to time......... There is gross delay in the disposal of pending files, leading to serious dissatisfaction in the public mind about the effectiveness of court process for ventilating the grievances of citizens.

Having studied this problem in depth, the Commission proposes to make certain radical recommendations to the Union Government in the belief that, if the said recommendations are implemented, the problem of delay may be solved at least to some extent.

In attacking the problem of delay in judicial administration which inevitably leads to the accumulation of arrears, two factors have to be considered. The first factor is human. Judicial process must be constantly conscious of its obligation to the community to render judicial verdicts at whatever stages the proceedings may be pending, without delay..........

The other factor is procedural. It involves the consideration, *inter alia*, of the propriety and necessity of several appeals and revisions which are at present contemplated in litigation which takes different forms and falls in different categories."

It is not for me to comment on the recommendations of such an eminent body, but two fundamental factors need emphasis. The court process, with its artificial rules, escalating appeals and many mystiques is sometimes a nightmare, not a sanctuary. Secondly, readiness to reform the judicial system and its functional methodology is sense and science. FRANKFURTER has noted:

"..... framers of judiciary Act are not required to be seers, and great judiciary Acts, unlike great poems, are not written for all times."

We need not be scared even if reform of the justice-system demands Constitutional changes. After all, the Constitution and the laws are for man and not the reverse and the good of our generation may justify transmutation, although monkeying and donkeying with great documents is a game history will not forgive and our national leadership will, in its wisdom, avoid. Our founding faith is justice to the people and that is the touchstone too for amendatory programmes. Three special areas stand out boldly in this context. Industrial law, taxation law and service disputes are not for generalists but for specialists. They brook no slow-motion judicial exercise and time is of the essence of justice. Today, the procedural law in these areas is baffling, prolonged and, expertise-wise, unsatisfactory. Therefore, the regular court-system being kept out of these fields is a recognition of the special skills needed by the subject-matter— not no confidence in courts. It is a superstition to fancy that the robes are the mantle of omniscience and it is realism to accept the judicial institution as arcane and archaic in some aspects. Nevertheless, the judge is a specialist in some sense. He has cultivated a bias against bias, refuses to be swayed by sensationalism, practises objectivity and has no direct interest in the dispute. These professional graces are essential to a refined adjudicatory ethos. So, may be, it is worth considering whether composite tribunals with experts in the field but presided over by serving judges should not prove more satisfactory as the apex level, provided the choice of personnel is done without politicking and with an eye on integrity and social philosophy. In *Carew & Co.*[1], in a separate opinion, I indicated:

> "While judicial review, at least on processual issues, is the hallmark of fair dealing with rights of persons in a republic, there are expanding areas of economic and technological codes where the adjudicator has to tread warily and pause circumspectly, especially because the expertise needed to unlock the statute is oridinarily unavailable to the judicial process and the subject-matter is too sensitive and fundamental for the uninstructed in the special field to handle with confidence.........It is well-known that back-door techniques, and corporate conspiracies in the economic sense but with innocent legal veneer, have been used by oligopolistic organisations and mere juridical verbalism cannot give the Court the clue unless there is insightful understanding of the subject, which, in specialised fields like industrial economics is beyond the normal ken or investigation of the Court or the area of traditional jurisprudence."

The Law Commission of India, in its 58th Report, has collected the data, discussed the pros and cons and avoided daring adventures.

I need hardly say that the decision of a body, with a High Court Judge or a Supreme Court Judge presiding, should be invulnerable to attack under Article 226. Otherwise, the whole object of the change will be stultified.

Another suggestion worth considering is whether Article 136 should suffer the same jurisdictional limitations of Article 133 or not. You tell the High Court today not to certify a case as fit for appeal to the Supreme Court save where the question is of general public importance which needs to be decided by the Supreme Court of India and stultify this restraint by writing into Article 136 an uninhibited omnipotence for granting special leave. This is a tentative point for full discussion. I have no settled view. The Supreme Court must ordinarily be reserved for supreme legal issues and not to bait every defeated litigant into bankrupting himself and opponent. Of course, the State has set a bad example by going in for indiscriminate litigation upto the Supreme Court. The Supreme Court criticised this aspect — but the vice persists. In *Dilbagh Rai*[2] the Court said:

> "In this country the State is the largest litigant to-day and the huge expenditure involved makes a big draft on the public exchequer. In the

1. (1975) 2 SCC 791 (804).
2. (1974) 3 SCC 554 (561).

context of expanding dimensions of State activity and responsibility, is it unfair to expect, finer sense and sensibility in its litigation policy, the absence of which, in the present case, has led the Railway callously and cantankerously to resist an action by its own employee a small man, by urging a mere technical plea which has been pursued right upto the summit Court here and has been negatived in the judgment just pronounced? Instances of this type are legion as is evidenced by the fact that the Law Commission of India in a recent report (Law Commission of India, 54th Report — Civil Procedure Code) on amendments to the Civil Procedure Code has suggested the deletion of section 80, finding that wholesome provision hardly ever utilised by Government, and has gone further to provide a special procedure for Government litigation to highlight the need for an activist policy of just settlement of claims where the State is a party. It is not right for a welfare State like ours to be Janus-faced and while formulating the humanist project of legal aid to the poor, contest the claims of poor employees under its pleading limitation and the like."

Earlier, the Kerala High Court had laid down in similar lines[1]:

> "....it must be remembered that the State is no ordinary party trying to win a case against one of its own citizens by hook or crook for the State's interest is to meet honest claims, vindicate a substantial defence and never to score a technical point or overreach a weaker party to avoid a just liability or secure an unfair advantage, simply because legal devices provide such an opportunity. The State is a virtuous litigant and looks with' unconcern on immoral forensic success so that if on the merits the case is weak, government shows a willingness to settle the dispute regardless of prestige and other lesser motivations which move private parties to fight in court. The lay-out on litigation costs and executive time by the State and its agencies is so staggering these days because of the large amount of litigation in which it is involved that a positive and wholesome policy of cutting back on the volume of law suits by the twin methods of not being tempted into forensic show downs where a reasonable adjustment is feasible and ever offering to extinguish a pending proceeding on just terms, giving the legal mentors of government some initiative and authority in this behalf.........."

The colour and rhythm of the legal system must be correlated to the raw Indian social condition. CARDOZO's insight aptly applies to us too:

> "The social interest served by symmetry or certainty must then be balanced against the social interest served by equity, fairness or other elements of social welfare."

1. (1971) Ker LJ 723.

"..... the great generalities of the Constitution have a content and significance that vary from age to age."

Once we have consensus on this sensitive subject of Law and Social Change, DEAN POUND leads kindly light:

> "Indeed fundamental changes have been taking place in our legal system almost unnoticed and a shifting was in progress in our case law from the individualistic justice of the 19th century which was passed so significantly in the name of legal justice, to the social justice of today even before the change in our legislative policy became so marked."

My learned colleague Shri Justice FAZAL ALI, in an address to the Judiciary, said the same tone[1]:

> "Let judicial thought be not a dead letter or an engine of oppression to the people but it should serve as an instrument of changing law and custom inherent in the society."

There is strength in the submission that our civil procedure and criminal procedure remain cumbersome, the administrative tribunals are sometimes running amok and there is need for a resurgent administrative law. Many more items on the inventory of urgent legal change may be reeled off, but governments are too static to respond. For example, the 47th Report of the Law Commission of India (1972) on the Trial and Punishment of Social and Economic Offences, observed:

> "At the end of the enquiry we felt that time has now arrived when Government should take suitable steps to study in depth the important question of evolving one common code dealing comprehensively in one place with all social and economic offences. We venture to think that it would be useful to make a similar study in regard to different tax laws. As our report indicates, we have evolved a rule of evidence pertaining to the shifting of onus in respect of socio-economic offences, but have refrained from recommending that the said rule should be applied to the tax laws on the ground that the tax laws are far too complex and complicated and lack stability. We feel that it is necessary that a study in depth of the tax laws should be made with a view to codify all the laws in one common code which would be simple, clear and stable. These questions, however, fall outside the purview of our enquiry. Nevertheless, we thought it was our duty to invite the attention of the Government to them." (para. 3.35).

Lost words after 4 years! Resurrection is a hopeful feeling in the current wave of awareness of need for change.

---

1. Inaugural address at the Seminar sponsored by the Jammu & Kashmir Judicial Officers' Training Institute, June 14, 1975.

I merely mention two more items and I am done. The rules of statutory construction we use in the post-Silver Jubilee era of Independence are the repertorie of canons of pre-Victorian English vintage! There is so much weightage for the vested interests, presumptions in favour of the past, sound proofing of the system from legislative and public debates, that even England of today and America are wondering whether this 'old wine' is any good. Our own judges, in lectures and seminars, have espoused the need for new canons of statutory construction. Each law has body and soul, the letter and the reason of the law. Indians regard the soul as governing the body. We must have a new Act for Interpretation of Statutes, updated and sensible. Fettered by precedents, largely based on English Common Law, we are stagnating. We are in new, free generation, with very radical goals. Blind adherence to old precedents when circumstances have changed and 'the needs of the community are vastly different' can do a considerable amount of harm. 'When a precedent has outlived its usefulness, it is better to say so and the community will have the benefit of a clear-cut change in principle, of a decision based on modern requirements or based on sounder logic'. In a period of rapid social, political and economic change in which our country is consciously planning development, in a context where substantial rational law making is better than legalisms, the law of precedents requires a second look so that socially conscious jurisprudence may not be stalled. Likewise, time-consuming arguments and trials must be cut short if judicial time is to be maximised for judicial work. Way back in 1957 one of the subjects seriously mooted at the All-India Law Ministers' Conference was to reduce the hours of argument but substitute that with carefully prepared briefs. It is doubtful if any country in the world allows so much time for trial of witnesses or oral arguments as India does. It is apt to repeat the words of Judge BRIAN MCKENNA:

> "The fault is that the rules of our procedure which by their discouragement of written argument make possible extensively protracted hearings in open court. Those responsible might think more of changing them. In civil cases a written argument supplemented by a short oral discussion, would sometimes save a great deal of time."

Another spinal weakness of our system is the proliferation of litigation on account of the absence of mechanism to bring the courts and the legislatures together. Whenever difficulties are noticed in a law during forensic debate, the simplest thing to avoid complications is to amend the law. New experiments are the sign of life and law reform in this direction is good to improve the system of legality. Lord Chancellor WESTBURY long ago said:

> "The first thing, then, that strikes every member of our profession who directs his mind beyond the daily practical necessity of the cases which come before him is, that we have no machinery for noting, arranging, generalising and deducing conclusions from the

observations which every scientific mind could naturally make on the way in which the law is worked in the country..........Why is there not a body of men in this country whose duty it is to collect a body of judicial statistics, or, in more common phrase, make the necessary experiments to see how far the law is fitted to the exigencies of society, the necessities of the times, the growth of wealth and the progress of mankind?"

Way back in 1921, BENJAMIN N. CARDOZO addressed the Association of the Bar of the City of New York and proposed an agency to mediate between the courts and the legislature. In characteristically beautiful prose he said:

"The Courts are not helped as they could and ought to be in the adaptation of law to justice. The reason they are not helped is because there is no one whose business it is to give warning that help is needed.........We must have a courier who will carry the tidings of distress...........Today courts and legislature work in separation and aloofness. The penalty is paid both in the wasted effort of production and in the lowered quality of the product. On the one side, the judges, left to fight against anachronism and injustice by the methods of judge-made law, are distracted by the conflicting promptings of justice and logic, of consistency and mercy, and the output of their labors bears the tokens of the strain. On the other side, the legislature, informed only casually and intermittently of the needs and problems of the courts, without expert or responsible or disinterested or systematic advice as to the workings of one rule or another, patches the fabric here and there, and mars often when it would mend. Legislature and courts move on in proud and silent isolation. Some agency must be found to mediate between them."

Another procedural problem to make our system viable has been indicated by jurists and even by the Supreme Court in more than one case.

In *Dhabolkar*[1] one of us explained the conceptual basis of 'person aggrieved' and, after a review of the legal literature, British and American, referred to the element of *actio popularis*, public interest litigation, class actions etc., and concluded that in a developing country like ours this pattern of public oriented litigation better fulfils the rule of law if it is to run close to the rule of life. Again in *Newabganj Sugar Mills*[2] the Court ruled:

"In this justice situation conventional procedures of each small claimant being left to litigate for his little sum from the miller or wholesaler is to write off the remedy and allow the illgotten wealth to be in the coffers of the wrongdoer (who got the charter to charge high from a court order). Nor is the seemingly sweet suggestion, that a representative action under Order 1, rule 8, C.P.C., be instituted on

1. (1976) 1 SC R 306.
2. (1976) 1 SCC 120 (122).

behalf of the class of consumers, feasible. Who is to start? Against whom? How is he to meet the huge litigative costs and how long (O Lord, how long!) is he to wait with long-drawn-out trial procedures, appeal, second appeal, special appeal, and Supreme Court appeal? For, on the other side is the miller with the millions to be coughed up!

The handling of small claims is probably the most deplorable feature of the administration of civil justice and yet small claims are in many respects more significant than large ones, involving large numbers and inter-class disputes. If the confidence of the community in the justice-system, especially consumer protection, is to be created, radical reform of the processual law is needed now and here."

The point that emerges is that when a large number of people are involved and the claim of each is small, class-actions are a sovereign remedy, speaking processually.

Judicial inventiveness, amendment of the relevant Civil and Criminal Codes and encouragement of consumerism and test litigation are important areas for innovation. Victims of crimes need protection in court, and a host of other simplifying measures are implied in Processual Justice to the People. This part of my plea for reform is best concluded by quoting from — *The Statesman Limited*[1]:

"There is a tragic touch in processual protraction as this little *lis* lasting a whole decade pathetically illustrates. Such lingering legal machinery is by passed by both sides in practice largely because, by sheer slow-motion, it denies relief when needed and drives parties to seek remedies by direct action or political intervention. What elegant *alibi* can there be for the routine charter of demands put forward in the middle of 1966, ripening into an industrial reference in November 1966 after a flare-up of illegal strike and failure of conciliation, taking around 3 years for rendering a short award and a little over 5 years for reviewing it in this Court? Law-makers, whose vocal concern for industrial peace and constitutional promises for the working class is being put to the test by failure in the field, will, we hope, alert themselves. Labour litigation can be a curse or dread where one side is weak, as here, and has not been able to hire legal services but has been made good by *amicus curiae* and the other side, regardless of cost, is anxious to settle some principle, as counsel for the appellant impressed on us."

* * * *

"One is led to wonder why there should have been so much delay, but the blame, if any, has to be shared between the State Government and the Tribunal."

1. Civil Appeal No. 232 of 1970, decided 22-1-1976.

Another area of change. Sophisticated concepts of relevancy and proof, herasies about hearsay and sanctity of oral testimony are counter-productive in our climate. Many statutes expressly exclude the Evidence Act now. Much more honest is to vitalise the law of Evidence by drastic revision in accord with our specific social conditions without sacrifice of justice. The Evidence Act looks like a fearful calamity and so the Law Commission may well simplify the law putting more trust in the sense and conscience of the judge than the protection of the subtle printed word. Decolonisation of the legal process, in many areas, is urgent if the random and haphazard accumulation of centuries made more murky by heaps of case-law were not to defeat the main goal of law — Justice.

We are in a democratic age dedicated to economic growth and people's welfare. Courts have a role but also a responsibility. Vigilance and the know-how about wise control are the desiderata. My views are found in a separate opinion delivered in *Carew & Co*[1]. After all judicial correction has a functional role when a power is vested in the Executive. Even minor minions may abuse, as is obvious from Lord HALE'S speech in the House of Lords[2]:

> "A constable can wander about a field; see a shapely young lady handling a net; arrest her on reasonable grounds of suspicion for pinching a blue butterfly; search her in her country clothing on the spot.........All the constable has to show is that he has reasonable cause. Well, many people have reasonable cause for searching young ladies."

Voices from the streets, the platforms and sometimes from the Houses and the ink from political critics and social scientists, have not spared the Indian judiciary which, when all is said and done, is a noble instrument of abiding objectivity and unpressurised independence. For all the epithets hurled at us we yet remain the calmest, unpolluted society of professional men whose activist presence makes it feasible for free men with faith in the rule of law to govern themselves without benefit of kings and dictators. Being so, Law is very much the marvel and sometimes the mystery of the democratic world. Even so a passing reference to judicial independence in the context of a developing society may serve as an alert signal.

American researchers have traced the social identity and attitudinal affinities of legislators and judges. Why the paramount progressive principles set out in Part IV make headway steadily backwards in some areas of legislation can best be explained by the social milieu of the people's representatives? What ROBERT MARTIN sharply states about judges, if applied to India, makes a case for more women, more *harijans*, more left-oriented persons on the judicial tiers and the professional cadres so that the decision-

---

1. (1975) 2 SCC 791.
2. Hansard, June 20, 1975, H.L. Vol. 361, Col. 1092, debate on the Wild Creatures and Wild Plants Protection Bill.

making instrument may command more institutional confidence. R. MARTIN, in *'Personal Freedom and the Law'*, is blunt[1]:

> "We must also ask whether the whole concept of the independent judiciary is illusory. Judges are members of the ruling class by birth or assimilation (regardless of what that class may be) and hired employees of the State who depend ultimately on the coercive power of the executive for the enforcement of their decisions. To disregard these conditions in an attempt to be totally independent would be meaningless."

This view was quoted by R. SEIDMAN, in *Ohio State Law Journal*, but his comment about African Judges is worth reading by Indian lawmen:

> "The judiciary as a whole depends for its ultimate support upon the goodwill with which it is regarded. It is the most fragile branch of government. It lacks a constituency that perceives itself as represented by it, and it lacks guns in default of legitimacy."

My submission is that the Law and its agencies must communicate with the common people, maintain public relations, argue for law reform, oversee social welfare schemes like National Legal Services Projects and act with such integrity and independence that Caesar's wife is above suspicion. New traditions independent of anglophonic styles are growing *sub silentio*. Once we have colleges for judges, orientation courses, rapport with the community at large and the judicial eye on the court revolution (as happened in American history), the robes will be revered in a new sense as sentinels of freedom.

My last thought, perhaps a twin thought, is the proposal for a Law Day when all brands of law men will meet and discuss the state of the justice-system in the nation and for a Judicature Society which will cover all the judicial families and function with the sole object of promoting effective administration of justice, through literary or mass media contributions, seminars, conferences, consultancy services and studies into the management of court systems. In a republic, the justice-system is no cloistered virtue, but the underwriter of the dynamic rule of law. Lord Devlin said, talking of the British legal system:

> "If our business methods were as antiquated as our legal methods, we should be a bankrupt country. There is need for a comprehensive inquiry into the roots of our procedure, backed by a determination to adapt to fit the conditions of the Welfare State."

Chief Justice WARREN BURGER, addressing the American Bar Association in 1970, said:

---

1. From Judicial Review and Fundamental Freedoms in Anglophonic Independent Africa by Robert B. Seidman — Ohio State Law Journal, Vol. 35, 1974, p. 840.

> "In the final third of the century we are still trying to operate the courts with fundamentally the same basic methods, the same procedures and the same machinery, ROSCOE POUND said were not good enough in 1906. In the super-market age we are trying to operate the courts with cracker-barrel corner grocer methods and equipment — vintage 1900."

Creative intelligence must use the full legal potential to see that India produces a just society through law.

That crying need impels a string of interrogations, with self-implied answers, as a fitting finale to this lecture. Why should our court methodology keep its out-moded ways while it can, without injury to its solemnity, adopt modern business management technology? Why should our legal system not institute a Research and Development Wing and incorporate big changes in the working processes, and for correct orientation, start a national college for judges and allied agencies? Why can't we provide facilities for the public in the court system and form forensic councils for court centres where the Bench, the Bar and the People will have opportunities for conversation on the toning up of justice administration? Why not there be a systematic rendering of an annual report to the nation in social depth, at District, State and Central levels about the litigative pathology, the legislative ambiguities and failings, the poor implementation of laws at the executive level, the need for social-political campaigning to make welfare legislation effective in action? Why can't the Indicative and Legislative Branches meet and exchange views at Seminars and Conferences? Is a post-audit of the performance of law and Social Change in terms of Part IV of the Constitution feasible and desirable? Politics — good politics — must do backseat driving, but law must be at the wheel. Social welfare work must pioneer, pilot and organise the law ways, since legality in a democracy must be strengthened by auxiliary forces — *a la* dowry and family planning. In short, it is time we go back to the basic proposition that Law is at the end of the tether. R.W.M. Dias, in a thought that will arrest Indian jurists, says[1]:

> "In a country like Britain, which has remained comparatively stable, it has been easy to preserve the philosophy of analytical positivism in which the science of law is abstracted from social, moral and other value-considerations. .... But when tensions begin to convulse the very surface of national life, jurists, let alone judges, are compelled to make conscious decisions as to which way to steer if shipwreck is to be avoided."

I am painfully alive to my juridical unorthodoxy and unlettered audacity. The old school may anathematize my thoughts as an exhibition of ignorance, a tomb over the inner temple of legal justice. I have often been

---

1. Cambridge Law Journal, 1972 B Jubilee Volume, p. 293.

spiked for heathen diction, but I ask forgiveness on the plea that to overcome a multi-dimensional legal langour, to set the sight of petrified jurisprudes and priests of law, a multi dimensional, semi-profane language is needed. Lawyers cannot long survive amidst mass misery as cunning craftsmen but only as fluent artistes. We want not ambivalent politics veneered by dazzling slogans and sepulchred law dressed in double-think statutes; we want not the unedifying and illusory spectacle of self-advertising merchants of political progressivism criticising allegedly reactionary judiciary. The desideratum is for law-makers and law dispensers to forge in the smithy of the nation's soul a healing art of justice affecting the bleeding reality of Indian life. That is the unsung epic of law and Social Change; that is the humanist's quest to salvage one-fifth of the race; that is the life-force of democratic legality, the central occupation of freedom-fighter, judge and jurist. Have we not reached the watershed of precipitous change for us to perceive that juris-conscience is the mainspring of jurisprudence? Can India not be cured of rural primitivism and urban exploitation by the jural-social-economic measures, remembering Franklin D. Roosevelt who quoted an English Judge to say: 'Necessitous men are not free men and, turning his guns on 'economic royalists', went on, 'Better the occasional faults of a government frozen in the ice of its own indifference? Our lawmen's ascetic error, meditating in the caves of Indo-Anglian courts and our law-makers' sound and fury in legislative chambers as *alibi* for neglect of nine-tenths of the nation ill-housed, ill-clad, ill-nourished, waiting for a New Legal Deal, must end. Justice must bind their festering wounds. I regard the project for law's use as a tool for social transformation that will make living death on urban pavements and ugly squalor pervading villages a thing of the past, as necessitous. This is no recondite prospect but a definite basis for a kind of India attainable in our own time. We need a single-point programme of Development Law — without which even the well-intentioned 20-point programme of kindred national reconstruction plans will boomerang as broken words. That single, spiritual, all-important point is simply that law — the Bench and the Bar and, importantly, the Legislature — shall live with the poor, work for the poor and listen to the poor, shall abolish the promissory distance between law and life. Our dedication must be to that New Legal Deal reverencing higher values, refusing to play dice with justice and giving up the politics of Jekyll and Hyde. The frail men's frail man, whom we piously call the Father of the Nation, packed all this profundity into his *Hind Swaraj*. Let the spark of service burn into legal flame and we would have redeemed, in some measure, our tryst with destiny. And the *aware* lawyer, I beseech, shall not help toll the legal knell of social justice! If the validity of a social order is the commonweal, our legal system will become *ultra vires* if the People cannot stand it. The new harmony of the three branches of the government provides the healthy amity unavoidable for the nation's progress.

It is a fine and flattering thought for lawyers to feel, their larger role of nation-building according to the rule of law. Shri K.P.S. MENON, that ever delectable emeritus diplomat, recounted the story of three stone-cutters. Asked what they were doing, one of them said: 'I am cutting stone'. Another said: 'I am earning my livelihood'. And the third said: 'I am building a cathedral'. In our daily labours of law and justice, the vision of the cathedral of a society of equity spiritualizes our profession. This confluence makes the large legal profession, not the janitors of litigative law but the moulders of social justice. Only then, law finds an identity in disciplined nation-building, lawyer a constituency in his people's four freedoms and legality a commitment to the country's weal. This inner enlightenment is the inauguration of Law India, socially relevant, fearlessly forward-looking. And, if Law were God, the rebuke of Rabindranath is still relevant:

> "Leave this chanting and singing and telling of beads!
>
> Whom dost thou worship in this lonely dark corner of a temple with doors all shut?.........
>
> He is there where the tiller is tilling the hard ground and where the path-maker is breaking stones.......
>
> Put off thy holy mantle and even like him come down on the dusty soil!"

NAV BHARAT— MILES TO GO AND PROMISES TO KEEP

Law is a social science and operates as an engineering adventure geared to people's material well-being. Justice confronts new social, economic, political and cultural problems and law weaves 'fresh woods and pastures new' to restore equity and justice. The rule of law runs close to the rule of life. And when Life undergoes metamorphosis under the impact of serendipitous technology with its startling wonders, novel discoveries reshaping our way of life and methods of work, wealth and happiness also suffer mutation. Technology has no heart. The rich harvest huge profit while the weak and poor diminish or perish. Two worlds emerge. The Gandhian concept of development rejected the idea that it should aim primarily at the creation of material wealth or the satisfaction of insatiable, endlessly multiplied needs. 'In so far as we have made the modern materialistic craze our goal', he wrote, 'so far are we going downhill in the path of progress.'

The New World Order demands fruitful changes because science and technology force inventions and innovations never conceived of before. Greed vulgarizes the appetite of tycoons and we are going downhill in morality and acquisition gluttony. Cosmos and chaos clash and produce disaster and imperialist rivalries compete victimizing the masses, **unless** everything from the nuclear fission to catastrophic explosion comes under United Nations' absolute humanist regulation. Inevitably, the compulsions of survival drive to battle for positive forensic juridical thinking, people oriented, not balvic-empty new paradigm discover new parameters, principles, methodologies and theories to obviate terrorisms and carnages and to revolutionize a just system the World Order. International law, because Big Powers become a law unto themselves, is now a vanishing point of humanist jurisprudence. Today, the new Axis Powers hardly listen to the United Nations or the Great Charter or their functional operations. And yet, the WHO, UNESCO, UNICEF and other global instrumentalities are unique in their universal source and wise use of Nature's resource. It is a pity President Bush ignores the U.N. and attacks any country by playing the role of global policing, keeping other nations in timid silence. Taciturnity is traumatic humiliation and toxic delinquency when international crime is committed by self-righteous invasion in violation of world law by aggressive

Big Powers. The U.N. and other national instruments must insist on security, sovereignty and tranquility which alone can facilitate a better deal for assuring civilized destiny for every member of the comity of nations. Mankind has a deep divinity and integrity so necessary for its superlative Future and astral ascent. Bharat is Gandhian, halcyon and never barbaric. When any power defiles International Law, breaches 'panchasheel' among nations and intimidates the sovereignty of other peaceful countries India must stand for peace and heaven. Silence is guilt where there is a duty to speak. (Who first used the atom bomb on Hiroshima and still corners nuclear bomb monopoly?) We are no longer free nor a leader of NAM if any megalomanic super power terrorizes and occupies, with all its invincible armoury, any non-belligerent country and weak armoury. Americans are a great people and a world wonder with a marvel of Declaration of Independence. That noble nation, with Abraham Lincoln, Waldo Emerson, Henri David Thoreau and Martin Luther King Jr. commands my homage. Our friendly relations currently embrace the U.S., Russia, China, Asia and Europe. Our heritage, history and glory shape our present Gandhi-Nehru worldview. The universe is in a realistic sense and shall not yield a unipolar pressure.

Today the proprietariat seeks to liquidate the proletariat by show of force or coercive moves. The dominant agenda of the U.S. mega-MNCs and the ruling classes is global colonisation.

Why are we, with our universal cultural glory, still vastly prostrate, para-colonial and victims of dependencia syndrome? The billions remain backward, over-awed and exploited by the barbarity of the exotic billionaire Proprietariat, who hold the world as their own. We have 'miles to go' and 'promises to keep' if the new century is to redeem our justice, dignity and the freedom of the downtrodden peoples. These are poignant thoughts, pensive, negative celebrations but even education, hospitals and shelter are beyond entry to a majority. This is a malignant reality and painful veracity. Let us strive, struggle and adopt swadeshi with patriotic import policy and agrarian development and surely 2020 A.D. will fulfill President Kalam's vision of Nav Bharat.

THE GERONTIC AGE AND SUNSET STAGE OF INDIAN LIFE

The Constitution of India has made the entire people the sharers of resources and power of the country. Therefore the elders of India in their growing numbers are title-holders of the wealth of the nation. Article 21 puts the right to life as the foremost human right enforceable by the court as a fundamental right. This provision has to be read with article 41, which mandates the State to give public assistance in cases of "old age, sickness and disablement". Article 51A emphasises the spirit of common brotherhood, compassion and humanism. The jurisprudence of the Constitution thus leaves no doubt that senior citizens are an integral part of Indian humanity, have a role to play in nation- building and receiving the benefits of decent life until one dies in dignity.

Once this view of those who reach the evening of life is recognised, there is an obligation on State and Society to look after those who are unable to make life livable with the basic needs satisfied to provide reasonable pensions, old age homes, medical relief and access to facilities of rest and leisure, including libraries and centres of games suitable to the conditions of failing health. Old age is visited by infirmities, physical and mental, and in its extreme form may afflict the victims with dementia and Alzheimer's disease. These helpless, hapless humans are not mere objects of pity or charity. The State is Trustee of these growing numbers of gray-haired brothers and sisters. Women need more help and this is implicit in gender justice and geriatrics which is part of medical relief. My conviction is that philanthropy by society, justice by the State and self-help to the extent possible deserve express statutory legitimacy.

We are passing through years of stress and distress and entering a new millennium with a notable social feature *viz.* the disintegration of the joint family and the infliction of the nuclear family system. Parents are left alone with their sons and daughters seeking employment in far off places and foreign lands. What do the lonely survivors do in such situations? Our social order, expressed in article 38, protects the welfare of the people regardless of age and sex, region and religion, poverty and wealth. The health and strength of men and women are the concern of our Republic. The command of the State may be summed up as a duty to render unto the old what they need for basic sustenance and decent living.

There is a positive dimension to the issue of senior citizens which should find an important place in the *national policy on elderly citizens*. The accumulated experience gathered by senior citizens in various capacities are a great resource to be utilised by the country. For instance, lawyers who are well past 60 do excellent work in the field of law and justice. Judges who retire from the higher courts do a tremendous lot of work in the field of arbitration and offering consultations although the fees charged by them deserve to be controlled and regulated. Politicians and statesman who are well past 60 or 70 or even 80 years of age are still contributing their wisdom for the country's political progress. Similarly, those who have retired from the Defence Forces are capable of advising the nation in its security. Likewise, in various avocation and services, a vast number of 'superannuated' people have stored up a rich experience. The nation has a right and duty to utilise their services in such manner that they do not block younger people rising to high positions but yet pour their capabilities in advising and other situations. In the field of running charitable institutions, in tendering advise in the medical, legal, engineering, teaching, artistic and other professional areas post-hectagenerian abilities can be pressed into service. Winston Churchill won World War II although he had retired according to the conventional standards. Gandhiji and Nehru and hundreds of others in our own country were marvellous examples of great patriotism in the development of the nation. Leadership at the bar and belong to the old and, therefore, a system must be drawn up by appropriated plan. This applies to men and women, professionals and politicians, educationists and artists. I plead for a comprehensive National Plan covering all the aspects I have stated before, so that until the last breath every Indian capable of help to his/her motherland may be given an opportunity to fulfill functional service and be taken care of as a signified citizen of Bharat.

SAINT OF SECULARISM—UNIFORM CIVIL CODE

There is a misapprehension among certain sections of the Islamic community that the question of enacting a uniform civil code to cover all the religious communities instead of individual personal laws is of recent origin. But the idea has a history of its own. It found reflection even in the Constituent Assembly. The late Mr. Ismail, who was the then leader of the Muslim League in the Constituent Assembly, argued strongly against the enactment of a uniform civil code asserting that that would tantamount to overriding and undermining Islamic Personal Laws. However, leaders like Mr. Nazruddin Ahamed welcomed the move for the enactment of common civil code. He told the Assembly:

"I submit that the interference in these matters should be gradual and must progress with the advance of time. I have no doubt that a stage would come when the civil law would be uniform. But then that time had not yet come" and he added:

> "As I have already submitted, the goal should be towards a uniform civil code but it should be gradual and with the consent of the people concerned."

Alladi Krishnaswamy Iyer, who also took part in the debate refuted fears that a common civil code would endanger the cause of any religion.

However, the debate assumed new proportions in the nineteen eighties following the award in the Shah Bano's case and the enactment of a special law, purportedly to protect the interests of the Islamic community. The fall out of this action was the renewal of the demand for a uniform civil code. Among those who ardently advocated the enactment of such a civil code was Krishna Iyer who felt that everyone should be equal before the law. That stance of Justice Iyer led some sections of the Islamic community to come to the conclusion that he was biased against their community, a belief without foundation. Nothing could be further from the truth. Rather than terming it as a belief born out of ignorance of the mind of Krishna Iyer, it would be more appropriate to say that these Muslims had been misled into this belief by vested interests. It is rarely that one could see a secular humanist like Krishna Iyer.

His views could be assessed from the following statement:

> "Our Republic is secular in constitutional texture. Its watchword is fraternity, steeped in equality. Our religious pluralism is conditioned by free and friendly relations and guarantees of non-discrimination based on religion. In constitutional law, we have solemn secular values. But in living fact, religious rivalries, fatal feuds and flames of caste-based feudalism destroy that human solidarity which is basic to Indian unity."

Here Krishna Iyer expressed his anguish at the status of secularism, its reality and the intolerance among communities. He expresses this regret in the following words:

> "Religious fundamentalism has become a deadly evil and our politics has been fatally polluted. Many organisations, Hindu, Muslim, and Christian have assumed menacing proportions, because of their utter disregard for our democratic secularity."

He condemns unequivocally the religious fundamentalism of all hues, communalism and decadent politics which operate diametrically opposed to the concept of secularism. Those who are unable to digest this bitter truth, cast aspersions at him saying that he is a communalist.

Krishna Iyer is not a person who had suffered narrow thinking or developed insular views. On the contrary his approach has always been broad based and is one which eschews communal or religious considerations. He had never failed to search for the sterling philosophies of every faith and hail the merits of each religion nor had he pulled his punches when there were attributes in religions which ran counter to the humanistic concept of secularism. Reading his writings and listening to his speeches, one is amazed at the commitment to and indepth understanding of Krishna Iyer of various religious philosophies. Commenting on the foreword that he had written to the text 'Nahjul Balegha', authored by the Islamic intellectual Dr. S.M. Shakeel Akhtar, an Islamic intellectual he has this to say about Krishna Iyer.

> "It is a matter for conjecture if even ulemas would have had the indepth knowledge about Islam as Krishna Iyer had imbibed. It is more than clear that he had studied the various texts of Islam and speaks of that religion with authority. In fact his comparative study of religion far surpasses even that of those who claim to have devoted their entire life on the study of religions."

The beastly acts of some of those in Pakistan and Bangladesh who claim to follow the precepts of Islam who began destroying the Hindu temples and places of worship in retaliation against the destruction of the Babri Mosque by a mob of barbaric fundamentalists, caused untold anguish among all right thinking Muslims in the country, who bent their heads in shame. If those who indulged in these senseless acts of retaliation had reacted in the manner that Bible enjoins: "Lord, forgive them for they know not what they do", then they could have been considered devout and true followers of Islam. But they had sullied the image of Islam. They are those who know not what Islam stands for. They are those who had failed to understand the philosophy of Hazrat Imam Ali, son-in-law of Prophet Mohamed who said: "When you gain power over your adversary pardon him by way of thanks for being able to over power him". Krishna Iyer who had an indepth understanding of the philosophy of Imam Ali, and had written and spoken about him extensively comments:

> "Rulers of the desert sands and tribal hordes were often cruel and despotic.
>
> "But Ali, the Caliph and ruler, was of different mould. He assured the safety and security of his subjects and allowed even religious freedom (to Armenian Christians). Amity in the community and justice without arrogance were the hallmark of his governance.
>
> "He ordered that the non-Muslim priests should be treated with due respect, their monasteries should be protected and they should be allowed to carry on their lectures, teachings, preaching and religious ceremonies unhindered, and even if they wanted to build their places of worship, then fallow and ownerless land was allotted to them.
>
> "Hazrat Ali may be a leading light of Islam; but he was also a beacon light for the human race, if only we can look at him without religious bigotry and obscurantist blinkers. If you care to read in gentle spirit and tolerant mood the last sermon of the Holy Prophet of Islam and then study the life and work of Hazrat Ali you will realise that this eloquent successor did visualise and actualise the sublime message intended, beyond the Islamic flock, for the whole human race. The social order implicit in the last message of Islam's holy founder breathes magnanimity and righteousness, fair dealing and working principles of life for the people on the earth and not an omnipotence in the sky for chant and prayer only. The global appeal of Islam is not as a rival to other religions but as the limitless light of a star from afar merging its luminosity in similar sheen from other stellar sources, since there is a unity in divinity and universality in spirituality. Not bleeding swords but light within the bosom that lift the human race to its highest divine fulfilment."

He clarifies succinctly, the truth between the Muslims and non-Muslims, in achieving self-realisation, true divinity and says:

> "The Hindus exalt *gyana* (true knowledge) as a route to the highest realisation. Veda itself means knowledge. The Bible also emphasises the 'Word, the Book, and urges; 'know ye the truth and Truth Shall make you free'. Now come to Imam Ali. Repeatedly, he stresses the

significance of knowledge and here makes no difference between Muslims and non-Muslims.

"From his many sayings about knowledge, it may be rightly inferred that knowledge is itself freedom for it saves people from ignorance which is the cause of man's slavery to false beliefs, unfounded fear of nature and his superiors. It is at the same time a key to attain and safeguard freedom accorded to human beings. The Qur'an is unique among the scriptures in encouraging the believers to acquire knowledge and to verify the fundamentals of faith rationally. There are 704 Qur'anic verses in which either the word 'ilm' or its derivations are used. Book, an essential aid of 'ilm', occurs in the Qur'an 230 times, while the total number of verses in which words related to *kitab* and *kataba* have occurred is 319. The Qur'an itself is mentioned as *kitab* on 81 occasions in its text. It is not possible in this brief article to quote even a few of the relevant Qur'anic verses and the sayings of Ali. However, it would not be out of place to point out the right to acquire knowledge and freedom of enquiry forms an essential part of the laws and guiding principles governing human rights in Islam. In this matter no distinction is made between Islamic and non-Islamic sources and Muslim and non-Muslim teachers.

"Science and knowledge have a teleological goal. Islam insists (and humanists everywhere do likewise) that science and advances thro' discoveries and more knowledge must be humanised, not satanised (vide atom bomb and chemical warfare)".

And about Islam he says:

> "The uplift of women and emancipation of slaves, economic justice to the oppressed and other have-nots like petty peasants and landless labourers, orphans, widows and old people claimed IslamÕs conscience. Zakat and Sadaqah are sharing of wealth with the needy.
>
> "Islamic humanism brings it closer to other religions. Respect for women, prohibition of alcoholic beverages, gambling, foul food, sexual promiscuity, usury and the like. On the whole, one may proceed on the assumption that the gracious Imam Ali and his sermons and teachings are reinforcement of the cultural heritage of humanity".

On the question misunderstanding about the Islam, Krishna Iyer quotes:

> "There is misunderstanding about Islamic hostility to non-Muslims.
>
> "As the Qur'an has taken special care of non-Muslims in the matter of their legal rights, it accords them full freedom in the matters of faith, economic activity, property, social security and the preservation of their culture and traditions".

While discussing about Prophets he compares Bhagavat Gita with Islamic texts:

"On the subject of sending Prophets from time to time when evil is on the ascendant and the good needs to be salvaged, the Bhagavat Gita of the Hindus has an affirmative proposition. Compare that with the teaching of Shi'ism:

"Shi'ism believes that God, in order to guide His creatures and lead them from the darkness of ignorance and misery to the light of knowledge and happiness, has sent a number of prophets, for God has created man for felicity and happiness and has created the means for the attainment of this end in the existence of the universe itself.

"Sending prophets is also with the purpose of perfecting this goal. That is why the teachings of the Prophets and the divine laws are always the supplement for creating organisation of human being. Any law which is opposed to the primordial and creation nature of man is surely not revealed by God."

Krishna Iyer also believed that:

"Islam, if I may humbly submit, must open up dialogue with other religions of the West and the East, since our indivisible world is the home of all and Islam stands for submission to the Supreme Power (Allah, the Merciful) and for the well-being of all created beings everywhere. Therefore, a new dignified, principled process of cultural communication must begin with stress on the common values for a better world. We are one in a soulful sense and must be tolerant members of a world brotherhood, welded together by unity in divinity and amity in diversity".

Why these people who lack such indepth understanding of Islam dare to taint him as anti-Muslim passes understanding. Is it because he views Islam with equanimity? Do they know not what they are doing? Only their conscience could answer this question. When the question was raised among some Muslim friends as to why they considered Krishna Iyer anti-Muslim, their reply was, "Krishna Iyer is demanding a common civil code in place of the Shariat law. In *Shah Bano* case, when the Supreme Court upheld section 125 of the Code of Criminal Procedure, he raised his voice in support of Shah Bano Begum".

The reasons are not far to seek. Many Muslim brethren are still ignorant of one factor in that they fail to identify the true image of those self-proclaimed leaders, the modern day messiahs of Muslims who claim that they were the guardians of Islam, but who are in reality selfish and self-centred, lacking knowledge of the tenets of this great religion. What the Prophet detested most was divorce. He who declared that Muslim men could marry four wives, said so due to exigencies of circumstances. Many males had been killed in the holy wars and women outnumbered men in the Islamic countries. But this concession was not without a proviso. He also warned that men who marry four women should treat every one of them alike, only then and then only could they marry four women. Today is it possible to marry more than one wife and maintain all of them and also to treat everyone equally?

Here, we would like to go along with what Dr. K.R. Noori, in his book 'The Running Commentary of the Holy Quran' says in the preface:

> "Belief in Islam does not mean mere confession of the existence of something. It really means the translation of the faith into action. Words without deeds carry no meaning in Islam. Therefore the term 'believe and do good' has been used like a phrase all over the Quran. Belief in something means that man should inculcate the qualities or carry out the prompting or guidances of that thing in his action. Belief in Allah means that besides acknowledgment of the existence of the Author of the universe, we are to show obedience to his commandments......"

The above statement and the *ayyats* as well as the clarification of the Islamic intellectual Noori make it clear that a husband of a divorced Muslim woman is duty bound to provide maintenance to her. But when the judgment in the *Shah Bano's* case was delivered Islamic leaders went into fits of rage condemning the judgment. Many Islamic countries had accepted the provision of maintenance to divorcee women as Koranic *fatwa* but only India has this phenomenon suffered at the hands of pseudo Islamic leaders. The rights of women were sacrificed on the altar of ballot boxes.

These views of the Islamic friends are thoughts that had been foisted in their minds. God has nowhere said that women should be treated as serfs or be bereft of all rights. Whenever the word common civil code is mentioned, an apprehension surfaces in the mind of the Muslims whether they would be forced to follow Hindu laws. Their basic fear is that since they were a minority, whether there would be danger from the majority community, that if they did not raise their voice loud and clear now, they would be compelled to forfeit all their rights; the common civil code was a facade to impose on the minorities the demands of the Bharatiya Janata Party, Shiv Sena, Bajrang Dal, Viswa Hindu Parishad and other organisations of majority communities with a view to suppress Muslims, Christians and the weaker sections of society by this coterie of the so-called majority communal organisations.

When Krishna Iyer talks of secularism, he views:

> "The basis of secularism is that in all civil matters including what may be called family laws, common citizenship postulates common family law. Discrimination between the sexes based on religion also violates secularism".

Robert Ingersal once wrote with fire:

> "There will never be generation of great men until there has been a generation of free women: of free mothers".

Are our sisters, Shah Banos, Roop Kanwars and the Mary Roys free women? Are they treated as equals? Do our Hindu, Muslim, Christian, Sikh or sisters from other communities enjoy equal civil rights such as for marriage, divorce, guardianship and inheritance? These are the questions that Krishna Iyer raises earning the ire of some Muslims.

Emphasising the need for a common civil code, Krishna Iyer tenders some very practical suggestions. He says:

"Parliament, without pusillanimity and appeasement tendencies towards Hindu, Muslim or Christian bigotry, must enact, as a first instalment, an enforceable Indian Familial Human Rights Act. Here many concepts of Hindu Law may suffer sea change. So also Muslim and Christian. Illustratively, all guardianship provisions in all religion-rooted family laws are for the father and the mother is discriminated against. Hindus have no place for the women in the joint family regarding agricultural property in our agricultural country.

"Irretrievable breakdown of marriage is good ground for divorce. But in spite of amendments to the Hindu code total breakdown has not yet been recognized. Even the adoption law is antique and unjust. The laws of pratiloma marriage and rights of the illegitimate child need overhaul. Under the Indian Divorce Act which governs all Indian Christians, the provision for divorce is discriminatory against women and outrageous. The Muslim law of marriage and divorce has facets more secular and attractive than what is contained in the Hindu and the Christian legislations. It follows that when a non-discriminatory uniform code of a universal character is enacted, we may borrow some provisions from the Muslim Law, if they are good, and apply them to Hindus and Christians and so on. A common code is an eclectic adventure in legislation and it may be that what is good in Muslim law may be picked up because it is more progressive. Suffice it to say at this stage that we may limit the legislation relating to marriage and its dissolution, equality of rights and responsibilities of spouses during coverture, inheritance on a just and equal basis where men and women are involved, and equal parental rights and duties in matters relating to their children.

"Two questions of tactics may be considered. When it is argued that a code may amount to the imposition by the majority community of its legal provisions on the minorities, the answer is that such a family code will be based upon many factors. What is best and just may find a place in the code and the portions from international declarations and covenants and principles in this field found in the legislations of socialist countries may be aptly incorporated.

"The second question is as to whether, as a matter of strategy, we should make family law as facultative in the first instance. We may, like in the Special Marriage Act, draw up a complete family code based on considerations of social justice but make their application optional. Certain portions which are fundamental, as in the case of Human Rights of the sexes, may be made binding. But other portions may not be held binding in the first instance, leaving it to the parties to opt for the application of such legislation. This is an experiment which may be flexibly undertaken, guided by a radical humanism and practical acceptability.

"Another intermediate measure is worth a trial. A progressive Islamic Code drafted by eminent Muslim jurists may be a good idea. Similarly, a progressive code for Christians. We have one for Hindus although that may require up-dating improvement. Once we have progressive family laws for the major religions and care is taken to have more or less similar provisions for other religions of minorities, then we reach a stage where social justice will illumine these separate family codes. The largest minority in the country, perhaps the weakest too, is Indian women, whatever the religion, they have to be served by legislative social justice in the matter of family affairs. Thus we reach a stage where Hindu, Islamic and Christian code more or less with similar provisions may pave the way for a uniform code for all. That will be the finest hour of family jurisprudence in our land of divisive religions and separatist family laws."

In these views, is there any phrase which is inimical to the interest of Islam, Christianity or Hinduism? Krishna Iyer's only lament is that people with masked face, try to render women without any rights. Politicians who have their eyes on the vote bank may say something now and another thing later. But statesmen would only be interested in the welfare of the people at all times and everywhere. Krishna Iyer is the foremost statesman that this country had seen in this century. Thus it is that his soul upholds the rights of women and leads the people as Saint of Secularism.

PROGRESSIVE INDUSTRIAL JURISPRUDENCE

"Now the capitalist system buys children and young persons under age, previously, the workman sold his own labour, which he disposed of nominally as a free agent. Now he sells his wife and child. He has become a share dealer".

—Karl Marx

How true to the Indian situation, where the worker has to sell not only his labour but his soul as well to keep his body and soul and that of his family together. To them industrial justice had been a distant dream never to be realised. The pathetic plight of peasants and the plantation workers, the suffering of industrial workers, the agonies of agricultural workers, the tragedy of those in the unorganised sector, the trauma of rural workers and others of their ilk are beyond description as if they were not part of 'We the people of India'.

If the peasants demand half a measure of rice as extra wages, their huts would be set on fire. Even minor skirmishes would be given a communal colouring. If industrial workers raise their voice, goondas and the police would join together to maintain the 'peace' of the capitalist. If the workers prompted by hunger raise the banner of revolt, they will not get food but would be rewarded with lathi. Their masters would make an indepth analysis of the Indian Penal Code, and rejoice at its provisions. If the worker goes to the courts in search of succour, the judiciary would dispense justice after the worker is dead.

Mr. K. Chanduru, advocate of the Madras High Court, very clearly and movingly illustrates the plight of the workers in the tale of woe of Sambunath Mukherjee, in an article in the Tamil weekly 'Junior Vikatan'. It is pertinent to quote the article here:

The case of Sambunath Mukherjee was as follows:

"Sambunath Mukherjee was an employee of a cotton mill in Delhi. He was dismissed from his employment on 24.8.65. on the ground that the name of an employee could be removed from the register if he was absent for more than eight days together. Sambunath Mukherjee had absented himself continuously for only seven days. But the employers not taking note of this position summarily and illegally dismissed him.

"He filed a case before the Labour Tribunal and it held in his favour. But the management challenged this decision by filing an appeal writ before the Delhi High Court. Again the management lost its case and then it sought an appeal before a division Bench of two judges of the High Court and here too the Bench held in favour of the worker. But the management without abiding by these decisions preferred an appeal before the Supreme Court and judgment was delivered in 1977 after a lapse of 12 years. The judges who heard the case confirmed the award of the Labour Court and dismissed the employer's plea with costs.

However, without reinstating Sambunath Mukherjee, the management held that he had reached the age of retirement and therefore he cannot be reinstated. The worker once again filed a plea before the Supreme Court and the Court allowing the plea directed the management to deposit the money due to Sambunath Mukherjee in Court. That was in 1981 and the judges tried to seek free legal aid for the worker. But the worker said that he needed no lawyers and that he would himself argue the case following which the Supreme Court ordered the Labour Court itself to conduct an inquiry.

The Labour Court sought an answer to the question if there was a permanent order in regard to the retirement age of employees in cotton mills, if not what was the quantum of wages that was due to the worker. After inquiry the Labour Court informed the Supreme Court that there was no standing order in regard to the retirement age of the workers in cotton mills. The Supreme Court took up the case for hearing on 28.9.94 but Sambunath Mukherjee was not present in Court. He had passed away. A shocked Supreme Court directed that the money due to him be paid to his widow.

There are thousands of Sambunath Mukherjees who had fought for 20 long years but were not there to benefit from the final order.

In that case the Supreme Court observed thus: This is the story of a worker written in tears, of a worker who had suffered enormous trauma, confining his miseries and bearing the tortures and finally succumbing to a mirage in the quest of justice and paying the price with his life.

"Every day the factory whistle shrieked tremulously in the grimy, greasy air above the workers' settlement. And in obedience to its summons saline people, roused before sleep had refreshed their muscle, came scuttling out of their little grey houses like frightened cockroaches.

"In the evening, when the setting sun found weary reflection in the windows of the houses, the factory expelled the people from the stone bowels as though they were so much slag and they climbed the street again.

"The day had been devoured by the factory, whose machines sucked up as much of the workers' strength as they needed. The day was streak out, having not a trace, and man had advanced one more step towards his grave".

Maxim Gorky in his classic "Mother", graphically describes the plight of the real worker. If Maxim Gorky had spoken through his "Mother", Charles Kingsley reflects the same thoughts in his novel that came out in 1848, where he states:

> "Here lies your inequity: you have given the labourer nothing but his daily food—not even his lodgings; the pigs were not stinted of their wash to pay for their sty room, the man was; and his wages, thanks to your competitive system, were beaten down deliberately and conscientiously (for was it not according to political economy, and the laws there of ?) to the minimum on which he could or would work. Without the hope or the possibility of saving a farthing."

This scenario is duplicated in India today. We who claim ourselves as a Socialist Republic, are more than satisfied by Articles 38 (2), 39, 41, 43 of the Constitution that we have adopted, by only committing it on paper in black and white.

Krishna Iyer who entered the brick red edifice in Tilak Marg, fashioned to uphold the principles laid down by the political Constitution, had developed an urge to give meaning, content and life to those Articles in the Constitution which dictated the socio-economic justice, as a follow up to the introduction to the Constitution by Justice Gajendragadkar, in this country. Krishna Iyer laid the foundation for a revolutionary industrial jurisprudence. He explained how law should be interpreted and to whom, meaningfully.

Since there was no clear definition as to what an institution called industry was, in the Industrial Disputes Act thousands of workers were affected. As a means to provide all of them relief, Krishna Iyer delivered a clear judgment in *Bangalore Water Supply and Sewerage Board* v. *Rajappa* defining what an industry was. That judgment said:

"The rather zigzag course of the landmark cases and the tangled web of judicial thought have perplexed one branch of Industrial Law, resulting from obfuscation of the basic concept of 'industry' under the Industrial Disputes Act, 1947 (for short, the Act). This bizarre situation, 30 years after the Act was passed and industrialization had advanced on a national scale, could not be allowed to continue longer. So, the urgent need for an authoritative resolution of this confused position which has survived—indeed, has been accentuated by—the judgment of the six-member Bench in *Management of Safdar Jung Hospital, New Delhi* v. *Kuldip Singh Sethi*, (1971) 1 SCR 177: (AIR 1970 SC 1407), if we may say so with deep respect, has led to a reference to a larger Bench of this die-hard dispute as to what an 'industry' under section 2 (i) means.

"Legalese and logomarchy have the genius to inject mystique into common words, alienating the laity in effect from the rule of law. What is the common worker or ordinary employer to do if he is bewildered by a definitional dilemma and is unsure whether his enterprise—say, a hospital, a university, a library, a service club, a local body, a research institute, a pinjarapole, a chamber of commerce, a Gandhi Ashram—is an industry at all? Natural meaning is nervous of acceptance in court, where the meaning of meanings is lost in uncertain erudition and cases have even cancelled each other out while reading meaning.

"Esoterica is anathema for law affecting the common man in the commerce of life, and so the starting point for our discussion is the determination to go by the plain, not the possible, sense of the words used in the definition, informed by the context and purpose of the statute, illumined by its scheme and setting and conceptually coloured by what is an industry at the current developmental stage in our country. In our system of precedents our endeavour must be, as urged by counsel, to reconcile prior pronouncements, if possible, and to reconsider the question altogether, if necessary. There are no absolutes in law since life, which it serves, is relative. What is an industry in Amercia or the Soviet Union may not be one in India and even in our country what was not an industry decades ago may well be one now. Our judgment here has no pontifical flavour but seeks to serve the future hour till changes in the law or in industrial culture occur.

"Law, especially industrial law, which regulates the rights and remedies of the working class, unfamiliar with the sophistications of definitions and shower of decisions, unable to secure expert legal opinion, what with poverty pricing them out of the justice market and denying them the staying power to withstand the multi-decked litigative process, de facto denies social justice if legal drafting is vagarious, definitions indefinite and court rulings contradictory. Is it possible, that the legislative chambers are too preoccupied with other pressing business to listen to court signals calling for clarification of ambiguous clauses? A careful, prompt amendment of section 2(j) would have pre-empted this docket explosion before tribunals and courts. This Court, perhaps more than the legislative and executive branches, is deeply concerned with law's delays and to devise a prompt delivery system of social justice.

"This obiter exercise is in discharge of the Court's obligation to inform the community in our developing country where to look for the faults in the legal order and how to take meaningful corrective measures. The courts too have a constituency—the nation and a manifesto—the Constitution. This is the validation of this divagation.

"Another sobering sign. In a world of relativity where law and life interlace, a search for absolutes is a self-condemned exercise. Legal concepts, ergo, are relativist, and to miss this rule of change and developmental stage is to interpret oneself into error.

"Yet a third signpost. The functional focus of this industrial legislation and the social perspective of Part IV of the Paramount Law drive us to hold that the dual goals of the Act are contentment of workers and peace in the industry and judicial interpretation should be geared to their fulfilment, not their frustration. A worker-oriented statute must receive a construction where, conceptually, the keynote thought must be the worker and the community, as the Constitution has shown concern for them, *inter alia*, in Articles 38, 39, and 43.

"A look at the definition, dictionary in hand decisions in head and Constitution at heart, leads to some sure characteristics of an 'industry', narrowing down the twilit zone of turbid controversy. An industry is a continuity, is an organized activity, is a purposeful pursuit—not any isolated adventure, desultory excursion or casual, fleeting engagement motivelessly undertaken. Such is the common feature of a trade, business, calling, manufacture—mechanical or handicraft-based-service, employment, industrial occupation or avocation. For those who know English and are not given to the luxury of splitting semantic hairs, this conclusion argues itself.

"The expression 'undertaking' cannot be torn off the words whose company it keeps. If birds of a feather flock together and *noscitur a sociis* is a common sense guide to construction, undertaking, must be read down to conform to the restrictive characteristic shared by the society of words before and after. Nobody will torture 'undertaking' in section 2(j) to mean meditation or mushaira which are spiritual and aesthetic undertakings. Wide meanings must fall in line and discordance must be excluded from a sound system.

"Likewise, an 'industry' cannot exist without co-operative endeavour between employer and employee. No employer, no industry, no employee, no industry not as a dogmatic proposition in economics but as an articulate major premise of the definition and the scheme of the Act, and as a necessary postulate of industrial disputes and statutory resolution thereof.

"An industry is not a futility but geared to utilities in which the community has concern. And in this mundane world where law lives now, economic utilities—material goods and services, not transcendental flights nor intangible achievements—are the functional focus of industry. Therefore, no temporal utilities, no statutory industry, is axiomatic. If society, in its advance, experiences subtler realities and assigns values to them, jurisprudence may reach out to such collective good. Today, not tomorrow, is the first charge of pragmatic law of western heritage. So we are confined to material, not ethereal end products.

"The relevant constitutional entry speaks of industrial and labour disputes (Entry 22, List III, Schedule VII). The preamble to the Act refers to the investigation and settlement of industrial disputes. The definition of industry has to be decoded in this background and our holding is reinforced by the fact that industrial peace, collective bargaining, strikes and lock-outs, industrial adjudications, works committees of employers and employees and the like cannot be organised, systematic operations and collectivity of workmen co-operating with their employer in producing goods and services for community. The betterment of the workmen's lot, the avoidance of outbreaks blocking production and just and speedy settlement of disputes concern the community. In trade and business, goods and services are for the community, not for self-consumption.

"Here we have to be cautious not to fall into the trap of definitional expansionism bordering on reduction *ad absurdum* nor to truncate the obvious amplitude of the provision to fit it into our mental mould of beliefs and prejudices or social philosophy conditioned by class interests. Subjective wish shall not be father to the forensic thought, if credibility with a pluralist community is a value to be cherished.

"Even so, this legislation has something to do with social justice between the 'haves' and the 'have-nots', and naive, fugitive and illogical cut-backs on the import of 'industry' may do injustice to the benignant enactment. Avoiding Scylla and Charybdis we proceed to decipher the fuller import of the definition. To sum up, the personality of the whole statute, be it remembered, has a welfare basis, it being a beneficial legislation which protects labour, promotes their contentment and regulates situations of crisis and tension where production may be imperilled by untenable strikes and blackmail lock-outs.

"The mechanism of the Act is geared to conferment of regulated benefits to workmen and resolution, according to a sympathetic rule of law, of the conflicts, actual or potential, between managements and workmen. Its goal is amelioration of the conditions of workers, tempered by a practical sense of peaceful co-existence, to the benefit of both—not a neutral position but restraints on *laissez faire* and concern for the welfare of the weaker lot. Empathy with the statute is necessary to understand not merely its spirit, but also its sense. One of the vital concepts on which the whole statute is built, is 'industry' and when we approach the definition in section 2(j), we must be informed by these values. This certainly does not mean that we should strain the language of the definition to import into it what we regard as desirable in an industrial legislation, for we are not legislating de novo but construing an existing Act. Crusading for a new type of legislation with dynamic ideas or humanist justice and industrial harmony cannot be under the umbrella of interpreting an old, imperfect enactment. Nevertheless, statutory diction speaks for today and tomorrow; words are semantic seeds to serve the future hour. Moreover, as earlier highlighted, it is legitimate to project the value-set of the Constitution, especially Part IV, in reading the meaning of even a pre-Constitution statute. The paramount law is paramount and Part IV sets out Directive Principles of State Policy which must guide the judiciary, like other instrumentalities, in interpreting all legislation. Statutory construction is not a petrified process and the old bottle may, to the extent language and realism permit be filled with new wine. Of course, the bottle should not break or lose shape.

"A pluralist society with a capitalist backbone, notwithstanding the innocuous adjective 'Socialist' added to the Republic by the Constitution (42nd Amendment Act, 1976) regards profit-making as a sacrosanct value. Elitist professionalism and industrialism is sensitive to the 'worker' menace and inclines to exclude such sound and fury as 'labour unrest' from its sanctified precincts by judicially de-industrialising the activities of professional men and interest groups to the extent feasible. Governments, in a mixed economy, share some of the habits of thought of the dominant class and doctrines like sovereign functions, which pull out economic enterprises run by them, come in handy. The latent love for club life and charitable devices are escapist institutions bred by clever capitalism and hierarchical social structure, shows up as inhibitions transumuted as doctrines, interpretatively carving out immunities from the 'industrial' demands of labour by labelling many enterprises as 'non-industries'. Universities, clubs, institutes, manufactories and establishments managed by eleemosynary or holy entities, are instances. To objectify doctrinally subjective consternation is casuistry.

"A counter-critic, on the other hand, may acidly contend that if judicial interpretation, uninformed by life's realities, were to go wild, every home will be, not a quiet castle but tumultuous industry, every research unit will grind to a halt, every god will face new demands, every service club willl be the venue of rumble and every charity choked off by brewing unrest and the salt of the earth as well as the lowliest and the last will suffer. Counsel for the appellants struck this pessimistic note. Is it not obvious from these rival thought ways that law is value-loaded, that social philosophy is an inarticulate interpretative tool? This is inescapable in any school of jurisprudence.

"We would only add that a developing country is anxious to preserve the smooth flow of goods and services, and interdict undue exploitation and, towards those ends, labour legislation is enacted and must receive liberal construction to fulfil its role.

"Our endeavour in this decision is to provide such working principles. This Court, within a few years of the enactment of the salutary statute, explained the benign sweep of industry in *Banerji* (AIR 1953 SC 58) which served as beacon in later years—*Ahmedabad Textile Research* (AIR 1961 SC 484) and acted on it. *Hospital Mazdoor Sabha* (AIR 1960 SC 610) and *Nagpur Corporation* (AIR 1960 SC 675) marched in its sheen. The law shed steady light on industrial inter-relations and the country's tribunals and courts settled down to evolve a progressive labour jurisprudence, burying the bad memories of *laissez faire* and bitter struggles in this field and nourishing new sprouts of legality fertilised by the seminal ratio in Banerji. Indeed, every great judgment is not merely an adjudication of an existing lis but an appeal addressed by the present to the emerging future. And here the future responded, harmonising with the humanscape hopefully projected by Part IV of the Constitution. But the drama of a nation's life, especially when it confronts die-hard forces, develops situations of imbroglio and tendencies to back-track. And law quibbles where life wobbles. Judges only read signs and translate symbols in the national sky. So ensued an era of islands of exception dredged up by judicial process. Great clubs were privileged out, liberal professions swarm to safety, educational institutions, vast and small, were helped out, diverse charities, disinclined to be charitable to their own weaker workmen, made pious pleas and philanthropic appeals to be extricated. A procession of decisions—*Solicitors'* case (AIR 1962 SC 1080), *University of Delhi* (AIR 1963 SC 1873), *Gymkhana Club of India* (AIR 1968 SC 554), *Cricket Club of India* (AIR 1969 SC 276), *Chartered Accountants* (1963-1 LLJ 567); (AIR 1963 Cal. 310) climaxed by Safdarjung (AIR 1970 SC 1407) carved out sanctuaries. The six-member Bench—the largest which sat on this court—conceptually to reconstruct 'industry', affirmed and reversed, held profit motive irrelevant but upheld charitable service as exemptive, and in its lights and shadows, judicial thinking became ambivalent and industrial jurisprudence landed itself in a legal quagmire. Pinjrapoles sought salvation and succeeded in principle (*Bombay Pinjrapole*), Chambers of Commerce fought and failed, hospitals battled to victory (*Dhanrajgiriji Hospital*) (AIR 1975 SC 2032), Standards Institute made a vain bid to extricate (*I.S.I.* case) (AIR 1976 SC 145), research institutes, at the High Court level, waged and won non-industry status in Madras and Kerala. The murky legal sky paralysed tribunals and courts and administrations, and then came, in consequence, this reference to a larger Bench of seven judges.

'Industry', as defined in section 2(j) and explained in *Banerji* (AIR 1953 SC 58) has a wide import.

(a) Where (i) systematic activity, (ii) organized by co-operation between employer and employee (the direct and substantial element is chimerical), (iii) for the production and/or distribution of goods and services calculated to satisfy human wants and wishes (not spiritual or religious but inclusive of material things or services geared to celestical bliss, *i.e.*, making, on a large scale prasad or food) *prima facie*, there is an 'industry' in that enterprise.

(b) Absence of profit motive or gainful objective is irrelevant, be the venture in the public, joint, private or other sector.

(c) The true focus is functional and the decisive test is the nature of the activity with special emphasis on the employer-employee relations.

(d) If the organization is a trade or business, it does not cease to be one because of philanthropy animating the undertaking.

"Although section 2(j) uses words of the widest amplitude in its two limbs their meaning cannot be magnified to overreach itself.

(a) 'Undertaking' must suffer a contextual and associational shrinkage as explained in *Banerji* and in this judgment; so also, service, calling and the like. This yields the inference that all organized activity possessing the triple elements in I (supra), although nor trade or business, may still be 'industry' provided the nature of the activity, *viz.*, the employer-employee basis, bears resemblance to what we find in trade or business. This takes us into the fold 'industry' undertakings, calling and services, adventures, analogous to the carrying on of trade or business. All features, other than the methodology of carrying on the activity, *viz.*, in organizing the co-operation between employer and employee, may be dissimilar. It does not matter, if on the employment terms there is analogy.

"III. Application of these guidelines should not stop short of their logical reach be invocation of creeds, cults or inner sense of incongruity or outer sense of motivation for or resultant of the economic operations. The ideology of the Act being industrial peace, regulation and resolution of industrial disputes between employer and workmen, the range of this statutory ideology must inform the reach of the statutory definition. Nothing less, nothing more.

"(a) The consequences are (i) professions, (ii) clubs, (iii) educational institutions, (iv) co-operatives, (v) research institutes, (vi) charitable projects, and (viii) other kindred adventures, if they fulfil the triple tests listed in I (supra), cannot be exempted from the scope of section 2(j).

"(b) A restricted category of professions, clubs, co-operatives and even gurukulas and little research labs, may qualify for exemption if, in simple ventures, substantially and, going by the dominant nature criterion, substantively, no employees are entertained but in minimal matters, marginal employed are hired without destroying the non-employee character of the unit.

"(c) If, in a pious or altruistic mission many employ themselves, free or for small honoraria or like return, mainly drawn by sharing in the purpose or cause, such as lawyers volunteering to run a free legal services clinic or doctors serving in their spare hours in a free medical centre or ashramites working at the bidding of the holiness, divinity or like central personality, and the services are supplied free or at nominal cost and those who serve are not engaged for remuneration or on the basis of master and servant relationship, then, the institution is not an industry even if stray servants, manual or technical, are hired. Such eleemosynary or like undertakings alone are exempt—not other generosity, compassion, developmental passion or project.

IV. The dominant nature test

"(a) Where a complex of activities, some of which qualify for exemption, others not, involves employees on the total undertaking, some of whom are not 'workmen' as in the *University of Delhi* case (AIR 1963 SC 1873) or some departments are not productive of goods and services if isolated, even then, the predominant nature of the services and the integrated nature of the departments as explained in the *Corporation of Nagpur* (AIR 1960 SC 675) will be the true test. The whole undertaking will be 'industry' although those who are not 'workmen' by definition may not benefit by the status.

(b) Notwithstanding the previous clauses, sovereign functions, strictly understood, (alone) qualify for exemption, not the welfare activities or economic adventures undertaken by government or statutory bodies.

(c) Even in departments discharging sovereign functions, if there are units which are industries and they are substantially severable, then they can be considered to come within section 2(j).

(d) Constitutional and competently enacted legislative provisions may well remove from the scope of the Act categories which otherwise may be covered thereby.

"We overrule *Safdarjung* (AIR 1970 SC 1407), *Solicitors* case (AIR 1968 SC 554), *Delhi University* (AIR 1963 SC 1873), *Dhanrajgiriji Hospital* (AIR 1975 SC 2032) and other rulings whose ratio runs counter to the principles enunciated above, and Hospital Mazdoor Sabha (AIR 1960 SC 610) is hereby rehabilitated".

Krishna Iyer who defined what an industry was, in order to explain the two important components of the unit, namely the employer-employee, made use of *Royal Talkies, Hyderabad* v. *Employees Insurance Corporation's* case to set his seal by way of judgment. Employers never volunteer to provide anything to the workers. They would at times be masters at the art of subterfuge to deny the workers what is their due. Like the women beedi workers being denied their statutory entitlements by their employers who issue the passbooks in the names of their husbands, employers in industrial units who classify their workers not as workers but as contractors or sub-contractors and thus make use of the loopholes in the law to sacrifice them on the altar of convenience. In the *Royal Talkies'* case the owners, instead of employing persons directly to be in charge of the canteen and cycle stand, employed them through contractors. However, they were entitled to all the benefits and social securities that the normal employee of the theatre is entitled to according to Krishna Iyer. In this instance the owners of the theatre become the principal employers.

In that Krishna Iyer held:

"The reach and range of the definition is apparently wide and deliberately transcends pure contractual relationships. We are in the field of labour jurisprudence, welfare legislation and statutory construction which must have due regard to Part IV of the Constitution. A teleological approach and social perspective must play upon the interpretative process.

"Now here is a break-up of section 2(j). The clause contains two substantive parts. Unless the person employed qualifies under both, he is not an 'employee'. Firstly, he must be employed "in or in connection with" the work of an establishment. The expression "in connection with the work of an establishment" ropes in a wide variety of workmen who may not be employed in the establishment but may be engaged only in connection with the work of the establishment. Some nexus must exist between the establishment and the work of the employee but it may be a loose connection. 'In connection with the work of an establishment' only postulates some connection between what the employee does and the work of the establishment. He may not do anything directly for the establishment; he may not do anything statutorily obligatory in the establishment; he may not even do anything which is primary or necessary for the survival or smooth running of the establishment or integral to the adventure. It is enough if the employee does some work which is ancillary, incidental or has relevance to or link with the object of the establishment. Surely, an amenity or facility for the customers who frequent the establishment has connection with the work of the establishment. The question is not whether without that amenity or facility the establishment cannot be carried on, but whether such amenity or facility, even peripheral may be, has not a link with the establishment. Illustrations may not be exhaustive but may be informative. Taking the present case, an establishment like a cinema theatre is not bound to run a canteen or keep a cycle stand (in Andhra Pradesh) but no one will deny that a canteen service, a toilet service, a car park or cycle stand, a booth for sale of catchy film literature on actors, song hits and the like, surely have connection with the cinema theatre and even further the venture.

"All that the statute requires is that the work should not be irrelevant to the purpose of the establishment. It is sufficient if it is incidental to it. A thing is incidental to another if it merely appertains to something else as primary. Surely, such work should not be extraneous or contrary to the purpose of the establishment but need not be integral to it either. Much depends on time and place, habits and appetites, ordinary expectations and social circumstances. In our view, clearly the two operations in the present case, namely, keeping a cycle stand and running a canteen are incidental or adjuncts to the primary purpose of the theatre.

"Contract workers are those unenviable souls who are kicked both by the employers and the contractors. The questions often arise as to whose employees they are. Is their relationship with the employer limited to that of the contractor or do the relationship go further? Outwardly, only the contractor is presented as the person dealing with the contract worker. But in reality even the employer who enters into a contract with the contractor has his connections with the worker. He is obliged to protect the welfare of the industry and its workers".

In *Hussain Bai* v. *Alath Factory Tozhilali Union*, Krishna Iyer observed:

"Who is an employee, in Labour Law? That is the short, die-hard question raised here.

"Indian Justice, beyond Atlantic liberalism, has a rule of law which runs to the aid of the rule of life. And life, in conditions of poverty aplently, is not livelihood, and livelihood is work with wages. Raw societal realities, not finespun legal niceties, not competitive market economics but complex protective principles, shape the law when the weaker, working class sector needs succour for livelihood through labour.

"The true test may, with brevity, be indicated once again. Where a worker or group of workers labour to produce goods or services and these goods or services are for the business of another, that other is, in fact, the employer. He has economic control over the workers' subsistence, skill, and continued employment. If he, for any reason, chokes off, the worker is virtually laid off. The presence of intermediate contractors with whom alone the workers have immediate or direct relationship ex contract is of no consequence when, on lifting the veil or looking at the conspectus of factors governing employment, we discern the naked truth, though draped in different perfect paper arrangement, that the real employer is the management, not the real immediate contractor. Myriad devices, half-hidden in fold after fold of legal form depending on the degree of concealment needed, the type of industry, the local conditions and the like, may be resorted to when labour legislation casts welfare obligations on the real employer, based on Articles 38, 39, 42, 43 and 43A of the Constitution. The court must be astute to avoid the mischief and achieve the purpose of the law and not be misled by the maya of legal appearances.

"If the livelihood of the workmen substantially depends on labour rendered to produce goods and services for the benefit and satisfaction of an enterprise, the absence of direct relationship or the presence of dubious intermediaries or the make-believe trappings of detachment from the management cannot snap the real-life bond. The story may vary but the inference defies ingenuity. The liability cannot be shaken off."

Krishna Iyer gave new interpretations to the provisions of the Industrial Disputes Act and other laws dealing with this matter. Through his judgments he provided relief to the poor workers, when their legitimate dues were denied or when they were served with quit notices. One such awards which was very hotly debated all over the country in seminars and workshops was the *State Bank* v. *N. Sunderamoney* judgment, in which he observed:

"It is but fair to add an implied but important foot-note that while exercising the wider power under Article 136 this Court must have due regard to the constitutional limitations on Article 133(1) and owe allegiance to those restraints save in exceptional cases.

"The skiagram of the employment order must now be studied to ascertain which of the rival meanings counsel have pressed deserves preference. Statutory construction, when courts consider welfare legislation with an economic 'justice bias', cannot turn on cold print glorified as grammatical construction but on teleological purpose and protective intendment. Here sections 25F, 25B and 2(oo) have a workers' mission and the input of part IV of the Constitution also underscores this benignant approach. While canons of traditional sanctity cannot wholly govern, courts cannot go haywire in interpreting provisions, ignoring the text and context. With these guidelines before us, we seek to decode the implications of the order of appointment. But before doing so, an analysis of the legal components of section 25F will facilitate the diagnostic task.

"To retrench is to cut down. You cannot retrench without trenching or cutting. But dictionaries are not dictators of statutory construction where the benignant mood of a law and, more emphatically, the definition clause furnish a different denotation. Section 2(oo) is the master of the situation and the Court cannot truncate its amplitude.

"A break-down of section 2(oo) unmistakably expands the semantics of retrenchment. "Termination for any reason whatsoever" are the key words. Whatever the reason, every termination spells retrenchment.

"Words of multiple import have to be winnowed judicially to suit the social philosophy of the statute. So screened, we hold that the transitive and intransitive sense are covered in the current context. Moreover, an employer terminates employment not merely by passing an order as the service runs. He can do so by writing a composite order, one giving employment and the other ending or limiting it. A separate, subsequent determination is not the sole magnetic pull of the provision. A pre-emptive provision to terminate is struck by the same vice as the post-appointment termination. Dexterity of diction cannot defeat the articulated conscience of the provision.

"Had the State Bank known the law and acted on it, half-a month's pay would have concluded the story. But that did not happen. And now, some years have passed and the Bank has to pay, for no service rendered. Even so, hard cases cannot make bad law. Reinstatement is the necessary relief that follows."

In *Western India Match Co.* v. *III Industrial Tribunal*, the second petitioner had been granted long leave by his employer because he was ill. But when he returned to work on November 5, 1963, discontinued him from employment. The industrial tribunal which adjudicated the case, held that the action of the employers who had granted leave to the worker due to necessity cannot now discontinue his services. This was upheld by the High Court. The Western India Match Co. appealed to the Supreme Court against this order under section 136 of the Constitution.

In that case Krishna Iyer held:

"The courts below held, and quite rightly in our view, that since the employee was all along on leave granted by the employer no question of incapacity or being incapacitated from properly discharging his duties arose. It is obvious that when an employee is on leave he is not called upon to discharge any duties and therefore the question of the capacity to discharge duties does not call for consideration. The clause relied upon comes into play only when an employee who has to discharge his duties fails to do so and the employer makes a judgment of the situation and comes to the conclusion that it is on account of an incapacity which will last longer than two months that the failure to discharge his duties has arisen. We are, therefore, satisfied that the clause could not have been invoked and the termination of service was bad in law.

"We must remember the general principle that the act of the court should not injure any party. The length of the proceeding in this Court from 1971 to 1977 is the inevitable consequence of the backlog in this Court and not blameable on either side. In such a situation, we must so mould the relief as not to prejudice either party bearing in mind the equities of the case. We think that it would to fair, having regard to the overall circumstances of the case, that till the date of reinstatement, which we fix as December 1, 1971, the Management will pay the employee 50% of the wages including the benefits that he may be eligible for had he continued in service from the date of High Court's judgment to 30th November, 1971 with interest at 7% per annum."

In a society which has converted itself into a speeding machinery, the worker in order to earn his sustenance has to sacrifice his labour, blood and sweat. Employers maintain that capital is what they invest, bank loans and the share holdings of partners. Therefore, they take up the position that they are the foundation and the pillars of the industry, who decide the destiny of the undertakings. Their investments and the machinery alone would never cause the capital to multiply. Only the productivity of the worker, his sweat and blood alone could increase the profits multifold and make any venture viable. But to expect a wage commensurate with his job, is nothing more than a mirage as far as the workers are concerned.

One factory could multiply into many because of the workers application, but his poverty and hunger remain his constant companions. The soaring prices of essential items, the increase in the house rents every year, the capitation one has to pay to admit his child to a school, the appalling conditions where the worker has to struggle for even one meal a day are compulsions which make him demand a higher wage. But the answer is often lock-out and if the employer has political clout, then the police and goondas are let loose on him. This is the position of the worker today. Having waited patiently and more patiently, bending low to the extent of making him a hunchback, harbouring fear at the face of oppression, if he raises his voice to demand justice what he gets is not justice but jail, dismissal and continuing tragedies. The Gujarat Steel Tubes Co. was not different to this stereotype pattern. It employed goondas to deal with the workers who placed reasonable demands before their employers. The goondas let loose violence on the workers. Unable to withstand this onslaught, the workers decided on self defence. The result was that the entire work force of 835 persons were dismissed. Gujarat Steels wrote a new chapter in the history of industrial disputes. This dispute which was referred to the labour tribunal, went to the High Court and then landed at the Supreme Court. It came up before a Bench comprising Justices V.R. Krishna Iyer, D.A. Desai and A.D. Ghosal.

Krishna Iyer delivered the judgment on behalf of his brother judge Justice Desai and himself in which he said:

"The Management, in our view, did punish its 835 workmen when it discharged them for reasons of misconduct set out in separate but integrated proceedings, even though, with legal finesse, the formal order was phrased in harmless verbalism. But fine words butter no parsnips, and law, in its intelligent honesty, must be blunt and when it sees a spade, must call it a spade. The action taken under the general law or the standing orders, was illegal in the absence of individualised charge-sheets, proper hearing and personalised punishment, if found guilty. None of these steps having been taken, the discharge orders were still-born. But the Management could, as in this case it did, offer to make out the delinquency of the employees and the arbitrator had, in such cases, the full jurisdiction to adjudge de novo both guilt and punishment. We hold that section 11A does take in an arbitrator too, and, in this case, the arbitral reference, apart from section 11A, is plenary in scope.

"In the second chapter of our sum-up the first thing we decide is that Article 226, however restrictive in practice, is a power wide enough, in all conscience, to be a friend in need when the summons comes in a crisis from a victim of injustice; and, more importantly, this extraordinary reserve power is unsheathed to grant final relief without necessary recourse to a remand. What the tribunal may, in its discretion do the High Court too, under Article 226, can, if facts compel, do. Secondly, we hold that the Award suffers from a fundamental flaw that it equates an illegal and unjustified strike with brazen misconduct by every workman without so much as identification of the charge against each, the part of each, the punishment for each after adverting to the gravamen of his misconduct meriting dismissal.

Passive participation in a strike which is both illegal and unjustified does not *ipso facto* invite dismissal or punitive discharge. There must be active individual excess such as master minding the unjustified aspects of the strike, *e.g.*, violence, sabotage or other reprehensible role. Absence of such gravamen in the accusation, the extreme economic penalty of discharge is wrong. An indicator of the absence of such grievous guilt is that the Management, after stating in strong terms all the sins of the workmen, took back over 400 of them as they trickled back slowly and beyond the time set, with continuity of service suggestive of the dubiety of the inflated accusations and awareness of the minor role of the mass of workmen in the lingering strike. Furthermore, even though all sanctions short of punitive discharge may be employed by a Management, in our current conditions of massive unemployment, low wages and high cost of living, disastrous impact on numerous families, is of such sensitive social concern that, save in exceptional situations, the law will inhibit such a lethal step for the peace of the Industry, the welfare of the workmen and the broader justice that transcends transient disputes. The human dimensions have decisional relevance. We hold the discharge orders, though approved by the Arbitrator, invalid.

"We cannot ignore a few raw realities since law is not dogmatics but pragmatics, without temporising on principle. The Management's limitations in absorbing all the large number of discharged employees all at once when, steel, the raw material, is scarce, is a problem. Likewise, their inability to pay huge sums by way of back wages or otherwise, without crippling the progress of the industry, cannot be overlooked but cannot be overplayed after *Hindustan Tin Works* (AIR 1979 SC 75).

"Moreover, rationalisation of re-absorption of the removed workmen requires attention to the classification of permanent workmen and their casual counterparts. Every proposal must be bottomed on the basic economic fact that the beneficiaries are from the many below the destitution line. This Court has, in a very different context though has drawn attention to the Gandhian guideline:

"Whenever you are in doubt... apply the following test. Recall the face of the poorest and the weakest man whom you may have seen, and ask yourself, if the step you contemplate is going to be of any use to him". It is apt here.

"We are concerned with 400 workmen, some of whom have been claimed by death or other irreversible causesÑcasualties of litigative longevity ! 370 workmen are left behind, of whom 239 are admittedly permanent. We have already stated that 100, out of them, are probably fixed up elsewhere. So, we exclude them and direct that the remaining 139 alone will be reinstated. A list of the aforesaid 100 workmen will be furnished to the Management by the Sabha within two weeks from today. That shall be accepted as correct and final.

"We concluded the arguments on August 3, 1979 and on the eve of the closure of counsel's submissions certain inconclusive settlement proposals were discussed. We, therefore, consider August 3, 1979 as a pivotal point in the calendar with reference to which the final relief may be moulded. We direct that the 100 workmen for whom reinstatement is being refused will be treated as in service until August 3, 1979 on which date they will be deemed to have been retrenched. We direct this step with a view to pragmatise the situation in working out the equities. These 100 will draw all terminal benefits plus 75 per cent of the back wages. This scaling down of back pay is consistent with the assumption that somewhere in the past they had secured alternative employment. The long years and the large sum payable also persuade us to make this minor cut. Of course, in addition, they will be entitled to retrenchment benefits under section 25F of the Act, and one month's notice pay.

"The reinstated casuals (74 of them) will be put back, as casuals but will be confirmed within six months from the date of rejoining since it is meaningless to keep them as casual labourers when they are, by sheer length of service, on the regular rolls.

"50 per cent of the amount that becomes payable to each workman under the directions herein above given will be paid on or before March 31, 1980, and the balance on or before September 30, 1980, and till then the amount will carry interest at the rate of 10 per cent", the Bench decreed.

Bonus

Another aspect which is a constant irritation in the employer-employee relations is the payment of bonus. This issue has been canvassed in various labour tribunals courts and finally at the Apex Court.

The capital of the employer and the sweat of the employee tend towards productivity and to earn profits in the production market. This profit is apportioned into many items and one of them constitutes the bonus paid to the workers. The Bonus Act of 1965 provides for the payment of bonus on the basis of profits or production. It is natural for institution of integrity to pay fair bonus, while unscrupulous ones seek to deny bonus to their workers by falsifying figures to show losses. Though it is the practice of some production units to pay the bonus after computing the annual accounts, others pay special bonus or pay customary bonus during traditional festivals. In *Mumbai Kamkar Sabha, Bombay* v. *M/s. Abdul Bhai, Byjulla Bhai,* and in *Hukumchand Jute Mill* v. *2nd Labour Tribunal,* Krishna Iyer upheld the practice of customary bonus. In the *Mumbai Kamkar Sabha* case he held:

"As we progress on the secular road, may be the Republic Day or the Independence Day or the Founder's Day may well become the occasion for customary bonus. The crucial question is not whether there is a festival which suckles the bonus and the custom. What is legally telling is whether by an urbroken flow of annual payments a custom or usage has flowered, so that a right to bonus based thereon can be predicated. The custom itself precipitates from and is proved by the periodic payments induced, by the sentiment of the pleasing occasion, creating a mutual consciousness, after a ripening passage of time, of an obligation to pay and a legitimate expectation to receive. We are, therefore, satisfied that the omission to mention the name of a festival, as a matter of pleading, does not detract from the claim of customary bonus.

"The Object and Reasons of the Bonus Act indicate that the subject matter of the statute is the question of payment of bonus based on profit to employees employed in establishments.

"Where an employer has paid any puja bonus or other customary bonus, he will be entitled to deduct the amount of bonus so paid from the amount of bonus payable by him under the Act. Of course, if the customary bonus is thus recognised statutorily and, if in any instance it happens to be much higher than the bonus payable under the Act, there is no provision totally cutting off the customary bonus. The provision for deduction in section 17 on the other hand indicates the independent existence of customary bonus although, to some extent, its quantum is adjustable towards statutory bonus. Again, section 34 provides for giving effect to the Bonus Act thus:

"It is clear further from the long title of the Bonus Act of 1965 that it seeks to provide for bonus to persons employed in certain establishments not in all establishments. Moreover, customary bonus does not require calculation of profits, available surplus because it is a payment founded on long usage and justified often by spending on festivals and the Act, gives no guidance to fix the quantum of festival bonus; nor does it expressly wish such a usage. The conclusion seems to be fairly clear, unless we strain judicial sympathy contrariwise, that the Bonus Act dealt with only profit bonus and matters connected therewith and did not govern customary, traditional or contractual bonus.

"We hold that the Bonus Act speaks, and speaks as a whole Code, on the sole subject of profit-based bonus but is silent on, and cannot therefore annihilate by implication, other distinct and different kinds of bonus such as the one oriented on custom. We confess that the gravitational pull on judicial construction, of Part IV of the Constitution, has to some extent, influenced our choice.

"The findings we have reached may now be formally set down. We hold that the Bonus Act (as it stood in 1965) does not bar claims to customary bonus or those based on conditions of service. Secondly we repel the plea of *res judicata*. There is no merit in the view that the Industrial Tribunal has no jurisdiction to try the dispute referred to it. We set aside the award and direct the Tribunal to decide on the merits the subject-matter of the dispute referred to it by the State Government".

"Roscoe Pound's words are jurisprudentially apt:

"'Law is more than a set of abstract norms or legal order. It is a process of balancing conflicting interests and securing the satisfaction of the maximum wants with the minimum friction'. And, Paton has set the tone for Part IV of our Constitution to be used as background music, if we may say so.

'The law itself cannot be impartial... for its very raisen d'etre is to prefer one social interest to another'.

"Every industrial dispute has a potential for large scale breach of the peace when the factories and workmen affected are numerous. But the general unrest induced by industrial demands and resistance may, on critical occasions, blow up unless timely action to defuse is taken. This measure has necessarily to be at the administrative level, since the judicial process is prone to suffer fròm slow motion.

"The working class, though a weaker class, when organised, is militant. Their privations are too desperate to stand delay. Policy formulation by Government takes time, involves consultation; adjudication involves long hearing and appeal upon appeal.

"The real purpose of the combination is the crucial test between innocence and injury.

As far as Krishna Iyer was concerned Industrial Law meant that, it should ensure industrial peace, develop a consensus to settle disputes through reconciliation. On many occasion he had said "Marx and Mahatma regarded the workers as a spiritual human being, not a marketable commodity, and entrepreneurs as organisers for social good, not maximisers of private wealth by exploitation of man by man."

"A new wave of nationalism in production and humanism in consumption must be the note to be struck, the rhythm to be pulsed, if industrial harmony—that urgent desideratum—were to prevail. We are a Socialist Republic and Social Justice is the national signature tune. We are hungry and poor and need all the resources even to survive. Within this parameters our norms of profit and wages and management partnerships must be worked out. This is the law of life and life of the law. This is social justice in its relatively and industrial justice where men matters. I stress this human side because among the billion 'absolute poor' of the earth over 250 million are warehoused in India as flotsam, jetsams and dire destitutes, men and women and children. In Tagore's words, they are 'the eternal tenants in an extortionate world'. Industrial equity, justice and good conscience must be read in this context" Krishna Iyer observed and held:

"The ugly reality is that we have unsocial socialists and anti-socialist politicians. We have planners whose stock is too low. We have 'feudal' capitalists devoid of even professional skills and denying the familiar lines of fossil management, with graduation in opportunist politics and corrupt tactics. We have workers who have no ideology nor trade union training and, on occasion, play capitalism from the other end or think that extremism is sound and fury is good polity. 'A progressive discipline, a fresh dialogue, a programme of realism-nationalism-humanism must be forged with focus on more production, more equity in the share of profits, more respect for each other, more social concernÑin short, more patriotism in industry...

"Harmony in industry as in other national affairs, is music from the heart, not forced notes with the whip hand. The labour union, once faith is created and goodwill smiles on both sides, will take care of the quality and quantity of the productivity because they have stakes in the size of the cake. The development-cum-distribution orientation above will orchestrate industrial relations, not Kilkeny fights of futility;

"In those lands where 'Marx is Christ', the will of the workers controls the entire economy. Socialist economics means workers economics. Fundamentals of Soviet law provide for workers participation in the management of industry" says, Justice Hari Swaroop.

Krishna Iyer felt if employers and employees work together, if workers get the democratic right to participate in the administration, and described it thus, "the working class participation in a management is the beginning of the end of industrial bonded labour".

In the case of some, the very mention of the name Krishna Iyer causes a rise in temperature and ups the blood pressure. They suffer the illusion that he is anti-capitalist. But Krishna Iyer never failed to appreciate the reasonable problems of the proprietary class and in providing relief as he did in protecting the welfare of the working class, and their rights. He was only concerned about social justice and condemned wherever it was denied and applauded wherever it was upheld.

BLANKET BAN ON STRIKES BY LABOUR—A JUDICIAL EXCESS?

A serendipitous pronouncement by a Division Bench of the Supreme Court declaring is as it does, regarded by critics as a curial aberration, a broad-spectrum ban on Labour's right to strike without investigating the grave grievances of the employees over a hundred thousand strong, which the State Government, in alleged intransigence, ignored, leading to the menacingly militant lightning strike. The Court, in its wisdom, disposed of the matter without discharging its adjudicatory function of examining the central issue under challenge *viz.* the vires of the bizarre, blitz Ordinance dismissing into the streets, with Draconian severity and stunning celerity, the lakh and odd staff members, sans enquiry under Article 311, sans chance to make representations. The Court, however, was eloquent about the disruptive, illegal, iniquitous, anti-social and unconstitutional dimensions of strikes generally which, the Bench felt, held the public to ransom. In an impassioned purple passage, the learned judges observed:

> *Strike as a weapon is mostly misused which results in chaos and total maladministration. Strike affects the society as a whole and particularly when two lakhs employees go on strike enmasse, the entire administration comes to a grinding halt. In the case of strike by a teacher, entire educational system suffers; many students are prevented from appearing in their exams which ultimately affect their whole career. In case of strike by Doctors, Innocent patients suffer, in case of strike by employees of transport services, entire movement of the society comes to a stand still; business is adversely affected and number of persons find it difficult to attend to their work, to move from one place to another or one city to another. On occasions, public properties are destroyed or damaged and finally this creates bitterness among public against those who are on strike.*

This is powerful prose but is it legal hermeneutics or jural exegetics carrying judicial authority, or hardly anything more than an emphatic expression of chaos and distress caused by strikes, a view which many may share because of the indiscriminate infliction of social disruption by negligible, irresponsible and disorderly elements unaccountable to anyone and measured by the anarchy they generate. Indeed, the irrational frequency and impertinent frivolity of intimidatory strikes are self-defeating operations which sound trade unionism never sponsors. But are all strikes illegal, immoral, unjust or liable to be suppressed by State authoritarianism, employer reprisal or judicial allergy by angry negation of writ relief? My personal regard for the two judges on the *Rangarajan Bench* and the institutional reverence for the Supreme Court, the hallowed home of the human rights guarantee, social justice, jurisprudential creativity and curial remediation (of which I was a humble member long ago) persuades me to critique respectfully but ratiocinatively the *Rangarajan ruling* which *seems* to hold all strikes as productive of havoc in a democratic society and *bete noire* and menace to public interest. To critique is not to carp but to correctively comment in good faith. Trade unions are a legitimate, lawful instrument of the working class and strikes, under necessitous circumstances, are a strategic weapon which has legal sanction under just conditions.

Lord Atkin, in one of his classic judgments, observed what every member of the judiciary in the Commonwealth and elsewhere will do well to remember:

> *Whether the authority and position of an individual judge, or the due administration of justice, is concerned, no wrong is committed by any member of the public who exercise the ordinary right of criticizing, in good faith, in private or public, the public act done in the seat of justice. The path of criticism is a public way; the wrong-headed are permitted to err therein; provided that members of the public abstain from imputing improper motives to those taking part in the administration of justice, and are genuinely exercising a right of criticism, and not acting in malice or attempting to impair the administration of justice, they are immune. Justice is not a cloistered virtue; she must be allowed to suffer the scrutiny and respectful, even though outspoken, comments of ordinary men.* (Judges P-114)

After all Judge Jerome Frank of the U.S. Court of Appeal sensibly explained:

> *In a democracy, it can ever be unwise to acquaint the public with the truth about the workings of any branch of government. It is wholly undemocratic to treat the public as children who are unable to accept the inescapable shortcomings of man-made institutions.... The best way to bring about the elimination of those shortcomings of our judicial system which are capable of being eliminated is to have all our citizens informed as to how that system now functions. It is a mistake, therefore, to try to establish and maintain, through ignorance, public esteem for our courts.* (Judges, P-205)

The overwhelming majority of our judges do a difficult job fairly well, commanding confidence of the people. Nevertheless, as judge Cardozo elegantly observed, in his book The Nature of the Judicial Process, social philosophy does not pass the judges by. Unwitting infiltration of class bias may creep into their overt impartiality. Professor J.A.G. Griffith, in his book

The Politics of the Judiciary, gave reasons to hold that judges, being but human, may not be immune to class bias, never intentional but subconscious in their surrender to partiality. He quotes Winston Churchill whom I reproduce instructively:

> *The courts hold justly a high, and I think, unequalled pre-eminence in the respect of the world in criminal cases, and in civil cases between man and man, no doubt, they deserve and command the respect and admiration of all classes of the community, but where class issues are involved, it is impossible to pretend that the courts command the same degree of general confidence. On the contrary, they do not, and a very large number of our population have been led to the opinion that they are, unconsciously, no doubt, biased. (Hon. Members: 'No, no', 'Withdraw' and interruption)*
>
> *The Secretary of State for the Home Department (Mr. W.S. Churchill) on the second reading of the Trade Unions (No.2) Bill, 1911 (26) H.C. Deb. Col. 1022) (The Politics of the Judiciary, P-173)*

Lord Justice Scrutton made a similar point:

> *The habits you are trained in, the people with whom you mix, lead to your having a certain class of ideas of such a nature that, when you have to deal with other ideas, you do not give as sound and accurate judgments as you would wish. This is one of the great difficulties at present with Labour. Labour says 'Where are your impartial Judges? They all move in the same circle as the employers, and they are all educated and nursed in the same ideas as the employers. How can a labour man or a trade unionist get impartial justice?' It is very difficult sometimes to be sure that you have put yourself into a thoroughly impartial position between two disputants, one of your own class and one not of your class.*
>
> *Lord Justice Scrutton in an address delivered to the University of Cambridge Law Society on 18 November 1920 (1 Cambridge Law Journal, p. 8). (The Politics of the Judiciary, P-173)*

Does it ring a bell in the bosoms of Indian brethren on the high bench? Our Constitution and Court have a vision which the Crown and Law Britannia do not possess.

Did not Lord Atkin in *Liversidge* v. *Anderson* hold the House of Lords: 'In this case, I have listened to arguments which might have been addressed acceptably to the court of King's Bench in the times of Charles-I'. Therefore, arguments at the Bar sometimes condition the conclusions of the Bench and public reaction and jurists' evaluation may be reflected in a reconsideration of the law laid down in a decided case. Law never stand still. It is in this liberal spirit and with a constructive purpose that I 'wash in acid' the ratio in *Rangarajan* and the anti-strike dicta of the Bench.

With due deference, I dissent from the macro-negative proposition based on broad assumptions and expressed in paragraph twelve of the judgment.

'Now coming to the question of right to strike, whether Fundamental Statutory Equitable. Moral Right—in our view, no such right exists with the Government employees.' The court's dicta, as pointed out in a passage earlier in this paper, have gone beyond Government servants and condemned strikes as unjustified 'on any equitable ground'. In a mood of benignant philosophy, the court counsels Labour on its patriotic duty.

> *In the prevailing situation, apart from being conscious of rights, we have to be fully aware of our duties, responsibilities and effective methods for discharging the same. For redressing their grievances, instead of going on strike, if employees do some more work honestly, diligently and efficiently, such gesture would not only be appreciated by the authority but also by people at large. The reason being, in a democracy even though they are Government employees, they are part and parcel of governing body and owe duty to the Society. (Para 21)*

This moral message, with a pulpit touch, reads like a judicial addition to Jesus' Ten Commandments. This hortative mantra is a spiritual mandate that workers of the world unite; when you have demands to gain from Government or other employer, *work harder, produce more* and *win the Management's heart!* No doubt, our country will be transformed if ministers travel less and work more, if Secretaries visit Delhi less and dispose of files more without paper-logging, if public offices slumber less and devote to duty more, if judges hear with more business-like thoroughness, bring down the appalling backlog of dockets and pronounce judgments to the point without prolonged procrastination. Indian judges have a tough job flooded by escalating litigation and medieval methodology.

In this very case, having tactfully and gracefully terminated the dismissal order using the good offices of K.K. Venugopal, a creative, compassionate counsel, the dubious incursion into ambiguous Labour law was perhaps obiter and superogatory. What did counsel, a battery of them, all eminent, do in countering the harsh criticism of strikes? The judgment is silent about their submissions on 'strike jurisprudence'. With curial cynicism, working class leaders and labour lawyers may pardonably be pejorative against this jurisprudence which may be more at home in President Reagan's country and bring solace to Super-Conservative Mrs. Thatcher and may be to multinational corporations (MNCs) who are allergic to the presence of labour as a menace creating unrest.

Our judges on the high bench are aware not only that India is a socialist Republic but that several provisions of Part IV of the Constitution like Articles 41 to 43A, which are 'fundamental in the governance of the country' have welfare of workers at heart. Indeed, the learned judges persuaded the Government to take the dismissed workers back as a measure of urgent relief. That shows the concern of the courts for employees. What is hurtful to labour jurisprudence is the castigation of all strikes as vicious. Were we colonial, perhaps the conspiracy theory of strikes might have passed unquestioned. Not so now in Gandhi country. Why, in England of today, trade union law has nullified the view that strikes are conspiracies. There are situations where the Management is unreasonably recalcitrant and turns down just claims of workers. An observation by Lord Denning, in a dissenting judgment, is relevant. I excerpt a part:

> *Here we have to consider the right to demonstrate and the right to protest on matters of public concern. These are rights which it is in the public interest individuals should possess; and, indeed, that they should exercise without impediment so long as no wrongful act is done. It is often the only means by which grievances can be brought to the knowledge of those in authority—at any rate with such impact as to gain a remedy. Our history is full of warnings against suppression of these rights. (The Politics of the Judiciary, P-146)*

Freedom of speech and freedom of association are not mere abstractions nor purposeless inanities. Collective action is implicit in these basic freedoms. In express terms, there is no freedom to strike writ into the Constitution. But collective bargaining for legitimate causes is best served by a creative combination of speech and association, of course, without breach of law and order or transgression of other people's human rights. Once this perspective, sanctioned by constitutional initiative, is correctly and curatively interpreted, industrial jurisprudence becomes a process where both managements and workers have rights. When claims are justly made based on the contribution of labour to the progressive profit making capacity of the Industry an arbitrary refusal even to discuss may lead to tension which may mount to the point of peaceful, though militant expression by collective withdrawal from work, otherwise called strike. This is more to strengthen the demand than to destroy the industry or to disturb the peace of the community. Strikes are not a noxious novelty of Indian Trade Unions, but have been in every country where industrialization has been a part of organized production. Those who are familiar with the International Labour Organization are not jittery about strikes.

A profusion of citations may be avoided by a reference to *B.R. Singh's case* (1989 SCC 710) where Justice Ahamedi, speaking for the Bench, observed:

> *The right to form associations or unions is a fundamental right under Article 19(1)(c) of the Constitution. Section 8 of the Trade Unions Act provides for registration of a trade union if all the requirements of the said enactment are fulfilled. The right to form associations and unions and provide for their registration was recognized obviously for conferring certain rights on trade unions. The necessity to form unions is obviously for voicing the demands and grievances of labour. Trade unionists act as mouthpieces of labour. The strength of a trade union depends on its membership. Therefore,*

> *trade unions with sufficient membership strength are able to bargain more effectively reduced if it is not permitted to demonstrate. Strike in a given situation is only a form of demonstration. There are different modes of demonstrations, e.g., go-slow, sit-in, work-to rule, absenteeism, etc., and strike is one such mode of demonstration by workers for their rights. The right to demonstrate and, therefore, the right to strike is an important weapon in the armoury of the workers. This right has been recognized by almost all democratic countries. Though not raised to the high pedestal of a fundamental right, it is recognized as a mode of redress for resolving the grievances of workers. But the right to strike is not absolute under our industrial jurisprudence and restrictions have been placed on it.*
>
> *(1989) 4 Supreme Court Cases 710 para 15)*

The right to strike and the conditions under which it should be exercised are found in the Industrial Disputes Act. Indeed, the Bench, in *B.R. Singh case,* was dealing with a strike in a Public Sector organisation and the court, on an overall view of the facts and circumstances of the case, held:

> *Keeping the interest of the institution in mind and bearing in mind the economic hardships that the labour would suffer if the impugned orders are not set aside, we think that it would be desirable to restore the peace by directing the reinstatement of the workers. (1989) 4 Supreme Court Cases 710 para 22)*

A Bench of seven judges, in the *Bangalore Water Supply and Sewerage Board* case, considered in great detail the meaning of the word *Industry*. A passage from the leading judgment therein is relevant: 'The International Labour Organization has had occasion to consider freedom of association for labour as a primary right and collective bargaining *followed by strikes, if necessary,* as a derivative right.' In para 62 of the ruling, the Court refers to the *Corporation of Nagpur case* where the Education Department of Government was brought within the conception of Industry. A plethora of case-law relied on in the leading judgment (in the *Bangalore Water Supply etc.* case) takes the view that even a hospital run by Government is an industry. Industry implies employers and employees, demands and denials of claims, strikes and lock-outs and industrial adjudication. Therefore, to exclude the idea of strike from the scope of legality is naïve.

It is not without significance that in *Gujarat Steel Tube* case (1980 2 SCC 593) the majority on the bench held that it was a fundamental flaw to equate illegal with unjust strikes. A strike may be illegal by a technical violation, but need not be necessarily unjustified. All that I mean is that a token illegality does not make the strike a gross act of injustice. It is surprising that the dubious legality of the Ordinance, extraordinary in its character and timing, had not awakened the court's jurisdiction into considering the constitutionality of the executive legislation affecting a colossal number of public servants. Some day, some bench of the Apex Court may be conscientised into scanning the constitutional jurisprudence of Ordinance Raj.

In the USA where 'hire and fire' is the rule, strikes are considered economic terrorism by the mega-corporate controllerate of the U.S. economy. Industrial jurisprudence is labour-friendly in India. Our Constitution, with social justice and industrial equity writ large, shapes labour law. Our robed brethren offer a dignified place to Labour as almost a partner in the productive process.

Criticisms apart, the judges in the *Rangarajan* case need a meed of praise for restoring instantly most of the employees who were sacked by an ireful Government, although it baffles me that Government employees for helping themselves back into office have had to apologize and undertake not to strike ever thereafter. This condition is an ad hoc humiliation which I presume the court never meant.

An Afterword

In the provocative context of the contra-strike pronouncement, the learned Attorney General, with alacrity and authority, repudiated the theory that the right to strike is anathematic. This historic right cannot run riot nor turn berserk but, within socially sensitive bounds and liberal legal limits, has a permissible home in Indian jurisprudence. We are not a totalitarian State nor subject to Corporate Employer authoritarianism.

I never mean a pejorative reflection on the high bench. The learned judges, with a sense of relief after having secured reinstatement for the bulk of employees, relaxed into a censorious frown and presented a certain point of view not integral to the relief sought or the arguments at the bar. The Court is supreme but not infallible. In a Preface of lovely brevity, Justice Kirpal has rightly stated (in a semi-centennial publication by the Supreme Court):

> *Many a time, the Court has changed its mind and adapted the law and Constitution to suit India's need. If its work has been appreciated, it has not always escaped criticism. ....*
>
> *We would like to believe that the Supreme Court has gone about its task less conscious of its supremacy and more warily with the intuition that the Court, though final, is fallible. (Supreme But Not Infallible)*

Rangarajan is a case where the Court, though *pro tem* final, is perhaps fallible.

SOCIETY, LAW AND SCIENCE

I hold in my hand a book on jurisprudence, which is heavy but also weighty. Heavy because it contains well over 400 pages and weighty because the voluminous and luminous pages open vistas for jurisprudence altogether beyond the ken of commonplace text book writers in law.

Justice J.S. Verma, in a brief but penetrating foreword, has indicated the quintessence of Katju's book titled Law in the Scientific Era. A reader with juristic appetite and avant-garde guard vision will accept the need for radical re-orientation of the theory of law and concept of justice in their ultramodern developments and novel dimensions. As randomly paged through the book of Katju I realized the truth of Abraham Lincoln's statement: *The dogmas of the quote past are longer adequate to the stormy present.* Indeed when life marches, law cannot lag behind. Therefore, Indian law cannot afford to remain feudal or Victorian or even Nehruvian or Marxian. Jurisprudence has to be dynamic and of current relevance Friedmann has pointed out:

> *It would be tragic if the law were so petrified as to be unable to respond to the unending challenge of evolutionary or revolutionary changes in society.*

Roscoe Pound, adopting a similar perspective, observed "all the social sciences must be co-workers, and emphatically, all must be co-workers with jurisprudence".

Lord's Scarman in his Hamlyn lectures struck a similar note:

> *A learned and cautious English Judge like Sir LESLIE SCARMAN has developed the new dimension of English Law, distinguishing change which develops and strengthens the system from change which develops and strengthens the system from change which destroys it. This pregnant presage is a caveat for us too:*
>
> *"I shall endeavour to show that there are in the contemporary world challenges, social, political and economic, which, if the system cannot meet them, will destroy it. These challenges are not created by lawyers; they certainly cannot be suppressed by lawyers: they have to be met either by discarding or by adjusting the legal system. Which is to be?"................"For instance, the common law was exceedingly taciturn for centuries on the subject of the duty of care and the tort of negligence.*

Pressurised by the developing industrialisation and urbanisation of society in the nineteenth century, the judges, using as a precedent the ancient action on the case, developed the substantive law of negligence, thereby without the intervention of the Parliamentary legislative process providing a legal right to compensation for personal injuries caused by the fault of another................ "A law of torts, a land law, and a family law, conceived on common law principles, however, admirable in substance, cannot effectively protect the general public or the weak, the poor, the aged and the sick. To satisfy the conscience of the nation the state has had to move into the empty spaces of the law, the deserts and hill country left uncultivated by distributive justice, and there to make provision for society as a whole, and for those not strong enough to provide for themselves. Thus the welfare state is challenging the relevance, or at least the adequacy, of the common law's concepts and classifications. Fault, trespass, property, even marriage, are now seen to be an insecure base for the development of a law suited to the needs of our society. Family life has been freed from the tyranny of the husband and its obligations buttressed by the state : social security is available on the basis of need and as of right : the use of land, sea and air are controlled in the interests not of property but of society anxious to protect its environment: ....

Changes in law and justice when social developments outstrip the *status quo*. It is thus clear that with the rapid strides science and technology make at a global level. Law cannot remain insular and aloof clinging to ancient precedents but must keep pace with the leap forward at a like pace.

Justice Katju, with a brilliant flair, has in a challenging mood produced for popular and juristic critique a new theory in the field of jurisprudence so that law, *living* law, may grapple with the modern world order which has pushed behind former theories and made a quantum jump to be a relevant instrument of governance in the 21st century. In the earlier days of classical positivism, of Bentham and Austin, the perspective and the process of law did not have a structure or form which could become a partner of social justice in contemporary conditions. But when social and economic order changed, the mechanical facets of the classical positivists became obsolete. Sociological jurisprudence, founded by Roscoe Pound and other radicals who followed him, stressed social and economic reality and widened the scope of jurisprudence. Statutory law responded with new legislation and judges ceased to be passive agents handcuffed by dated precedents. Sociological jurisprudence arms a judge with tremendous powers of creative hermeneutics so that advances through activism could make the court a potent instrument of social engineering. Of course, some judges, still remain static, status quoist while others use gudge powers to creatively transform the social order. In Katju's words:

After all, arming judges with wide discretionary legislative powers solves few problems. There are all kinds of judges, scientific and unscientific, intelligent and dull, active and passive. To give all power to judges is thus a superficial solution to the problems of the modern world.

The theory of dynamic positivism which the author is presenting in this book adopts the correct points in classical positivism (the distinction between ('Is' and 'Ought') and in sociological jurisprudence (treating law as part of the social reality), avoids the defect in both, and takes the subject of jurisprudence to an altogether higher level than as yet achieved (see the Chapter entitled 'Classical Positivism and Dynamic Positivism').

The reader must also be activist and the jurist, who is lawyer, judge or academic, must also be possessed of noetic dynamism. Then alone the message of Justice Katju will reach out to change imitate jurisprudence and generate law adapted to the scientific era. I agree with the thesis of Katju, although I would not like to surrender social justice at the alter of globalization, liberalization and privatization in their perverted Orwellian semantic. There is a crisis in jurisprudence in our country because there is a tension of the tenses.

Jurisprudence is a social science and cannot be unscientific, outdated or submissive to conquest by neo-imperialist, corporate-dominated economic order. However, there is no doubt that classical positivism is no longer current coin. But sociological jurisprudence, if refined and sharpened to meet the challenges of recolonisation, has a revolutionary role to play.

I deeply appreciate Justice Katju's valuable study. He has produced a remarkable *textbook* and not merely a collection of adventurist essays. He deals with the origin and development of law, investigates natural law in a successful effort and takes a look at the shape of law in the future. A whole chapter devoted to Roscoe Pound's Jurisprudence and also corresponding theories in continental Europe enlivens the book. The present controversy about the pure theory of law still polemical in Anglo-Saxon jurisprudence but uninteresting to the *Sanatana Dharma* Schools in India, finds a place in this book.

What is remarkable about Katju's vistaramic vision of jurisprudence is that he moves on to law in the scientific era, law, religion and politics, law and justice in their deeper nexus, and the welfare state, of course, he deals with judicial legislation which is becoming significantly successful in the social justice era we live in and the corrupt operations who control power.

It is difficult for me to discuss in detail the diverse chapters of the book. But imagine Katju discussing the Indian economy and the role of the Indian judiciary. He proceeds to consider what is very relevant today, namely, the nature and problems of space law, air law and their application to Indian Sovereignty. In getting into the 21st century, Katju has not forgotten to deal with the *mimansa* principles of interpretation and also the challenges before the under-developed nations.

A venial touch of vanity has persuaded Justice Katju to add quite a number of his judgment in Part II of the volume. However, each judgment has a tale to tell, a lesson to teach and a social issue to discuss and decide. Public interest litigation is neither anathema nor allergy to Katju J. but is an opportunity for judicial effort at transformation of the social order. I conclude by saying Amen to the last sentence in the Preface to the book *"it is submitted that Dynamic Positivism will be the jurisprudence of the scientific era"*. Do remember, dear author and reader, that law is but the means and justice the end; and so, the legal instrument should resist global subversion by the tycoons of the world's Impoverished Incorporated.

SCIENCE, RELIGION AND THE DHARMA OF SOCIAL DEVELOPMENT

Science without Religion is lame; Religion without Science is blind, said Einstein. The developmental potential of *homo sapiens* is best advanced only through a dynamic synthesis of the spiritual and material values so that their positive interaction may promote the Infinite lying latent in every person and waiting to be released thro' the process of higher consciousness. Indeed, science discovers the profound secrets of Nature and Religion manifests the divinity in man. There is no antithesis between science and spirituality and their *modus vivendi* is necessary. Both are engaged in the search for Truth following different paths but do meet and illumine the universe that dwells within and without the human being. Science sans humanism may turn savage and must therefore be directed towards noble purposes and religion, bereft of righteousness and compassion for all Creations, may become barbaric and destructive defeating the glorious goal of self-realisation which makes the whole world Kin. In this context, we have to device ways and means of reaching truth and justice, values which are inalienable, if progress of all mankind is our tryst with destiny.

Science breeds technology and together holds out hope of human happiness worldwide. If misdirected, technology promotes thanatology or science of death. The glory of technology shines when its discoveries liberate humans from dogmas and obscurantisms and transforms society as a haven of joy and security, the fullness of faculties and scientific social order where egalite is writ large in the face of the world order. On the contrary, if satanic distortion possesses the scientist and technologist and his inventions are used to kill and conquer, to make profit and enslave people, the laboratory of discovery incarnates as cannibalism and exploitation of weaker sections victimised by powerful corporations and hegemonic, military states through inhuman globalisation. The choice between science for betterment of humanity and grave peril and incurable suffering of society depends upon wisdom and compassion versus wickedness and torturesome grab of wealth, with greed of the powerful dominating the needs of the victimised vast.

Let me quote a graphic portrait of contrast from Will Durant's Pleasures of Philosophy':

Here is an old man on the bed of death, harassed with helpless friends and wailing relatives. What a terrible sight it is—this thin frame with loosened and cracking flesh, this toothless mouth in a bloodless face, this tongue that cannot speak, these eyes that cannot see! To this pass youth has come, after all its hopes and trials; to this pass middle age, after all its torment and its toil. To this pass health and strength and joyous rivalry; this arm once struck great blows and fought for victory in virile games. To this pass knowledge, science, wisdom: for seventy years this man with pain and effort gathered knowledge; his brain became the storehouse of a varied experience, the center of a thousand subtleties of thought and deed; his heart through suffering learned gentleness as his mind learned understanding; seventy years he grew from an animal into a man capable of seeking truth and creating beauty. But death is upon him, poisoning him, choking him, congealing his blood gripping his heart, bursting his brain, rattling in his throat. Death wins.

Outside on the green boughs birds twitter, and Chantecler sings his hymn to the sun. Light streams across the fields; buds open and stalks confidently lift their heads; the sap mounts in the trees. Here are children: what is it that makes them so joyous, running madly over the dew-wet grass, laughing, calling, pursuing, eluding, panting for breath, inexhaustible? What energy, what spirit and happiness! What do they care about death? They will learn and grow and love and struggle and create, and lift life up one little notch, perhaps, before they die. And when they pass they will cheat death with children, with parental care that will make their offspring finer than themselves. There in the garden's twilight lovers pass, thinking themselves unseen; their quiet words mingle with the murmur of insects calling to their mates; the ancient hunger speaks through eager and through lowered eyes, and a noble madness courses through clasped hands and touching lips. Life wins.

The march of science is thus fraught with disaster or charged with sublime prospects, the decisive factor being the benign or malign direction it is put to. The agenda of the human future has to be drawn up by the world's thinkers and statesmen, its Bertrand Russels and Mahatma Gandhi's if our biosphere is to be the home of *homo sapiens*, spiraling to higher levels of perfection and cosmic harmony. The world can come to an end with massive miseries, macro-diseases and wildest bombs inflicting a sort of globoshima or gassasination. Development, in its noble dimensions, comes from the sound judgment on science policy and use of technology. The role of religion and *dharma* comes into play at this critical stage.

The outer space and environment, the exploration of Nature and the explosion of technology fall within the sphere of research. Even the mind and brain and their material side, including psychic and psychosomatic changes, fall for scientific study. Science, in its search for Truth, plays on the superficial level, occasionally penetrating the mysterious universe and the deeper dimensions of life and its inner processes. Truth, in its garment of materialism, is its jurisdiction, now and then great scientists unveiling the externals and peeping into the wonders beyond its normal jurisdiction and guessing, as philosophy does, at Creation and its imponderables. The artist of the Absolute paints Relativity and science and its lancet and lab grapple with the technology of the stars and skies, planets and global forces. The atom is within its sphere of operation; the *atman* is too deep for it to reach or touch. That is the task of philosophy, religion and spiritual vision. And yet philosophy (and religion) must cognize the findings of science if it is to feel its way to Reality. Will Durant writes:

> *The sciences are the windows through which philosophy sees the world, they are the senses of which it is the soul; without it their knowledge is as chaotically helpless as sensations that come to a disordered mind, making an idiot's lore. Spencer was right: philosophy is the most generalized knowledge. But he was wrong: it is not merely knowledge; it implies that difficult and elevated vision in which mere knowledge is lifted up into a total view that orders and clarifies the confusion of desire; it involves that strangely different quality called wisdom.*
>
> *Without science philosophy is impotent; for how can wisdom grow except on knowledge fairly won, with honest observation and research, and recorded and charted by impartial minds? Without science philosophy become decadent and dishonest, isolated from the flow of human growth, and falling more and more into the dreary futility of scholasticism. But without philosophy science is not merely helpless, it is destructive and devastating.*

Philosophy is a different route to Truth and Light, even as Religion, in its spiritual ascent, gravitates towards God, not in its theological crudity but in the Gandhian definition that Truth is God. God is a process, so is science. The more we dive into the ocean of Truth, the more pearls we gain and the more stones we drop. Religion, like science, renews itself as fresh dawns bring new sights and majestic visions. "Lead us from Darkness to Light; from Untruth to Truth" is a vedic saying which brings together science and religion, both being experiments with Truth. Every great scientist chasing the Absolute is religious; every saint gaining glimpses of the Grand Reality is a scientist of the Spirit. God is everywhere and science sees new Light everywhere. Listen to Walt Whitman:

> *I believe a leaf of grass is no less than the*
> *journey work of the stars.*
> *In the faces of men and women I see God, and in my*
> *Own face in the glass,*
> *I find letters from God dropt in the street, and every*
> *One is sign'd by God's name.*

What is Truth? The profoundest interrogation that confronts humanity has to be answered daily if existence is to possess sanity and not be lost in lunacy. So we enter the interface of *dharma* which is the lodestar that leads kindly light amidst the chaos in the cosmos. *Dharma* is righteousness, non-violence, duty, truth and divinity, all rolled into one.

The world today is in the grip of terror and horror, having been witness to two bloodiest wars and gruesome and ghastly violations of human rights. Hitler died by suicide but the grim prospect of torture and violent eruptions, killing unjustly hundreds of thousands of humans, still luridly survives, what with the United Nations Declarations and Resolutions laying down golden rules of jurisprudence. It has been rightly said that international law is the vanishing point of jurisprudence. That is why we find magnificent instrument of humanism and justice emanating from the United Nations, but the Super Power and lesser powers ignoring the obligations under these humane prescriptions with a touch of tyranny and despotic soi-disant global policing authority. Even in various States, dictatorship dwells dreadfully and democracy, with its thin veneer of people's Government, despises human rights and uses sovereignty as a cover for breaches of peace, security and the rule of law. Thus we find the world of contradiction, societies jettisoning the imperative of civilization and the State, which is obliged to protect the people trembles over rights. In this poignant scenario, we need to reconcile the apparent misuse and abuse of power and the *dharmic* obligation to prevent human rights violations. Science and Technology become weapons in the hands of the ruling class while injustice and suffering become the lot of the common masses. In such a strange and savage age in which we live, the necessity for *dharma* to control abuse of power and to restore truth, righteousness and justice, becomes an operational principle geared to the transformation of society. The Hindu culture of ancient vintage has developed the idea of *dharma* which is a beautiful blend of truthfulness and righteous justice and the rule of law which governs all, rulers and ruled alike. Legal literature of ancient India, called *dharma shasthras* contains the quintessence of truth and justice. *Dharma* is not static, but dynamic and collective harmony in human society, adapted from time to time to changing values. Perhaps the commandments which Christianity preaches and the "Quran" teaches also may be apprehended by the expression *dharma*, in its wider semantic sweep. But it is for the United Nations to articulate opposition to discrimination, abuse of power and other vulgarities and asuric forces by issuing declarations, covenants, resolutions and principles. In short, *dharma*, the conscience of mankind is an interface between science and religion. But to sustain political and socio-economic order, *dharma* comes to our rescue. In the golden days of the past, during periods of challenges and crises, the large Indian community used to fall back upon *dharma*, which bound kings and subjects alike. This is jurisprudence in its finest hour, and demands of science to promote human values and of all religions to prohibit superstitions obdurate obscurantism and other macro-monstrosities. *Dharma* is a science of celestial ideas of divine vision, of social harmony and of the preservation of the humblest humans, the lowliest, the lowest and the last. *Antayajas* (Dr. Ambedkar) and *Antyodaya* (Gandhi) come within the complex of *manava dharma*. It is this concept of integral humanism that is timeless and harmonious that luminously manages to extinguish chaos, distinguish between right and wrong and strives to nourish a social order which our founding fathers have spelt out in article 38 of the Constitution. The millennium that is close to us will be great only if democracy, in its social, economic and political structure, becomes a reality for all mankind. On the contrary, Corporate cannibals seek to inaugurate 'hellennium,' westoxicated with money-manic, diabolic vulgarities and values, making life for the vast populace everywhere a struggle against torture, a battle for survival and a stressful period of despair. Everyone who desiderates a global golden age governed by the dynamic rule of law must therefore opt for the jurisprudence of *dharma* (without any pejorative implications of particular religions) and divinisation of humanity.

CONCLUSION

A vistaramic vision of science and religion yields deeper perceptions than have been articulated in the past. A humanist synthesis and secular-sacred cross-fertilization may well be the new solution for a crime-riven society. *Dharma* is the nexus which tames science and humanises religion, though operating in dual dimensions. Moral values sustained by transformation into legal directives may well be the necessary route to an orderly society striving to accomplish it through a new functional mutuality. I would love to end this essay by quoting from an address by Lord Denning to the Law Society's National Conference:

> *When you look upon these scientific achievements, then look back for a moment on our world today, what do we see? Crime, increasing everywhere; sin, disgraceful sin, increasing everywhere, pollution, noisome pollution, increasing everywhere; corruption, corroding corruption, increasing everywhere. When we see this, surely we recall the words of 2,000 years ago. 'What doth it profit a man if he gains the whole world and loses his own soul?*

COMMITTEES AND COMMISSIONS OF BRITISH INDIAN VINTAGE

Post-Independence India, in its heritage of colonial culture, has clung to Committees and Commissions of British Indian vintage; and the currently bathetic proliferation of these institutions has rendered them illusory panaceas, pathological profusion of high cost, slow speed, Tammamy taint and no meaningful action for public good. The choice, the process, the product and the greed of retired judges to manipulate, make this methodology a dubious game. This Committee-Commission syndrome has its accommodative uses for defeated politicians and corrupt businessmen ready to buy a position at hidden prices. And whenever a vociferous grievance likely to damage a party in power has to be silenced, the strategy to save the criminal and the Administration is to appoint a Commission and then forget all about it. As for the noise making masses a commission is opium. There are judicial commissions, ombudsmanic commissions, Human Rights Commissions, Women's Commissions, and *ad hoc* Inquiry Commissions and Myriad Chameleon Commissions. Of course, the Constitution itself has sanctioned a plethora of them; and other statutory commissions are a tribe on the increase. Committees are fewer but are escalating in numbers. Whenever Government finds itself in a politically inconvenient situation, the remedy for the malady is a Committee. The appetite for committees and commissions grows since even bankrupt administrations guilty of culpable deviances can provide a cover, postpone the evil day and pack the Committee or Commission with pliable members. The difference between a Commission and a Committee is more verbal than real, more status-conscious than functional, more statutory than created by the Executive. There is no uniformity in nomenclature as, for instance, the Constitution Reform Commission, which is purely a creation of a transient Ministry, and yet within it there are many Committees (not sub-commissions). A semantic serendipity is the Kerala Ombudsman for overseeing panchayats' functionalism. The demand for sitting judges as Commissions to pull political clustnuts out of the fire is an abuse of judicial credibility and when the Report is politically unfavourable it is buried and rejected or no fruitful action taken. In short, committees, though less pompous, are often stratagems motivated by escapism or designed to achieve unholy objectives through the decent device of committees. The Indian experience of Commissions and Committees has largely been an expensive futility, institutional illusion or rogue process as a cover-up to gain political or economic end or hidden agenda by the backdoor.

It is not my purpose to condemn all Commissions or Committees but to enter a caveat to use wisdom, statesmanship and concern for the nation's interests, dismissing political expediency and corrupt objectives, even a wee-bit, when deciding on a Commission or Committee, choosing its composition, terms of Reference and determination to take action on the Recommendations. At this point, we may go back to the legacy of Commissioner methodology and its history in pre-Independence India which constitute the four volumes work under review here. The mintage of this instrument of plural member wisdom is British and its vintage belongs to the British Indian era of the early nineteenth century. Administration may become chaos in the cosmos unless policies are based on principles, governance is guided by democratic fundamentals and collective notices of experienced persons leads lay ministers and mindless masses along correct lines. The mental-moral and pragmatic processes must precede governmental action and relevant legislation. So no democracy can dispense with an antecedent expert examination because of the complexities and variegated ground realities of society; and that is the *raison d'etre of* Commissions in England, and Committees, called Royal Commissions with their roots in the regal regime at the beginning of the second millennium. This instrumentality, as a sophisticated tool, came into frequent use in the thirties of the nineteenth century. Naturally, imperial India also had its share of such investigative bodies. Mittal Publications have taken great pains and invested research labours in producing four volumes including quite a few of the important Committees and Commissions between 1836 and 1947. A boon for a researcher, rare material for a student of the comparative history of pre-Indian and post-Indian Commissions and a valuable insight into the history and policy of British rule in Viceregal times. One need not be allergic to everything – British Indian, in which case our bureaucracy, judiciary, and civil administrative structure, which still retain the paper-logged and hierarchical, systemic infirmities and philosophy of 'the white man's burden' may have to be regarded as anathematic.

The very concept of Commissions and Committees has merits, if wisely used, and has demerits and deceptions if misused with *mala fides*. Anyway, Free India is slave to the Commission opium. Popular clamour for judicial enquiry even for tremendous trifles is another folly which delays and defeats regular legal proceedings and benefits the Commissioner judge if he is indolent or retired, and what is worse, the villain will gain from the delay since evidence will evaporate. The dilatory Report may or may not be published at the pleasure of Government or acted upon according to its mood or interest. The report is not even probative material in a civil or criminal court. In short, Commissions and Committees are a gamble if freedom of information for the public is defeated or distorted save in a few exceptional cases.

Let us look at the British Indian experience from 1836 to 1947 covered by the four volumes divided into four periods. The Whigs, when in power in British politics, stood for limited monarchy, liberal Parliament and social values. They were willing to experiment with Commissions and Committees at home and in India.

Royal Commissions galore secured access to British India and facilitated better understanding of the impact of the alien administration on the people. Two important Committees, whose findings are included in Volume One, are significant. Since imperial security had high priority, the two Committees were concerned with Prison Discipline (1838) and Jail Conditions (1864). The rebellion of 1857, a shock to the foreign rulers, led to the Special Ordinance Commission (1874). The Fainine Commission (1878) and two Commissions on salt manufacture and allied issues are purposeful. Alas, even today, prison justice, salt supplies, famine, health and education are pathetic problems. Time stands still, suffering persists and pachydermic rulers are comfortable. The rationale behind these enquiries is simple. Maladies must be diagnosed before remedies are prescribed and then alone will administrative action help. Imperialism did not believe in soft justice. The British introduced afflictive punishments in jails and one who reads the ruling in *Sunil Batra* on Prison Reform and the Report of 1836 on Prison discipline together will soon realize the humanist winds of *Sunil* as against the blood and iron of Jail injustice recommended by the Pre-Independence Committee. Even so, it is informative to go through the Terms of Reference, Recommendations and other contents which present the horror of punitive processes, with a touch of humanity here and there. As 'penitentiary' literature, it is interesting reading; but if compassion is a cultural component of sentencing the British heart muscles are made of savage cells. 'Deterrent' prescription, if harsh, misses reformatory justice; and the advance India has made, if any, in jail reforms, has to be assessed in the light of the British Indian Committee Report. We too had a National Jail Reforms Commission but, in pensive mood, I feel that we have hardly done justice to that and other reports on custodial justice. Incarceratory humanism has miles to go if jail realism is to keep faith with the Constitution. Let us proceed. Anees Chishti, in an instructive Introduction observes:

> *That the findings and recommendations of a Commission of Enquiry are primarily of an advisory nature and it is not mandatory for the appointing government to implement the recommendations of these bodies has been a constant source of disappointment to aggrieved sections that are concerned with the issues that lead to or cause the appointment of an investigating agency. This issue should be debated thoroughly and the need for some*

> *mandatory status being given to the recommendations of Commissions and Committees has to be highlighted forcefully. Legislation to this effect is indeed a desirable step, but that does not seem to be very easy to achieve. In independent India itself where an open and democratic system of governance exists, the voice of the people, particularly the exhortations of the Press to the government to implement recommendations of its Commissions and Committees from time to time, such implementation is found to be often not complied with. And, one can imagine, what degree of arbitrariness might be associated with picking and choosing of recommendations for implementation by an alien government governing India in case some of the recommendations of an investigating body were unpalatable to the foreign rulers.*

The vast reforms I made in Kerala in 1957 as minister and prescribed as rule of law from the Supreme Court as judge, makes me wonder why even the jail-going ministers keep prisons even now hell! Oscar Wilde's lines on prison life is good for the new Indian millennium: 'Something was dead in each of us, and what was dead was Hope'. The truth is that the British meant business when Royal Commissions were set up but Indian rulers rarely took Commissions seriously or set them up to escape Opposition criticism or public anger. The gap between intentions and actions, *vis a vis* Commissions if closely studied over the years, revealed how implementation lagged behind the professed objectives. Even Parliamentary Commissions in India, when tested on the touchstone of action taken, had a sorry tale to tell.

Chishti, in his illuminating opening, explains the nuances of distinction between Committees and Commissions, which, I consider, has no uniform application but does help know the scope and status of these enquiries. Let me quote:

> *A study of the nature and coverage of the Commissions and Committees of the boom period would reveal the true motivation behind their appointments. They were appointed to know the lacunae in the administration of the country by the British, particularly after a firm notice had been served on the British masters of India by the rebellious Indians in 1857. Only after detecting the shortcomings, the loose ends could be tightened, be they in the management of prisons, the operation of the penal code, sale of and tax on salt, the famines that could be the cause of unrest, different areas of the economy, the crucial sector of education, the conditions in the matter of narcotics, or even tackling health issues like Plague, Kala-Azar or Leprosy where success could create favourable public opinion about the alien government among the people, at least in the consequential urban areas.*

If, indeed, I take volume after volume and critique them separately, my angry analysis and your tolerable patience will outrage the editor who struggles with space. So I compress the review but remind the reader that rare material, rarer marshalling and rarest of all, presenting the essential parts of the anatomy of each Report hard to get even for an industrious research are packed into the pages without hiking the price. What a large range of subjects like Delhi Town Planning, Tuberculosis in India, Decentralisation in India (1907), Army Organisation and Expenditure in India, Railway Commission, Indian Universities, Leprosy in India, Opium, Labour Enquiry Commission (1895) Indian Education and so on. What a Vistarama! admirable and Imperial history from a different angle!

I endorse Chishti's concluding expectations:

> *It is hoped that the contemporary researchers would make a positive use of these reports and benefit from their findings, keeping in view, all the time, the colonial biases that might be a significant feature of these reports.*

Fine thought. But in our era of bibliophobia reading is low priority unless it be linked to pornos, casteist mythos or narco-thanatos.

CABINET SANS CONFIDENCE OF HOUSE—A CABAL IN POWER OR PRO TEM CARETAKER BY COURTESY—SOME CONSTITUTIONAL PERCEPTIONS

India is passing through many crises, material, moral, military and miscellaneous. One of the critical and portentous dilemmas turns on the current constitutional imbroglio relating to the restraints on the role of the cabinet which, having lost the confidence motion in the House of the People, continues as a precarious *locum tenens* until the imminent next election, on the strength of the President's 'pleasure' as a pro tem Caretaker Government. Minority Governments sustained by support from the Opposition are becoming common at the Centre and in the States, in India and other democracies. In a world which is rapidly changing and throwing up issues of great moment we cannot blink at the broad parameters and pragmatic principles Caretaker Governments must accept. Presently, our country is in the grip of constitutional contretemps and other ominous issues. I confine myself to the constitutional limitations. Unless reasonably just solutions are found by jurists our democracy may be derailed, the rule of law hijacked and the governance of the country may prove to be authoritarian, unaccountable and illegitimate.

Our founding fathers had patterned our Republic on the Westminster style with a President who is more like a constitutional head of State, mostly a ceremonial figure, with some authority, and a Cabinet answerable to Parliament substantially embodying the conventions of the British Constitution. The Council of Ministers rules and the President reigns, if one may express the constitutional profile in a general way. "The President, like the King, has not merely been constitutionally romanticised but actually vested with a pervasive and persuasive role. While he plays such a role, he is not a rival centre of power in any sense and must abide by and act on the advice tendered by his Ministers except in a narrow territory which is sometimes slippery."

In *Samsher Singh*'s case, (1974 SCC 8310) the powers of the President and the Prime Minister have been discussed at length in the separate but concurring judgment of Krishna Iyer J with whom Bhagwati J concurred. "The law of our Constitution, any student of Indian political history and of comparative constitutional systems will agree, is partly eclectic but primarily an Indo- Anglian version of the Westminster model with quasi-federal adaptations, historical modifications, geo-political mutations and home-spun traditions – basically a blended brew of the British Parliamentary system, and the Government of India Act, 1935 and near-American, nomenclature-wise and in some other respects.

Not the Potomac, but the Tames, fertilises the flow of the Yamuna, if we may adopt a riverine imagery. In this thesis we are fortified by precedents of this Court, strengthened by Constituent Assembly proceedings and reinforced by the actual working of the organs involved for about a 'silver jubilee' span of time."

Granville Austin has pointed out: "The (Constituent) Assembly chose a slightly modified version of the British Cabinet system. India was to have a President, indirectly elected for a term of five years, who would be a constitutional head of State in the manner of the Monarch in England ..... As in England, there was to be a Council of Ministers, headed by the Prime Minister and collectively responsible to Parliament, to aid and advise the head of State. The President was to be the nominal head of the Executive; the Prime Minister the real head." Sri. Alladi Krishnaswamy Iyer explained to the Assembly the position of the President *vis-à-vis* the Cabinet thus: "It was provided in the Constitution . . . . that the Council of Ministers would be collectively responsible to the House of the People. If a President stood in the way of the Council of Ministers discharging that responsibility, he would be guilty of violation of the Constitution and would even be liable for impeachment. It was, therefore, merely a euphemistic way of saying that the President had to be guided by the advice of his Ministers. The Council of Ministers were collectively responsible to the House of the People, answerable to the House in regard to the Budget, all legislation and *indeed for every matter connected with the administration of the country.* There was therefore no necessity for setting out in detail in an article of the Constitution what the functions and incidents of responsible Government would be.

Dr. Ambedkar's comprehensive statement introducing the Draft Constitution on November 4, 1948 is scintillating. He said:

> *In the Draft Constitution there is placed at the head of the Indian Union a functionary who is called the President of the Union. The title of this functionary reminds one of the President of the United States. But beyond identity of names there is nothing in common between the form of Government prevalent in America and the form of Government proposed under the Draft Constitution. Under the Draft Constitution the President occupies the same position as the King under the English Constitution. He is the head of the State but not the Executive. He represents the nation but*

does not rule the nation. He is the symbol of the nation. His place in the administration is that of a ceremonial device on a seal by which the nation's decisions are made known. Under the American Constitution the President has under him Secretaries in charge of different departments. In like manner the President of the Indian Union will have under him Ministers in charge of different departments of administration. Here again there is a fundamental difference between the two. The President of the United States is not bound to accept any advice tendered to him by any of his Secretaries. The President of the Indian Union will be generally bound by the advice of his Ministers. He can do nothing contrary to their advice nor can he do anything without their advice. The President of the United States can dismiss any Secretary at any time. The President of the Indian Union has no power to do so long as his Ministers command a majority in Parliament.

Dr. Ambedkar emphatically asserted in the Assembly that the President will be bound to accept the advice of the Ministers. *In fact, he cannot act without the advice of his Ministers.* It is true that even Dr. Rajendra Prasad and Sri Munshi had doubts about the success of such a scheme. Sri Munshi stated: "During the framing of the Constitution, we all dreamt that we would make a success of Parliamentary democracy and the British Cabinet system. *It must be confessed that this experiment has failed. If I had to make a choice again, I would vote for the Presidential form of Government,* so that, whenever the politicians fail the country, there is at least one strong organ of the State capable of tiding over the crisis."

Sri B.N. Rau, who was the constitutional advisor at the time of the framing of the Constitution, has observed that the Parliamentary system of Government in India, with periodic elections, *Parliamentary control of Ministers* and a constitutional Monarch at the head, was part of our cultural heritage from the days of Manu and Kautilya, has met the familiar arguments urged to invest powers in the President as against the Council of Ministers. In an article, published in 1957, captioned *To what extent is the President under the Indian Constitution required, in the discharge of his functions, to act upon the advice of his Ministers,* he has dealt with the relevant articles and the usual considerations put forward to reject the theory of a symbolic presidency.

Sir Ivor Jennings, a reputed British Jurist, has endorsed the view that tho' the President has vast powers vested in him, going literally, but history must provide the *modus vivendi* as between the cabinet and the Rashtrapathi. In an article entitled Crown and Commonwealth in Asia he, however, wrote:

Dr. Rajendra Prasad seems to have been following British conventions with some fidelity; but there is nothing in the Constitution which requires him or his successors to do so, and one of them may well say that he is not bound by the constitutional practices followed in a foreign monarchy and that he proposes to carry out the law and the law alone.

The tyranny of literality in interpreting the constitutional text may lead to dangerous consequences and stifle the soul of democracy for which the struggle for freedom was waged. This aspect has been dealt with in *Samsher Singh*'s case and deserves to be repeated for the sake of clarity of understanding about the structural basics of our Constitution. I quote from that ruling: " In Felix Frankfurter's phrase, this is the "gloss which life has written" on our constitutional clauses, and the Court, true to its function, must try to reflect that gloss by balancing in its ruling the origin, formulation, and growth of a constitutional structure denying judicial aid to undermining the democratic substance of Cabinet Government. A coup can be constitutionally envisioned by an erroneously literal interpretation of the living words of the Organic Law. Prof. Allen Glendhill, we must warn ourselves, wrote:

Let us assume that a President has been elected who has successfully concealed his ambition to establish an authoritarian system of Government. One-fourth of the Members of a House of Parliament, suddenly aware of the danger, give notice of a motion to impeach the President. Before the fourteen days, within which it can be moved, the President dissolves Parliament; a new House must be elected but it need not meet for six months. He dismisses the Ministers and appoints others of his own choice, who for six months need not be Members of Parliament and during that period he can legislate by ordinance. He can issue a Proclamation of Emergency, legislate on any subject and deprive the States of their shares in the proceeds of distributable taxes. He can issue directions to States calculated to provoke disobedience and then suspend the States' Constitutions. He can use the armed forces in support of the civil power. He can promulgate preventive detention ordinances and imprison his opponents.

Again, that learned jurist has commented:

> *The Constitution vests the executive power of the Union in the President and provides that all executive action shall be taken in his name. The President is also given many powers, shortly to be discussed, but the last fourteen years have shown the world that India is a Parliamentary democracy in which Ministers decide policy and carry on Government, but the Constitution does not say in as many words that the President must act on Ministerial advice; what it says is that there shall be a Council of Ministers to aid and advise the President; no court may inquire into the question whether any, and if so what, advice was tendered to the President. What the Constitution contemplates is that normally the Government shall be carried on by a committee of Ministers selected from the elected representatives of the people, but it recognises that circumstances may arise in which that system may break down, so it is desirable that there should be some authority empowered to continue the Government and set about restoring Parliamentary Government as soon as possible. It is for this reason that Constitution legally vests the executive power on the President.*

> *We cannot allow a "confusion of vision" to creep into our constitutional interpretation because political scientists notice grave short-comings in the electoral process, social workers complain of corrupt misuse of power by parties in office or the ordinary people find legislators indifferent and ineffective. After all, any social scientist will agree that in a rapidly changing and inter-acting world the technology of government by the people has to be a continuous process of readjustment and fresh experiment. As Judges, we only essay a creative understanding of the constitutional complex, not a programme for possible innovations.*

The overwhelming weight of judicial authority makes the proposition that India has adopted the Cabinet system of the Westminster model. To sum up, the President cannot exercise power without the aid and advice of the Council of Ministers. Likewise the Cabinet is answerable to the Parliament and when it fails there, it must resign and cease to enjoy constitutional authority to govern. "The omnipotence of the President and of the Governor at State level – is euphemistically inscribed in the pages of our Fundamental Law with the obvious intent that even where express conferment of power or functions is written into the articles, such business has to be disposed of decisively by the Ministry answerable to the Legislature and through it vicariously to the people, thus vindicating our democracy instead of surrendering it to a single summit soul whose deification is incompatible with the basis of our political architecture-lest national elections become but Dead Sea fruits, legislative organs become labels full of sound and fury signifying nothing and the Council of Ministers put in a quandary of responsibility to the House of the People and submission to the personal decision of the head of State. A Parliamentary-style Republic like ours could not have conceptualised its self-liquidation by this process.

Samsher Singh's case concludes:

> *We declare the law of this branch of our Constitution to be that the President and Governor, custodians of all executive and other powers under various articles shall, by virtue of these provisions, exercise their formal constitutional powers only upon and in accordance with the advice of their Ministers save in a few well-known exceptional situations. Without being dogmatic or exhaustive, these situations relate to (a) the choice of Prime Minister (Chief Minister), restricted though this choice is by the paramount consideration that he should command a majority in the House; (b) the dismissal of a Government which has lost its majority in the House, but refuses to quit office; (c) the dissolution of the House where an appeal to the country is necessitous, although in this area the head of State should avoid getting involved in politics and must be advised by his Prime Minister (Chief Minister) who will eventually take the responsibility for the step. We do not examine in detail the constitutional proprieties in these predicaments except to utter the caution that even here the action must be compelled by the peril*

to democracy and the appeal to the House or to the country must become blatantly obligatory.

The exalted status of the President, not withstanding, the true jural fundamental is set out in Samsher Singh: "The omnipotence of the President and of the Governor at State level – is euphemistically inscribed in the pages of our Fundamental Law with the obvious intent that even where express conferment of power or functions is written into the articles, such business has to be disposed of decisively by the Ministry answerable to the Legislature and through it vicariously to the people, thus vindicating our democracy instead of surrendering it to a single summit soul whose deification is incompatible with the basics of our political architecture." Otherwise the Cabinet will be in a quandary of responsibility to the House of the People and submission to the personal decision of the head of State.

The next issue setforth for consideration is to ascertain whether the President is only a Ceremonial Glory or has, *in fact,* strategic powers to act of his own in special situations. His solemn oath, as the highest functionary is not frothy phraseology but sanctions action geared "to preserve, protest and defend the Constitution and devote himself to the service and well-being of the people of India." Moreover, under article 78, he has the right to demand information from the Prime Minister covering any aspect of Government. This is a constitutional power, which cannot be derogated from by the Cabinet. There is no secrecy regarding any information, however sensitive it be. The President, like the Crown in England, has the right "to the consulted, to encourage and to warn". Acting on Ministerial advice does not necessarily mean immediate acceptance of the Ministry's resolves. The President can state all his objections to any proposed course of action and ask his Ministers in Council, if necessary, to reconsider the matter. It is only in the last resort that he must accept their final advice. In grave situations and extraordinary exigencies where democracy and its paramountcy are in imminent jeopardy, the Rashtrapati may defend the nation invoking his great oath, in the rarest of rare cases, compelled by the magnitude of the peril and the profundity of the impact on the basic structure.

Even when a war involves the nation or other matter of great moment shakes the people about corruption among Ministers and minions, the President has the privilege of compelling transparency and surrender of facts, however strategic, they be. There is no iron curtain between the President and the Cabinet.

Shamsher Singh substantiates its reasoning thus: "The President of India is *not* at all a glorified cipher. He represents the majesty of the State, is at the apex, though only symbolically, and has rapport with the people and parties, being above politics. His vigilant presence makes for good government if only he uses, what Bagehot described as "the right to be consulted, to warn and encourage". Indeed, article 78, wisely used, keeps the President in close touch with the Prime Minister on matters of national importance and policy significance, and there is no doubt that the imprint of his personality may chasten and correct the political Government, although the actual exercise of the functions entrusted to him by law is in effect and in law carried on by his duly appointed mentors, *i.e.*, the Prime Minister and his colleagues. In short, the President, like the King, has not merely been constitutionally romanticised but actually vested with a pervasive and persuasive role. Political theorists are quite conversant with the dynamic role of the Crown, which keeps away from politics and power and yet influences both. While he plays such a role, he is not a rival centre of power in any sense and must abide by and act on the advice tendered by his Ministers except in a narrow territory which is sometimes slippery".

All these propositions proceed on the basic thesis that there is a House, which is a controllorate over the Cabinet, which must command the confidence of the Commons. Subject to this effective discipline, the Ministers govern in the name of the President, except in certain exceptional situations. For example, in *J.P. Metter*'s case, the Supreme Court held that the *President had exclusive power to determine the age of a judge* when it was in dispute. The Cabinet has to keep its hands off and cannot advice the President as to the age of the judge. Why? Because the independence of the judiciary will vanish, if the Ministry can advice the President on the dispute. That is why the Executive has no voice in matters connected with judges, including their age. The President is the sole authority there and may consult the Chief Justice of India.

As in the case of the age of judges, there is an exception in the case of disqualification of members of Legislatures where the Cabinet cannot advise the President. "In *Brundaban Nayak* v. *Election Commission* another sensitive situation relating to the functions of the President (Article 103) and the Governor (Article 192) arose. It is a sacred principle of our democracy, like the independence of the Judiciary, that decisions on the disqualifications of Members of Assemblies should be unbiased. While formally the power to decide a dispute in this behalf is vested in the President and the Governor under articles 103 and 192, respectively, it would be a travesty of impartiality if such decision were to be made on the aid and advice of a Ministry which is essentially chosen from a party or combination of parties. How can a political activist with party loyalty in our pluralistic society judge a cause in which he has deep concern? Therefore, the Constitution has made the Election Commission the real arbiter in the dispute". As future shocks spring suddenly where the vitals of democracy, constitutional basics *et al* desiderate Presidential judgment, the Cabinet may not issue ukases over-ruling or by-passing the Rashtrapati.

Another well-known exception to the Cabinet's voice prevailing over the President's view is the issue of sanction to prosecute a Minister. The Court has rightly ruled that the Cabinet cannot advise the President in such a matter. How preposterous it would be for the Rashtrapati to be obligatorily bound by the ministry about one of its members being prosecuted for a crime *prima facie* made out! Thus when new challenges shoot up, the dogmas of Cabinet power, good for the quiet past, may not handcuff the President in the turbulent and malignant present, if the spinal, seminal novelty and riddlesome character of the decisional matter justly desiderates the independent judgement of the President.

A distantly relevant instance of importance may strengthen the point that the Cabinet is dispowered to advice the President *viz.* the appointment of judges. The Supreme Court has the sole power to choose, the Law Ministry merely processes the names and the President acts as recommended by the Chief Justice. The Prime Minister has forfeited this valuable authority thanks to a High Bench Holding (with which I do not personally agree). The Supreme Court is final not because it is infallible. It is infallible because it is final.

Another observation is noteworthy. While Alladi, a leading jurist and statesman and activist in the Constituent Assembly, expanded the amplitude of the Cabinet's plenary power, Justice Alladi Kuppuswami (the son) argued for a more positive presidential intervention. He gave the instance of President Venkatraman refusing Shanti Bhushan's request for sanction to prosecute Rajiv Gandhi for corruption. (Incidentally, the same President declined to assent to a Bill improving parliamentarians' pension because of a basic flaw in the introduction of a money Bill). Anyway, the pro-Presidential slant of former Chief Justice Alladi Kuupuswami runs thus: "As in the past, there will be occasions in the future when the President has to act on his own without being aided and advised by the Council of Ministers. Thus, he need not be a figurehead or a rubber-stamp as visualized by the framers of the Constitution." This broad proposition is overdrawn and the Rashtrapati Bhavan has to accept more circumspection and circumscription and self-limitation because what is at stake is the parliamentary system.

Let us shift our focus to a case where the House has been dissolved. In *U.N.R. Rao*'s case (1971) 2 SCC 63, this point was discussed with lucidity and learned authority by Sikri C.J. "The Constituent Assembly did not choose the presidential system of Government. If we were to give effect to this contention of the appellant we would be changing the whole concept of the Executive. It would mean that the President need not have a Prime Minister and Ministers to aid and advise in the exercise of his functions. As there would be no 'Council of Ministers' nobody would be responsible to the House of the People. With the aid of advisers he would be able to rule the country at least till he is impeached under article 61.

The appellant urges that the House of the People having been dissolved this clause cannot be complied with. According to him it follows from the provisions of this clause that it was contemplated that on the dissolution of the House of People the Prime Minister and the other Ministers must resign or be dismissed by the President and the President must carry on the Government as best as he can with the aid of the Services. As we have shown above, article 74(1) is mandatory and, therefore, the President cannot exercise power without the aid and advice of the Council of Ministers. We must then harmonise the provisions of article 75(3) with article 74(1) and article 75(2). Article 75(3) brings into existence what is usually called 'responsible Government'. In other words, the Council of Ministers must enjoy the confidence of the House of People. While the House of People is not dissolved under article 82(2)(b) article 75(3) has full operation. But when it is dissolved the Council of Ministers cannot naturally enjoy the confidence of the House of People. Nobody has said that the Council of Ministers do not enjoy the confidence of the House of People when it is prorogued. In the context therefore, this clause must be read as meaning that article 75(3) only applies when the House of People does not stand dissolved or prorogued". In short, even when the House is in suspended animation (prorogued) or dissolved, the President acts thro' his Cabinet, not using insulated, unaccountable power with a fuehrer potential. The rulings thus result in the President having to govern *only* with a Cabinet to rule, even when the House is dissolved. A ministry sans the House is conceivable but the tenure is not full-blooded as representing the people since the Parliament is under eclipse.

Imagine a more aggravated span of unaccountable national administration. Constitutionally speaking, a Cabinet which loses the Confidence of the Lok Sabha instantly exits as the mandatory fundamental of collective responsibility to the Lok Sabha snaps (article 75(3) and survival after death is not a constitutional phenomenon. True, showing the door to Prime Minister and Co. when a confidence vote collapses will leave a vacuum, which is a constitutional anathema. To keep in office a ministry after the House has expressed lack of faith is bete noire. Equally allergic is to leave the President the solo ruler. The only way to cut the Gordian Knot is to search for a balancing of the clashing principles more in keeping with the highest courts seminal ratio. Better the President and a Council rather than a solitary throne is the direction of judicial wisdom, perhaps.

CARETAKER CABINET – CONSTITUTIONAL PARAMETERS

When a House runs out its course the President requests the Government to continue to enable the holding of elections and bringing a new House into being. This is a straight-forwarded case of a Caretaker Ministry. The plenary executive authority of a Council of Ministers which commands the confidence of the elected surrogates is morally and politically higher as it carries the people with it in larger measure than a lame duck lack-luster locum cabinet as an interregnum by courtesy of the Rashtrapati for routine management of State business. A lesser breed of Caretaker Cabinet is a creature of exigency. Where the Lok Sabha has voted out a Ministry but no alternative majority leader is in sight, the President, by constitutional compulsion, has to run the country through a Council of Ministers (as per the rulings of the Supreme Court), must make-do with a transient team as a stop-gap arrangement until the early poll is held. Necessity is the mother of invention and a reluctant category of Caretaker coterie is put in place. Such situations are rare and tenurial brevity is must be writ large on its bosom. Indeed, the basic rule of responsibility to Parliament stands negated in this anomalous instance because the House has already rejected a Confidence Motion. A rootless Cabinet with no House to control and worse, with the stigma of a negation of confidence expressed explicitly, is more a formal compliance, a euphemism for a Cabinet.

Does such a doubly debilitated Government possess the large executive authority and total parliamentary accountability of a regular Cabinet whose Prime Minister, by the credential of House majority, is the leader? Morally and politically no. But constitutional diction cannot exhaustively express answer for every bizarre or freak development lying in the womb of the future.

We function under the Constitution but the Constitution is what the judges say it is. From this perspective, we have to abide by the Supreme Court's pronouncement, read with article 141 of the Constitution. As has been long ago observed by Dixon J. "The task of expounding a Constitution is crucially different from that of construing a statute. A statute defines present rights and obligations. It is easily enacted and easily repealed. A Constitution, by contrast, is drafted with an eye to the future. Its function is to provide a continuing framework for the legitimate exercise of governmental power and, when joined by a Charter of Rights, for the unlimiting protection of individual rights and liberties. Once enacted, its provisions can't easily be repealed or amended. It must, therefore, be capable of growth and development over time to meet new social, political and historical realities often unimagined by its framers. The judiciary is the guardian of the Constitution and must, in interpreting its provisions, bear these conditions in mind."(*Hunter et al* v. *The Southam Inc.*, 1984 11 DLR 641 at 649 per Dickson J.). The creative realism and imaginative progressivism of the Judiciary make a Constitution work better and brighter in the future. There are competing theories of interpretive approaches like the literal theory, the purposive theory and the teleological or value – coherent theory. The *sui generis* nature of constitutional construction is now well accepted in the judicial universe. Less rigidity and more generosity is needed when discovering meaning in the Constitution, as distinguished from an ordinary statute. It is the Constitution and not the parliament, which is supreme, and the court must remember its duty to protect and uphold the Constitution, rather than be swayed by parliamentary expressions and passions. To emphasise my point I may as well quote from a South African ruling where Frowneman J emphasised the need for judges to adopt a radical mind-set in response to the needs of the people's march towards the millenium of Human Justice. The Learned Judge wrote: (the Indian Judges must also remember, in the light of the Preambular pledge,) "In a constitutional system based on parliamentary sovereignty it makes good sense to start from the premise of seeking the "intention of the legislature" in statutory interpretation, because the interpreting Judge's value judgment of the content of the statute, is theoretically at least, irrelevant... The interpretative notion of ascertaining the "intention of the Legislature" does not apply in a system of judicial review based on the supremacy of the Constitution, for the simple reason that the Constitution is sovereign and not the Legislature... The interpretation of the Constitution will be directed at ascertaining the foundational values inherent in the Constitution, whilst the interpretation of the particular legislation will be directed at ascertaining whether the legislation is capable of an interpretation which conforms with the fundamental values or principles of the Constitution. Constitutional interpretation in this sense is thus primarily concerned with the recognition and application of constitutional values and not with a search to find the literal meaning of statutes." Paramountacy belongs to the Paramount Parchment. Supreme Court Judges of the US had often done service to the nation by this remarkable approach and interpretive philosophy. "It is surprising but true that many of the principles of constitutional liberty most prized by Americans were created, not by the founders but by the Supreme Court during this century. At the very least, the understandings that have given those principles their current life are very recent creations. Indeed, for most of the country's history the liberties chartered in our Bill of Rights were sharply circumscribed. The overriding reason for there modern Supreme Court... A return to a narrowly described "original understanding" would result in the elimination, in one bold stroke, of many constitutional safeguards." Bhagwati J. expressed the same thought " It must be remembered that a Constitution is a totally different kind of enactment than an ordinary statute. It is an organic instrument defining and regulating the power structure and power relationship: it embodies the hopes and aspirations of the people; it projects certain basic values and it sets out certain objectives and goals. It cannot, therefore, be interpreted like any ordinary statute. It must be interpreted creatively and imaginatively with a view to advancing the constitutional values and spelling out and strengthening the basic human rights of the large masses of the people..."

A resume of the discussion leads to the logical conclusion that although textually the Constitution does not use the expression Caretaker Council of Ministers, Judges have to think through the foundational proposition of parliamentarism. A Ministry, with a House to invigilate, is the normal rule. But when the House is under eclipse a Caretaker Ministry takes over. A

Caretaker is less than a Prime Minister commanding a majority. And when the House has voted out a Ministry for want of confidence, there is a graded inequality in the Status and quantum of Exclusive power *vis-a-vis* the President, in whom the Constitution, in so many words, vests all Executive Authority. It follows that a Government censured by the new House, but surviving for a short spell during the presidential 'pleasure' needed for the re-incarnation of the House through the hustings, cannot arrogate to itself what belongs to a majority leader-cum-Prime Minister sitting on the commanding height of the House.

The only question then is what can the Caretaker Ministers do – and cannot. This is a grey area and depends on circumstances, crises, national consensus and presidential vigilance. One thing is certain. Major policy changes of a serious character cannot be undertaken. Similarly a reversal of policies of great moment accepted in the past with the silent or express assent of the House cannot be reversed or even materially modified. That is stultifying the House. Any drastic measure, which is fround upon by the displeasure of the President, is violative of constitutional propriety. Likewise, when a grave danger suddenly descends on the nation the absence of the House must be partially made up for by consultation with the former members of parliament or leading parties. It must be noted that parliament includes *the two Houses and the President*. Therefore, when the Loksabha is dissolved, the two other entities remain. So much so, crucial decisions call for consultation by the pro tem Executive. To consult the Rajyasabha and the President himself is fair. Not to do this minimal compliance by a cabinet which exists by survival after death is unjust. They should not shy from the Rajyasabha or the political parties. *Ipse dixits* of the Cabinet cannot carry the same authority as in a normal case. These are tentative suggestions and depend upon urgencies and national or international conditions. Do avoid a grammar of constitutional anarchy by grammatical construction or pettifogging argument missing the grand mission and founding vision of the Constitution created by "We the People of India".

POSTSCRIPT

There is a current controversy about even calling the Rajya Sabha to discuss the nation's macabre Kargil battles and the high level communications between the Pak P.M. as well as the U.S. President plus taking into confidence the people thro' the Upper House and receive feed back, criticisms and insistence on Governmental transparency and people's right to know about the war strategy and the mobilisation of patriotic readiness to defend the motherland by blood, toil, tears and sweat, as well as energising our farms and factories. Elimination of corruption, hoarding and profiteering must end and the law must be harsh. Extravance, wasteful paraphernalia and public prodigality must be banished. After all, P.M. and Co., are not even members of Parliament but bare citizens holding office during the pleasure of the President who is a high functionary, although chosen by indirect election. Debate is the self-critical correction by the nation and no argument of demoralisation of the Defense Forces can have democratic validity.

Before concluding, it would be interesting to notice how Prime Minister Winston Churchill, in the later stages of the War, formed a Government which and which he regarded as a National Administration but which was in his own words a Caretaker Government. Thus we have a glorious instance of a Caretaker Government in Britain during World War II. Although that Coalition had a majority in the House, even that Government did not retreat from debate in the Parliament. There was a vote of censure at a time when the British Forces where losing and retreating. Churchill did not avoid the debate and was severely criticized as incompetent. Nevertheless the daring democratic Churchill faced the charges against him and wound up the debate thus:

> *This long debate has now reached its final stage. What a remarkable example it has been of the unbridled freedom of our Parliamentary institutions in time of war! Everything that could be thought of or raked up has been used to weaken confidence in the Government, has been used to prove that Ministers are incompetent and to weaken their confidence in themselves, to make the Army distrust the backing it is getting from the civil power, to make the workmen lose confidence in the weapons they are striving so hard to make, to present the government as a set of nonentities over whom the Prime Minister towers, and then to undermine him in his own heart, and, if possible, before the eyes of the nation. All this poured out by cable and radio to all parts of the world, to the distress of all our friends and to the delight of all our foes! I am in favour of this freedom, which no other country would use, or dare to use, in times of mortal peril such as those through which we are passing."*

If this is the model of democratic functioning during the World War by Great Britain there is no justification to avoid a debate in the Rajya Sabha over Kargil and allied matters, especially when the Government is not a majority party but a lingering coterie censured out of office. I have great reverence for the Prime Minister but I have no appreciation for one who will not take the surviving remnant of Parliament into confidence. The right to know is a people's fundamental. The duty to be responsive to the House which still is an integral parliamentary instrument is non-negotiable. Kargil cannot stifle people's investigative, invigilatory and information-extracting right. Presidential activism has to quicken the high office of a constitutional sentinel on the *qui vive*.

The Kargil intrusion by Pakistan gave a grave shock to the national territorial integrity. And when the Ministry, already disapproved by the Lok Sabha, wears the cloak of power on the slender 'pleasure' of the President, its fundamental accountability to the People of India has to be vicariously discharged by calling the Rajya Sabha and present the full facts and get a feed back from the Upper House. The President could ask the limping Cabinet to 'advise' him to summon the Rajya Sabha. If the Ministry evades or avoids, the President's paramount duty to defend democracy under the residuary use of presidential 'pleasure' to direct the Prime Minister to report to the nation through the Rajya Sabha cannot be abdicated. A recalcitrant Cabinet can *be replaced by another* since the present team itself does not possess that imperative of our democracy of responsibility to the Lok Sabha. Those who 'strut and fret their hour upon the stage', till the next poll elected a set of players, cannot risk the President's displeasure. And there is no need to apprehend any refusal from the Prime Minister and his companions who are good democrats, seasoned statesmen and constitutional actors.

If a feeble cabinet without parliamentary credibility acts in excess of routine business or tends to transgress by doing or undoing policies which may gravely impact on the nation controversially or irreversibly, the Rashtrapati cannot be silent. When a Caretaker Cabinet with brevity of authority breaches its bourne the President has a role. If M.Ps., by far a majority in the last Lok Sabha, request the President to summon the Rajya Sabha he will be less than fair to the people if he keeps quiet waiting for the Ministry's initiative. There are under our Constitution, as explained in *Samsher Singh* and in Seervai's classic on the Constitution, *special exceptions to the absolutism of a Cabinet.* Transparency, accountability and responsive policy changes are not on holiday, merely because the Lok Sabha is dissolved. Nay, it is a fortiori case. Searvai, as I understand his views from his book, also exalts the President's position to jettison the Ministry if it rejects an obvious constitutional obligation. The President, when great democratic urgencies arise and is transfixed between a defiant Cabinet and an extraordinary crisis where a national inquest through the Rajya Sabha is a democratic desideratum, must act.

The pro tem operators of the constitutional process must remember Disraeli's great words: 'All power is a trust – that we are accountable for its exercise – that, from the people, and for the people, all springs, and all must exist'. Of course, now that the poll process has commenced, adventurism, populism and opportunism have no legal life.

'Know ye the truth and the truth shall make you free' is a biblical version of the right of the citizen in a Republic. Truth is subversive and secrecy is often the mark of unveracity.

QUO VADIS PARLIAMENTARY PANDEMONIC PROCESS?

Our Founding Fathers wrote into the Constitution a parliamentary system. The Parliament is a grand inquest of the nation, the great auditor and ombudsman of the Executive, the final arbiter, policy monitor and destiny designer of the people. Edmond Burke once observed—

> *Parliament is not a congress of ambassadors from different and hostile interests; which interests each must maintain, as an agent and advocate, against other agents and advocates; but* ***parliament is a deliberative assembly of one nation, with one interest, that of the whole****; where, not local purposes, not local prejudices ought to guide, but the general good, resulting from the general reason of the whole.*

The members deliberate, debate and discuss with reasoned arguments, dissect with political lancets autopsy with accuracy and expose every wrong and crime done to the country's social, economic and cultural autonomy with focus on the betterment of 'We, the People of India'. The two Houses are the most august institutions representing a billion Indians, with a certain gravity, dignity, solemnity, responsibility and complete commitment to the country's progress, not party's power grab or victory in verbal velocity or volume. Values of high moment, corruption of shocking dimensions, legislative bills of constitutional dimension, global issues which affect Bharat-Kashmir and other critical problems and treaties claim every hour of the Houses while sitting and transacting serious business. That is Parliament's noble purpose and public trust. The misdirection and misappropriation of this national time and institutional session is a shock and shame and stultification of the sovereignty of the people by its own surrogates. Only under the severest provocation, facing national insult or attack, confronted by the country's dangers to integrity, quacked and rocked by Himalayan crises does the house set aside its supreme purpose of decision by debate and victory by convincing argument. To do less is to forfeit the *raison de'etre* of Parliament itself and writing it off as an operational nullity. Even in these rare instances, not withdrawal from Parliament but demand for debate at these matters of moment is this panacea. Taciturn retreat is contempt of the House. Babels, bedlams bullying and brow-beating, jujitsu-like gesticulating, culminating in leaps into the well of the House downing by din its business or walk out with and fury paralysing parliamentary functionalism these 'sublime to the ridiculous' acrobatics is preposterous. We, in India, in the long-ago past have had such great spells of speech and spelt binding oratory. The wonder of democratic debate is best expressed by a single instance from the House of Commons. World War II was in progress and Britain, in the then early stages, was beating retreat from some fronts. Then came a motion by statesmen of the Opposition using their persuasive skills against Winston Churchill, the Prime Minister. The powerful speeches from the opposition ended and Prime Minister Churchill rose to reply to defend Britain's military misfortunes and daring advance ahead. In matchless eloquence Sir Winston fought back:

> *This long debate has now reached its final stage.* ***What a remarkable example it as been of the unbridled freedom of our Parliamentary institutions in time of war!*** *Everything that could be thought of or raked up has been used to weaken confidence in the Government, has been used to prove that Ministers are incompetent and to weaken their confidence in themselves, to make the Army distrust the backing it is getting from the civil power, to make the workmen lose confidence in the weapons they are striving so hard to make, to present the Government as a set of nonentities over whom the Prime Minister towers, and then to undermine him in his own heart, and, if possible, before the eyes of the nation. All this poured out by cable and radio to all parts of the world, to the distress of all our friends and to the delight of all our foes! I am* ***in favour of this freedom,*** *which no other country would use, or dare to use in times of mortal peril such as those through which we are passing. But the story must not end there, and I make now my appeal to the House of Commons to make sure that it does not end there.*

The House supported the heroic leadership of the Prime Minister. That debate, at a time when the nation had its worst days of the war, proved that what parliament could do was to dissect expose, urge and becomingly uphold the glory of debate despite the mortal peril of a crisis.

We, in India, also had great days in parliament and assemblies. I remember, as member of the Madras Legislative Assembly, participating in orations and perorations in battles of words and blistering replies. But in the early 50s, with Rajaji as Chief Minister and Sri. T. Prakasam as the Leader of the Opposition we did not convert the House into a noisy wresling ring with bouts and display of para-violence. Once, right in the beginning of the first session, there was a walk-out when Sri Prakasam protested against the Governor's address. When the House assembled next day (fading memory!) a motion of censure was brought by Rajaji for the contempt of the House by the Opposition's walking out demonstration. Now the scenario has suffered asphyxiation. What prevails too frequently is zoological, with jungly simian exercises. Sad, sad indeed. The House adjourns, amidst shouts, transacting no business, reassembles, recommences the deafening scenes and repeats of the same process ensues day after day. What I emphasize is not merely the extra-ordinary waste of the public money (MPs are paid well) which is considerable but the insult and humiliation, the shock and shamelessness showered, which make the finest institution of Parliament a limping futility held hostage, defeating the Constitution and disenchanting the vast masses who look for action against corruption and for good Administration. Every proposition of Government can be countered by contradiction in debate. Every guilty conduct or gaffe of the Ministers can be torn to pieces in the loud transparency of the House. Every rogue, rascal and freebooter in the country, every predator, grabber and swindler from the public exchequer can be, and ought to be, criticised in sharp diction shaking up the nation to what catastrophe and GATTastrophe, the country is being dragged into. A token walk-out may perhaps be understood as a technical protest but hours and hours, days and days and seasons after seasons, cannot be sacrificed Government is really rescued from exposure by this negative locomotion. Walk-out achieves nothing save epileptic excitement for the media plus a sense of impotence for presiding greats and inconsequence for the Houses. Argument cannot substitute by any locomotion. The speechless citizenry who are the silent majority in the country are victims of this functional futility unlimited. What pathetic, bathetic impairs! Issues there are where Government must hold or change course. *Tehelka* is a national shock and political crime. In the budget session everything under the sun may come under actinic critique and Ciceronian surgery! Wlak-out is escapist. Policies there are which betray the nation and its resources. Betrayals there are which surrender our sovereignty and facilitate recolonisation. But these acts and omissions must be brought to light through the great instrument of parliament. The one means that democracy allows defeat is by speech and by demand to dismiss by Government by vote inside or people's upheaval through the process of public education, mass mobilisation and, in India, by Gandhian *satyagraha* or by judicial writ by proof corruption of Ministers. On the contrary, walkouts facilitate a guilty Government to get through its business after the bally hoo is over. Many Bills can be passed without legitimate criticism when the Opposition benches are empty. Walt Whitman warned against these antics: 'Where the populace rise at once against the never-ending audacity of elected persons". Therefore, I entreat all the political parties to use the Parliament to full purpose, patriotic action and devotion to the defense of the country's interest. A Convention against stunning stridency, blocking business and boycotting the House must be developed as a decency.

Before I conclude, I must here record my appreciation of a measure to arrest corruption. *Tehelka* is not last or least corrupt act. The Minister for Law and Justice Shri. Arun Jaitley a sound lawyer, good parliamentarian and efficient Minister for having has achieved the limited beginning of seeking and securing approval of the Central Cabinet for the Lokpal Bill which will cover, I assume, the Prime Minister down to the minions of the State. We need a Lokpal, against Party bosses—a lesson from *Tehelka* and some parties becoming Big Business and Politicos Unincorporated—independent and powerful, fearless and totally free from bias. Kerala, unfortunately has a curious Lok Ayukt with no *suo motu* jurisdiction which is full of flaws and weakness built-in, so that it is example of frustration of its objective. The Lokpal Bill, I hope will appear in the Houses for debate and not for walk-out or share its predecessor. I impress upon the people of the country, the NGO's, the political parties and social activists to press for the passage of this Bill with wide jurisdiction and effective jurisprudence. A Government can be truly democratic only if its operations can be transparent and ombudsmanic and engineered by a powerful instrumentality.

A Concluding Caveat

John Pilger quotes Napoleon Bonaparte under the heading 'A CULTURAL CHERNOBYL'. "There is only one thing in this world, and that is to keep acquiring money and more money, power and more power. All the rest is meaningless." Alas, this miasmatic mantra is currently the Indian politicians Dharma. Do you know Roman Rolland reminded us "France fell because there was corruption without indignation". 'Sathyameva Jayathe' is our national opium if Parliament is condemned into comatose or bellicose mood constantly, democratic governance becomes a rope of sand. I conclude with a poignant quote. "The conditions which surround us best justify our co-operation; we meet in the midst of a nation brought to the verge of moral, political and material ruin-Corruption dominates the ballot box, the legislatures, the Congress, and touches even the ermine of the Bench' (Populist Party Preamble 1892). Does it a ring a bell as we watch our pervasive corruption and democratic mafia nexus with politics?

Perhaps we may add that some of our panchayats belong to the host of polluted institutions. "Among a people generally corrupt liberty cannot long last". (Burke). Our Penal code and criminal laws face an open challenge, a determine threat and unconstitutional intimidation by political parties who dare to denounce debate and unpatriotically assert that Parliament shall not be permitted from working and the people shall thereby be denied the benefit of a functional Parliament. This perhaps is the 'most kindest cut of all', silencing the voice of the representatives of a billion Indians—Is this a crime? a traitor's success?, or a contra-constitutional Opposition reducing the Indian Republic into a deaf, dumb orphan with none to protest, resist or call to order the challenger. Imagine this felonious feat to happen to all the counts in the country with no judge, no writ, no command or contempt power! Will India survive? This Operation Jettison is terrorism to the nation for which our generation must answer before long.

The Treasury Bench, because of a brute majority cannot deny a J.P.C. But, it is bizarre to have a judicial commission a JPC and a criminal investigation simultaneously. Their purposes may partly overlap but are different processes. The sooner the criminals are prosecuted the gladder the people will feel that justice has been done. Here we must have a system of independent investigation, independent prosecutors and some Indian Judge Sirica to speed up the trial and convict the guilty politicians. The rule of law is in peril if the law limps, the police shuffle and suffer the dependencia syndrome acting under orders from the Home Ministry, and the judge, day in and day out, calls for case diaries or otherwise interrupt or distort investigations. The Nixon trial is a lesson for the Indian system. *Tehelka* is a crime and the court must deal with it. When we remember that once before the FIR was sought to be shot down by Council for the prosecution, the then Law Minister and, alas, the robed gentleman on the Bench. Will *Tehelka* will face such a shame?

A grave suspicion

I read in The Hindu that 'no police investigation in *Tehelka* because a Commission has been appointed'. This alibi is a cover-up. A public enquiry by a judge is geared to wider purposes, its Report may or may not be published and its focus does not zero-in on a particular crime with a prosecution in mind. A police investigation is sharp, leads to arrests, recording magisterial statements and the culpable persons punished soon. When an offense is *prima facie* committed no Cabinet can inhibit an investigation. The Criminal Procedure Code governs; No Cabinet, cabal or clique, can subvert this legal imperative. Otherwise, every Commission will be an escape route for every political felon. Why should and how could, police investigation be inhibited when the Code commands it? What is the real motive for stalling investigation? A riddle wrapped in a mystery inside an enigma? Or a plain but lame game plan to stultify criminal justice?

Quo Vadis India?

BEST (?) BY THE BEST ONLY?

Supreme but not infallible is the truthful title of a semi-centennial publication by the Supreme Court of India about itself. Fallible it is, but because it is final too, the remedy for its institutional errors, when they are grave, has to be by Constitutional Amendment. To err is human. One such errant situation had arisen where the Supreme Court, has wrested the power of appointment of the members of the High Courts and Supreme Court from the Executive altogether. That only judges are the best judges to select the best as judges without even sharing the power with the President is a proposition explainable not on the Constitution, which expressly denies this monopoly in the text and in the Constituent Assembly proceedings. Two judges have disagreed but seven, forming the majority gained an arithmetic victory. But that is the law since the Constitution is what the judges say it is, even if the ruling be by a sharp division.

The world over, the power to appoint judges—and judges wield vast power—is either with the Executive or in consultation with the top judicial echelons but never to the exclusion of the executive. Independence of the Indian judiciary, depending on this 'untouchability' factor, is a strange allergy, notwithstanding the judges asking for favours from the Executive like luxury cars, fine furnished bungalows, police escorts, state guest status, free trips with family, and other perks and pomp. Judicial independence is made of sterner stuff as America's great judges have demonstrated. Lord Atkin and his kind in the United Kingdom have provided through luminous instances and Indian heroes and martyrs in robes have earlier blazed the train. The Constitution is clear. In simple Anglo-Saxon, it lays down that the appointment of the higher judiciary, shall be by the president 'after consultation with' the Chief Justice of India and such other judges as he may 'deem necessary'. To 'consult' is not to surrender, nor concur. And yet, alleged high principle, certainly not self interest, their Lordships discovered in Art. 124 the opposite of what Dr. Ambedkar emphatically asserted was the intent and sense of the Constitutional provision.

Independence of the judiciary is absolutely basic to democracy and it needs no judicial rhetoric to drive home the point. Our founding fathers have made sufficient provision, consistent with pragmatic limitations, to defend the forensic institutions against executive, legislative or other interference. In theory, the judiciary has neither the purse nor the sword, as part of its institutionals authority but reading the Constitution, together with the guaranteed retirement age and contempt power, I have no hesitation to hold that, the Indian judiciary is freer than any other high curial organ, including the mighty Law Lords in the U.K. and the robed brethren in the U.S.A.

The fundamental issue is as to whether the total functional autonomy of the judiciary is liable to be influenced by the appointing authority being the President, that is the Prime Minister. There are great institutions, which call for independent operation like the Comptroller and Auditor General and the Election Commission, but the incumbents thereof, are appointed by the nation's Chief Executive. For over 50 years the higher judiciary in India has been selected in consultation with the Chief Justice and appointed by the President according to the Prime Minister's choice. Is it conceivable for any judge of the Supreme Court to hold that the CAGs and the CEOs, the judges of the High Courts and the Supreme Court, who technically owe their selection to the Prime Minister or the Cabinet, were pliable tools in the hands of the Government? It would be libel to suggest so. It would be unveracious to vilify all the great judges of India whose performance has won international laurels to condemn them as suppliant surrogates. If the Chief Justice of India and some of his colleagues were to be given the power to select, does it mean that the selectees would be stooges of the Chief Justice who himself, having been appointed by the President, would be supple to oblige Government interest since, in his time he must have been an appointee of the President. The several judges who by majority, (*The Second Judges Case*) ruled that the Chief Justice of the India must have the right of primacy were themselves in their time chosen by the Prime Minister and yet dared to challenges his impartiality and integrity. Chief Justices are also human and cannot be exalted into quasi-divine status. It is unfortunate that 'consultation' used in the Constitution has been exaggerated beyond the limits of 'ordinary lexical definition.' I am unhappy to disagree with the view. The administration of justice is of such paramount importance in our Human Rights era that the process of appointment should be so exalted that the selectee is the best choice. The Constitution assigns the highest place to justice; and justices occupy the highest place in the Constitutional scheme. There is no doubt, therefore, that the methodology of appointment should measure up to the invioble majesty of the office and the high value of justice delivery itself to the people as a whole.

Having said all this, the Judges will remember that the Constitution is above them. There has been widespread demand that judicial appointments are far too paramount to be left to the judges themselves and that a National Commission, which accords high judicial participation, but admits of the higher echelons of the Executive and perhaps other relevant outstanding elements, may be the appropriate machinery. The Constitution 67th

Amendment Bill, 1990 was introduced to provide an institutional framework for such a commission. In many countries mutual consultation has been the convention. The recent National Commission to Review the Working of the Constitution, adopting an immoderately moderate attitude, has suggested formation of a committee.

CONSTITUTIONAL CONUNDRUM OF A CARETAKER GOVERNMENT

Kargil was an invasive shock for India. But it had to be handled by a Caretaker Government. From the time the confidence Motion was lost political legitimacy for the Council of Ministers vanished. But the President requested Sri Vajpayee, whose resignation was accepted to continue in office since a Ministry is a necessary presence under our constitutional order which substantially, adopts the Westminster paradigm. It is a confusion of constitutional vision to regard the Rashtrapati as the sole Supreme Executive of the nation under all circumstances. A paragraph from *Samshere Singh,* quoted as sound law by Seervai in his classic work, runs thus:

> *We declare the law of this branch of our Constitution to be that the President and Governor, custodians of all executive and other powers under various articles shall, by virtue of these provisions, exercise their formal constitutional powers only upon and in accordance with the advice of their Ministers save in a few well-known exceptional situations. Without being dogmatic or exhaustive, these situations relate to (a) the choice of Prime Minister (Chief Minister), restricted though this choice is by the paramount consideration that he should command a majority in the House; (b) the dismissal of a Government which has lost its majority in the House, but refuses to quit office; (c) the dissolution of the House where an appeal to the country is necessitous, although in this area the head of State should avoid getting involved in politics and must be advised by his Prime Minister (Chief Minister) who will eventually take the responsibility for the step. We do not examine in detail the constitutional proprieties in these predicaments except to utter the caution that even here the action must be compelled by the peril to democracy and the appeal to the House or to the country must become blatantly obligatory.*

All these propositions proceed on the basic thesis that there is a House, which is a controllorate over the Cabinet which must command the confidence of the Commons. Subject to this effective discipline, the Ministers govern in the name of the President, except in certain exceptional situations. For example, in *J.P. Mitter*'s case, the Supreme Court held that the *President had exclusive power to determine the age of a judge* when it was in dispute. The

Cabinet has to keep its hands off and cannot advice the President as to the age of the judge. Why? Because the independence of the judiciary will vanish, if the Ministry can advice the President on the dispute. That is why the Executive has no voice in matters connected with judges, including their age. The President is the sole authority there and may consult the Chief Justice of India.

As in the case of the age of judges, there is an exception in the case of disqualification of members of Legislatures where the Cabinet cannot advise the President. "In *Brundaban Nayak* v. *Election Commission* another sensitive situation relating to the functions of the President (Article 103) and the Governor (Article 192) arose. It is a sacred principle of our democracy, like the independence of the Judiciary, that decisions on the disqualifications of Members of Assemblies should be unbiased. While formally the power to decide a dispute in this behalf is vested in the President and the Governor under articles 103 and 192, respectively, it would be a travesty of impartiality if such decision were to be made on the aid and advice of a Ministry which is essentially chosen from a party or combination of parties. How can a political activist with party loyalty in our pluralistic society judge a cause in which he has deep concern? Therefore, the Constitution has made the Election Commission the real arbiter in the dispute".

Let us shift our focus to a case where the House has been dissolved. In *U.N.R. Rao*'s case (1971) 2 SCC 63, this point was discussed with lucidity and learned authority by Sikri C.J. "The Constituent Assembly did not choose the presidential system of Government. If we were to give effect to this contention of the appellant we would be changing the whole concept of the Executive. It would mean that the President need not have a Prime Minister and Ministers to aid and advise in the exercise of his functions. As there would be no 'Council of Ministers' nobody would be responsible to the House of the People.

The appellant urges that the House of the People having been dissolved this clause cannot be complied with. According to him it follows from the provisions of this clause that it was contemplated that on the dissolution of the House of People the Prime Minister and the other Ministers must resign or be dismissed by the President and the President must carry on the Government as best as he can with the aid of the Services. As we have shown above, article 74(1) is mandatory and, therefore, the President cannot exercise power without the aid and advice of the Council of Ministers. We must then harmonise the provisions of article 75(3) with article 74(1) and article 75(2). Article 75(3) brings into existence what is usually called 'responsible Government'. In other words, the Council of Ministers must enjoy the confidence of the House of People. While the House of People is not dissolved under article 82(2)(b) article 75(3) has full operation. But when it is dissolved the Council of Ministers cannot naturally enjoy the confidence of the House of People. Nobody has said that the Council of Ministers do not enjoy the confidence of the House of People when it is prorogued. In the context therefore, this clause must be read as meaning that article 75(3) only applies when the House of People does not stand dissolved or prorogued". In short, even when the House is in suspended animation (prorogued) or dissolved, the President acts thro' his Cabinet. The rulings thus result in the President, having to govern *only* with a Cabinet to rule, even when the House is dissolved. A ministry sans the House is conceivable but the tenure is not full-blooded as representing the people since the Parliament is under eclipse.

Imagine a more aggravated span of unaccountable national administration. Constitutionally speaking, a Cabinet which loses the Confidence of the Lok Sabha instantly exits as the mandatory fundamental of collective responsibility to the Lok Sabha snaps (article 75 (3) and survival after death is not a constitutional phenomenon. True, showing the door to Prime Minister and Co. when a confidence vote collapses will leave a vacuum, which is a constitutional anathema. To keep in office a ministry after the House has expressed lack of faith is bete noire. Equally allergic is to leave the President the solo ruler. The only way to cut the Gordian Knot is to search for a balancing of the clashing principles more in keeping with the highest court's seminal ratio. Better the President and a (crippled) Council rather than a solitary throne, is the direction of judicial wisdom, perhaps.

When a House runs out its course the President accepts the resignation but requests the Government to continue to enable the holding of elections and bringing a new House into being. This is a straight-forwarded case of a caretaker ministry. The plenary executive authority of a Council of Ministers which commands the confidence of the elected surrogates is morally and politically higher as it carries the people with it in larger measure than a lame duck lack-luster locum cabinet, as an interregnum, by courtesy of the Rashtrapati for routine management of State business. A lesser breed of Caretaker Cabinet is a creature of exigency. Where the Lok Sabha has voted out a Ministry but no alternative majority leader is in sight, the President, by constitutional compulsion, has to run the country through a Council of Ministers (as per the rulings of the Supreme Court), must make-do with a transient team as a stop-gap arrangement until the early poll is held. Necessity is the mother of invention and a reluctant category of Caretaker coterie is put in place. Such situations are rare and tenurial brevity is must be writ large on its bosom. Indeed, the basic rule of responsibility to Parliament stands negated in this anomalous instance because the House has already rejected a Confidence Motion. A rootless Cabinet with no House to control and worse, with the stigma of a negation of confidence expressed explicitly, is more a formal compliance, a euphemism for a Cabinet. In such a nationally exceptional spell the President is not toothless but may bite when strikingly deviant impropriety or arrogation is attempted by a Caretaker.

Does such a doubly debilitated Government possess the large executive authority of a regular Cabinet whose Prime Minister, by the credential of House majority, is the leader? Morally and politically no. But constitutional diction cannot exhaustively express gradations of power answer every bizarre or freak development lying in the womb of the future.

We function under the Constitution but the Constitution is what the judges say it is. From this perspective, we have to abide by the Supreme Court's pronouncement, read with article 141 of the Constitution. As has been long ago observed by Dixon J "The task of expounding a Constitution is crucially different from that of construing a statute. A statute defines present rights and obligations. It is easily enacted and easily repealed. A Constitution, by contrast, is drafted with an eye to the future. Its function is to provide a continuing framework for the legitimate exercise of governmental power and, when joined by a Charter of Rights, for the unlimiting protection of individual rights and liberties. Once enacted, its provisions can't easily be repealed or amended. It must, therefore, be capable of growth and development over time to meet new social, political and historical realities often unimagined by its framers. The judiciary is the guardian of the Constitution and must, in interpreting its provisions, bear these conditions in mind."(*Hunter et. al.* v. *The Southam Inc.*, 1984 11 DLR 641 at 649 per Dickson J.). The creative realism and imaginative progressivism of the Judiciary make a Constitution work better and brighter in the future.

When new challenges confront the country, the President must keep the constitutional process on sound democratic principle. Here, the imaginative genius of the court must help find out reconciliation where the President may invoke his ultimate authority to defend the Republic. The Cabinet may be there but it has lost the confidence of the House and so the President has to be more alert, activist and invigilatory. Alladi Kuppuswamy, a former Chief Justice, has observed:

> *As in the past, there will be occasions in the future when the President has to act on his own without being aided and advised by the Council of Ministers. Thus, he need not be a figurehead or a rubber-stamp as visualized by the framers of the Constitution.*

We get a constitutional clue to Presidential creativity where a Ministry composed of a group of good men who are not members of Parliament, but only a cabal called a Cabinet by courtesy are currently accountable to none except the corrective jurisdiction and accountability of jurisprudence of the court.

There has been a demand for calling the Rajya Sabha to discuss the nation's macabre Kargil battles and the high level communications between the Pak P.M. as well as the U.S. President plus taking into confidence the people thro' the Upper House and receive feed back through criticisms and insistence on Governmental transparency and people's right to know about the war strategy and the mobilisation of patriotic readiness to defend the motherland by blood, toil, tears and sweat. After all, P.M. and Co., are not even members of Parliament but bare citizens holding office during the pleasure of the President who is a high functionary, altho' chosen by indirect election. Debate is the self-critical correction by the nation and no argument of demoralisation of the Defense Forces can have democratic validity.

It would be interesting to notice how Prime Minister Winston Churchill, in the later stages of the War, formed a Government which and which he regarded as a National Administration but which was in his own words a Caretaker Government. Thus we have a glorious instance of a Caretaker Government in Britain during World War II. Although that Coalition had a majority in the House, even that Government did not retreat from debate in the Parliament. There was a vote of censure at a time when the British Forces where losing and retreating. Churchill did not avoid the debate and was severely criticized as incompetent. Nevertheless the daring democratic Churchill faced the charges against him and wound up the debate thus:

> *This long debate has now reached its final stage. What a remarkable example it has been of the unbridled freedom of our Parliamentary institutions in time of war! Everything that could be thought of or raked up has been used to weaken confidence in the Government, has been used to prove that Ministers are incompetent and to weaken their confidence in themselves, to make the Army distrust the backing it is getting from the civil power, to make the workmen lose confidence in the weapons they are striving so hard to make, to present the government as a set of nonentities over whom the Prime Minister towers, and then to undermine him in his own heart, and, if possible, before the eyes of the nation. All this poured out by cable and radio to all parts of the world, to the distress of all our friends and to the delight of all our foes! I am in favour of this freedom, which no other country would use, or dare to use, in times of mortal peril such as those through which we are passing.*

If this is the model of democratic functioning during the World War by Great Britain there is no justification to avoid a debate in the Rajya Sabha over Kargil and allied matters, especially when the Government is not of a majority party but a lingering coterie censured out of office. I have great reverence for the Prime Minister but I have no appreciation for one who will not take the surviving remnant of Parliament into confidence. The right to know is a people's fundamental. The duty to be responsive to the House which still is an integral parliamentary instrument is non-negotiable. Kargil cannot stifle people's investigative, invigilatory and information-extracting right. Presidential activism has to quicken the high office of a constitutional sentinel on the *qui vive.*

The Kargil intrusion by Pakistan gave a grave shock to the national territorial integrity. And when the Ministry, already disapproved by the Lok Sabha, wears the cloak of power on the slender 'pleasure' of the President, its fundamental accountability to the People of India has to be vicariously discharged by calling the Rajya Sabha and present the full facts and get a feed back from the Upper House. The President could ask the limping Cabinet to 'advise' him to summon the Rajya Sabha. If the Ministry evades or avoids, the President's paramount duty to defend democracy under the residuary use of presidential 'pleasure' to direct the Prime Minister to report to the nation through the Rajya Sabha cannot be abdicated. A recalcitrant Cabinet can *be replaced by another* since the present team itself does not possess that imperative of our democracy of responsibility to the Lok Sabha. Those who 'strut and fret their hour upon the stage', till the next poll elects a fresh set of players, cannot risk the President's displeasure. And there is no need to apprehend any refusal from the Prime Minister and his companions who are good democrats, seasoned statesmen and constitutional actors.

If a feeble cabinet without parliamentary credibility acts in excess of routine business or tends to transgress by doing or undoing policies which may gravely impact on the nation controversially or irreversibly, the Rashtrapati cannot be silent. When a caretaker cabinet with brevity of authority breaches its bourne the President has a role. If M.Ps., by far a majority in the last Lok Sabha, request the President to summon the Rajya Sabha he will be less than fair to the people if he keeps imense waiting for the Ministry's initiative. There are under our Constitution, as explained in *Sasmsher Singh* and in Seervai's classic on the Constitution, *special exceptions to the absolutism of a Cabinet.* Transparency, accountability and responsive policy changes are not on holiday, merely because the Lok Sabha is dissolved. Nay, it is a fortiori case. Seervai, as I understand his views from his book, also exalts the President's position to jettison the Ministry if it rejects an obvious constitutional obligation. The President, when great democratic urgencies arise and is transfixed between a defiant Cabinet and an extraordinary crisis where a national inquest through the Rajya Sabha is a democratic desideratum, must act.

The pro tem operators of the constitutional process must remember Disraeli's great words: 'All power is a trust – that we are accountable for its exercise – that, from the people, and for the people, all springs, and all must exist'. Of course, now that the poll process has commenced, adventurism, populism and opportunism have no legal life.

'Know ye the truth and the truth shall make you free', is a biblical version of the right of the citizen in a Republic. Truth is subversive and secrecy is often the mark of unveracity.

THE NOBLE PREAMBLE: WE HAVE PROMISES TO KEEP

Over a semi-centennial span ago We, the People of India, made a tryst with destiny to redeem every human being in our Republic from Poverty, Slavery, Inequality, Deprivation of Developmental Opportunity and Denial of Access to Justice in its well-known triune dimensions. More than five decades after, let us turn back to our nation's performance in an objective spirit of social audit and creative critique. The Indian humanscape, when Freedom dawned in August 1947, was vibrant with socialist hope of egalite, liberty and pursuit of happiness. As the 20th century was about to set and a new millennium was being midwifed by passage of time, the onward Nehruvian locomotion of people's progress took a reverse Manmohanomic direction with some authoritative estimate declaring, a decade after the Globalisation experiment, India to be the poorest country in the world. People's rosy expectations at the hour of Independence, darkened into indifference, indifference into blood and tears, which in turn, dismayed into the doom of despair. Of course, this sad scenario afflicted only the vast masses. The movement was zigzag and princelings, feudal elements, bourgeois sections and a noveau riche class emerged with consumerist appetite, imitative of the West and pejorative allergy to native culture. The great majority were harrowingly under-privileged and demanded alleviation of penury and elimination of unemployment and other privations. The antimony between the Proprietariat and the Proletariat deepened and hunger for socio-economic change hotted up. Meanwhile, human rights and democratic values, in their holistic dimensions, gained political voice and the Constitution largely reflected, given semantic radicalism, the militant desiderata of the deprived, preponderant population. We started well with the grand Preamble and the glorious verbiage of article 38 of the Constitution, setting the nation's sights socialist and secular, egalitarian and economically advanced. The crimson aspirations and libertarian transformation of the social order found finer expression through the early Constitutional Amendments, the reports of the left-oriented Planning Commission, nationalisation of Key industries, the creation of a public sector which was meant to occupy the commanding heights of the national economy, and a great stress on agrarian reform.

Judged by political rhetoric and stentorian polemics, our legislatures sounded radical and our courts, though at times darkly conservative, also supported progressive values. The Nehru-era was a proud beginning, notwithstanding *de facto* single Party politics, corruption in public life, misuse of Constitutional powers under article 356 and defeat at the hands of China. Indo-Soviet friendship, States reorganisation, independence of the judiciary and the stature of Jawahar as utterly secular, genuinely socialistic, keen on land reforms and leading the world movement for liberation of colonies and developmental march of the Non-Aligned Movement; were notable events which inspired confidence in the people about the realisation of the Indian revolution. But feudalism dies hard, colonial mentality resists constitutional liquidation and bureaucracy, habitually paper-logged and hierarchically structured, rarely bows out. So, Bharat continued to live simultaneously in several centuries.

Nehru, the leader of the Freedom Struggle, was a militant humanist but Nehru, the Prime Minister, was a Hamlet. His charisma suffered somewhat from the bar of limitation since his performance did not slough off the old world ethos or soft state syndrome. In nation-building civilian administration as supreme, the democratic order as basic and making socialist ideas and abolition of poverty with a vision and plan Nehru made headway and thereby strengthened liberty, equality and other fundamental rights of the lower layers of humanity.(The creamy layer and communal strata survived.) Secularism and socialism became vogue words even in high official circles and foreign economic infiltration or invasion were checked to some extent. Human Rights flourish only in such a milieu as Nehru verbally emphasised. A revolution needs cadres with political conviction and infrastructure deeply committed and a leadership defiant of imperialist powers and their next of kin who cunningly and corruptly do back-seat driving. Equality, liberty and other great freedoms summon echelons at all levels, including the professions, technical experts and visionaries with principled, planning pragmatism. Mao Tse Tung's two observations, absent under Nehru and the 'Leftists', but actively operational in New China, need recapitulation.

> *A revolution does not march in a straight line. It wanders where it can, retreats before superior forces, advances wherever it has room, attacks whenever the enemy retreats or bluffs and, above all, is possessed of enormous patience.*
>
> *Revolution is not a dinner party, nor an essay, nor a painting, nor a piece of embroidery; it cannot be advanced softly, gradually, carefully, considerately, respectfully, politely, plainly and modesty.*

The fatal failure of our fine Preamble and Nehru's red rose perspective have several causes. Etiologically perceived, the system was run by cadres and leaders for whom the common people hardly mattered and the 'old order' was preserved by a political and official elite conditioned by British *Raj* ethos and *Maharaja* bossism. The judicial fraternity too were of Indo-Anglian vintage. Left nomen-clature, largely fabricated for winning elections, left the populace cold since poverty alleviation, employment generation and people's participation were discovered by the have-nots to be abracadabra. Disenchantment with gubernatorial duplicity and judicial inaccessibility compounded by Anglo-philic erudition, created extremist militancy and terrorist estrangement Result: High sounding Liberty – Equality-Development – vocabulary on the one hand and pervasive privation, escalating unemployment and illiteracy unlimited on the other. Of course, periodic elections, reeking with corruption and counterfeit-ballots, was a simulacrum of democracy. True, Winston Churchill was right when he observed: 'At the bottom of tributes paid to democracy is the little man, in a little booth, with a little pencil making a little cross on a little bit of paper— no amount of rhetoric or voluminous discussion can diminish the overwhelming importance of the point'. The same anti-Indian Churchill opposed handing over Independence to Indian leaders whom he described as 'rogues, rascals and freebooters'. Both his powerful statements, in retrospect, after 50 years of booth-capturing game and dubious governance deserve serious debate *vis a vis* liberty, equality and other democratic values. The Preamble prised open the precious values of human dignity, access to social, political and economic justice as well as liberty and other fundamental rights. But while in the early decades measures were taken to build the basic structure necessary for social justice to be a reality, abuse of power and ubiquity of corrupt politics and judicial conservatism grew without let or hindrance. Executive authoritarianism and irresponsible parliamentarian arrogance slept together, with liberal diction about people's power and socialist pattern being the opium of the people.

How fragile is our working anarchy and oligarchy alias Indian democracy has been poignantly presented with lucid emphasis by Dr. Ambedkar in the Constituent Assembly. Our Constitution is a majestic instrument and if implemented in letter and spirit the present generation would be placed a happy Administration. But asked Ambedkar on 25th November 1949: 'What would happen to her (India's) independence?.........Will she lose it a second time?.......... What perturbs me greatly is the fact that not only India has once before lost her Independence but she lost it *by the infidelity and treachery of some of her own people*...... Will history repeat itself? We must be determined to defend our independence to the last drop of our blood.' Later, in the course of his address, he placed accent on social democracy beyond political democracy. He clarified that liberty cannot be divorced from equality and fraternity. Equality without liberty would kill individual initiative. Without fraternity, liberty and equality could not become a natural course of things. He admitted the complete absence in our society of genuine equality. The prophetic words he uttered are worth repeating more than half a century later because his fears are proving true now. "On the 26th January 1950 we are going to enter into a life of contradiction. In politics we will have equality and in social and economic life we will have inequality.......... How long shall we continue to live this life of contradiction?........ We will do so only by putting our political democracy in peril. We must resolve this contradiction....... or else those who suffer from inequality will blow up the structure of political democracy......' Common brotherhood, as against dichotomy among the people with caste and class division, is a *denial of fraternity*. Sans fraternity, 'equality and liberty will be no deeper than coats of paint.' A grammar of anarchy may be the consequence, he warned. All these prophetic portents are happening under our nose and the struggle for a new social order can be successful only by realization of the perils pointed out by the great Indian Ambedkar. The decadence of our democracy is mired by pathos and bathos because the victims are voiceless and Power is an illusion for them. Elite are the privileged and thus there is none to protest when India is being recolonised and its freedoms are formal under dependencia syndrome. We have formally under a Constitution but by the grace of world corporatecracy, with American hegemony. Gandhi Swadeshi is dead. Nehru socialism is under eclipse. The Constitution is comatose and the Courts are drowned in oceanic litigation. Dalits have none to lead and there is chaos in the cosmos. The court itself has changed its class character. EMS was punished for contempt when he pointed out the class character of the judiciary but today the judicial class has secured larger emoluments, more power over the other two branches that justice, especially social justice, is in precarious condition. The past projects itself into the present and the tryst with destiny made by Indian's cannot be betrayed. A recap of a few pregnant Nehru passages is pertinent here:

> *Freedom and power bring responsibility. That responsibility rests upon this Assembly, a sovereign body representing the sovereign people of India. Before the birth of freedom we have endured all the pains of labour and our hearts are heavy with the memory of this sorrow. Some those pains continue even now. Nevertheless the past is over and it is the future that beckons to us now.*
>
> *That future is not one of ease or resting but of incessant striving so that we might fulfil the pledges we have so often taken and the one we shall take today. The service of India means the service of the millions who suffer. It means the ending of poverty and ignorance and disease and inequality of opportunity. The ambition of the greatest man of our generation has been to wipe every tear from every eye. That may be beyond us but as long as there are tears and suffering, so long our work will not be over.*

What, has happened to India through the semi-centennial spell? A.K.Goalan was detained without trial. Is this personal liberty? And what did the Court do after marathon arguments? They, by majority vote, upheld this incarceration. The fate of liberty remains vulnerable. The Court has often approved deprivation of personal liberty even as late as TADA. I do feel that Freedom of the masses, political or economic, is not safe in the hands of the Republic. Proof? The disastrous Emergency validated by the Supreme Court and the despotic irrational imposition of President's Rule on nine States twice and the Court lending its wax and seal and signature, legitimising the jettisoning of provincial autonomy. Over hundred times the precious State, though limited, sovereignty was overthrown with no judicial assertion against this contra-constitutionality.

The creation of a socialist order is a tough task, a battle against unconscionable capitalism. A public sector and nationalisation, abolition of Princes' Privy Purses and planned development holding under restraint concentration of wealth to the detriment of the people and distributive justice promotive of basic needs of the dire poor—these are fundamental requisites to fulfill the goals of the Preamble. But the Court struck down Privy Purses Abolition, Bank Nationalisation, Kerala Agrarian Reform and other progressive legislations, even Constitutional Amendments to protect certain progressive statutes. Indeed, the Court was to be guardian of people's liberties and be the sentinel on the *qui vive.* But on several occasions the judiciary gave the impression of being the conscience - keeper of the capitalist class. However, times changed and access to justice, formerly a difficult and expensive process, became easier with Public Interest Litigation becoming a democratic judicial remedy. Corruption was fought, abuse of power was struck down and environmental protection assured by judicial oversight. Human rights received special concern from courts. Custodial trauma or death, molestation of women, bonded labour, child labour and other harassments inside lock-ups and prisons found the judges sensitive watch-dogs with punitive sternness. Indeed, the Judiciary played a great part in defending life and liberty and sentencing violators of Human Rights. This massive task was executed by the court with such firmness that abuse of power by the Executive was checked making the authoritarian governments tremble because the 'robed brethren' had jurisdiction to control and condemn misdeeds by even high functionaries. The presence of Human Rights Commissions at National and State levels, Women's Commissions and juvenile justice processes have strengthened the people's rights although full powers have not been confirmed. The struggle for a New Social Order made headway because many NGOs sprang to move the judiciary and NHRC with responsive writs issuing from the higher tribunals and recommendations from Commissions. Moreover, the Court began to use even U.N. instruments and the Directive Principles of State Policy as effective hermeneutic, humanitarian aids to read municipal laws humanely. Human Rights Jurisprudence was deepened and broadened and access to justice, what with PIL and judicial activism, was 'in widest commonalty spread'. Refugee law, anti-torture justice, gender justice, prison jurisprudence, children's rights, poverty jurisprudence and the like made the court the sanctuary of the weak and the asylum of the oppressed. Time was when, in Tennyson's lines, courts, unapproachable for the humble, were no longer hallowed but "where blind and naked Ignorance delivers brawling judgments, unashamed, on all things all day long". But those by-gone days are replaced and the new juristic time is : 'ring out the old, ring in the new'! Indeed, Tennyson versified, lovely fashion, (of Britain but now of India as well) :

A land of settled government,

A land of just and old renown,

Where Freedom slowly broadens down

From precedent to precedent.

Our Republic, with an ancient composite culture and modern socialist texture, suffered a value torture in the 90s of the 20th century. Socialism slumbered in the Constitution, secularism slowly lost its vigour and re-colonisation 'red in tooth and claw' pressured the Mughals in Delhi to abandon the marvellous values of humanism and compassion and substitute them with globalization, liberalisation, privatisation and marketisation. Gandhicidal, Nehrucidal, winds began to blow and a 'New Democracy', shaped by exotic forces and corporate compulsions, made Bharat an international mendicant and GATT victim. Indeed, a constitutional coup secretly, silently infiltrated intriguingly into our economic vitals. A bizarre change of heart and head with quislings in power made India Westoxicated. Today, dollar hunger of the rich dominates; and starvation and hunger of the poor has ceased to be a matter of grave concern. Patriotism, Swadeshi and self- reliance are on a long holiday. What once was anathema and allergy because it was imperialist is now darling as dollar adventurism, disguised as technological venture. The gap between the rich and the poor is widening. Glitteratti are glad and imports are in profusion. Agriculture is collapsing and rural indebtedness and suicides are escalating. 'Fair is foul and foul is fair.' In particular, contra-constitutional forces have stultified the Preamble.

> *Political chemeleons must quit if swaraj is to be stable. Without social justice, no social stability will last longer than the waves that break upon the Bench and are absorbed by the sands. Now we seek stability and secularity plus corruption free social order. Whose democracy? Whose stability? Whose social justice? We, the people of India must call the bluff and end the 'progress' baloney of the proprietariat. (Andhra University Law Journal P-5)*

The dynamic rule of law has to reassert itself charging forward with the Preamble as the goal. Currently an 'iron curtain' has descended on the land between the people in their miserable millions and the richer tycoons collaborating with MNCS and mafia corruption. 'Quit India' has a new dimension and progressive direction. Today, when the people must be educated about their grim future if we do not change course and become a self-reliant fraternity with social and economic democracy, we will fail in the long run. Even foreign lawyers will force themselves in! In my humble view, to delay the reassertion of the Constitution and its Preamble may lead to recolonisation. That shall not be. Law is for Life—of a billion Indian humans.

The Hidden Agenda of the New World Order is satirically yet truthfully expressed by Steinbeck in an oft quoted observation representing the current Indian lot of blood, toil tears and sweat. I quote Steinbeck so as to open the eyes of great jurists who live far away from hungry realities:

> *The fields were fruitful, and starving men moved on the roads. The granaries were full and the children of the poor grew up rachitic, and the pustules of pellagra swelled on their side. The great companies did not know that the line between hunger and anger is a thin line.(The Pocket Book of Quotations P-144)*

The Bench and the Bar, do awake and break the chains using Judge Power as the sword of We, the People of India.

CONSTITUTION OF INDIA—THE NATION'S SAFETY VALVE

The Indian Constitution is the cornerstone of a liberated nation. It lays the grand foundation of a great people's political edifice of governance. It projects the socio-economic vision of a generation emerging from a feudal culture, colonial domination and federal negation. It spells out the fundamental rights and socialistic aspirations of the vast masses long inhibited by an imperialist ethos. It creates a trinity of democratic instrumentalities with checks and balances, parliamentary in structure, quasi-federal in character. Endowed with adult franchise, empowered with periodic elections, provided with plural Parties, equipped with a unitive justice system with a uniquely supreme judicature at the apex which gives access to every citizen against injustice, the political stricture of the billion-strong Indian humanity is a paradigm of secular, socialist, democratic Republic.

An independent judiciary, an accountable Parliament at the Centre and like legislatures at the State level, a powerful Election Commission and fearless, critical Comptroller and Auditor General provide a paramountcy of democracy, at once responsible and responsive. Judicial review of State action, public finance auditable by a constitutional authority, obligation to seek fresh mandate through general elections with adult franchise, accountability, direct and indirect, to the people in several ways,—these are fundamental in the governance of the country. The people, though free, have fundamental duties mandated by Art.51A of the Constitution to exercise which, as in cases of environmental and ecological preservation, compassion for living creatures, protection of the value of *composite* culture, the authority of judicial writ power may be moved in aid. In the words of Dr. Ambedkar, winding up his speech moving the passage of the Draft Constitution, "I feel that it (the Constitution) is workable, it is flexible and it is strong enough to hold the country together both in peace time and in war time. Indeed, if I may say so, if things go wrong under the new Constitution the reason will not be that we had a bad Constitution. What we will have to say is, that Man was vile".

Stability does not mean immutability. Times change. Social conditions are altered by various factors. Each generation may differ in values from a previous generation. Therefore, realism dictates flexibility which implies amendability. Therefore, our Constitution (Art. 368) vests power in parliament to amend the Constitution but with more rigorous procedures than in passing ordinary legislation. Indeed, amendment of the Constitution, necessary in certain circumstances, has been provided for, blending pragmatism with special safeguards, avoiding rigidity, but facilitating flexibility. At this point it must be remembered that a mere majority cannot be allowed to tamper with the Constitution. Why? There are certain great values, which our founding fathers have regarded as paramount and inviolable. If those values can be jettisoned by a majority of Parliament a fanatical majority or absolutist party commanding huge numbers in the House may destroy democracy, secularity, independence of the judiciary and the rule of law itself. All constitutional safeguards and safety valves may become ephemeral, unless basic values are put beyond parliament's power to truncate. So it is that we have, as settled constitutional law, re-enforced by *Kesavananda Bharathi, Minerva Mills, Indira Nehru Gandhi, Bommai* and other cases, the doctrine of basic structure of the Constitution which is beyond mutation by the plenary power of Parliament. Thus the great fundamentals are immunised; at the same time variable values can be given validity by appropriate amendments. Indeed, the Constitution has undergone around seventy-eight effective amendments. What are the basic features of the Constitution which are outside the pale of amendment? The Rule of Law, for instance is one; equality before the law is another; secularism is a third; judicial review is a fourth. Even federalism and supreme sovereignty are substantially inviolable.

India is a pluralist society with a huge Hindu majority with subsidiary caste minorities, and a number of religious minorities with separate identity. To preserve our democracy and the confidence of the minorities, safeguards need to be incorporated and wisely therefore, protection and reservation for minorities, autonomy for religious communities and freedom for linguistic groups find a haven in the Constitution. Dr. Ambedkar, in the Constituent Assembly, has defended the provision of reservations and other safeguards. "To diehards who have developed a kind of fanaticism against minority protection I would like to say......one is that minorities are an explosive force which, if it erupts can blow up the whole fabric of the State." Therefore, he argued for a tolerant majority with respect for minority rights.

He quoted Grote, the historian of Greece:

> *The diffusion of constitutional morality, not merely among the majority of any community but through out the whole, is the indispensible condition of a Government at once free and peaceable; since even any powerful and obstinate minority may render the working of a free institution impracticable, without being strong enough to conquer ascendency for themselves.*

By constitutional morality Grote meant—a paramount reverence for the forms of the constitution, enforcing obedience to authority acting under and within these forms yet combined with the habit of open speech, of action, subject only to definite legal control, and unrestrained censure of those very authorities as to all their public acts combined too with a perfect confidence in the bosom of every citizen amidst the bitterness of party contest that the forms of the constitution will not be less sacred in the eyes of his opponents than in his own. (The Framing of India's Constitution-Vol-IV P-428)

A great safety value of Human Rights, constitutionally inscribed, is the power of judicial review even to the extent of correcting and invalidating executive and legislative excesses by binding writs Articles 13, 132, 226, 136, 141, 142 are some of the vital provisions which grant access to the people to move the court and seek redressal against injustice. Be you ever so high, the law is above you. This proposition must be read with the power of the independent judiciary, *viz.*, the law is what the judges say it is. Since judicial review is a basic feature of the Constitution, the citizen has inalienable power to defend himself. Of course, what are "basic features" depends on the pronouncements of the judiciary in their wisdom. Judicial independence is itself a basic feature of the Constitution.

Two questions remain before us. Who appoints judges? Who will correct judicial misconduct? Equally relevantly, the question arises, as Prof. Griffith (The Politics of Judiciary) points out, the social and political position, the class bias and communal influences of judges themselves may colour their objectivity and their social vision. A National Judicial Commission may perhaps be a partial answer. What should be the composition of such a Commission?

The concern on the issue is very succinctly expressed in a Private Member Constitution (Amendment) Bill, 1996 to amend articles 124, 217 etc. by Mr. V.N. Gadgil, Member of Parliament in Rajya Sabha on December 18, 1998. The salient points made in Mr. Gadgil's Bill are as under:

i. *The Constituent Assembly while providing for appointment of High Court and Supreme Court Judges in the Constitution did not intend that consent of the Chief Justice of India should be obtained. What was envisaged was only consultation with him. Dr. B.R. Ambedkar clearly expressed himself against a provision requiring concurrence of the President since according to him, Chief Justice after all "is a man with all his feelings, all the sentiments and all the prejudices which we, the common people have."*

ii. *The judgment of the Apex Court is based on distrust of Parliament and the Executive.*

iii. *Nowhere in the world there is a system where Judges themselves decide as to who will be the next Judge. One cannot be Judge in one's own cause. No Parliament should accept such a proposition.*

iv. In the United States, selection of Judges is a political process and Chief Justice or other Judges of the Supreme Court are neither informed nor consulted in the matter. In Britain, the proposal is made by the Lord Chancellor who is head of the judiciary but also Minister of the Crown. In Canada too, the power to appoint judges vests in the executive.

v. Independence of Judges is a myth. All judgments are not objective as Judges' own views do get reflected in the judgments.

A Judicial Commission which will have a mix of representative from the judiciary, executive and others has been advocated from time to time by many including the Law Commission of India (see 121st report) with a view to ensuring that judicial appointments at the level of High Court and Supreme Court Judges are made with the collective wisdom of a representative body rather than leaving the same to absolute or sole power of one wing of the State.

(The Constitution of India—Select issues and perceptions by Subhash Jain P-5/6)

In our democratic system, the strongest safety valve to protect our freedom is the exercise of adult franchise whereby every person, above age eighteen has the right to cast his vote at a general election held obligatorily by an independent Election Commission. This power of the people is the ultimate sanction to control the Executive and the Legislature. In Churchill's famous words:

> *At the bottom of all tributes paid to democracy is the little man, walking into a little booth, with a little pencil, making a little cross on a little bit of paper—no amount of rhetoric or voluminous discussion can possibly diminish the overwhelming importance of the point.*

In our cabinet system the council of ministers must command a majority in the House. This sanction is a protection against authoritarian regime. The historic Indira Gandhi debacle, after the Emergency span, demonstrates how effective elections are as a safety valve.

Freedom of expression, which covers freedom of the media, is a constitutional guarantee which properly exercised, will empower, as the Fourth Estate, the political opposition in the country and make Part III of the Constitution (Fundamental Rights) a living reality. Parties play a vital role in the operation of the democratic order. Even if a plurality of parties form Coalitions or Fronts they are answerable to the House and the House itself, functionally powerful, is a sentinel of people's liberty and an incorruptible responsive and responsible Government. The pity is that our legislatures are not functioning meaningfully and are often lost in 'sound and fury signifying nothing'.

The rule of law is a great principle which gives access to every aggrieved person to seek justice before an independent judiciary. However, litigation is expensive, backlogs colossal and final pronouncement of judgement so delayed that judicial justice becomes a mirage. Here again, judicial reform is a necessary measure which cannot wait longer because the situation is already nearing breakdown point.

The Constitution is a social document and economic instrument. Secularism is a guarantee and socialism is an imperative of our Republic. In this context, part IV and IV-A which deal with Directive Principles fundamental in the governance of the country as well as the provisions regarding Fundamental Duties, if taken seriously, will ensure life, liberty and the pursuit of happiness of every Indian a basic birthright. Above all is the judicial process, but it is in a lamentable crisis currently, so much so; we have miles to go before claiming that social justice is an enforceable, realizable credential of citizenship.

The salvation of Swaraj—every Indian human's right to dignity, development and democratic voice—depends on the creative, sensitive, sarvodaya spirit of our constitutional order.

> *It is well to remember the oft repeated passage from the last speech of Dr. B.R. Ambedkar in the Constituent Assembly on November 25, 1949 to the following effect:*
>
> *"....I feel, however good a Constitution may be, it is sure to turn out bad because those who are called to work it, happen to be a bad lot. However bad a Constitution may be, it may turn out to be good if those who are called to work it, happen to be a good lot. The working of the Constitution does not depend wholly upon the nature of the Constitution."*
>
> *Dr. Ambedkar further added:*
>
> *"The Constitution can provide only the organs of State such as the legislature, the executive and the judiciary. The factors on which the working of those organs of State depends are people and the political parties they will set up as their instruments to carry out their wishes and their politics. Who can say how the people of India and their parties will behave? Will they uphold constitutional methods of achieving their purposes...."*
>
> *(The Constitution of India—Select issues and perceptions by Subhash Jain P-12)*

The ultimate Safety Valve of our Republic rests, vests, in the last analysis, in the practical wisdom, social active and collective comity of "We the People of India".

INHUMANITY ON ADIVASI AND THEIR REHABILITATIVE STRATEGY— A KERALA FIASCO

The adivasi humanity of Kerala, as elsewhere, humble in numbers, homeless have-nots in status with negligible political clout and live in landless despair. The rule of law blinks at them and politicians of all parties betray them. This micro-community a little over one per cent. of the Kerala population, is victim of social deprivation, dubious promises and dishonourable existence. Are they Indians? Yes. Are they forest dwellers from ancient days? Yes. What is their distressing status today? *De facto* dishonoured by the State and *de jure* proffered jungle slices which do not exist these tribal communities are refugees without territory, not even a trace of what once belonged to them. The law plays hide and seek with these 'specially favoured' children of the Constitution. Driven by despair these less miserables have began to dare to demand rights. This militant mood may explode justly every day heedless of Khaki fury unless the adivasi land question is settled with justice, equity and good conscience weaving a jurisprudence which treats tribals as humans with title to survival. Kerala is an advanced State and if their destiny is terrorised travail, their lot in other parts of the country must be more pathetic. From a pan-Indian angle the current Kerala tribal crisis is an event and portent.

Adivasis are mostly *vanavasis*, forest-dwellers. They live in jungles, collect forest produce and own small cultivable lands, the green woods being their habitats. Their unlettered way of life, their naivete and artless ethos make them easy prey to exploitation by cunning settlers from the plains who rob the tribal proletariat of their patches, leaving these hoodwinked humans victims sans basic human rights, without which their survival is in conditions of shock and shame. The endemic social disease of alienation of adivasi holdings became an extermination operation too unconscionable for the State to tolerate without legislative intervention. So in action ceased to be an option.

In 1975 the Kerala legislature unanimously enacted The Kerala Scheduled Tribes (Restriction of Transfer of Lands and Restoration of Alienated Lands) Act. The legislation had a mission—the redemption of dispossessed, destitute tribals in distress. Had this Act been implemented with the social passion which drove the House into salvationary locomotion the tribal revolt which has now escalated into a mass upheaval could never have happened. Alas, this legislative manoeuver proved to be a dastardly double deception. It was the commission of a grave guilt, the corrupt culpability having tainted every political party. The tribal innocents were stabbed in the back by deliberate default in not notifying the law for years after being doped and duped by a statutory pretense of restoration of their gullibly alienated humble holdings. The people of the State who sympathised with the tribal proletariat were left with an illusion of land legislation which was allowed to slumber. The neo-settlers meanwhile developed the lands, defying the legislation and silencing Governments in turn by Fronts of *'radicals'* and *'democrats.'* In politics, nomenclature is Orwellian diction meaning the opposite of what it seems to say. Every party professed support, to adivasis; every party had opportunity to enforce the law while it was in office but not one did put back an acre of alienated land. The non-tribals settled on these lands, encroached on more neighbourhoods; and the forest-dwellers were disowned by the forests. To recover lost land from aliens and encroachers Government had to implement the law with passion for the cause, compassion for the powerless. The settlers, mostly Christian, had the Church with them. By their political numbers, well-organized under political flags, they could not be dislodged. The scattered adivasis, with a stillborn law in the statute book, had but futility and mockery. Imagine the seriousness of a Government which has been ruled by two rival Fronts, treating the law as all but dead. The rules were framed more than a decade later, and giving effect to them from January 1982 was mere jugglery with the calendar. The law was not implemented on the ground and so the adivasis wandered in the jungle with not a cent to claim as their own. Then came one Dr. P.Nallaambi Thera who filed O.P. No.8879/88 before the High Court seeking implementation of the Act. It is unfortunate that even the Marxist party-led government was guilty of insouciance. There were 8088 cases pending under the Act for restoration and yet orders were passed only in 1201 cases and alas, only in 3 cases actual restoration took place. The grossest contempt for the adivasi law and the adivasi right is thus loud and clear. Today the Left Front is violently vitriolic against the Congress government, but their performance while in power is a shameful chapter.

The High Court was more radical than the noisy political parties and directed Government to dispose off all pending restoration applications within a period of six months from 15-10-1993. The vocal socialism of all the parties, judged by their performance *vis a vis* the adivasi proletariat had lost the cosmetic crimson in practice. Despite the High Court directive, Government dawdled, delayed and deprived the tribals of their dues. Ultimately, the High Court ordered peremptory compliance. The lack of sincerity of the Left Front in power became manifest when instead of giving land under the 1975 Act as ordered by the High Court, a legislation largely scuttling the original Act was brought under guise of Amendment in 1996. The teasing illusion and promise of unreality held out to the adivasi ended with this Amendment. But a contradiction in history took place. The Marxist Bill was withheld assent by the President who was advised by the Congress Cabinet to do so. A student of dialectical materialism has much to explore in this curious anti-climax. The bankruptcy of socialist sympathy for the landless adivasi is evident from the fact that Government moved the High Court, time after time, to gain an opportunity to fulfill the obligations under the Act. Finally, the High Court granted time for Government to give right and justice to the tribal proletarian by 5-1-1999. Meanwhile, the dubious policy of the Government became apparent and a new bill, namely, the Kerala Restriction on Transfer by and Restoration of Land to Scheduled Tribes Bill 1999 was introduced before the Assembly. The tribals are political trivia, the settlers and the church and others who had seized adivasi land had tremendous political clout. Inevitably, the new bill of 1999 was enacted and the progressive bill of 1975 was repealed. The Meanwhile, litigative anfractuosities followed by petition in the High Court and the Supreme Court. Contempt proceedings were also instituted and the legal destiny of these proceedings depends on the final verdict of the appeal now pending in the Supreme Court.

A new chapter of nonviable commitments by the Chief Minister Antony of the UDF was made on 16th October, 2001 at a conference where Janu, a lady leader of the adivasis, took militant part. Five acres of land for every adivasi family as far as possible was the basic understanding. Wynad District is where the adivasis are hard hit in landless destitution. But Wynad Region is where under the 1971 Act vast extents of private forests were vested in the State compensation free. An affirmation was made that lands from these vested forests may be identified and allotted to landless adivasi folk, of course, after securing Central Government approval. The deplorable fact remains that most of the S.Ts are duped. The Kerala Private Forest Vesting and Assignment Act, 1971 was upheld as a measure of *agrarian reform.* Section ten of the Act obligate the State to assign vested forest land to property less tribals. In breach of the promise by the Chief Minister, and mindless of the constitutional urgency of land allotment after a procrastinated game of hide and seek, the State Government sought an option in inaction infuriating the tribal starvelings. Perhaps, the alibi was that a Central Forest Conservation Act was brought into force in 1980 and any assignment of forestland needed approval from the Central Government. Had the 1975 Act been implemented the 1980 unborn Central Act could hardly have been a hindrance. The problem now is to secure large extents of land to settle the landless wandering forest dwellers. The apparent impasse is not a deadlock, which cannot be surmounted, given the political will. Some measures which obviously occur may be considered in the context of the grave crisis which looms large over the whole State worked up with the confrontational fury of the adivasis escalating after the battle of Muthanga between the tribal intransigents and the police.

Who deprived the land of the tribals in yesteryears? The settlers from the plains mostly Travancoreans from the Christian belt. It is true they sold away their belongings at home and settled in large numbers dispossessing the tribal population by petty allurement and tricky operations. Gaining foothold, they expanded by encroachment. Of course, arriving with their culture and working hard on the hilly terrain they made improvements, cultivated crops, built homesteads, constructed schools and established churches. This civilising mission eclipsed the adivasi flock and the uprooted chunk of humanity became alien in their own land, desperate for source of survival and slaving for rightless existence. Historic justice may well warrant redistribution of lost land and rehabilitation of the rootless diaspora. The moral foundation of the 1975 Act is the re-taking from the aliens the alienated land for re-settlement but the intervening period of development where the settlers had, with blood and toil, added to the value of the land and created a new homeland became a reality which could not be wished away. At the same time the forlorn aboriginals ware a poignant territorial truth and morally and legally deserved re-instatement.

The obvious source of land for re-settling them was, therefore, re-taking reasonable slice from the plains people. Perhaps exceptions may have to be made to exclude from resumption church buildings, schools, essential community centers, and the like. Where there has been expansionist encroachment of adivasi land there is clear justification for evicting the occupants from such excess. There will be resistance, especially because the occupational community is politically powerful. Indeed the inexcusable delay of the State in implementing the 1975 Act and the legislative and the litigative strategies to undo the 1975 Act prove beyond reasonable doubt the culpable operations of the settlers over the goofy aboriginals. Today, when a crisis is brewing, the mood has to change, the mind- set has to become sterner and the commitment to restorative justice uncompromising. If this new locomotive of land redistribution were adopted without hanky-panky a substantial portion of land can be given back to the landless tribals.

Government can, on a warfooting, survey the encroachments, discover and recover the extra-land so occupied and, on just terms of compensation, give it back to the adivasi. Fifty committees spread all over Malabar *with adivasi representatives* and technical services of land surveyors can implement this operation in a few months time. Immediate orders must be passed vesting in the local tribals the encroached land. Will the Government, what with its commitment and legislative backing, undertake a blitz operation?

A brief chronicle of the tribal kinsman, with special reference to their habitant, may help understand the land grab victimisation and homeless helplessness which lead to adivasi desperation. Conditions became so distressing that in the 1950s the Dhebar Commission was appointed to go into the traumatic tribal situation. A land-mark report recommended legislation for prevention of alienation of tribal lands and restoration of alienated land back to the tribal. The states were dragging their feet because tribals were politically lightweight nitwits. However, during the Emergency, the Kerala Legislature enacted the 1975 Act a salvationary legislation which was a casualty in its implementation. However, the 'bio-diversity' charade was used as a new alibi to throw the tribals out of their natural habitats. Vested interests operate blowing up 'environment' to gain strangle-hold over forest land-eliminating aboriginals who have all along contributed as friends of the woods and integral part of forest preservation ethos. Indeed, the tribal human is part of bio-diversity and is its sentinel rather than its hostile. Based on this fundamental the Forest Policy Statement of 1988 was formulated, propounding the philosophy of 'symbiosis of tribal and forest', harmonising this duality. This ecological confluence of aboriginal and his forest milieu, if applied to Kerala adivasis and their arboreal haven, will happily resolve the present confrontation and clashes. The Forest Conservation Act, 1980 which is held out as a legislative taboo for the entry of tribals is an exaggerated hermeneutic distortion of the law rather than an embargo on user of forest as tribal habitat. There is an elitist antipathy in this interpretation. The welfare and survival of the tribal community resident in forests from ancient times is not considered by forest bureaucrats to be a 'forest purpose' under the 1980 Act, although construction of quarters, destruction of trees for provision of facility for comfortable official living, road and other amenities for the forest boses and echotourism are considered 'forest purpose'. To my mind, having read the 1980 Act and the explanation regarding forest purpose, I see no semantic sense in excluding the bare occupation of aboriginal in the wilds with an obligation to protect the trees, prevent braking up of the land and otherwise damaging the forest qua forest. The tribals can take the forest produce, live and watch against poachers and be the natural instrument of forest preservation. Joint committees with forest officials, tribal members and departmental watchdogs can be constituted in every forest to oversee forestry. The adivasi families may innocently live there, take natural forest produce and make a living without injury to the arboreal integrity. *No ownership* of forest may be given to the tribal, but the right to live there by leave and license, the right to take the customary forest produce and be on duty to see that wild animals do not destroy the forest and poachers do not trespass. Jaundiced environmentalism, which is allergic to tribal presence but is at home with game-hunters and personnel of Forest Departments, fussy environmentalists, professional photographers of wild life, and affluent holidayers in tours conducted by liberally staffed contingents of officials, agents and other hangers on Forest and Tourism Development Departments. Humanise your arboreal vision and viably operate the philosophy featured prominently in the 1988 Forest policy statement of *Symbiosis of Tribal and Forest*—do this creatively, and the adivasi is part of bio-diversity. Imagination is lacking in the bureaucrats when he reaches the definition of *'non-forest use'* in the 1980 Act with an uppish prejudice. In my humble submission, all the stranded adivasis of Kerala can be accommodated by adopting the above formula and constituting *joint management committees* with tribals and officials sitting together to guard our forests.

Large extents of forest were once private lands of Malabar landlords but were vested in the State by virtue of the Kerala Private Forests Vesting and Assignment Act, 1971. No compensation was provided and the High Court struck down the law as *ultra vires*. But the Supreme Court reversed the High Court, upheld the vesting on the score that it was an *agrarian reform measure*. Significantly the Supreme Court directed redistribution and assignment of half the vested lands to be assigned to landless tribal people, or exclusively to them in areas where they formed a substantial population. The court had cautioned that this re-distributive process should not remain a teasing illusion. If only this desideratum had been carried and diligently before the 1980 Forest Conversation Act there would have been no adivasi problem at all. This culpable failure has deprived the major stakeholder, namely the tribal, of his homeland. On the contrary, through various guidelines the State Government has declared these forests as reserved forests and sanctuaries for wild life preservation. Indeed, while driving out the tribals Government did not put into operation any massive afforestation programme. In recent times, there has been an explosive episode of land hungry adivasis trying to occupy whatever crumbs of land they could get but here the might of the State threw them out.

T. Madhava Menon, I.A.S., who had worked intimately among forest dwellers has narrated the chronicle of one police operation *vis a vis* the tribal population.

> *2.6.1. Kerala case. A glaring example of arbitrariness is seen in the Muthanga Forest, recently the scene of the violence against tribal people who had occupied portions of it. When the Nilgiri Biosphere Reserve was constituted, several forests falling within a pre-determined compass were included in it. In Muthanga, areas that had been clear-felled for planting eucalyptus for supply at subsidized prices to the defunct Gwalior Rayons Factory at Mavur near Calicut have also been included. This enterprise of planting eucalyptus failed and the area did not regenerate successfully with other species. It has been subject to annual fires, and is covered with Eupatorium and other weeds. But for administrative convenience, and for geographic contiguity, it has been included in the Reserve. It was this area*

that the tribal people occupied; they did so deliberately so that their occupation would cause the minimum ecological consequences, but the Government thought it was the unforgivable sin, and turned all their organized violence against the hapless tribal folk.

2.6.2. A larger significance. Nothing illustrates the validity of the thesis of symbiosis between tribal people and the forests better than the Muthanga case. The Forest Department had thoughtlessly clearfelled the area and planted eucalyptus there, an enterprise that failed. It had been unable to prevent annual fires, so that the natural vegetation could not re-establish itself. Even bamboo regeneration was not possible. The area became overrun with weeds. Obviously, it provided no forage or habitat suitable for a viable wild life population, except as a portion of migratory paths. The tribal people intuitively recognized the tract as one that required human presence and intervention for regeneration. Their occupation would inhibit wild life migration through the tract, and thus enable regeneration of some species that would otherwise invite browsing. The upper soil, hardened by repeated fires, could be broken up by human labour. The stage was set for the symbiosis of a human community capable of a technology of mild intervention so that the bio-productivity of the tract would be stored, if not to what was its original composition, to at least one of better value for humans and wild life than its present condition.

(Report on Tribal Land Rights)

The crying need of the hour is to give creative shape to tribal and forest in such manner that rehabilitation becomes a reality. One concrete proposal which I wish to place before the State legislature is to enact a Tribal Resettlement Act. This will have to be a case of carving out of vested forest under the 1971 Act necessary lands for providing tribal habitat. Forest is a subject in the Concurrent List of 7th Schedule of the Constitution. Therefore the State is well within its powers to legislate subject to Central assent. There is a good case to make. The Kerala State acquired vested forests under a statutory blitz which survived the Supreme Court scrutiny. In that very judgement the court had addressed itself to assignment of land to tribals. Secondly, there are Muthangas which are formally 'reserved forests or sanctuaries' but are woodless areas available for dwelling by adivasis. The best forests can be left intact but the marginal ones may be made available. Here again, my proposal is not to spare the neo-settlers and the Church who have grabbed lands in defiance of the 1975 Act. To evict them is a statutory duty that may not satisfy the entire needs of the tribals. That is why we must fall back on alternative resources of vested forests by special legislation. Humanism and compassion, history and geography, once seen in proper setting, will persuade the Central Government to the necessary constitutional assent. In the special project by way of legislation, sufficient conditions can be imposed to protect forest trees and to regenerate the fictitious forests, to inhibit damage to forests by wild animals and defend forests against poachers may also be Adivasi Rehabilitation Project. I would urge once again that Muthanga is more a message and a sign-post rather than an adivasi invasionary occupation as it is prejudicially presented. Operation Muthanga has a salvationary dimension.

Government must not lose a sense of priority in regard to land ownership. The first charge on land for sheer survival belongs to the aboriginal, the last claim, viewed from a value base, belongs to huge corporations. In Kerala, large (excessive) forest land.for alleged plantation and other purposes are with Big Business like the Tatas, the Gwalior Rayons etcetara. Those lands must instantly be taken over by the State and made over for adivasi occupation. This will relieve the scarcity situation a great deal without tears. All that is needed is for Government and the people to decide on whose side they are—with the needy tribal or the greedy corporation.

INDIAN POLICING—SOME SOCIAL DIMENSIONS

The criminal justice system is the conscience and foundation of the social order and, in turn, the basic structure of this system has two fundamental components. Of course, paramountcy belongs to the Judiciary. Why? Because, as St.Augustine put it, Justice being taken away then, what are Kingdoms but great robberies? For what are robberies themselves, but little kingdoms? (The City of God) Next to the judicature, probably more vital in certain respects, the police establishment plays a cardinal role on which hinges people's life, liberty and the pursuit of happiness in peace and security. Policing, like justicing, has therefore to be at the service of the people commanding the credibility of the community at large without fear or favour, affection or ill-will. Independence and accountability with commitment to the rule of law, are as much the non-negotiable qualities of the invigilating, investigating police force as of the 'robed brethren' on the bench. If the investigative process fails, if the police presence to guard law and order is not functionally successful, the adjudicatory apparatus collapses and our adversarial system of justice becomes dysfunctional. The safety of society, sans police integrity, accountability, transparency and efficiency, suffers illusion and unreality. Once we accept this critical proposition of the police process in people's protection, orderly development and creative participation in people's right to justice, we have to focus on the systemic flaws, performance failures and room for reform of the uniformed cadres and higher echelons so that the police paradigm may present a transformation rid of the evils which now beset the establishment. Police reform is too grave to neglect, too urgent to delay, too serious to be left to self-corrective strategies.

Chronic indifference to progressive reform may make police presence as good as absent. This will certainly fuel increase in social conflict and encourage crime, mafia operation, terrorist activity and vigilantism; and inhibit good governance and economic development. The whole criminal justice system is, with exceptions, currently obese, obsolescent, obscurantist and obnoxious. Overhauling is overdue but holistic measures and comprehensive correctives cannot be an excuse for not implementing feasible reforms to the immediate extent possible.

Initiatives from the Centre to catalyse police reform is a good beginning. There are many valuable reports of valiant Commissions at the national and State levels which slumber and gather dust because, apart from cosmetic changes, Governments rarely bother to undertake radical mutations. It is unpleasant to implement reforms because the political Governments with power appetite do not take kindly to the constitutional fundamental of insulating the police establishment from illegitimate political control and external interference. To be a Minister is to be able to manipulate police power and therefore this corrupt proclivity inhibits self-restraint and autonomy of the police service. It is necessary to stress without mincing words that the police are indeed accountable only to law and must be beyond clout or threat from any other oblique quarter. However, the present system has created such a deep subversion of the concept of independence and accountability that it requires a radical reorientation in the philosophy of police control and management. The political will to reform the police is presently beyond visibility. It must be created through public pressure, political campaign and judicial mandate.

A diagnostic approach to the present pathology of the police system is a good beginning. I have had experience of conducting many tough criminal cases while at the bar and have known the vices and weaknesses, the moral deviances and inhuman violations the police have indulged in during normal duties, investigative operations and stages of prosecution. The institution, as such, has great potential, as I have discovered while I was Home Minister in the Kerala State for a brief while (1957-59). I know the deterioration and excellence of that Establishment and, as judge, I have pronounced on the performance of the Police *a la* Nandini Satpathy case (AIR 1978 SC 1025) *et al.*

The police have their own problems and difficult situations without realising which criticism will be unjust. For instance, 'a policeman called to the scene of a crime must make an instant decision on what action he must take, then take it. A judge may be presented with the same set of facts a month later. He can take all the time he needs in deciding what to do about it. But not the policeman. He has to act and act now. (Bill Schipp) (Readers Digest Oct 1962 P-112). This does not mean that the police can be a law unto themselves under guise of urgency. However, as Roger J Traynor has lucidly expressed 'The great advantage of police compliance with the law is that it helps create an atmosphere conducive to a community in respect for officers of the law that in turn serve to promote their enforcement of the law. Once they set an example of lawful conduct they are in a position to set up lines of communication and to gain its support'. Police performance is thus a community asset promotive of the rule of law. At present, custodial abuse is often at the door of the police and investigative infallibility is rarely regarded as an attainment of the police. On the contrary, political interference, corrupt practices, third degree methods and fabrications of evidence are imputed to the police. Maybe, there are black sheep, but to generalise is to forget the presence of great policemen at every level. There are inadequacies in police equipment, training and culture. Commission after commission has pointed out the peculiar predicament of the police service caught in a dilemma between political bossism and legal obligation. Those who are generous to the finer police patriots will agree that—to borrow Churchill—'never in the field of human conflict was so much owed by so many to so few'. Crimes are escalating; society is deteriorating, politicians are interfering; power abuse is becoming a growing syndrome. At the same time, policing intelligence is on the wane; police violence is on the rise. A new sense of dignity and reverence for institutional reputation must develop from within the police establishment. Technology is rapidly advancing and canny criminals corner them, making the methods of crime technologically superior to police strategy. The integrity of the police establishment must also become unassailable and its credibility invincible so that court may not dismiss police processes unworthy of *prima facie* acceptance. All these and other matters of concern make it imperative that *avant garde,* progressive metamorphoses in police functionalism are the challenge of the time.

The ethos of the police must change. So too its eidos. Do remember that the police organisation in India was established after the Indian mutiny in 1857 to curb dissent, to enforce obedience and make loyalty for the foreign ruler the basic objective. Inevitably, this systemic cult engendered a pro-ruler, anti people culture. Since Independence, nothing radical has been done to infuse a progressive dynamism, a people-oriented democratisation and a versatile measure of professional excellence geared to national values. Commissions have been appointed, Reports submitted but not implemented. True, some initiatives have been taken like the National Police Commission of 1979-81, but the central issues and recommendations which the report emphasised remain slumbering far too long and the Police Act of 1861 needs to be replaced and modernised with ideological changes incorporated, so that the system may be in tune with the constitutional teleology and technological advances. The Rebeiro Committee and the Padmanabaiah Committee have made valuable proposals for reform. The late Inderjit Gupta (CPI leader), as Union Home Minister, took the initiative in 1997 to exhort the States to introduce police reform on the lines of the N.P.C. Indeed, all these are part of history and the police *modus operandi* is basically left without ideological or methodological modifications of a cardinal nature. The price of lethargy is that expectations from the police remain a frustration in practice. There is so much mistrust of the police among the people that an iron curtain has descended between the two Reforms cannot tarry.

Speaking generally, people regard the police as an inevitable evil, a ubiquitous need, a physical power whose proximity is desiderated for prestige and pomp. Sans police activism, chaos in the cosmos will be the grave risk. Crimes will be committed recklessly, absent the deterrent mobility of the State's armed might. If police intelligence does not detect and arrest criminal gangs and omnipresent mafia, if the investigative machinery does not bring to justice anti-social offenders with celerity, the syndrome of turbulence, social clashes and even terrorism well shock society into anarchy. Therefore, the police is people's inseparable friend. Then why mistrust him, malign him and condemn him as if khaki uniform is a sartorial virus or toxic professional disease. No, not at all. They are part of us, share our problems and will be our source of strength *once a progressive Police Reform Agenda becomes operational.*

Critical to our millennial march is the defense of human rights which are vulnerable to violations from many angles and we fall back on the sensitized police personnel for protection and preventive action.

What are the ground realities *vis a vis* the police in their conventional activities? Some hard evidence reads horrendous. ACHRI publication reports:

In 1999 alone, over 74322 complaints were received from the public against police personnel in the country. (Crime in India 1999)

> *In 1999-2000 the National Human Rights Commission received reports of 177 deaths in police custody, 1157 illegal detention and arrest', 1647 'false implication' and 5783 'other police excesses'. (NHRC Annual Report 2000)*
>
> *In addition, there are the recent incidents of what happened in Gujarat. There is strong evidence to show that the police force not only failed to handle the disturbances efficiently but showed partiality in dealing with the rioters. They were not merely indifferent but complicity involved in several incidents of violence targeted against the minority community in the state. Besides the loss of lives and property of the riot victims, the state has suffered an economic loss of over Rs. 3,000 crore.*

Although repetitively, let me emphasize the fundamentals with some supplementary thoughts.

The social order in a civilized society needs a Force to maintain public order and prevention of crime plus bringing the criminals, by prompt prosecution, to condign punishment. To ensure this process we need an organized body sensitive to human rights, beyond purchase or pressure and totally committed to a crime-free-society. Towards this end, the State must empower the police echelons and cadres, from top to bottom, to take preventive action, investigate crimes, impart confidence in the people about their security and, apart from defending the victim, to take punitive measures according to law. In this larger sense, the police represents the collective interests of the community *vis a vis* life; liberty and the pursuit of happiness. The functional fulfillment of the police duty requires non-interference by those in political authority, extraneous clout or coercion or even impractical, ill-informed and unwarranted judicial commands. Indeed, the measure of a society's stability depends on the autonomy, integrity and fearless performance of duty by the police hierarchy. Of course, broad parameters for the fulfillment of the objectives of the constitutional system will be laid down by legislation and general directives, consistently with constitutional imperatives and the laws. These may rightly be issued by the political government, which is ultimately answerable to the people who are the final political custodians of power and beneficiaries of the Welfare State. Within these boundaries, autonomy is enjoyed by the police force with its own internal discipline, control and command. Of course, judicial review is a constitutional corrective, which binds and guides and pronounces upon police action. Thus there is a controllerate to keep the police within bounds and a sanction for operation by the police of its duties and commitments. In this sense, the police is not merely the friend, philosopher and guide of the citizenry but also a stern engineer of the laws necessary for peace and security.

> *Just as the character and the quality of a country's police forces provide a touch-stone of spirit and quality of its government and civil administration, the 'police' provides a touch-stone of the quality and conduct of the people themselves. In short, a student of the political institution of any country desirous of understanding the 'ethos' of any country's Government can hardly do better than to make a close study of its police system, which will provide him with a good measuring rod of the actual extent to which its government is free or authoritarian.* (Coatman, John (1959)

The inevitable interrogation posed from ancient times is "who will police the police?" Generally speaking, there is an organisational pyramid and the Ministry at the top – which keeps the police in leash and guides its powers promotive of the welfare of the people and their peaceful life. It must always be remembered that the Constitution which is paramount vests in the Court the power of judicial review which is a basic feature of our Constitution. But judicial review is not teasing tinkering; and forensic excess harms successful investigation. Judicial oversight, with becoming restraint, comports with police dignity, autonomy and accountability.

Centres of research, hi-tech equipments which will beat the criminal's tricks and enable squads in uniform or in mufti to chase and trap the criminals, are necessary for efficiency. White Collar crimes, economic offences and dangerous proliferation of the underground criminal world compel the State to train a police force with ultra-modern machinery, methodology and manpower so that the most sophisticated and cunning of criminals cannot escape the coils of the police net. Most embarrassing situations arise when an Executive Boss or political heavy weight is himself the doer of crimes and, very rarely though, even a robed brother on the Bench plays truant and is a hidden abettor of criminals.

The police officers have to deal with crimes, which are too intricate unless trained adequately in specialised fields. He may have to interrogate, hypnotise, subject persons to psychic examination, dig up unsuspected places, enter and seize seemingly sacred spots and seek the assistance, during investigation, of medical specialties and call in aid experts in technology and even dogs with sixth sense or olfactory sharpness. Indeed, even prevention of crimes or identification of criminals summon versatile forms of training and know-how, without use of third degree methods, which is the current coin of the third world constabulary. Torture has to be avoided, molestation of women and children should be mercilessly rooted out and yet results must be produced so that the confidence of people in the police will be kept high even as the morale of the police is sustained.

A fundamentally different aspect deserves serious consideration. The police whose sacred task is search for truth is sometimes perverted into victimizing people on account of corrupt motives, outside pressures, pornomania and sadistic sex and torture. The result is that the credibility in the police is at stake. When the police become criminal the violence that they inflict escape punitive proceedings. So much so, it is essential to have a Vigilance Commission or other ombudsman to act immediately when police delinquency or criminality is brought to its notice. So it is important that apart from the long-winded judicial proceedings we must have an instant instrumentality, outside the police department, which will blitz into action when reports about the police violation come to its notice. Torture and rape, custodial molestation, illegal detention, unwarranted shadowing violative of basic privacy and roping in of innocent people in grave crimes are not uncommon. Even children are made to suffer mayhem and dalits are subjected to humiliation. Whenever peasants and workers organize strikes and demand rights, it happens the police are used to break strikes and deprive the tenants of their claims because mangements and landlords influence the police. So, certain guidelines are necessary to forbid such unjust police interference under guise of anticipated violence. Similarly the police connive at smuggling, blink at alcohol-based crimes and wink at like anti-social offences. Rackets by the mafia have often links with the police at various levels. In short, the role of the police is reversed and complicity in crimes by the police escalates since offenders are rich underground operators who buy up and grave crimes go undetected. If hawalawalas and their allies and bribe-givers and their go-betweens bribe the police and make them limpets and manipulate investigations, courts acquit and people are perplexed. Political pressure on the police thwarts straightforward investigation and the aggrieved are helpless and voiceless. Sometimes police documents are fabricated or tampered with. In all these cases there is need for an organization to guard the guards, to try offences by the police by an independent agency *a la* Vittal (and his web site) and insist upon compliance with constitutional guarantees. In *Nandini Satpathy* case, referred to earlier, many directions were given regarding the accused's right to counsel and forbidding excessive and torturesome interrogation of women in police stations. Hand-cuffing by the police, insultingly inflicting indignity on the victim is violation of human rights. These and other matters deserve special attention when reforms are under consideration.

A two-volume report by a Committee appointed by the H.R.D. Ministry, and chaired by me, on custodial justice to women contains concrete steps and practical recommendations but governments have paid no heed to those suggestions. The National Police Commission Report contains exhaustive recommendation but we are still governed by the British Indian vintage Police Act which is more than a century old. The Indian Republic and the Constitution's Preamble can promote a just social order only if there is radical reenactment of a progressive police code where women and children will receive special attention and the police force will undergo special courses in human rights and keep pace with updated judicial pronouncements. In this sense, a courier between the police and the judicairy is a systemic necessity. To dismiss the police with contempt or cynicism is irresponsible. To bring in a new spirit of humanism and constitutional responsibility in every police person, man or woman, is the task of the legislatures. Democracy is stable only if the police are conscientised, trained and treated, not as a gang of uniformed musclemen but as State functionaries mandated to maintain peace by legal means.

Victimology is burgeoning into an important branch of criminal jurisprudence. The present system which is adversarial and of Anglo-Saxon vintage, deals with a criminal case as a battle between a person accused of crime and the state which impersonally represents the people. The individual victim, the community which has suffered in a riot or clash, the relatives and other concerned persons who are affected by the occurrence are ignored. The police take charge of investigation. The victim has no voice, as of right, to compel the police to take evidence or to move the court to be heard through his prosecutor. The community, as such, though vitally affected in the public peace that is violated has no *locus standi* before the police or the judge nor is a claim for compensation maintainable at the instance of the victims save in an action in *tort*. Even after sentence is imposed, when parole is granted or suspension or reduction of sentence by way of commutation ordered, the victim is not heard as of right. This leads to gross injustice at times. We therefore need a developed system of victimological jurisprudence and legislation in that behalf. Police policy must make it obligatory to involve the victim community in the investigative and prosecutory operations.

Today, we live in an era of human rights in a wider sense than the individual aggrieved person. The police functionary has crime-free community responsibility far beyond particular crimes. Law and order, 'in widest commonalty spread', becomes his concern. Simmering disturbances, underground activities, foreign presence insidiously active, become the duty of the police person to discover before the explosion occurs. Intelligence, these days, is a highly specialised operation and demands skills, technologies and strategies sometimes too complex for lay persons to discern. Here is a field of specialisation for the police. Likewise, a course in human rights, what it means and how to resist their violation must be a compulsory course from the constabulary upwards. Third degree methods cannot be eliminated by more judicial rhetoric. A new culture has to be evolved, a new ethos has to be woven and a new drill has to become an exercise so that the policemen and police women by a humanised chemical change, truly become the collective defender of the social order.

Accountability of the Police

A basic feature of democracy is transparency coupled with accountability. Secrecy of operation and refusal to be accountable to the public amount to negation of the rule of law and respect for human rights.

All policing has to be brought in line with the requirements of democratic functioning and must take into account the fact that Indian citizens have constitutionally mandated fundamental rights and all instrumentalities of government must be accountable to the people.

The Victorian vintage Indian Police Act does not speak of the role of the police beyond law enforcement and does not recognize the need and responsibility of the Government to establish an effective and efficient system of democratic policing. State Police Acts passed after Independence are mostly modelled on the 1861 Police Act and there is little to distinguish them from colonial legislation. By contrast, the police Acts of UK, British Columbia and several other Commonwealth countries, make it a statutory responsibility of the government to set out objectives and performance targets for the police and clearly lay down how these responsibilities are to be discharged through a process of consultation. Similar provisions are found in the Police Act of South Africa and, in fact, the Constitution of South Africa envisions such responsibility on the state.

The presence of a lawyer when an accused is questioned or arrested promotes accountability because an advocate corrects police excess on the spot, prevents third degree and makes the uniformed authority answerable to legality. It must be remembered that the police, as a law enforcement agency, command far more physical power than any other public service agency and therefore the mechanism for accountability is all the more necessary. The weaponry the police carries, the large powers the police possesses under the Prevention of Terrorism Act, the Gunda Act and similar State laws demand a greater level of accountability from and invigilation of the police as a force. This sense of accountability has to be visible if it is to carry confidence with the public. That is why the presence of an advocate is a great safeguard. True, the advocate cannot be obstructive of interrogation or negative road blocks in the investigative discovery of truth.

Another dimension of accountability in the evaluation of police performance needs mention. The statistical test of number of conviction leads to distortion. Apart from the fact that the conviction rate is discreditably low as an efficient instrument, there is a tendency not to register cases, extract forced confessions. Facile use of third degree methods and other undesirable practices for detection escalate as easy methods of procuring conviction. Accountability, so long as this para terrorist process prevail, takes a long holiday. Therefore, more scientific and continuous assessment of police performance is to be formed to evaluate individual and collective performance. The National Police Commission has suggested independent directorates of police evaluation in every State. Another commission which deals with justice to women in custody (of which I was the Chairman) recommended the empowerment of responsible non-official organisations to enter and inspect places of police custody. There is no reason why representatives of the people and responsible agencies of the public with acceptable credentials should not be allowed to meet and ask for information, including the right to see persons in custody. This will largely promote openness and considerably let it down police abuse. Indeed, police-people interaction, public participation in crime prevention, common operation in situations of distress or commotion will bring the community into closer relations with the police and consequential elimination of extra-legal methods habitual with the police.

A major area of public dissatisfaction with the police arises from the inability of the public to follow the progress of reported crime and victims' complaints to police. At present, police feel themselves under no obligation to provide information to a victim or complainant about how the investigation is progressing. It should be made mandatory in law for the police to inform the complainant about the progress of the investigation. This will not only enhance accountability to the complainant as far as investigation is concerned, but also progressively build confidence that will bring in more willing public participation into policing.

The police process must possess a democratic culture if the Republic is to bear true faith and allegiance to the Constitution. Today, the situation is different, because police-public relations are soured by hostility and allergy. It would appear that in 1999-2000 the National Human Rights Commission received reports of 177 deaths in police custody. 1157 illegal detentions and arrests, 1646 false implications and 5783 other police exercises. These facts illustrate the current estrangement between the police and the people and stresses the need for healthier constructive police-community inter-action. Today there is lack of communication and accessibility between the police and the citizen and a new functional nexus must remove the mists of misunderstanding.

The basic premise of community policing, as Dr. Doel Mukerjee put it, lies in allowing the community to collaborate with the police force to perform various duties. These could include maintenance of peace and security, safety of citizens, law enforcement, crime control and orderly flow of traffic. If these functions are taken care of, it will leave ample time for the police to execute their remaining duties such as investigation of cases.

International experiments have also proven the viability of the community policing idea. In the UK, the new Police Act, it is claimed, gave a fresh image and responsibility to the beat constable making the bobby a household person in hamlets, in the back alleys and the big cities. More recently, the Police Act and the recent UK Police Reforms Bill, 2002, further entrenches the idea by requiring community consultation and providing scope for induction of Community Support Officers and Community Accreditation Schemes. In addition, the Reform Bill allows the Chief of Police in the UK to liaise with the business community of an area to supervise their employees in carrying out certain community safety functions.

Police liaison committee celebration of Annual Police Day, participation of police officers in community welfare activity and other pre bono operations are promotive of better relations and elimination of mistrust. It has been suggested that citizens' boards may be set up which may include advocates, business people, women's associations and retired judges who may work in close association with law enforcement agencies and keep a crime database. Meeting and discussing together issues of common concern may bridge the gap between the police and the people. What is needed is an attitudinal change on both sides, so that a creative camaraderie between the people and the constable may become a *modus vivendi.* Perhaps, statutory support may lend strength to this dynamic concept. After all, in our days of terrorism and crime explosion people-police activism is of socially therapeutic value.

CODA

What should be the nature of the structure which will bring together the public and the police? An advisory body with sentinel status in every district may do liaison service. Here, again, the presence of a retired judge to help such a committee of police public relation may be welcome. Similarly, a retired senior police officer on the committee may be salutory since he/she will bring the needed knowhow about police public problems. While the local MLA and MP may properly figure as people's representatives great care should be taken to exclude political, communal and other undesirable influences to sap or convert the credibility, integrity and impartiality of the committee. Surely, the committee's discussions should be frank and fair and fearless criticism of the police will enhance the work of the committee in ventilating general grievances and felt necessities bearing upon policing proper. The police too get an opportunity to communicate with the public. The party in power, or for that matter, any other powerful political group should not utilise the committee to shape the course of particular cases. Nor, indeed, should the committee have any power to pronounce on or steer the course of any individual case. The selection of the members of the committee may probably be made by the District Collector in active consultation with the seniormost judicial officer locally available and also the District Panchayat President.

The authority and responsibility of the Government *vis a vis* the police force must be regulated by statutory process, so that nothing lawless, dubious, arbitrary or oblique is done under guise of oral or written instruction, secretly making the police a political instrumentality or amenable to extraneous pressures and partiality.

Periodic professional courses in Human Rights and social justice must be imparted at every level of the police hierarchy by competent and seasoned organisations like the National Law School or Judicial Training Institute. The course must be based upon an agenda for community policing and the play of human rights in the daily dealings, involving the people and the police.

I suggest, with respect, that non-official bodies or highly respected personalities be given legal access to police officers to obtain information about matters of public concern *vis a vis* police operations. Another suggestion, which I found in Madison (USA), may be adapted so as to promote openness and reduce shady or secret methodology. Final year law students or those who are doing doctoral thesis in criminology may be given access, guided by a senior professor of the law school to visit police stations and offices at higher levels and acquaint themselves with the happenings inside. Not that confidential matters should be made available to the injury of investigations but that police offices be open to the public and nothing secretive, canny or dubious takes place. In short, such a procedure may strengthen the confidence of the people in police probity and processual rectitude.

The National Police Commission has recommended a draft Police Bill for consideration. That may have to be updated and brought in tune with the fundamental freedoms of the citizen and the victimological obligations of current jurisprudence. Today, the police is a suspect body. It need not be. Today, the police is regarded as an *armed force* not a *public service.* It need not be. Finally, policing must be given a high functional status, considerable technological training and constant subjection to invigilatory oversight by a statutory functionary with power to inquire and, in turn, submit public reports like any other public authority amenable to the rule of law. The Police are trustees of public peace and are under on fiduciary duty to the people.

Let me conclude with a sober quote:

> *Much about the moral fiber of a society can be learned from the way it deals with crime. It is not enough to treat criminals with as much compassion as we can, especially when this liberal spirit is carried to the excess of*

interfering with crime prevention as the courts have done. It's about time society showed a little moral strength by acknowledging that victims, real people, are hurt by crime and that it is to them that criminals owe their debt.
—Editorial, "Making Criminals Pay," The Wall Street Journal.

A CRIME,
A CRIME BY A CRUDE KHAKI CROWD

An old man in poor health was dragged by a khaki corps by house-breaking into the home of Karunanidhi in the wee hours after midnight, violating, according to the version of the former Chief Minister's side, all canons of decency, dignity and humanity, insolently and ignorantly ignoring the constitutional mandate in articles 21 and 51A (humanism and compassion) and the Supreme Court directives and the Penal Code provisions. If the eye will not lie, the television media luridly showed a ghastly scene of rude use of brute power by a crowd in uniform, the solitary valetudinarian, octogenarian victim in bed, struggling and crying—a scene of woe the like of which my eyes have never before seen, nor my heart conceived nor my pen or tongue could adequately tell. Inferentially, the cabal who commanded the crew was the Chief Executive. They merely carried out this savage circus. The Hindu editorial of Ist July diagnoses this Operation Traumata as political vendetta. Were it true, human rights in Gandhi country are on the cross, constitutional guarantees are but paper tiger and a barbaric blitz has possessed the police and the top echelons with unconscionable ease. Some Central Ministers have been taken into custody, with puerile impunity, paralysing, in part, the Union Government's functionalism. Police raj has over-powered the constitutional order and the rule of law has surrendered to a quasi-fascist syndrome. If allowed to run berserk, this authoritarian terrorism will make Bharat a bedlam. The nation must protest, the Courts must *suo motu* initiate action and the Union Cabinet must get its ministers freed forthwith and judicial enquiry ordered right now into these draconian doings by the top to bottom of ministers and minions. Prosecution for grave violation and grievous offence as a shocking abuse of power must be rushed through lest one billion Indians lose their credence in the legal system. The Indian Penal Code in section 166, or 321 to 326, (committing any violent act unwarranted and excessive in the circumstances) or violation of human rights by abuse or use of distressingly disproportionate force—these are criminal conduct punishable under the law. Sections 46 and 49 of the Criminal Procedure Code prohibit avoidable force for arrest. An old invalid with poor vision, sleeping in his bedroom, a respectable person twice a Chief Minister, does not need to be disturbed by *midnight* knock and dragged and roughed up. Why past midnight? Why a posse of police? The whole melodrama, *prima facie*, seems rudely insulting, insanely excessive and utterly lawless. Police power is a public trust and its brazen breach calls for condign punishment. In the *Nandini Satpathi* case I had ruled against abuse of police muscles—not fists but wits. The arrestee is entitled to know why, has right to counsel. The Supreme Court, in *D.K. Basu's* case (AIR 1997 SC 610), has given clear guidelines of which the police, who took Karunanidhi into custody, seem outrageously innocent. Any public-spirited body can move the High Court for right and justice on the basis of quasi-habeas corpus jurisprudence. Article 142 of the Constitution vests in the Supreme Court wide powers in order to assure doing of *complete justice;* and this power has been used *suo motu* to give relief instantly. Palpable injustice instantly invites this power and I wonder whether the Karunanidhi torture is not sufficiently shocking to invoke the said jurisdiction. Even otherwise, Article 32 and 226 are not slumbering provisions but spring into action so that fundamental rights and other human rights are not dead letter. Indeed, the gravamen of the charge takes on an aggravated form when we realise, as The Hindu Editorial suggests, that there is some conspiracy by a cabal of political-cum-bureaucratic operators behind this apparent outrage. The constitutional consternation that shocks and shames every citizen when political authoritarianism, through ukases and gun power, holds the freedoms of fellow Indians to ransom for political reasons.

The implications of the Chennai episode, including the reckless arrest of Central Ministers, are so grave that unless immediate steps against the offending group is taken, one day any State Chief Minister with political limpets and police bullies, may perpetrate a similar crime on our Prime Minister himself? Who is safe if the law sleeps and the judicial sentinel blinks away from the culprit and crime. Similarly, the National Human Rights Commission, to create confidence in the common people about the reality of guaranteed constitutional rights, must move with procedural celerity and punitive insistence. The issue at stake before one billion Indian humans is whether he or she has the right to life and liberty and other basic values writ in print (or water) by the Founding Fathers. Is the rule of law a teasing illusion or promise of unreality? Is torture police culture? If not, in the absence of the slightest suspicion of escape, can the police commit housebreak, inflict mayhem a gerontic gentleman in his sleep? The reputed Tamilnadu Police, I suspect, by their strange conduct, has spoiled India's Human Rights reputation in the comity of nations. So I write this piece. Mark Twain comes to mind:

> *It is by the goodness of God that in our country we have those three unspeakably precious things; freedom of speech, freedom of conscience, and the prudence never to practise either of them.*

I blush.

A CASE FOR NATIONAL PRISON POLICY

Our Constitution is on trial in our prison houses, our cultural credentials are tested behind stone walls and iron bars, our penal panaceas are in peril, what with the deterrent no-return and recidivist escalation despite long incarceration. The law cannot hang limp but must lash out to restore order, correct deviance and stabilise that personal integrity which is the best guarantee of behavioural normality and societal harmony. Barbarity in sentence and torture in prison are a trend, which aggravates the malady and so self-defeating that punitive cruelty is a curative futility and preventive disutility. From a practical range, criminologists have concluded that benumbing, long prison terms and inflictions within the walled campuses are ineffective drugs in the penological pharmacopoeia.

Therefore, a reformative philosophy, rehabilitative strategy, therapeutic prison treatment and enlivening of prisoner's personality through a technology of fostering the fullness of being such a creative art of social defense and correctional process activising fundamental guarantees of prisoner's rights, is hopeful not of national prison policy struck by the Constitution and the Court. This is my thesis but I must argue my case and establish the justice of this policy. Tersely put, the State must discover and engineer the highway to human rehabilitation and put it into practice in the prison system.

At this point we may begin with the basic question: Do we have a national prison justice policy? To be honest, the *Raj* had a prison programme at the services of its imperial policy, but the Republic, with all its boasts and all its hopes, has no penal policy, no prison, no humanism, no jail justice, even though almost every minister who was wielded power, regardless of party, has suffered incarceratory laptism. Regrettably, the judiciary has parrot-like, carried over precedents of Victorian vintage, being innocent of progressive penological thought and the nexus of constitutional values with prison praxis. Judicial illiterarcy about criminology, rehabilitative technology and of the court's responsibility in purposeful sentencing projects and restorative penitentiary procedures is appalling.

On the legislative front, the less said, the better. In a country where the majority of legislators have served a jail spell almost as a qualification for candidacy, is it not surprising that the Prisons Act, 1894, codifying the repressive policy of Whitehall, continues "red in tooth and claw", come freedom, come Constitution. The harassing and hamstringing traditions validated by Prison Manuals, are preserved thoughtlessly, decades after prisoner patriots assumed power (wearing a Gandhi cap is, under the Punjab Jail Manual, a Jail offence even now). Parliamentary apathy is matched by executive insouciance. Of course, at seminars and conferences, ghost speechwriters cover up minister's conscience with glittering inaugural exhortations and even policy formulations. And criminological workshops the academia's, never taken seriously by the politician, the bureaucrat, the judge and the warden who alone matter in executing prison justice. Thus, the battle for a national policy on prisons and imprisonment has been lost by apathy, insensitivity and 'eminent' ignorance.

The people—the political swashbucklers and professional jargon-mongers apart, are unaware, doped by hopes, and are inertly irresponsive to the sentencing mystiques. If only a human transformation inside the walled world of offenders were planned and executed, through a circumspect, yet intelligent project to invigorate benignly the inner man in custody, a crime-free society, why, a prisonless State may dawn in the distance, given creative courage and national vision in perspective of human values. This is not a moonly ideal but largely practical, as several social scientists and sublime pragmatists claim. I know, ever science has been an out caste. I may sound unorthodox but orthodoxy is the Bourbon of the world of thought. It learns not, neither can it forget.

Among the three alternatives, the retributive, the deterrent and the rehabilitative, modern penologists opt for the last with a sprinkling of the second. To be retributive is to claim an eye for an eye-and, logically, a murder for a murder, a rape for a rape, a reprisal barbarity for brutal burglary and so on. Soothing for the sadist, heartening to the little Hitler lingering in many bosoms, this form of blood-thirsty justice, which still is prevalent in a few countries, has become obsolete, what with the dignity and worth of the human person receiving better recognition in civilised societies responsive to the new international legal order. Not quite dead is *lex talionis*, as is evident from the lively controversy about death penalty.

Don C. Gibbons in his recent edition of "Society, Crime and Criminal Careers" writes: "What purpose does the infliction of suffering on law-breakers serve? Tappan has offered an incisive summary of the purposes of punishment. He notes that punishment is designed to achieve the goal of retribution or social retaliation against the offender. Punishment also involves incapacitation, which prevents the violator from misbehaving during the time he is being punished. Additionally, punishment supposed to have a deterrent effect, both on the law-breaker and on potential misbehaviours. Individual or specific deterrence may be achieved by intimidation of the person, frightening him against further misbehaviour, or it may be effected through reformation in which the law-breaker changes his deviant sentiments. General deterrence results from the warning offered to potential criminals by the example of punishment directed at a specific wrongdoer".

The theory that savagery must be fought by savagery dies hard and if that philosophy holds good, judges must welcome prison torture and police third degree. Anyway, these primitive strands of thinking, decked in different apparel, are found among judicial, legislative and executive agencies. Is this our penal policy? Then, do jail the delinquent in, gouge his eyes, publicly flog him, dismember his limbs and hang him to the delectation of ghoulish crowds. Blinding Bhagalpur justice par excellence.

British justice once hanged even children for petty offences and some great judges were unhappy when some in the long list of capital sentence offences were sought to be jettisoned. "Sir Rober Peel regarded it 'as a most dangerous experiment' when stealing £5 from a dwelling-house ceased to be a capital offence. Lord Ellenborough, the Lord Chief Justice of his day, thought transportation as a punishment for stealing 5s. from a shop was quite inadequate substitute for the death penalty, and the Solicitor-General, Sir William Garrow, argued passionately that the Government could not exist without the protection of drawing and quartering".

England has replaced the gallows by prisons, and a macabre mix of retaliatory cruelty, a deterrent confinement defiles prison management. In many countries, long terms behind bars, harsh and humiliating regimen like solitary confinement and fetters all over, deprivations of basic needs to deepen the punitive thrust became the "zoological" penal policy embittering the culprit. Wincfred A. Elken writes: "At the turn of the century, a government committee was set up to investigate the work of the prisons. What impressed its members was not the deterrent value of imprisonment, but the extent to which the prisoners were brutalized and demoralised by their experience. The prisons were in fact breeding grounds of crime.

"The deterrent theory seems in fact to lead to an inevitable dilemma. Crime continues in spite of punishment and the logical answer is to make the punishments even more severe. Ultimately the point is reached when the demoralisation produced by these punishments becomes too glaringly obvious and the administrators of justice, and the public, become sickened by what the law demands. Experience has in fact shown that the purely repressive punishments are neither necessary nor effective".

The champions of severity of infliction, corporal or in-prison, as possessing a deterrent potential have lost the battle by now, because crimes have been increasing despite heavy penalties. A variety of reasons render impotent these draconian penal prescriptions, including the venality of investigative agencies, the judicial distance between the first charge and final guild and the easy purchase of acquittals or light sentences, through clever lawyering, and the non-performance of the criminal justice system which is creaking crumbling, credibility-lacking instrumentality. Even the barbarities in some of the middle-East countries become bearable, except in stray dramatic cruelties, because bribery and other pressures buy off where the law's claws otherwise tear into the flesh. Even the stern socialist societies and their penal pharmaceuticals suffer failure, at least in part. Reams can be written, hours can be spoken, to prove the point that terror and horror, as punitive armoury, only debase justice but do not deter the culprit except marginally. Of course, society must emphatically express public denunciation for some types of crime through punishment but brutal deterrence is fiendish folly. It frightens, never refines; it wounds, never heals; it embitters him, never binds him to others; it burns the skin, never awakens the soul. It works on the animal in man but neglects the spirit within. And penal torture hardens the criminal while our objective is to socialise and redeem the individual. Radical humanism and progressive penology must gravitate towards the therapeutic processes, which heal and humanise, restore and socialise, reconcile punishment with dignity of personhood.

A SPECIAL NOTE ON PAROLE JURISPRUDENCE AND NARCOTIC CONVICTS

The criminal justice system has moved away from its harsher Draconian days to the reformatory humanitarian present. The parole process has been conceived of as a progressive device to humanise prisoners and reward them for good institutional conduct by a conditional release subject to procedural safeguards and obligation to return to prison. Penological confusion used to prevail that parole was like suspension of sentence. But this is a fallacy as the Supreme Court of India has explained in *Dadu* (2000) 8 SCC 437. The court categorically states:

> *6. Parole is not a suspension of the sentence. The convict continues to be serving the sentence despite granting of parole under the statute, rules, jail manual or the Government Orders. "Parole" means the release of a prisoner temporarily for a special purpose before the expiry of a sentence, on the promise of good behaviour and return to jail. It is a release from jail, prison or other internment after actually being in jail serving part of sentence.*
>
> *7. Grant of parole is essentially an executive function to be exercised within the limits prescribed in that behalf. It would not be open to the court to reduce the period of detention by admitting a detenu or convict on parole. The court cannot substitute the period of detention either by abridging or enlarging it. Dealing with the concept of parole and its effect on period of detention in a preventive detention matter, this Court in Poonam Lata v. M.L. Wadhawan held: (SCC p.354, para 8)*
>
> *It is a provisional release from confinement but is* deemed to be a part of the imprisonment. *Release on parole is a wing of the* reformative *process and is expected to provide opportunity to the prisoner to transform himself into a useful citizen. Parole is thus a grant of partial liberty of lessening of restrictions to a convict prisoner, but release on parole does not change the status of the prisoner. Rules are framed providing supervision by parole authorities of the convicts released on parole and in case of failure to perform the promise, the convict released on parole is directed to surrender to custody.*

Grant of parole is essentially on executive function Sethi, J. has clarified: 'parole has become an integral part of the English and American system of criminal justice intertwined with the evolution of changing attitude of the society towards crime and criminal'. The penal system now considered release on licence i.e., parole as an executive function.

In a Constitution Bench decision of the Supreme Court, the precise connotation in law of parole has been elucidated; 'parole ameliorates punishment by permitting convict to serve sentence outside the prison wall, but parole does not interrupt sentence'. During parole period there is no suspension of sentence, but the sentence is actually continuing to run during that period also".

Representations were made to the High Level Committee on Parole and Remission by certain aggrieved narcotics, praying for release on parole, notwithstanding section 32A of the Narcotic Drugs and Psychotropic Substances Act, 1985. They pointed out, and rightly, that they may be considered for release on parole since the Indian court 'in recent years made orders of release on parole on humanitarian condition'. In *Dadu,* after explaining the legal concept of parole as distinguished from bail or suspension of sentence the court, made an observation with lovely and lucent clarity.

> *It is thus clear that* parole did not amount to the suspension, *remission or commutation of sentences* which could be withheld under the garb of Section 32A of the Act. *Notwithstanding the provisions of the offending section,* a convict is entitled to parole, *subject however, to the conditions governing the grant of it under the statue, if any, or the jail manual or the government instructions. (2000) 8 SCCP-444 Para 11)*

Narcotic sentencees cannot, therefore, be denied parole since the court has stated, with specific reference to section 32A of the Act, 'notwithstanding the provision of the offending section, a convict is *entitled to parole,* subject, however, to relevant conditions governing the grant of it under the statute, if any, in the jail manual or Government instruction. One thing that follows from this crucial dictum of the court is that a narcotic convict has an equal title to parole which is a compassionate consideration. There is no specific statutory provision forbidding *parole* to narcotics.

The present 32A of the Act had ostensibly persuaded the Kerala Government to deny parole to narcotic prisoners. The rule is obviously the offshoot of the Act. Now that the Supreme Court has gone to the extent of striking down that part of 32A, which deprives judicial power to grant bail and *a fortiori* the grant of parole is an *entitlement,* subject to other conditions, the jail manual must be read down and the ban on parole to narcotic convicts deemed non est. With the tree falls the branch. In the light of the court ruling, denial of parole on the score that the prisoner is a sentencee under the Narcotic Act no longer holds good. The humanitarian philosophy of parole equally applies to this category of prisoners, especially after Dadu. If there be doubt, its benefit belongs to Freedom as parole, as a process is geared to a reformative goal.

Rule 452 BB (vi) deserves to be deleted now that the Supreme Court has spoken and the survival of the negation of parole to narcotic convicts is no longer sustainable. We recommend to Government repeal or deletion of that sub-rule and act as if the bar has been dropped. However, the other conditions regarding emergency leave and regular parole require compliance since the guidelines prescribed for grant of parole are just, fair and reasonable. There is a measure of discretion, within the parameters of the parole rules, vested in the executive; but arbitrariness on the part of the executive is allergy to the Constitution. Therefore care must be taken to comply with the remaining conditions that apply to all parolees most apply to narcotic convicts. It is unjust and arbitrary to reject parole *solely* because he is a narcotic convict. Since reformation is the object of parole there is no reason to differentiate between a narcotic convict and other criminal convicts. Articles 14 and 21 make it just, fair and reasonable to obliterate the narcotic invidiousness *vis a vis* parole decision.

Criteria for granting or denying parole and the terms of parole have been indicated in *Maru Ram's* case and in the extant jail rules as of now. This point needs emphasise because, among the various points in the criminal justice process, no point offered more opportunity for abuse and arbitrary exercise than parole release decisions. The courts do not take a "hands off" attitude towards such executive decision as is evident from the recent ruling of the recent Kerala High Court leading to the setting up of the High-level Committee.

Even in the United States, since the early 1970's; there has been an explosion in case-law on the parole release decisions with potential promise far greater accountability in this process. Sufficiency of reasons or frivolous reasons or absence of reasons has been the subject of judicial scrutiny. Sheldon Krantz, in his classic work **Corrections and Prisoner's Rights** (P-299), writes thus:

The court determined that the reason was insufficient after applying this test:

> *Can such a reason be so meaningful that a reviewing court can determine whether the Board has adopted and followed criteria that are appropriate, rational and consistent, and does it protect the inmate against arbitrary and capricious decisions or actions based upon impermissible considerations? 389 F.Supp. at 409.*
>
> *Thus, it appears that the giving of reasons requires both explicit criteria and facts indicating why the criteria were applied in a given way. This area obviously is in need of further development, however. It is clear that the giving of very general or abstract reasons would result in Childs amounting to a meaningless victory.*

In sum, the notion that parole is grace of the Executive has been eroded by decisions of the Supreme Court of the U.S., and the *constitutional right of the parolee,* when it touches his freedom, attracts procedural due process. Finally, the State always must remember that parole is a kind quasi-imprisonment geared to the ultimate object of humanization and socialization of a person under incarceration. Here the narcotic stands in the same footing as any other convict.

DEATH PENALTY

"The penalty is barbaric and inhuman in its effect, mental and physical, upon the condemned prisoner and is positively cruel. The condemned prisoner suffers excruciating long wait from the imposition of the sentence untill the actual infliction of death. It involves lingering death. The physical pain and suffering which the actual execution of the sentence of death involves is also no less cruel and inhuman. The death penalty is cruel and inhuman, disproportionate and excessive".

Former Chief Justice of the Supreme Court of India Justice P.N. Bhagwati made these comments while delivering a lecture at the eighth United Nations Congress on "Prevention of Crimes and Treatment of Offenders". He spelt out in no uncertain terms his opposition to the imposition of death penalty.

The International Human Rights Charter takes congnizance of the right of every individual to live. It also adds that "No one shall be subjected to torture or to cruel, inhuman or degrading treatment or punishment" with emphasis. But many countries have still not abolished death penalty.

"There will be crimes in India founded on the basis of Ahimsa ..... Like all other diseases, committing crime is also an ailment; a malady born out of the present social system. Therefore all crimes, including murders would be considered a disease and the perpetrator would be given treatment. The other question is if such an India would ever take shape?" (Gandhiji in Young India, 10.9.31. p. 255)

Those who trumpet and take pride that they are the heirs of Mahatma Gandhi set fire to this dream of the Apostle of Ahimsa, the very day they set alight his funeral pyre at Rajghat. All the prisons in the country have turned out to be houses of torture shattering the dream of Gandhiji that prisons should be treatment centres.

This nation which offered Buddha who preached universal compassion to the world, and in a country where 'political parties' and individuals alike advocate that not even an ant should be subject to torture, death penalty has not been ended. We pride ourselves claiming that we were the first people in the world to lead a civilized life but we have not given up the barbaric practice of hanging convicted murderers, until they are dead. Our pretensions of justice is monumental hypocrisy.

A paper presented by Amnesty International (International Secretariat), London, on "Civil and Political Rights, Protection of Personal Integrity and Abolition of Death Penalty" at the World Congress on Human Rights in 1990 in New Delhi, read:

"Countless men and women have been executed for the purpose of preventing crime, especially the crime of murder. Yet, study after study in diverse countries has failed to find convincing evidence that the death penalty has any unique capacity to deter others from committing particular crimes".

It added:

> "Nor is there evidence that the threat of the death penalty will prevent politically motivated crimes or acts of terror. If any thing, the possibility of political martyrdom through execution may encourage people to commit such crimes".

In the article "The Human Rights Flag Atop Prison Towers; A radical judicial medical conspiracy to rescue man from his cage" Krishna Iyer writes:

"I believe that:

a. Criminals are made, not born, are curably human, not irredeemably brutish.

b. Crime is a disease and most criminals are a kind of psychic patients. Therefore, such anti-social maladies must be healed by medico-legal recipes inside prisons or at centres ideologically oriented on hospitalisation goals and appropriately adapted to kindle, not kill, the suppressed social being behind bars or under supervision.

c. Judicial punitivity must be conditioned by the philosophy of reform, not retribution, and must be sublimated into remedial sentencing with social defence safeguards and mainstreaming procedures, not dreadful disciplines and incarceratory inflictions sadistically masked as deterrence but actually proved to be counter productive.

d. Medical humanism and clinical pragmatism, not traditional legal torture as magic healer, plus the non-negotiable character of the quintessential constitutional guarantees of human rights of sentences is the New Testament of Penology."

In his view he could not accept the concept that judicial murder was the answer for criminal murder, something which cannot be condoned. It was inhuman, he felt. When a man is sentenced to death there is no torture which could be compared to the one that he suffers not knowing if the sentence would be commuted or not.

In his report, the Rapporteur of the United Nations Committee on Torture, submitted to the United Nations Human Rights Commission in 1988, it was stated;

"Persons who have been sentenced to death have to wait for long periods before they know whether the sentence will be carried out or not" and "if the uncertainty ...... lasts several years ...., the psychological effect may be equated with severe mental suffering, often resulting in serious physical complaints........ It may be asked whether such a situation is reconcilable with the required respect for man's dignity and physical and mental health."

Justice Krishna Iyer had already given emphasis in 1974 itself to the views that the United Nations stressed in 1988. In the case of *Ediga Annamma* v. *State of Andhra Pradesh,* the District Sessions Judge had sentenced the accused to death on December 31, 1971. "We are now in February, 1974", Justice Krishna Iyer pointed out and that continued suffering of the heart would have good impact and commuted the death sentence into one of life imprisonment. In his order, he said:

"It may also be worth mentioning that, apart from her youth and womanhood, she has a young boy to look after. What may perhaps be an extrinsic factor but recognised by the court as of human significance in the sentencing context is the brooding horror of hanging which has been haunting the prisoner in her condemned cell for over two years. The Sessions Judge pronounced the death penalty on December 31, 1971, and we are now in February 1974. This prolonged agony has ameliorative impact according to the rulings of this Court.

"The unmistakeable shift in legislative emphasis is that life-imprisonment for murder is the rule and capital sentence the exception to be resorted to for reasons to be stated.

"We assume that a better world is one without legal knifing of life, given propitious social changes. Even so, to sublimate savagery in individual or society is a long experiment in spiritual chemistry where moral values, socio-economic conditions and legislative judgment have a role. Judicial activism can only be a signpost, a weathervane, no more. We think the penal direction in this jurisprudential journey points to life in prison normally, as against guillotine, gas chamber, electric chair, firing squad or hangman's rope. "Thou shalt not kill" is a slow commandment in law as in life, addressed to citizens as well as to States, in peace as in war. We make this survey to justify our general preference where section 302 keeps two options open and the question is of great moment.

"Let us crystallise the positive indicators against death sentence under Indian Law currently. Where the murderer is too young or too old, the clemency of penal justice helps him. Where the offender suffers from socio-economic, psychic or penal compulsions insufficient to attract a legal exception or to downgrade the crime into a lesser one, judicial commutation is permissible. Other general social pressures, warranting judicial notice, with an extenuating impact may, in special cases, induce the lesser penalty. Extraordinary features in the judicial process, that such as the death sentence has hung over the head of the culprit excruciatingly long, may persuade the Court to be compassionate. Likewise, if others involved in the crime and similarly situated have received the benefit of life-imprisonment or if the offence is only constructive, being under section 302 read with section 149, or again if the accused has acted suddenly under another's instigation, without premeditation, perhaps the court may humanely opt for life, even like where a just cause or real suspicion of wifely infidelity pushed the criminal into the crime. On the other hand, the weapons used and the manner of their use, the horrendous features of the crime and hapless state of the victim, and the like, steel the heart of the law for a sterner sentence. We cannot obviously feed into a judicial computer all such situations since they are astrological imponderables in an imperfect and undulating society. A legal policy on life or death cannot be left for *ad hoc* mood or individual predilection and so we have sought to objectify to the extent possible, abandoning retributive ruthlessness, amending the deterrent creed and accepting the trend against the extreme and irrevocable penalty of putting out life.

"Here, the criminal's social and personal factors are less harsh, her feminity and youth, her unbalanced sex and expulsion from the conjugal home and being the mother of a young boy—these individually inconclusive and cumulatively marginal facts and circumstances—tend towards the award of life-imprisonment. We realise the speculative nature of the correlation between crime and punishment in this case, as in many others, and conscious of fallibility dilute the death penalty. The larger thought that quick punishment, though only a life-term, is more deterrent than leisurely judicial death award with liberal interposition of executive clemency, and that stricter checking on illicit weapons by the police deters better as social defence against murderous violence than a distant death sentence, is not an extraneous component in a court verdict on form of punishment".

C.A. Balan, a Tamil activist who spent some time in a condemned cell describes vividly the mental agony of the man to be hanged and the procedure of judicial murder in his book "In the shadow of the gallows".

"The day after I was confined in the Condemned Block in the Coimbatore Central Jail, a person was executed. This was unabashed incident of premeditated murder. Man has no right to kill fellow man. But this was an event where that right is usurped to suspend a man from the gallows".

The ritual that precedes the execution is described thus:

> "The Chief Jailor would open the page which contains the details of the condemned prisoner whose account is being closed and ask him questions in order to check the entries. He will be asked for his name, that of his father, his village and other details. And after comparing the distinguishing marks on the body of the condemned man, he

would say, "My friend, the President has rejected your mercy plea. Therefore you will be hanged at 5.30 in the morning. Pray to God. If you want to pass on any information to your relatives or friends, I will make necessary arrangements. These messages could be transmitted by telegram or you can use the post cards or envelopes that I will provide. After all is it not the work of the Almighty? Worship him." He will then be hanged".

Again Balan says:

> "Some will cry aloud; they will blabber about many things. They will beg of anyone they see to rescue them from death. Tears will roll down in cascades from their eyes. The authorities will tell them to repeat the holy names of the Gods. But on realising that even Gods would not be able to save them, they will begin wailing once again. They will have no stamina even to stand up. The legs will totter. The whole body will feel weak, yes, that is the fear of death."

The final hor(r)oscope of the condemned prisoner read before him sometimes renders him mute. Sometimes it makes him cry aloud. At other times, it makes him sober and leads him to rotate the rosary. Whether one rotates the rosary, prostrates himself and prays repeatedly, and writes Ram, Ram a million times, once the hard-hearted juridicial administration had decreed that he be hanged by the neck till he is dead, neither Ram, Allah nor Jesus would and could come to his aid.

When it is said that a person is to be hanged by his neck, let us see how it is done. Again we seek the authority of Balan's book. He says:

> "The man to be hanged would be made to stand on a circle drawn on the trap door of the hanging platform. Suspended from a cross bar across two pillars would be a hemp rope at the end of which a ring would be attached. One end of the rope would be passed through the ring and the other tied to the cross bar. This noose would be placed around the neck of the condemned man. When he is brought to the gallows itself his hands would be pinioned at his back with manacles and leather straps. As soon as he is made to stand on the circle his leg also would be bound. He will not be able to move in any manner.
>
> "As soon as the prisoner stands on the circle and his legs are tied, the jailor would say 'ready' and the lever would be pulled making the man hurtle down into the pit and to eternity.
>
> "The space between the circle and the bottom of the pit or well is 18 feet. When the trap doors are opened the man falls into this well. His head would be two feet below the surface of the trap doors. Legs would not touch the ground. If one were to look at the gallows after the execution is over, only a taut rope could be seen. The figure that remains suspended would present a ghastly picture. The entire tongue would be hanging outside the executed man's mouth".

This murder committed by the state is justified as an action in the interests of the large section of the people. A murder is a murder by whatever name you call it. We are still living like barbarians and have not developed humanitarian character. Writing in the 'Harijan', opposing the death penalty, Gandhiji said:

> "Only God has the right to take away a life, because it is the God who gave life".

A bill introduced by Gaya Prasad Singh in the State Assembly in 1931, seeking the abolition of death penalty was defeated due to Government opposition. In 1956 Mukund Lal Agarwal, tabled a Bill in the Lok Sabha for the same purpose and it was opposed by the Government and was defeated. In 1958, Prithvi Raj Kapur introduced a bill in the Rajya Sabha urging the ending of the death penalty. This motion was withdrawn after debate. In 1961 Savithri Devi Nigam brought a similar Bill in the Rajya Sabha and was rejected after a debate.

But the motion introduced by Ragunath Singh in the Lok Sabha in 1962, calling for the abolition of death penatly, created an uproar in the House and assumed great importance.

This motion was withdrawn only after the Central Government gave an undertaking that the debate would be compiled and sent to the Law Commission to enable it to review the Indian Penal Code and the Criminal Procedure Code. As a result of this motion, the Law Commission presented a report on the death penalty. It urged the Government that India should not experiment with this acid test by removing death sentence.

Great leaders had raised their voice against death sentence. Mahatma Gandhi had said:

> "Destruction of individuals can never be a virtuous act. The evil-doers cannot be done to death. Today there is a movement afoot for the abolition of capital punishment and attempts are being made to convert prisons into hospitals, as if the prisoners are persons suffering from a disease."

People's leader Jayaprakash Narayan in a message sent to the conference against death sentence, held in Delhi had this to say:

> "To my mind it is ultimately a question of respect for life and human approach to those who commit grievous hurt to others. Death sentence is no remedy for such crimes. A more humane and constructive remedy is to remove the culprit concerned from the normal milieu and treat him as mental case. I am sure a large proportion of the murderers could be weaned away from their path and their mental condition sufficiently improved to become useful citizens. In a minority of cases, this may not be possible. They may be kept in prison houses till they die a natural death. This may cast a heavy economic burden on society than hanging. But I have no doubt

that a humane treatment even of a murderer will enhance man's dignity and make society more human". (On the Abolition of the Death Penalty, A.I., p. 13)

Krishna Iyer translated his beliefs and principles into reality. In fact as Law Minister in the Namboodiripad ministry, he had commuted the death sentences of convicts into life imprisonment. As a judge, he commuted the death sentences and imposed life sentence in *Rajendra Prasad* v. *State of Uttar Pradesh, Kunju Kunju Janarthanan* v. *State of Kerala* and *Shio Sankar Dubey* v. *Uttar Pradesh* cases. The fate of the noose hanging above the heads of these condemned men, was rewritten. The Bench which delivered the judgments in these three cases, described in an elaborate manner under what circumstances, and for what reasons this cruel death sentence could be imposed.

"Law must be honest to itself. Is it not true that some judges count the number of fatal wounds, some the nature of the weapons used, others count the corpses or the degree of horror and yet others look into the age or sex of the offender and even the lapse of time between the trial court's award of death sentence and the final disposal of the appeal. With some judges, motives, provocations primary or constructive guilt, mental disturbance and old feuds, the savagery of the murderous moment or the plan which has preceded the killing, the social milieu, the sublimated class complex and other odd factors enter the sentencing calculus. Stranger still, a good sentence of death by the trial court is sometimes upset by the Supreme Court because of law's delays. Courts have even directed execution of murderers who are mental cases; who do not fall within the McNaughten rules, because of the insane fury of the slaughter. A big margin of subjectivism, a preference for old English precedents, theories of modern penology, behavioural emphasis or social antecedents, judicial hubris or human rights perspectives, criminological literacy or fanatical reverence for outworn social philosophers buried in the debris of time except as part of history—this plurality of forces plays a part in swinging the pendulum of sentencing justice erratically.

"The twists and turns in sentencing pattern and the under-emphasis on the sentence's circumstances in decided cases make an indepth investigations, of the 'principles' justifying the award of death sentence a constitutional duty of conscience. This Court must extricate, until Parliament legislates, the death sentence sector from judicial subjectivism and consequent uncertainty.

"It is fair to mention that the humanistic inperatives of the Indian Constitution, as paramount to the punitive strategy of the Penal Code, have hardly been explored by courts in this field of 'life or death' at the hands of the law.

"The main focus of our judgment is on this poignant gap in 'human rights jurisprudence' within the limits of the Penal Code, impregnated by the

Constitution. To put it pithily, a world order voicing the worth of the human person, a cultural legacy charged with compassion, an interpretative liberation from colonial callousness to life and liberty, a concern for social justice as setting the sights of individual justice, interact with the inherited text of the Penal Code to yield the goals desiderated by the Preamble and Articles 14, 19, and 21.

"Let us leave 'law' a while and begin with drawing the backdrop with a lurid brush. Every sombre dawn a human being is hanged by the legal process, the flag of humane justice shall be hung half-mast, such is the symbolic reverence the land of Gandhi should pay to human life haltered up by lethal law.

"We approach the resolution of the punishment predicament in a manner at once legal, logical and criminological and impregnated with values constitutional. Therefore, we will first study the significant legislative developments in the two interacting codes and related parliamentary essays at change. Where broad conclusions emerge from such an investigation, constitutional reinforcement may be sought. Since the Constitution is paramount and pramountcy is paramountcy, its expansive humanism must overpower traditional 'terrorism' in the practice of sentencing. When this stage is reached and formulation of guidelines made, we will consider the criminological foundations of theories of jurisprudence of our cultural cosmos. Finally, we will set down the salient cynosures for judges in their day-to-day labours.

"Primarily we seek guidelines from the two Codes, in the omnipresence and omnipotence of the over-arching Constitution. The Indian cultural current also counts and so does our spiritual chemistry, based on divinity in everyone, catalysed by the Buddha, Gandhi compassion. 'Every saint has a past and every sinner a future strikes a note of reformatory potential even in the most ghastly crime. This axiom is a vote against death and hope in life'.

"But 'murder most foul' is not the test, speaking scientifically. The doer may be a patriot, a revolutionary, a weak victim of an overpowering passion who, given better environment, may be a good citizen, a good administrator, a good husband, a great saint. What was Valmiki once? And that sublime spiritual star, Shri Aurobindo, tried once for murder but by history's fortune acquitted.

"The only correct approach is to read into section 302, I.P.C. and section 354 (3), Cr.P.C., the human rights and humane trends in the Constitution. So examined, the right to life and to fundamental freedoms is deprived when he is hanged to death, his dignity is defiled when his neck is noosed and strangled.

"The dignity of the individual shall not be desecrated by infliction of atrocious death sentence merely because there is a murder proved although crying circumstances demand the lesser penalty. To exemplify, supposing a boy of fifteen incited by his elder brothers, chases with them a murderer of their father and after hours of search confronts the villain and vivisects him in blood-thirsty beastiality. Do you hang the boy, blind to his dignity and tenderness intertwined?

"So, we search for guidelines within section 302, I.P.C. read with section 354, Cr. P.C., and find that, ordinarily, for murder a life-term is appropriate save where 'special reasons' are found for resort to total extinction of the right to life and farewell to fundamental rights. Public order and social security must demand it. That is to say, the sacrifice of a life is sanctioned only if otherwise public interest, social defence and public order would be smashed irretrievably. Social justice is rooted in spiritual justice and regards individual dignity and human divinty with sensitivity.

"You cannot inflict degrading punishment since the Preamble speaks of dignity of the individual. To stone a man to death is lynch law which breaches human dignity and is unreasonable under Article 19 and unusually cruel and arbitrary under Article 14. Luckily, our country is free from that barbarity legally.

"Likewise, if a man is a murderer, so hardened, so blood-thirsty, that within the prison and without, he makes no bones about killing others or carries on a prosperous business in cadavers, then he becomes a candidate for death sentence. If psychoanalysts and psychiatrists find him irredeemable in the responsible run of time, then his being alive will involve more lives being lost at his hands. If, however, he can be reformed in a few years' time by proper techniques of treatment, imprisonment for life is good enough. But, on the other hand, if he is far too hardened that it has become his second nature to murder, society cannot experiment with correctional strategy, for, when he comes out of jail, he may kill others. Such an incurable murderer deserves to be executed under the law as it stands. Difficult to imagine though, but even the bizarre may happen. The social setting, the individual factors and like imponderables still remain to be spelt out. While the world is spiralling spiritually towards a society without State-sanctioned homicide, a narrow category may under current Indian societal distortions deserve death penalty although realistically the law is held at bay by corporate criminals killing people through economic, product, environmental and like crimes.

"Our culture is at stake, our Karuna is threatened, our Constitution is brought into contempt by a cavalier indifference to the deep reverence for life and a superstitious offering of human sacrifice to propitiate the Goddess of justice.

"There is yet another consideration of grave moment which must weigh with the court, vowed to uphold Justice—Social, Economic and Political. Who by and large, are the men whom the gallows swallow? The white-collar criminals and the corporate criminals whose wilful economic and environmental crimes inflict mass deaths or who hire assassins and murder by remote control? Rarely. With a few exceptions, they hardly fear the halter. The feuding villager, heady with country liquour, the striking workers desperate with defeat, the political dissenter and sacrificing liberator intent on changing the social order from satanic misrule, the waifs and strays whom society has hardened by neglect into street toughs, or the poor householder—husband or wife—driven by dire necessity or burst of tantrums—it is this person who is the morning meal of the macabre executioner.

"Historically speaking, capital sentence perhaps has a class bias and colour bar, even as criminal law barks at both but bites the proletariat to defend the proprietariat, a reason which, incidentally, explains why corporate criminals including top executives who, by subtle processes, account for slow or sudden killing of large numbers by adulteration, smuggling, cornering, pollution and other invisible operations, are not on the wanted list and their offending operations which directly derive profit from mafia and white-collar crimes are not visited with death penalty, while relatively lesser delinquencies have, in statutory and forensic rhetoric, deserved the extreme penalty. Penal law is not what the printed text professes but what the prison cell and the condemned man testify.

"The retributive theory has had its day and is no longer valid. Deterrence and reformation are the primary social goals which make deprivation of life and liberty reasonable as penal panacea.

"The current ethos, with its strong emphasis on human right and against death penalty, together with the ancient strains of culture spanning the period from Buddha to Gandhi must ethically inform the concept of social justice which is a paramount principle and cultural paradigm of our Constitution.

"'Special reasons' necessary for imposing death penalty must relate, not to the crime as such but to the criminal. The crime may be shocking and yet the criminal may not deserve death penalty. The crime may be less shocking than other murders and yet the callous criminal, *e.g.*, a lethal economic offender, may be jeopardizing societal existence by his act of murder. Likewise, a hardened murderer or dacoit or armed robber who kills and relishes killing and raping and murdering to such an extent that he is beyond rehabilitation within a reasonable period according to current psychotherapy or curative techniques, may deserve the terminal sentence. Society survives by security for ordinary life. If officers enjoined to defend the peace are treacherously killed to facilitate perpetuation of murderous and often plunderous crimes, social justice steps in to demand death penalty dependant on the totality of circumstances.

"We must always have the brooding thought that there is a divinity in every man and that none is beyond redemption. But death penalty, still on our code, is the last step in a narrow category where, within a responable spell, the murderer is not likely to be cured and tends to murder others, even within the prison or immediately on release, if left alive—a king cobra which, by chronic habit, knows only to sting to death unless defanged if possible. The patience of society must be tempered by the prudence of social security and that is the limited justification for deprivation of fundamental rights by extinguishment of the whole human being. The extreme penalty can be invoked only in extreme situations.

"Those reasons and the evidence in support of them would provide the special reasons according to the State which impel capital punishment. It would be open to the accused to rebut this evidence either by submissions or if need be, by leading evidence. At that stage, the only consideration relevant for the purpose of determining the quantum of punishment would be the consideration bearing on the question of sentence alone and not on the validity of the verdict of guilty. After considering the submissions and evidence it would be for the court with its extreme judicious approach and bearing in mind the question that the extreme penalty is more an exception, to determine what would be the appropriate sentence. This would ensure a proper appreciation of vital considerations entering judical verdict for determining the quantum of sentence".

In *Rajendra Prasad's* case, Krishna Iyer quotes the verse of Oscar Wilde:

"The vilest deeds, like poison weeds,
Bloom within prison air;
It is only what is good in Man
That wastes and withers there".

Prasad's prison term never 'cured' him. Who bothered about cure? The blame for the second murder is partly on this neglect.

"Nothing on record suggests that Rajendra Prasad was beyond redemption; nothing on record hints at any such attempt inside the prison. Lock-up of a criminal for long years behind stone walls and iron bars, with drills of breaking the morale, will not change the prisoner for the better. Recidivism is an index of prison failure, in most cases. Anyway, Rajendra showed no incurable disposition to violent outbursts against his fellowmen. We see no special reason, to hang him out of corporeal existence. But while awarding him life imprisonment instead, we direct for him mental-moral healing courses through suitable work, acceptable meditational techniques and psychotherapic drills to regain his humanity and dignity. Prisons are not human warehouses but humane retrieval homes.

"This convict has had the hanging agony hanging over his head since 1973, with near-solitary confinement to boot! He must, by now, be more a vegetable than a person and hanging vegetable is not death penalty. This is an additional ground for our reduction."

In *Kunju Kunju Janardhana's* case he asked:

"Is Janardanan a social security risk, altogether beyond salvage by therapeutic life sentence? If he is, the pall must fall on his cadavar. If not, life must burn on" and adds, "So viewed, no material, save juridical wrath and grief, is discernible to invoke social justice and revoke his fundamental right to life. A course of anti-aphrodisiac treatment or willing castration is a better recipe for this hypersexed human than outright death sentence.

"Sentencing is a delicate process, not a blind man's buff. We commute the death sentence to life imprisonment".

In *Dubey's* case, he observed: "It is illegal to award capital sentence without considering the correctional possibilities inside prison. Anger, even judicial anger, solves no problem but creates many."

In *Noel Riley* v. *Attorney General (UK)*, on the question of whether the delayed execution of a sentence of death by hanging could be described as inhuman or degrading punishment; Lord Scarman and Lord Brightman who gave the minority opinion, after referring to the British Practice and *Fuman* v. *Georgia, People* v. *Chessman, People* v. *Andison, Ediga Annamma* v. *State of Andhra Pradesh, Rajendra Prasad* v. *State of Uttar Pradesh and Tyrer* v. *United Kingdom* said:

"It is no exaggeration, therefore, to say that the jurisprudence of the civilised world, much of which is derived from common law principles and the prohibition against cruel and unusual punishment in the English Bill of Rights has recognised and acknowledged that prolonged delay in executing a sentence of death can make the punishment when it comes, inhuman and degrading. As the Supreme Court of California commented in *Anderson's* case (supra) it is cruel and has dehumanising effects. Sentence of death is one thing; sentence of death followed by lengthy imprisonment prior to execution is another.

"It is of course true that a period of anguish and suffering is an inevitable consequence of sentence of death. But a prolongation of it beyond the time necessary for appeal and consideration of reprieve is not. And it is no answer to say that the man will struggle to stay alive. In truth, it is this ineradicable human desire which makes prolongation inhuman and degrading. The anguish of alternating hope and despair, the agony of uncertainty, the consequences of such suffering on the mental, emotional, and physical integrity and health of the individual are vividly described in the evidence of the effect of the delay in the circumstances of these five cases. We need not rehearse the facts, which are not in dispute. We do not doubt that the appellants have proved that they have been subjected to a cruel and dehumanising experience."

In 1982, when Krishna Iyer was in Mentrora Hertfordshire in England, in connection with some conference, Lord Scarman of Privy Council wrote a letter to him which read:

6th October 1982

Dear Judge,

I am sending you a copy of the Privy Council Appeal Judgement from Jamaica. The case is *Riley* v. *The Attorney General.* You will see that Lord Brightman and myself in our dissenting opinion made very great use of some observations of yours in the Supreme Court.

Yours sincerely,

Leslie Scarman

This shows that Krishna Iyer's judgments were appreciated even outside India, especially among English judges. The saying goes that a prophet is not honoured in his own country. True he was invited by the Amnesty International to co-inaugurate with the then Sweden's Prime Minister Olaf Palme, the International Conference against Death Sentence at Stockholm, where he passionately urged global abolition of capital penalty.

DEATH SENTENCE ON DEATH SENTENCE

Capital punishment for murder is writ in the Indian Penal Code under Macaulay's creative ability. This terrorist provision of death penalty has been abolished in many countries for more than half the world, including the United Kingdom and Israel. This sanguinary gap still exists between the horror of punitive hanging and the savage terror of formal reformatory prison term. I believe in India's finer values and so advocate the altruist, **ahimsa**, of alternative life-life in jail. If he transforms his life, turns a new leaf and becomes a **Valmiki**, the abolition of death sentence refines the sentence into a good human. My thesis is **From Macaulay to Mahatma.** When I was minister for Law and Home I did persuade the Central Home Minister Pantji to exercise the clemency power (Article 72).

In Edigma Annama [(1974) 4 SCC 443] and Rajendra Prasad [(1979) 3 SCC 646] (affirmed in Maruram case) in all of which I wrote the governing judgment against the capital penalty. Death sentence was commuted judicialy into life imprisonment. When these cases were reconsidered by a Constitution Bench the judges substantially upheld my approach but modified the ratio by holding that in the rarest of rare cases death sentence was permissible. In sum, death sentence has given a long idle holiday never to come into operation again save in extremist cases of satanic and irredeemably inhuman criminal cases. This grave and gory jurisdiction can be exercised only if the court's punitive conscience is shocked. Were I to have my way I would have adopted what I have described in my judgments as **Operation Valmiki.** It is a proud and compassionate movement for me to recollect the receipt of a personal letter written to me by the great judge Lord Scarman where he says that he was deeply moved by my ruling in **Rajendra Prasad** and that he had followed it in a dissenting Privy Council pronouncement. The most grievous homicide in the recent period taking away the life of one of the greatest British Generals (who was India's last Viceroy, Lord Mountbatten) lost his life in a most horrendous act of explosion. The magnificient Mountbatten was assassinated by a deliberate explosion by a hostile Irish enemy Thomas McMahon. He was **not sentenced to death in Briton** for this heinous crime. Thomas McMahon was sentenced to life in prison for the murder. McMahon was released in 1998 under the **Good Friday Agreement.** If any human life is judicially hanged for a hateful crime the flag of humanity hangs low in the name of compassion and respect for the divinity that sustains universality. It is noteworthy that the Universal Declaration of Human Rights has declared against death sentence.

Save in the rarest of rare cases too diabolic to be restore the criminal's human dignity, the sublime power of clemency, vested in the Governor and the President shall fulfill itself by ever saving life, never by slaughtering what God has created.

TERRORISM: IS POTO FAIL SAFE JURAL SWORD?

On December 13, 2001 happened Free India's most shocking event—a diabolic shoot-out by treacherous Pakistani terrorists on the noblest symbol of Bharat's Secular Socialist Democratic Republic—a sudden though abortive savagery on the hallowed circular mansion by a suicide squad, the like of which no eye ever before had foreseen, no heart ever had dreamt would violate the sublime parliamentary precincts, no patriotic tongue could have, without raging passion, adequately told. This dastardly deed, in broad daylight, with vehicular transportation driving through the main entrance with firearms and explosives cleverly concealed, is a daring challenge to the nation, its unity, security and sovereignty which desiderates a deeper autopsy than police investigation, a profounder introspection which transcends Party polemic and a preventive, punitive pharmacopoeia beyond pettifogging POTO I or II and politicking vendetta. A grave malady summons the people in entirety to stand together for a national remedy, mobilising the common masses, secular forces and communal bosses in a do-or-die spirit, without making cheap capital out of lamentable lapses in intelligence and other flaws in an angry cross-fire, or opportunist attempt to score populist points or battle to belittle the Opposition's sensible criticisms. Parliamentary debate, in its sublime heights, is a nobler exchange than adventurist babel and acrimonious scrimmage. The dignity and dialectic of debate, not sound and fury signifying nothing, shall inform the solemn proceedings. A high standard and veracious, vocal duel with focus on terrorism as the country's cunning enemy shall be the highlight. When a house is on fire do you steal valuables or fight together to extinguish the foul flame? Pakistan is provoking us for war with 'nuclear' arrogance and US alliance and Chinese goodwill. America is dubious *vis-a-vis* India, as ever before. Let us beware of black sheep and guard our own unity now endangered by fissiparous politics, camouflaged communal agendas and stratagems of divisive defections. A British illustration of great debate in the House will drive home my point. There was a time when, in the early stages of World War II, British forces were on the retreat and a Censure Motion was tabled in the Commons, supported by the ablest Opposition.

Winston Churchill, the War-time Prime Minister writes:

I followed this powerful speech in winding up the debate. The House was crammed. Naturally I made every point which occurred to me.

This long debate has now reached its final stage. What a remarkable example it has been of the unbridled freedom of our parliamentary institutions in time of war! Everything that could be thought of or raked up has been used to weaken confidence in the Government, has been used to prove that Ministers are incompetent and to weaken their confidence in themselves, to make the Army distrust the backing it is getting from the civil power, to make the workmen lose confidence in the weapons they are striving so hard to make, to present the Government as a set of non-entities over whom the Prime Minister towers, and then to undermine him in his own heart, and, if possible, before the eyes of the nation. All this poured out by cable and radio to all parts of the world, to the distress of all our friends and to the delight of all our foes. I am in favour of this freedom, which no other country would use, or dare to use in times of mortal peril such as those through which we are passing.

Our Houses must impress the country with this debating gravity and critical ability, not indulge in slanging matches, gesticulatory antics or leap to the well of the House failing oral argument. For sure, POTO is impotent because the grave crime occurred in the teeth of nascent POTO already in force. Its futility was demonstrated by five Pakistani blow-up-blackguards *driving in through the main entrance.*

Kuldip Nayyar, who was present when the deadly tragedy was being enacted has told us, in a contemporaneous write-up, that one NDA member of Parliament remarked: now that the terrorist menace is right here in the House you will approve of POTO. Kuldip Nayyar wondered how the Hon'ble member was not aware that POTO was already operational and failed to change the daylight terror by a bunch of Pakistani hell-bent on barbarous butchery.

Recently an iron legislation less ferocious than POTO was sought to be put through in the British Parliament. The House of Lords defeated the bill notwithstanding the Home Secretary accusing the opponents of 'sabotage' and of 'systematic wrecking' of the legislation meant to put down terrorists. The Lords, however, battled against the bill holding that those who believed in democracy, and relished the privilege of living in a democratic State, must surely stand by the things which characterised such a State, such as the rule of law, the right to a fair trial, and appeal to the court against actions of Government. They were deeply skeptical about a rag-bag of new offenses making up a package of emergency legislation. If democracy were to survive, legislation which kills its vital values cannot be the salvationery route.

There is unanimity that terrorism is dangerous and its ubiquity makes the menace a cause for consternation. But under guise of anti-terrorist enactment everything precious in our Constitutionally sanctified criminal justice catena cannot be subverted. The United Nations High Commissioner for Human Rights Mary Robinson, warned Governments *'that measures to eradicate terrorism must not lead to excessive curbs on human rights and fundamental freedoms'. (UN Newsletter)*

The other leaders of the West also joined a statement which reads:

> *"While we recognize that the threat of terrorism requires specific measures, we call on all governments to refrain from any excessive steps which would violate fundamental freedoms and undermine legitimate dissent," the statement said. In pursuing the objective of eradicating terrorism, it is essential that States strictly adhere to their international obligations to uphold human rights and fundamental freedoms.*

They also stressed that some rights may not be derogated from, under any circumstances. These include the right to life, freedom of thought, conscience and religion, freedom from torture or cruel, inhuman or degrading treatment, and the principles of precision and non-retroactivity of criminal law except where a later law imposes a lighter penalty.

In Gandhi India the integral link between ends and means argues itself. POTO is pretence, an otiose measure suppressive of human rights and fair trial and generative of police raj syndrome. The British did quit India but does the ghost of Rowlatt stalk the Home Ministry still? POTO remotely reminds one of Pol Pot, world's worst killer terror of Cambodia. It vividly revives memories of the dark days of macabre Emergency, of the MISA, TADA, NASA and the still surviving Goonda Act of Tamil Nadu. Some ministers now in power were victims of the Emergency and yet, when the legal terror of POTO stains the statute book with blood and iron, they suffer from amnesia. But one remembers Shakespeare: 'Man, proud man, drest in a little brief authority,.......like an angry ape plays such fantastic tricks as make angles weep!' Those who now 'strut and fret the hour' forget their future and fate of oblivion. The rule of law digs its grave when Unlaw, attired as law, sneaks into the statute book. The writing on the wall is clear. Don't seek refuge in court rulings only. Did not the Emergency find the Apex Court say Amen to legislative terrorism, only to be rejected at the next election after all the spilling of people's blood and tears? Did not TADA torture incarcerate countless innocents but only one per cent, of those behind bars were convicted? TADA too formally found the Supreme Court say O.K.; and yet it died by lapse of time. We want statesmen on the Bench, in the House and the country round to make our Republic 'a land of settled government, a land of just and old renown, where Freedom slowly broadens down from precedent to precedent'. Alas, let us not move in reverse gear.

Terrorism must be fought by a whole people mobilised as a locomotive against lawless violence unconscionably springing on innocent humans. But police terrorism – a POTO-placebo – is not a remedy in the pharmacopoeia of the Rule of Law. Don't we have, even now the NASA (National Security Act) the Armed Forces Special Powers Act, the Disturbed Area Act, the Special Courts Act, the Unlawful Activities (Prevention) Act and what not, supplementing the two great Codes? 'Rajiv Gandhi's killers were sentenced to death under the ordinary law, not the TADA', says Kuldip Nayyar. POTO is powerless against the communalists who demolished the Babri mosque nor against the mini-Bin Ladens and Veerappans and those of their ilk, lingering in hide-outs, powerless for the police or even the army to chase and seize. But thousands in a thousand places will suffer if police minions and politicized ministers are vaguely and vagariously armed by legislation to act lawlessly. O, Lord, Now the Law is dead—Rest in peace! Six months in custody and the police suspect having to disprove that he is a terrorist, is a dying declaration of the Rule of Law. 'Terrorism', so widely overdrawn, becomes a terror even for ordinary criticism to be made. The police enjoy larger power to suspect and seize property, to arrest citizens if they have 'reason to believe' and it is well-known in our corrupt system that the police however have a variety of 'reasons to believe' against a person, man or woman. Bail being ruled out, the provisional prosecutor and judge is the police minion. POTO is not patriotism. It is the death sentence on democratic freedom. We cannot salvage democracy by jettisoning its very values. You can't preserve people's raj by succedaneum of police raj. You are never free when you are ever in fear of police custody. It is the paramount need of the hour not to confuse between POTO totalitarianism and non-conformist patriotism. The National Human Rights Commission, with substantial reasons, has opposed the fundamentalism of POTO I and II. What is needed is revamping the Intelligence Process updating their equipment, empowerment of the police with modern gadgetry and training and educating the people about the terrorist tactics. Latest crime-detection technology, astute training and other infrastructural toning up are more important than the violent definitions in a contra-constitutional POTO. Professional ballyhoo in Parliament may help hide governmental blunders which need to be thrashed out by biting criticism and convincing rationality. Of course, the object must be not to score points in deafening debate or creating hysterical hijacking of the House through hubristic hooliganism but to serve the country, to strengthen government to eliminate terrorist threats and to rouse people's nationalism. The urgent desideratum is a full and frank investigation into our systemic failures and to augment a democratic invigilation to defend the nation regardless of obfuscatory notions of governmental infallibility and ruling party prestige. We must fight terrorism at all costs but 'barbarisation' and 'briberisation' will be counter-productive. Mobilize the masses, tell them the perils and India will win without the dependensia syndrome from across the Atantic.

THE POTO PROCESS AS INSTRUMENT OF OR AGAINST TERRORISM

Terrorism, in its catastrophic reality, is a grim, gory, violent violation of life, limb and liberty and so, with the might and main of society and state, must be fought outright mobilising the people and all national resources. But camouflaged as 'terrorist act' by ersatz legal fiction if other motivated *mareechas* manage to sneak into the definition and suppress democratic dissent, it is a deception and hoax and which deserves to suffer suffocation at the legislative inception. The Prevention of Terrorism Act (POTO for short) captiously invoking anti-terrorist sentiment, defines 'terrorist act' vaguely and vegariously and, if enforced by rogues in uniform, may achieve the silence of the grave, not the vibrance of the Republic. While I wholly share the concern of every patriot to damn, and defeat terrorism 'red in tooth and claw', I apprehend the hand of foreign Corporates and Bank-Fund Power, routed diplomatically by American sources, to burke articulation of critical thought if it hurts Big Business, as the root reason for this flabby, ferocious POTO process.

A Random Reflection

Global corporate power hell-bent on world market capture, necessarily expects popular upheaval from the Third World when victimized, as now, by foreign predatory operations (with the abetment of GATT and WTO, *a la* the recent foreign car parts imports ruling against India). Democracy survives by dissent, and at times by protests with sound and fury a wee-bit slanting towards vocal duel. India is as Galbraith put it, a functioning anarchy. Our Parliament daily demonstrates a yen to be a babel. Freedom of expression, the oxygen of Fundamental Rights, is freedom to differ, even demonstratively. Silencing critical voices by legislative gag is the device to mug or muzzle free speech and keep enforced peace. Who wants such commanded tranquility except MNCs who demand undeterred right to occupy commanding heights of our economy. Joseph Stiglitz, who was the Chief economist of the World Bank (and later a Nobel Prize winner) has gone on record that the IMF-World Bank imposed "reform" would bring about *"social unrest"*. They offer their own solution too. "Put down rioters with political resolve". Third World farmers commit suicide by the legion because of GATT—WTO policies? The answer must be: Put down the survivors with political resolve. They don't care", Stiglitiz says about the big corporations he has worked with, "if people live or die". 'In the final stages of the World Bank's package comes what Stiglitiz calls, "the IMF riot". After all, corporations have no soul to be damned nor body to be burnt but have insatiable hunger for profits and unlimited markets to rob. So the Bank-Fund has a vested interest in *peaceful pillage.* They dub social unrest as, *quasi-*terrorism. Do battle against terrorism, by legal process and ban mobilised masses but by police baton calling those who protest against the policy of globophilia as terrorist by liberalising the definition of 'terrorist act'. Thus it is plain that the US Government and the Bank-Fund duo, facilitating the operations of the world's major corporates, have a predominant interest in keeping India and other democracies statutorily obedient, POTO-mute and incapable to offer vocal hostility. If protest, justified or not, takes on a threatening turn, it should be suppressed by labelling it 'terrorism', the vogue word to trample down opposition. In short, *to end internal dissent or disturbance against MNCs is itself an end* and the *means* towards that end may be legislatively legitimated as Operation Anti-terrorism incarnating as POTO's flabby, inflated provisions. Those who oppose GATT, WTO and cunning World Bank strategy may be branded Terrorists. No *more arguments.* Maybe, only 1% court conviction, as in—TADA, but till then custodial silence! Those who support the foreign exploitative infiltration, aided by cabals, compradors, quislings and limpets of Big-Business wear the anti-terrorist mask! 'Private tyrannies' (Noam Chomsky's phrase), draped as MNCs, have provoked negative popular action in escalating measure, with indigenous, especially small scale industries and traditional agriculture and natural resources suffering a collapse syndrome (despite billions of dollars spent by Corporates for marketing the 'capitalist story'). In the Uncle Sam lexicon, terrorism means all that hurts the interests of the Global Proprietariat, Corporate Establishment and supportive vested interests. The pressure from US and its dominant clientele desiderates the suppression, statutorily, of any kind of violent or non-violent 'insurgency' against subjugation of the people's economic interests and national green politics. The logic is that the great yankee appetite to win markets and consequent concern in keeping Indian people's swadeshi noises at bay, through appropriate legislation drawn up very widely to cover every opposition to foreign predation dubbing it as affect *Indian 'security'*! Has not POTO, thus viewed, a nexus between World Bank designs and MNC manoeuvres and the Indian Administration's unquenchable thirst for a law against people's protest? POTO is suspect proxy legislation to hamstring human rights agitation. What is the motive? The foreign caravan will pass but the swaraj dogs shall not bark! POTO will arrest, even shoot! *Real* diabolic terrorism needs to be burst but sham terrorism, with illegitimate lexical latitude, is a shame.

Can it be that, among other reasons, the hasty repetition of POTO, dubiously bypassing the Parliament session, is due to suggestions from across the Atlantic? Strike dumb the rising escalating peasant-proletariat revolt but call it a danger to (dollar) national security. Else, why this fanatical hurry and nascent fury, over-expanding the Law Commission's limited draft, overruling the objection of the National Human Rights Commission and all Opposition? Read section 3(1) *'any act...or by any other means, whatsoever....in such a manner as to cause or likely to cause....any other persons..."* The sky is the limit. The definitional universe of 'terrorist act' is over-inclusive and ropes in plural meanings too arbitrary to stand the test of responsible restraint under Articles 14, 19 and 21 of the Constitution. The drafting trick is to begin with something terrible and then, by a sly device, tediously expand the provision by diluted words, at each remove a wider net to catch, till at last even fund collection for any purpose remotely linked to a recondite objective broadly mentioned in section 3(1), is POTO-culpable. Fancifully over-broad, beyond the rational parameters of 'endangering the unity, integrity, security or sovereignty of the nation. Too far-fetched and fails the *Maneka Gandhi* test, of being limited to 'just, fair and reasonable' parameters.

There is legal terrorism in disguise in the device of drafting the clause with an appealingly *shocking* beginning and cannily broadening it to catch even minimally noxious, tremendous trifles. At the end of the journey, the sweep of the Act puts everyone in peril. No man is free if the police-man suspects him/her not merely of attempt or abetment but also an alleged *preparatory* act.

There is another cute and cunning provision relating to *'confession before a police officer"*. Indian jurisprudence has so far been justly reluctant to receive confessions to the police. But now such 'confessions', even through electronic device, shall be admissible in the trial of a confessor. A goofy guarantee is added to put sceptics at ease. It is naive and gullible to provide—as has been done—that the police officer shall record the confession after warning appropriately or *in an atmosphere free from threat.* Is this realistic? For this we need the incarnation of a new uniformed race. What is more bizarre and incredible is the curious caution that the 'confession' shall be *re-recorded* within 48 hours before a Magistrate. Is it not preposterous to conceive that an accused who made a confession (under concealed police threat) will change in a fit of judicial assurance? He will merely repeat parrot-like before the Magistrate his 'police confession', especially because the prisoner/ accused is under police surveillance all the time. This judicial smoke-screen never makes for a voluntary admission and, under POTO, a profusion of 'statutory terrorist' convictions will shower, based on police confessions, duly encored before a Magistrate. These convictions, if only dissected in detail, will reveal the maiming of the fundamentals of our criminal justice system. The Emergency is a bad dream, the TADA is a legislative bully, now buried. POTO is of the same breed.

The wild pen of the POTO draftsman makes 'preparation' (an elusive will-o'-the wisp or imaginary doubt) also a crime. Harum-scarum draft bill, if passed, harms the dignity and renown of the House. POTO, unless *radically humanised, severely pruned* and *refined into a 'just fair piece'* will make the House the laughing stock of freedom-lovers across democracies and the 'unlaw' law as the vanishing point of criminal justice, beware! Police raj and POTO regime are neighbours and should not disgrace our corpus juris.

The definitional dexterity and lexical laxity of 'terrorist act' makes the Ordinance itself a contribution to terrorist methodology. How devastating to make police power, acting on suspicion, so vast! Who is safe from this new despotism—including the present ministers, once they cease 'to strut and fret the hour' of their power and fall foul of their successor team!

LEGAL TERRORISM—THE MENACE

We have had illegal terrorism before and after Independence. Now we have a *new incarnation*—terrorism *by law,* using Orwellian double-speak of 'law to prevent (read promote) terrorism'. 'Fair is foul and foul is fair'.

The illegitimacy of the Ordinance process falls for notice first. Where some measure is so urgently needed that it cannot await the meeting of Parliament, an exceptional provision to meet an emergency situation is the *raison de'tre* of Ordinance promulgation by the Executive. If this *sine qua non* is absent, the resort to this rare constitutional instrumentality is a fraud on power. In this case, no imperative of imminent action is present and the new brand of 'terrorism' is indefensible even procedurally, independently of the *substantive* arbitrariness. Personal liberty is too precious to be derogable on dubious grounds on which the obviously draconian measure is founded. When reckless illiberalism is writ large on the face of the enactment, the scrutiny of its legality also has to be too stern and searching to be scared into cowardly surrender merely because of patriotic phrases like unity, integrity, security or sovereignty of India or other deadful diction like terrorism, bomb, dynamite, and explosive which may create terror in a panicky or pusillanimous judiciary. Fundamental freedoms inscribed in Part III desiderate a bold barricade by the court if Constitutional guarantees are not to collapse like a pack of cards, frightened by intimidatory statutory vocabulary. And when the law is so overdrawn in awesome breadth that even innocent acts may fall within the law's culpable spell, the High Bench must call the bluff and not be bullied. Those now in power know the earlier darker days. A liberal Prime Minister, a homespun Home Minister, a persecuted Defence Minister, a luminous Law Minister, and the traumatic experience of Emergency, MISA, NASA, TADA plus plus—and but yet the pity of it! POTO raj. Parliamentarians, you have a paramount duty, beyond the inscrutable face of the Coalition sphinx, to 'We, the People of India' the ultimate political sovereign. Finally, we forget at our peril Lord Atkin's lasting warning: Even amidst the clash of arms the laws shall not be silent'.

(Laws mean here, I presume, not executive authoritarianism wrapped in parliamentary print but those finer fundamentals of civilised jurisprudence India is proud of). Justice Anand in *D.K. Basu's* case, has observed what is personal liberty *vis-a-vis* the State's commanding terrorism:

> 32. *The response of the American Supreme Court to such an issue in* Miranda v. Arizona, *is instructive. The Court said:*
>
> "*A recurrent argument, made in these cases is that society's need for interrogation outweighs the privilege. This argument is not unfamiliar to this court.* [*See e.g., Chambers* v. *Florida,* US at pp. 240-41: L Ed at p. 724: 60 S Ct 472 (1940)]. *The whole thrust of our foregoing discussion demonstrates that the Constitution has prescribed the rights of the individual when confronted with the power of Government when it provided in the Fifth Amendment that an individual cannot be compelled to be a witness against himself. That right cannot be abridged.*"
>
> 33. *There can be no gainsaying that freedom of an individual must yield to the security of the State. The right of preventive detention of individuals in the interest of security of the State in various situations prescribed under different statutes has been upheld by the courts. The right to interrogate the detenus, culprits or arrests in the interest of the nation, must take precedence over an individual's right to personal liberty. The Latin maxim* salus populi suprema lex *(the safety of the people is the supreme law) and* salus republicae suprema lex *(safety of the State is the supreme law) coexist and are not only important and relevant but lie at the heart of the doctrine that the welfare of an individual must yield to that of the community. The action of the State, however, must be "right, just and fair". Using any form of torture for extracting any kind of information would neither be "right nor just nor fair" and, therefore, would be impermissible, being offensive to Article 21. Such a crime-suspect must be interrogated—indeed subjected to sustained and scientific interrogation—determined in accordance with the provisions of law. He cannot, however, be tortured of subjected to third-degree methods or eliminated with a view to elicit information, extract confession or derive knowledge about his accomplices, weapons etc. His constitutional right cannot be abridged in the manner permitted by law, though in the very nature of things there would be qualitative difference in the method of interrogation of such a person as compared to an ordinary criminal. Challenge of terrorism must be met with innovative ideas and approach. State terrorism is no answer to combat terrorism. State terrorism would only provide legitimacy to "terrorism". That would be bad for the State, the community and above all for the rule of law. The State must, therefore, ensure that various agencies deployed by it for combating terrorism act within the bounds of law and not become law unto*

themselves. That the terrorist has violated human rights of innocent citizens may render him liable to punishment but it cannot justify the violation of his human rights except in the manner permitted by law. Need, therefore, is to develop scientific methods of investigation and train the investigators properly to interrogate to meet the challenge.

[(1997) SCC 434/435]

The worth of the human personality is the final audit of the rule of law.

VEERAPPACRACY AND AN ORAL OBITER

'Moderation is a fatal thing. Nothing succeeds like excess' (Oscar Wilde). This sting came to mind when I found the Media blare with eclat an acid oral obiter emanating from a Bench of the Supreme Court; that if the Government is unable to tackle the bandit it should quit and make way for somebody who can do it' (news report). *Who can do it?* The judges with their writ or wit? Are we rewriting the Constitution by providing a new ground beyond article 356 to the effect that if the court holds that a Government has failed to arrest a terrorist the Government must get out? Failure to fulfill a legal obligation is a bad thing but the Constitutional functionary may not be thrown out of office for that reason. Otherwise, judges who do not deliver judgments for years after arguments are over or Governors or President who do not sign a Bill passed by a legislature for months may face a fatal consequence. Judges making obiter remarks may have to remember that while it makes great headlines it also humilitates Chief Ministers and others. The same logic, when turned on them, may lead to unpleasant consequences. Bowen L.J. once observed 'I believe that obiter dicta, like the proverbial chickens of destiny, come home to roost, sooner or later, in a very uncomfortable way to the Judges who have uttered them and are a great source of embarrassment in future cases.' Sardonic *ipse dixits* are a sweat delight from the Bench to make but how unhappy the victim who has to swallow the pejorative! (Did the media, out for levitous publicity, exaggerate irresponsibly a jocular slip, blowing it up as great directive?) When the Veerappan matter elicited the sharp rebuke from the highest court as hyped by the Press, there were two distinct reactions among the people. Most people were relieved that some one said it. How long, how long shall one terrorist hold a beloved human hostage successfully, outlaw himself and flout the criminal law with two or three important Governments, with different parties in power in succession! Could they not and did not bring to book a brigand, thus impotently failing in its duty to protect from death and destruction a large number of innocent officials and common people and thus establish a Veerocratic domain? He kidnaps, kills, terrorises the police and the law lies dead! Apparently, this is an abdication of governance and must be remembered by the people at the next polls. If every Party or Front during its spell of power is guilty of this omission or delinquent misrule what can the community do? Live in perennial panic? A judicial writ may remain unexecuted if Government after Government lets down the law. *Salutations to the judges who have insisted on the sovereign function of the rule of law as an imperative obligation of the Administration.* Can a State surrender and put a people in perennial peril? I felt happy when the court condemned this gubernatorial gaffe and administrative imbecility? Be you ever so high, Veerappan, the law is above you! So far the people's response to the court's observation raised the dignity of the rule of law as a basic feature of the Constitution. But could the robed brethren, with a touch of authoritarian exercise, also say that the Government should 'quit' and some one else put in place? All the parties of Karnataka, including the Opposition, are reportedly behind the Chief Minister. Who then will be sworn in as Chief Minister on the judicial mandate to arrest Veerappan? None indeed. That is the despair of the scenario': If you move the army with the aid of the Centre, which for all these years, remained indifferent on Constitutional technicality of jurisdiction while hyperactive in West Bengal, Veerappan may be caught. But on the cards are the prospect of Rajkumar becoming a casualty. That prospect may trigger a terrible scene of violence against Tamils in Karnataka the like of which, as in the case of Cauvery riots, did prove this portent. Mobs in fury are a law unto themselves. We witnessed it in the 1984 riots in Delhi with Sikhs slaughtered and buildings burned down with the police unable or unwilling to control the communal massacre. Could the Supreme Court arrest this mass catastrophe or did it direct the Prime Minister to resign so that some one else could take his place and bring order and peace in the capital? When the partition of India brought in its wake blood and tears on a scale history has never known before, did the eminent judges ask Nehru and Patel to quit for some one else to take over? Judicial bravado solves no problem but the glory of the judiciary evident in the *Veerappan* case (as in the case of *Marbury* v. *Madison*) is to enter a caveat to the country about constitutional fundamentals and paramount sovereign duties to the people sans which jungle rule will jettison the jejune Executive. I hold the humble view that our judges of the highest court have, by and large, though marred occasionally, performed creditably but it is good for the Bench not to humiliate other equally important branches of the State struggling to tackle a tricky, delicate, dangerous imbroglio. The Supreme Court is final not because it is infallible. It is infallible because it is final; and an obiter binds none, not even the one who made it. Judges sit on a hallowed Bench and perform sublime functions. And so it is that 'We, the People of India' look to the Apex Bench for ultimate justice. But judicial realism, diplomacy and statesmanship are integral to sapient justicing. The greatest Chief Justice of the most powerful court in the strongest country in the world was Chief Justice Marshall. But President Andrew Jackson, "amidst the speculation over whether he would enforce the Court's decree, was reported to have said, John Marshall has made his decision. Now let *him* enforce it." After all, minus power of the purse or sword, what sustains 'the least dangerous branch' is the people's overwhelming faith in the great court. The Court is neither the Super-Executive nor Third Chamber. Archibald Cox explains how Nixon obeyed judge Sirica and resigned, having been returned as President with the largest majority, because the highest court held against him:

> *Constitutionalism works, our liberties are protected, and our society is free because officials, individuals, and the people as a whole realize that liberty for the weak depends upon the rule of law and the rule of law depends upon voluntary compliance. When the test comes, that realization must be strong enough for the people to rise up, morally and politically, and overwhelm the offender. The roots of constitutionalism lie in the hearts of the people.(P15)*

Watergate Tapes has a lesson for us. 'We, the People' make the court the Everest of power and judges must display a blend of restraint and power, realism and intrepidity. Archibald Cox argues:

> *Why do the people support constitutionalism and the rule of law, and, as their instrument, the courts? Will the support continue?(P25)*

Law binds the judges as well as the judged. My proposition is *that ex cathedra* utterances, even of judges, must be tempered and not provocative, pragmatic, perceptive, sensitive, not ivory-towered. Theoretically, it is O.K. to redicule the Veerappan bregandage (Dr. Dhavan's phrase) and failing to arrest him (or, for that matter LTTE Prabhakaran), nothing is left of effective governance. That is myopic jurisprudence of exaggeration. It is like asserting that if astronomical heaps of arrears of cases are not *now* liquidated, nothing is left of judicial justice. But if the administrator is confronted with the gruesome realities of keeping the peace when large mobs run berserk, irrationally infuriated, engineered by linguistic insanity and limited police force to control their fury, the judges must have imagination to visualize the Government's difficulties. I have been, as Home Minister of Kerala, through such a crisis as Operation Overthrow (1959) tacitly backed by Central political leadership and coalition of communal forces and political cabals. To shoot is easy. But how many? In the Cauvery riots in Karnataka or the Bombay riots or Sikhs slaughtered in Delhi, will the panacea of "get out" and someone else will take over, be viable? What happened during Partition? Nehru and Patel resigning, who would have taken over? Administrative incompetence matched by judicial laze hubris and inadequate appreciation of ground realities—What can be the recipe? When people turn loony what rage and ravage follows? *O judgement, thou art fled to brutish beasts, and men have lost their reason (Shakespeare).*

The withdrawal of cases, as a legal problem, did trouble me and brother Chinnappa Reddy in the *George Fernandez* case. We took a view informed by principled pragmatism. We were perhaps right or may be wrong. I have great confidence in the capable Bench, which heard the recent Veerappan syndrome litigation. None but the mad will back the bully brigand. But imagine the sleepless nights of the Chief Ministers in handling the sequel to an armed move, with the Cine Star as hostage and a fleeing wounded Tamil population and political fall-outs, too vast, vicious and vagarious. Administrative strategy, where mass massacre, mob fury and other felonious factors and inter-state stress and strain are involved, summons sensitive statesmanship, not textbook scholarship. A sensitive measure of discretion must be conceded. I don't plead for Veerappan jurisprudence or Krishna-Karunanidhi concessions *ad nauseam* or for lawless state impotence but do urge the Court to grant room for play of executive prudence, balancing of forces and relevant, though extraordinary, conscientious activism. These are riddles wrapped in mysteries too imponderable for readymade or fast food solutions. Law and Life, with overall vision and wisdom, is Justice. I wholly agree that the humiliation inflicted by Veerappan on two impotent State governments for several years (and what about the Centre under article 355 in its failure of duty to help Karnataka, whatever the party in power, as well as non-issue of directives under article 365 for abdication by the State to carry out article 21 rights of the people) deserves judicial rebuke. I hail the Supreme Court for exposing the States and insisting on people's human rights as the highest value *vis a vis* Veerappan and the precious life of the Cine Star. An aside. What has the Supreme Court done on the nearly half-a-century old *Babri Masjid* case pending in Lucknow and what did it do when barbaric violation of its order took place virtually before its eyes? How sadistic to be sardonic for robed brethren!

Why beholdest thou the mote that is in thy brother's eye,
but considerest not the beam that is in thine own eye?

Judge Learned Hand has rightly said that on every court wall must be written Cromwell's words: 'In the bowel's of Christ, think it possible that you might be mistaken.' I glorify the Supreme Court for reminding the Executive about the shock and shame of our nation, which bends and bows before a whiskered villain and his criminal horde. But the 'quit' quip is quack placebo. The constitutional pharmacopoeia contains no 'quit' command vested in the judiciary. Great is the court, which rejects the State's absurd move of 'stoop to conquer'. Never forget that many Veerappans hide in the five-star jungles of our glitteratti cities. Catch them red-handed in their hawala operations and politico-criminal nexus.

The law locks up both man and woman.
Who steals the goose from off the common?
But let the greater felon loose
Who steals the common from the goose.

One last word about the print media. The media, (not all), mindless of public panic or with appetite for vicious sensation or thoughtless of humiliation inflicted on tensed up administrators extravagantly machinate casual incidents into macro-events with publicity pleasure leading to mass mischief. Many a random remark from the Bench or the House is blown up as sensational diet for next day's news sheet by soap bubble journalism engaged in competitive trivialisation. Alas, serious issues go by default? Mark you, the reporter's pen can hit harder than a gun. That noble profession of journalism is a trustee, a fiduciary power, fearless but sober. My hunch may be wrong but the *obiter* from the Bench was exaggerated beyond bounds, if I may put my point pardonably sharply to drive home a viewpoint. In a heated hearing a judge may make a random remark relevant in the context of the battle of arguments. But the Press is unjust to the court to pick up a stray observation and magnify because it is good meat for the next morning!

The surrender syndrome, scared by a villain flourising in his arboreal hide-out is not merely a picture of pathos and bathos but the beginning of constitutional collapse, unless fool-proof *strategies,* operated with blitz success, over-power the *stratagems* of a brazen law-breaker negotiating on equal terms with Chief Ministers. Alas, the law is dead! Rest in peace! No, never, if the Republic lives, and it does.

INDIVIDUAL FREEDOM

"Necessity is the plea for every infringement of human freedom. It is the argument of tyrants; it is the creed of slaves."

William Pitt

What poignant portrayal by Pitt over 200 years ago which rings true even today, if only with greater emphasis where individual freedom is sought to be curbed in the name of necessity. Does freedom connote, breaking the shackles of foreigners and becoming serfs of swadeshis? While the Constitution was drafted the clause relating to the right of individual freedom was debated from April 21, 1947 up to November 3, 1949, when it was given final shape and submitted to the President of the Republic for his assent. Dr. Baba Saheb Ambedkar completed the task initiated by B.N. Rao. In the new draft, Articles 15 to 21 were given new meaning and content.

> "No person shall be deprived of his life or personal liberty except according to the procedures established by law." Since our founding fathers considered personal liberty as of paramount importance, they declared it as a fundamental right. There was a long debate as to whether the phrase should be "procedure established by law" or "due process" and ultimately it was decided that it should be "process established by law".

Article 19 of our Constitution deals with rights such as freedom of speech and expression, right to assemble, to form associations and unions, to move freely throughout the country, to practise any profession, etc. etc.

Article 21 guarantees that no person shall be deprived of his life or liberty except according to procedure established by law. Article 22 speaks about protection against arrest and detention.

Articles 21 and 22 are the Magna Carta of our personal liberty but fade when it comes to reality.

Mr. A.K. Gopalan, a forefront leader of the Communist Party of India, was brutally beaten up by the Kannanur Jail authorities when he hoisted the National Flag on the day of Indian Independence, that is on August 15, 1947. He was one who actively took part in the freedom struggle as a Congressman and later changed into a Communist. He was a great martyr. He had been in jail from 1947. Each time when he came out, he would again be taken into custody on one charge or other.

While still in detention under the order of the Madras Presidency, on 1st March, 1950, Gopalan was served with an order made under section 3 (1) of the Preventive Detention Act. He challenged the legality of this order contending that Preventive Detention Act was unconstitutional contravening the provisions of Articles 21 and 22.

Supreme Court observed that the expression "personal liberty" means liberty relating to or concerning the person, not the body of the individual.

This writ of habeas corpus against the detention of A.K.G. made history.

On reading this strange judgment, the thoughts of Tolstoy that "Slavery has been abolished. Rome has abolished it. America had abolished it. Russia had abolished it—on paper" must have coursed through the mind of A.K.G and it is possible that he may have concurred with Tolstoy that India had also abolished it—"but on paper".

In *Kharak Singh* v. *State of Uttar Pradesh*, wider meaning was given to the phrase "personal liberty", by the Supreme Court. Kharak Singh was arrested in a case of dacoity and acquitted by the courts. The police who did not know the meaning of human dignity, kept Kharak Singh under surveillance even after his acquittal, in terms of the police rules. He was forced to inform the police whenever he went out and his whereabouts and when he would return. They had the inhuman habit of knocking at the door of Kharak Singh's house at night almost every day to ascertain if he was at home, which affected the personal liberty, dignity and privacy of Kharak Singh. The domiciliary visits were done under Regulation 236 of the U.P. Police Regulations, which authorised policemen to visit the house of the any former accused at night to make sure that he was at home. Kharak Singh had challenged the U.P. Police regulations on the ground that the domiciliary visits by the police to his house at nights interfered with his personal liberty and was violative of the fundamental rights enshrined in the Constitution.

The Supreme Court upheld the contention of the petitioner that domiciliary visits violated his personal liberty. The Supreme Court observed:

> "Having regard to the terms of Article 19 (1), we must take it that the expression is used as not to include the right to move about being excluded, its narrowest interpretation would be Article 21 which comprehences nothing more than freedom from physical restraint of freedom from confinement within the bounds of a prison. We do not hold that the term was intended to bear only this narrow interpretation, but on the other hand consider that "personal liberty" is used in the Article as a compendious term to include within itself all varieties of rights which go to make up the personal liberties of man, other than those dealt within the several clauses of Article 19 (1)...."

In Kharak Singh's case, Justice Subbha Rao said:

> "Psychological restraints are more effective than the physical ones. As such any interference with the right to privacy would also be a breach of personal liberty.

"Right of an individual to be free from restriction and encroachments are directly imposed or indirectly brought about by calculated measures."

This concept was further exemplified in the celebrated case of Maneka Gandhi, wife of the late Sanjay Gandhi, second son of Indira Gandhi.

Maneka Gandhi was issued a passport on June 1, 1976, under the Passport Act, 1967. On the 4th of July 1977, Maneka Gandhi received a letter dated 2nd July, 1977, from the Regional Passport Officer, Delhi intimating to her that it was decided by the Government of India to impound her passport under section 10 (3) of the Act "in public interest". Maneka Gandhi was required to surrender her passport within seven days from the receipt of the letter. Maneka Gandhi immediately addressed a letter to the Regional Passport Officer requesting him to furnish a copy of the statement of reasons for making the order as provided in section 10(5) of the Act. A reply was sent by the Government of India, Ministry of External Affairs on 6th July, 1977 stating inter alia that the Government has decided "in the interest of the general public" not to furnish her a copy of the statement of reasons for the making of the order. Maneka Gandhi then filed the writ petition challenging the action of the Government in impounding her passport and declining to give reasons for doing so.

Article 21 of our Constitution has acquired new and broad dimension after Justice P.N. Bhagwati and Justice V.R. Krishna Iyer's judgment in Maneka Gandhi's case. It has totally over ruled A.K. Gopalan's case. This historic landmark judgment dealt with all aspects with authority in Krishna Iyer's characteristic style and language. In that case the Court held that mere prescription of some kind of procedure cannot ever meet the mandates of Article 21, Justice Krishna Iyer the only Judge who often quotes the cyclonic Sadhu, Swami Vivekananda in his judgments, sought support from modern India's greatest saint.

Krishna Iyer observed:

"India is India because Indians, our ancients had journeyed through the wide world for commerce, spiritual and material, regardless of physical or mental frontiers". And when this precious heritage of free trade in ideas and goods, association and expression, migration and home-coming, now crystallised in Fundamental Human rights, is alleged to be hamstrung by hubristic authority, my sensitivity lifts the veil of silence. Such is my justification for breaking judicial lock-jaw to express sharply the juristic perspective and philosophy behind the practical necessities and possible dangers that society and citizenry may face if the clauses of our Constitution are not bestirred into court action when a charge of unjustified handcuffs on free speech and unreasonable fetters on right of exit is made through the executive power of passport impoundment.

"Remember, even democracies have experiened executive lawlessness and eclipse of liberty on the one hand and "subversive" use of freedoms by tycoons and saboteurs on the other, and then the summons to judges comes from the Constitution, overriding the necessary deference to government and seeing in perspective, and overseeing in effective operation the enjoyment of the "great rights".

"Let us grasp the permissible restraints on personal liberty, one of the facets of which is the right of exit beyond one's country. The sublime sweep of the subject of personal liberty must come within our ken if we are to do justice to the constitutional limitations which may, legitimately, be imposed on its exercise. Speaking briefly, the architects of our Founding Document, (and their forerunners) many of whom were frontline fighters for national freedom, were lofty humanists who were profoundly spiritual and deeply secular, enriched by vintage values and revolutionary urges and, above all, experientially conscious of the deadening impact of the colonial screening of Indians going abroad and historically sensitive to the struggle for liberation being waged from foreign lands. And their testament is our asset.

"Let me first define my terms. By "personal freedom" I mean the freedom of every law-abiding citizen to think what he will, to say what he will, and to go where he will on his lawful avocations without let or hindrance from any other persons. Despite all the great changes that have come about in the other freedoms, this freedom has in our country remained intact.

"The freedom of movement is the very essence of our free society, setting us apart. Like the right of assembly and the right of association, it often makes all other rights meaningful—knowing, stuyding, arguing, exploring, conversing, observing and even thinking. Once the right to travel is curtailed, all other rights suffer, just as when curfew or home detention is placed on a person.

"America is of course sovereign, but her sovereignty is woven in an international web that makes her one of the family of nations. The ties with all the continents are close as well, as culturally. Our concerns are planetary beyond sunrises and sunsets. Citizenship implicates us in those problems and perplexities, as well as in domestic ones. We cannot exercise and enjoy citizenship in world perspective without the right to travel abroad.

"Men suspected of Communist leanings in America had poor chance of passport at one time; and politicians in power in that country have gone to the extreme extent of stigmatising one of the greatest Chief Justices of their country as near Communist. Earl Warren has, in his autobiography recorded:

> "Senator Joseph McCarthy once said on the floor of the Senate, "I will not say that Earl Warren is a Communist, but I will say he is the best friend of Communism in the United States".

"The Indian panorama from the migrant yore to tourist flow is an expression of the will to explore the infinite, to promote understanding of the universe, to export human expertise and development of every resource. Thus the humble pride of patriotic heritage would have been pre-empted had the ancient kings and medieval rulers banished foreign travel as our imperial masters nearly did. And to look at the little letters of the text of Part III de hors the Discovery of India and the Destiny of Bharat or the divinity of the soul and the dignity of the person highlighted in the Preamble unduly obsessed with individual aberrations of yesteryears or vague hunches leading to current fears, is a persilanimous (sic) exercise in constitutional perception.

"My idea as to the key-note of our national downfall is that we do not mix with other nations—that is the one and sole cause. We never had the opportunity to compare notes. We were Kupamandukas (frogs in a well).

"... If you want to become equal with the Englishman or the American, you will have to teach as well as to learn, and you have plenty yet to teach to the world for centuries to come".

Swami Vivekananda

"The right to travel is a part of "liberty" of which the citizen cannot be deprived of without due process of law under the Fifth Amendment. In Anglo Saxon law that right was emerging at least as early as the Magna Carta. Travel abroad, like travel within the country, may be necessary for a livelihood. It may be as close to the heart of the individual as the choice of what he eats, or wears, or reads. Freedom of movement is basic in our scheme of values". (*Kent* v. *Dulls*, 357 US 116: (1958) 2 L.Ed 2d 1204)

"To sum up, personal liberty makes for the worth of the human person. Travel makes liberty worthwile. Life is a terrestrial opportunity for unfolding personality, rising to higher status, moving to fresh woods and reaching out to reality which makes our earthly journey a true fulfilment—not a tale told by an idiot full of sound and fury signifying nothing, but a fine frenzy rolling between heaven and earth. The spirit of Man is at the root of Article 21. Absent liberty, other freedoms are frozen.

"What is fundamental is life and liberty. What is procedural is the manner of its exercise. This quality of fairness in the process is emphasised by the strong word "established" which means "settled firmly" not wantonly or whimsically. If it is rooted in the legal consciousness of the community, it becomes "established" procedure. And "Law" leaves little doubt that it is normally regarded as just since law is the means and justice is the end.

"Procedural safeguards are the indispensable essence of liberty. In fact, the history of personal liberty is writ large. The history of procedural safeguards and right to a hearing has a human rights ring. In India because of poverty and illiteracy, the people are unable to protect and defend their rights: observance of fundamental rights is not regarded as good politics and their transgression as bad politics. It sometimes pensively reflect that people's militant awareness of rights and duties is a surer constitutional assurance of governmental respect and response than the sound and fury of "question hour" and the slow and unsure delivery of court writ. "Community consciousness and the Indian Constitution" is a fascinating subject of sociological relevance in many areas.

"It is a mark of interpretative respect for the higher norms that our founding fathers held dear in affecting the dearest rights of life and liberty so to read Article 21 as to result in a human order lined with human Justice. And running right through Articles 19 and 14 is present in this principle of reasonable procedure in different shades. A certain normative harmony among the Articles is thus attained, and I hold Article 21 bears in its bosom the construction of fair procedure legislatively sanctioned. No Passport Officer shall be mini-Caesar nor Minister incarnate Caesar in a system where the rule of law reigns supreme.

" My clear conclusion on Article 21 is that liberty of locomotion into alien territory cannot be unjustly forbidden by the Establishment and passport legislation must take processual provisions which accord with fair norms, free from extraneous pressure and, by and large complying with natural justice. Unilateral arbitrariness, police dossiers, faceless affiants, behind-the back materials, oblique motives and the inscrutable face of an official sphinx do not fill the "fairness" bill, subject of course, to just exceptions and critical contexts. This minimum once abandoned, the police state slowly builds up which saps the finer substance of our constitutional jurisprudence. Not party but principle and policy are the key-stone of our Republic.

"Let us not forget that Article 21 clubs life with liberty and when we interpret the colour and content of "procedure established by law" we must be alive to the deadly peril of life being deprived without minimal processual justice, legislative callousness despising "hearing" and fair opportunities of defence. And this realization once sanctioned, its exercise will swell till the basic freedom is flooded out. Hark back to Article 10 of the Universal Declaration to realize that human rights have but a verbal hollow if the protective armour of audi alteram partem is deleted. When such pleas are urged in the familiar name of pragmatism public interest or national security, courts are on trial and must prove that civil liberties are not mere rhetorical material for lip service but the obligatory essence of our hard-won freedom.

"Phoney freedom is not worth the word and this ruling of ours is not confined to the petitioner but to the hungry job seeker, nun and nurse, mason and carpenter, welder and fitter and above all political dissenter. The last category detested as unreasonable, defies the Establishment's tendency to enforce through conformity but is the resource of social change.

"Under our constitutional order, the price of daring dissent shall not be passport forfeit.

"The impugned legislation, sections 5, 6 and 10, especially, must be tested even under Article 21 on canons of processual justice to the people outlined above. Hearing is obligatory-meaningful hearing flexible and realistic, according to circumstances, but not ritualistic and wooden. In exceptional cases and emergency situations, interim masures may be taken, to avoid the mischief of the passportee becoming an escapee before the hearing begins, "Bolt the stables after the horse has been stolen" is not a command of natural justice. But soon after the provisional seizure, a reasonable hearing must follow, to minimise procedural prejudice. And when a prompt final order is made against the applicant or passport holder the reasons must be disclosed to him almost invariably save in those dangerous cases where irreparable injury will ensue to the State. A Government which revels in secrecy in the field of people's liberty not only acts against democratic decency, but busies itself with its own burial. That is the writing on the wall if history were teacher, memory our mentor and decline of liberty not our unwitting endeavour. Public power must rarely hide its heart in an open society and system.

"I now skip Article 14, since I agree fully with all that my learned brother Bhagwati, J., has said. That Article has a pervasive processual potency and versatile quality, egalitarian in its soul and allergic to discriminatory diktats. Equality is the antithesis of arbitrariness (annex cathedra ipse dixit) is the ally of demagogic authoritarianism. Our knight errants of "executive excesses"—if we may use a current cliche—can fall in love with the Dame of Despotism, legislative or administrative. If this Court gives in here, it gives up the ghost. And so it is that I insist on the dynamics of limitations on fundamental freedoms as implying the rule of law; "Be you ever so high, the law is above you".

"A minor pebble was thrown to produce a little ripple. It was feebly suggested that the right to travel abroad cannot be guaranteed by the State because it has no extra-territorial jurisdiction in foreign lands. This is a misconception of the point pressed before us. Nobody contends that India should interfere with other countries and their sovereignty to ensure free movement of Indians in those countries. What is meant is that the Government of India should not prevent by any sanctions it has over its citizens from moving within any other country if that other country has no objection to their travelling within its territory. It is difficult to understand how one can misunderstand the obvious.

"More importantly, restraints are permissible only to the extent they have nexus with the approved object. For instance, in a wide sense, the interests of the general public are served by a family planning programme but it may be constitutional impertinence to insist that passport may be refused if sterilisation certificates were not produced.

"Restraints are necessary and validly made by statute, but to paint with an over-broad brush power to blanket-ban travel abroad is to sweep overly and invade illicitly. The law of fear cannot reign where the proportionate danger is containable. It is a balancing process, not over-weighted one way or the other.

"What characterises the existence and eclipse of the right of exit? "Breathes there the man with soul so dead" who if he leaves, will not return to his own "native land"? Then, why restrict? The question, presented so simplistically, may still have overtones of security sensitivity and sovereignty complexity and other internal and external factors, and that is why the case which we are deciding has spread the canvas wide. I must express a pensive reflection, sparked off by submissions at the Bar, that, regardless of the "civil liberty" credentials or otherwise of a particular Government and mindless of the finer phraseology of a restrictive legislation, eternal vigilance by the superior judiciary and the enlightened activists who are the catalysts of the community, is the perpetual price of the preservation of every freedom we cherish. For, if unchecked, "the greater the power, the more dangerous the abuse". To deny freedom of travel or exit to one untenably is to deny it to any or many likewise, and the right to say "aye" or "nay" to any potential traveller should, therefore, not rest with the minions or masters of Government without being gently and benignly censored by constitutionally sanctioned legislative norms if the reality of liberty is not to be drowned in the hysteria of the hour or the hubris of power. It is never trite to repeat that "where laws end tyranny begins", and law becomes in-law even if it is legitimated by three legislative readings and one assent, if it is not in accord with constitutional provisions, beyond abridgment by the two branches of Government. In the context of scany expressions like "security", "public order", "public interest" and "friendly foreign relations", we must warn ourselves that not verbal labels but real values are the governing considerations in the exploration and adjudication of constitutional prescriptions and proscriptions. Governments come and go, but the fundamental rights of the people cannot be subject to the wishful value sets of political regimes of the passing day.

"Free speech may similarly be hit by restriction on a campaigner for liberation of colonial peoples or against genocide before the United Nations Organisation. Refusal in such cases is hit on the head by negation of a national passport and can be rescued only by compliance with the relevant saving provisions in Article 19 (2), (4) or (6).

" Supposing a lawyer or doctor, expert or exporter, missionary or guru has to visit a foreign country professionally or on a speaking assignment, he is effectively disabled from discharging his pursuit if passport is refused. There the direct effect, the necessary consequence, the immediate impact of the embargo on grant of passport (or its subsequent impounding or revocation) is the infringement of the right to expression or profession. Such infraction is unconstitutional unless the relevant part of Article 19(2) to (6) is complied with. In dealing with fundamental freedom substantial justification alone will bring the law under the exceptions. National security, sovereignty, public order and public interest must be of such a high degree as to offer a great threat. These concepts should not be devalued to suit the hyper-sensitivity of the executive of minimal threats to the State. Our nation is not so pusillanimous or precarious as to fall or founder if some miscreants pelt stones at its fair face from foreign countries. The dogs may bark, but the caravan will pass. And the danger to a party in power is not the same as rocking the security or sovereignty of the State. Sometimes, a petulant Government which forces silence may act unconstitutionally to forbid criticism from afar, even if necessary for the good of the State. The perspective of free criticism with its limits for free people everywhere, all true patriots will concur, is eloquently spelt out by Sir Winston Churchill on the historic Censure Motion in the House of Commons as Britain was reeling under attack at the hands of Hitlerite hordes:

"This long debate has now reached its final stage. What a remarkable example it has been of the unbridled freedom of our Parliamentary institutions in time of war! Everything that could be thought of or raked up has been used to weaken confidence in the Government, has been used to prove that Ministers are incompetent and to weaken their confidence in themselves, to make the army distrust the backing it is getting from the civil power, to make workmen lose confidence in the weapons they are striving so hard to make, to present the Government as a set of nonentities over whom the Prime Minister towers, and then to undermine him in his own heart, and if possible, before the eyes of the nation. All this poured out by cable and radio to all parts of the world, to the distress of all our friends and to the delight of all our foes! I am in favour of this freedom, which no other country would use, or dare to use, in times of mortal peril such as those through which we are passing".

"Our country, with all its hopes, all its tears and all its fears, must never forget that freedom is recreated year by year, that "freedom is as freedom does, that we have gained a Republic "if we can keep it" and that the watershed between a police state and a people's raj is located partly through its passport policy. Today, a poor man in this poor country despairs of getting a passport because of invariable police enquiry, insistence on property requirement and other avoidable procedural obstacles. And if a system of secret informers, police dossiers, faceless whisperers and political tale-bearers, conceptualished and institutionalised "in public interest", comes to stay, civil liberty is legicidally, constitutionalisedÑa consummation constantly to be resisted. The merits of a particular case apart, the policing of a people's right of exit or entry is fraught with peril to liberty unless policy is precise, operationally respectful of recognised values and harassment proof."

Krishna Iyer aware of the every day unconstitutionalities in police stations expounded the norms for ensuring protection to a person, accused or having the possibility of being fabricated as accused of an offence, from the interrogative coercion of the police. In the question of women, Krishna Iyer showed great concern to safeguard the personal freedom and personal liberty of the women. As rightly stated by Justice Hari Swaroop:

"Krishna Iyer apprehends great danger when a woman is taken to a police station for interrogation. The threatening atmosphere of the police station by itself can create a fear complex and may act as a tool of coercion. This may be termed as environmental coercion and coercion of this category can certainly be present in other places, too, but for historical reasons it can be presumed to exist to a high degree in a police station where the use of third degree methods is not unknown. In a male dominated police station the women will certainly need great protection, and that is why the law places checks on the police power to summon a women to a police station for interrogation".

In the case of *Nandini Satpathy* v. *P.L. Dani*, Krishna Iyer observed:

"In this case, a higher level police officer, ignorantly insisting on a woman appearing at the police station, in flagrant contravention of the wholesome proviso to section 160 (1) of the Cr. P.C. Such deviance must be visited with prompt punishment since policemen may not be a law unto themselves expecting others to obey the law. The wages of indifference is reprimand, of intransigence disciplinary action. If the alibi is that the Sessions Court had directed the accused to appear at the police station, that is no absolution for a police officer from disobedience of the law.

"The policy of the law is that each individual, accused included, by virtue of his guaranteed dignity, has a right to a private enclave where he may lead a free life without overbearing investigatory invasion or even crypto-coercion. The protean forms of gendarme duress assumes the environmental pressures of police presence, compounded by incommunicado confinement and psychic exhaustion, torturesome interrogation and physical menaces and other ingenious, sophisticated procedures—the condition, mental, physical, cultural and social, of the accused, the length of its conduct and a variety of like circumstances, will go into the pathology of coerced para-confessional answers. The benefit of doubt, where reasonable doubt exists, must go in favour of the accused.

"On the other hand, if there is any mode of pressure, subtle or crude, mental or physical, direct or indirect, but sufficiently substantial, applied by the policeman for obtaining information from an accused strongly suggestive of guilt, it becomes "compelled testimony", violative of Article 20(3).

"A police officer is clearly a person in authority. Insistence on answering is a form of pressure especially in the atmosphere of the police station unless certain safeguards erasing duress are adhered to. Frequent threats of prosecution if there is failure to answer may take on the complexion of undue pressure violating Article 20 (3). Legal penalty may by itself not amount to duress but the manner of mentioning it to the victim of interrogation may introduce an element of tension and tone of command perilously hovering near compulsion.

"We hold further that the accused person cannot be forced to answer questions merely because the answers thereto are not implicative when viewed in isolation and confined to that particular case. He is entitled to keep his mouth shut if the answer sought has a reasonable prospect of exposing him to guilt in some other accusation actual or imminent, even though the investigation underway is not with reference to that. We have already explained that in determining the incriminatory character of an answer, the accused is entitled to considerÑand the court while adjudging will take note of—the setting, the totality of circumstances, the equation, personal and social, which have a bearing on making an answer substantially innocent but in effect guilty in import. However, fanciful claims, unreasonable apprehensions and vague possibilities cannot be the hiding ground for an accused person. He is bound to answer where there is no clear tendency to criminate.

"The right to consult an advocate of his choice shall not be denied to any person who is arrested. This does not mean that persons who are not under arrest or custody can be denied that right. The spirit and sense of Article 22 (1) is that it is fundamental to the rule of law that the services of a lawyer shall be available for consultation to any accused person under circumstances of near-custodial interrogation. Moreover, the observance of the right against self-incrimination is best promoted by conceding to the accused the right to consult a legal practitioner of his choice.

"Lawyer's presence is a constitutional claim in some circumstances in our country also, and, in the context of Article 20(3), is an assurance of awareness and observance of the right to silence. The Miranda's case, (1966) 384 US 436 has insisted that if an accused person asks for lawyer's assistance, at the stage of interrogation, it shall be granted before commencing or continuing with the questioning. We think that Article 20(3) and Article 22(1) may, in a way, be telescoped by making it prudent for the police to permit the advocate of the accused, if there be one, to be present at the time he is examined. If an accused person expresses the wish to have his lawyer by his side when his examination goes on, this facility shall not be denied, without being exposed to the serious reproof that involuntary self-crimination secured in secrecy and by coercing the will, was the project.

"The symbiotic need to preserve the immunity without stifling legitimate investigation persuades us to indicate that after an examination of the accused, where a lawyer of his choice is not available, the police official must take him to a magistrate, doctor or other willing and responsible non-partisan official or non-official and allow a secluded audience where he may unburden himself beyond the view of the police and tell whether he has suffered duress, which should be followed by judicial or some other custody for him where the police cannot reach him. The co-locutor may briefly record the relevant conversation and communicate it not to the police but to the nearest magistrate. Pilot projects on this pattern may yield experience to guide the practical processes of implementing Article 20(3). We do not mandate but strongly suggest.

"To ensure this free will by inbuilt structural changes is the desideratum. Short-run remedies apart, long-run recipes must be innovated whereby fists are replaced by wits, ignorance by awareness, "third degree" by civilized tools and technology. The factotum policeman who does everything from a guard of honour to traffic patrol to subtle detection is an obsolescent survival. Special training, special legal courses, technological and other detective updating, are important. An aware policeman is the best social asset towards crimelessness. The consciousness of the official as much as of the community is the healing hope for a crime-ridden society. Judge centred remedies don't work in the absence of community centered rights. All these add up to separation of investigatory personnel from the general mass and in service specialisation of many hues on a scientific basis. This should be done vertically and horizontally. More importantly, the policeman must be released from addiction to coercion and be sensitized to constitutional values," the judgment added.

That individual freedom assumed top priority in the thinking of Krishna Iyer is amplified by the above judgments. Whether on the Bench of the Apex Court, High Court, Law Comission or as Minister and legislator, he had articulated this commitment and that is why even today when individual freedom is in peril, people seek his intervention, as a lodestar for guidance and he has disappointed none.

IN THIS LAND OF DARIDRANARAYANANS

In a class, property oriented society, civil laws permit the detention of a person in a civil prison if he fails to satisfy the demand of a debt-creditor. The founding fathers of our Constitution highly valued the personal liberty as a fundamental right under our Constitution. Here in the conflict between the Constitution and Code of Civil Procedure. Decree for money creates only a civil liability, whereas Article 21 of our Constitution and Article 11 of the International Covenant on Civil and Political Rights uphold the dignity of the human personality. Article 11 of the International Covenant on Civil and Political Rights clearly spells out:

> "No one shall be imprisoned merely on the ground of inability to fulfill a contractual obligation".

In Krishna Iyer's view, the right to personal liberty is supreme. In *Jolly George Varghese* v. *Bank of Cochin,* Krishna Iyer observed:

"This litigation has secured special leave from us because it involves a profound issue of constitutional and international law and offers a challenge to the nascent champions of human rights in India whose politicised preoccupation has forsaken the civil debtor whose personal liberty is imperilled by the judicial process itself, thanks to section 51 (Proviso) and Order 21, rule 37, Code of Civil Procedure. Here is an appeal by judgment-debtors—the appellants whose personal freedom is in peril because a court warrant for arrest and detention in the civil prison is chasing them for non-payment of an amount due to a bank—the respondent, which has reined into a decree and has not yet been discharged. Is such deprivation of liberty illegal?

"From the perspective of international law the question posed is whether it is right to enforce a contractual liability by imprisoning a debtor in the teeth of Article 11 of the International Covenant on Civil and Political Rights. The Article reads:

"No one shall be imprisoned merely on the ground of inability to fulfill a contractual obligation'. An apercu of Article 21 of the Constitution suggests the question whether it is fair procedure to deprive a person of his personal liberty merely because he has not discharged his contractual liability in the face of the constitutional protection of life and liberty as expounded and expanded by a chain of rulings or this Court beginning with *Maneka Gandhi's* case.

"Right at the beginning we may take up the bearing of Article 11 on the law that is to be applied by an Indian Court when there is a specific provision in the Code of Civil Procedure authorising detention for non-payment of a decree debt. The Covenant bans imprisonment merely for not discharging a decree debt. Unless there be some other vice or *mens rea* apart from failure to foot the decree, international law frowns on holding the debtor's person in civil prison, as hostage by the court. India is now a signatory to this Covenant and Article 51(c) of the Constitution obligates the State to "foster respect for international law and treaty obligations in the dealings of organised peoples with one another.

"The march of civilization has been a story of progressive subordination of property rights to personal freedom, and a by-product of this subordination finds noble expression in the declaration that "No one shall be imprisoned merely on the ground of inability to fulfill a contractual obligation". This revolutionary change in the regard for the human person is spanned by the possible shock that a resuscitated Shylock would suffer if a modern Daniel were to come to judgment when the former asks the pound of flesh from Antonio's bosom according to the tenor of the bond, by flatly refusing the mayhem on the debtor, because the inability of an impecunious to oblige shall not imperil his liberty or person under the new dispensation proclaimed by the Universal Declaration of Human Rights. Viewed in this progressive perspective, we may examine whether there is any conflict between section 51, C.P.C. and Article 11 of the International Covenants quoted above. As already indicated by me, this latter provision only interdicts imprisonment if that is sought solely on the ground of inability to fulfill the obligation. Section 51 also declares that if the debtors has no means to pay he cannot be arrested and detained.

"Equally meaningful is the import of Article 21 of the Constitution in the context of imprisonment for non-payment of debts. The high value of human dignity and the worth of the human person enshrined in Article 21, read with Articles 14 and 19, obligates the State not to incarcerate except under law which is fair, just and reasonable in its procedural essence.

"It is too obvious to need elaboration that to cast a person in prison because of his poverty and consequent inability to meet his contractual liability is appalling. To be poor, in this land of "Daridra Narayanans" (land of poverty) is no crime and to recover debts by the procedure of putting one in prison is too flagrantly violative of Article 21 unless there is proof of the minimal fairness of his wilful failure to pay inspite of his sufficient means and absence of more terribly pressing claims on his means such as medical bills to treat cancer or other grave illness. Unreasonableness and unfairness in such a procedure is inferable from Article 11 of the Covenant. But this is precisely the interpretation we have put on the proviso to section 51, C.P.C. and the lethal blow of Article 21 cannot strike down the provision, as now interpreted.

"The words which hurt are 'or has had since the date of the decree, the means to pay the amount of the decree'. This implies, superficially read that if at any time after the passing of an old decree the judgment-debtor had come by some 'resources' and had not discharged the decree, he could be detained in prison even though at that later point of time he was found to be penniless. This is not a sound position apart from being inhuman going by the standards of Article 11 (of the Covenant) and Article 21 of the Constitution. The simple default to discharge is not enough. There must be some element of bad faith beyond mere indifference to pay, some deliberate or recussant disposition in the past or, alternatively current means to pay the decree or a substantial part of it. The provision emphasises the need to establish not mere omission to pay but an attitude of refusal on demand verging on dishonest disowning of the obligation under the decree. Here considerations of the debtor's other pressing needs and straitened circumstances will play prominently. We would have, by this construction sauced law with justice, harmonised section 51 with the Covenant and the Constitution," the order said.

'Saucing law with justice' has been the philosophy of Krishna Iyer and this thread can be noticed in all his judgments. If one goes rigidly by the dictates of the law, notwithstanding other factors to the contrary, justice will continue to remain an unacheivable dream for the 'Daridranarayanans', many of whom will be forced to spend their time in civil prisons for failure to fulfill a contractual obligation. Thanks to Krishna Iyer this Damocle's sword had ceased hanging from above the heads of the poor.

BAIL AND THE POOR

"A person is not in prison because he is guilty. He is not in prison because he has been punished. He is not in prison because there was apprehension that he would escape before release. The only reason why he is in prison is that he is poor."

—Lyndon B. Johnson

The then President of America

In life Justice is as dear as the commodities for which one has to pay a heavy price before and after the national budget. Justice has to be bought in the (in) justice market paying an exorbitant price. The stark naked fact is that the have-nots, the poor, the penury stricken and those wallowing in unfathomable depths of poverty have only to lose something every time they go before the justice market and have no power or wealth to gain anything.

Be it a rickshaw puller who has to sign documents every time a case is put off or if due to force of circumstances the very presiding magistrate stands before the signing clerk, nothing would move unless Rs. 25 or more are shelled out. Only if the litigant bribes and the bargain is met would his case be called in the morning. Otherwise he would have to languish throughout the day in courts. God forbid if he is late by a few minutes, a warrant would be issued for his arrest.

There is a pithy proverb which says that to a person who is afraid, everything would appear like an apparition. So is the apparition of justice. Often the guilty go scot free while the innocent is brought into the web of law. To a policeman, the poor are *de facto* criminals. They (the police) do not countenance dirty or crumpled clothes. Even if Mahatma Gandhi is resurrected and walks along the streets today in his "naked fakir" garb, he would be arrested by the police on suspicion.

The misfortune of our country is that the innocents who are arrested, the undertrials are not aware as to why they were being arrested, or when they would be released. Those who are not sure of their next meal, those who are so poor that they have no money to buy tickets while travelling in trains, those who are engaged in minor aberrations like fighting in the streets for a beedi are those who are apprehended and sent to prisons. They are convicted and sent to prisons for one or two months while the undertrials with their wings clipped spend months (sometime even years) together in the jails.

Are the poor not entitled to bail? Who could answer in the negative? If the person could engage an eminent lawyer from the legal market, if he could present two sureties who are acceptable to the court, if he could oil the palms of the village administrative officer to certify that the sureties could be relied upon and that they have assets in the form of properties, then he could come out on bail. Often the so called leaders of the people inveigle the gullible men that they should participate in rallies, go on thousand kilometer pada yatra towards Chennai or storm Delhi to win their rights and demands. The innocents reach these destinations in the cheapest possible mode of transport while those who sounded the call, fly by planes or travel in air-conditioned comfort of railway coaches. The unsuspecting common man, who goes to these distant places and gets stranded is considered a criminal and taken to courts by the policemen. In such strange places where could the poor Karuppan and Khanshiram go in search of sureties to release them on bail?

Though the Code of Criminal Procedure stipulates crimes which are bailable and non-bailable, there is confusion because there is no proper definition of "bail" which clearly spells out the meaning of this term. This was succinctly illustrated in *Motiram's* case. Motiram, one of the innumerable persons who remain deaf and dumb mutes in jails as undertrials. He sought bail from the magistrate and the latter ordered the release of Motiram, a mason on a bond for Rs. 10,000. However, the magistrate refused to accept Motiram's brother as surety since, all his assets were in another State. The Supreme Court could release a person on bail under the Code of Criminal Procedure on his own bond. He could either be an undertrial or even a convicted criminal who has filed an appeal.

Even a destitute's life is lit up occasionally by some illuminating luck. When *Motiram's* case came before Justice Krishna Iyer, he said that the court was shocked that the magistrate had fixed a sum of Rs. 10,000 for bail of a poor mason and held that the benefit of the doubt should be given to the magistrate who had failed to understand these nuances of poverty and added that if the law was not to betray the poor, many laws including those of bail should be repealed.

In *Niranjan Singh's* case, Krishna Iyer in his order said:

> "The blood-curdling plot disclosed in the complaint is that pursuant to a conspiracy the brother of the complainant was waylaid by the police party on August 27, 1978 as he was proceeding to Shirdi. He had with him some gold ornaments and cash. He was caught and removed from the truck in which he was travelling, tied with a rope to a neem tree nearby, thus rendering him a motionless target to a macabre shooting. One of the sub-inspectors fired two shots from his revolver on the chest of the victim at close range and killed him instantaneously. The policemen, having perpetrated this villainy,

vanished from the scene. No action was taken by the State against the criminals. How could they, when the preservers of the peace and investigators of crime themselves become planned executors of murders? The victim's brother was an advocate and he filed a private complaint. The learned Magistrate ordered an inquiry under section 202, Cr. P.C., took oral evidence of witnesses at some length and held; "Thus taking an overall survey of evidence produced before me, I am of the opinion that there are sufficient grounds to proceed against all the accused for the offences under sections 302, 323, 342 read with section 34, I.P.C."

"The story of encounters during arrest and unwitting injuries resulting in casualties, sometimes become a mask to hide easy liquidation of human life by heartless policemen when some one allergic to authority resists their vices. The police have the advantage that they prepare the preliminary record which may "kill" the case against them. This disquieting syndrome of policemen committing crimes of killing and making up perfect paperwork cases of innocent discharge of duty should not be ruled out when courts examine rival versions. Indeed, we must emphasise that the trial Judge shall not be influenced by what we have said and shall confine himself to the evidence in the case when adjudging the guilt of the accused. We were constrained to make the observations above because the Sessions Judge, quite unwarrantedly, discussed at prolix length the probabilities of the police party's exculpatory case and held:

> "So it is reasonable to hold that there was a scuffle and resistance offered by the victim, Amarjeet Singh before shots were fired at his person by the accused No. 1".

"Detailed examination of the evidence and elaborate documentation of the merits should be avoided while passing orders on bail applications. No party should have the impression that his case has been prejudiced. To be satisfied about a *prima facie* case is needed but it is not the same as an exhaustive exploration of the merits in the order itself.

"Grant of bail is within the jurisdiction of the Sessions Judge but the court must not, in grave cases, gullibly dismiss the possibility of accused who are policemen intimidating the witnesses with cavalier ease. In our country, intimidation by policemen, when they are themselves accused of offences, is not an unknown phenomenon and the judicial process will carry credibility with the community only if it views impartially and with common sense the pros and cons, undeterred by the psychic pressure of police presence as indictees.

"We agree that, in our view, an outlaw cannot ask for the benefit of law and he who flees justice cannot claim justice. But here the position is different. The accused were not absconding but had appeared and surrendered before the Sessions Judge. Judicial jurisdiction arises only when persons are already in custody and seek the process of the court to be enlarged. We agree that no person accused of an offence can move the court for bail under section 439, Cr. P.C. unless he is in custody.

"We conclude this order on a note of anguish. The complainant has been protesting against the State's bias and police threats. We must remember that a democratic State is the custodian of people's interests and not only police interests. Then how come this that the team of ten policemen against whom a Magistrate, after due enquiry, found a case to be proceeded with and grave charges, including for murder, were framed continue on duty without so much as being suspended from service until disposal of the pending sessions trial? On whose side is the State? The rule of law is not a one-way traffic and the authority of the State is not for the police and against the people. A responsible Government, responsive to appearances of justice, would have placed police officers against whom serious charges had been framed by a criminal court, under suspension unless exceptional circumstances suggesting a contrary course exists."

Thus it was Krishna Iyer's view that bail should be the order and jail the exception and where the applicant for bail is poor, the law should show latitude in fixing the quantum of bail amount. He also desiderated that when the accused in cases are policemen they should be treated not differently from other criminals.

WHY THIS NEGATION OF EDUCATION FOR HAVE-NOT HUMANITY?

The Constitution, in its Preamble and Fundamental Rights Part, has inscribed the right to life with egalite and social justice to every person who is a member of the grand collective, We, the People of India, as a guaranteed right and paramount value. The authoritative interpretation by the Supreme Court which is final and binding on the country's institutions, holds that dignity and equality of status and opportunity are integral to the *right to life* and that education is a cardinal component of human dignity and, therefore, of the basic structure of the Constitution. It follows, as a *fundamental State obligation* that each Indian, be his socio-economic station high or humble, has a just right to a fair level of education sans social, financial, regional, religious discrimination or purchasing power. Remember, the Preamble which has a semantic bearing on the meaning of meanings in understanding the spirit and sense of the 'right to life', 'secularism' and 'equality before the law'. The expression 'socialist' is the next neighbour of 'secular' and qualifies 'democratic Republic', and 'equal protection of the laws'. So much so, that the '*socialist* Republic' concept, with its ideological dynamics inscribed in the Preamble is no idle adjective but has the power to sensitize the words and thoughts of the other provisions. So viewed, the right to 'education' derives an ideational activism which judicial construction cannot burke or jettison based on the sub-conscious impact of the dubious mantra of 'privatization', an aggressive product of imperialism with its currently global conditioning of mental-moral locomotion. An integrated value-vision, while exercising the curial art of constitutional construction, obligates the court to measure the semantic dimensions of diction in paramount documents, taking care to remember that the Preamble, Articles 14 and 21 are inviolable, being part of the basic structure of our Founding Deed. I esteem the erudite brethren of the High Bench which enjoys supremacy; but contradictory pronouncements has landed the rule of law in a jural imbroglio and consequent difficulties to the nation as a whole whose massive demographic sector consists of *daridra narayanas*.

Courts have given unwitting currency and authority to counterfeit meaning to the right to education by holding *de facto* that education is an industry, a saleable commodity, a business—now Big Business—where possible future investment and reasonable profit are relevant in computing and inflating admission fees and disguised capitation fee from students. They seem to forget the fundamentals inspiring the economic justice concept, writ into the Constitution, which alone gives judge's power controlled by its humanist philosophy which contradicts commercializing and colonialising of 'education'. It is good that a college for judges has been started to refine and refresh them, *inter alia*, in the country's socio-economic condition and swaraj as people's educative emancipation.

Commercialisation of Higher Education

Commercialisation of the right to education may tend towards cadaverisation of the constitutional right to *life in dignity*. Today the State is so indifferent to the lowest rising to the highest level of education that admission even to L.K.G. is often possible only on payment of ten thousand rupees as a condition, covert or overt. Who but the corrupt can afford? Admission to the medical colleges involves concealed, disingenuously rationalised capitation fee which can be a fancy sum of Rupees forty lakhs, obviously beyond the reach of even ordinarily well-to-do Indians. Thirty or forty lakhs of rupees for admission to the MBBS is claimed to enjoy judicial sanction, according to private managements who demand monopoly of all seats. No honest judge or minister can gain entrance for his son or daughter in a medical, engineering or other challenging course depending on his salary alone. Thus, this century will hear testimony to Bharat divided, the few rich with their children enjoying higher education and later professional corruption and demand of large dowry to make good the early heavy investment, and on the other hand, the millions of minions and have-nots, bonded labour, jobless proletariat sans any education, employment, slowly losing faith in Swaraj. Big Business Houses will operate 'higher education' colleges as a commercial adventure with money power over State institutions. Terrorism, corruption and foreign exploitation will find fertile fresh woods and pastures a new. India that is Bharat will suffer from a culture of dependencia syndrome and exotic mania. The prospects are grim and the portent is a national educational policy promotive of colonization. In tune with privatization in vital developmental domains fatal to Independence and self-reliance, may have to face traumatic decline, paving the way for *open sesame* to plutophilic forces and pathological futurology. The State is denigrating the public sector and advocating withdrawal from all fundamental activities, including education. Management of our nation is steadily but wilfully getting into the hands of a rich ruling class under foreign domination. Beware, the world's proletariat will not spare the *sub silentio* State terrorism of the Proprietariat with their hidden agendas. Do we create a huge dissenting majority to resist the Western—pressured 'monoculture of the mind', desiderating an 'insurrection of subjugated knowledge' against the dominant knowledge and pseudo-developmental technology of post-industrial capitalism. (*Vide* Vandana Shiva's writings). I do not dogmatise without violence and denigration of participative government. The State may revise its policy, the Court may, as it has done before, reverse its interpretation to save the nation, and the rich may realize the futility of estranging a vast populace. We must defend *poorna swaraj*. 'In the democracies, this means the courage to clear away the ideological rubble that smoothers independence of mind and leads to self-censorship. This is not without risk. 'If one tells the truth,' wrote Oscar Wilde, 'one is sure sooner or later to be found out'. It is a freedom we are in danger of losing without even knowing it. For when there is no longer anyone speaking out, who will be the last voice? (John Pilger)

A final caveat of history before I close: An august deprivation and privation may drive a people into despair and cannibal culture and or slave—suicide syndrome. Democracy, then, becomes barbaric and society suffers in status into menagerie. The root cause, as a dialectical diagnosis reveals, is negation of equal opportunity, social justice and suppression of dignity and access to education!

STATE EXTRAVAGANZA AND BANKRUPTCY OF TREASURY*

India, a Socialist Republic going by the Constitutional Preamble, and possessing a plenitude of natural resources and heritage of profound wisdom is currently feudal, colonial and ubiquitously backward and bankrupt. Kerala is a lovely province with rich potential for remarkable development, highly literate and rich in human harmony and religious plurality with marginal communal friction and felonious feuds. Among the rarest of the rare, geographically speaking, is Kerala with the Western Ghats and the Arabian Sea bounding the green beauty of the hills and vales and enlivening the biosphere with equable climate and fortyfour charming rivers many backwaters. The population however is high while the State is sweet but small. Every Finance Minister of the State, Left or Right, in power has been grumbling about the grim budget situation and monetary doldrums. However, it is a paradox that luxury is writ large, developmental pretentions paraded and agrarian prosperity with rubber and peeper and other medicinal plants and vegetation flourish in Nature, while alcoholism and drug menace are endangering the health of the people. Onam day this year Rs.130 crores worth of liquor is reported to have been consumed. Gold shop everywhere, glittering bazaar with crowds around proving consumerism beyond the means of the people generally star hotels and fashion shops busy everywhere. They borrow or rob and live gluttonous lives, eventually commit suicide or land up in prison because of debts, clashes, raids, terrorism and corruption everywhere. Society deteriorates into a base berserk system where morality has no place in public life and humanity suffer a gory syndrome. This ethos of consumerism and 'affluenza' had reached outrageous propositions and has affected as a disease even Governments and public institutions. In this context, we come across P.W.Ds as department of expenditure terrorism vandalism. House wife parsimony or husbandry economy rarely inhibits the reckless excesses habitual to the P.W.D. They make their own rules of lavish spend-thrift laxity and generous self-help. Everywhere, the PWD is a prodigious obesity, while vandalism beyond the control of ministers, even Finance Ministers is

* January 27, 2007.

its liberal unscrupulousness. Indeed, Rajaji, among the wisest and the most seasoned administrator of our time described the PWD as **public enemy number one.** I shall give but one instance. The Tellicherry Government Brannon College had a ramshackle building divided by the highway. It was so bad that the Madras University (Tellicherry and Malabar were part of Madras province until November 1956) threatened to disaffiliate the college unless a new building was constructed. The Madras Government pleaded financial inability. They wanted people's contribution in part. I was an MLA (Madras) at that time and was chosen to be President of a people's committee to raise some funds. Our resources were poor and the peril of disaffiliation compelled me to complain to Kamaraj, the then Chief Minister, to grant the required money of Rs.17 lakhs which was the huge estimate of the PWD.(largely by standards of those days) Kamaraj flatly challenged this excessive estimate and said that another first grade college privately owned (the Zamorin's college), had been inaugurated by him a few months earlier. He had enquired about the cost and the management had told him that the excellent building had cost only Rs.6 lakhs. My Government will give your committee 6 lakhs to build the Brannon College, bypassing the PWD. I informed the education secretary Sri. Gopalaswamy I.C.S about this conversation. He immediately sent for the Chief Engineer and appraised him of Kamaraj having mentioned to me that the PWD estimate was far too excessive and would be ignored. Krishna Iyer's committee would instead take over the construction. What a shock and shame, said Gopalaswamy to the Chief Engineer. Immediately the Chief Engineer returned to his office and came back with a more moderate estimate of Rs.11 lakhs. This shows that the PWD has its own way of boosting public expenditure and other public institutions. They spend exaggeratedly including a significant element of unaccountable extras. Mosquitoes and ugly pathological heaps of filth are a menace and mayhem to Kochi and all over Kerala. When I question about the environmental threat and ubiquitous ugliness Mayor pleaded lack of funds. The Finance Minister has always been pleading State borrowings and—Treasury deficit. But it would appear that the PWD has a traditional system of annual repair of all Government buildings (maintenance) and the sums were usually inflated and uneconomical with none to question them about the rigidly colossal expenditure. Whenever people's project were put up to be executed there was no money in the budget, but when big public buildings had to be repaired the expenditure was horrendous. In this strain, the PWD spent Rs.17 lakhs to repair the Marxist Home Minister's potential residence. (Otherwise he was, as a Marxist residing in humbler accommodation.). Similar large sums for the bungalow of other ministers. Do remember that Marxists are committed to fighting for the poor in privations, and selling an example of austerity, never of ostentation. EMS as the first Chief Minister of Kerala drew a salary of Rs.350/- although the statutorily sanctioned salary permitted him a higher sum and weak in the official quarters without wasting money on PWD repair. So did I. Economy and thrift as surrogacy is a minister puritans style of life in a poor country is what is expected of communists whose fundamental policy is abolition of poverty and wise parsimony of public expenditure so that, on basic needs of life, there may be equality or equity. Luxury is allergy for administrators in power if they have a socialist conviction. Money must be spent to provide the poor with essential needs, like shelter, education and good health. If the malignant mosquito whose bite terminates life for want of immediate treatment in hospital Government is culpable because enough hospitals, doctors and medicine to save life, at least from mosquitoes, even if it involves high investment is a shame if costly lay-out on travels, telephones and obviable police escort is a Leftist extravagance we face defeat before special mosquitoes kill but boast of battles against Musharaff. The extraordinary extravagance of previous Ministries is no alibi. It is allergy to the have-not millions if even LKG and tattered shelter are bafflingly beyond indigent India Unlimited. MPs and MLAs and judges draw huge emoluments and perks, not to speak of two crores for MP for local patronage. We need a revolution, Gandhian and Nehruvian, socialist and secular. But how can it happen when the Ruling Power and Opposition Coalition, the leading media and Corporate Controllerate are undiluted bourgeosie! The have-not sector of Indian humanity shall not forgive those in power Left or Right if they do not implement Article 14 (Equality) and Article 21 (the Right to Life) in its fullest sense.

INDUSTRIALIZE AND PERISH*

Modernisation is axiomatically through industrialization according to capitalist dogma. Appropriate technology reconciles progress through industry with employment of labour. Super capitalists with focus on hyper profit adopt gluttonous technology whereby accumulation of wealth with the least Labour is achieved, the hunger of the masses and the decline of agriculture be disregard and national policy being regarded as **industrialize or perish**. Mega-corporates particularly foreign and imitatively colossal and naitive destroy agricultural development and consume in the basic thesis that industrial production is the principle source of wealth for any country. India is an agricultural country but unemployment multiplies and the masses are left hungry when the main source of employment are agriculture hardly survives. Such land has a potential for profitable cultivation. Since traditional commodities do not withstand competition with industry or commercial crops which become big business technology reduces the need for Labour promotes appetite for wealth and man becomes poor value augmenting starvation. Fundamentally the craze for wealth through hi-tech industry generates economic disaster. If our country cares for Gandhiji, if India lives in its villages, if a billion Indians matter more than 23 millionaires a conceptual reversal of vision and values is necessary. I am not against industrialization. As such, wealth multiplication in a few hands throwing voiceless millions as worthless commodities. The proletariat must survive and flourish and shall not surrender to the syndrome of proprietariat monopoly.

It is from this angle that I agree with Sumit Chakrabarty and company who campaign against the acquisition of 1000 acres of green prosperity in favour of a giant company for starting a car industry which will run and run over and destroy agriculture and humanity as a nation's treasure. Gandhiji taught us fundamentals of development.

Gandhiji wrote:

> *The Gandhian concept of development rejected the idea that it should aim primarily at the creation of material wealth or the satisfaction of insatiable,*

* December 6, 2006.

endlessly multiplied needs. 'In so far as we have made the modern materialistic craze our goal,' he wrote, 'so far are we going downhill in the path of progress.' *(Third World Tomorrow P-19)*

Nehru tried to reconcile rural development with necessary industries. But a perverse economic terrorism since 1991 made India a victim of the western winds which particularly yankee. India today is rapidly dying and its villages suffer desertification and starvation, of course by a process of recolonisation we are becoming foreign automobile manufacturers and dumping around for five star consumerism. India can never be regarded as a developed country. So long as it is a prisoner of dependencia syndrome and dehumanized progress 'where wealth accumulates and men decay'. It is unfortunate that Leftist Government should use statutory machinery to acquire thousand acres of fertile land from common farmers to be made over to one of the most powerful industrial concerns in the country. Marxist party becomes a misnomer if ordinary landholders are to be deprived of their lands by the State in favour of huge companies. Karl Marx stands betrayed when a party with his name uses the State possess to benefit a large company depriving rich land from peasants while infertile or barrel lands are available for an industrial enterprise. Even otherwise manufacture of cars, construction of huge roads when the State has scarce resources and poverty plagues the people and jobless malady stares the economy. Marx once wrote:

> *The philosophers have only interpreted the world in various ways; the point is to change it.*

If the State has the will to restore the acquired lands it is perfectly possible to add a provision to the land acquisition act that all lands are statutorily seized and made over to private enterprises will be vested in the owners if moved within a specific period for such return on repayment of compensation if in the opinion of the state the land was acquired against the will of the owners. This will do social justice, a basic principle of equity.

ARBITRATION—CERTAIN ARBITRARY ASPECTS*

Our courts are suffocated by mounting arrears of cases. The chances of their disposal within a reasonable time are rare. The clients who have to go to court have no hope of getting justice in their lifetime. Therefore suggestions have been made to arbitration as an alternative to litigation but experience shows that this remedy is worse than the malady. Let us examine the merits and demerits of arbitration as a process of getting cheap early justice.

The realities of court pendencies demonstrate that judges cannot disposes of the heavy arrears. The Ayodhya case where once Babari Masjid stood has been before the Lucknow bench for nearly half a century. There are other instances of outrageous delays in other court in India. Is arbitral method a solution at all? No is my answer. Judges are plentifully appointed according to Parkinson's Law and Peter Principle. A new method of appointment of judges is necessary.

The Chief Justice of India while in Kochi the other day pleaded that cases be settled by mediation, which will lessen the load of the courts, which are heavily loaded by mounting arrears of dockets. Indeed no one will disagree with the proposition. Our judges have much to account for to the people who find litigation most expensive, multi-docketed, gambling in result and on the whole victims of extravagant expensive astrological syndrome. Poor people as Indians are can hardly afford a legal system, which will bankrupt the parties and baffle the verdicts especially because of the dilatory curial process and the highly costly lawyers fees and the overall corruption of the system escalating and not diminishing. The quality of the judges and the diminishing commitments to the community at large and the absence of devotion to the values expressly mentioned in the Preamble to the Constitution such as socialism, secularism and a sense of realism about the agrarian and urban destitution. The very selection of judges has no scientific or socially realist basis and often reminds a public critic of Parkinson's Laws and Peter Principle. No voice of the jurists or the enlightened elite among the

* January 8, 2007.

public is heard. Consequently there is chaos in the judicative operation, which will continue until a revolutionary change and creative restructuring, in harmony with the raw Indian condition take place. The reconstructing of a dynamic modern legal system in tune with dialectical materialism pledged with spiritual material and moral values (or Dharma) is the desideratum. The distance is long, the roadblocks are many and the vest interests are barriers. The cultural transformation demands mass participation and jurists with the vision of creating Law India with a sense of swarajya and without primitive feudalism, colonialism and Yankee biased geo-colonialism.

The alternative of arbitration to reduce case-laws accumulation has proved to be a remedy that aggravates the malady because of dreadful delay, heavy financial investment and unsatisfactory performance and judicial indiscipline which are subject to costly judicial scrutiny is absence. The Chief Justices of India have often been emphasizing the calamity of Himalayan arrears of dockets, which makes the court system untouchable and unapproachable for the common human sector. Arbitration is a nice word but a noxious process. Its formalities and farfetched health resort venues are forbiddingly expensive. If only the arbitrators, who are retired judges, levy fees equal to their last drawn salaries together with their pensions it would be a service; but now the venues chosen are luxurious hill stations. The whole process turns into an inevitable plutocratic pleasures. They charge fantastic fees outrageous when compared to their salaries. These affluenza sick arbitrators are a law unto themselves. Work for a few hours, punctuated by procrastinating postings and exhausting the resources of the disputants. Indeed, arbitration as a judicial process has become an extraordinary racket. A simplified inexpensive accessible methodology of settlement is easy to devise but money is the focus of the retired judges, settlement is never on their socially constructive goal. The finest hour of bringing parties together is never on their agenda. The whole system of arbitration is a luxurious operation of lucrative windfall for retired judges who make more income in a few years of arbitration than they have made in their whole judicial career. A creative realistic humane arbitration law and recruitment of judges whose commitment to economic justice and not inflated lucre is what we need. Remember, we are in indigent India and swaraj with swadeshi demands a totally new arbitration calculus. Generally speaking, judicial experience free of corruption is a valuable social asset, never freebooters or mere Mammon devotees. A research into the subject of arbitration law in action is a necessity followed by a creative informal justice oriented economic process with rules of austerity and good behaviour binding on the bench and the bar.

Perhaps better than arbitration is mutual settlement assisted by lawyers on both side. There must be settlement bodies appointed by the High Court of impartial persons with integrity. They must at least three. If all the three agree on a settlement its must be binding. One revision to the high court will be alone and no proceeding to the Supreme Court is permissible except where the Advocate General or Attorney General certifies it as fit. I conclude by two famous quotes:

> *I must say that, as a litigant, I should dread a lawsuit beyondAlmost anything else short of sickness and of death.* (Learned Hand)
>
> *Discourage litigation. Persuade your neighbors to compromise whenever you can. Point out to them how the nominal winner is often a real loser—in fees, expenses, and waste of time. As a peace-maker the lawyer has a superior opportunity of being a good man.* (Abraham Lincoln)

PATENT LAW—PATENTLY UNFAIR?

'Where knowledge is free-
Into that heaven of freedom,
My father, let my country awake'

This fragment from the Gitanjali is the universal culture of our country where knowledge is free, and sacredly so. Secrecy of information and monopoly of discovery is allergy to our heritage and the Constitution mandates the fundamental duty 'to value and preserve the rich heritage of our composite culture' and Patents are contrary to the idiom of our ancient wisdom. Nevertheless, India like other countries, has adopted the jurisprudence of patents in a manner which leaves a wide margin for openness and protects the health and progress of the people. This law of patents of 1970 has stood the test of time and has eclectic validity. Patent Laws, however, have come under the greedy avidity of monopoly appetite by developed countries whose pressure to exploit discoveries to the maximum monetary advantage was lead to cornering proclivities. The Patents Act, 1970, a patriotic measure, is now under challenge in the age of Intellectual Property Rights (IPR). There is a contradiction between the profit hunger of developed market economies and the social necessity of developing countries of protecting public health and access to medicine. The North has, somehow, managed to manipulate the Final Act of the Uruguay Round of Trade Negotiations—a Round which incorporates an unhealthy provision in the shape of Agreement on Trade Related aspects of Intellectual Property Rights (TRIPS). India weakly and meekly ratified this Final Act and thereby committed itself to implement the TRIPS provisions. The harsh monopoly under the TRIPS Agreement hurts India's Pharmaceuticals, energy, petro-chemical, seed, micro-organisms and so on. The ill-effects of this regime are enormous. It is designed to further enrich already rich multinationals and cripple the knowledge bases, productive capacity and, indeed, the individual research endeavors of countries of the South. The Final Act came into force on January 1, 1995 and since then, controversy has raged around TRIPS in public fora and at official gatherings. The last ministerial conference of the WTO which debated the issue was held in November, 2001 resulting in two Doha ministerial declarations. Even earlier, international developments led to the enactment of Patents Amendment Act, 1999 providing for Mail Box to entertain product patent applications for pharmaceuticals, plus. The 1999 Act permits grant of Exclusive Marketing Rights (EMRs) to the patent applicants. The 1970 Act deals with process patents while the TRIPS includes, importantly, the concept of product patent which has deleterious implications on the Indian pharmaceutical industry and, consequently, the availability and fair price line of drugs and medicines. Access to health, which is a fundamental right (Article 21 of the Constitution), comes into play and any legislation in India must show grave concern for people's health and their reasonable right to secure remedies under just conditions. Thereafter, in alleged fulfilment of the TRIPS obligation, the Patent (Second Amendment Bill), 1999, was introduced in December that year. That Bill was referred to a Joint Parliamentary Committee, which has since submitted its report to the Rajya Sabha on December 10, 2001. The Bill, as reported, will be debated by both the Houses. Meanwhile, the Doha Ministerial Conference Declarations (WTO) on the TRIPS Agreement bearing on Public Health and allied matters has been issued with submissive compliance with and substantial relevance to the provisions of the TRIPS Agreement. The flexibilities of Doha Declaration may come up for consideration before the nation and the two Houses. It is therefore appropriate to investigate matters of moment relating to the jurisprudence of patents from the primary angle of people's health, which claims paramountcy in the light of Article 21 as interpreted by the Supreme Court. If the Right to Health is fundamental, as integral to the Right to Life, any legislation by Parliament has to abide by this criterion. Does the Bill, now pending, reflect the spirit of the Doha Declaration and meet the Indian people's constitutional right to health? Currently, between the North and the South there is a Drug Divide which needs to be bridged so that global pharmaceutical wealth, with access to the poor, may build a health haven for humble humanity in Developing Countries. This issue gains great significance as the global campaign against profiteering by gargantuan pharma giants rages. Health activists as well as drug companies in India gear up to fight the battle over TRIPS *vis-a-vis* patents legislation. Let us examine the Doha Declaration and the light it throws upon the future of patent legislation.

The revised Parliamentary Bill fails to cognize Doha and hardly meets the aspirations and urgencies of our people in matters like import technology, impact on Research and Development investments, local technological innovations, bio-piracy, defense of indigenous vintage knowledge and materials, pharmaceutical advance within India, consumer protection against run-away prices, which is the be-setting sin of monopolies, and so on. The dangerous journey, invasive of Indian pharmaceutical wonder, began with the Dunkel Draft Text, decades old, continues even after Doha Declaration and the nation must awake to the potential disaster of a legislative surrender by India to the cannibalism of global mega-corporates. Social activists, political polemists, avant-garde jurists and the people-oriented media must mobilise parliamentary opinion before it is too late. The nation's health is in peril. Billions on publicity will be spent by the North to make Truth a Casualty.

A TRIPS CLOSE-UP

A human rights perspective comports with TRIPS objectives, unless distorted. Patent provisions patently unfair to the poor must be repudiated, as the primary purpose of TRIPS is social justice. Adulteration of the Patents Act, 1970, beyond the survival interests of the masses, will be violative of the basic features of the Constitution and betrayal of the tryst with destiny. We, the people of India, made as Independence dawned.

Articles 7 and 8, as the conscience of the TRIPS treaty, must receive magnanimous and benignant interpretation 'in a manner conducive to social and economic welfare'.

Article 8 (1) runs thus:

> *Members may, in formulating or amending their national laws and regulations, adopt measures necessary to protect public health and nutrition, and to promote the public interest in sectors of vital importance to their socio-economic and technological development, provided that such measures are consistent with the provisions of this Agreement.*

One more provision in the TRIPS strategy desiderates vigilant scrutiny. Article 27(1), in its vicious expansionism and extravagant internationalism, makes patentable a wide range of subject-matter disastrously favourable to MNCs. This requires judicious 'reading down' and severe operational truncation. It reads, in its maddening globalism, patentable subject-matter thus:

> *Patents shall be available for any inventions, whether products or processes, in all fields of technology, provided that they are new, involve an inventive step and are capable of industrial application. Patents shall be available and patent rights enjoyable without discrimination as to the place of invention, the field of technology and whether products are imported or locally produced.*

Anything under the sun, products or processes, made inside or outside the country, seemingly inventive and gleamingly or novel/simulating industrial application, and technological in its complexion, is patentable—too wide a monopoly canvas and too noxious to be in our national interest. Parliament must, in its sovereign power and responsible concern, prune and pare down the blanket obesity of patentability. And here Article 27(2) and (3) will help in large measure, given the Parliament's Will to whittle down the scope of the subject-matter. The two sub-articles may be read here with focus on the exclusionary locus which those words yield in their semantic sweep

Article 27(2) run:

Members may exclude from patentability inventions, the prevention within their territory of the commercial exploitation of which is necessary to protect ordure public or morality, including to protect human, animal or plant life or health or to avoid serious prejudice to the environment, provided that such exclusion is not made merely because the exploitation is prohibited by domestic law.

Article 27(3) stipulates:

Members may also exclude from patentability:

(a) *diagnostic, therapeutic and surgical methods for the treatment of humans or animals;*

(b) *plants and animals other than micro-organisms, and essentially biological processes for the production of plants or animals other than non-biological and microbiological processes. However, Members shall provide for the protection of plant varieties either by patents or by an effective sui generis system or by any combination thereof. The provisions of this sub-paragraph shall be reviewed four years after the entry into force of the Agreement Establishing the MTO.*

There is thus broad jurisdiction and burning justification to non-patentise, in the name of public order, morality, health and environment, many items injurious to our pharma flowerage. The elimination contemplated by Article 27(3) is wide enough to spread out conceptually to forbid bio-piracy, promote plant protection and deny inventive novelty to the world of ayurvedic wealth and of other indigenous systems, including tribal medicine. The sky is the limit provided our politicians are robustly independent, resolutely nationalist and culturally committed to swadeshi in its vintage amplitude. Mark you, so immense is our ancient medicinal pluralism and diverse innovative practices. The dynamics of interpretation and the dialectic of peopled health needs are a challenge to our law-makers in the formulation of patent law principles.

While there are several sinister matters we have to guard against in the TRIPS-obedient Amendments I stress two horrendous aberrations we have to beware of. One of them is the pernicious idea that India grant patent but the patent holder need not work the patent in our country on the bizarre fiction that import of patented goods will be treated as compliance. Indians cannot produce because the foreigner is the patentee. Nor does the latter produce here because he imports the article, which will be deemed to be sufficient. This surrender to a foreign patent holder is opposed to morality, public conscience and the homely availability so necessary for native health. Sans these minimal safeguards, our patents legislation may latently risk the nation's developmental destination and gravely imperil the country's social justice commitment.

Compulsory licensing, a benignant mandate of the 1970 Act, should not be jettisoned since TRIPS shall be incompatible with national interest and the health care obligation of the vast masses below the poverty line. In this context, the minimum that we can incorporate is a provision like the compulsory licenses article in the Brazilian Patent Law. Articles 68 and 69 are enough to show the green signal. Of course, Indianised provisions to suit native conditions may well be in order after Doha where India has presented its social justice.

An imaginative legislature, with concern for the pathetic populace, the lowliest and the last, cannot but vastly explore the potential of Article 8(1) and incorporate measures mandatorily protective of the people's access to modern pharmacopoeia and consistent with the indigent economic condition of the Indian people. To fail here is to betray the social justice testament that binds us. Parliamentary patriotism is on test in this Patents Amendment Bill.

POSTSCRIPT

Murasoli Maran, our Commerce Minister, in an excellent paper published on the eve of the Doha Meet referred to the architecture of international trade which deserved to be fundamentally recast by developing nations. He warned that the powerful US pharmaceuticals industry was one of the most active and strong lobbies arguing for the expansion and strengthening of patent protection with its predatory operation in disguise. Bio-piracy is the subject of theft of intellectual rights of the poor by the rich, which must be forbidden by Indian Law. The world today, as Maran points out, is divided not by ideology but by technology. The theology of IPR is robbery of traditional Indian drugs and medicines, patentise them and sell them back at soaring prices. We must remember that what we need is help not from WTO (which stands for the barons of pharmaceuticals) but from the WHO (which stands for the health for all in our sick universe). India, at Doha, agreed to drop from the Declaration the word "public interest". Dr. Hamled of CIPLA wonders why India accepted such a deletion. India has about 58 million diabetics, 40 million asthmatics and 40 million Hepatitis B patients. These are continents of diseases as large as the population of some countries. In India, every disease is a national emergency, unlike other countries. Health in India is a permanent emergency. So, why was the term public interest left out of the declaration? Anyway, we must fully stand by the people and use the flexibility provision in the Doha declaration that 'the TRIPS Agreement does not and should not prevent members from taking measures to protect public health'. For this, the Agreement can and should be interpreted and implemented in a manner supportive of WTO Members' right to protect public health and, in particular, to promote access to medicines for all. Doha Declaration reaffirms the right of WTO members to use, to the full, the provisions in the TRIPS Agreement, which provide flexibility.

In sum, Parliament must remember that under the Doha Declaration 'each Member has the right to determine what constitutes a national emergency or other circumstances of extreme urgency'. What can represent a national emergency or other circumstances of extreme urgency must be imparted semantic sweep. This should be the focus of the debate in the House on behalf of 'We the people of India'.

HUMAN HEALTH AND PATENT LAW

The deleteriousness of TRIPs, in relation to health and social justice, cannot be wished away by Parliament since Right to Life, a basic feature and constitutional guarantee, cannot be truncated or trampled upon. So too social justice and right to development in its distributive dimension.

Dear life in good health and free from disease is the foremost human right and is a constitutional fundamental. The humbler the Indian human, the higher the state's duty to protect the person. In this perspective we may have to examine the impact of TRIPs (Trade-Related Intellectual Property Rights) Agreement on Indian corpus *juris vis-a-vis* the right to life guaranteed under Article 21 of the Constitution, read with Article 14.

Public health laws, national drug policy and the patent system are intensely inter-related. This was explained by Prime Minister Indira Gandhi while speaking at the World Health Assembly in Geneva on May 6, 1981. In her words:

> *Affluent societies are spending vast sums of money understandably on the search for new products and processes to alleviate suffering and to prolong life. In the process, the drug manufacture has become a powerful industry.*

She added, on the parent system:

> *My idea of a better ordered world is one in which medical discoveries would be free of patents and there would be no profiteering from life or death.*

In this historic session, the participating countries unanimously adopted a resolution for "Global Strategy on Health for All". Since then there have been laudable contributions by science and technology to tackle successfully many health problem areas. While there is a substantial unfinished agenda on the health front, new and formidable challenges have been thrown up by an unequal treaty on all-pervasive economic and social aspects by the Final Act embodying the results of the Uruguay Round negotiations. In particular, the TRIPs agreement is the most contentious part of the Final Act. The aim of this agreement is to enforce globally tough standards in respect of several forms of intellectual property, which include patents, trade marks, protection of undisclosed information, and so on, forgetting the goals expressed by Indira Gandhi in regard to freeing of medical discoveries from the patent system. (B.K. Keayla)

Going to the fundamentals, what is a patent?

A patent is a monopoly right granted by a state to a person to exploit and benefit from the invention patented by him for a particular period. Thereafter, it passes into the public domain. According to Justice Rajagopala Ayyangar's report submitted in 1959, which report constitutes the basis for the Indian Patents Act, 1970, "The theory upon which the patent system is based is that the opportunity of acquiring exclusive rights in an invention stimulates technical progress in four ways, first, that it encourages research and invention; second, that it induces an inventor to disclose his discoveries instead of keeping them as a trade secret; third, that it offers a reward for the expenses of developing inventions to the stage at which they are commercially practicable; and fourth, that it provides an inducement to invest capital in new lines of production which might not appear profitable if many competing producers embarked on them simultaneously. Manufacturers would not be prepared to develop and produce important machinery if others could get the results of their work with impunity." To the same effect is the decision of the Supreme Court in *Vishwanath Prasad* v. *Hindustan Metal Industries,* 1979 (2) SCC 511 (Justice Jeevan Reddy).

In a cultural milieu where "knowledge is free", and is transmitted from generation to generation as a duty, it is incongrous to convert discoveries into "cash and carry" vulgarity but that is the perversion under pressure from Western Big Business. "Intellectual Property Rights" conceptually belongs to this moneymanic bigorry and TRIPs is the patent of this morally indefensible but virtually glorified anathema, Even so, in human affairs, minor adjustments, without forsaking fundamentals, may be necessary for peaceful co-existence. Even the TRIPs text partially acknowledges this aspect.

It is ironic but interesting to recall Thomas Jefferson's words:

> *"If nature has made any one thing less susceptible than all others of exclusive property, it is the action of the thinking power called an idea... No one possesses the less, because every other possesses the whole of it. He who receives an idea from me, receives instruction himself without lessening mine; as he who lights his taper at mine, receives light without darkening me." In Jefferson's vision, there are no barriers to the acquisition of knowledge. Nobody owns it, everybody partakes of it — and the world becomes richer.*

Alas, his country is the most venal violator to this value.

Our cultural cornerstone, the Rigveda mandates: "Let noble thoughts come to us from every side." Patenting intellect or its products is sacrilegious and a social outrage:

> *The trouble with the law is that it does not differentiate between the incentives needed to invest in different kinds of technologies. It accords as much protection to an idea thought up in the bath as to a drug that may have taken many years and hundreds of millions of dollars to move from*

conception to market-place. Even Jeff Bezos, founder of the Internet retailer Amazon.com and the holder of several business-method patents, has suggested in an open letter posted on the Internet that software and business-method patents should have a shorter life than other patents - say, three to five years.

The deleteriousness of TRIPs, in relation to health and social justice, cannot be wished away by Parliament since the right to life, a basic feature and constitutional guarantee intractable by parliamentary majority, cannot be truncated or trampled upon. So too social justice and right to development in its distributive dimension. While in form and phraseology the World Trade Organisation (WTO) - the successor to the General Agreement on Tariffs and Trade (GATT) - was set up to ensure more free trade, in actual fact the TRIPs Treaty catalyses monopolies, inhibits competition and freezes the initiatives of Indian scientists and technologists in producing cheaper and better products through more facile and finer processes. The TRIPs Agreement, in its restrictive provisions, saborages developmental objectives and creative quantum leaps by countries like India which have intellectual potential and actual successes in the field but suffer from inhibitions through TRIPs taboos and GATT handcuffs.

The specious plea that foreign technology will flow into India if product patent is legalised, is a patent unreality. Wisely, the Indian Parliament currently grants only *process* patents although hasty, harmful mutations are under way. Under TRIPs, monopolies are strengthened and the prices of pharmaceuticals are apt to jump, leaving the poor and their Right to Life to fatal Domestic enterprises have to encounter unequal competition on an uneven playing field with gargantuan corporations with their publicity power, glamour and clout. In short, the interests of Indian consumers and producers will be a casualty if the patent law of India, so carefully crafted, is to suffer mayhem by parliamentary self-infliction under exotic pressure and/or an insufficient understanding of the partners if products of all kinds are thrown open for patentisation. "Health for all", an undertaking made by India internationally, will be a victim of surrender to TRIPs pressure. Beware! The poor shall not spare but would rather dare in despair.

The Union Government is moving the *new amendments apparently under the TRIPs Circean spell,* although I hold the view that by a people-oriented interpretation and national resistance, based on grim realities, we can salvage a substantial portion of our existing statute. Let me recall Articles 7 and 8 of the TRIPs Agreement:

Article 7 Objectives—The protection and enforcement of intellectual property rights should contribute to the promotion of technological innovation and to the transfer and dissemination of technology, to the mutual advantage of producers and users of technological knowledge and in a manner conducive to social and economic welfare, and to a balance of rights and obligations.

Article 8 Principles—(1) Members may, in formulating or amending their national laws and regulations, adopt measures necessary to protect public health and nutrition, and to promote the public interest in sectors of vital importance to their socio-economic and technological development, provided that such measures are consistent with the provisions of this Agreement.

(2) Appropriate measures, provided that they are consistent with the provisions of this Agreement, may be needed to prevent the abuse of intellectual property rights by right-holders or the resort to practices which unreasonably restrain trade or adversely affect the international transfer of technology.

Justice B.P. Jeevan Reddy, in a lucid lecture, explains a vital difference between Process Patent and Product Patent.

"Patents are of two kinds - product parents and process patents. If the result of a new process is a new article or a better article or a cheaper article than that produced by an old method, that process is patentable and is called the process patent. In other words, a new and the alternative method of arriving at the same result, irrespective of whether that result is better or cheaper, is patentable. As against this a product patent means the grant of a monopoly right to produce that product which necessarily means preventing any other person from producing the same product, whether improved or otherwise, and even by adopting a different or new process, for the period of patent. The Rajagopala Ayyangar Committee advisably and wisely, if I may say so with respect, recommended for providing legal protection only *to process patents and not to product patents."*

The battle between *process* patent and *product* patent can be largely eliminated by a stiff Indian stance. Value of life, law and order, moral standards and cultural heritage are inviolable and non-negotiable. Whole rural communities will break the amended patent law when confronted by starvation and death as a consequence. Trips versus Terrorism is apt to be the dialectical contradiction. The choice is obvious. The 1970 Act, with humanist concern, makes compassionate exclusions. Let me quote Justice Jeevan Reddy:

"While defining the expression 'medicine or drug' in such expansive terms, the Act took care to exclude several matters from the purview of "invention". Section 3 sets out matters which cannot be treated as inventions. Among the matters so excluded in section 3 are "(h) a method of agriculture or horticulture; (i) any process for the medicinal, surgical, curative, prophylactic or other treatment of human beings or any process for a similar treatment of animals or plants to render them free of disease or to increase their economic value or that of their products. Almost 90 per cent of the drugs and medicines produced in the world are produced by about ten multinational corporations in the world located in the USA, Germany, Switzerland, the U.K. and probably the Netherlands. These multinational

companies say that they are constantly inventing new medicines to treat human and animal ailments and plant diseases. They say that they have to and have been spending billions of dollars on research, that only a few of the products into which research is conducted prove to be successful from a commercial point of view and that to enable them to carry on this research activity it is essential that they should be allowed to have a patent for the product invented by them so as to reimburse themselves for the cost of research undertaken by them. Since their products are sold all over the world, they prefer uniform patent laws, that is, product patents, modelled upon the patent laws of the advanced countries. In short, they want to impose product patents on all those countries where it does not exist - and India is one of them.

"At this juncture, I may point out to a popular but true example illustrating the consequences of the product patent system and the process patent system. Glaxo is one of the multinationals. It manufactures, inter alia, *'zenetac', an antacid medicine. It manufactures the said medicine in India, in the U.K. and in the U.S.A. A ten-tablet strip of zenetac costs in India a little above seven rupees, in England it costs more than three hundred rupees and in the USA it costs more than eight hundred rupees. Even in Pakistan it is sold for around one hundred and twenty rupees. You may immediately ask why is Glaxo selling the very same medicine in India at such a cheap price and why is it selling the same in USA at more than hundred times the price in India. That is because in India we do not have product patent. The absence of a product patent has enabled any number of Indian pharmaceutical companies to manufacture antacid tablets with the same properties by different processes, processes which are both cheaper and, may be, better."*

Product patent is a death sentence on indigenous pharmaceuticals. The blunder of signing the Uruguay Round (as later conceded by some Ministers) is an anti-people sell-out. One thing is certain. Any product, to be patentable, needs the triple qualities of (a) novelty (previously unkonwn to the public) (b) non-obviousness (containing sufficient innovativeness to merit protection) and (c) industrial applicability for usefulness. By one broad stroke, all ayurvedic drugs; adivasi recipes, alternative native, medicines, naturopathy, magnetotherapy and yoga therapy, from Charaka and Susruta and Patanjali downwards, familiar in various parts of India and therefore no novelty at all, can be out of the pale of patents. Minimal changes which have nothing to do with the core of it, but impart glittering appearance, attractive packing and sexy advertising magic, cannot be treated as establishing novelty. Ultra-modern manipulation of ancient vintage Indian medicine cannot be fobbed off as patentable merely by using dazzling brand name baloney. Already American pharmaceuticals are taking patents for neem, tulasi, gooseberry and what not? This is a fraud and a scam, not legally permissible.

Dr. Vedaraman, a super-specialist in this legal branch, suggests that the section 2(1) "Invention" has been understood to mean "an invention which must involve an *important technical advancement of considerable economic significance*" in relation to prior art of the matter existing in the public domain on the date of application. Tweedledom to tweedledee is too trivial an innovation.

Process patents are already in our statute although, philosophically speaking, *knowledge is universal and free.* Advance of civilisation or march of science is nor decided by rushing to patents offices. It is doing violence to cultural values to measure prosperity by a profusion of patents. Even assuming that intellectual property (a divine gift) is monopolisable, larger opportunities to make products in the public interest must prevail over vulture-culture greed and profit through patents, sacrificing humanitarian considerations. Life-saving methods must not be market-controlled commodities or services. The worth of the human person is so high that the maximum enlargement of easy availability of such products and process must be legally permissible.

Viewing TRIPs from this megabenevolent angle, Articles 7 and 8 can be liberalised hermaneutically and thereby we may drop the injurious amendments to the Patents Act. When a patent-holder monopolises and practices exclusivity and secrecy so as to contradict "the promotion of innovation", he obstructs dissemination of technology and thus violates Article 7. His operation is not conducive to social and economic welfare. So a specific provision *against* patents whose result will be a socio-economic barrier to India's research and discovery of new pharmaceutical advances is fair. The West cannot claim legitimacy for a stranglehold on Indian progress, using patent right as an iron curtain. Law is for life, science is for "man" and the dignity and worth of the human person shall not suffer "patent servitude". Let us not forsake United Nations fundamentals.

Article 8(1) quoted above has great potential for whittling down the scope for patents which involve life, health and social development vital for the people so pervasively poor as Indians, stricken with ill-health and nutritionally miserable. To exploit sickness and peril to life merely to pamper monopolists is to betray constitutional mandates and global human rights. We cannot allow MNC quislings in Bharar. Ours is a socialistic pattern of society. We have high infant and maternal mortality, famine conditions and fatal syndromes, to cure which medical supplies are an urgent necessity to across the nation. But where is the will to resist predator-corporate power and redeem the tryst with the nearly five hundred hungry million humans? Our patriotic parliamentarians will (must) decline to outrage the conscience of a sixth of mankind through nescience or pusillanimity and invite rebellion against MNC tyranny.

Members (like India, for instance) "may, in formulating or amending their national laws adopt measures necessary to protect public health and nutrition, and to promote the public interest in sectors of vital importance to their socio-economic and technological development". This is TRIPs text. Given semantic sympathy, we can press everything needed to protect and preserve public health, nutrition as well as public interest and technological development, and make drugs to remedy the proliferating maladies victimising the masses and thus save the 1970 Act almost *in toto* as falling within the permissive spaces of TRIPs. Of course, the battle raging round product versus process patent remains, although I take the view that, having grave regard to the grim state of health, fatal diseases, prevalence of penury and inviolable Budda-Gandhi tradition of compassion, the rejection of restrictive *product patent* is reasonable. The Preamble and basic features of the Constitution bind and command this step. Abuse of intellectual property rights by rights-holders and unreasonable restraint on trade and other adverse ploys affecting national concerns can be checked under Article 8(2). Why not dare and do, sustaining the present law, instead of amendments being made to suit corporate palate and pocket?

Article 27(2) gives scope for saving our patent law from corporate claws. The text reads:

> *Members may exclude from patentability inventions, the prevention within their territory of the commercial exploitation of which is necessary to protect order public or morality, including to protect human, animal or plant life or health or to avoid serious prejudice to the environment, provided that such exclusion is not made merely because the exploitation is prohibited by domestic law.*

Let me present a set of interrogatories:

> *Patents in India for goods manufactured outside and imported? Sky-high prices for drugs and commodities needed by poor people in large numbers in our Socialist Republic without state control? Over-publicised goods with erotically appealing and addictive methodology to cerate craving? Manufacture of vicious but tempting consumer items - the Coke craving and Mcdonalds magic which harm health in the long run - may become "the opium of the people", eventually leading to cancer deaths, suicides, bankruptcies, divorces, social disorder, morally degenerative and traditionally obnoxious merchandise, made and sold with malignant monopoly, creating law and order problems, violation of hygiene and the like? No, never! These exotic goods and services are bete noire for the composite cultural heritage of India (Article 51A) and incompatible with social justice basic to our Constitution. To grant a monopoly by way of patent within India, without obliging the producer to manufacture within our country but to import and exploit the market, free from competing Indians, is egregious, absurd and anti-India. The concession of patent must be conditioned by the obligation to make the goods here. Let me cite Sir Robert Reed:*

> *Nothing can be more absurd or more outrageous than that a foreign patentee can come here and get a patent and use it, not for the purpose of encouraging industries of this country but to prevent our people (from) doing otherwise what they would do. To allow our laws to be used to give preference to foreign enterprise is to my mind ridiculous.*

To manufacture cheap outside, import and sell at any price in our market *preventing by law* indigenous producers is almost a definition of colonisation by a foreign power entering India, forbid Indians making the goods but offer a monopoly market. Why concede this dog-in-the-manger strategy? This is a textbook case of the violation of Article 19(1)g and 19(6) of the Constitution. This straragem, it legislatively approved, is a shock and shame and proof of *conquest by patent.* Articles 14 (equal protection of the law), 19 (right to any trade or business) and 21 (right to life in good health) stand stultified if such glaring inequality between Indian products (denied patent) and foreign import of any commodity granted exclusive selling rights with no special benefit to the Indian consumer. This is gross inequality writ large, arbitrary, with no rational nexus to the well-being of "We, the People of India.... (Article 14).

Similarly, Article 19 is unreasonably transgressed. To refuse the non-patentee the right to manufacture the same product, the restriction must be justified constitutionally by reasonable grounds relatable to public interest. For the surrender of a non-patentee's Article 19 rights, what is the substantial public interest for Indians? No other ground save that MNC Might is Right. And "the most unkindest cut of all" is that by the grant of parents on even agriculture, pharmaceuticals and essential items necessary for the life of the community, Article 21 - the right to life, health, shelter - is frustrated.

Can free trade warrant trading away our freedom? But that is the result if the bill goes through as introduced.

However, by interpretative enlargement, Article 27(2) of TRIPs can be turned to India's advantage by exclusion from patentability any invention on grounds of "*order public* or morality." Non-patentability, so as to protect human, animal or plant life or health or to avoid prejudice to the environment, is valid under TRIPs. So a large area of manufacture can be kept out of bounds for patents, having regard to Hindu religious sentiment of Vedic vintage, with its worshipful concern for plants and animals, ecology and environment.

The government has moved the Patents Amendment Bill proposing to amend the Patents Act 39 of 1970 which, in the past, has been a major success in the legislative field for the promotion of the health of the people and the advancement of industry and agriculture. Assuming that some amendments are necessary, how far do the amending provisions stand the scrutiny of reasonableness and constitutional compatibility?

TRIPS must be read down as its broad objective is:

1. "to ensure that developing countries... secure a share in the growth in international trade commensurate with the needs of their economic development". To quote a statement made by the government in an international forum, "developed countries have utilised the WTO system to obtain legitimacy for their own ptotectionist policies", and they continue with their trade barriers. So I urge Parliament to reject WTO super-sovereign hold.
2. Members may, in formulating or amending their national laws and regulations, adopt measures necessary to protect public health and nutrition, and to promote the public interest in sectors of vital importance to their socio-economic and "technological development, provided that such measure are consistent with the provisions of this Agreement".

We have room for interpretive benevolence:

A report produced for the United Nations Development Programme (UNDP) says that TRIPS was signed before most governments and people understood the social and economic implications of parents. Third World TRIPs must be protected: Union Law Minister (The Hindu Business Line, February 12, 2000). The Minister stated that the rights of the poor and developing countries must be safeguarded while enforcing TRIPs laws. He also added that "although India was taking to a free market society, India had a constitutional obligation to provide assistance to the poor".

WHO DAP Series No. 7 (Health Economics and Drugs) has recommended that any drug on the WHO Model List of Essential Drugs should be the object of a compulsory licence for public health reasons. The WHO report also states that a certain number of 'sensitive' provisions of the TRIPs agreement, particularly the general principles concerning the protection of health, the obligation to work the patent locally, anti-competitive practices, and the exclusive marketing rights conferred during the period of transition, will necessarily be subject to interpretation in their application.

A throughtful quote from a paper by B.K. Keayla, an expert on Patentisation:

The raw materials from India were exported and value-added finished goods a monopolistic prices were sold in Indian markets. The industry was dominated by MNCs. They were reaping enormous profits from the Indian markets. An American Senate Committee, headed by Senator Kefauver, stated in 1959 in its report that the prices of drugs in India were "amongst the highest in the world.

The 1970 Patents Act helped the development of the industry through certain salient provisions.

These included the exclusion of certain fields basic to India's economy and the well-being of the Indian people from patentability; the denial of product patents in some other important areas such as drugs and pharmaceuticals and agro-chemicals, provision of a shorter period of patent protection: importation not being treated as working of a patent; the compulsory licensing and licence of right to ensure working and dissemination of technologies and the fixing of a ceiling on royalties on the sub-licensing of patents. Thus balancing of rights and obligations and ensuring that patent monopolies are not established. Because of these features, Indian industry, during the post 1970 period after the new parent system was introduced, progressed quite satisfactorily.

The number of producers in India rose from 5,000 to 24,000, and prices came down. India should not be tripped or trapped by TRIPs. TRIPs as the West construes it is a death warrant for the lowly, the lost and the last who have no wherewithal to buy hiked high-priced medicines when hit by lethal illness.

This prefarory caveat serves as the nationalist perspective for a critique of the new legislative essay.

The patent system legally ensures the working of the patent in the country, which grants the patent rights. Imports beyond a specified period are being regarded as abuse of patent rights and for this reason the imports are being used as one of the reasons for the grant of sub-licensing to others. A system of compulsory licensing has thus been provided in national laws. Compulsory licences are granted by the national governments for upholding the public interest.

In India, automatic licensing of rights has also been provided for certain products in the public interest for ensuring working of patents in a competitive environment. This right is mainly available for chemicals-based products like pharmaceuticals. As regards the term of the patent, it varies from country to country. India has had only 5 to 7 year terms for process patents for pharmaceuticals and other chemical-based products and 14 years for other products, whereas the U.S. held a uniform term of 17 years for all patents and now it has changed to 20 years because of TRIPs.

The TRIPs patent system now seeks uniform patent laws for all member countries of the WTO although their economics vary vastly.

According to the U.S. Supreme Court, "it is undeniably true that the limited and temporary monopoly granted to inventors was never designed for their exclusive profit or advantage, the benefit to the public or community at large was another and doubleness to the primary object in granting and securing that monopoly". (Quoted in Vaughan 1956, 32). But now this objective is being totally ignored in providing a global, strong patent system in TRIPs. (Keayla).

The Patents Act, 1970 has encouraged the manufacture of bulk drugs and formulations in India and the emergence of a very strong national pharmaceutical industry. The positive environment provided by the Act has resulted in much lower prices in India than elsewhere in the world. The prices are five to 30 times higher in countries which have product patent.

The above scenario is directly related to the "patent system" as practised in these countries. It is the same enterprise which is charging highly differential prices in different countries as it is possible to exploit the markets on the consideration of the extent of patent monopoly available.

More appropriately, let me draw the attention of the people of India, particularly the parliamentarians and party leaders, to the consequences of the Treaties entered into, costing us the essence of *swaraj* itself. The WTO is an assault on India's sovereignty. India is now Treaty bound to lift perhaps all quantitative restrictions on imports and all non-tariff restrictions on such imports. What a pity that constitutionally we have bidden farewell to constitutional values by reducing customs duty sharply to facilitate free trade for lawful loot. Food and food products, milk and milk products (with the largest cattle population we have in the country) agricultural products, including cotton and rubber, industrial goods, manufactured elsewhere at cheaper cost to flood our markets and starve our rural and urban people—is this socialist, Gandhian economics? Our public sector is being dismantled and our private sector will pine away and perish or be absorbed by MNCs. Small-scale industries are all on their way to the grave. In short, we are to suffer foreign domination and are all on our way to recolonisation. This I call GATTastrophe.

Let us not worry about MNC pharmaceutical withdrawals if we do not oblige them with patent law for products. Dr. Dinesh Patel of the Indian Drug Manufacturers Association (IDMA), an expert in the field, has stated:

> *Many of the well-known discoveries by international pharmaceutical companies, are mere molecular manipulations of existing patented drugs.*

He pointed out:

> *In the case of Terracycline, an antibiotic, Pfizer had modified its molecule to create and promote a new drug Oxycterracycline. This was further developed to Doxycycline, then Doxycycline Hicalte, again by molecular manipulation. Interestingly, all these drugs enjoyed patent protection. Now, Doxycycline Hicalte is marketed at Rs. 10 per tablet, while the same product is sold by Indian manufacturers at Rs. 2 per tablet. This kind of monopolistic situation created by multinationals would get stronger after India goes in for product patent law. Right now, the process patent law prevalent in India has created a level playing field, ruling out monopolistic situations arising from molecular manipulations.*

A global study will reveal the skulduggery of the MNCs and the Indian indigent will be forgotten by his own surrogates if product patent is granted to keep transnational corporations in exploitative good humour.

A plea in anguish to Parliament members from a layperson with concern to preserve the jurisprudence of human health for Indians; you, as proud India's humble servants, should oppose and defeat the bill before Parliament, I am sure that the two Houses, the Health Ministry, the Prime Minister and the plural parties in our country will collectively ensure the sovereign right of Indians to battle against foreign pharmaceuticals' invasion at least to save the life and health of India's teeming millions. If you stand by the poor and defend the current Law of Patents 1970, that will be parliament's finest hour! With patriotic confidence in your unreserved support, I conclude.

PEOPLE'S COMMISSION ON PERVERSION OF OUR PATENT LAWS

When the economic history of Independent India comes to be written with the vision and passion of the Founding Fathers of our Constitution, the perversion of our excellent Patents Act 1970 and the subversion of our national interests through GATT treaties will be condemned as brazen betrayal of people's concerns committing the country to global corporate commands. This humiliating syndrome has been called GATTastrophe and Operation Recolonisation. The Report of the People's Commission on Patent Law for India, which is the book under review, exposes, stage by stage, the shameful story of the Government of India's unfortunate surrender and political cover-up landing the nation in a situation where people's battles for winning back Patent Swaraj, inside parliament and through campaigns outside, are necessitous.

Patents are monopolies and monopolies are evil unless regulated by law designed to serve social justice, national interests and pragmatic considerations. Patents have come to stay the world over and India inherited a colonial system which was overthrown by a fine piece of legislation—the Indian Patents Act, 1970—based on the brilliant, balanced Ayyangar Commission Report. Public interest was in the forefront but foreign patent holders also had a fair deal. The Americans held the largest number of patents under the 1970 Act. The philosophy of the Indian legislation is that patents are granted to promote inventions to be worked in this country on a commercial scale without undue delay. Only *process* patents, not *product* patents for food, medicine and agro-chemicals. No profit from pain and suffering and no patents for living matter and other vital items of national concern. Public interest mechanisms like compulsory licensing, licenses of right and revocation, these and other pro bono provisions made the Indian Act a glory that benefited the people, stimulated native pharmaceuticals and saved the health of the nation from the grab rapacity of foreign corporate operators. Says Keayla, who has a life-long record of study of Indian pharmaceutical jurisprudence and commitment to Indian humanity, has authoritatively stressed, with facts and figures, how our benign law kept prices down *vis a vis* Pakistan, UK, USA *et al.* It is because of our patent system that the price differential is so favourable for us.

Had not the 1970 Act arrested prices of medicines and given incentives for phenomenal pharmaceutical development India would have been in a crisis instead of being the lowest in relation to the glaring differences in product patent regimes. Likewise the availability of new products and medicines from indigenous sources would have been hard had our dependence on imports been the main source. The truth is that the finest hour of pharmaceutical jurisprudence arrived with the 1970 Act but the decline and fall of health for all began with the Uruguay Round of GATT and the Dunkel Draft Text. The right to medical care for the humblest human is integral to the Alma Ata Declaration (1979) in which India, among 134 nations, pledged urgent action and the resolution of the 38th World Health Assembly gave this promise practical shape.

Nevertheless, American pressure mounted, Uruguay Round negotiations made September 1986 the beginning of the end of the great days of Indian Patent Law. GATTastrophe, if one may express the Patent Law tragedy graphically, found the Indian Government a *soft State.* Indeed, Government was playing hide and seek with Parliament and pretended to be resistant to the retaliatory threat of the U.S. Trade Act (Super 301 and Special 301). This was evasive comedy and contradictory. There was public opinion mounting against Government's surrender to the Dunkel Draft. Indeed, in between, the Gujral Departmental Related Parliamentary Standing Committee on Commerce in its Third Report (1993-94) was critical of Government's ambivalence.

Alas, at Marrakesh (1994) without parliamentary approval the Central Executive signed away India's commercial independence. The deed was done, the WTO treaty was signed—sans serious parliamentary debate. Government ratified the Final Act of GATT and the 'fifth act' of the tragedy was completed. Any important international treaty innocent of parliamentary ratification is guilty of sabotage of democracy—a fundamental flaw overlooked by our Founding Fathers while framing the Constitution. The Constitution Review Committee headed by Justice Venkitachaliah has drawn attention to this basic blemish. Anyway, the Marrakesh signature of 1994 obligated India to implement TRIPS, trade related Intellectual Property Rights (IPR) Agreement. Thus the nationwide opposition to TRIPS became futile and the struggle was to salvage people's rights as much as possible out of the traumatic TRIPS patent system. Government went ahead with The Patent Amendment Ordinance, 1994. The bill to replace the ordinance was opposed but passed in the Lok Sabha where the Government had a majority. However, in the Rajya Sabha, Government had no majority and so the bill was referred to a Select Committee of the House. Meanwhile political events, consequent on the dissolution of the Lok Sabha in May 1996, led to the lapse of the bill. During the budget session of Parliament in March 1999 a bill was passed varying the provisions Act of 1970. A subsequent parliamentary committee of both houses submitted a report and a fresh bill as revised was finally passed in May 2002, with 64 amendments. The discussion in parliament was powerful and voiced on the floor of the House the importance of affordability, accessibility, and availability of drugs to all sections of society. Vain words!

The passage of the bill is not the last word on the law and the life of the people. Creative criticism cannot be silenced until Patents Jurisprudence comes to human terms with social justice. Murassoli Maran at Doha demanded deep concern for the welfare of the Indian people while interpreting and applying the TRIPS agreement. We must begin the battle for change. Parliament must speak for US, not for the U.S. The present People's Commission is an expression of this desideratum. Headed by Sri I.K. Gujral this eminent collective of intellectuals is a powerful mission capable of informing public opinion and illumining parliamentary cerebration. Look at the composition. Gujral's great experience, Dr. Yusuf Hamied's specialisation par excellence, Rajiv Dhavan's superlative juristic expertise and the distinguished participation of Muchkund Dubey, Ashok Parthasarathy and Yash Pal command compelling attention. The wisdom of the commission has resulted in positive recommendations of an extensive nature and I am sure the whole problem of patents may have to be subjected to luminous re-examination.

Dr. Yusuf Hamied, Managing Director, CIPLA is a pharmaceutical celebrity and humanist researcher whose universally recognised contribution to the curative dimension of AIDS deserves tribute. Each member of the People's Commission is an excellent choice. Let us listen to them.

One weighty view of the Commission needs emphatic mention.

> *India is a vast and poor country. Our Constitution in its Preamble provides that India is a Sovereign Socialist Secular Democratic Republic. It is thus obligatory on the part of the government that the people of the country are directly or indirectly apprised of the major economic issues. The people of the country have to be taken into confidence and there should be no question of maintaining any secrecy about the handling of WTO issues. A system has to be devised whereby people are able to debate and also there is debate in parliament to ensure arriving at national consensus on such issues.*
>
> *(Report of the Peoples' Commission Patent Laws for India, P-110)*

Articles 73 and 253 (the relevant treaty provisions) have to be so exercised by the Union Government as to bring the treaty *under the Constitution, not over it.* You cannot barter away the sovereignty of People of India by entering into a treaty making the country a vassal or colony of another. Such a treaty would be repugnant to the basic features of the Constitution.

Eventhough, the Patent (Second Amendment) Act, 2002 has been passed into law in May 2002, the plenary power of Parliament is not exhausted and the Supreme Court power to pronounce any provision of the treaty violative of the basic structure of the Constitution may still be exercised.

It must be remembered, as the commission reminds us:

> *TRIPs itself leaves open many matters for future consideration. Secondly, more importantly, treaties evolve and change over time in response to exigent needs. Before 1994, the international patent regime was very different from that which emerged under the aegis of the WTO treaty. A decade is a long time in such matters, India needs to approach the WTO and TRIPs with wide angled lenses so that the long term perspective is as much as they affect India's national interest and the interest of other nations is also not overlooked. (Report of the Peoples' Commission Patent Laws for India, P-92)*

The scope of patentability is a core issue. Article 27 of the TRIPS agreement covers not merely an inventive step but capability of industrial application. The Indian parliament can read down the meaning of 'invention' in such manner that it serves national interest. India is passing through a scenario of transition from process to product patent which has great relevance to pharma industry. All our ayurvedic wealth, herbal medicines and tribal recipes involve no novelty to an Indian and should not be available for patentisation under the western illusion of glittering packages and trivial tampering, to produce a seeming dilution and claiming the right to a patent.

Compulsory licensing system is extremely important to ensure the role of domestic enterprises to provide adequate availability of patented products. India's provision of licensing of right under the 1970 Act helped a great deal. The pharma industry has prices lowest in the world. The Commission has made flexible recommendations in formulating its compulsory licencing system.

The term of patents for twenty years is too long, taking the practical view that products become obsolete sooner. Therefore, we must insist on a shorter period suggested by realism. Pricing of patented products is very relevant for a country like India. Therefore, prices of patented products need to be regulated to safeguard the interests of the poor. Already seventy per cent. of the population cannot reach medicines. Therefore, affordable prices should be our slogan, so that the vast masses are not priced out of the market. Other recommendations of the Commission need expert examination. The Minister of Commerce and Industry has indicated that there will be another bill *viz.* the Patent (3rd Amendment) Bill which will be introduced before 1-1-2005. This is an occasion when a comprehensive study of the lacunae in the existing system and the necessity for flexibility in various provisions may be considered closely. Indian legislation must serve Indian reality *vis a vis* health resources and access, especially in times of emergencies.

> *8.31 The Doha Ministerial Declaration of November 2001 has already laid down a comprehensive work programme. Based on our past experience of Uruguay Round of GATT negotiations it would be in fitness of things if the*

> *new issues are first debated in Parliament. The government can prepare approach papers on various issues and then the same could be presented for debate in Parliament and if need be also in the State Legislative Assemblies. The constitutional provision is extremely important for the democratic system to survive in this country. Report of the Peoples' Commission on Patent Laws for India, P-112)*

The right to life of billion-strong Indian humanity—We, the People of India—is the ultimate accountability of our Indian Democratic Republic. People first, TRIPS next.

DON'T BE TRAPPED BY TRIPS

The Bretton Woods Conference (1944) inaugurated a fresh drive, imparted a new dimension and generated a paradigm shift *vis a vis* the western leaders by a switch in Weltanschauung from Global Military Supremacy to a World Trade Dominancy. War or Peace, the focus was on greedy grab of global business. A materialist metamorphosis, from bleeding conquests by wars under various pretexts to gobbling up markets by bullying ploys, trade traps and treaties under threats—that is the blitz-striking success. Resources of weaker nations are currently under a predatory process of glowing globalisation minted to mean, according to Orwellian double-speak 'rob-grab globocracy by Gargantuan xenophilic Corporatocracy. Kleptocracy is the locomotive for launching Operation Big Business. The Hidden Agenda behind the Bretton Woods voodoos, such as IMF, World Bank, Multilateral Trade Negotiations has been commercial subjugation of nations by bizarre methods like IPR and other mystic acronyms. The most important and intriguing development during the GATT process was the Uruguay Round of Multilateral Trade Negotiations. What was won was a great advance by manipulating the serendipitous inclusion of TRIPS in the Punta Del Este (Uruguay Round). Naive nations like India gave in to knave *quasi*-imperial *arm-twisting*. Some of our team, one suspects, spoke *not for us* but *for the U.S.*, according to critics—a la V.C. Shukla. To-day, some of them are in the WTO camp! Why? How? Defection or affection?

TRIPS is the offspring of GATT and is the product of seven long years of dialogues and negotiations from September 1986 to December 1993. These dubious confabulations and diplomatic pressures were formally finished in April 1994 at Marrakesh, Morocco. TRIPs came into force on January 1, 1995 with the establishment of the WTO. The GATT, with imperious authority governs global trade, and the international instrumentality which rules from a super-sovereign height is the WTO. Many statesmen of the Third World have condemned GATT as GATTastrophe, while the Indian Establishment, with a procession of Prime Ministers and Finance and Commerce Ministers have made make-believe dissents, but obeyed the WTO. In short, notwithstanding victimisation of the masses, deepening poverty and unemployment and mobilisation of opposition by NGOs and social activists, the World Corporate Might marches on. 'The dogs may bark, the caravan will pass', is the cavalier mood of the GATT 'junta' drawn from the ruling class.

Among the most controversial of the GATT treaties is TRIPS—the V-weapon in Operation Globalisation. 'The tryst to wipe every tear from every eye' made by Prime Minister Nehru when India celebrated its Freedom is forgotten and Imperial acronyms like TRIPs, TRIMs, TRIS, WIPO, MAI and what not, dominate Cabinets, Parliaments and perhaps even the Judicature. Quo Vadis Indian Socialistic Democracy, Sovereignty and Constitutional Supremacy? These are the dialectics, dilemmas and challenges which demand debate, not 'zero hour' sound and fury nor polemic pandemonium. The spinal issues of great moment go by default. Political parties, with babels and bedlams, exaggerate local and regional tremendous trifles inside and outside the House—a scenario of pathos and bathos, while xenophilic policies and legislations and obliging anti-people, pro-MNC budgetary mutations get implemented without protest. While Opposition Parties, apart from strident stalemates, do no eloquent, dialectical, people-oriented inquests, TRIPs and other fatal treaties are executed, by the Treasury Bench, behind the people's backs. So India succumbs to GATTastrophe and TRIPs syndrome. Trading Indian Economic Freedom for Trade-Related IPRs is *re-colonisation*!

Now to the odyssey of Intellectual Property Rights. Jayashree Watal's book on IPR is all about this enigmatic theme. TRIPs has the inscrutable face of the sphinx. East and West interpret this treaty as suits their interests and WTO resoles disputes often in favour of the North. 'Fair is foul and foul is fair'—depends on who is West and who is East.

> *Intellectual property rights (IPRs) are legal rights governing the use of creations of the human mind. This term covers a bundle of rights, such as patents, trade-marks or copyrights, each different in scope and duration with a different purpose and effect. The mundane object generally is to exclude third parties from exploiting protected subject-matter without explicit authorization of the right holder, for a certain duration of time. Monopoly, sans humanism, is the essence of patents without fear of loss or control over their use. Do IPRs help creative and inventive activity of orderly marketing of proprietary goods and services? No, alas, no.*

What a pity, today, the world is macro-victim of MNCs which corner, through patents, life-saving drugs. They hold humanity to ransom! India has an excellent legislation which serves industrial and agricultural advance, promotes people's health and is subject to State control in public interest. Our pharmaceutical progress is phenomenal and our law of patents is *compassion in action*. We may be soon tripped by TRIPS in many ways and so our parliamentarians have to be on their guard with vigilant humanism, as each clause of the Amending Bill is passed.

The author, who was involved in the Uruguay Process, sums up tersely the anatomy of TRIPS. (the quote is long but its content is cardinal).

Apart from being the first international intellectual property agreement to dramatically increase the level of minimum standards of such law, TRIPS is also the first international property law agreement—

- *that obliges in a undertaking new standards on as many as seven types of IPRs (namely, copyrights and related rights, trademarks, geographical indications, industrial designs, patents, layout designs of integrated circuits, and undisclosed information) for a many as 138 countries/territories (as on July 2000).*
- *To be inclined as a part of the rules governing in multilateral trading system, thus marrying trade law and jurisprudence with intellectual property law, particular making applicable the swifts.*
- *Throughout this book the terms developed countries or South are loosely used to define the crucial difference between those who demanded rules on strengthened IPR protection in the global trading system and those who opposed them. The picture is complicated as national interested differ with particular sectors and particular IPRs. These complication influenced the positions of different countries during these negotiations.*
- *If protection of client varieties is taken separately. The only substantive area of intellectual property left out is utility models, which are a weaker form of patents, sometime referred to as pity patents in this area, member of the WTO are free to legislate under the overall framework laid down in the Paris Convention.*
- *For example, the concept of most-favoured-nation treatment has been extended to IPRs under TRIPS. Also, some parts of the TRIPS text uses language identical to that used in JATT, 1947. Consequently, the first panel and the effective dispute settlement process of the WTO, which can impose trade penalties on members violating the agreement.*
- *That includes fairly detailed standards for domestic enforcement of IPRs both internally and at the border.*
- *That obliges protection of new type of IPRs even in developed countries, of which at least one, undisposed information, has never been the subject of any multilateral agreement before, and another, protection for integrated circuit designs, had no effective international treaty, while others like planned variety protection or performers' rights, were geographically limited.*
- *That covers new subject matter under existing types of intellectual property, at least for some developing countries, such as protect patents for food, pharmaceuticals, chemicals, microorganisms or copyright protection for software,*
- *That creates new categories of rights under existing types intellectual property of the majority of the WTO members such as rental right for*

computer programmes and sound regarding(and for films under certain circumstances) under copyright and related rights, higher level of protection for geographical indications for wines and spirits, reversal of burden of proof for process patentees, and

- *That incorporates a text on the control of anti-competitive practices in the licensing of IPRs in a binding treaty.*

We have, as of 1970, an excellent Patent Law. Process patent, not product patent, restrictions in public interest and life-saving drugs and agriculture are of special concern. Brevity of patent term and compulsory licensing are in public interest. Process patent law, with a human face, is allergy to GATT geared to greed, even as product patent has a pick-pocket proclivity, forbidding rival research. This value contradiction is inevitable when MNCs operate for mega-profits and *our* Constitution desiderates social justice.

Jayashree Watal has chosen to dwell at length on TRIPs, scholarly fashion, of course, with a Westward slant wrapped in academic apparel. The agony of impact on Indian masses hardly troubles bosoms of pro-WTO intellectuals. Her book makes indispensable reading for all those involved in intellectual property rights, pro-TRIPs litigants and lawyers, jurists and MNC propagandist puppeteers. This painstaking book does credit to the author's presentation, although I, as reviewer, must confess that I am critical of TRIPs as destructive of India's development. The competence of the author has added value since she was participating in the formative Uruguay operations. Our Parliament is currently discussing amendments to patent law. It is tragic to jettison that precious legislation of 1970; but under evil pressure from semi-imperial forces, Parliament is yielding at the expense of the people of India. Even so, *Article 7* sets out a seemingly noble objective. It provides explicitly that the protection and enforcement of intellectual property rights should contribute to the *promotion of technological innovation* and for purposes conducive to social and economic welfare. Why not explore the farthest frontiers of these words with semantic amplitude? *Article 8* permits adoption of measures 'necessary to protect public health and to promote the public interest in sectors of vital importance to their socio-economic and technological development'. The battle for 'patent; justice is supported by this broad phraseology. Article 27, dealing with patentable subject-matter, allows members to exclude from patentability inventions, the prevention within their territory of the commercial exploitation of which is necessary *to protect ordre public or morality, including to protect human, animal or plant life or health or to avoid serious prejudice to the environment.* Vast is the meaning if your heart is with the people. These provisions, if imaginatively, humanistically and compassionately construed with hermeneutic harmony promotive of the Preamble to our Constitution, may go a long way to save many of our present provisions and reject the vicious ambition of Big Corporations 'red in tooth and claw'. Our constitutional values are paramount and I insist that our jurists and law makers, our judges and academics, should give priority to humanity than to dollaroniat. The law of patents is not the vanishing point of humanist jurisprudence but serves to solace the life and suffering of the people of Bharat.

I wish our MPs presented the kindly side of the case—sans noisy walk-outs. As an Indian aware of ground realities, certain damaging dimensions of TRIPS could have been exposed by Jayashree Watal. Her book is factual, true, but the plea for the humble humans goes by default.

Many people in our country are not familiar with the new developments in the modern science of biotechnology. In a chapter titled Plants, Genes and Bio-diversity. Jayashree has much instructive material to offer. TRIPS and its relevance to biotechnology are discussed with clarity. She rightly points out that the U.S. belief that anything under the sun made by man except human being was patentable is egregious. Indian readers will be interested to read Articles 7, 8 and 27.3 (b) of TRIPS, which set some useful parameters.

But what is the definition of a microorganism. Here again is disputed area. It is instructive to read the description in Chapter 5 on this subject. Watal takes the position—

> *However, given the existing technological gap between developed and developing countries under the capital-intensive nature of product development, the best way forward for developing countries seems to be collaboration and not confrontation.* *(Page 183 of the book)*

I am not sure whether surrender is an easy solution to a problem so intricate and affecting the interests of a billion Indians.

Copyright and related rights have come in for through examination in the book. So too, trademarks and geographical indications. To deal with them in detail will take more space than a review can permit. Nevertheless, I must emphasize the importance to India of geographical indications—a la basmati rice.

TRIPS is really a conquest by patent of developing countries. WTO has effective mechanisms for monitoring and ensuring compliance with TRIPs standards. Generally speaking, the dispute settlement mechanism of WTO may not favour India or like countries when pitted against American might or like MNC giants. The fight is likely to be rough, resulting in an exchange of difficult concessions between the 'demandeuse' and others. The struggle to modify TRIPs in favour of developing countries is an urgent necessity but boneless Ministers and spagetti-spine politicians leading Third World Countries must stand up with guts to battle for their rights.

One concluding caveat. Jayashree's industrious process and persuasive product deserve study. But her readers must remember that there are critics who hold that TRIPS harbours Hidden Agendas dangerous to our swaraj.

WTO HO!

Fair is foul, and foul is fair
Hover through the fog and filthy air (Shakespeare Macbeth)

Long years ago we made a tryst with destiny, and now the time comes when we shall redeem our pledge, not wholly or in full measure, but very substantially. At the stroke of the midnight hour, when the world sleeps, India will awake to life and freedom. A moment comes, which comes but rarely in history, when we step out from the old to the new, when an age ends, and when the soul of a nation, long suppressed, finds utterance. It is fitting that at this solemn moment we take the pledge of dedication to the service of India and her people and to the still larger cause of humanity.

(Framing of India's Constitution p-558)

This grand prose, this sublime pledge, this noble national commitment reinforced by the constellation of solemn promises enshrined in the Constitution—these are not mere glorious diction but inviolable values inscribed in the suprema lex, not by moral midgets and political charlatans but by the finest minds with patriotic fervour. They are fundamental sentiments establishing a profound compact with the entire people of India and the generations of humans who had longed for long to be liberated from political, economic, social and cultural bondage. That vision which was the foundation of our total revolution demanded a sense of history and of destiny, a dimension of people's democracy and a vibrant will never, never to surrender to feudal and colonial forces and ever, ever to battle for *poorna swaraj* in its meaning of meanings, not cunning of cabals, Quislings of corruption and the great vulgar middle class and yuppies crazily suffering from consumerist syndrome. And yet, a great betrayal of Bharat's masses is rapidly riding forward, making a disaster wear the apparel of victory, shattering what little had been achieved, disintegrating by design what socialistic achievements had been made. Now 'foul is fair', socialism and secularism are anathema and India has Unpeople, We, the People having been invisibly eliminated. The vintage words of Napoleon Bonaparte are now the basic feature of governance:

There is only one thing in this world, and that is to keep acquiring money and more money, power and more power. All the rest is meaningless. (*Pilger p-445*)

We have manufacture of foreign cars, importation of fashionable goods and gadgets, fast food services, five-star lifestyle invitations for exploitative foreign investments and a glut of glossy technological goods appealing to the appetite of the glitteratti. 'Westoxication' goes to the head and reckless borrowings, regardless of ability to repay, are freely undertaken. The whole policy of self-reliance, sobre *swadeshi* and development through appropriate technology with a view to live within the means and resources of the country—these values have been jettisoned. To scuttle the shop of ship of State with xenophelic temptation has a traitor's touch. Gandhiji had cautioned against insatiable, endlessly multiplied needs. 'In so far as we have made the modern materialistic craze our goal so far are we going downhill in the path of progress.' But Gandhiyan values lie buried five fathoms deep and MNCs with their tantalizing tactics have won 'open sesame' from the Mughals in Delhi. 16 years of Nehruvian regime with a Planning Commission geared to democratic socialist transformation, creation of a public sector to occupy the commanding heights of the economy, promotion of agrarian reforms, green revolution and brown revolution and blue revolution—these and other developmental emphases on rural masses have met with their Waterloo with the greedy globalisation grab ideology took over. Small-scale industries are waiting for their grave increasing unemployment is virtually encouraged by bringing in TNCs high-tech minionising work force. The poor and their privation have no relevance to the new-fangled concept of 'progress'. Growth without distributive justice is the dominant economics on which the development methods are now based. True, long ago, Winston Churchill said: Beware, beware I say, on the gleaming wings of science what is showered as blessings will throw humanity back to the stone age.' I am quoting from memory but the essential sense is made out:

What is Development for the Third World

The purpose of development should not be to develop things, but to develop Men.

In the early years of independence in the Third World, right up to the end of the First Development Decade in 1970, a single model dominated the thinking and efforts of developing countries, development agencies and aid donors alike. Development, all but a few radical spirits agreed, involved following the yellow brick road painted by Western societies towards an Oz of industrialisation and consumerism. All countries should be striving for a society of skyscrapers, with televisions in every home, cars in every garage and combine harvesters in the fields, with everyone working in humming factories and carpeted offices.

(Third World Tomorrow p-23)

Time was when generations of law graduates were taught that international law was the vanishing point of jurisprudence. The truth of today is that jurisprudence is the vanishing point of international treaties designed to aid and abet powerful M.N.Cs. hungering to gain entry for predatory operations. GATT is one such treaty of global operation. Its nidus and sanctions are not Conventions and World Court pronouncements but the Might of Great Powers deemed as global Right. M.N.Cs., largely America Inc., control the New World Economic Order with the weaker nations having little options to reject the commands of Capitol Hill and White House and other mini-imperialisms disguised as treaties with seemingly fair enforcement mechanisms. Way back in 1918, Woodrow Wilson, campaigning for U.S. Presidency, said:

> The masters of the Government of the United States are the combined capitalists and manufacturers of the United States, it is written over every intimate page of the record of Congress, it is written all through the history of conferences at the White House, that the suggestions of economic policy have come from one source, not from many sources.... The Government of the United States at present is a foster child of the special interests.
>
> *(America Inc. p-29)*

And what is the major motivation of World Capitalist Corporates? In the words of Napolean Bonaparte:

> There is only one thing in this world, and that is to keep acquiring money and more money, power and more power. All the rest is meaningless. *(Hidden Agendas p-445)*

After World War II, the U.S. with other Big Powers decided to gain the same imperial goal by a paradigm shift. At the Bretton Woods Conference, instead of the World Military Order, was woven, with the gun primed to shoot if necessary, the World Trade Order. This new global business strategy was cannily spun, among others, primarily through several rounds of delicate negotiations winning nascent and soft states. Persuasion, when sufficient, pressure when necessary, and quasi-military measures and minatory methods when alternatives did not work! And surrender syndrome of developing nations helped the progress of the global game. Corruption purchased conquest, often without military hardware. A blend of militant diplomacy, trade embargo and other dubious stratagems were in the Big Business armoury. Markets, not men, mattered for Corporations which had no body to be burnt nor soul to be damned.

Do not deceive your conscience by the illusion that UNO was ready at Manhattan to defend freedoms of all nations and human rights of the peoples of the earth. For America two voices were there. First, as key player in the UNO with 188 members—a constellation of stars, big and small, twinkling like an omnipotence in the sky—and the other a hungry, angry collective corporate Gargantua conquering market after market using such verbal blossoms and Orwellian double-speak like Globalisation, Liberalisation and Privatisation. Right at the beginning, (1948) this U.S.

moral contradiction was evident. Let me quote from Pilger's book Hidden Agendas:

Everyone has the right to work, to just and favourable conditions of work and to protection for himself and his family (and) an existence worthy of human dignity... everyone has the right to a standard of living adequate for the health and well being of himself and his family, including food, clothing, housing and medical care.

Universal Declaration of Human Rights, 1948

We have 50 per cent of the world's wealth, but only 6.3 per cent of its population. In this situation, our real job in the coming period is to devise a pattern of realtionships which permit us to maintain this position of disparity. To do so, we have to dispense with all sentimentality... we should cease thinking about human rights, the raising of living standards and democratisation. *George Kennan, US Cold War planner, 1948*

Making noises for peace, security, anti-child labour and civil and political rights but undermining both through stratagems robbing the markets of the world—such has been the Yankee yen for capture of world markets. (Raeganomics). The locomotive of this Janus-faced economics, otherwise called Reganomics is at the heart of GATT. While trade negotiations were in progress through several rounds, mini-military operations were also in progress. The message of American Might kept in sheath to be unsheathed whenever its expansionist (market) Right was in jeopardy is clear from contemporary history.

After World War II, a sense of global Manifest Destiny came to dominate United States policies. Between 1945 and the late 1980s, the United States militarily intervened more than 200 times into the internal, sovereign affairs of well over 100 "third world" countries, causing directly or indirectly the murders of 20-25 million human beings and the maimings of at least that many. (On Third World Legs by Brian Willson).

Many military supplies, (arming the world is a major industry) hot battles instigations for wars have been going on with imperial terrorism as latent resource.

India with its concern and compassion, while dealing with America Inc. for which people are visible only in terms of markets and profits, must read American President Eisenhower:

Every gun that is made, every warship launched, every rocket fired signifies-in the final sense-a theft from those who hunger and are not fed, those who are cold and are not clothed. This world in arms is not spending money alone. It is spending the sweat of its labourers, the genius of its scientists, the hopes of its children.

The price of one British Aerospace Hawk is roughly the amount needed to provide 1.5 million people in the Third World with fresh water for life. (Pilger)

At the Uruguay Round of Multilateral Trade Negotiations something bizarre happened. The cunning phrase Trade-Related Intellectual Property Rights—what a sophisticated imperial acronym TRIPs—became a point of American pressure for inclusion in the GATT. Some countries like India were disinclined to yield to this sinister suggestion. But in the end, as usual, the Indian Government gave in. TRIPs became part of GATT.

Trade is business, barter and promotion of exchange of goods on a fair playing field. It has nothing to do with intellectual exercises, discoveries of science and other noetic achievements of human talent in the laboratory or farm and field and factory. The brain is no saleable commodity but God-given gift and is the wealth of humanity. It is creation of the mind, not a material commodity or physical service. It is creation of the mind. Galelio, Copernicus, Newton and Einstein did not produce merchandise; nor indeed did Patanali, Adi Sankara or Jesus or the yogis or the priestly scientists seek money for discovery or invention or even innovation. Knowledge is free and only then mankind gets into 'that heavens of freedom' which Indian culture symbolized. Glorious is the march of civilization through wider horizons of thought but sacrilege it is to talk of Socrates, Plato, the Buddha and Rama as traders and dealers or commercial operators in intuitive, intellectual, philosophical or materially bountiful flashes of wisdom meant for the consummation of universal happiness. Did Karl Marx produce market stuff (or IP) out of Das Capital or struggle to devise a revolutionary process to break the chains of the world's have-nots who had a right to be free.

The goal of the World Powers is globalisation of markets through monopolisation and exploitation, liberalisation of access to every country and its resources so as to carry them away and also to dump U.S. goods and services by the force of seeming international treaties and claiming the right to privatization and wreck every country's public sector and social justice projects. The Hidden Agenda is obvious if discerningly perceived. Conquest by patents, occupation of the commanding heights of the economies of the Third World and liquidation of socialism as an ideology and as a culture, and impose an alternative project of uncontrolled appetite for privatization geared to Profit Grab Universal.

A CONSTITUTIONAL CAVEAT

GATT is a calamity if the Constitution of India has validity. The Preamble promises social justice, equal opportunity, human dignity and other values which make homo sapiens an evolutionary pinnacle. The right to life includes the right to dignity, health, education, shelter, food and equal opportunity for development. Part III guarantees on wealth of human rights and Part IV frowns upon concentration of wealth to the detriment of the community and advocates distributive justice, rights of the child and so on. These are basic features even as federalism is, subject to certain limitations. India lives in her villages and agriculture, ecology and environmental salubriousness are a high priority. From Stockholm to Rio de Janeiro, India has had integrated those values. The Alma Ata Declaration, relating to health for all, is implicit in our Constitution. The weaker sections of the community are a special concern and commitment of the Constitution. Thus we have, as the Paramount Law, a procession of inviolable imperatives of human worth. Not all the members of Parliament nor all cabinets in the country can undo the basic structures and features of the Constitution as outlined above. It is necessary to emphasise the obvious instead of investigating the abstruse. Adopting this stance, if we examine the GATT along with the other imperial acronyms like TRIPs and TRIMS, we may arguably hold that all the present manoeuvre and legislative gambits under compulsion from WTO as contra-constitutional gaffe. Such a coup on the constitution has to be rejected and the highest court in the land must have the functional celerity, diamond-hard integrity and hermeneutic illumination to tell the other instrumentalities of the Constitution about the GATT as an illegal locomotive, violative of the Suprema Lex.

The American Constitution and other Constitutions like those of South Africa and South Korea plus plus provide for international treaties having to be ratified by the highest legislature. This is implicit in parliamentary supremacy and I would dare to hold that the Indian Cabinet could do only what Parliament generally approve. The Cabinet is not a cabal sitting high as a third chamber of the House. A single minister signing away India's swaraj or swadeshi or self-reliance, away from Lok Sabha and Rajya Sabha, is egregious effrontery. It is supreme. It is a pity that our ministers not only sign international treaties but humiliatingly make entreaties to Big Powers for investments and carry away our agricultural resources as well as other assets on their terms. Indian rulers are no bone less wonders nor mere spaghetti spines. Indians must stand up and their governments should not consent to recolonisation for a few pieces of corrupt silver.

FUTURE SHOCK OR BETTER TOMORROW

Indians made a historic tryst with destiny when Bharat, in full realisation of the penurious privations of the vast masses, resolved to wipe every tear from every eye if not in full but in substantial measure. I behold, alas, in the scenario of the sunset decade of our bizarre century a brazen betrayal of that solemn tryst and a tragic reversal of the patriotic resolve of We, the People of India, enshrined in the Preamble to the Constitution which forms the basic feature of that Paramount Parchment inviolable even by Parliament acting nem con. Who bothers about Parliament when even GATT and WTO was never discussed and approval sought and yet the Finance Ministry obsequiously implements defeat of confidence, come motion come Election (what a contrast that the frenetic Clinton call to the world to sign the CTBT collapsed on the Capitol Hill!). The Supreme Court, the other corrective constitutional instrument, sometimes wears the inscrutable face of a sphinx and often times pronounces on issues of national moment once in a blue moon. So, the Executive *de facto* runs wild like John Gilpin on the horse with no meaningful controllerate in the House, Court or Fourth Estate. The theory of checks and the theory of balances is illusory and sovereignty of the billion strong populace feebly expressed at the hustings is but 'sound and fury signifying nothing.' The raw reality of our democracy is that the Cabinet rules, the President reigns, legislature babels, the parties have wheeler-dealer deals and the vast victim masses look at the Administration with awe or react with epileptic demonstrations since official secrecy and ministerial ukases are for them only 'riddles wrapped in a mystery instead an enigma.' This is New Democracy guided by private economic tyrannies, respectably christened M.N.Cs. John Filger explains : "True democracy is expressed not on Georgian tablets but in Articles 23 and 25 of the 1948 Universal Declaration of Human Rights. These say that everybody has the right to life and to a decent life: a right not only to employment. But to decent pay, decent working conditions, 'the right to form and join trade unions', the right to a proper home and the right to feel secure, 'in sickness, disability, widowhood, old age': the right to dignity. Nowadays, this is a subversive document, to be perverted and circumvented.

New Democracy is now the way. 'First and foremost,' wrote Peter Gowan, 'a New Democracy is run by strong capitalist proprietors funding the political process and offering electors a choice of leaders who share opinions on most things but have different styles of leadership.... This guarantees that public policy stays politically correct. At the same time New Democracy makes it easier for multinationals to advance their influence and for the "global" (*i.e.* Western) media to shape public opinion. [In this way] we get leaders in the target country who "want what we want". Hence there is no need to use the big stick...'"

The Berlin Wall has fallen. The Great Wall of China is being scaled. The Himalayas is no mountain but an invitation for occupation. Elections are a façade. Ten per cent of the total adult population can usurp power by electronic poll arithmetic and call itself majority rule. The Cabinet becomes a Cabal. The two major parties, with a minor difference and much noise have the same Westoxicated agenda. Whoever may win, *Pax Americana* governs.

At this stage, I revert to the Nehru peroration of August 1947. "The future beckons to us. Whither do we go and what shall be our endeavour? To bring freedom and opportunity to the common man, to the peasants and workers of India, to fight and end poverty and ignorance and disease; to build up a prosperous democratic and progressive nation, and to create social, economic and political institutions which will ensure justice and fullness of life to every man and woman.

Dr. Ambedkar, in the Constituent Assembly, referred to the hollow political democracy of 'one man one vote' and bitingly added: 'On the social plane, we have in India a society based on the principles of graded inequality which means elevation of some and degradation for others. On the economic plane, we have a society in which there are some who have immense wealth as against many who live in abject poverty.' "How long shall we continue to live this life of contradictions? How long shall we continue to deny equality in our social and economic life? If we continue to deny it for long, we will do so only by putting our political democracy in peril. We must remove this contradiction at the earliest possible moment or else those who suffer from the inequality will blow up the structure of political democracy which this Assembly has so laboriously built up." Baba Saheb warned, referring to the marginalised masses and the socio-economic chasm: "the sooner room is made for the realization of their aspiration the better for the few, the better for the country, the better for the maintenance of its independence and the better for the continuance of its democratic structure."

Gandhiji deplored the dire poverty of the Indian people and when approached for a message on the auspicious Independence Day said poignantly "I have run dry". He wrote about the Constructive Programme thus: "It means the levelling down of the few rich in whose hands is concentrated the bulk of the nation's wealth on the one hand, and the levelling up of the semi-starved, naked millions persists. The contrast between the palaces of New Delhi and the miserable hovels of the poor labouring class nearby, cannot last one day in a free India in which the poor will enjoy the same power as the richest in the land. A violent and bloody revolution is a certainty one day, unless there is a voluntary abdication of riches and the power that riches give and sharing them for the common good."

Right from the start, through the Independence Struggle, Indians have been demanding a socialistic pattern of society. Dr. Ambedkar explained in the Assembly Part IV of the Constitution in its socialistic dimension. Nehru had stressed the need for a socialist vision for the solution of India's problems of poverty and unemployment. The Supreme Court, in more than one case, particularly in the *Nakara* case, emphasized the socialist content of our Constitution. Moreover, in several rulings, the radical urgency of abolition of poverty and actualization of distributive justice has been the refrain of the Supreme Court pronouncements. Indeed the *right to life* has been interpreted by the Court as the foremost human right and has held the explaining the meaning of article 21 to include life with dignity access to good health, shelter and livelihood for every Indian.

The Planning Commission has been engaged in the functional formulation of policies, which would strengthen the socialist base of the country's economy, its *swadeshi* character and self-reliant strategies. The public sector has been regarded as the route to the social destination of the nation and so it has been so designed as to occupy the commanding heights of the economy. The Supreme Court, accepting the submission of the State, has up-hold nationalisation of steel and coal and the public distribution system. In sum, the court has endorsed the social justice essence on Parts III and IV which have to be read as integral to constitutional manifesto of India's economy. Any arbitrary act on the part of the Executive deviant from the fundamentals of the Constitution, as above explained, is *ultra viras* (read closely the Maneka Gandhi ruling). Public Interest Litigation and Social Action gaining access to the forensic process has made the Supreme Court the macro-instrumentality to monitor violations of constitutional values. It is now settled law that Executive Functionalism which is not just, fare and reasonable' is with article 14, 19 and 21. Social justice is the *sine qua non* of constitutional validity. What, in *daridra narayana* country, is social justice? Without doubt, the basic needs of livelihood and dignity for 'the butcher, baker and the candlestick maker' (Justice Vivian Bose) the bonded labourer, destitute gender, forlorn tribal and forsaken masses. Judicially speaking to jettison their interests and fashion 'blue blood' policies is betrayal of the Constitution and violation of the oath of office. Politically speaking, invitation of dollar colonialism paving the way for surrender of economic sovereignty is subtle subversion and cunning coup by a cabal, disguised as Cabinet, by Parties draped in different political costumes but playing the same game whose name is neo-colonialism Yankee brand.

The mission of the Founding Deed is inviolable and has been complied with haltingly and dubiously until the late 80's. Our export import policies, our country's availability foreign investments and our entire financial structure and foreign relations have been conditioned by these Gandhian-nehruvian-constitutional imperatives. Indeed, ministries of various parties and coalitions have taken oath by the Constitution as interpreted by the Court, indicating a certain hermeneutic harmony and Minister after Minister has claimed Gandhiji as the Father of the Nation, Ambedkar and Nehru as builders of modern India. The Cabinet, each time, professed the acceptance of the wisdom of Part IV and the Preamble, which explicitly creates a Socialist Democratic Republic. But in 1991, (seeds were sown late in the 80's with Rajiv Gandhi's ideological imbroglio and ambiguous reference to the summons of the 21st century) a sharp U turn was taken *without consultation with parliament dissemination among the people and indifferent to the mandate of the Constitution.* This *tour de force* created chaos in the constitutional cosmos, using euphemistic jargon such as globalisation, liberalisation and privatization. Indeed, Orwellian double speak gained official currency and the World Bank – IMF Axis dominated the economic structure obligating Bharat to obey Raeganomics. Some call it Manmohanomics, others see its reincarnation in Chidambaromics and finally, the swadeshi-committed, poverty-sensitive behold an anti-people, xenophobic in Sinhanomics!

A sardonic sum up may perhaps be with the corporate propriety abated by quislings and fifth colounist should make up a few hundred millions of the middle class enjoy the west oriented five star friendly life. While himalayan heap of the proletariat has nothing to blood toil tears and sweat. The diagnosis of the sinister syndrome is no part to seek a boldness wonders in the Finance Ministry and the corrupt coteries in the business of administration. Support the callous marketisation and the glitteratti's fascination for globalisation has made the people of India unpeople, alliance to the resources of their own country and hopes kindled by Independence having darkened into despair.

TRANSNATIONAL CORPORATIONS AND PIRACY OF AYURVEDIC HERITAGE

Introductory

The General Agreement on Trade and Tariffs (GATT) was launched in 1948 with the creative objective of promoting fair international trade relations and tariff reduction so that the goal of global justice in commerce and business may be achieved among member nations the world over. However, the leopard cannot change its spots nor super-capitalist powers miss opportunities to exploit the developing nations shedding their imperialist appetites.

The treaties of TRIPS, TRIMS and TRIS eventually led to the creation of the WTO which is the international instrumentality now in force. This organization and its North-biased operation have made it clear that the South is in the grip of Gattastrophe and neo-colonialism. From Seattle to Doha to Cancun it has become plain that the developing countries have to face victimization from the developed countries. That apart, multi-national corporations are proving a menace to the wealth of the South in other ways. India, in particular, has to safeguard its vast, unique and world-famous pharmaceutical wealth by appropriate strategies.

Defense of Ayurveda against Piracy and Patency

The Uruguay Round of GATT Negotiations concluded in 1993 and the World Trade Organization (WTO) came into being in 1995. This global legal authority, with its imperial slant, controls the commercial destiny of East and West, North and South. Its jurisdiction is international in operation and its jurisprudence subjugates the South to benefit the North with an apparent veneer of judicial neutrality. The agreement on Trade Related Intellectual Property Rights (TRIPs) governs all types of Intellectual Property Rights (IPR) including grant of patents.

Conquest of markets everywhere through technologies as well as by capturing product patents is a master-strategy of Multi-National Corporations (MNCs). Indian intellectual property, in the ancient field of ayurveda, may come under the skullduggery of MNCs using the dubious device of piracy and patenting of ayurvedic pharmaceuticals. Our pliable

Central Government may repeatedly amend the 1970 Act and Indian ayurveda may well become an exotic MNC pharmacopoeia. The accessibility and affordability and authenticity of ayurvedic medicines will be adversely affected if the patent laws are so changed by the cunning and clout of MNCs to bring them in line with their interests. In this context, we must remember our *constitutionally* mandated *fundamental duty*, under Art. 51A(f) to 'value and *preserve* the rich heritage of our composite culture'. Our medicinal legacy, a few thousand years old, is ayurveda, derived from the Maharshis and supplemented by tribal medicals and other plural systems native to the soil. It will be a betrayal of fundamental right to life (Art.21) and duty if we allow insidious invasion by macro-corporates committing piracy of our ancient formulations and drug wonders, with a view to practise 'golden deer' packagery, and thereby alienate Indian producers of ayurvedic pharmaceuticals from their own country. This is not a theoretical apprehension but an operative misappropriation against which sovereign India, as the defender of its people's health, must take preemptive steps. Swaraj jurisprudence, with sensitive nationalism and concern for the health of the people, must use parliamentary legislation and WTO litigation, to defend our unique system of medicine from conquest by patent—a peril to ignore which is to jettison our priceless pharmacopeial asset well known globally for its curative glory. In this context, the nation must conscientize itself so that patents cannot be granted of any ayurvedic or tribal medicine since it *involves no invention* but belongs to India's widely known indigenous materia medica. Insidious foreign invasion and stealthy transmission of our drug wonders can never be novelty, invention or creative innovation, a sine qua non of patent claim.

We may note at this point that neither TRIPS nor other international agreements will bind the Indian people unless national legislation is made in implementation. It is useful to note that the U.S. law specifically stipulates that no provision of the WTO, inconsistent with any law of the United States, shall have effect. In the U.K., treaties are not accepted until given effect to by Parliament. It is thus open to the Indian Parliament to make a comprehensive legislation protecting ayurveda and other native systems of medicine from inroads by foreign countries. The indigenous medical knowledge of India must be insulated from piracy and patents. Of course, India will be under increasing pressure from U.S. and Europe to further amend its patent laws not to exclude ayurvedic drugs. Demands for green medicines, instead of synthetic products, are escalating in the western world. Sales of plant based drugs rose from $4.5 billion in 1980 to $15.5 billion in 1990. Similar increases in other countries are noticeable. 50% of the world's estimated plant species are in tropical rain forests and India is world's richest bio-diversity hotspot and is now a prey of bio-quarry and bio-piracy. In the interest of our country it is basic nationalism to make effective legislation against injury to ayurvedic system of medicines. Our vast bio-diversity and well-developed indigenous medicine system developed through generations shall not be bartered away thoughtlessly as if we are a colony and the North is an imperial power.

Independently of this argument, our national leaders must remember that *health for all is an international commitment by India* and that guarantee must override any other international agreements advocated by powerful corporations hungry for markets. The right to medical care for the humblest human is integral to the Alma Ata Declaration (1979) in which India, among 134 nations, pledged urgent action. A recent session in August 2000 of the sub-commission of U.N. Commission on human rights has concluded that the TRIPS agreement constitutes contravention of international human rights law. The implementation of the TRIPS does not adequately reflect concern for the *right to health of the people.* Parliament has a solemn obligation to protect the fundamental right to life under Article 21, of every Indian. Western medicine, now that product patents are included by amendment in the Patent law, will rise in price sky high. In this view it is just, fair and reasonable and consistent with international human rights law to legislatively defend the native systems of medicine against piracy and patentisation.

Already Germany and other countries are committing covert robbery of our herbal therapy and bio-diversity. They are taking patents in their country on the view that patents in their country, because of TRIPS provisions, will bind our country. India must, with all emphatic opposition, resist the application in our country or elsewhere the validity of patents of ayurvedic drugs. Even under the existing patents law, no patent can be granted unless there is a clear *case of invention* claimed by the patentee. It is outrageous that any German can claim any *invention* of an ayurvedic drug. So also of herbal medicines popular all over India. What we have to do is to drive home the point that ayurveda, siddha, unani and tribal medicines are not secret therapies, never German serendipities, but public property available to anyone who reads the relevant texts and meets any medical practitioner of the system. A data base, comprehensive in scope, plenary in planned presentation, collected with painstaking investigation and made available with appropriate sources and references to anyone interested, will defeat the pretense of any foreigner who urges a phoney plea of *discovery.*

Apart from drugs and medicinal herbs, there are a wealth of medical treatments by way of oil massage, eye exercises and yoga practices which are fantastic in their curative benefits. Kerala has a glorious tradition in these therapeutic procedures. Tamil Nadu has an excellent native orthopaedic system with special oils and ointments. So too Kerala. These cannot be smuggled and patented. To claim that our life-saving indigenous drugs now open to numbers of native physicians as inventions is a therapeutic outrage. Glittering packaging and minor manipulations do not sustain a patent claim.

Our pharmacology is part of our sovereignty and it is public property beyond the pale of patent jurisprudence. Our case against such patentisation must be fought before the W.T.O. The recent controversy of patent for cotton seeds, turmeric powder, neem extract, basmati rice and others, and securing of patent by M.N.Cs. for common place items like dosai, idli, pullao, curry etc has brought out the fact that we have foreign foes who will fight even for frivolous and fraudulent patents. Indigenous therapeutics, herbalist heritage and publicly owned treasure house of medical knowledge, now in peril of deprivation, must awaken Parliament into nationalist legislation. To exclude patents based on traditional/indigenous knowledge and essentially derived products and processes from such knowledge, has been the stand of the Government of India *vis a vis* Article 273(b) of TRIPs agreement Parliament must hasten with adequate legislation to make this claim a legal reality.

Coda

Negative hostility to foreign surreptitious operations and patentisation is not enough. Our Governments and native pharmacologists, vaidyas and custodians of ancient Indian therapeutics orally transmitted from generation to generation must collect all these processes and products, document them, popularize their use and modernize their qualitative and quantitative availability in capsules and bottles and other traditional containers and market them attractively. Our pharmacology is a rare treasure house which can benefit humanity if preserved, pooled together presentably and protected from adulteration and pilferage and betrayal for a few pieces of silver or dollars.

Maharshi Mahesh Yogi is making ayurveda internationally known as a great gift of India to humanity. There is an Ayurvedic University in London founded and run by Dr. Varier (belonging to Kerala). There are a few distinguished ayurvedic treatment centers in India, particularly Kerala, where scrupulous attention is paid to authentic herbal medicine and massage methodology. But the new menace of foreign invasion, money-oriented and packaging glitter, may have to be resisted by appropriate national legislation.

Swaraj has a pharmacopic dimension derived from sages and tribals and enriched by ages of practice and progressive changes but emphatically insisting on purity of drugs and methodologies.

GENDER JUSTICE

Ours is a sacred soil where women are venerated as Shakthi and Goddess. There are more women deities in our pantheon than male divinities. Nevertheless, we squeeze the life out of infant girl immediately after birth. Even before the umbilical cord that links the womb to the infant is severed, life is snuffed out of the new born by administering cactus milk or by forcing a paddy seed into its mouth. In the land of the birth of Jhansi Rani, Kasturba Gandhi, Indira Gandhi and Lakshmi and in a country where Mother Teresa dwelt, where everyone speaks of compassion to animals, where movements are launched against cow slaughter, when it comes to the question of female child the attitude passes understanding. Female infanticide is more the rule than exception in many areas of the country. Moved by this social tragedy the poet portrays the plight poignantly:

To mother,

In this beautiful earth is there no air, for me to breathe? my mother.

How did the cactus juice find its way into your comforting breasts?

The dream you cherished was it not for a male child?

Though I germinated in your womb I am alien Cactus sap and paddy seed are convulsing my throat, sapping my life.

Mother, don't you think I am dead.

When you killed me, you laid on the bier your motherhood,

father's manliness, the affection of grandma to eternal sleep.

I am ashamed my mother for blossoming in a tree with humanism dead.

These lines from the verses of poet Vannachirahu are whip lashes for the barbarism that had taken deep root in us. The horrendous phenomenon of female infanticide is not confined to Usilampatti and Salem in Tamil Nadu alone. It has now become a national phenomenon spreading even to Punjab. The Tamil writer and Deputy Inspector-General of Police Ms. Thilakavathi, writes that those who belong to the Bedi community in Punjab are called "kurimars". This means, the killers of daughters. She adds that girl child is murdered and buried with sugar candy in the mouth and cotton in the palms. "Eat the candy and weave the cotton. But do not come back" is the meaning of song that they sing on the occasion. The lines are:

Kurkayen punitha thone, Apna ayen, bhaiya yahankalen.

For centuries women had remained slaves, suffering oppression and untold atrocities. Seetha, the consort of Rama, whom we worship as a goddess, was chanting only the name of Rama, when she was kept as prisoner in Sri Lanka and performed penance. But when she was released after the war and they returned to Ayodhya, to prove her chastity she was asked to undergo a baptism of fire, according to the well known legend.

The incident is still fresh in our minds, when a journalist of the Indian Express bought a woman in a weekly fair in Madhya Pradesh and produced her before the highest temple of the Indian Judiciary, the Supreme Court and told the Court, "You speak of human rights. Here I have produced before you a woman whom I purchased in the open market".

In the State of Karnataka, the system of Devadasis still continues at the Ellamma temple. Dalit youths who objected to women being stripped naked and taken to the tank for a bath and being brought back without a stich of clothing were attacked and charged with creating law and order problems. Can these incidents be obliterated from our minds?

The practice of women committing sati on the funeral pyre of their dead husbands still continues. Is it not a fact that people take pride in building a temple for a woman who committed sati?

The Equal Remuneration Act only remains ornamental in our statute books. Aren't women still considered beauty manikins, advertising models and emotionless objects? The unwritten law is one kind of justice for men and another for women. It is common knowledge as to what the status of women is under Article 14 of the Constitution which stipulates that men and women are equal but pales into insignificance before the case of Muthamma.

Muthamma joined the Indian Foreign Service. But was penalised only because she was a woman. Commenting on the atrocities that she had to suffer, Krishna Iyer burst out:

> ".................. one of the reason for the petitioner's supersession is the long standing practice of hostile discrimination against women. Even at the very threshold when the petitioner qualified for the Union Public Services at the time of her interview, the Chairman of the U.P.S.C. tried to persuade (dissuade?) the petitioner from joining the Foreign Service. On a subsequent occasion he personally informed the petitioner that he had used his influence as Chairman to give minimum marks in the viva. At the time of entry into the Foreign Service, the petitioner had also to give an undertaking that if she were to get married, she would resign from the service.
>
> "Then on numerous occasions the petitioner had to face the consequences of being a woman and thus suffered discrimination though the Constitution, specifically under Article 15 prohibits discrimination on grounds of religion, race, caste, sex or place of birth

and Article 14 of the Constitution provides the principles of equality before law.

"That members of the Appointments Committee of the Union Cabinet and the respondent No. 2 are basically prejudiced against women as a group. The Prime Minister of India has been reported in the Press as having stated—it will not be irrelevant here to mention that most of the women who are in the service at senior levels are being very systematically selected for posts which have traditionally been assigned a very low priority by the Ministry".

Muthamma of Indian Foreign Service knocked at the doors of the Supreme Court seeking redress for the injustice meted out to her. The Supreme Court admitted the petition and it came up for hearing before Justice Krishna Iyer and Justice P.N. Singhal. Justice Krishna Iyer delivered the judgment in which he said:

"The credibility of constitutional mandates shall not be shaken by governmental action or inaction but it is the effect of the grievance of Miss Muthamma that sex prejudice against Indian womanhood pervades the service rules even a third of a century after Freedom. There is some basis for the charge of bias in the rules and this makes the ominous indifference of the executive bringing about the banishment of discrimination in the heritage of service rules. If high officials lose hopes of equal justice under the rules, the legal lot of the little Indian, already priced out of the expensive judicial market, is best left to guess. This disturbing thought induces us to make a few observations about the two inpugned rules which appear prima facie, discriminatory against the female of the species in public service and have surprisingly survived so long, presumably, because servants to Government are afraid to challenge unconstitutional rule-making by the Administration.

"If a fragment of these assertions were true, unconstitutionality is writ large in the administrative psyche and masculine hubris which is anathema for Part III haunts the echelons in the concerned Ministry. If there be such gender injustice in action, it deserves scrupulous attention from the summit so as to obliterate such tendency.

"Discrimination against woman, in traumatic transparency, is found in this rule. If a woman member shall obtain the permission of Government before she marries, the same risk is run by Government if a male member contracts a marriage. If the family and domestic commitments of a woman member of the Service is likely to come in the way of efficient discharge of duties, a similar situation may well arise in the case of a male member. In these days of nuclear families, inter-continental marriages and unconventional behaviour, one fails to understand the naked bias against the gentler of the species. Rule 10 of the Indian Foreign Service (Recruitment Cadre, Seniority and Promotion) Rules, 1961, run in the same prejudicial strain: 1 to (3) states:

" No married woman shall be entitled as of right to be appointed to the service".

"At the first blush this rule is in defiance of Article 16. If a married man has a right, a married woman, other things being equal, stands on no worse footing. This misogynous posture is a hangover of the masculine culture of manacling the weaker sex forgetting how our struggle for national freedom was also a battle against woman's thraldom. Freedom is indivisible, so is Justice. That our founding faith enshrined in Articles 14 and 16 should have been tragically ignored vis-a-vis half of India's humanity, viz., our women, is a sad reflection on the distance between Constitution in the book and law in action. And if the executive as the surrogate of Parliament, makes rules in the teeth of Part III, especially when high political office, even diplomatic assignment has been filled by women, the inference of die-hard allergy to gender parity is inevitable.

"We do not mean to universalise or dogmatise that men and woman are equal in all occupations and all situations and do not exclude the need to pragmatise where the requirements of particular employment, the sensitivities of sex or the peculiarities of societal sectors or the handicaps of either sex may compel selectivity. But save where the differentiation is demonstrable, the rule of equality must govern.

"The sense of injustice rankles and should be obliterated so that every servant in strategic position gives of his or her best to the country.

"What we do wish to impress upon Government is the need to overhaul all Service Rules to remove the stain of sex discrimination, without waiting for ad hoc inspiration from writ petitions or gender charity".

At the end of the judgment he said "We dismiss the petition but not the problem" in his own inimitable way so that it would sound loud and clear to those who mattered.

A few years after he delivered the judgment in the Muthamma case, Krishna Iyer met Jagat Mehta, who was the Foreign Secretary at the time of the case. Recalling the discussion that he had with the Foreign Secretary, Krishna Iyer remarks:

"Later on, Jagat Mehta who was then the Foreign Secretary, met me in Mussouri. I am just giving you an anecdote to show how things get deep and we do not resist them. Jagat Mehta told me one day, "Well you thought, Muthamma was a woman and on gender prejudice I did not promote her. I myself was a victim. My wife was a foreign service girl. And when she married me she had to resign".

In a capitalist society women are considered mere chattels or merchandise. Wittingly or otherwise they are forced into the flesh trade. Some women abducted or inveigled by immoral men and with the connivance of the moneyed coterie are compelled to become commercial sex workers and are consigned to the hell called brothels. Here too the woman becomes the personal property of the broker who purchased her. She has to sleep with every one at any time the broker dictates. She has to submit herself to the sadistic pleasures of the client. She had to allow herself to cruel sex practices and orgies of the wolves in human garb, suffer burns, beastly attacks, unnatural activities for all of which she would be rewarded with fatal diseases. This is the status of prostitutes who are euphemistically called commercial sex workers. They are also like machinery. They satiate the sex hunger of many men every day, they become tired in both body and soul and when they lose their charm and become old they are thrown on to the streets.

Krishna Iyer paid great attention from the beginning to the abolition of prostitution. When he was a Minister, he launched a programme towards this end and he recalls it:

"Let me tell you how once I was Home Minister of the Kerala State some 35 years ago and had the opportunity to enforce the Suppression of Immoral Traffic Act (SITA), I felt that society's active involvement was a sine qua non for success of welfare measures and the whole police force, suspect on illusory and real grounds, could not go it alone. So we organised public meetings where leading political and public figures and labour leaders participated. I appealed to the working class to co-operate and offered police protection for Dharna in red light streets. It worked with partial success. I ordered a blitz raid on notorious hotels and government owned travellers Bungalows. The catch was not bad. But once a district police officer, when asked to raid a dubious hotel, was hesitant saying supposing 'I find a top police officer or politician on the offending bed and I decided to arrest and prosecute, you perhaps, would have ceased to be Minister and I would be made mince meat of by the top echelons of the civil services, who will save my family?', he asked.

Again on some other occasion,

> "In Andhra Pradesh, a senior police officer, for registering a sex related case against a Minister was victimised and the worst of it is that Judges are not serious about a campaign for women's liberation and sex sanitation, as if they were sky-masters above society."

When Krishna Iyer was elevated to Supreme Court, a criminal appeal came before him. It was a case under Suppression of Immoral Traffic Act. Krishna Iyer concerned about the plight of the women of this great nation, reflected it in C.J. *Vasvani* v. *State of West Bengal.*

"The scene is the Isias Bar, 15, Free School Street, Calcutta. A hall of enchantment extends nocturnal invitation to have a nice time with svelte sylphs. The entrance fee is but a paltry of Rs. 15/- per man and inside is served animating liquor. Scantily clad female flesh of sweet seventeen or thereabouts flit about or sit on laps, to the heady tune of band music. They solicit carnal custom, and the willing male victims pay Rs. 30, choose whom they fancy, drink together and, taking leave of decencies, indulge in promiscuous sex exercise legally described as "operation prostitution'. The stage is busy with many men and girls moving into rooms, lavatories and chambers. The curtain rises and a raiding party of police and excise officers surprise this critic company drowned in drink and damsels.

"Oftentimes, a bar or restaurant is a euphemism for a brothel and the socialites, unsuspectedly and without stich, satisfy their sex in these respectably labelled houses patronised by even prestigious dignitaries and opulent businessmen.

"Section 3 punishes persons who keep brothels, sub-section (3) of section 3 lays down that notwithstanding any other law any lease, under which such premises are held or occupied at the time of the commission of the offence, shall become void and inoperative with effect from the date of the said conviction. It is plain therefore that the consequence of a conviction under section 3 is the invalidation of the lease of the premises where the brothel is run. The logical consequence must be that the occupier must be thrown out of the prostitutional premises.

"We are in the International Women's Year—a circumstance meaningful socially, but not relevant legally. Even so, it is time to tighten up this statute and we may permit ourselves a few concluding observations, hopefully. May be, there are other provisions of the Act which have contributed to its dismal failure in the field and the legislature must, in the International Year of Women, protect the virtue of the weaker sex from the purchasing power of the takers of virginity who sip from every flower and change every hour.

"No nation, with all its boasts, and all its hopes, can ever morally be clean till all its women are really free—free to live without sale of their young flesh to lascivious wealth or commercialising their luscious figures. India, to redeem this "gender justice" and to proscribe prostitution whereby rich men buy poor women through houses of vice, has salved its social conscience by enacting the Act. But the law is so ill-drafted and lacunose that few who follow "the most ancient profession in the world" have been frightened into virtue and the customers of wine-cum-women are catered to respectably in bars, hotels and night-clubs in sophisticated and subtle ways, especially in our cities".

The "stridhan" assets which were given to the bridegroom by the feudal land owning class later assumed the nomenclature of dowry. This dowry system was intended to indicate the affluence of the feudal landlords or to offer gifts to the bride groom. Today it has taken cancerous shape and has become a permanent feature in even the lives of the working class.

Kidwai, a writer of repute, who recently interviewed the trainees to the Indian Adminstrative Service, who will be manning the bureaucratic machinery of the country and deciding the destiny of the poor, at the

Mussorie IAS training centre has made shocking revelations in his article. According to him an IAS officer in Andhra Pradesh is eligible for dowry upto Rs. two crores. The same situation prevails in North India. Many young IAS cadres took pride in this fact and felt there was nothing to feel ashamed about in accepting dowry. Can even the gods rewrite the destiny of India, hereafter? No one knows.

In the *Somnath's* case in which the husband was accused of burning his bride, Krishna Iyer said:

> "Wife burning—that atrocious species of murder horrendously escalating in some parts of this country is the shocking crime proved, according to two courts, by the prosecution in this case. Concurrent findings of fact cannot be disturbed save on enormity of improbability which we are unable to see in the present case. The three dying declarations corroborated by other circumstances are sufficient in our view to bring home the offence. Counsel has sought to discredit these declarations relevant under section 32 of the Indian Evidence Act forgetting that they are the groaning utterances of a dying woman in the grip of dreadful agony which cannot be judged by the standards of fullness of particulars which witnesses may give in other situations. To discredit such dying declarations for shortfalls here or there or even in many places is unrealistic, unnatural and unconscionable if, basically there is credibility. The terrible event in this case has taken place in the house and in the presence of the husband who has been convicted. We hardly see any reason for interfering with this conviction, and would have been shocked ourselves if any other course had been adopted either by the trial court or by the High Court. Gender Justice has a high place in Indian criminal jurisprudence".

In *Narotam Singh* v. *State of Punjab*, Krishna Iyer said:

> "The law of crimes perverts itself on occasions into the crime of law if narrow legalism overwhelms social justice. This criticism applies to the field of penology as well, and so the finer, more perceptive and sociologically relevant approach to punishment, when crime has been proved, is to take a holistic, realistic and humanistic size-up action as to promote rehabilitation without offending community conscience.
>
> "Discrepancies do not necessarily demolish testimony; delay does not necessarily spell unveracity and tortured technicalities do not necessarily upset conviction when the Court has had a perspicacious, sensitive and correctly oriented view of the evidence and probabilities to reach the conclusion it did. Proof of guilt is sustained despite little infirmities, tossing peccadilloes and peripheral probative shortfalls. The "sacred cows" of shadowy doubts and marginal mistakes, processual or other, cannot deter the Court from punishing crime where it has been sensibly and substantially brought home. By these

guidelines, the conviction of the appellant must stand, although we do not detain ourselves to discuss the details of the evidence.

"We incorporate the settlement as part of this judgment as an annexure. The solution reached by the compromise seems reasonable. The masculine offender pays Rs. 40,000/- to the victim wife". This sum will clearly take care of her future and be a sufficient reparation. We also award costs in a sum of Rs. 5,000/-. The compensation for his sexual aberration and breaking up of the matrimonial home will instill a correctional responsibility on the man. At the same time, his acquittal, following upon the composition, will hopefully save his business, and avert the hurtful jail term. The consent to divorce by the complainant will put asunder in law the marital tie which in fact has long ago sundered. Thus, the parties will be free to live in separate amity and form fresh alliances—lasting, not fleeting. This conspectus of consequences has persuaded us to grant leave to compound and do justice to the actors in the tragedy and to society generally. The triumph won after necessary travail, as in this case, has our approval and also on the sad lady and the misguided man. Will this order open a better chapter for both? The book of life often has hopeful parts in the later sober pages.

"It is distressing that dowry or bride price should be married to felicity with feudal cruetly in India, largely because the anti-dowry law sleeps on the statute book and social consciousness is not mobilised to ban effectually its vicious survival. Law, hanging limp, is a slur on the executive charged with its enforcement and the traumatic consequences are illustrated by this very case. Will the Administration awake to the urgency of a campaign so that the people may become participants in the observance of social welfare legislation."

India is neither Hindustan nor Islamistan. We have accepted India as a secular State and not as a religious State. It was the confluence of the blood of various communities and their sacrifices that have made it possible for us to breathe the air of independence. The argument that one law for one community, another for another religious community is untenable and unacceptable contention. Section 125 of the Code of Criminal Procedure enables a person who is unable to maintain herself to obtain maintenance from her husband, mother, father or children. This section 125 extends an arm of help to prevent a person becoming destitute and orphan. This section providing for maintenance assumes importance in the context of the concept that it is loss of self-respect for person to remain destitute for want of a source of sustenance.

In recent times the voice of religious fanatics has been to be heard loud, strident and hoarse. Our present day leaders with an eye on the vote bank have genuflected under the call of the religious fanatics. So long as a Hindu, a Muslim, a Christian, a Parsee, a Sikh, a Buddhist or a Jew breathes the Indian air, his religious text is only the Indian Constitution. Anyone who contravenes this norm cannot be considered as a human being much less an Indian. Every religion calls upon its followers to respect their motherland and its laws.

To argue that only the Shariat law has relevance here and that the Code of Criminal Procedure is inapplicable does not bear any credibility. No religion, no god would have dictated that his children and women should be treated like slaves and destitutes. These arguments and debates are the outcome of the people with insular thinking who had interpolated these clauses.

Krishna Iyer showed great anxiety to restore all the rights to women.

In *Shahulhameedu* v. *Subaida Beevi*, Krishna Iyer said:

> "The starting point of all this argument that the Muslim Law actively permits multi-marriages is itself open to serious doubt, as I will presently show. Moreover, it is distressing for a Court to discriminate against Muslim women who have for ages been subjected to several social disabilities clamped down on them in the name of personal laws. It is surprising that dubious religious interpretations with values valid in a bygone age are being enforced in the current times by civil courts in our professedly secular State when those values have become mere legal superstitions, if not anathema for the community at large, out of a false sense of solicitude to a fancied section of society. The Indian Constitution directs that the State should endeavour to have a uniform civil code applicable to the entire Indian humanity and, indeed, when motivated by a high public policy, section 488 of the Code of Criminal Procedure has made such a law, it would be improper for an Indian court to exclude any section of the community born and bred up on Indian earth from the benefits of that law, importing religious privilege of a somewhat obscurantist order. I have no doubt that it behoves the courts in India to enforce section 488(3) of the Code of Criminal Procedure in favour of Indian women, Hindu, Muslim or other. I will be failing in my duty if I accede to the argument of the petitioner that Muslim women should be denied the advantage of para. 2 of the proviso to section 488(3).

"The Holy Koran in Chapter IV, Verse 3, frequently relied upon as supporting polygamy says:

> "And if you fear that you cannot do justice to orphans, marry such women as seem good to you, two, or three, or four; but if you fear that you will not do justice, then (marry) only one or that which your right hand possesses. This is more proper that you may not do injustice'.

"It is admitted on all hands that this Chapter was revealed to guide the Muslims under the conditions which followed the battle of Uhud." (The Holy Quran by Maulana Muhammad Ali).

In (Chapter IV, Verse 129), the Koran says:

> "Ye are never able To be fair and just As between women, Even if it is Your ardent desire."

"It follows from these passages that the Koranic injunction has to be understood in the perspective of prevalent unrestricted polygamy and in the context of the battle in which most males perished, leaving many females or orphans and that the Holy Prophet himself recognised the difficulty of treating two or more wives with equal justice and, in such a situation, directed that an individual should have only one wife. In short, the Koran enjoined monogamy upon Muslims and departure therefrom as an exception. That is why, in the true spirit of the Koran, a number of Muslim countries have codified the personal law wherein the practice of polygamy has been either totally prohibited or severely restricted (Syria, Tunisia, Morocco, Pakistan, Iran, the Islamic Republics of the Soviet Union are some of the Muslim countries that may be remembered in this context).

"A. Yusuf Ali in his commentary on the Holy Quran has pointed out with reference to the original text, in its proper context, that the Prophet first strictly limited the unrestricted number of wives of the "Times of Ignorance" to a maximum of four, "provided you could treat them with perfect equality in immaterial things as well as in affection and in material things'. As this condition is most difficult to fulfil, the recommendation was understood to be towards the practice of monogamy.

"Irrespective of the decree declining maintenance or declaring that she is not entitled thereto for the reason that she refuses to live with her polygamous husband, the Criminal Court can and must order maintenance".

In *Bai Tahira* v. *Ali Hussain Fissali maintenance* case, Krishna Iyer held:

"In this appeal, by special leave, we are called upon to interpret a benign provision enacted to ameliorate the economic condition of neglected wives and discarded divorcees, namely, section 125, Cr. P.C. Welfare laws must be so read as to be effective delivery systems of the salutary objects sought to be served by the legislature and when the beneficiaries are the weaker sections, like destitute women, the spirit of Article 15(3) of the Constitution must belight the meaning of the section. The Constitution is a pervasive omnipresence brooding over the meaning and transforming the values of every measure. So, section 125 and sister clauses must receive a compassionate expansion of sense that the words used permit.

"We hold that every divorcee, otherwise eligible, is entitled to the benefit of maintenance allowance and the dissolution of the marriage makes no difference to this right under the current Code. In the normal course, an order for maintenance must follow, the quantum having been determined by the learned magistrate at the trial level.

"The meaning of meanings is derived from values in a given society and its legal system. Article 15(3) has compelling, compassionate relevance in the context of section 125 and the benefit of doubt, if any, in statutory interpretation belongs to the ill-used wife and the derelict divorcee. This social perspective granted, the resolution of all the disputes projected is easy. Surely, Parliament, in keeping with Article 15(3) and deliberate by design, made a special provision to help women in distress, cast away by divorce. Protection against moral and material abandonment manifest in Article 39 is part of social and economic justice, specificated in Article 38, fulfillment of which is fundamental to the governance of the country (Article 37). From this point of vantage, we must view the printed text of the particular code.

"The next submission is that the absence of mutual consent to live separately must be made out if the hurdle of section 125(4) is to be overcome. We see hardly any force in this plea. The compulsive conclusion from a divorce by a husband and his provision of a separate residence as evidenced by the consent decree fills the bill. Do divorcees have to prove mutual consent to live apart? Divorce, painfully implies that the husband orders her out of the conjugal home. If law has nexus with life this argument is still-born.

"The last defence, based on mehar payment, merits more serious attention. The contractual limb of the contention must easily fail. The consent decree of 1962 resolved all disputes and settled all claims then available. But here is a new statutory right created as a projection of public policy by the Code of 1973, which could not have been in the contemplation of the parties when in 1962, they entered into a contract to adjust their then mutual rights. No settlement of claims which does not have the special statutory right of the divorcee under section 125 can operate to negate that claim.

"Nor can section 127 rescue the respondent from his obligation. Payment of mehar money, as a customary discharge, is within the cognisance of that provision. But what was the amount of mehar? Rs. 5000/-, interest from which could not keep the woman's body and soul together for a day, even in that city where 40% of the population are reported to live on pavements, unless she was ready to sell her body and give up her soul! The point must be clearly understood that the scheme of the complex of provisions in Chapter IX has a special purpose. Ill-used wives and desperate divorcees shall not be driven to material and moral dereliction to seek sanctuary in the streets. This traumatic horror animates the amplitude of section 127, where the husband, by customary payment at the time of divorce, and subsequent series of recurrent doles is contra-indicated and the husband is liberated. This is the teleological interpretation, the sociological decoding of the text of section 127. The keynote thought is adequacy of payment which will take reasonable care of her maintenance.

"The legal sanctity of the payment is certified by the fulfilment of the social obligation, not by a ritual exercise rooted in custom. No construction which leads to frustration of the statutory project can secure validation if the court is to pay true homage to the Constitution. The only just construction of the section is that Parliament intended that divorcees should not derive a double benefit. If the first payment by way of mehar or ordained by custom has a reasonable relation to the object and is a capitalised substitute for the order under section 125 not mathematically but fairly then section 127(3)(b) subserves the goal and relieves the obligor, not protanto but wholly. The purpose of the payment "under any customary or personal law" must be to obviate destitution of the divorcee and to provide her with wherewithal to maintain herself. The whole scheme of section 127(3)(b) is manifestly to recognise the substitute maintenance arrangement by lump sum payment organised by the custom of the community or the personal law of the parties. There must be a rational relation between the sum so paid and its potential as provision, for maintenance; to interpret otherwise is to stultify the project. Law is dynamic and its meaning cannot be pedantic but purposeful. The proposition, therefore, is that no husband can claim under section 127(3)(b) absolution from his obligation under section 125 towards a divorced wife except on proof of payment of a sum stipulated, by customary or personal law whose quantum is more or less sufficient to do duty for maintenance allowance.

In *Fuzlumbi* v. *Khader Vali*, Krishna Iyer held:.

"If her plea has substance, social justice has been jettisoned but judicial process and a just and lawful claim due to a woman in distress has been denied heartlessly and lawlessly. We say "heartlessly", because no sensitive judge with empathy for the weaker sex could have callously cancelled an order for a monthly allowance already made in her favour, as has been done here. We say 'lawlessly' because no disciplined judge bound by the decision of this Court which lays down the law for the nation under Article 141 of the Constitution could have defied the crystal clear ruling of this Court in *Bai Tahira* v. *Ali Hussain Fissalli Chothia*, (1979) 2 SCC 316: AIR 1979 SC 362 by the disingenuous process of distinguishing the decision. We are surprised by this process of getting round the rule in Bai Tahira's case (supra) by the artful art of concocting a distinction without difference. The Sessions Court and the High Court, who had before them the pronouncement of the Supreme Court, chopped legal logic to circumvent it. Reading their 'reasoning' we are left to exclaim how the high Bench argued itself out of Bai Tahira's case by discovering the strange difference.

"We must first remember that section 125-127 is a secular code deliberately designed to protect destitute women, who are victims of neglect during marriage and after divorce. It is rooted in the State's responsibility for the welfare of the weaker sections of women and children and is not confined to members of one religion or region, but the whole community of womanhood.

"The payment of an amount, customary or other, contemplated by the measure must insert the intent of preventing destitution and providing a sum which is more or less the present worth of the monthly maintenance allowances the divorcee may need until death or remarriage overtake her. The policy of the law abhors neglected wives and destitute divorcees and section 127(3)(b) takes care to avoid double payment, one under custom at the time of divorce and another under section 125.

"Whatever the facts of a particular case, the Code, by enacting sections 125 to 127, charges the court with the humane obligation of enforcing maintenance or its just equivalent to ill-used wives and castaway ex-wives, only if the woman has received voluntarily a sum at the time of divorce, sufficient to keep her going according to the circumstances of the parties.

"Neither personal law nor other salvationary plea will hold against the policy of public law pervading section 127(3)(b) as much as it does section 125. So a farthing is no substitute for a fortune nor naive consent equivalent to intelligent acceptance."

This stance of Krishna Iyer laid the foundation for similar judgments in later years by the courts, setting many precedents. Though some religious fundamentalists have felt that Krishna Iyer's interpretations of the Holy Texts of Koran was biased in favour of the women, nothing could be further from the truth as it is clear that he was prompted more by justice to women than any other consideration.

A VIBRANT VISION AND MILITANT MISSION

Empowerment, egalite and dignity of women are the desiderata of contemporary womanhood, long subject to undeservedly humiliating inferiority of status, discrimination in civil and political rights and subordination in developmental opportunities. Women are human and, as of right, a radical transformation in women's position is just, fair and necessary to put an end to the current invidiously arbitrary situation. To actualise this dynamic dimension of women's upgradation we need planned action which, in turn, must result in a project for change sufficiently comprehensive to meet the challenges in the civil, political, cultural, social and economic dimensions. That is why a vibrant vision which inspires a militant mission, is necessary. Civilised humanity considers the norms of equality and liberty as the basis of just society. The notion of equality has many nuances even as the vice of discrimination operates in many fields. The Universal Declaration of human rights adopted by the United Nations way back in 1948, claims that all human beings are born free and equal in dignity and rights. This egalitarian versatility postulates not merely equality of opportunity in social and economic affairs but realistic unfoldment of personality in all faculties. Only then is it possible to feel that womanhood has gained an environment wherein her worth can blossom as a full human being. The holistic development of man and woman is impossible without social justice which protects the weak and inhibits the strong and in a gender dimension makes the woman no less than the man.

Global jurisprudence, through various Conventions, Declarations, Resolutions and other instruments, has affirmed that the female of the species shall not be invidiously treated from foetal state to final exit, from the cradle to the grave. The world's largest conference where women's rights found full acceptance and special consideration for womanhood was treated as integral part of the equalisation process was the Beijing Declaration, ratified by India. It binds and obligates initiation of national laws to incorporate the Beijing decisions. What is equally important is that international legal instruments, ratified by nations, enable the courts to read into municipal laws, the larger jurisprudence evolved at the global level. Thus a variety of universal instruments which deal with the girl child, with status of women and with gender discrimination have become invisibly part of India's justice system. The Supreme Court of India and the High Courts have used these International Instruments in interpretation of Indian Laws and in applying those principles where there is vacant space in the India *corpus juris*. In short, we have a universal gender jurisprudence applicable to India and beneficial to Indian women consisting of international instruments, Indian statutes and case-law which judicially bind.

Indian constitutional jurisprudence has emphatically accepted equality of station and opportunity and prohibits discrimination on the basis of sex. Article 14 of the Constitution, proclaiming equality before the law, goes beyond that bare equality through judicial interpretation. Women as a class are different from men as a class in so far as they are entitled to special treatment as a class. Article 15, not merely frowns on discrimination against women but permits especially favourable treatment to women based upon the social realism that they are weaker in economic and social status. The special disabilities of women can be counteracted by special provisions in their favour. The truth is that the fair sex has had an unfair deal in law and life and therefore legal activism at the judicial and legislative levels need to abolish the shameful inequality, indelible stain and incurable wound which is the lot of Indian womanhood. In *Muthamma's* case (1979 SC 1868) the Supreme Court condemned a rule of victimisation of women in the Foreign Service Rules. The court said, "discrimination against woman in traumatic transparency is found in this rule". The court struck down the Rule as naked bias and violation of equality. In short, not merely is equality guaranteed but discrimination in favour of women has found favour with the Constitution and the court. Protective discrimination supportive of women is a permissive classification under the Constitution. Special laws can be made and have been made in favour of women and children. Women's physical structure and performance of maternal functions places her at a disadvantage in the struggle for subsistence and her physical wellbeing becomes a matter of public concern in order to preserve the strength and vigour of the race.

Disabilities and Discriminatory treatment Women undergo

Globally speaking, civil and political rights, social and economic rights, cultural and gender rights have been unfair to womanhood. Indeed, human rights are not fully enjoyed even now by our daughters, sisters and mothers. It is heartening that the United Nations, in its great instruments, has upheld gender dignity and egalite. It is equally gratifying that the Indian Constitution has, in various provisions, shown special compassion for the weaker sex. We must be proud that our constitutional jurisprudence unreservedly grants equal status and guarantees equal opportunities to both sexes. We live at a time when Kalpana Chawla has blazed the trail to demonstrate that a woman can excel even in space travel (although the second experiment ended tragically). There is none in India who does not agree with the proposition that woman, if given unbiased environment, can perform in every field with signal success what men may claim they can. We, therefore, proceed from the fundamental fact that socially and politically woman must have equal rights. The reality is a different story and so women have to fight on every front as sisters and daughters, as wives and mothers, as partners in public affairs, as heirs under succession law and economic equals in every field of human activity, not for condescension nor concession but social justice and equal recognition. This is integral to the gender vision of the nation sans which slavery in disguise may still be the feminine fate. The rule of law is not fair unless the rule of life so transforms women's status as to be equal with that of men and opens up equal opportunity for women in every walk of life. Suffrage is necessary but the ballot alone not win power for the subject gender. So it is that we have to go beyond the vote to actualisation of equality as a social reality. The glory of the equal gender becomes a fact of history only when, from an angle of pragmatism and jurisprudence, it can be demonstrated that the aspirations of womanhood, regardless of religion, region, caste and creed, are not inhibited, but are promoted, by the sex factor. The mensuration of gender justice is not in international instruments, constitutional provisions and political platitudes but in the dynamics of life itself.

Our statute book, in some measure, supports equal rights but truth to tell, invidious discrimination weakens women's potential. It is heartening however, that the higher judiciary has been gender-friendly, has upheld constitutional equality and has exposed the practice of inequality against women. Nevertheless, there is much in the law which is lawless if equality is the test. There is much in politics that reveals prejudice because her very presence in Parliament or public office is negligible although by numerical strength equal power must be shared by both sexes.

Woman and the Law

In constitutional theory there is equality but diehard discrimination harms the claim of women in matrimonial life and divorce rights, in guardianship law, in succession and inheritance laws. Special provision protective against discrimination is distances away. Even in executive matters there is bias against woman. Just one instance, *Muthamma's* case, out of many:

The writ by Miss Muthamma, a senior member of Indian Foreign Service, speaks a story which makes one wonder whether Articles 14 and 16 belong to myth or reality. It was a unique example of sex discrimination *ultra vires* Articles 14 and 16 of the Constitution of India. Rule 8(2) of the Indian Foreign Services Rules, 1961 provided that "*a woman member* of the Service shall obtain the permission of the Government in writing before her marriage is solemnized. At any time after marriage, a woman member of the service may be required to resign from service, if the Government is satisfied that her family and domestic commitments are likely to come in way of the due and efficient discharging of duties...." "Discrimination against woman, in traumatic transparency, is found in this rule.... In these days of nuclear families inter-continental marriages and unconventional behaviour one fails to understand the naked bias against the gender of the species". Both the rules were declared violative of the principle of equality and held discriminatory. (*C.B. Muthamma* v. *Union of India*, AIR 1979 SC 868)

The political presence of Indian woman-hood either as legislators or as ministers is grossly inadequate. Considerable noise was made promising at least 1/3rd of the membership of the House to women. But this tantalising proposition suffers procrastination with no hope of implementation. In many political parties and trade unions the situation is no different. If woman is to matter, a change in her representation in public life is a *sine qua non*. In the professions, women's competence notwithstanding, they have no proportionate standing. Few woman lawyers, why? Few women judges, why? Very few women professors, why? Scarce is the presence of abundantly available women,—*a la* Kiran Bedi, in the police force or other strategic walks of life. Surely there is invisible discrimination and the process of social justice *vis-a-vis* women is iniquitous. In sum, there is a fundamental distortion which demands correction. Occupational injustice coupled with the burden of motherhood, house wife functionalism and other inevitable chores, aggravates her iniquitous fate. There is therefore need for a campaign for gender justice in plural dimensions if equality of the sexes is not to be abracadabra.

In law, there is the room for grievance. Family law, whichever the religion, is tilted against the woman. In Hindu law, where discrimination was writ large, statutory reform has gone a long way in doing justice. There is still room for making law equal in favour of the Hindu woman even now. Christian women patently suffer from discrimination. Luckily, the Travancore Christian Succession Act and the Cochin Christian Succession Act have been struck down by the court. Still, in the matter of inheritance, the law is not fair because implementation of the Supreme Court ruling in *Mary Roy's* case is resisted. In Islam the situation is worse. Orthodox Islamic opinion protects clamping down pardha on woman and banishing her to the kitchen and bedroom. This is being perpetuated despite constitutional equality. Even regarding maintenance to divorced woman, *Shah Bano* case notwithstanding, there is legislative discrimination although the court has interpretatively ameliorated the lot of the forsaken partner. Talaq is trauma for the victim even like the 'four wives privilege'.

The girl child is the Cinderella of law and life. She is neglected and survives under adverse conditions. She suffers dowry terrorism and even Sati homicide. Law, in its majestic equality has not helped her at school or place of employment. Sex has become a sombre liability. We have to rewrite the law to defend Helen, Fazulin Bi and Sita to secure what is their due. Her heroic exploits thrill the world but women are looked down upon as less than equal. A comprehensive gender code which assures equal opportunity and equal protection as indefeasible norms of justice. This masculine world must change its ethos and eidos. The gender sector has to wage a battle for a fair deal. In this context, the courts come out with flying colours because judicial pronouncements have challengingly upheld women's claims through girlhood and womanhood. A few leading cases may be an apt illustration of the great vision the judges have projected. Case-law, in profound value-set, can be cited to support how the judges have, by their powerful pen, salvaged women from their parlous lot.

Way back in December 1969 a judge of the Kerala High Court (Krishna Iyer, J) rejected the argument that a Muslim woman was not entitled to claim maintenance on the distressing ground that her husband has discarded her and married a second wife. The plea that Islam provided for four wives for every Muslim male was exposed as fallacious and section 499 of the Criminal Procedure Code granting maintenance to a neglected wife was applied. Here is a part of the head note in that case:

> *Section 488 provides a summary remedy and is applicable to all persons belonging to all religions and has no relationship with the personal law of the parties. It is distressing for a Court to discriminate against Muslim women who have for ages been subjected to several social disabilities clamped down on them in the name of personal laws. The Indian Constitution directs that the State should endeavour to have a uniform civil code applicable to the entire Indian humanity and, indeed, when motivated by high public policy. Section 488 of the Criminal Procedure Code has made such a law, it would be improper for an Indian Court to exclude any section of the community born and bred upon Indian earth from the benefits of that law, importing religious privilege of a somewhat obscurantis order. It behoves the Courts in India to enforce section 488(3) in favour of Indian women, Hindu, Muslim or other. It follows that Muslim women should not be denied the advantage of para 2 of the proviso to section 488(3). There is hardly any doubt that neither the reliance on Art. 25 of the Constitution of India nor the refuge under the sanctions of the Koran can save a Muslim husband from meeting his statutory obligation under section 488. (K.L.T 1970 p-4)*

In another Muslim matrimonial case the court (same Judge) upheld a woman's claim to divorce in a case of total breakdown of wedlock. It may be useful to excerpt from the head note the following proposition strengthening the women's case:

> *Modern legal systems are veering round to the view that while no party can be permitted to benefit by his own wrong conduct and obtain divorce, pleading a break-down of marriage, public interest demands that formal ending of marriages which remain marriages in name only is but right. When an intolerable situation has been reached, the partners living separate and apart for a substantial time, an inference may be drawn that the marriage has*

broken down in fact and so should be ended by law. This trend in the field of matrimonial law is manifesting itself in the Commonwealth countries these days. This principle is of Quoranic vintage.

Muhammedan Law—Divorce—When to be granted—Dissolution of Muslim Marriage Act (1939), section 2(ix)—Applicability.

The sanctity of marriage is preserved not merely by the morality that permeates it, but by the reality that holds the family together; one without the other spells a breakdown; and so the ground for divorce may well be made out if there is a total irreconcilability between the spouse. The Muslim law, independently of Act 8 of 1939, accepts this ground for dissolution of marriage. (KLT 1971 p. 664)

A string of cases abbreviated but bringing out the essential concern of the Court may now be given:

1. *State of Maharashtra* v. *Chander Prakash Kewalchand Jain,* (1990) (1) SCC 550 this case dealt with the rape of a newly married girl—the Supreme Court observed that the prosecutrix cannot be put on par with the accomplice. She being a victim of the crime, not only is she a competent witness, her evidence should carry the same weight as said, "ordinarily the evidence of the prosecutrix who does not lack understanding must be accepted. To insist on corroboration except in the rarest of rare cases is to equate a woman who is a victim of the lust of another with an accomplice to a crime and thereby insult womanhood."
2. *State of Maharashtra* v. *Madhukar Naain Mardikar,* JT 1990 [4] SCC 169, the Supreme Court held that even a woman of easy virtue is entitled to protect her person. Her evidence cannot be thrown koberboard on that count. The Court expressed its unhappiness over the manner in which the investigation by the police was casual and defective.
3. *Government of A.P.* v. *P.B. Vijayakumar,* 1995 (3) SCALE 163 – Reservation of posts for women has been upheld under Art. 15[3] though Art. 16 does not specifically provide for such reservation for women.
4. *Vishaka* v. *State of Rajasthan,* 1997 (6) SCC 241 relying upon CEDAW and the country's official commitment to it, in addition to the Constitutional mandate, the Supreme Court has laid down guidelines to be followed by employees to prevent sexual harassment of women employees. The guidelines are mandatory till they are replaced by legislation.
5. *Mangatmul* v. *Punni Devi,* 1995 (5) SCALE 199, the Supreme Court said "Maintenance as we see it necessarily must encompass a provision for residence. Maintenance is given so that the lady can

live in the manner more or less to which she was accustomed. The concept of maintenance must, therefore, include provision for food and clothing and the like and take into account the basic need of a roof over the head. Provision for residence may be made either by giving a lump sum in money or property in lieu thereof".

6. *Saleem Basha* v. *Mumtaz Begum*, CRL R.C. No. 1000+999 of 1995-decided on 22-4-1998. Judge S.M. Siddickk of the Madras High Court said, "Quran discourages divorce—it permits only after pre-divorce conference attempting for reconciliation" and mediation by both parties. Reference was made to the case of *Fazlenb* v. *K. Khader*, AIR 1980 SC 1730, Justice Krishna Iyer speaking before the Supreme Court quoted CJ Behard Islam—an elaborate judgment replete with quotes from the Holy Quran has exposed the error of early English authors and judges who dealt with Talaq in Muslim law as good even if pronounced at whim or tantrum by the husband........in the absence of serious reasons, no man can justify a divorce either in the eye of religion or the law. If he abandons his wife or puts her away in simple caprice, he draws upon himself the divine anger, for the curse of God, said the Prophet, rests on him who repudiates his wife capriciously.

Actions that outraged the modesty of female employees constitute sexual harassment and it is importantly laid down by the judges that physical contact may be absent but still sexual harassment may take place. The court imported international instruments in imparting a liberal approach to the issue.

1999 (1) SCALE 57, AIR 1999 SC 625, [2000] 1 LRC 563, (1999) 2 CHRLD 455

The respondent was removed from his post as an employee of the appellant council after the relevant disciplinary authorities found him guilty of sexually harassing X, a junior employee. He filed a writ petition before the High Court challenging his dismissal. A single judge allowed the petition, finding that the respondent's dismissal was unjustified on the grounds that he had only tried to molest X and had not actually established any physical contact with her. The appellant was ordered to reinstate him. The Division Bench of the High Court upheld this decision and the appellant appealed to the Supreme Court. The appellant, *inter alia,* relied upon the fundamental rights to equality (Art. 14) and life and liberty (Art. 21), as well as India's international obligations under the Convention on the Elimination of All Forms of Discrimination against Women, the International Covenant on Economic, Social and Cultural Rights (ICESCR) and the Beijing Declaration.

In allowing the appeal, it was held that:

1. In the absence of procedural irregularity, the High Court was wrong to interfere with the findings of fact recorded by

disciplinary authorities and with the punishment which they imposed. It is a well-settled principle that, in exercising the power of judicial review, the court is not concerned with the correctness of findings of fact which are reasonably supported by evidence, but with the decision-making process itself (*Union of India* v. *Parma Nanda,* (1989) 2 SCC 177 (Ind SC); *B.C. Chaturvedi* v. *Union of India,* (1995) 6 SCC 749 (Ind SC); and *Government of Tamil Nadu* v. *A. Rajapandian,* (1995) 1 SCC 216 (Ind SC) followed).

2. Sexual harassment is a form of sex discrimination projected through direct or implied unwelcome sexual advances, requests for sexual favours and other verbal or physical conduct by the female employee may affect her employment, unreasonably interfere with her performance at work and create an intimidating or hostile working environment for her (dicta of Verma, J. in *Vishaka* v. *State of Rajasthan,* (1997) 6 SCC 241, [1999] 2 CHRLD 202 (Ind SC) followed).
3. Each incident of sexual harassment in the workplace is incompatible with the dignity and honour of women and violates the fundamental rights to equality, life and liberty.
4. The respondent's behaviour did not cease to be outrageous for want of physical contact and the observations made by the High Court to the effect that the respondent did not actually molest X because he did not establish such contact with her are unacceptable. The courts should examine all the evidence to determine the genuineness of the complaint and should rely on the evidence of a credible victim.
5. The respondent's conduct offended against morality, decency and X's modesty. It constituted an act unbecoming of the good conduct and behaviour expected from a superior employee and undoubtedly amounted to sexual harassment. It follows that the punishment imposed on the respondent was commensurate with the gravity of his objectionable behaviour and there was no justification for the High Court to interfere with it. Any reduction in punishment is bound to have a demoralising effect on women employees and is a retrograde step.

   The courts are obliged to give due regard to international conventions and norms when construing domestic laws particularly when they are consistent and where there is a void in domestic law. Moreover, the Convention on the Elimination of All Forms of Discrimination against Women, ICESCR and the Beijing Declaration impose obligations on India to gender-sensitive its laws.

Expression

Women

Depictions of social evils allowed where they advanced film's serious message

Supreme Court 1 May 1996

A.H. Ahmadi, CJI, S.P. Bharucha, J, B.N. Kirpal, J, (1996) 4 SCC 1: AIR 1996 SC 1846: (1997) 3 LRC 1

The film *'Bandit Queen'* deals with the real life story of PD, a poor, lower caste rural girl who is brutalised by her husband, the upper caste community and the police and is transformed into a revengeful bandit. The film contains scenes including female frontal nudity, a bare male posterior, rape, violence and generally strong language. The Appellate Censorship Tribunal unanimously upheld the film's 'A' certification (*i.e.* for adult viewing only) without requiring the cuts which had been sought by the Censorship Board. When the fim opened for public viewing, the first respondent, a member of the upper caste community depicted in the film, filed a writ petition before the Delhi High Court seeking a ban of the film on the ground that it depicted members of his community as rapists and the portrayal of PD was 'a slur on the womanhood of India'. The writ petition was allowed by a single judge, who quashed the certificate granted to the film and suspended its screening until the Censorship Board carried out modifications and excisions in terms of his order. This decision was upheld by the Division Bench of the High Court. The appellants appealed to the Supreme Court.

In allowing the appeals and restoring the film's 'A' certificate, it was held that:

6. The censorship guidelines under section 5B of the Cinematograph Act, 1952, which echo the constitutional restrictions on the guarantee of freedom of expression (Art. 19(2)), are broad standards that cannot be read as one would read a statute. The film certification authorities are required to be responsive to the values and contemporary standards of society while ensuring that artistic expression and creative freedom are not unduly curbed. The film must be judged in its entirety from the point of view of its overall impact (*K.A. Abbas* v. *Union of India,* (1970) 2 SCC 780 (Ind SC); *Raj Kapoor* v. *State,* (1980) 1 SCC 43 (Ind SC), *Samaresh Bise* v. *Amal Mitra,* (1985) 4 SCC 289 (Ind SC) and *State of Bihar* v. *Shailabala Devi,* (1952) SCR 654 (Ind SC) considered).

7. No film that extols or encourages a social evil is permissible but a film that illustrates the consequences of a social evil necessarily

must show that social evil. The scenes of nudity and rape and use of expletives in the film, permitted by the Tribunal, were in aid of the theme of the film showing the psychological and physical effect of rape and violence on a village child. They were intended not to arouse prurient or lascivious thoughts but revulsion against the perpetrators and pity for the victim.

8. The court should recognise the message of a serious film and the test that should be applied to the individual scenes is whether they advance the message. If they do they should be left alone, with only the caution of an 'A' certificate. Adult Indian citizens as a whole may be relied upon to comprehend intelligently the message and react to it, not to the possible titillation of some particular scene.
9. Whether the depiction of a social evil is necessary is best left to the sensibilities of the expert Tribunal which gauges public reactions to films. Except in cases of a stark breach of the guidelines, the Tribunal should be permitted to go about its task.
10. Nakedness does not always arouse the baser instinct. The guidelines permit scenes of sexual scene where PD is humiliated, stripped naked, paraded and made to draw from a well within a circle of a hundred men was intended by those who stripped her to demean her. The scene was central to the powerful human story and its effect could hardly have been better conveyed than by showing the scene explicitly. It helps to explain PD's rage and vendetta against the society that had heaped indignities upon her.
11. The rape scene also helps to explain why PD became what she did. Rape is crude and its crudity is what the rapist's bouncing bare posterior is meant to illustrate. Rape and sex are not being glorified in the film. On the contrary, it shows the terrible and terrifying effect rape can have on the victim.
12. Too much need not be made of a few swear words the like of which can be heard every day in every city, town and village street. No adult would be tempted to use them because they are used in this film.

Bodhisattwa Gautam v. *Subhra Chakraborty*

Family remedies women

Interim award made to rape victim pending acused's trial

Supreme Court 15 Dec 1995

Kuldip Singh, J. v. *Saghir Ahmad, J.*, (1996) 1 SCC 490: AIR 1996 SC 922: (1995) 2 CHRLD 159

The Respondent alleged that the appellant induced her to have sexual intercourse with him by giving her false assurances of marriage. She claimed that when she subsequently became pregnant the respondent agreed to marry her secretly, despite knowing that the marriage was not valid, but later insisted that she have an abortion. She became pregnant again a few months later and underwent another abortion allegedly at the appellant's insistence. The respondent claimed that, having spent several years cohabiting together, the appellant finally abandoned her. The appellant was charged with committing various criminal offences under the Indian Penal Code and filed a petition to quash the proceedings. The High Court dismissed the petition and the appellant sought special leave to appeal to the Supreme Court. In refusing leave to appeal, the Supreme Court considered whether any further order could be passed compelling the appellant to pay maintenance to the respondent pending the resolution of the criminal proceedings against him. The appellant submitted that he should not be burdened with the liability of paying maintenance to the respondent as he was unemployed. Under Art. 32 of the Constitution, the Supreme Court has the jurisdiction to enforce fundamental rights, including the right to life (Art. 21). In ordering the appellant to pay interim compensation to the respondent pending the resolution of the criminal proceedings against him, it was held that:

13. Fundamental rights can be enforced even against private bodies and individuals.
14. It is not necessary, for the exercise of the Supreme Court's jurisdiction under Art. 32, that the person who is the victim of the violation of his or her fundamental right should personally approach the court. The court can itself take cognizance of the matter and proceed *suo motu* or on a petition of any public-spirited individual.
15. Rape is a crime against basic human rights and is also violative of the victim's most cherished fundamental right, namely, the right to life.
16. *Delhi Domestic Working Women's Forum* v. *Union of India,* (1995) 1 SCC 14 (Ind SC) recognises a rape victim's right to compensation by providing that it shall be awarded by the court on conviction of the offender, subject to the finalisation of a Criminal Injuries Compensation scheme by the Central Government. On the basis of the principles set out in that case, the court's jurisdiction to award interim compensation shall be treated as part of their overall jurisdiction to try rape offences and this power should be included in the above scheme.

17. The Supreme Court has, in any event, the inherent jurisdiction to pass any order it considers fit and proper in the interests of justice or in order to do complete justice between the parties.
18. The court is *prima facie* satisfied as to the truth of the serious allegations made by the respondent and accordingly orders the appellant to pay to the respondent Rs. 1000 (approximately US $ 27, as at 15 December, 1995) every month as interim compensation pending the resolution of the criminal proceedings against him. The appellant shall also pay arrears of compensation at the same rate from the date on which the complaint was filed by the respondent to the present date.

Observation

The right to life means more than mere animal existence; it means the right to live with human dignity and includes, therefore, all those aspects which go to make a life meaningful, complete and worth living.

Valiant has been the role of the judiciary in the vindication of gender justice. But case-law, creative, imaginative and gender friendly, has its logic and limitation. Judges cannot make law but only interpret it and decide specific cases and controversies within defined bounds although in that process they do make law interstitually. But legislation is essentially a wider function covering vaster spaces and free to weave fabrics of fundamental mutation. So it is substantive codification, radical in transformation of the social order, that we need, an *avant-garde* operation parliament must perform. Magnificently as the judiciary has acted, they have not and could not usurp legislative functions. It follows that while paying a tribute to the progress achieved by the Bench we still need a *great gender code* to render unto womanhood empowerment, which is her due. Subjection over centuries must be manumitted, not only by judicial daring but by legislative liberation. Operation Empowerment is legislation in action and goes beyond the passive declaration of equality of the sexes. Grant power to the subjugated sector, make her independence a source of strength, install her in seats where power resides and generate in her, a suppressed half of humanity, that confidence, courage and capacity which will sustain her worth and dignity so as to enhance the human resources of our generation to the common advantage of the world community. No society is free until the last girl child and the last damsel in distress is free. That is the dynamics and dialectics of our age, rewriting vintage subordination, restoring to our vast sister sector the victory of empowerment which belongs to her by human rights culture. Brave new Bharat belongs equally to sister and brother in power, property and pursuit of happiness. That is the militant vision social justice and cosmic jurisprudence project. Coda: We are active partners and march together. We have a world to conquer.

ALCOHOLISM—A SYNDROME OF PLURAL PATHOLOGIES

Gandhiji, dubiously described as the father of the Nation, was a humanist crusader for prohibition and soulful opponent of alcoholism. When India became free, swaraj made it a political imperative to use the State against consumption of alcohol. When Rajaji became the Chief Minister of Madras he discovered that taxes levied on intoxicating beverages were part of the unrighteous revenues and if State exactions from marketing liquor and drugs were forsaken the public treasury had to be replenished to make up the tax loss by other innocent means. For this purpose he introduced sales tax. If prohibition was to succeed and the consequent loss of revenue compensated, sales tax had to be imposed not excessively, but for the limited purpose of balancing the budget. The scheme worked well and manufacture and sale of neera or sweet toddy proved popular. Drinking is a dangerous habit and the West revels in it. In India, Gujarat has abolished alcoholism and has not become bankrupt, but largely under foreign influence liquor bars have sprung up, clubs have made it a fashion to serve alcoholic drinks. The State, governed by the Congress, Marxists or other coalitions thrive on morally guilty duty levied on manufacture and sale of liquor unconscionably licenses and levies fees; and each year, more licenses and heavier duties become the addiction of finance ministers in their budgets. It is now a creed, as it were, of Finance Ministers, to derive large revenues from intoxicating substances. Today, the state is seeking to survive financially, relying on alcoholism as dependensia syndrome. How grave a menace to a state is this vice has to be seriously considered by every patriot who reveres Gandhiji and has concern for the life and health of the people, rich and poor, and for the law and order of State and society. A Finance Minister whose onetime budget boozes on taxes and levies is a felonious abettor of lethal consumer of drugs and drinks and is no sober rule but intoxicated enemy of the people. What a vicarious breach of constitutional morality.

Time was when some political parties like the Congress believed in Prohibition, but now politics whatever the hue, is wet in fiscal policy; and allergy to alcohol is absent vis a vis any party. Article 47 of the Constitution obligates the state to take measures for raising the level of nutrition and standard of living of the people as among its primary duties, in particular, it has been emphasized that the State shall endeavour to bring about prohibition of consumption of intoxicating drinks and of drugs injurious to health. Of course, medicinal uses are exempted. Even though Article 47 is only a directive principle **it is fundamental in the governance of the country** (Article 37). Our politics is inebriate and intoxicated, our Government is tipsy and boozy and naturally, our bureaucracy is addicted to moral drugs and drinks because of the deleterious revenue it brings. From the constitutional angle and political mandate of the Father of the Nation one might accuse the state and their ministers of toxic breach of the Republic's basic text. If only our Republic had insulated the billions and billionaires from drugs and drunkenness the health and wealth of the people would have been far finer.

Abraham Lincoln was a *teetotaler*. Of course, Gandhiji too. Bernard Shaw, Dr. Johnson and every other great man I have heard of has been allergic to alcoholism. Hospitals and cancer centers are full of alcoholic patients and courts are full of alcohol-induced crimes. The right to life,—a foremost fundamental, is in peril. Peace at home and in the streets is in toxic travesty. Purity of character, free from corruption commands anti-alcoholic; anti-drug imperative. Islam is against alcohol; so too higher religions which are true to divinity. Humanity has a future only if intoxicating substances are totally taboo. Efficiency in every walk of life, integrity in every professional activity, every humane commitment and selflessness in society and a somber world order informed by social justice, can be possible only if alcoholism becomes *bete noire*.

There is global apprehension of terrorism but if the liquor habit is utterly abolished along with narcotic consumption, terrorism will die a natural death since drunken violence most often triggers deadly attacks. It is a tragedy that even Marxist leaders who stand for the liberation of the exploited sector, when they are in power, rely on revenue from alcohol sales. Kerala is a notorious example of the Congress-led party in power raising fees and taxes by encouraging toddy shops and foreign liquor taverns knowing fully well that the fatal fluid pauperizes families, inflicts social disaster and causes a variety of diseases and noxious vices. The Marxist-led regime has shockingly escalated this source. It is a shame that in Kerala the rich and the poor drink themselves to death and the Congress and Marxists manage their budget by exploiting more licenses, bars and toddy parlours. Are Governments themselves vicariously drunk and aware of all alcoholic affluenza and disasters raised cling to this intoxicating process?

Is there no moral order or ethical integrity what with the paramountcy of Article 37 read with Article 47 made 'fundamental' in the governance of the country? The violation of Arts. 21, 37 and 47 (right to life) which results in the break-down of the Constitution? Is the Council of Ministers above law so as to jettison the anti-alcoholic creed of the suprema lex? Why surrender to the press and popularity and the 'drink' pressure of the proprietariat, corrupting society and sinking peace and security in the chaos syndrome.

Jawaharlal Nehru, when confronted with an alcoholic challenge of our ambassadors, gave a corrective lesson which the present Prime Minister of India must adopt. The Supreme Court, in one of its rulings has quoted him approvingly:

33. 'In India some genteel socialites have argued for the diplomatic pay-off from drinks and Nehru has negatived it:

Not only does the health of a nation suffer from this (alcoholism), but there is a tendency to increase conflicts both in the national and the international sphere.

I must say that I do not agree with the statement that is sometimes made—even by our ambassadors—that drinks attract people to parties and if there are no drinks served people will not come. I have quite frankly told them that if people are only attracted by drinks, you had better keep away such people from our missions.... I do not believe in this kind of diplomacy which depends on drinking....and, if we have to indulge in that kind of diplomacy, others have had more training in it and are likely to win.' (SCC 1978 P-572 Para 33)

Alcoholism is an invitation for many pathological and penurious invasions on society. Once the habit has won over the person's psyche he becomes a victim and succumbs to many vices and diseases. Alcoholic toxicity makes the habitual consumer a chronic menace of tipsiness. When he begins drinking, first he becomes jocose, slowly he becomes bellicose, then lachrymose and finally comatose. His last lap is in the liver cancer ward or prison bars. Each peg invites the next noxious dose. And then the corrupt sip and so on. Administration puts no limitation on quantum of bottles and drinkers are proselytized into drunkards and create companions. Street fights, domestic quarrels, divorces, terrorism and what not, are multiplied by consumption of this deleterious drink. The sanity of society, the sobriety of politics, the compassion and fraternity of humanity, law and order in the community suffer sacrifice unless prohibition becomes a generally accepted virtue. Violence, disease, domestic discord, divorce, communal carnage, homicides, suicides, traffic accidents and many diseases are caused by drugs and intoxicating fluids. Kerala, *alas*, is a cornucopia of booziness, bankruptcy and social disaster. And the architect of the budget encourages pubs, chubs and toddy parlours criminally neglecting the grave disasters.

A Third World country like India can be restored to social justice and welfare state only if we banish the alcoholic-drug addict bestiality, physical, moral and spiritual. Here is a quote from Aldous Huxley:

'Then brim the bowl with atrabilious liquor!
We'll pledge our Empire vast across the flood;
For Blood, as all men know, than water's thicker,
But water's wider, thank the Lord, than Blood.'

PROHIBITION—A CONGRESS CREED, TRAVESTIED BY KERALA PREMIER

Politicians are after the purchase of the media at alcoholic price for democratic popularity. Recent reports bruited about in the Malayalam media the tidings that the Congress Chief Minister served alcohol in Delhi to the media at a dinner—Five star fashion, although he is a seasoned member of the Congress whose creed is absolute allergy to alcohol. If liquor flow at a bankrupt Chief Minister's party what sense of Gandhism or constitutional loyalty can this indigent administration claim in vain as Article 47 inscribed as a directive principle of state policy 'endeavour to bring about prohibition of the consumption except for medicinal purposes of intoxicating drinks............'

If the salt lost their savour wherewith shall they be salted. (Bible)

Is there no moral order or integrity with the paramount notwithstanding Article 37 which obligates with Article 47 read with Article 37 is made 'fundamental' in the governance of the country? Is the Chief Minister above law and have Congressmen jettisoned the anti-alcoholic creed of the party to buy up the goodwill of the press and popularity that this corrupting measure was adopted? Such myopic devices intoxicate and demoralize the common people.

Jawaharlal Nehru when confronted with an alcoholic situation gave a corrective lesson which the Prime Minister of India must adopt even as the Supreme Court has quoted him approvingly:

> *"In India some genteel socialites have argued for the diplomatic pay-off from drinks and Nehru has negatived it:*
>
> > *Not only does the health of a nation suffer from this (alcoholism), but there is a tendency to increase conflicts both in the national and the international sphere.*
> >
> > *I must say that I do not agree with the statement that is sometimes made—even by our ambassadors—that drinks attract people to parties and if there are no drinks served people will not come. I have quite frankly told them that if people are only attracted by drinks, you had better keep away such people from our missions.... I do not believe in this kind of diplomacy which depends on drinking....and, if we have to*

indulge in that kind of diplomacy, others have had more training in it and are likely to win.

Of course, the struggle for Swaraj went beyond political liberation and demanded social transformation. Redemption from drink evil was woven into this militant movement and Gandhiji was the expression of this mission:

I hold drink to be more damnable than thieving and perhaps even prostitution. It is not often the parent to both? I ask you to join the country in sweeping out of existence the drink revenue and abolishing the liquor shops.

Let me, therefore, re-declare my faith in undiluted prohibition before I land myself in deeper water. If I was appointed dictator for one hour for all India, the first thing I would do would be to close without compensation all the liquor shops, destroy all the toddy palms such as I know them in Gujarat, compel factory owners to produce humane conditions for their workmen and open refreshment and recreation rooms where these workmen would get innocent drinks and equally innocent amusements. I would close down the factories if the owners pleaded for want of funds.

It has been a plank in the national programme since 1920. It is coming, therefore, in due fulfilment of the national will definitely expressed nearly twenty years ago."

Sociological journey to interpretive destination.

This long excursion may justly be brought to a close by an oft repeated but constitutionally relevant quotation from Field, J. irresistibly attractive for fine-spun feeling and requisite expression:

> *'There is in this position an assumption of a fact which does not exist, that when the liquors are taken in excess the injuries are confined to the party offending. The injury, if it is true, first falls upon him in his health, which the habit undermines; in his morals, which it weakens; and in the self-abasement which it creates. But as it leads to neglect of business and waste of property and general demoralization, it affects those who are immediately connected with and dependent upon him. By the general concurrence of opinion of every civilized and Christian community, there are few sources of crime and misery to society equal to the dram shop, where intoxicating liquors, in small quantities, to be drunk at the time, are sold indiscriminately to all parties applying. The statistics of every State show a greater amount of crime and misery attributable to the use of ardent spirits obtained at those retail liquor saloons than to any other source. The sale of such liquors in this way has therefore, been, at all legislative regulation. Not only may a licence be exacted from the keeper of the saloon before a glass of his liquors can be thus disposed of, but restrictions may be imposed as to the class of persons to whom they may be sold, and the hours of the day, and the days of the week,*

> *on which the saloons may be opened. Their sale in that form may be absolutely prohibited. It is a question of public expediency and public morality and not of federal law. The police power of the State is fully competent to regulate the business to mitigate its evil or to suppress it entirely. There is no inherent right in a citizen to thus sell intoxicating liquors by retail; it is not a privilege of a citizen of the State or of a citizen of the United States. As it is a business attended with danger to the community, it may as already said, be entirely prohibited or be permitted under such conditions as will limit to the utmost its evils. The manner and extent of regulation rest in the discretion of the Governing authority. That authority may vest in such officers as it may deem proper and power of passing upon applications for permission to carry it on and to issue licenses for that purpose. It is a matter of legislative will only.'"* (SCC 1978)

If Nehru's noetics have value, Oommen Chandy whom I respect for many other reasons is a riddle wrapped in a mystery inside an enigma.

ENVIRONMENTAL MALADIES AND JUDICIAL REMEDIES

The integral yoga of life and law is the key to environmental justice. The judges have a vital role to play in winning the war against the pollution of the biosphere and defending the eco-system sans which survival of the human species will be a hollow hope and hi-tech dope. The right to life is the foremost human right but you need pure air, potable water and non-noxious food. Thus the jurisprudence of environment *vis-à-vis* basic human rights is of paramount importance if society is to live without deleterious invasions. Nature is compassionate and promotive of universal happiness provided advances in science and technology do not wound ecology or violate the environment. So in our age of rapid technological conquests, victimising Nature and borrowing 'westoxicated' imitation of pollutive technology, geared to profit-greedy toxic processes, regardless of grave injury to living Creation, there is great need to enact and enforce laws sensitive to preservation of the delicate balance necessitated by eco-friendliness. The jural compulsions and judicial function to police and protect the values of Life cannot be neglected except at lethal peril to society. Developing countries forget the ancestral heritage of Nature worship and reverence to that harmony which sustains the universe on its spiritual-material foundations. The fundamental significance of environment is no longer a scientist's esoterica but a common man's life-saving concern and jurist's curative commitment. Law is not a narrow, punitive function of sovereignty but a social science with a larger welfare objective. Indeed, judges too, in their professional orthodoxy and dogma of *locus standi,* find themselves obsolete and so have begun to awaken themselves to the great social engineering and stern legal policing expected of them even as pollution is furiously escalating, industrial mafia is merrily making money thro' contamination of soil, air and water, politicians are corruptly inactive in arresting toxic processes and the masses are pathologically perishing. However, judicial statesmen, with wider vision and profound humanism, are invigorating environmental law and justice. The finest hour of forensic functionalism arrives when judicial activism, catalyses the law and fulfills its mission of ensuring conservation of Nature. Not all judges rise to this creative height. It needs scholarship, wide reading, dynamism and people-oriented passion to transform the text of the statute into operative reality of society. Justice Ashok Desai's handy volume on Environmental Jurisprudence proves he belongs to the scholarly category. I am myself an environmental fundamentalist balancing growth with justice, technology with eco-amity and granting priority for humanity over profit-grab propensity. Desai, I discover, is a battler for a non-noxious biosphere. May his tribe increase!

Justice Desai has, in his book, gone to the ancient roots of environmental theology in all the religions, probed the spiritual values from the *Upanishads* and *Atharva Veda* and with a rare eclecticism dwelt on the teachings of Lord Buddha, Mahaveera and the *ayaat* of the Merciful Allah. A passage from his book thrills me:

> *These bounties of Nature from Allah are entrusted to man as a trust for his upliftment and betterment of other creations. These bounties are shielded and protected by an environment through which filter down the light and energy from the sun, the beauty and grace of the moon and the navigating guidance of the stars and the planets tracing their destination in the firmament.*

Christ was for all-embracing love and kindness, even as Kautilya (300 B.C) mandated protection of the environment. The author has painstakingly brought out the reverence of religions for Nature. Thus profound perception of anti-pollution is a distinct Desai contribution to the environmental literature. Science and technology are means, not ends, and cannot suppress or surpass the sublime harmony of Creation we behold in Nature. The violence and vulgarity, which became a bye-product of the industrial revolution, obliterated the happy fusion of science and human well-being, and the arrogance and money-manic vice of the savage in man repressed the *rule of Nature* to achieve the *rule over Nature.* In the words of Martin Luther King Jr. 'the means by which we live have out distanced the ends for which we live. Our scientific power has outrun our spiritual power. We have guided missiles and misguided men'.

> *Our century, before it expires, has a choice to make. It faces a Hamlotian dilemma. To be, or not to be: that is the question – if we care or dare at least to frame the question and fact the problem. I mean here not the nuclear terror in the hands of some of whom one holds mankind to horrendous ransom. Human survival is menaced by another equally homicidal missile euphemistically described as environmental pollution. If I may mint an odd expression, 'thanatology through technology' is the Frankenstein's monster that Science and Industry, promising global progress, have created. If dehumanized industrialization, with all its profit – hungry vulgarity and its ecological insensitivity, invades Nature without enlightened resistance from society and poisons or depletes all the resources of land, water and air, the crucifixion of humanity is a certainty and the resurrection of the race a lost*

possibility unless we begin the battle for human values against barbarity incorporated, right now. Today is late; Tomorrow may be too late. (Desai at page 280 quoting me)

Ashok A. Desai has done a lot of lucubration in preparing this learned work, judging by the profusion of quotations and vistarama of coverage. Being a senior judge, his words carry weight and I wish others of his tribe on the Bench, instead of getting paper-logged, did some research and reading which will enrich their court pronouncements beyond the blinkers of cited precedents and obsession with backlog of dockets. Judges must constantly conscientise themselves, while dealing with environmental litigation, that "we owe it to our ancestors to preserve entire those rights, which they have delivered to our care: we owe it to our posterity not to suffer their dearest inheritance to be destroyed". Judges (and lawyers) are trustees of the human estate, the world's great heritage; and the robes have a fiduciary responsibility obligating the use of writ power to restrain and regulate modern industry and technology so that progress is not perverted into high profits of some to the environmental injury of the many. Development needs to be re-defined to forbid mass disaster and a code of environmental ethic must be enforceably clamped down on pollutive industry and agriculture. The Third World has no tomorrow if it is fatally infatuated with the deadly dope of glitteratti life-style and afflicted by the disease of affluenza. I often quote, because of the power of his words, Winston Churchill who had warned us about the terrorism of reckless technology: "The dark ages may return – the stone age may return on the gleaming wings of science; and what might now shower immeasurable blessings upon mankind may even bring about its total destruction. Beware I say! Time may be short."

Ashok Desai, aware of the grim portents of worldwide pollution has expanded his attention to our ancient reverence for and warning against violation of Nature. The emergence of environmental jurisprudence, its development from the Stockholm Conference to the Rio de Janeiro Summit, the Club of Rome and so on are rightly dealt with. The Gandhian perspective has been ignored by Indian politically corrupt ignoramuses in power who refuse to learn the lessons of the Union Carbide tragedy – Bhoposhima and gassasination, as I called it. The Constitutional provisions and legislative enactments and the story of judicial activism in environmental protection have been addressed by the author. Necessarily, public interest litigation has been discussed and the Court's drive to apply the Polluter Must Pay principle has claimed the learned author's specific notice.

Justice Desai takes a look at the 21st century prospects for a pollution-free world. He deals with the 'war for water', the chaos in the legislative cosmos and the reversion to the Gandhian wisdom to correct the current toxic technology running amok. P.V. Narasimha Rao, addressing a Delhi Conference in 1994, regretted: 'When legislation is passed, but not enforced, the society goes into absolute disarray. Legislation is a weapon, if it gets blunted and observed only in breach, how to change the society? Where legislation fails, the gun takes over." The great polluters of the earth are America Inc. followed by the other G-7 Corporates. The jurist in Justice Desai has done me the honour – unmerited, if I may humbly add – of quoting me more than once:

> *Justice Krishna Iyer has an ardent belief and puts it thus" "Finally let me emphasise again that legislation must envision positive action and not stop with policing the pollution. A national environmental policy and ecological plan must be promoted by law so that Man and Nature love and live in harmony. We must disprove W.S. Gilbert: 'Man is Nature's sole mistake.*

By 2000 A.D. do we enter the Millenium or 'Hellenium'? With optimism, the author concludes with a quote from Prof. Nayak:

> *If present trends continue, the world in 2000 will be less crowded (though more populated), less polluted, more stable ecologically and less vulnerable to resource-supply disruption than the world we live in now. Stresses involving population, resources and environment will be less in future than now. The world's people will be richer in most ways than they are today. The outlook for food and other necessities of life will be better... Life for most people on earth will be less precarious economically than it is now.*

The reader may be assured of the profusion of quotations, appropriate and therefore deserving to be appropriated. A good volume on a vital branch of jurisprudence written by a learned judge with industry, integrity and encyclopedic amplitude must find its place in all law libraries.

I must not conceal my pessimism, even as our political leaders seem to surrender to global corporate power, for reasons obvious but must be avoided from public mention.

Mikhail Gorbachev once wrote, what is pregnant with meaning, to the International Life Institute:

> *Present-day science and technology offer an opportunity to beautify, in the full sense of the word, life on Earth, to create conditions for the all-round development of every individual. But it is the very creations of the human mind and human hands that threaten the very existence of the human race. What a crying contradiction! We want science to cease to be the servant of two masters-life and death. We want it to serve life only.*

This desideratum is feasible provided the Gargantuan Global Corporates which are the macro-pickpockets with meretricious marcecha strategies, are caught by environmental law and taught not to corrupt the political Controllerate (ministers and minions, beurocrats and technocrats) on pain of penal consequences. Pollution has reached a peak point where 'to be or not to be' is an imminent interrogation.

WOUNDED NATURE *VS.* HUMAN FUTURE

Divinity is manifestation of humanity and creative plurality. Jurisprudence 'in its cosmic dimension assumes its majesty and glows in its glory only when this magnificent subject from its micro to macro vision embraces the infinite aspects. It has been said most wisely. How comprehensive the rule of law is luminously expansive. If dharma in its parameters reaches out to creative wonder the subject of my lecture is vistaramic as explained above.

Having due regard to the several considerations involved, I chose a subject of current relevance and poignant portent ,"*Wounded Nature* v. *Human Future*". Nature is bleeding, amidst hi-tech glitter and profit-hungry adventures while our future is flickering and our survival somber, what with Man's torturous inhumanity to Nature and avaricious injury to culture.

Let me write a prefatory note before I begin the discussion. A holistic vision of Creation, which itself is the manifestation of the Absolute (taking in, as it does, the Unmanifest and the Manifest), is the spiritual legacy of ancient Indian vintage. So it is that the Constitution, in Article 51A, mandates compassion for all creation, promotion of humanism and harmony and protection of natural environment and ecology. This sublime ideology embraces all Nature, organic and inorganic matter and human and other species, each being a part of an integral whole. *Esa Vasyam idam sarvam* (God inhabits all creations) is the vedic wisdom,—a vision of the unity in divinity, diversity, and the happy synthesis of materialism and spiritual universality. Pluralism, in its phenomenal existentialism, is not negated but subsumed in the unitive perception of plurality as a play of the Supreme in its evolutionary spiral. In a broad perspective, Nature is the material manifestation of *Brahman,* and the human is the highest life form in this progressive process, the long march of the *Atman,* in human embodiment, towards the Infinite Absolute which is the celestial destination defined by different religions in divergent ways. Materialists, using dialectical tools, read through the contradictions in the Manifest, a struggle towards higher synthesis. But scientists and religionists agree that Nature is too sacred and inviolable to be traumatized by ecologically and environmentally hostile technology and hedonist thanatology. A finer harmony between nature and man is the basic condition of human survival and advance towards a better world. This is scientific sanity, unity in divinity and dynamic modus vivendi between development and human aspiration for happiness. The integral yoga of nature and man is thus fundamental to civilization and gross distortion of this beautiful balance will claim a painful price from humanity. This profound realization is the creedal essence of ecology, environment, conservation of nature and sustainable development. Such a revolutionary vision is the locomotive of human progress, this prolegomenon serves to explain the theme of my Lecture: "*Wounded Nature* v. *Human Future*".

The advocacy of wild life preservation, animal rights, vegetarianism and environmental protection have their roots in a new ethic of universal compassion inscribed long ago in the rock pillars of Emperor Asoka. The opposition to a host of insensitive operations such as sealing, whaling, wild life hunting, cattle slaughter, fur garments mid luxuries in diet and dress involving cruelty to creatures, animal experimentation for cosmetics and curative guinea pig methods can be traced to a vibrant humanism and green movements which transcend the coarse, unconscionable hungers of the savage stand in still lingering human personhood.

There is a spiritual connection between environmental and animal rights and harvesting of seals and other hunting operations carried to commercial excess. The following quote is typical of the ecology, economy and ideology connectivity that is gaining ground as part of the green campaign:

> *"A spiritual bond between Native hunter and animals is certainly implied in the invocations and allusions made by many environmentalists (see, for instance Udall 1962) to the deeper ecological understanding of native peoples. The best-known example of environmentalist – native kinship if found in the literature distributed by the Greenpeace.*
>
> *An ancient North American Indian legend predicts that when the Earth has been ravaged and the animals killed, a tribe of people from all races, creeds and colours would put their faith in deeds, not words, to make the land green again. They would be called 'The Warriors of the Rainbow', protectors of the environment".*[1]

This higher perception of cosmic holism and social and moral interaction creates the reality of a single cognitive community and cultural identity that is the essence of egocentrism. Protest movements against commercial exploitation of seals and killing of other wild life are fuelled by a new awareness of justice for humbler sub-humans as the conscience of compassion for all living creatures—'regardless of whether it affects human beings, non-human beings or the Earth herself'. In sum, homosapiens, to be worthy of his spiritual - ethical status, must shed his carnivorous, morally callous appetite which is vulgar, vicious and too violent to be consistent with the values which mark the milestones of progress. In lines of penetrating, simplicity, Coleridge versified:

---

1. George Wenzel, *Animal Rights Human Rights*, 1984, p. 134.

"He prayeth well, who loveth well
Both man and bird and beast".[1]

This is not a return to crude Nature worship nor primitive animistic pantheism but a refinement of the soul which resists the materialistic corrupt consumerist indulgence masked as pursuit of happiness. What is at risk is finer humanness, consonance with Nature and commitment to future generations which are the first charge on our power to use natural resources. Our glorious global future lies, not in a reversion to promitivism and asceticism and hands-off nature and its abundant bounties, but in a lovely, lively balance which sustains material development without ravishment of nature, pollution of environment and extermination of ecological excellence.

> *"We owe it to our ancestors to preserve entire those rights which they have delivered to our care: we owe it to our posterity not to suffer their dearest inheritance to be destroyed".*[2]

Our Constitution has mandated that, "The State shall endeavour to protect and improve the environment and to safeguard the forests and wild life of the country".[3]

Again, in another provision, writ in strong diction is the command:

> *"It shall be the duty of every citizen of India... to protect and improve the natural environment including forests, lakes, rivers and wild life, and to have compassion for living creatures".*[4]

The future is not a beggar eating what left-overs the present leaves on the table but the rightful heir to the bequeathment of the estate preserved prudently as trustee.

The biosphere sustains us all. To preserve it is the path to progress. To pollute it is the route to ruin—may be today, may be tomorrow. Survival through suicide is the nostrum of those who wish us to wink at pollution as the necessary price of progress. Humanism and law must call the bluff. To muddle and bungle, to omit and abet, the rape of the earth is to dig the grave of humanity.

Justice to Nature is investment in life's unsullied joy:

"There is a pleasure in the pathless woods,
There is rapture on the lonely shore,
There is society where none intrudes,
By the deep sea, and music in its roar;
I love not Man the less, but Nature more,
From these our interviews".[5]

---

1. 'The Ancient Mariner', Part VII.
2. Junius, Letters: Public Advertiser, 1769-71.
3. The Constitution of India, Article 48A.
4. The Constitution of India, Article 51A(g).
5. Byron, "Childe Harold's Pilgrimage", C.I. Stanza 179.

Man is nature's best promise and worst enemy. The ancients have stated that God sleeps in the mineral, awakens in the vegetable, walks in the animal and thinks in man. The sublime prospect that unfurls before civilization through the advances of science is darkened by the devastating misuse of technology to poison and pollute the biosphere and thereby to hold humanity in terrible peril of total liquidation of the life process. Man blinded by myopic profit-making, is matricidal towards Mother Earth and is rapidly making himself an endangered species. India, notwithstanding its primitive rurality and worship of cows, ice, eagles, peacocks, rivers, trees and plants, is violently violating ecological ethics. The compassion of the Buddha and the non-violence of Gandhi stand terribly travestied by the processes of pollution in India that is Bharat.

The unconscionable industrialization, the unpardonable deforestation and the inhuman extermination of living species betray an exploitative brutality and anti-social appetite for profit and pleasure incompatible with humanism and conservationism. The *Rig Veda* praises the beauty of the dawn (ushas) and worships Nature in all its glory. And yet today a bath in the *Yamuna* and *Ganga* is a sin against bodily health, not a salvation for the soul. So polluted and noxious are these 'Holy' waters now that the words of Rev. Martin Luther King Jr. that our scientific power has outrun our spiritual power and that we have guided missiles and misguided men.

Unsocial industrialism and socialist India

Opening wide ajar the doors into Indian industrial space to the multinationals and other corporates without a Code of Conduct, environmental safeguards and social accountability and safety enforceable by law effectively is the gravest danger confronting the Nation today. Such a policy placatory corporate power, foreign or indigenous, is fraught with 'Union Carbide syndrome', fatal environmental pollution, lawless ecological injuries and yuppee-yankee cultural subversions, apart from deforestation and even defiance of Indian Justice whose arms may fail to reach corporate giants headquartered abroad. Human health is in peril because of noxious industrial operations of gargantuan MNCs. Even otherwise, the Central Government is somnolescent about environmental preservation, notwithstanding the Constitution. Two illustrations among hundreds I cite from that sensitive environmentalist Maneka Gandhi:

> *"I can give you a number of examples where the absence of proper vision has created very grave problems for the society. Take for instance the PVC fire in Delhi which was been proved to be carcinogenic. Every Delhiite runs a 50 per cent greater chance of cancer at the moment".*
>
> *"Take the case of aluminium foils. Aluminium comes from bauxite which is mined at tiger sanctuaries. Are encroached upon? Are we not going to create a situation where the species will get extinct?"*[1]

1. Interview with Maneka Gandhi, Sunday Communicator dated 20-8-1995.

Do remember that given an absent and ineffective environmental disaster jurisprudence and forensic infrastructure, we are going to face many more tragic Bhopal assassinations. As Maneka Gandhi mentioned:

> *"Our government thinks that the unemployment problem in the country will get solved when these multinationals set up a number of industries here. The fact is, they are not going to set up labour-oriented industries in the first place to solve the unemployment problem. Secondly, they are not interested in setting up their factories in under-developed areas. The third and the most important danger is, they are coming out with those projects which are banned in their countries for environmental reasons. In effect, we are giving a red carpet welcome to those industries which have been banned in the developed countries. They will pollute the entire atmosphere and we will be compelled to drink polluted water and breathe polluted air. If these indiscriminate sanctions for environmentally hazardous industries continue, India will be doomed forever. We cannot allow that to happen".*[1]

Imagine the culpable governmental failure when we remember the Stockholm Conference and Resolutions.

The United Nations General Assembly passed a Resolution on December 15, 1972, emphasizing the need for active co-operation among the States in the field of human environment. The Resolution has designated June 5, as the World Environment day and has urged Governments and Organizations in the United Nations system to undertake on that day every year world wide activities reaffirming their concern for the preservation and enhancement of the environment. On the same day another resolution was passed which provided for institutional and financial arrangements for international environmental co-operation. Among others, provisions were made for establishing a Governing Council for Environmental Programme, Environment Secretariat and Environment Fund.

Indira Gandhi, impressed by Stockholm sought to revolutionize legislatively the environmental safety of the Indian biosphere. Many laws were made, but when pitted against corporate power, laws failed to act and courts in their innocence acquit the guilty ignorantly. The situation is a deepening crisis even in America compounded by official secrecy. Ralph Nader in an old writing, observes about the US:

> *"A burgeoning technology is giving corporations more power than they choose to exercise responsibly. Witness, for example, the domestic chemical and biological warfare called, too charitably pollution. Concentration of economic power develops momentums of abuse in political, social, educational and union areas. Laws and antitrust and regulatory frameworks have been symbols rather than arms of democratic governing, while the corporate regulates control the public regulators".*[2]

---

1. Interview with Maneka Gandhi, Sunday Communicator dated 20-8-1995.
2. Introduction, Morton Mintz and Jerry S. Cohen, Amrica Inc. (1972), p. 14.

Business depredators are too big for the law as the U.C.C. Bhopal tragedy proved. Violations are on the rapidly rising, scale of escalation. As for India, the best commentary on the impotency of anti-pollution Justice is the fact that the Supreme Court has recently directed, "The Central Pollution Control Board to serve notice on the 8378 noxious units, asking them to shift out of the National Capital Region".[1]

Harinder Singh writes in a renowned newspaper on 30th April, 1995:

> *"The first thing that strikes a first-comer to Delhi is the variety of pollution – a unique mix of noise and nose-shattering fumes hit him straight in the face, leaving him more than flabbergasted. For the Capital of India, said to be the third-most polluted city in the world (though some call it even worse than the Mexico City), is the earth's very own version of limbo, if not hell.*
>
> *It all began with Delhi attracting all kinds of petty traders from across the north India, leading, over a period of time, to the creation of a wholesale market, renowned as one-stop shop for all the cheap goods. As the next logical step, a host of very small industrial units sprung up in the city to cater to the needs of the wholesale market. And this put Delhi well on its way to acquiring the status of a polluted city.*
>
> *Along the way, every nook and corner of the city became 'infested' with such riches bringing manufacturing units. Even though the city administration tried to keep a step ahead of the proliferating units by setting up various industrial areas, it all proved futile: new units kept on springing up (literally) in non-conforming areas. Today the situation is such that these units contribute around 10 to 12 per cent to the total pollution.*
>
> *Though the persons concerned – ministers, bureaucrats, etc.—made all the right kind of noises, it was not until M.C. Mehta, the renowned environmental lawyer, filed a public interest litigation (PIL) before the Supreme Court that the things began moving. Acting on it, the Apex Court, on March 24, directed the Central Pollution Control Board (CPCB) to serve notices on the 8.038 noxious units, asking them to shift out of the National Capital Region".*[2]

Vehicular Pollution in Delhi with its 28 lakh automobiles pollute with black fumes the city's streets and nothing has yet been done to arrest this corrupt asphyxiation of the air. Delhi's denizens would soon have to work around with oxygen bags for sheer survival, all because pollution is profit and purity is a little expensive. Corporate power in Delhi, as in Washington D.C. can overpower. The reason is best given by a blunt statement by Woodrow Wilson long ago:

> *"The masters of the government of the United States are the combined capitalists and manufacturers of the United States... It is written over every*

1. *M.C. Mehta* v. *Union of India,* 1995 (4) SCALE 789.
2. The Financial Express, 30th April, 1995.

> *intimate page of the record of Congress, it is written all through the history of Congress, it is written all through the history of conferences at the White House, that the suggestions of economic policy have come from one source, not from many sources... The government of the United States at present is a foster child of the special interests".*[1]

We live in a world of depletion of natural resources, of desertification, of air pollution, of dangerous radiation, of chemical breakfasts, lunches and dinners more noxious than nutritious. Nature is 'in tears, while exploitation of resources is exasperating as our callous century advances, nature, wounded, retreats. This great contradiction is growing; and now, with CATTASTROPHE accompanied and the Uruguary, Round completed, MNCs have open sesame everywhere. Their rapacious activities have involved all of nature's sub-systems—the biosphere, atmosphere, hydrosphere and lithosphere—inflicting mortal wounds on 'homosphere' where humans live. Science will become the enemy of progress, the balance between man and nature, is shaken. Sustainable development, therefore, must restrain the terrorism of technology. Winston Churchill once warned, in a different context, of the insane consequences of excessive industrialization through homo-lethal, market-manic technology:

> *"The dark ages may return – the stone age may return on the gleaming wings of science; and what might now shower immeasurable material blessings upon mankind may even bring about its total destruction. Beware, I say! Time may be short".*[2]

The Third World is the worst victim, but the First World is also in peril. Ecology and environment, so necessary for human survival, are being wounded fatally leaving our human future in grave danger. A major culprit is capitalism's moneyocratic cannibalism. Even socialist States, with constitutional injunctions to protect nature, bring about disaster through callous industrialization and technological deprivation. The Third World with its poverty, air pollution by soot and rotting garbage fumes and filth, the absence of water supply systems and even toilets and shelter contribute to violation of nature, especially in the absence of ventilation in houses, over-crowding of human and animal co-existence in shocking rurality. While socialist States (none are now left!) have better aliveness to conservation of nature, capitalist countries are ecologically reckless and environmentally deleterious. President Theodore Roosevelt warned arrogant Americans:

> *"The natural resources of our country are in danger of exhaustion if we permit the old wasteful methods of exploiting them longer to continue... The time has come to inquire seriously what will happen when our forests are gone, when the coal, the iron, the oil, and the gas are exhausted, when the soils shall have been still further impoverished and washed into the streams,*

1. The New Freedom, 1913, pp. 57-58.
2. As quoted in Krishna Iyer V.R., Environmental Protection and Legal Control, 1992, p. 13.

polluting the rivers, denuding the fields, and obstructing navigation. It is time for us now as a nation to exercise the same reasonable foresight in dealing with our great natural resources that would be shown by any prudent man in conserving and wisely using the property which contains the assurance of well-being for himself and his children".[1]

In the late 1960s, Stewart Udall, the then Secretary of the Interior (America), sharply rebuked his countrymen:

"This nation leads the world in wealth and power, but also leads in the degradation of the human habitat. We have the most automobiles and the worst junkyards. We are the most mobile people on earth and we endure the worst congestion. We produce the most energy and have the foulest air. Our factories pour out more products and our rivers carry the heaviest loads of pollution".[2]

By the 1970s, an American moved to the Moon, but his launching pad lay, on a field of garbage. Ronald Reagan, then Governor of California told his electorate:

"There is no subject more on our minds than the preservation of our environment and the absolute necessity of waging an all-out war against the debauching of that environment".[3]

Grigori Khozin, the Soviet Journalist quoted reports from the U.S. and said:

"In the early 1970s, as a result of a continuous deterioration in the quality of the working environment and of increased pollution at US factories, at least 1,00,000 people were dying every year and another 3,90,000 were being seriously disabled. In the Federal Republic of Germany, the number of people suffering from hearing defects due to factory noise in the 1960s rose 13.5 times compared with the previous decade; and the number of industrial workers suffering from skin diseases has been growing fast. In Sweden, an examination of workers employed in copper smelting works showed an increasing number of deaths due to cancer of the lungs, blood disease, cirrhosis of the liver and cardio-vascular disease. Medical men are alarmed at the continuous growth of hereditary diseases and even deformities among working-class children".[4]

Many violations by *Corporations of the* laws concerning air and water pollution resulted in fines, but the ecological damage was not arrested. The West European countries also breached nature conservation. Grigori Khozin turns the lens on nature being reduced into a junkyard for all sorts of wastes. For instance:

"In the Reserve Mining Company alone has been daily pumping 67,000 tons of waste products containing dangerous elements into Lake Superior -

1. James Rathlesberger (Ed.), The Politics of Devastation, 1972, pp. 5, 7-8.
2. As quoted in Grigori Khozin, Big Business Against Nature, 1984, p. 18.
3. As quoted in Grigori Khozin, Big Business Against Nature, 1984, p. 19.
4. As quoted in Grigori Khozin, Big Business Against Nature, pp. 19, 20.

one of the world's largest fresh water lakes (one-twelfth of all the reserves of clean fresh water on Earth). Special conferences convened by the public, court rulings, strict government orders, and even attempts to close down the plant have all failed to force the owners to abandon such 'commercial activity', which brings in an estimated daily profit of 14,000 - 24,000 dollars".[1]

Pointing out that *many rivers in the West* are industrially polluted, Khozin takes the example of the Rhine and says:

"... every year waters of the Rhine pour into the North Sea 41 tons of mercury, 140 tons of arsenic, 1,700 tons of lead, 1,600 tons of copper, 13,100 tons of zinc, and 20 million tons of salts".[2]

Limitless impurities have polluted most of the rivers and lakes of the US and, in the air, heavy toxic and other matter harmful to health threaten human life. US corporations experiment with chemical compounds geared to maximum and immediate profit and, in the bargain, spread toxic, carcinogenic and other harmful elements. Capitalism has no body to be burnt, nor soul to be damned. Industrialism even in socialist lands inflicts injury to environment and human life although to a lesser degree. The catalyst of capitalist industry is large profits, ecological havoc caused being of little consequence to its conscience. Agricultural production as an industrial operation, using chemical fertilizers and pesticides and consuming much power, has turned hostile to human health.

Forests are 'lungs' or oxygen factories which sustain life. But the great forests of all continents are vanishing at a dangerous pace and the deforestation-desertification syndrome is a terrible menace to human progress.[3]

Industrial wastes are often highly noxious and the 'advanced' countries corruptly transfer these sources of pollution to Third World countries. Developing nations are seduced into dismantling congenial plants and projects of appropriate technology and the politicians ad compradors of these weaker countries have a honeymoon with big corporations of the North. In the guise of covering the technological gap, corporations of capitalist countries build 'polluter' plants and consumer lollipops, imitative of the exotic Western lifestyle, in the territory of developing nations. When there is an outcry against these 'recolonisation' processes, propagandist unveracity on a big scale is used to take environmental and other evil fallouts as the inevitable price of 'progress'. Thus a fatalist acceptance is induced by

1. As quoted in Grigori Khozin, Big Business Against Nature, p. 20.
2. As quoted in Grigori Khozin, Big Business Against Nature, pp. 22, 23.
3. As quoted in Grigori Khozin, Big Business Against Nature, 1984, p. 26. In the capitalist countries monopolies control the forest resources (in Sweden 75 per cent of the forests are privately owned, in Austria 74 per cent, in Great Britain 69 per cent, in the United States 68 per cent, in France 64 per cent, in Italy 61 per cent, in Japan 57 per cent and in West Germany 41 per cent, and they lay claim to the unlimited use of the forest resources of other countries as well, especially those of the developing nations.

drugging the people with false fairy tales about technological blessings. Affluent consumerism, hi-tech developmentalism and macroindebtedness are the troika which pushes Indian political economy 'into conquering Nature callous to consequences.

Today, with the collapse of Communist Kremlin and Crimson East Europe, and the ghastly, goofy thesis of exploitative market-friendliness, liberalization and globalization – Orwellian Newspeak – the South, including India, is jettisoning its Gandhi-Nehru heritage and, in simian fashion, adopting policies ruinous to the poor millions and narcotizing the creamy layers through imported hi-tech from outside. To interdict import of hazardous, environmentally obnoxious ad cost-wise and otherwise objectionable plants, machines, collaborations and transfers is a hard job since MNCs have great clout with soft States and dubious rulers. They have Super-Power and G-7 pressure on their side to open up markets for foreign 'corporates' ignoring native capacities!

What the world does not know adequately is that big corporations are empires in themselves and can conquer the economies of lesser nations and can control the U.S. Presidency itself. Big business is private government, buys up mass media, manufactures news and views and conceals corporate crimes of robbery of nature, violation of the biosphere and adulteration of food and drink in secret making the consumer a victim. Misinformation about pollutive products apart, the power to prevent and punish giant producers from wounding Nature so as to defend the human future rests on the politicians who run the State apparatus. But the politician is an investment for Big Business and his voice is muted. Listen!

> *"The concentration of economic power, opinion power and political power creates a sort of closed loop. Politicians must raise money from corporations in order to pay the networks the enormous cost of television time. Corporate advertisers call the network tune. And the networks must curry favour with the successful politicians to assure their franchise. The open society seems to be closing - not by conspiracy, but by this mutual dependence".*[1]

The moneyocracy (Corporate Carnivores) contribute to legislators who, as *quid pro quo*, consent, sub rosa, never to use public power to protect public interest when large corporations pollute for profit and kill for more dividends. Open government and public accountability are myths wherever Big Business operates. This is a universal proposition best stated with poignant felicity by Alexander Solzhenitsyn in a letter to Russian Writers' union:

> *"Just the same, it is time to remember that the first thing we belong to is humanity. And humanity is separated from the animal world by thought and speech and they should naturally be free. If they are fettered, we go back to being animals. Publicity and openness, honest and complete – that is the*

1. Kingman Brewster, Jr. as quoted in America Inc., 1972, p. 195.

prime condition for the health of every society, and ours, too. The man who does not want them in our country is indifferent to his fatherland and thinks only about his own gain. The man who does not want publicity and openness for his fatherland does not cleanse it of its diseases, but to drive them inside, so they may rot there".[1]

Open government and free information are the first casualty when corporate power operates against Nature in their felonious art of concealment and illicit control of political government. The pity of it is that in India (and the Third World) the foreign media and transnational companies let politicians fight over communal and other issues, while the Finance, Commerce, Agriculture and Power Ministries and ministers and millions go to sleep or go slow while Big Business, robs natural resources without protest noises and drug the public through buying up the empathies of opinion-makers, and media bosses. Whenever these corporate empires poison our biosphere to aggrandise themselves, they, in business interest, administer long sleeping doses to the Justice System so that litigative pyrotechnics may not create popular consternation. They divert legislators into internal quarrels and brickbats while MNCs cunningly colonise and carry away our natural wealth or cash in on our mines, bio-diversity and 'patent' their own prosperity contra-constitutionally, leaving judges and lawyers to worry about long-pending, never-ending Everest high docket arrears.

These long aberrations have intimate relevance to India too. The world is a village and poisonous proximity makes violence to Nature somewhere the victimization of people everywhere. And our natural resources and people's survival are in peril if we slumber over or admire the investmental infiltration and dark dacoity of billionaire businesses as victory, misled by 'official' versions and media marijuana. The great concern worldwide over conservation of Nature and the human future is grimly evident from the global deliberations in Ruo, Vienna and Copenhagen, in the felicitous diction of Dr. Singhvi, "A Tale of Three cities".[2]

Nature-friendly strategies of human advance are categorical imperatives. The responsibility for resource conservation lies mainly with the industry, not only because it is a major user of resources and a major polluter of the environment, but also because of its vast experience in producing useful products from natural materials, its ability for innovation, and its efficient organizational structure.

Nikita Moisseyev, a Soviet scientist writes, with wisdom and farsighted prospects, about our task to-day:

"The growing might of modern industrial civilisation increases not only man's power over nature but also nature's power over man – his dependence

1. Kingman Brewster, Jr. as quoted in America Inc., 1972, p. 107 (as quoted).
2. The Rede Lecture 1993 in University of Cambridge.

on the state of the biosphere. And man may easily cross the fatal threshold which marks the beginning of an unknown and unpredictable evolution of the natural environment in which there may be no place left for him. But the development of powerful technical capacities is accompanied by the development of science which opens up new vistas of progress, points out dangers and suggests ways of finding compromise solutions designed to avoid a catastrophe.

The first results obtained in this new line of research are already impressive, for they indicate new, alternative approaches to the present-day global situation and ways of civilisation's further development. Regrettably, these problems are being tackled today by small and separate groups of scientists whose work is almost unknown to the broad public, sometimes even to those on whom global decisions depend. It is necessary, therefore, to unite the efforts of scientists working in different fields.

When I say 'scientists' I do not mean only mathematicians, geophysicists, biologists and other 'natural scientists'. Our colleagues in the humanities can also play a big role. The fact is that natural scientists can indicate the limitations imposed by nature on human activity, but any restrictions or bans relating to human activity can only be put into practice by people. Here is where economists, sociologists and other scholars should take over and show how the spontaneous solution of contradictions must give way to institutions of accord. They should explain to people that the world today is quite different from what it was at the beginning and even in the middle of the 20th century. This means in effect that mankind faces the onset of an epoch that needs new ethics and new morals".[1]

What is advocated is not a primitive preservation of Nature by adopting a policy of strict 'birth control' over industry, preventing modernization altogether. The plea is for socially sensitive and sagacious production process where nature, like a mother, will help human advance, but will not tolerate stabbing her for sucking material blood instead of nutritious milk. After all, the biosphere is the environment of our life, it is the 'Nature' which surrounds us. The integral yoga of human survival and technological development assumes grave dimensions when we understand the implications of the contradiction between conservation, represented by the green movement, and hi-tech excesses promoted by MNCs with profit-oriented gold rush. It follows that to maintain a sustainable human order for India and the world, we must arrest irresponsible industrialization, lest the crucifixion of humanity be the penalty for Nature-callous adventurism. An aware statesmanship, *vis-a-vis* environment, ecology and nature friendliness, quote figures which are too moderate because more damage has been done since, you will do well to realize, that every year 16,000 million tones, of oxygen are burnt up and that 24,000 million tones of carbon dioxide are

1. Man, Nature and the Future of Our Civilisation, 1987, pp. 92-93.

discharged into the atmosphere. The pollution of rivers, lakes, seas and oceans has reached a dangerous level, with about 50 per cent of all the pollution of the biosphere being caused by the United States, which has less than six per cent of the world's population. More macabre will be our future if we are blind to the perils to the biosphere through unchecked pollution. But the picture is not all that bleak. Why? If there is social will and scientific talent, what is dismissed as waste may bless us as a resource.

The management of environmental pollution through creative strategies is a feasible prospect and we need not despair if sensitized statesmanship takes control of industrial growth and agricultural production. On an earlier occasion, when I had addressed the theme of "Waste into Wealth Operation" at a Conference organized by the Internationally renowned NEERI, I had advocated a positive approach to the issue:

> *"A constructive approach to pollution prevention and waste conversion pays dividends. Environment, and therefore, sustainable development must occupy a high place in the overall planning process. No system of production and consumption can sustain itself unless the residuals and wastes produced therefrom are assimilated through pragmatic management of the environment's carrying capacity, in keeping with the basic tenets of ecology. If pollution gets the better of the system, the victim will necessarily be society itself. Pollution prevention and resources conservation are two sides of the same coin".*[1]

One need not be an advocate of ascetic simplicity in the name of nature-friendly piety. Progress in science and technology can lead to rational and restrained regimes which will make life happy. The objection is to the immoral motto of maximum profit for corporate enterprises because the doomsday scenario will certainly visit the planet if science does not heed the need not to bleed nature. Toxic technology with terrorist thanatology is a grave danger to people's survival.

Humanitarian consideration must forbid undue exploitation of nature's resources and the democratic sense of distributive justice must halt the First World's money-manic enterprises from depredation of the natural resources of the Third World. Of course, under IMF indoctrination and MNC opiumisation, India and like countries happily believe the opposite of the real situation. The aggressive exploitation of our resource, despising the socialist complexion of our Republic and the caution of appropriate technology, which is the economic message we have adopted since freedom, may spell collapse of our structure.

Unfortunately, the glamorous glorification by the engineers of the New Economic Policy of the foreign investors in appropriate consumerist areas - the coke culture - successfully strangle people-oriented economic sanity,

1. Inaugural address on February 25, 1995, Conference on Appropriate Waste Management Technologies for Developing Countries, p. 7.

tighten thought control and shape opinion formation, the vast poor - the voiceless poor-being ignored and the unemployed numbers, swelling year after year, marginalised. What is the most important feature of India today is that there is no freedom of information of the operation of Government and of the foreign enterprises and no effective consultation when plants and factories, which adversely affect environment and ecology, are set up. Secrecy is becoming the rule of Indian official life. The CAG and Parliament having little time to probe into the darker sides of dubious contacts, the computerised process and the anti-human ascendancies of profit keeps down transparency. The social environment in a paper-logged Government makes the administration a dictatorship of files, keeping even the Ministers half-informed about what is actually taking place. Knowledge, so far as the public is concerned, is a forbidden fruit and even the courts are not informed about the truth. Small wonder the human future is bleak and a kind of Cassandra's curse makes competent foretellers of our fate receive tidings of dangers ahead with disbelief. We want progress, but without tears. We want freedom from permit raj and handcuffing regulations of the economy, but, conservation of Nature, when life faces the dilemma of "to be or not to be", should be the conscience of community good. For, Nature, under torture, may, in a rage of reprisal, rupture progress.

We, of the Third World, need more greening of our developmental projects, greening of our political perspectives, greening of our environment and greening of our people's consciousness before the red rage of people in pain rise and dethrone elite power at the polls. The Eco-greens seek to protect the natural world from toxic wastes, radiation, air pollution as well as promoting eco-friendly development, use of renewable-resource technology for energy and industry. We want ecological reformers whose holistic vision is radical, conservationist, furiously anti-pollutionist and pro-ecological and who regard the politics of macro-economic power, the real enemies of the New World Human Order. Commercial whaling, seal culling, dumping of toxic and radio-active wastes and manufacturing hazardous substances potentially harmful to health, contaminating environment and even doing genetic in tooth and claw will kill life in the long run if Big Business, with focus on the Almighty Dollar, ignore the conservation constitutionally mandated by Articles 48A[1] and 51A.[2] Grass-roots greens are growing in India, Sundarlal Bahaguna and Medha Patkar being conspicuous among masses of have-nots and handicapped, economic pariahs and the proletariat who have nothing to lose except their lives.

A little deviation, to drive home the Gandhian nexus with Nature and Development tuned to Third World ethos—and economic—demographic realities, Gandhi had the courage to warn against development based on

1. *Supra*, n. 5
2. *Supra*, n. 6.

industrial giantism and foreign technological domination. Modern machinery and technology had a tendency for concentration and centralization of wealth and power. The Constitution of India with its socialistic bias and orientation in regeneration of villages of destination conceptually accepted the Gandhian developmental model. The insatiable urge for amassing wealth takes the nation downhill in the path of progress.

If growth with justice is the path towards progress which is nature friendly we need a transformation in developmental thoughts with reverence for nature. Writes Paul Harrison, in what he calls a report from the battlefront in the war against poverty:

> *"One of the most distasteful aspects of the Western model of development has been its appalling arrogance, in the face both of nature and of traditional cultures. The rape of the earth has been central to the past progress of Western industrialism; the plunder and waste of irreplaceable resources, the poisoning or destruction of fragile ecosystems, the belief that man can mould nature with no need to take account of nature's reactions to such a violation. Disdain for traditional cultures and social system was a fundamental characteristic of all modern European empires, and this attitude spread to the new ruling elites who had adopted Western ways. As a result one development project after another triggered irreversible changes in local habitats. And the whole development process did not build on the foundations of traditional society but fell on it like a nuclear bomb and blew it apart.*
>
> *The concept of eco-development, or ecologically sound development, has been developed by the United Nations Environment Programme. Its basic principles are simple. Development should respect the local ecosystem. It should conserve resources, using renewable resources wherever possible. It should minimize waste and recycle as much as it can. And it should respect local, social and cultural patterns, by involving the local population in deciding on the style and pace of development".*[1]

Basically, development must be designed as a process of distributive justice when there is appalling poverty. A mad race to close the wealth gap with the West is as futile and foolish as the arms race. Social justice is nature-friendly while the hi-tech dehumanised race for more and more rapes the earth for pleasures and profits. If India is to obey the Gandhian-Nehruvian values of the Constitution, we have to re-think our New Economic Policy and tighten our belts determined not to surrender to the North. Here is the point of confluence between the Mahatma, Ambedkar, Nehru and the Green Movement, all of them being enveloped in the Supreme Buddha teaching of *ahimsa and antyodaya.*

Bigness has a seductive appeal. Why? Because inexorably economic power controls political power. The process fattens on itself and demolishes

1. The Third World Tomorrow, 1980, pp. 38-39.

democratic criticism by buying up the fourth estate. Those who own or control the mass media and macro industrial enterprises can work havoc with nature and environment safety and social justice rendering freedom of information a mirage. That is why Justice Douglas observed:

> *"Industrialized power should be decentralized. It should be scattered into many hands so that the fortune of the people will not be dependent on the whim or caprice, the political prejudice, the emotional stability of a few self-appointed men. The fact that they are not vicious men, but respectable and social-minded is irrelevant. That is the philosophy and command of the Sherman Act. It was founded on a theory of hostility to the concentration in private hands of power so great that only a government of the people should have it".*[1]

We owe it to our Founding Fathers to reject mammoth projects at once globalised and privatised and controlled by those who are beyond Indian Justice. The core creed is best expressed by E.M. Forster in his "Towards End":

> *"It is the vice of a vulgar mind to be thrilled by bigness, to think that a thousand square miles are a thousand times more wonderful than one square mile, and that a million square miles are almost the same as heaven".*[1]

The Indian greens may be ideologically economic iconoclasts in the eyes of the New Establishment. The Gandhians and Ambedkarites, Nehruites and greens, and many others, believe that the New Investment rush and technological passion are tomorrow's Frankenstein monster namely the MNCs recolonisation of India. Green economic thought for the Third World demands:

> *"...the development of appropriate, labour-intensive technologies, fundamental and reform, and a shift from industrialization and export-orientation towards increasing self-reliance. They also propose to establish a realistic, future-oriented price structure of nature resources that will give Third World countries the means for their own development, instead of forcing them to sell off their resources cheaply, merely to ensure their short-term survival. Finally, the Greens support South-South relationships, affirming that 'the people of the Third World themselves will find the solution to their problems'. The Green Economic Programme contains not only specific proposals for ecological, social, and economic measures, but also suggestions for financing these measures".*[2]

Recent industrial tragedies *like the Union Carbide catastrophe,* the Basle disaster, the Chernobyl Nuclear Power Plant collapse, the Three Mile Island near-disaster, are among the other many unpublicised hazardous events, which are portents to send signals regarding grave risks to the good earth

---

1. As quoted in America Inc., 1972, p. 447.
2. Charlene Spretnak and Fritj of Capra, Green Politics: The Global Promise, 1984, p. 97.

from adventurist industrializations. The World Bank has issued guidelines for identifying and controlling major hazard installations in developing countries and yet in our 'sound-proof' policy making rooms industrialization with a pachydermic disposition towards environment is considered by the economic planners as equivalent to development, making little distinction between technology and thanatology (science of death). Corporate interests invariably take precedence over the health and safety of workers and of the community.

The corporate tendency to down-play hazards is an art of misinformation. The Third World Governments, even after the UCC experience, have not insisted on a legally enforceable code of conduct for MNCs nor draft charter of rights for workers of denizens.

Agriculture itself is being industrialised under pressure from the North. World Hunger is, alas, Big Business.

Big Agri-business Corporations operate within Third World countries promise, green revolutions, manipulate seeds through genetic control, produce more grain to make their gains, but before long create an agricultural slavery. Pest management through pesticides which are dangerous and fertilizers sold at great price which in the long run destroy the soil cumulatively land up agriculturists in a chemical trap. A myth was created that corporate agri-business is good for the Third World. In truth fertilizers and pesticides dumped on the Third World enter the food chain, wind up in human tissue and produce grave health hazards. In short, using the scarcity scare, India and like countries are victims of the 'poison business' promoted by the US and G-7 countries under guise of greater benefits.

The new menace of the GATT (Gattastrophe) is patentisation by the advanced countries forcing India to abandon its nationally beneficial and rationally just law of patents and to adopt American prescriptions in this field of law. Products of bio-diversity abundant and essential for the life of the people are robbed by the West using the patent process. Neem for instance, is a herb of many uses for Indians, but the West is patentising neem products thereby preventing Indians from using India's natural wealth. Other instances of our bio-diversity becoming bio-scarcity are not available, but our Government is ready to jettison the life-saving and nationally inalienable genetic wealth to foreign firms thereby negotiating the people's right to life.

Degradation of Nature follows upon destruction of the plant world. How many species have been eliminated by Man by his rapacious operations! We are still left with a number of plants, invaluable for human health and happiness. Herbs and trees grant us fuel, food, wood, medicines, manures, fodder and even industrial raw material. We must worship the tree because we survive through their environmental contribution. If we wipe out forests, cut away herbal plants, fail to preserve herbariums, rare plant species and do research to discover their best uses and therapeutic advantages we are the losers in the long run. So we must have a cooperative culture where happy coexistence of minerals, plants, animals and humans is promoted. Environment and development has this dimension.

Useful tree species growing wild is capable of medicinal values, properly researched. For instance bael tree has many medicinal uses:

> *"Bael tree has many medicinal uses. The leaves, fruits and roots find medicinal applications. In eye diseases, the juice of the leaves is poured into the eyes and the paste of the leaves is applied over the eye lids. In Odema and chest pain, steam bath with the leaves is given. The juice of the leaves with black pepper is used in the treatment of jaundice. It is also prescribed in heart diseases. The juice of the leaves is given in cases of chest pain, cough and bronchitis. It is also effective in diabetes mellitus and in uterine inflammation.*
>
> *The unripe fruit is used in loss of appetite, diarrhoea etc. Mixed with sugar it is given in cases of bacillus dysentery and piles. The ripe fruit is also used for such purposes. The pulp of ripe fruit is aromatic and cooling. It is laxative and cures indigestion. It is a good source of vitamins, particularly riboflavin, minerals and carbohydrates. The root is commonly used in the treatment of rheumatic disease, mental disease and sleeplessness. It is also used to cure intermittent fever".*[1]

Oil palm development in India has great potential, provided you identify suitable areas for cultivation. Likewise coconut cultivation is extremely useful because of the anti-carcinogenic and anti-microbial qualities of coconut oil. There are many other uses of coconut oil which have come recently under close study. New methods of improving coconut farming such as conservation and use of organic sources may help reduce costs and increase productivity. Examples like these are many and this boon of a tree can be multiplied through strong extension systems. In short nature friendly farming has great promise in our country. But the facts are cruelly contrary. Take the instance of enlightened Kerala. The rich bio-reserve and scenic beauty of Periyar Wild Life Sanctuary is a matter of national pride.

One of the leading newspapers[2] reported the present malady of the bio-reserve:

> *"The picture of heads of wild elephants moving majestically along the lakeside in the background of lush green forest is so familiar to us through the glossy posters of the tourism department, that it has become almost the visual symbol of Thekkady itself... The Kokkarakandam and Perakkad areas of the Thekkady range, which form parts of the sanctuary, had sandal forests just two years ago. But today there are hardly any sandal trees left. In May*

1. Tree World, a monthly newsletter, September, 1995.
2. The Hindu, 1st September, 1995.

this year, nearly 100 trees were cut down and taken away. The poachers even cut trees from the roadside hardly 50 feet away from the Range Officer's residence. It was only then that the authorities noticed the felling...

The 'Vayana' trees which are valued for their bark used in large-scale agarbathy production are no longer to be seen in the forest. The illegal bark collectors strip the trees bare and they die. One person can debark one tree a day and usually a group of 15 is engaged for the work, says a shop owner at Thekkady. This means 15 trees were destroyed daily. The department officials plead their inability to book the culprits. They say there are not enough staff or vehicles. Also if a culprit is caught political pressure is brought on them to compound the case and let him free. There are a number of compounded cases in the range".

The human enemies of nature defy the law, because they are government-friendly. Are we, of this generation, safe trustees of the great estate of Nature? Rio notwithstanding, we are not.

The failure of the existing paradigm and the danger of opening up large economic space for corporate industry and agri-business is fraught with danger to nature and human life. Therefore, a new international legal regime is urgently called for if the people are to have their right to life assured against macro-accidents and ultra-hazardous activities. To begin with, the agenda of legal defense of human life must draft a code of international liability so that people's safety may gain priority. Special considerations for developing countries, with a new jurisdiction and jurisprudence, must be formulated. Transnational litigations must become simpler and easier of recourse. The Indian Supreme Court in *M.C. Mehta* v. *Union of India,*[1] adopted the principle of absolute liability for all activities which are "hazardous or inherently dangerous".[2] A 'negligence' theory of liability is no longer adequate to meet the challenges of transnational corporations. The foundation for a new international justice with easy access to enforcement force and ready recovery of compensation is a necessary concomitant of the new economic policy and the dangerous implications therein. One view presented by Ayesha Kadwani runs thus:

"When the risk of harm from an activity is transnational in character, major in degree and cannot be eliminated by the exercise of reasonable care, the state must be held strictly liable and originally responsible for consequent injury. The transnationally harzardous nature of a given activity may be determined by way of a contextual multiple factor analysis. It centers on ascertaining whether a significant risk of transnational damage exists, not in the sense of a high probability of minor damage but of severe damage associated even with very low probability. The hazardous nature may be further compounded by lack of State compliance with any incumbent duty of

1. AIR 1987 SC 1086.
2. AIR 1987 SC 1086 (1099).

prior information and consultation. Transnational industrial accidents should therefore be treated as ultra hazardous activities justifying the application of a principle of absolute liability under national law. Such liability should attach jointly to the State and to the industrial enterprise in the facilities of which the accident has occurred.

A crucial element in allocating liability for transnational industrial accidents must be prevention. Such liability must be strict and indeed absolute. A strict liability standard will force industries and nations to weigh the benefit of a polluting activity against the injury caused by pollution. The main rationale for absolute international liability "should be to minimize the possibility of injurious consequences and to provide adequate redress where injurious consequences do occur" [Report of the International Law Commission, 35 U.N. GAOR, Supp. (No. 10), U.N. Doc. A/35/10 (1980), p. 365]. While States are increasingly willing to seek agreements about measures of prevention, they are generally unwilling to accept a direct linkage between preventing measures and liability for damage".[1]

Agriculture and Nature

One may briefly revisit the area of agri-business. Using organic manure for growing grains, India was raising its food supply in a self-reliant direction. The US popularised the use of pesticides tempting underdeveloped countries with export crop possibilities:

> *"An underdeveloped country, moreover, easily gets locked into producing more and more export crops, in part to earn foreign exchange to pay for more and more imported pesticides. Pesticides lead to an agricultural environment requiring more pesticides, as we will explain. The diminishing financial returns per acre that result often step up the pressure to devote even more land to export crops. The entire process bypasses the need of local people for food".*
>
> *"Pesticides usage in underdeveloped countries is concentrated in little export-oriented enclaves that are functionally mere extensions of the agricultural systems of the industrial countries. In these enclaves pesticides are commonly applied so intensively that environmental scientists are given the "opportunity" to study the effects of extreme chemical farming".*[2]

The fact is that insecticides and other heavy pesticide doses did more harm than good. Plant-eating pests outnumbered their predators, the result being the defeat of pesticides despite expensive poison in the field. It must be remembered that half of the pesticides exported from the US is the Third World and often times people were getting sick because of pesticide use in agriculture. Litigation against the manufacturer for blurred vision, speech

---

1. Transnational Industrial Accident as Ultra Hazardous Activities in David Dembo et. A. (Eds.), Nothing to Lose But Our Lives, (1988), pp. 142-143.
2. Francis Moore Lappe and Joseph Collins, Food First, (1978), p. 61.

and memory blocks, nervous system disorders and the like have affected the American exporters:

> *"With low levels of literacy, meager extension services, and heavy company propaganda about the chemicals' benefits, farmers in the Third World cannot be expected to appreciate the hazards of an apparently innocuous white power".*[1]

Nevertheless, air-planes drop pesticides which are deadly sometimes. They enter into the food chains and windup in human tissues. This chemical drug has affected nature adversely and the food of the people fatally. The poison business despite life endangering hazards is continuing because of propaganda. In the *'Food First'*, the authors have completely exposed the bogus poison business for crops and gold courses and poison for beauty used for colouring fruits and vegetables to look attractive. The chemical companies put pressure to keep people ignorant about pesticidal dangers:

> *"The massive increase in pesticide use is not because of the pressure of hungry people's need for food... lack of pesticides is not what is keeping them hungry. The real threat is that pesticide technology is in the hands of few corporations that will profit only if they can continue to make farmers and "concerned" people everywhere believe that our very survival depends on the indiscriminate use of their products".*[2]

The truth is that the pesticide myth has the silent blessings of our Government which should have stopped their import long ago. Likewise, the ballyhoo about chemical fertilisers is fraudulent because organic manure available at home is far better than imported chemicals. In that, the author says:

> *"Chemical fertiliser must, therefore, never be thought of as a substitute for organic sources. First, all sources of organic matter should be mobilised and returned to the soil. Then, for countries like China and Algeria with petroleum available to produce chemical fertiliser, developing and using that potential can make sense. (Furthermore, even though China is making a big push to utilise its petroleum for fertiliser, 70 per cent of its fertiliser is still from organic sources, enough to guarantee sufficient food production)".*[3]

The total dependence of Third World agriculture on First World monopolies must end, if nature and agriculture must come together. Indeed, the following observations are instructive when we consider local alternatives to imported chemicals:

> *"Take fertiliser. First of all we must keep in mind that shifting from monoculture to a variety of crops and instituting crop rotation will, as first*

---

1. Francis Moore Lappe and Joseph Collins, Food First, (1978), p. 65. A research term in Pakistan in 1974 reported that one customer, lacking a suitable container, unwrapped his turban, poured a granular pesticide therein, and replaced it on his head for transport.
2. Francis Moore Lappe and Joseph Collins, Food First, (1978), p. 75.
3. Francis Moore Lappe and Joseph Collins, Food First, (1978), p. 163.

steps, reduce the need for fertiliser. More important, however, the local potential for producing fertiliser from indigenous waste material is estimated to represent six to eight times the amount of nutrients in costly, largely imported, chemical fertilisers actually used by the underdeveloped countries. This energy and fertiliser potential can be tapped right at the village level, using materials that are often wasted.

The fertiliser produced through the biogas technique is many times richer in nutrients than the waster products that went into it. By fermenting the village wastes of 500 human beings and 250 cattle, a biogas "plant" can supply the average cropped land of a typical Asian village with two and one half times the present nitrogen applied in the form of chemical fertilisers. Moreover, it can supply almost double the present daily energy needs of the village for cooking, water pumping, electricity, and industries".[1]

Neem, earlier mentioned by me, as insecticide is available locally, and remember, it is an eco-friendly botanical pesticide. *Neem* is nature's bitter boon and if used widely defends agriculture batter from pests. Curious but true is the fact of conserving spiders to protect crops:

"Spiders are predators of pests like thrips, caterpillars, aphids, plant bugs, leaf hoppers, flies, etc. Their importance as pest control agents is not a recent discovery. On the contrary, their value has been acknowledged by farmers from time immemorial. Several ancient books on agriculture mention their importance. In China, even to the present day many elderly people in villages take the number of spiders in a field as a measure of its potential agricultural productivity. Fields abundant in spiders, prior to the introduction of chemical pesticide are now witnessing a change in the scenario. In addition to killing pests, these chemicals are also taking a heavy toll on useful insects. Preservation of spiders necessitates abandoning of these pesticides, or spot treatment and rational use of the same. Once pesticides are kept away from the fields, spiders invariably take shelter in the fields, feed on the pests and add to the productivity".[2]

It is true that chemical fertilisers can increase yields but they cannot maintain or enhance the soil's organic matter which is the ultimate key to fertility. Organic matter maintains the porous soil structure, provides superior water holding capacity (critical during droughts) and allows oxygen to penetrate for use by soil organisms that break down manure, crop residues, and other organic matter. Seventy per cent. of China's fertilisers come from organic sources; why not India too? We should not be victimised by propaganda baloney of Fertiliser Corporations.

Yet another eco-friendly methodology has great potential. It is the way of transforming waste into wealth. India will belong to the world of waste

---

1. Francis Moore Lappe and Joseph Collins, Food First, (1978), pp. 482, 483.
2. Pesticide Post, Vol. 3, 3 May, 1995.

if we do not recycle the accumulating waste. The wealth of waste will easily bless the country's industry if only political ignorance, social prejudice and sluggish industrialism give way to a new 'waste to wealth' operation, at once reducing pollution, re-enforcing conservation of nature and promoting eco-balance as an imperative. Garbage, if treated becomes power. Now, it produces plagues. Popular participation in making riches from rags is a measure we can and must utilise.

Environmental code and court

More than judge-made law and broad constitutional commands we need nature conservation—specific statutory outfits wherewith to confront environmental criminality and tort culpability. Of course, on-going programmes for judges from the trial to the Apex Court are very necessary to make for forensic nature-friendly adjudications.

A comprehensive legislation expressing the nation's stem determination to stamp our industrial pollution is a State obligation. Currently, the law is lame and the Bhopal tragedy has luridly revealed the shocking incompetence of our legal system and the shameful shortfalls in judicial jurisdiction and absence of 'disaster jurisprudence'. The Supreme Court of India, faced with this new terror, expanded on the Environment Protection Act, 1986, and insisted on a national policy and a code of ethics *vis-a-vis* industrial pollution. Moreover, we need mobile environmental courts since pollution is all over the rural and urban and on-the-spot justice is best.

I have no doubt, NEERI, party fills the bill in defending people's life from pollutive lethality. The new millennium, with all its boasts and all its hopes, can never really host humanity on the planet in the coming century, if expert institutions with commitment like NEERI, catalyse resistance to industrial wastes and contaminants and other developmentally deceptive but actually dangerous technologies. Sometime ago, I wrote what I think is here an apt quote:

> *"We need environment law societies, conservation organisations, informed intellectuals, independent scientists and mass mobilisation organs well informed on industrial pollution. A comprehensive code must provide for all these anti-pollution operations fighting Corporate Almighty. This is a vital policy position if the State is to take the danger of pollution by industry seriously".*[1]

The story of humanity is a perennial process with its advances and retreats, its triumphs and defeats. Now Life wins with achievements, but again, Death gains dark victories. What is puzzlesome is that in the small planet we eat each other in cannibalistic appetite, not by flesh being cooked *tandoori* fashion, as allegedly happened once in New Delhi, but by sucking people's economic blood to add riches and revel in sensual pleasure. Such a

1. V.R. Krishna Iyer, Environment Protection and Legal Defence, (1993), p. 139.

system besmirches our country because it betrays the cultural heritage Love which Jesus preached, the power of non-violence which Gandhiji permeated, every spiritual cell of his physical being, and all the vision and wisdom the sages and seers, prophets and revolutionaries lustrously gifted to our generation. Enlightenment is own inalienable, universal, millennial possession, with every human's partner in this precious treasure.

But where are we? Science marched forward, lightened our labours. Brightened our lovely lives. Dreams of prosperity and pleasure came true. But alongside came Satan challenging the divine in the human, using technology to conquer and kill, to corner wealth and sink in sex and drug and, in the bargain, the savage prevailed over the sage. The 'White Man' reappeared in history as Corporate Power and, backed by the Juggernaut of Super-Power, began to exploit all resources condemning all but the creamy layer to blood, toil, tears and sweat. The maxim of this immoral, incorporated, Power (Private) Limited was and is Business as Usual.

The intoxication of material advance, drugged by desire for more and armed with modern technology, began to torture Nature reckless of consequences, polluted environment to profiteer, mindless of the boomerang effect, exterminated ecology and bruised bio-diversity with gluttonous intent. Then came the criminal challenge to Nature and its indispensable role in human welfare. You may rush to the moor but shall not be a loon in your self-hypnotised selfishness! And yet, it is Private Multinationals Incorporated which ravish Nature in search of rapist pleasure; but the sentence of death, for their crime, is visited on humanity unlimited and generations unborn. So, the dialectic of Mother Earth under technological siege and heady, hedonist lust with Epicurean urge, is that our fish will perish, our water will no longer be potable, our air dangerous to breathe, our food chemically poisoned, our eyes and ears become dysfunctional, our body invite AID syndrome and cancer from skin to soul and our dear earth forbidden for habitation, having eaten the forbidden fruit of technological induced thanatos.

> *Our minerals, animals and humankind have a unity in divinity and each has a dharma to discard which is to deserve future shock.*

The universality of the calamity of intoxicated macro-pollutive projects, industrial and agricultural, is well brought out by Cheen Yoke Ling in a recent article titled "Economic Boom takes a heavy toll in Environment". They ring a bell for every sensitive Indian and so I quote excerpts from it:

> *"Protest against a dam to be built on prime farm land led to the killing of four villagers on the island of Madura, off Eastern Java. More than one million farmers in North-East Thailand were faced with massive displacement to make way for large-scale tree plantations to supply pulp for the global paper industry. Defence of ancestral lands against logging in Sarawak, Malaysia saw more than 400 indigenous villagers arrested since 1987. Indigenous women who decry toxic pesticide poisoning in the*

Philippines were threatened with a lawsuit by Hoechst, one of the world's biggest chemical transnational corporations".

"The changes have been traumatic for the environment and local populations. Structural shifts in resource use and perceptions of nature, and escalating materialism among a growing urban middle class are driving to the surface fundamental clashes between those who benefit from economic success and those who are victimised. A familiar lament of farmers and indigenous peoples is "Our land, our forest are more than what you see. They are our life, our spirit. We are only guardians". The equally familiar reaction is "These selfish and ignorant people are obstacles to development". In that confrontation, Non-Governmental Organisations and peoples' movements (those of farmers, fishermen, indigenous peoples) have emerged. Their roles range from mediators to protagonists".

"Sadly, the lessons are not learnt, and we find that the same short-term exploitation continues in Malaysia and Indonesia. Consequently, water shortage and water pollution caused by industrial/urban growth are on the rise. NGOs and even some officials in the region anticipate deeper water crisis in the next decade.

In the farming communities, time-tested traditional systems of agriculture have been largely displaced by the promised technological miracle of the Green Revolution. The result is a wiping out of seeds diversity from farms, a growing dependence on chemicals which do not work but instead injure and even kill farmers and agricultural workers, soil made infertile by the use of chemicals and machinery, and huge irrigation and drainage systems which are failing".[1]

What we need is to conquer this pest of "Progress", this menace to human advance is for the NGOs to fight the vice and sensitive scientists join together to launch a campaign of enlightened opposition to the insanity of neo development engineered by MNCs:

"Environmentalists argue, with strong documented evidence, that megadams have an unmitigated record of problems. Local populations refuse to be displaced. The Pak Moon dam in Thailand, the Nipah dam on Madura island and the revived Bakum dam in Sarawak are but some hot spots of contention.

Where agriculture is promoted, it is inevitably export-looking, too. Monoculture crops (oil palm, cocoa, trees for pulp), horticulture, exotic fruit and vegetable production as well as aquaculture open up environmentally sensitive areas such as forests and wetlands. These projects also threaten local food production and marginalise small farmers and fishermen.

In Malaysia, the clearing of forest in a watershed in the Kinta Highlands for growing temperate flowers for export, and the clear cutting of 5,000 acres

---

1. Indian Communicator, 5th October, 1995.

of inact pert swamp forest in Pahang for the world's largest eel farm owned by a Taiwanese company, hit the national news in 1993. Local fishermen and NGOs in Southern Thailand have been fighting for the last few years against large-scale shrimp culture which is leaving in its wake environmental disasters and impoverished coastal communities".[1]

Even golf as earlier mentioned by me is a game that goes against common people:

"The latest area of conflict is golf course and resort development. Rapid industrialisation in South-East Asia inevitably brings with it recreational facilities which are an obsession with the Japanese investors who are major players in the region's growth. Golf courses and related tourism development have created land conflicts with local rural people, destruction of forests, coral reefs and other sensitive environments as well as water contamination from sewage and the massive amounts of toxic chemicals used for greens. These projects also promote an elitist lifestyle at the expense of the needs of poor people and the environment, and as more business deals are struck on golf courses than in boardrooms, the rising elite of South-East Asia is fast adopting a similar lifestyle.

This trend is the subject of growing protest. In Singapore, plans to build a golf course in a reservoir catchment area were dropped. Public protest following complaints of safety hazards by pilots in Malaysia resulted in the halting of night golfing near the Subang International Airport. The Department of Environment is, for the first time, taking to court a golf course developer who did not conduct an environmental impact assessment before bulldozing forest in Fraser's Hill, causing tremendous soil erosion.

In Indonesia, a coalition of NGOs is working with affected communities to prevent golf course construction on farmlands and environmentally sensitive areas. New regulations were enacted in Java in May 1993, but construction of approved projects continued. Protest by farmers, human rights activists and lawyers were met with arrests and harassment".[1]

It is thus apparent that humanity is being victimised in its ecological and environmental dimensions by a creamy layer of humanity, corrupted by the passion for pleasure and the fashion for high life.

At this point, I turn to a lecture—delectable, elegantly worded and pregnant with grave portent—delivered by Dr. L.M. Singhvi titled, with characteristic flavour, "A Tale of Three Cities", which has touched a poignant chord in me reminding me of the contrast in Indian's human categories.[2]

Of course there are 'White' Indians, – a fifty of our population who claim that we are in the best of times and there are dark Indians—over five

1. Indian Communicator, 5th October, 1995.
2. *Supra.* n. 23

hundred million in number—who sorrowingly say it is the worst of times. Some put faith in the new era of the MNC entry. The poor are shocked to see prices of essentials rise sky-high. Inevitable, I am fascinated by the aptness of a Charles Dickens' quote, from *A Tale of Two Cities*. To my mind, the passage applies to the white Indian - dark Indian contradiction. Here is the delectably worded Dickensian dialectic. Although he said it about London and Paris, about 1775, I repeat it for India, 1995:

> *"It was the best of times, it was the worst of times, it was the age of wisdom, it was the age of foolishness, it was the epoch of belief, it was the epoch of incredulity, it was the season of light, it was the season of darkness, it was the spring of hope, it was the winter of despair, we had everything before us, we had nothing before us, we were all going direct to Heaven, we were all going direct the other way".*

When scientists with concern for the human future, statesmen with far sight for the next generation and sage thinkers with commitment for the ages ahead ponder beyond myopic political midgets, they will discover that the Stockholm Conference of the Seventies had stressed Nature but the greed of the rich countries paid no heed to the needs of preserving Nature, judged by the deeds and projects by which 'advanced' technology is tearing up the earth and the biosphere. The United Nations, by several instruments, has prescribed and proscribed various measures hoping that planetary patriotism would control corporate terrorism against nature. Nevertheless, the erosion of environmental values has to be arrested if the world process is to hold out a happy promise. Dr. Singhvi, in his felicitous speech, polished his presentation on this point:

> *"The tale of the first of my three cities did not really begin in Rio. Nor did it begin with the UN Conference on Environment and Development also known as Earth Summit in June 1992. It had begun ever since and each time human beings perceived their shared tenancy of Planet Earth, their membership of the human family and their future. And it is an endless tale. In a sense it began in 1972 in Stockholm which was quite unlike Rio. The seeds for the harvest in Rio were sown in Stockholm. In twenty years, propitious and somewhat modest beginning made in Stockholm had become a mighty movement enlivened by a new found sense of the oneness of our world, and its common future".*[1]

The ancient Upanishads had told us of human unity, of all Creation enjoying a holistic indivisibility and of a total togetherness in mutual reverence if the Earth were to be our home. The West violated this wisdom until scientists and statesmen beheld the grave threat. This hereafter of humanity, when futurologists got scared, forced the nations to convene, under the auspices of the United Nations, the Earth Summit at Rio de Janerio.

1. *Supra*, n. 23. p. 7.

With a sense of sublime patriotism, with vibrant universalism, we may look at the ancient wisdom manifest in reverence for all of Nature's Creation. Hinduism, if I may venture in all humility has emphasised the communion with the Earth and has taught us in its panentheistic (as distinct from pantheistic) world view, the sacramentalism of St. Francis of Assisi as well as the echo philosophy of Western thinkers.

Contrary to the carmalism of current times in the stirring opening of Ishopanishad. *G. Naganathan, a theosophist quotes and remarks:*

> *"The entire universe and everything in it, animate and inanimate, is His. Let us not cover anything. Let us treat everything around us reverently, as custodians. We have no charter for dominion. All wealth is commonwealth. Let us enjoy but neither hoard nor kill. The humble frog has as much right to live as we.*
>
> *Following the Hindu's reverential approach to every aspect of life is the creation of a phalanx of minor and major divinities, or deities or Devatas, though no other religion has been more forthright and clear on the ultimate nature of the one and only Reality. Each deity presides over a certain function, has a certain consort, uses a particular vehicle, giving them a concrete aspect that appeals to less spiritually sophisticated lay people. All these insignia have a deep philosophical symbolism. What might interest us presently is that all these vehicles are mostly drawn from the world of animals, birds, and even reptiles. For example, Brahma has a swan, Vishnu has a garuda, a type of eagle, Siva rides a bull, Ganesh a mouse, Subrahmanya a peacock, and so on. The idea is only to emphasise the kinship with animals. Trees have the divinity Vanadevata. War is presided over by the Goddess Chamundi riding a lion. Sound has a divinity, the Nadabrahmam. The Goddess Saraswathi presides over music and arts. Lakshmi sitting on a lotus deals with wealth. Parvathi, the consort of Siva, rules the entire Nature. All these divinities serve to consecrate every aspect of daily life. The whole pantheon serves to emphasise the one ultimate Reality".*[1]

The Brihad-aranyaka lifts ecology to sublime dignity in one of its early stanzas:

> *"He who dwells in all beings and is within all beings, whom all beings do not know, whose body all beings are, who controls all beings from within—He is thy Self, the controller within, the immortal".*

One may conclude this noble thought with a vedic prayer which pleads for total concord with the Universe:

> *"Peace of sky, peace of mid-region, peace of earth,*
> *Peace of water, peace of plants, peace of trees,*
> *Peace of all Gods, peace of Brahman,*

1. Animal Welfare and Nature: Hindu scriptual Perspectives, 1989, p. 2.

Peace of the Universe,

Peace of peace; May that peace come to me". – Yajur Veda.

When history was boasting of the pinnacle of civilised opulence in our times, the scientists realised mankind was precipitously perched on the brink of disaster, devastation, destruction and dark annihilation. And so, the agenda of the Earth Summit discussed the subject, "Wounded Nature Human Future", if I may put it that way. Dr. Singhvi, with lawyerly advocacy and brilliant study, presented the crisis of humanity in his Rede Lecture:

> *"The Report of the World Commission on Environment and Development titled, "Our Common Future" had pointed out in 1987 lapses of environmental neglect and degradation and the perils of developmental failures. It pointed out that in terms of absolute numbers there were more hungry people in the world than ever before; their numbers were increasing even though global production had increased faster than the population growth. It pointed out that the number of those who lacked fuel to cook and warm themselves were increasing and the gap between the rich and poor nations was widening. It also pointed out that each year some six million hectares of productive dryland was turning into worthless desert and more than 11 million hectares of forest were destroyed. During the 1970s, twice as many people suffered each year from natural disasters as during the 1960s. In the 1960s, some 18.5 million people were affected annually by drought and 5.2 million by floods; in 1970s correspondingly 24.4 million by floods; in 1970s correspondingly 24.4 million and 15.4 million people were affected annually. Numbers of victims of cyclones and earthquakes also increased considerably. Worse still we have persisted in a profligate use of Earth's finite resources and have continued to precipitate global warming and climate change by excessive burning of fossil fuels, denude the forest cover of the Earth, cause desertification and extreme scarcity of water, necessitate shifting of agricultural areas, raise sea levels, flood coastal cities, submerge low-lying islands and disrupt national economies. Pollution is rampant. There is a criminal dumping of industrial waste. The plantet's protective ozone shield is on the brink of depletion. Toxic substances poison the human food chain and the underground water tables. The world's bio-diversity is being progressively destroyed. We have already transgressed the tolerance limits of benign Nature and the dangers are clear and present. As the UN Commission had concluded, the environmental crisis, the development crisis and the energy crisis are all one and the crisis is global. The crisis can no longer be contained in national compartments or labelled leisurely under neat traditional classifications".*[1]

The urgent case for a dynamic harmony among human beings, North and South, and Nature, from the earth to outer space, is grimly obvious, and

1. *Supra*, n. 23, pp. 8-9.

so, the new concept of sustainable development, a creative *modus vivendi* and a new equity, flexibility and spirit of unity, became the empasis and main thrust of the Rio Declaration and Agenda 21 adopted at that city.

Nikhil Chakravartty, elder statesman among Indian journalists, observed about the Rio finale:

> *"What is the message that has come from Rio? The massive gathering at the Earth Summit with the unprecedented turnout of various denominations of activists from all parts of the world, gave it a truly global character which no other international gathering of the past could claim".*[1]

Rio leaves mankind with a macabre prospect and clear mandate, even as Stockholm marks a conscientising event and epochal message. Today, the problem of environment is universally accepted as central to the survival of living Earth.

This grave concern accompanied by a great commitment is a positive achievement at the end of 12 days of oral skirmishes, play of forces, and voices of peoples, commencing from 3rd June, 1992. This Summit, *vis-a-vis* environmental challenges, was constructive in many dimensions. The balance-sheet of this marathon meet where as many as 115 Heads of States and Governments and a while lot of other nations took part, organising conferences, and crystalising, through instruments and documentations, clearer perspectives and firmer objectives with supportive action plans is in mankind's favour. UNCED was, after all, a tremendous triumph, whatever its shortcomings. Rome was not built in a day. But 'the undone vast' makes our future vulnerable.

The 27-point Rio Declaration claimed general consensus. Even the former US President Bush felt compelled to present himself at Rio and offer his views on the three tough issues of forestry, funding and convention on biological diversity. The countries of the G-77 group, which has stalwarts like Prime Minister Hamathir Mohammed, took strong stances on issues like cutting down of emission of carbon monoxide and other pollutants by the US and other industrial countries. Fortunately, the pressure built up at the Summit imparted a new vision even to the nations of the north like Germany, Japan, France and Britain, unmindful of the hostile attitude of hegemonist US so as to sign the Convention on biological diversity. There was tension on the issue of forests. The Americans wanted to globalise the forest wealth of the South while the American woodlands like in Texas were sought to be kept out of the purview of the treaty. The Third World fought back and Kamal Nath, the Indian environment minister, saw through the game as his observations reveal: "The US finds it more profitable to have forests in India than Texas". Finally, the principles on forestry were adopted unanimously. The North was the main polluter and must atone for the guilt

1. Mainstream, Hube 27, 1992, p. 7.

by paying for the clean-up. Trees, it was recognised, were more than a giver of oxygen, but were a multi-purpose blessing. India worships since our ancients were wiser than our West-polluted generation. But our barons of the woods are timber-felling our Future.

Two basic principles emerge from Rio. Firstly, the human beings are the centre of sustainable development and secondly, that an interdependence and indivisibility with global expansiveness is a must when we speak of development and environment. The song of Rio is the reality of harmony, justly based on universal compassion and fundamental fraternity. A series of accords were signed proving, "we are the world; we are the children" – a song sung at the same time by the young in all the Nations to save the hungry in Africa. The Rio Summit is a new manifesto for mankind.

Among the lessons of the Earth Summit Conference what the world must learn are the following:

1. The North, comprising 20 per cent of the world's population and consuming 80 per cent of its reserves (the US consumes the lion's share), is reluctant to take any initiative to save humanity from environmental degradation and the adversities of under-development. Have the 'haves' ever in history shared with the 'have-nots' a holistic strategy to make all humanity a global brotherhood in development, environment and ecology, save under the sole force of cosmic collective conscience which is the locomotive of history?
2. Victory comes once the South stands together and awareness dawns on the North that the Earth is environmentally indivisible.
3. The prognosis is bright if the nations, weak and strong, present a united front against eco-imperialism.
4. Finally, as the Brazilian President underscored on the eve of the Rio Summit: "You can't have an environmentally healthy planet in a world that is socially unjust".
5. Have the nations any recipe for success? Such a viable proposal is what Mahathir Mohammed made:

> *A global fund, financed by national contributions assessed on the basis of population and carbon dioxide emissions, would be created to assure the success of this vast effort at reforestation and new forestation. Such a project would not only solve, at least partially, one of the world's most important environmental problems, it would also exemplify an approach to saving the Earth through cooperative efforts that are fair and just for all, not merely for the North.*

A new global order must build a justice-informed society.

Environment, ecology, population, poverty and life in luxury, all have an impact on the escalating global disorder. In this context, we must remember the World Population Day (July 10th) because it is a day to celebrate humanity, to look back and consider human achievements, and also to look forward to the new kind of world our children will inherit.

True we have made a mammoth step forward on paper. What is guaranteed against G-7 treachery and criminal abetment by Third World politicians who look for the next election and not the next generation? I must conclude with a sad note from Robert Frost:[1]

"The woods are lovely, dark, and deep,
But I have promises to keep,
And miles to go before I sleep,
And miles to go before I sleep".

---

1. "Stopping by Woods on a Snowy Evening" in C.T. Thomas (Ed.), Twentieth Century Verse: An Anglo-American Anthology, 1986, p. 110-111.

ANIMAL CITIZEN

Copy of appeal made by Justice Shri V.R. Krishna Iyer, Vice-Chairman, Animal Welfare Board of India, to the Prime Minister of India, for banning export of frogs' legs.

Dear Prime Minister,

We wish to draw your compassionate consideration to an agonising issue which disturbs the conscience of all those who love living and have sensitive regard for our ahimsa heritage. The specific subject which we beseech you to examine is the ban on export of frogs' legs dismembered while the bleeding creature is alive and conscious.

The French have protected their frogs from extinction by law but India and Bangladesh supply frogs' legs. An estimated 70 million frogs a year are cut in twain and legs shipped abroad from India—in insufferable cruelty on a massive scale inflicted on innocent amphibians which, incidentally, are ecologically invaluable for our country's economy and national health.

Frogs are our friends as ecologists and sensitives of social health are aware. May we quote in support from famous humanist, Mr. Whiting:

> *"The large hungry frogs are really the best friends that the peasant farmers have, for they eat close on their own body-weight of insects and other crop pests each day, as well as carriers of waterborne diseases which afflict the farmers' cattle. They also control the insects that carry malaria and encephalitis now devastatingly on the increase".*

Annually Indian Business exports over 10,000 tons of live frogs:

> *"Ecologically these frogs would have eaten over 10,000 tonnes of crop pests PER DAY during the monsoon season, had they been left alive in the rice paddies and coconut gardens".*

The gains made by these cruel export tycoons are more than cancelled out by the vast health hazards to the common people. Writes Whites:

> *"At this time an agricultural research project led by Dr. A.G. Joshi of Bombay Natural History Society found that the spread of disease and damage to crops was increasingly due to the wholesale destruction of frogs. The £ $5^1/_2$ million in foreign exchange obtained from frogs' legs export was offset by a £ 13 million bill for imported pesticides to replace the frogs. Many of these*

broad spectrum insecticides are so dangerous to the operator and to the environment that their use in the Western World has been banned. The pesticides also affect the frogs' spawning grounds adversely. Frogs also control fresh-water fish parasites, thereby helping to maintain healthy fish stocks. Insect-borne diseases of cattle are on the increase.

A frequent topic in the press is the alarming increase in deaths from malaria and encephalitis, both mosquito borne diseases".

We humbly submit that the nation suffers more enormous, though invisible, losses than the heartless exporters seem to net. It is a fatal folly to permit this ecological disaster for the private profit of a few.

We may now briefly project the excruciating process in the words of White who is a great animal lover:

> *"The catchers – men and children – carry torches, the light from which dazzles the frogs so that they can be caught. Some are hunted with sticks. As they are caught, they are dropped into gunny sacks. Depending on their size, between 100 and 300 may be bundled into the gunny-bags before taken by bicycle or bus to the collecting centre. "20% may be dead when they arrive at the factory after having been humped and crushed for ten hours or more in the gunny sacks".*

Some are skinned alive, the leather being used for watchstraps and purses. The majority are *cut into two through their middles by being thrust against a fixed curving knife. The leg halves will be frozen, the writhing torsos tossed into a heap to die, minutes later.* Amphibians take longer to die than mammals:

> *"Apart from the cruelty, the lack of food hygiene causes concern. Flies settle thickly on the cut legs. Those that have died hours earlier are starting to putrify in the heat. The ice they are packed in is "local" water often unfit for drinking.*
>
> *In 1973 the USA temporarily banned the import of frogs' legs from India....."*
>
> *"The scenes show the frogs being taken from the gunny sacks the day following capture. Two or three attempts are made to cut through the lower abdomen. The operator stretches them horizontally in each hand and pushes them against a Datri, the traditional Indian cooking knife which has a curved blade fixed vertically to a plank held by a foot to the ground".*

The torso is tossed aside into a twitching bloody pile of moving limbs and gasping mouths to die painfully slowly.

> "The dismembered legs have the long-webbed toes chopped off and are dropped into a bucket. *Later the now putrifying legs are transported in sacks of dirty ice to the factory".*

Living frogs agonies in pain as they are cut in twain, their legs are dismembered and the webbed toes chopped off the legs and artless rural girls, for a bare living, do the skinning and packing. This unspeakable cruelty to speechless creature is a outrage on our *ahimsa* culture and an assassination of the spiritual remains of the Father of the Nation. In the name of humanism, we beg of you to ban this trade in torture and profit from vivisected limbs.

We plead with you, to respect the values of the Constitution and enforce the *fundamental duties Part IVA imposes on all Indians.* Dollar earnings by outraging the Constitution are illegal, immoral and unworthy of our national honour. In this connection, it may be apposite to read Article 51A:

"It shall be the duty of every citizen of India—

(f) to value and preserve the rich heritage of our composite culture;

(g) to protect and improve the natural environment and to have compassion for living creatures;

(h) to develop humanism".

To hack, in manner most foul, helpless millions of living creatures ecologically helpful to man and his healthful environs for a mess of business pottage stultifies the mandate of the Constitution to show compassion to living creatures, travesties the cultural testament from Buddha to Gandhi and involves the nation in health hazards by destroying Nature's balance and immunity system.

May we emphasize that the frog slaughter is a crime against Section 11(a) and (b) of the Prevention of Cruelty to Animals Act, 1960 and Part IVA of the Constitution? Compassionate people, in vast numbers, who are deeply moved by the spirit of Karuna towards all created beings are shocked and shamed by the vivisectionist violence and the pathological callousness behind the mass frogicide.

While cows and pigs rouse man's religious passion to butcher each other and Administrator's concern to extinguish such confrontations, there is another brutality of savage dimensions silently perpetrated in our fields and farms and factories, by a heartless brood of dollar-franc maniacs, on croaking creatures in excruciating pain. We urge you, well-meaning, quick-acting and uninhibited Primer Minister, to intervene and interdict this barbarity and defend humanistically a fundamental duty (Article 51A).

We close on a note of hope and speak for the voteless, voiceless, never-the-less, living amphibians.

A Plea for Universal Declaration of the rights of nature

An issue of fundamental significance and universal relevance needs to be brought into the consciousness of the World community. Ecology and environment, life in every form and evolution, have certain harmony and integrality that makes all creation kin. Spiritually speaking, the quintessence of the environmental movement, in its widest sweep, is that everything belongs to the Supreme Self and performs its *Karma* with a functional nexus. In practical terms, there is a purpose for everything in Nature too sacred to be destroyed. Eknath Easwaran has exquisitely expressed this idea which I may excerpt here:

> *"Nobody has any right to pollute the air, water, or seas, to cut down forests, or to wash away the topsoil. We do not own the earth. We are just transients who have been entrusted to leave the earth a little better than we found it. This is everybody's job; nobody is exempt from it and, in this sense, nobody is unemployed.*
>
> *"It follows that our environmental crisis demands that every one of us play a useful part, in our own way, to improve the environment wherever we live. If a person fails to do that, even if he makes a lot of money or if he wins a prestigious prize, the Buddha would say, "You haven't done what you have to do".*
>
> *"When you have done what you have to do, you will feel very secure, very fulfilled. As you discover the self in your own heart, you discover it simultaneously everywhere, in the people and creatures around you. You will feel very much at home in this universe. You don't need to take my word for it. Try it and see for yourself". ("Your Life is your message" by Eknath Easwaran, Nilgiri Press, USA - p. 92-93).*

Ahimsa of Gandhi or 'love thy neighbour' of Jesus proceed on the basic law of our being, the truth of our nature and our innate desire for peace, justice, order, freedom and personal dignity. This *advaidic* vision is the soul of our cultural heritage; and when we meditate with this unitive understanding, the mountains, the oceans, the forests and all living forms and inorganic things look divine. God (or call him by whatever name you like) sleeps in the mineral, wakes in the vegetable, walks in the animal, thinks in man and reaches realisation when the human ascent and the divine descent meet. If we are able to gain this *vistaramic* perspective, peace on earth becomes an easy essay to achieve. In the words of Adlai Stevenson, the human race is a family; men are brothers; all wars are civil wars. Such a holistic perception, makes the whole world kin and promotes a new world order alive with a sublime presence.

The U.N. Conference on Environment and Development and the Declaration made at Rio de Janeiro emanate from these spiritual depths. The order of Nature is itself a manifestation of this conceptual globalisation. The time has come for the nations and peoples everywhere to adopt the order of Nature as the cornerstone of the New World Human Order.

The philosophy of the Order may be tersely expressed thus:

Nature is made up of an inanimate terrestrial, aerial and aquatic ensemble, on the one hand and an animate vegetable, animal and human habitat, on the other hand.

'The human species must consider itself an element of the terrestrial habitat and must respect coexistence and symbiosis. Any failure to respect these is an attack on Nature, prejudicial to the whole ensemble of inanimate and animate beings.

'The actions to be rewarded concern, in particular, the safeguarding of the natural environment, the struggle against genocidal pollution, the safeguarding of the vegetable and animal species, animal protection, the teaching of the relations between humans and non-humans, the fight against speciesism and more generally, all actions tending to render efficient the Universal Declaration of the Rights of Animals, the Universal Declaration of the Rights of Plants and the Universal Declaration of the Rights of Nature which is drafted by Prof. Georges Heuse. The declarations and the Order of Nature will stimulate the perception of the cosmic integral Unity in human species.

There is no international nor national order comparable to the Order of Nature; the existing orders regard human beings as humans, and not as members of the community of Nature. The Order of Nature will be considered as the first supranational Order and the first planetary model.'

This Vedic vision of the Indian seers of ancient vintage is our proud heritage. The radiant light of this world of harmony and non-violence must persuade all humanity to adopt what Prof. Heuse, President of the World Foundation of Quality of Life, has called the Universal Declaration of the Rights of Nature. Animal Welfare, plant culture, organic and inorganic chemistry of existence find fulfilment only when everyone is conscientised into acceptance of the Universal Declaration of the Rights of Nature. The text of the Declaration is shown in the Annexure. This declaration was drafted by Prof. Georges Heuse (Belgium), President of the World Foundation for the Quality of Life (University of Ghent), author of the Universal Declaration of the Rights of Animals (1972) and proclaimed on 15th October, 1978 at UNESCO. I advocate the adoption of this declaration by Bharat of the Buddha and Gandhi and inspire humanity world-wide to attain harmony with everything everywhere.

Mobilise people's compassion to activise animal welfare legislation

The universality of divinity is a fundamental faith of Indian humanity rooted in the Rig Veda and manifest in the spiritual core of all religions. "The ancients have stated that God sleeps in the mineral, awakens in the vegetable, walks in the animal and thinks in man". The unity that runs thro' Creation is thus a basic truth. Nature has thus an integral relation with *animalia* and *homo sapiens* is an inseverable part of the evolutionary spiral, the highest peak of ecological ascent. The ecological and environmental preservation is vital for life to survive on earth. These great values are reflected in our Constitution, a rare good fortune and a binding recognition. The State and the citizen are duty bound to promote and preserve ecology and environment as mandated by Arts. 48A and 51A.

Justice to animal citizens is as basic to humanism as social justice is to an exploited people. You are no true Hindu, Buddhist, Jain, Parsi, Christian or Muslim if you do not accept the indivisible unity of Creation and the power of the invisible Creator. So it is that love of animals, in the widest connotation, is integral to the divine vision. Be you secular or spiritual, ecological fundamentals compel us to a compassionate relationship with our sub-human brethren. Here, indeed, is the starting point of the deeper awareness of the harmony of Nature, *Karuna* and *Ahimsa* as a part of our cultural heritage.

The philosophical perspective of Animal Welfare is thus part and parcel of our cultural heritage. Every time cruelty is practised on man or beast or bird or insect, we do violence to the Buddha and Mahavira. Every torture on an animal and every export of animals is a sin to the memory of the founders of Bharatiya Samskar.

Rukmini Devi, that gracious lady who symbolised kindness to animals in her person, moved Jawaharlal Nehru to pass a legislation and thus we have to-day the Prevention of Cruelty to Animals Act, 1960.

Laws are decorative pieces on the Statute Book unless there are powerful movements supportive of their provisions. The anatomy of the 1960 Act has powers and, functions and infrastructure and has the funding and control of the Government. Cruelty to animals is an offence and experimentation on animals is regulated but not abolished. Performing animals in circuses and otherwise for exhibition imply torture and so the Act has provisions for policing such performances and exhibitions with a view to prevent cruelty. With all this and one or two later amendments, cruel practices are continuing in the land where the cow is sacred, compassion is a constitutional duty but torturesome entertainment, bleeding, butchery, animal sacrifice and other forms of cruelty are still extant. Sans people's movement, cruelty to animals will never, cease.

Monkeys were exported for terribly cruel experimentation abroad but because of the agitation and propaganda led by Rukmini Devi, the Central Government banned this brutal export. I wonder whether, in the present hunger for acquisition of foreign exchange, the Government of our Republic, which casts a fundamental duty of compassion to all living creatures, may revive the despatch of frog and cattle meat and even monkeys, forgetting that the image of Indian culture depends not on the dollars earned by exports but by the values we cherish and the homage we pay to the Founding Fathers of Bharat's Samskar.

There are other ways of inflicting cruelties on animals, including non-vegetarian food and attractive dresses and other fancy goods. How true is the PETA appeal! The People for the Ethical Treatment of Animals (PETA), argues:

"If we want to help animals, the most important place to start is with our own lifestyles.

What we eat, wear and use has a direct impact on the lives and deaths of animals. Every time we visit the grocery store, the pharmacy, or go shopping for sweaters or shoes, we vote with our consumer dollars for or against animal suffering.

Here's how a few changes in our buying habits can help thousands of animals.

The most direct contact most people have with animals is at mealtime—they eat them.

No, we don't need animal products to live a healthy life."

Leonardo Da Vinci is worth a quote:

"From an early age, I have abjured the use of meat, and the time will come when men will look upon the murder of animals as they look upon the murder of men".

Now that the western winds are blowing and the consumerist craze is growing, there is a new peril to our animal brethren. For instance:

"The fur industry wages war on wildlife, the lucrative leather market bolsters the cattle industry, and wool comes from sheep who suffer unanaesthetized tooth grinding, tail cutting and unskilled shearing. Angora is made from the hair of rabbits bred for a fast-growing intensive confinement industry.

By choosing products made with canvas, cotton, nylon, acrylic and other materials, we can clothe ourselves beautifully without endorsing cruelty.

The more we realize that animals have real lives like our own, the more courage we have to inform others. Most people prefer not to be associated with animal suffering, but may not know the facts. Our silence must not contribute to their ignorance."

Animals, said Henry Beston, an author-naturalist, are "other nations, caught with ourselves in the net of life and time". Like us they too fear pain and death. To torture them and derive delight by cruel sport, soft flesh and caging birds and lions is heartless imperialism and brutal exploitation. Animal's fur skin or flesh do not add to our inner joy but yet we like the feel, look and taste of these pieces of animals even though without these sordid additives, life can be healthier and lovelier.

A pamphlet titled: 'How Killing Them is Really Killing Us' instructively tells truths we should not hide.

"Public health and safety are jeopardized because researchers, encouraged by the multi-billion dollar animal supply industry, are reluctant to break away from old fashioned, unreliable and costly animal testing methods.

Fifteen thousand children were born with severe deformities because Thalidomide, a sedative prescribed to pregnant women, was found "safe" after extensive animal testing. More sophisticated non-animal tests showed Thalidomide dangerous to the development of the fetus. Recently, E-Feral and Diethylstilbestrol have caused serious side effects and death in humans.

> *Many alternatives, such as highly developed computer and mathematical models, cell and tissue cultures, already exist. Emphasis must be placed on discovering and perfecting other alternatives."*

Tender calves are delicate meat. So too are dog's meat and snakes (skinned alive) and cockroaches and insects eaten in some odd countries practising crimson ideologies. To be carnivorous is to be cannibalistic, since man too is animal. But even in America, the exemplar for mundane pleasures, an awakening is discernible.

Meat is extremely high in saturated fats and in cholesterol, which accumulates in arterial walls and is a major factor in heart attacks.

Large amounts of antibiotics, growth stimulants and chemicals must be fed to meat animals now reared in crowded indoor environments. These chemicals are passed on to meat eaters, weakening human defenses against disease and rendering once helpful drugs useless.

The kidneys of a moderate meat eater must work three times harder than those of a vegetarian to deal with excess toxic wastes found in meat.

During World War II, Denmark and other Scandinavian countries were forced to switch to a non-meat diet due to the food blockade. Mortality rates for males dropped 34%, a world record. With the post-war return to meat eating the rate returned to "normal".

Current animal protection legislation merely protects animals from suffering and dying in public view and from becoming extinct. The differences between other species and ours do not justify prejudicial treatment, slavery and slaughter. The price of changing our habits is, at worst, inconvenience during adjustment. The benefits are to the other animals, our own health and vitality, world hunger and the whole ecosystem.

Truly, history will judge the worth of our "civilization" less by our technological accomplishments than by the way we treat our fellow beings."

'PETA' has a poignant poem on animals in labs which must move our heart if we have any.

> *"Unseen they suffer,*
> *Unheard they cry,*
> *In agony they linger,*
> *In loneliness they die."*

Animal experiments which are becoming more popular and more cruel are a source of severe suffering for innocent animals like mice, rabbits, guinea pigs and monkeys; and now a grave danger has arisen with patents being available in the U.S. for living species and genetic engineering becoming a source for scientific discoveries for mutations. Food, to look attractive and plentiful, draws on the liberal use of agro-chemicals; many of which are toxic, and their toxicity is assessed in laboratory animals. We must discourage the use of such products and encourage the need for safety by buying organically raised crops.

"By buying free range eggs, free range poultry, and meat from non-intensively reared livestock, we encourage the use of systems that are less dependent on animal-tested drugs and vaccines - as well as being more humane".

Likewise, we should avoid processed foods and those with artificial additives. Clothing and household fabrics, cosmetics and toiletries and other attractive consumer items involve, at some early stage, cruelty to animals in chemical experiments. Cruelty-free culture is safe, cheap, and dignified.

Drugs in various forms are being developed and tested in laboratory animals.

Ayurveda, Homeopathy, Unani, Siddha, Acupuncture, Naturopathy, Herbalism, Spiritual healing and other indigenous methods of cure do not involve animal experimentation. Therefore, it is a scientific superstition to insist on animal-experimented curatives. There are alternative therapies. There is a further factor to be remembered. What may work in an animal may not work in a human. More research in new organic foods, herbal cosmetics and other therapeutics can avoid cruelties to our sub-human species.

These days, killing of animals for food is accepted as an inevitable evil. This is not valid, but until people everywhere abjure meat and accept vegetarianism, slaughter houses will persist.

If there is no way of banning killing, abattoirs using minimum violence must be insisted on. Man, in his march towards higher culture and consciousness, has evolved agriculture as against hunting. The question is whether, so long as there is meat eating, we should reduce the pain of killing and make meat hygienic. But if the object is to build macro-size abattoirs to slaughter scientifically on a large scale, it may lead to the elimination of our cattle wealth, thus depleting a large animal resource for earning foreign exchange. This is a perversion of the spiritual essence of our culture and the "PCA Act of 1960". While we should fight animal sacrifice, we must conserve animal wealth in the spirit of Article 48 which casts an obligation on the State to organise agriculture and animal husbandry on modern and scientific lines and to preserve and improve the breeds and to prohibit the slaughter of cows and calves and other milch and drought cattle.

Abattoirs produce meat and meat-eating is prone to cause cancer and other diseases; and the traumatic terminal phase of the animal will add to the toxicity of the butchered beast or bird. The bacteria in raw or cooked meat eventually punish the eater. So it is that vegetarianism is becoming worldwide. Moreover, 16 kgs of foodgrains are needed for the animal body, to add 1 kg. of weight. So we deny grains for human food for boosting animal weight for heavier export and foreign exchange. However clean and well-kept the abattoir, the cattle dragged for slaughter knows by instinct its end, resists and runs and the gory agony and helpless curse in its pathetic eyes make the meat a medium of misery visited on the eater, innocent *tho' he be.*

Nor am I charmed by the cow protection groups who never spend a copper to feed neglected street cattle nor contribute to animal welfare but create religious tension and communal explosion. National interests and people's health are best promoted by habits of diet on organic-manured food and cultivation of aversion for meat for reasons of health, kindness and *satvic* development. Food and character interact.

Dairy products, so good for growth and health, necessitate preserving cattle wealth and improving their breed. We are reaching self-sufficiency in this field, thanks to Operation Flood and Dr. Kurien. Now to import milk powder or dairy products and kill our cows and buffaloes for export of meat is double dependency. Fresh milk, good for medicine, especially goat's milk, may tragically vanish under the globalisation dispensation! How myopic a policy of surrender to MNCs and petro-dollars!

> *"Among the ruminants, the goat in India has unique qualities like small size, clean habits, maintenance of low-grade ration, particularly roughages which are usually not used by other animals and converting such roughage into high-protein milk and meat absorbed from diverse ecological resources, with other advantages like early maturity, smaller gestation period, prolificacy (twins, triplets and even quadruplets are common), short interlactation interval and wide range of adaptability. Its milk being easily digestible is recommended for infants, the old and invalids.*

It is an ideal animal for those with meagre resources like small and marginal farmers, especially those in the drought-prone areas, and even for the landless. It browses intermittently, quickly moves from shrub to shrub and never destroys the natural vegetation cover as some bigger animals like cattle and buffaloes do. This animal, which efficiently converts the natural vegetation into milk and meat is however wrongly conceived as an animal of denudation of forest cover leading to soil erosion and deforestation. On the other hand, it uses the minimum natural vegetation, without much wastage, to produce meat and milk with maximum protein. In India, as large portions of arable land are marginal in quality, having no irrigation facility, and marginal and small holders and landless are large in number, the goat has an ideal situation for survival and growth, where crop husbandry is not possible or uneconomic and where the masses of the poor have no alternative source of living, the goat supports the survival of the weaker sections of the population." (H.R. Kalia and A.R. Rajpurohit, 1985).

Another significant factor often treated with contempt, calling India as still in the bullock cart age, is the indifference to the drought force and power output of the varieties of draught animals available in the country like bullocks and buffaloes, donkeys and camels, mules and even elephants. If only we utilise the animal power of India, especially in the country side, studies show that fuel shortage and import of oil will disappear. Indeed, the West-biased attitude is the villain of the peace. Similarly, the use of bio-gas, compost and fertilisers, where cattle contribute much raw mass, is being overlooked. China did and does use bio-gas in a big way. Our energy crisis originates in power alienation from native resources.

There are many more uses of animalia, especially since India is blessed with animal abundance. What we need more than prevention of cruelty to animals, is promotion of utility through animals. The 'discovery of India' is never complete until we weave a lively fraternity between the human and animal species.

It is a profound and fascinating thought, in keeping with the new World Human Order, that we give life to a new Universal Animal Order which will be a symbiosis of living Creation with a cosmic dimension.

In a wider vision we must inaugurate a new movement for a Universal Declaration of the Rights of Animals.

All that I have spoken up to now relates to a new pluralism of human and animal mutuality. We have legislations and sacred texts, but the stark question is that in our materialist world with consumerist appetite the animal world and its happiness is drowned in the sadistic delights and dietary pleasures, compounding our savage past and our *asuric* present. To conquer these gargantuan vices and to restore the moral spiritual fibre of humanity we need mobilisation of popular opinion, conscientisation of human conduct and campaigns on a lofty scale harnessing social action groups and organising kindness clubs everywhere. High on the agenda of the nation must be the methodology of awakening and mobilising through mass action, sans which law will be dead letter and the Animal Welfare Board an apparatus without animation.

A tearing and raging campaign by NGOs is the only passionate alternative. We must reach schools, teach college students and publicise cruelty to animals as horrendous inhumanity through our media. Villagers may listen for a while but the winds of consumerist change are corrupting the minds of good people. So the task is hard, pamphleteering is necessary; exhibitions of animals in agony in cages and zoos, in circuses and pet-shops must brought luridly to the notice of civilized sections.

Governments must be pressurized to do the right thing lest India's image and cultural heritage suffer severe damage. Let us not betray the generations from the Buddha to Gandhi. Our tryst with destiny, made when India awoke to Independence, included an imperative that the nation will 'wipe every tear from every eye'. This applies to our animal brethren, parrots, doves and other birds with broken wings to be sold as pets or for delicate dish, lions and tigers cramped and doped in small cages and even elephants and bears brutally treated to perform impossible feats. Let us begin the crusade for compassion and we must win because our case is just.

The Spiritual Dimension of the Animal Citizen

Wrote William Blake:

"A dog starv'd at his master's gate
Predicts the ruin of the State,
A horse misus'd upon the road
Calls to Heaven for human blood.
Each outcry of the hunted hare
A fibre from the brain does tear,
A skylark wounded in the wing,
A cherubim does cease to sing".

Yes, elsewhere, Blake wrote an inspired piece on that creature 'The Lamb':

"Little Lamb, who made thee?
Dost thou know who made thee?
Gave thee life, and bid thee feed,
by the stream and o'er the mead;
Gave thee clothing of delight,
Softest clothing, woolly, bright;
Gave thee such a tender voice,
Making all the vales rejoice?

Poets have a sensitive soul and when we wish to soar to sublime heights let us turn to them. With a vision of all Creation, Walt Whitman poetized:

"I think I could turn and live with animals, they are so placid and self-contain'd,
I stand and look at them long and long.
They do not lie awake in the dark and weep for their sins,
They do not make me sick discussing their duty to God,
Not one is dissatisfied, not one is demented with the mania of owning things,

Not one kneels to another, nor to his kind that lived thousands of years ago,

Nor one is respectable or unhappy over the whole earth".

How glorious is bio-diversity in its range of versatile beauty, variegated wonder and unity in divinity! He who does not feel a togetherness in this dimension is deficient in higher culture or deeper religion.

Compassion for and fellowship with life, whatever its form, a feel for every spark of divinity whatever its form, a feel for every spark of divinity whatever its evolutionary gradation, makes the whole world kin. More explicitly, S.T. Coleridge told us of God and identity of all of us with that supreme, universal Being whom the sages called Brahman. I have often felt that all creation is the individualised manifestation of Cosmic Power, be it plant, beast or man. "The ancients have stated that God sleeps in the mineral, awakens in the vegetable, walks in the animal and thinks in man. [Psychic Exploration - A Challenge for Science - Edited by John White - Page 681]

The lines of Coleride are here:

"He prayeth well, who leveth well
Both man and bird and beast.
He prayeth best, who loveth best
All things both great and small;
For the dear God who loveth us,
He made and loveth all".

The beautiful divinisation and ecological integration gives meaning to our constitutional obligation (Article 51A) of compassion to all living creatures. To my mind, this expansion of consciousness is the spiritual foundation for animal welfare and the recognition of animal citizenship. Gandhiji, like St. Francis of Assisi, was able to see a brotherhood among Humans, Animals and Birds.

Profound is the thought, solace to the soul is the joy of life in all its forms. Such is the validation of all that we do to defend the Order of Nature as an inviolable creed.

The savage in man having lived a hunter's life in the past, dies hard and takes delight in flesh-food forgetting that some life has been killed to make for this carnivorous palate.

Smt. Indira Gandhi spoke sensitively when she warned that "the survival of man is dependant on the survival of animal and plant life". The dynamic unity of ecological species is best brought out by Dr. Yogesh Kumar Arora in an article written in 1987:

> *"Some years ago, the World Health Organisation took up a programme of DDT spraying on Borneo in an effort to control the mosquitoes. It proved very effective but destroyed wasps. These wasps preyed on caterpillars which ate the thatched roofs. So as a direct result of the mosquito control*

programmes, the hut roofs collapsed. Similarly, DDT spraying to kill house flies resulted in the death of small lizards - geckoes - which preyed on the former. The dead lizards were eaten by cats, which began to die. Eventually, this led to an enormous increase in the rat population, which not only began to invade the houses and consume the food but also spread plague. Finally cats were parachuted into remote Bornean villages to restore the ecological balance.

In South Africa, a campaign was waged against hippopotamuses. The result was a rapid increase in a debilitating disease called Schistosomiasis, caused by a snail-carried parasite that attacks the human liver. Without the hippos, which served as natural bulldozers, the rivers silted up, the snails proliferated, and Schistosomiasis became a great health hazard.

Buffalo hunters and U.S. Army slaughtered the bull buffalo or bison herds so recklessly thereby 1900, the 60,000,000 bisons that once roamed the continent were almost wiped out. Finally, only few wild bisons were left in the entire United States. Cattle and sheep replaced bison for commercial reasons. But the ecology differed. The buffalos roamed freely allowing grasses to renew themselves but the new owners of the land fenced the pastures. The domestic animals stayed in one place eating the grasses and then the roots. The grasslands were thus destroyed".

The Hindu venerates Vishnu, Siva, Saraswati, Karthikeya and Krishna together with the Eagle (Garuda), the Bull (Nandi), the Swan, the Peacock and the Cow. Even trees are worshipped, not out of superstition, but because of supra-rational understanding. Today the grosser materialism which has possessed the five-star culinary culture is leading to wiping out of various species. A Report to former USA President Jimmy Carter says:

> *"Hundreds of thousands of species - perhaps as many as 20 per cent of all species on earth will be irretrievably lost as their habitats vanish".*

The cruelty towards living creatures, particularly the cattle, driven hundreds of miles, beaten as they walk, is insufferable and the slaughter produces unhealthy meat and stink and releases pathogenic microbes. Animal products are exported for foreign exchange, but the soul of Man is lost in the bargain. Another type of cruelty flourishes with none to protest.

> *"Approximately 10 million birds are taken from wild every year. Perhaps half die before they even reach their destination. Two of the biggest traders are Senegal and India. Between 1970 and 1980 India exported nearly 15 million birds.*

Many experts believe that if this process continues at its present rate the whole ecological balance could be affected".

Life, dear life, God's life deserves fraternal love. That is the spiritual foundation of material prosperity:

"The caterpillar on the leaf
Repeats to thee thy mother's grief.
Kill not the moth nor butterfly,
For the Last Judgment draweth nigh".

A song from *Narmada Bachao Andolan* moves our tears with compassion for creation

Whose are the forests and the land?
Ours, they are ours.
Whose the wood, the fuel?
Ours, they are ours.
Whose, the flowers and the grass?
Ours, they are ours.
Whose the cow, the cattle?
Ours, they are ours.
Whose are the bomboo groves?
Ours, they are ours.

The best ever said with acid pen is by Bernard Shaw:

Darwin taught us not that all men were monkeys once
But that some monkeys have no tails now.

SLAUGHTER OF CAMEL VERSUS JUDICIAL COMPASSION

Life is sacred even of animals. Sacrifice of living creatures is satanic and never hallowed even if offered in holy dedication. In India, 'Gandhi Country', the value of life and the villainy of torture are hostile to each other being judged by the high moral order which govern our Constitution. Today we have the constitutional mandate of Chapter IV (A) which commands as a fundamental duty compassion for living creatures (Article 51A (g)). Therefore killing camel can never be condoned as a religious performance, be it Hindu, Christian or Muslim. Under these circumstances our tryst with the Constitution commands abolition of the barbarity of killing camels. The other day the media carried the news that around one hundred and fifty camels were butchered in Tamil Nadu on the Id day. A single judge of the Madras High Court had granted stay of this massacre, but a division bench vacated that stay forgetting its humanist duty of preserving animal life. I would regard this an unfortunate violation of the Constitution notwithstanding the implicit forensic sanction.

Fundamental duties are inscribed in Article 51A of the Constitution which obligates 'compassion for living creatures'. A camel is a living creature entitled to compassion. No religion shall justify sacrifice of a living creature because it is an act of terrorism, inhumanity and unconstitutionality. Maybe a camel gives huge quantity and its carcass may feed many, but the Constitution of India forbids sacrificing animals by express provision in Article 51A (g). There is statutory prohibition of cruelty to animals punishable under the law. Now there is a fundamental duty making compassion for living creatures a positive act of humanism. It is interesting to note that a practice which prevailed in the desert land of Arabia cannot be treated as a divine act in India where, according to Mahatma Gandhi, Ahimsa is the golden rule, reinforced by a profound provision making compassion a fundamental duty. Recently, an incident that took place in Kerala is of value in this context. Two camels were brought to Kerala, apparently with the purpose of slaughtering them and eating their meat. The Collector (who is the District Magistrate) banned that vicious project and saved their life. This was compassion in action. But a barbaric massacre of hundreds of camels has been reported in the newspapers as part of Id ceremony because the High Court, tragic to say, vacated the stay. Atrocious! with no court, government nor humanist institution respecting the Constitution should have allowed. I regard it as a grave guilt to ignore law and the Constitution with none to protest nor prosecute. The Constitution has failed, notwithstanding the fundamental diction in Article 51A.

The Constitution binds the State and it is a betrayal of Suprema Lex not to enforce 51A by appropriate legislations and executive action to make compassion to living creatures a reality. Law is what **law does**, not what **law says**.

We live in an era of grim violence. Human life has lost its value and even numberless lives are being massacred every day regardless of international law, human rights concern and wars without United Nation's sanctions. Indeed, the massacres for which the United States is responsible are a savage catastrophe for which history has no precedent. When World War II reached its final stages the President of the U.S (Truman) used atomic weapons with no justification killing countless people in Hiroshima and Nagasaki. The World Order, even after the United Nations and the Great Charter had come into existence, has been showing little concern for massive casualty of humanity. Small wonder, living creatures have little value and are mercilessly wiped out. Lord Buddha and Emperor Asoka stood for kindness and mercy and tender disposition towards living creatures. Our Constitution has expressed these values particularly in Article 51A(g). Our Republic must necessarily protect life by effective legislation. Camels are useful animals and harmless creatures, not carcasses for gluttonous meat. If Law India is to be conscientious in its commitment to the Constitution Parliament must awake and enact a comprehensive code which will empower the citizenry to eradicate willful terrorism depriving innocent animals of their Right to Life. Our culture is in peril if hundreds of camels in one State alone (Tamil Nadu) are cut to pieces under the pretension of sacrifice to God.

Hitler committed horrendous inhumanity and gory genocide. The great charter and the United Nations were expected to extinguish the savage atrocities of World War II. Alas, the cosmos has now surrendered to chaos, nuclear brutality and war weapons have been cornered by Big Powers particularly the U.S. The unipolar world is holding almost every country under its subjugation. The time has come for mankind to revive the supreme value and vision implicit in the great statement 'God sleeps in the mineral, wakes in the vegetables, **walks in the animal** and thinks in man'.

RIVERS, A NATIONAL TREASURE; THEIR WASTE AND POLLUTION, A NATIONAL CRIME*

Water is a divine gift to humanity, so necessary for life's survival and serves a multitude of social uses. From the Ganga to Kaveri we have, across the country, an abundance of this precious natural resource. When I was a minister in charge of Irrigation and Electricity (1957-59), I thought it a high priority to prepare a masterplan of the water resources of Kerala. When it was ready, I presented it to the then Prime Minister Jawaharlal Nehru who greeted the idea as a great accomplishment. He desired me to utilize the waters fully and not waste this boundless bounty which otherwise would empty itself in the Arabian Sea, Bay of Bengal or Indian Ocean. Hydel projects for electricity generation are the least expensive while atomic power the most expensive and radio-active. Nehru told me that I should start a large number of minor irrigation and electricity projects, and referred as an example, to the collective farms of the then Soviet Union. I did start a number of lift irrigation projects, and otherwise tried to put to use diverse aqua projects having due regard to people's local needs. Kerala has 44 rivers (big and small) and water falls capable of irrigation and power. I insisted on people's participation and labour, (I called it Sramdan) which came voluntarily and abundantly. This productive contribution and working people's organized democratic share were largely drawn from the local villages which gave the villagers a sense of possession and **gram swaraj**. This is economic democracy which I used with rare joy even for village electrification, of course, with the active operation of engineers. Given some training rural youth can substantially play a creative role even on electricity distribution. I wonder whether any of my successors in office has cared to read the master plan of water resources of Kerala, lost as they were in communalism and faction politics and vote magnetism. Constructive nation building is not in their agenda. No other State in India, to my knowledge, has prepared a similar master plan. The late great Dr. K.L. Rao, a superb minister in charge of energy, once told me that no other State had done what my engineers had under my direction. Dr. Rao himself had advocated an All

* December 26, 2006.

India grid but this grand mega-idea, on Rao's death, was never pursued. Imagine the glory of Ganga-Caveri water wonder creating a dynamic aquatic Indian unity! Plan with a national goal is the basis of scientific engineering, to enrich the country's resources and alas! We have failed to harvest even rainwater so urgently needed for cultivation and drinking water. Our aquatic boon falling from heaven goes by neglect into rivers and channels polluting public sources, taps and domesting supplies. How I wish the nation did harness the water resources of India and planned their use for the villages, urban taps, tanks and the desert areas of Bharat. It is a gesture of patriotic pride that way back in the seventies, I, with EMS, reached a fruitful water treaty giving surplus Kerala waters we had, sufficient to spare, to Tamil Nadu (Kamaraj and C. Subramaniam). I consulted all parties and the Institution of Engineers before finalizing this unique Agreement. India's water resources belong to Indian humanity. Swaraj, in this nationalist dimension, is our supreme strength. Not power-hungry but statesman alone can circumvent petty quarrels and work out profound aqua-communions.

A Supplementary note On Mullaperiyar

Water dispute is an ugly display of failure to solve the problem of inter-state sharing of water according to each state's social needs by hostility and absurdity. The solution of Mullaperiyar has worked for a century on the basis of aqua-based social justice, arrived at by humane engineering, not by inter-state rivalry and grab-water chauvinism. Why not choose three or five excellent hydel engineers of the country with expertise in water uses, in agriculture and other potable purposes. They may make on-the-spot enquiries. They will request all information, meet people on both sides, study soil condition in both the states, and the versatile advantages of cultivation and other social and economic dimensions of agrarian benefits to both states. Let the two States using the perspectival approach of common Indian grain wealth. Never adopt acrimonious attitude as if it is a battle between two countries. A court is incompetent to do justice without the serious study by concerned experts and agriculturists. Our judges are laypersons and without deep investigation life's rural realities, they cannot do the country good. Representative agriculturists from both sides must form a **joint committee** and advise the engineering specialists so that water uses can be put to the best common use. Patriotism is not politicking; nationalism is not divisive challenges. Indian humanity Tamil or Malayalee, is one. Who gets more water is not the issue. More production with more water utilized in a planned process is the wealth of both the States. Kerala-Tamil Nadu have a common swadeshi interest and swaraj resources. We are a happy fraternity with the finest functionally rational irrigation.

RIVER JURISPRUDENCE AND INTER-STATE WATERS

A country like India has a billion- strong humanity and, necessarily, water becomes an indispensable factor for sheer survival, individual and national. The late Dr. K.L. Rao, who was minister for Irrigation at the Center, suggested a national water grid whereby the multitude of rivers which provide abundance of aquatic wealth could be utilized with nationally designed engineering strategies and humanitarian objectives promotive of agriculture, inland navigation, social uses and, more than all, domestic needs like drinking water. With Rao's exit, the idea also withered and what we have today is water disputes, politically fighting State, destabilizing developments, violating the values of justice, unity and fraternity, which are fundamental for the Nation's progress. The Cauvery River, like the Krishna River, is rich in developmental potential and catalyzes agriculture and industry, given a master plan of the water resources and the best way to utilize them without negative competition and acrimonious rivalry. The primary objective of maximizing the river advantages to the community must be to the welfare of the people as a whole without polemics and pollution. Viewed through parochial patriotism the dispute will lead to inter-state instability, aggravation of mutual hostility, litigative discord, popular violence and violation of material benefits shared justly by the community, regardless of State geography. Today, on the contrary, inter-state rivers take on belligerent dimensions and two or more states battle for water rights as if they are different countries at war. What a shame that nationalism has committed hara-kiri over water justice.

Law is for life and water resources must be for people without political divisiveness. Kannada, Kerala and Tamilnadu are integral parts of India and everyone there is an Indian. The whole approach to the Cauvery controversy has been divisively different. Harmony needs unified vision and Indian humanity and happiness are a common mission. If more rice grows in Tanjore fields the harvest feeds neighbouring areas. If a Kannadiga starves because of drought a sensitive Tamil weeps. Kerala employs so many jobless Tamils as brothers. We are one on soil and in water. We are federal and our fraternity is our solidarity. We are one from adivasi and kuchela to the high caste and Kubera.

Indian humanity lives on unity and social justice, shared resources gifted by Nature and the bounty of green wonder from Kanyakumari to Everest. Likewise, river water, indifferent to political geography, belongs to every Indian as a member of our Socialist Democratic Republic (*vide* the Preamble). **'We, the People of India'**, have a common claim to the economies of Bharat in its basic natural wealth. In this view, how do we solve the distribution of Cauvery? Not by fighting or faction nor by fanatic obscurantism. The three States, through their ministers, must meet as members of the Southern zone and the Central symbol, the Prime Minister, must preside to discuss the distribution issue as a matter of social justice and common prosperity. A Zonal Commission must be set up by Constitutional Amendment where the three States will have representatives and the Central presence will have a valid voice. The dominant determinant will be not the extent of territory or political sound and fury but the social and economic contribution to the wealth of the community attributable to the irrigation facility covered by the command area of the Cauvery River. This depends on the annual rainfall and the cultivable lands which prosper with the strategic use of water. Pollution from industries should be prevented. Social uses by the common people must be safeguarded. Irrigation and electricity too are significant factors if properly planned and exploited. State boundaries are not relevant as the productive uses from the flow of water promises the people who are part of the Indian Union. On the contrary, political irritation and fragmentation of the beneficial flow spoil the rich potential of Cauvery. A composite Commission which I contemplate has no political polemics but constructive reward and must have leading agriculturists on its panel. Excellent engineers with expertise in hydroelectric utilization of water must have a governing voice. This collective body will sit periodically, study dispassionately and distribute justly the waters that flow from the Coorg heights, with streams as tributaries and riparian claims, of the three states, taking note of waterfalls from hills which may replenish the total resource. When they—statesman, engineers and agriculturists—together take a decision about distribution without bureaucratic bouts and parochial rivalries and factory pollution spoiling the aquatic purity of the Cauvery, the verdict of the Zonal Commission of the three States must accept it. If there be a surviving controversy a special bench of the Supreme Court should sit in the South with expert advisers, hear concerned persons with full access to justice. That judgment must, in all grace, be accepted by all the States.

The judiciary does not possess river engineering skill nor modern agricultural-irrigational technology. Necessarily, river disputes end in political scrambles. Justice must seek conciliation as a solution. The court should not undertake what judges are not equipped with. In this process each state must speak in one voice and internecine party struggles should not mar fair projects. Such a positive approach demands statesmanship, not narrow polemical perspectives. For a rational negotiation the concerned

States must prepare master plans of their water resources so that alternatives can be explored. Secondly, non-political engineers and agricultural specialists should be involved in seeking constructive conclusions. The Institution of Engineers is a fruitful, creative organization. I speak with some experience in the matter. While I was Irrigation Minister of Kerala, (1957-59) a master plan of the water resources of Kerala was got prepared which I presented to Prime Minister Nehru. He congratulated me and I implemented the findings in part. I regret to say, though, my successor ministers in Kerala hardly studied the Report which sleeps until today. Tamil Nadu or Karnataka has no such master plan yet. I plead to the engineering community and the statesmen of the three States to use their vision in constructive patriotism and humanist nationalism. Surely they can produce a Cauvery paradigm without litigation and avoid dissatisfaction among the politicians and agri-community. The present situation is mired by obdurate controversies and public agitations. There is at least one instance where EMS and I (as irrigation minister)—settled a water dispute with Tamil Nadu represented by Kamaraj and C. Subramanyam and both States were benefited by that agreement. The politicians have failed us now and the Centre woefully blinks at the issue absent federal nationalism. Why? It is a riddle wrapped in a mystery inside an enigma.

HYDEL POWER PROJECTS AND PERIL TO HUMAN SURVIVAL

Material advance in the modern world depends largely on the multiple uses of electricity. Nuclear power was considered a great source but after the terrible Russian disaster and the near-catastrophe in America avoided by a lucky last-minute discovery of a fault in the Three-Mile Island plant in the U.S, many progressive countries have given-up reliance on atomic power generation as carrying a latent risk and otherwise very costly. The menace of the atom notwithstanding, India has been tempted to use this technology ignoring the grave dangers of radiation involved in this process. Hydroelectric power is cheaper and safer and so, where water resources are available, without violation of ecology and environmental safety, hydel power plants have become popular and thermal alternatives have been resorted to where coal and like facilities are the blessings of Nature enjoyed by some nations. Even wind power and tidal energy have been developed despite the cost and difficulties of production. Where water resources like rivers and huge waterfalls from mountain regions are Nature's gifts, the State has naturally run after such methodology. But this appeal is fraught with serious disadvantages dangerous disregard of ecological and environmental factors. Myopic approaches by semi-literate administrations are sometimes unmindful of the values of ecology and environment with the result that hydel plants with large dams and big canals inflict irreparable damage to long-term interest of the people. Earth sciences are very important in this context. Prime Minister Indira Gandhi realized this significance and the Constitution was amended to stress the vulnerability of Nature and the necessity of compliance with ecological and environmental factors. Dr. M.G.K. Menon, a great scientist and adviser to the Central Government, insisted on examining projects from the above point of view. That is how the scientists of Kerala fought their way successfully to preserve the integrity of the world-famous Silent Valley which would have been victim of hydel projects and robbery of its unique forest wealth, the beneficiaries being wealthy commercial interests, which are a growing *mafia* menace unconcerned with the rare treasure of Nature. Article 48A and Part IVA of the Constitution have a supremacy in Development. Lesser considerations of augmenting electricity and industry may attract small minds in power influenced by tycoons and moneymaking Big Business is not to decide national governance of our Republic. Statesmen, with a vision and for long-term benefits of generations, will never surrender to the syndrome of promoting commerce and industry for the prosperity of the creamy layer. Industrialize or perish, the capitalist giants would agree. If ecological and environmental criteria are forsaken, industrialize and perish would be Nature's retort. The agrarian poor, with a pittance of land, have no voice as against the powerful urban factory-owners and merchants with political influence. Green fields, rich forests which are the sanctuary of rare species of birds, peasants who are the backbone of food self-sufficiency and jungles with wild animals and rivers which die dry if polluted or deprived of sand beds will disappear to be replaced by ugly concrete skyscapers of business magnates who spread lethal chemicals in the air, water and the natural soil, punishing with disease the billions of villagers and making the few billionaires roll in wealth and luxury with Westoxicated technological terrorism. To whom does India or Kerala belong? What is patriotism and development?

The U.N. in a Conference had defined development as follows:

> *Development must be designed, even at the humblest level, as a process of ensuring the advancement of man through his own endeavours, says UNESCO. The multiplication of material wealth has to be dethroned as the purpose of development. "The goal of development should be not to develop things, but to develop man," says Cocoyoc. 'Development must be aimed at the spiritual, moral and material advancement of the whole human being, both as a member of society and from the point of view of individual fulfillment,' says UNESCO.*

Similarly ecology means the study of the interaction of living organisms with their physical, biological, and chemical environment. The ecological movement of the 1960s onwards has argued that people must live within the limitations of the Earth's finite supply of resources, and that humanity is very much dependent on its environment. The Indian Constitution on a sensitive provision in Article 48A states 'The State shall endeavour to protect and improve the environment and to safeguard the forests and wild life of the country'. This is a fundamental obligation of the State since its violation has fatal implications. Article 51A(g) creates a fundamental duty in every individual to obey the mandates of environment and ecology. It follows that no project which damnifies environment should be permitted. Article 14, (social economic equality) 21 (right to life), 48A and 51A(g) read together is a Constitutional Code of functional imperatives. The Silent Valley which was vulnerable to deforestation on the basis of project proposals was salvaged by the immunity the Central Government gave. No project can be executed if it imperils forests and rivers and wild animals. Big dams are a threat to arboreal abundance. Cutting trees on a large scale is an evil doing, which spoil the soil, and affects rainfall.

The issue of power generation schemes required for hi-tech projects fall under the ban since they may adversely affect the natural resources, agricultural progress and people's survival. This problem has come-up sharply in Kerala where the Pathrakadavu project is being ambiguously advocated by the Minister for Power and opposed by an activist section who consider it deleterious ecologically. Any power scheme will inevitably involve substantial injury to the forest wealth of Palakkad and may defy the command of the Constitutional Code spelt out above. Pathrakadavu is quite adjacent to what has been preserved so long as a rare asset of Nature. The Chief Minister had, while he was a leader of the Opposition opposed this scheme proposed by the then UDF Government and now he is inclined to take the same negative view. His resistance must prevail. There is no doubt that when a dam is constructed and ancillary works are undertaken the Silent Valley may have to suffer a new menace if you have constitutional sensitivity to ecology. Indeed, what is a treasure like the Silent Valley or adjacent forests cannot be sacrificed for the sake of a power project. Kerala has unexploited water sources, hills and valleys which generate wind power and a long coast-line which if explored from the hidel power angle may be a lasting source of electric energy. Once the Pathrakadavu project is taken up by contractors or even the PWD the Silent Valley and the excellent natural forests will be in peril of survival whatever the Government may promise. The Central Government also with its privatization inclination cannot be trusted with this opinion where public policy of preservation of forests is at stake. Rajaji while he was Chief Minister of Madras long ago described the PWD as public enemy number one. Today Governments are considerably controlled by powerful private corporations. Under no circumstances therefore should Pathrakadavu or other dubious schemes which are constitutionally culpable be undertaken. Never be a traitor to the future or be hostile to the ecological command of the Constitution.

WATER, THE GREATEST GIFT OF LIFE AND THE HARSHEST MILLENNIAL CRISIS

A semi-centennial span of years ago I happened to be a Minister in the Kerala State. A plural bunch of portfolios, assigned to me by Chief Minister EMS, included Irrigation and Power which together covered the water resources of the state. I thought it fit to approach the issue of using Kerala's abundant water resources scientifically by careful study and innovative methodology, through expert engineers. Based on that comprehensive compilation it would be sensible to plan and construct projects, irrigational and hydel. A master-plan was so prepared and in later months and years, quite a few minor and medium irrigation schemes were started and executed with the enthusiastic participation of the people whose manual and skilled contribution did play a democratic role. How soul-stirring to lead people in constructive schemes with participative pleasure. Likewise, electricity project, exploiting an excellent, waterfall was also conceived by me and commenced. Curiously that electricity project was completed taking a few years. There again, the people welcomed the dam construction with great gusto. People's passion and élan are powerful resources. They insisted that *I should switch on* the formal ceremonial completion because the whole hydel concept was mine. The gratitude of the local community is profound. There was also a sense of pride in the process, but I too was excited because the common people who had no source of electricity had now a chance to get power at their doorstep. However, when the time for inauguration came and the local people asked me to perform the 'switch on' ritual I had already become a judge of the High Court of Kerala. Appreciating the sentiment of the people I consented and with the help of the engineers and the government I did the fulfillment of what I had begun years ago. Thus I had the patriotic pleasure of switching on the Kuttiyadi project. The basis, of course, was the master plan of the water resources of Kerala. In those days, for everything good or great, Jawaharlal Nehru was the inspiration. So I presented the Master Plan to him at a big public function in Delhi. He spoke in luminous and lucid words what a constructive approach should be like when water, a glorious gift of nature, was to be utilized for irrigation, power and other social uses. With this introduction, I give below my foreword to the Report written in 1958 at the presentation to the Prime Minister:

Our ancients from the Vedic days worshipped the great rivers of the country because they either blessed the fields with their fertile flows (and were placated by song). In a superstitious age mighty forces of nature were deified and offered prayers. In an age of science the powers of Nature are imprisoned for the service of man. Today, in modern India, where a free people are rebuilding their national economy, we think in terms of training and taming our rivers and harnessing the waters to beneficent use. Kerala, with her backward agricultural economy, is also struggling to surge forward by exploiting her natural resources fully. Naturally, her rich river resources, properly utilized, are capable of producing abundant wealth. At this juncture when we are striving hard to develop our resources all over the country, it is our bounden duty to evolve a sound and co-ordinated water utilization programme—a long range, integrated plan covering the assessment of our over-all hydro resources in the river basins as also of the water required to irrigate the available lands in each basin, a study of the possibility of utilizing surplus waters for irrigation by transfer to neighbouring valleys, a survey of our hydro-electric potential, the drawing up of a flood control programme, the investigation of inland navigational prospects, in short the formulation of a comprehensive multi-purpose and co-ordinated plan for the optimum use of the water resources of Kerala to build up the nation's economy.

We have heavy rainfall, copious mountainous catchments and over 40 rivers, big and small, spanning the State. But now the tragic course of these rapid torrents erodes the soil, floods the lands on the flanks washing themselves waste into the sea without proper exploitation. By careful planning and application of science, by the construction of a series of reservoirs, canals, flood banks, tunnels and other measures of water transfusion and conservancy, the rivers of Kerala might well, in future, transmute the fields and gardens into golden harvests, accelerate the industrial development of the State, what with the abundant hydro-electric power that may be generated and facilitate the development of a long water transport system from one end to the other of the State.

We have to evolve a water policy, *viz.*, a development programme for the survey and utilization of the available waters precipitating in our territory, the main purpose of such a policy being to make our rivers an increasingly constructive and many-sided contributor to the well-being of the people at large. In implementation of this water policy, a water plan must be forged which will co-ordinate the principal needs of the State to be served by these rivers and integrate the schemes in this behalf. To put it in a nutshell, comprehensive Master Plan for the utilization of our river waters is a *sine qua non* for

> the progress of Kerala. The preparation of such a pre-plan is a gigantic job, the first stage of which has just been completed by our patriotic engineers. Now we can go forward, with a clear vision and greater vigour, to formulate specific schemes and projects which when executed in the course of coming years will spell plenty both in food production and power generation, not to speak of other advantages like water transport and drinking water supply. We will, henceforth, face the future with confidence and banish our 'deficit' mentality. Science in combination with the patriotic enterprise of our engineers and people will be able to order the angry floods into good behaviour and extirpate the curses of drought and salinity and to produce conditions where industry and agriculture will flourish, thanks to a correct water plan and water policy. The Master Plan which is presented in this heavy volume must be studied by the common people so that they may become conscious of the store of water wealth we have, for it is only an enlightened and enthusiastic people who can produce big changes, possessed by a developmental frenzy.

Dr. K.L. Rao was the Central Minister, an outstanding Engineer who had encouraged me, a lawyer by profession, in my exceedingly interesting and creative vision and operation. He told me, more than once, that my work in this regard was a pioneering effort and stroke of wonder; and that to his knowledge no other state had prepared a master plan for their water resources. Development is a catchy word, but requires a vision and a mission. It stands for deep study and commitment to the people—not the wealthy tycoons and latifundists, but the small peasantry whose thirst for agricultural production and facilities therefor are made available by the state. Mega-technology, with hidden agendas of the rich, keep villages barren and peasantry unemployed. 'Small is beautiful' said the great economist Schumacher about Ganahiji's agrarian Democracy of development lays emphasis on the common people, the agrarian women and hardworking tillers, not the kulaks and MNCs who hire at their price the humble folk who starve if no work is offered. Economic justice is not high-tech, shower shared by tycoons but the millions in their masses with muscles and brains but empty bellies and vain search without work. Indian humanity means, in constitutional terms, 'We, the People of India". Then the 'haves' buy fast food and rob the nation's resources the have-nots diminish and perish. We must battle for the Brave New Bharat no longer a colony, and win by blood, sweat and toil, swaraj which is the humblest humans birthright.

Another instance. Nelliampathi is a high-range health resort, lush and lovely, breezy and rich with orange plantations. It is the beautiful source of a deep river of precipitous enchantment, but going waste leaving the proximate villages deprived from the cool flow. Absent any pool, women had to carry kilometers of water—what a curse!—although Nemmara gram could get water at home if only the hospitable Pothundi wonder stream could be exploited by a hydel scheme into a project for the people. Once I visited this charming salubrious mini-mountain glory and when I saw the sun bright and the wind blow. I decided that the river shall be transformed into a dam and bless the neighbouring villages. I was minister for Irrigation and my imagination made engineers convert purposeless descent of wasted waters into a constructive irrigation development. I was intoxicated with the irrigation potential in contrast to the parched homes and women carrying big pots on bent backs. So the engineers agreed we build a Pothundi scheme. I felt happy because creative projects with waters supplied by Nature are God's divine presence even if the project be designed at heavy cost. Service to humans is more celestial than all the worshipful chants, poojas and prayers! Even a weed has value, so too a sullied stream, given the creative capacity to convert waste into wealth. Emerson one said : What is a weed? A plant whose virtues have not been discovered. Pothundi is precious aqua-power once technology transformed neglected stream.

Harvesting Nature's resources is socially dynamic patriotism. Total use of water, available as boundless bounty, without wasting them into the ocean is a national obligation. Alas, Kerala, in its prodigality, hardly harvests what monsoons shower on our land. Every panchayat, town and city denies drinking water to the poor. Why? We have no aqua-statesmanship—No vision of the wealth of water. Do you know that every five-star hotel, even sky-high concrete peak, with extravagant apartments, is a prodigal denial of drinking water to the have-not humans below waiting for potfuls of water trickling from scarce public pumps.

PLACHIMADA PATRIOTISM—TOXICOLA TERRORISM

The right to life is a foremost human right sans which societal survival ceases to exist. Air, water, outer space and everything without which generations of Creation cannot exist is universal asset, indefeasible wealth of the world.

Humanity needs water for a hundred reasons and so civilized progress is inconceivable without potable aqua. Indeed, the need for water world-wide and for ages, is ever so necessary that it is no exaggeration to consider the vision of the future of the human species as too fundamental to be diminished even a wee bit in importance.

The habitable countries, globally spread, struggle for sources of water, air and what not today, that the dire need for collecting and preserving every ounce of potable water and breathable air is humanity's highest priority. Under such circumstances every drop of rain has to be harvested, every well of water has to be conserved and every pool or pond has to be preserved as humanity's universal reservoir without unjust reservation.

Water is never a private asset and ever a universal property. Every person born on the planet has thus an imperative claim to a just quantum of people's share of social uses of water. Every village, every town, every rural corner belongs to the world; and no monopoly, no cornering, no profiteering, no racketeering is permissible since homo sapiens cannot live without that gift of nature called water in as pure a form as what keeps life a human process. *The right to life is integral to the Universal Declaration of Human Rights. This is ancient non-negotiable jurisprudence.*

In this context, it is planetary patriotism, humanist nationalism, universal desideratum to insist on physical-moral, civilization equity, and non-negotiable imperative to demand and grant Nature's gift of water. Every village in India, every use of social water, has a human claim, a moral mandate, an equitable samaritarianism. This is *Gramswaraj,* village self-sufficiency and habitat humanism. Viewed in this social justice perspective and humanitarian *wettanschuung (vision of life),* greedy globalisation of water as cornered wealth by Gargantuan corporates and planet-wide rapacious processes have to be subjected to social justice, humanitarian control of water resources and fair sharing of basic needs like water. Cadaverous corporates of the world's water resources by tactics of thanatonic terrorism is gross inhumanity. Parch our rivers, dry our underground storage, wipe out our global ecology and inhibit green environment of flowing water and collective dams to make money, and you are guilty of carnage and massive monstrosity.

Water is infinite power and humanity is its owner. 'I came, I saw and I was conquered' said Franklin D Roosevelt as he inaugurated the Hoover Dam (30 Sep., 1935)

A universal vision of water in infinite quantum is a human wonder sans which mankind survival has serious limitation. It is appropriate to begin with what great visionaries have looked at with worldwide prospects. Let me quote from a classic work:

> *I Came, I saw and I was conquered.*
>
> *President Franklin D. Roosevelt at Hoover Dam inauguration ceremony, 30 September, 1935*
>
> *Hoover Dam, an astonishingly graceful curve of concrete pushing back the Colorado River to fill its deep canyon on the Arizona-Nevada border, unleashed the big dam era. Wallace Stegner, the great novelist and essayist of the US West, was overawed when he visited the 221-metre-high dam in 1946, a decade after its completion:*
>
> *It is certainly one of the world's wonders, that sweeping cliff of concrete, those impetuous elevators, the labyrinth of tunnels, the huge power stations. Everything about the dam is marked by the immense smooth efficient beauty that seems peculiarly American.*

To many other writers, leaders, engineers, bureaucrats, nationalist and revolutionaries of the subsequent six decades, big dams have been potent symbols of both patriotic pride and the conquest of nature by human ingenuity. Providers of electric power, water and food; tamers of floods; greeners of the desert; guarantors of national independence—for most of our century, dams, the largest single structures built by humanity, have symbolized progress, whether that amorphous concept be the creation of capitalist wealth, the spreading of the fruits of socialism, or the great march of communism.

At the opening of the Nangal Canal in the Punjab in 1954, Pandit Jawaharlal Nehru, the first Prime Minister of India, described his 'strange exhilaration and excitement' at seeing the canal and the construction site of the Bhakra Dam. Nehru expressed his awe through nationalism mixed with religious reverence:

> *What a stupendous, magnificent work—a work which only that nation can take up which has faith and boldness! .... it has become symbol of a nation's will to march forward with strength, determination and courage..... as I walked around the (dam) site I thought that these days the biggest temple and mosque and gurdwara is the place where man works for the good of mankind.*

Which place can be greater than this, Bhakra-Nagal, where thousands and lakhs (Hundreds of thousands) of men have worked, have shed their blood and sweat and laid down their lives as well? Where can be a greater and holier place than this, which we can regard as higher?

Massive dams are much more than simply machines to generate electricity and store water. They are concrete, rock and earth expressions of the dominant ideology of the technological age: icons of economic development and scientific progress to match nuclear bombs and motor cars. The builders of Hoover were advised by an architect to strip the dam of planned ornamentation in order to accentuate the visual power of its colossal concrete face.

The ecology and politics of large dams can gain practical dimension and dialectical directions only by humanitarian jurisprudence.

(Silenced Rivers by Patrick Mc Cully, Page 1-3)

The rule of law runs close to the rule of life and the Indian Constitution, in its humanist vision, has made environmental-ecological preservation a fundamental value. Rivers which are the source of potable and well water, sands that sustain riverbeds, river banks, greenery, bridges, coastal beaches which contain rare minerals and offshore sea beds which protect the littoral stretches, are a precious natural resource indispensable for human survival. Coastal seabeds if dredged for sand by builders may be deleterious to fishing wealth on which the fishing communities depend for livelihood. It follows that rivers, sands and coastal water have communal uses too cardinal to be neglected and too fundamental to be commercialized. Indeed, the higher jurisprudence of Article 21 of the Constitution (right to life) embraces the protection and preservation of Nature's gift without which life ceases to be viable and human rights become a *simulacrum*.

The Stockholm Declaration of United Nations on Human Environment evidences this seminal proposition:

16. The natural resources of the earth, including the air, water, land, flora and fauna and especially representative samples of natural system, must be safeguarded for the benefit of present and future generations through careful planning or management, as appropriate. .... Nature conservation including wildlife must therefore receive importance in planning for economic development.

17. In *State of Tamil Nadu* v. *Hind Stone*, AIR 1981 SC 711 it has been observed as follows:

"Rivers, forests, minerals and such other resources constitute a nation's natural wealth. These resources are not to be frittered away and exhausted by any one generation. Every generation owes a duty to all succeeding generations to develop and conserve the natural resources of the nation in the best possible way. It is in the interest of mankind. It is in the interest of the nation."

18. During the Summit in Rio de Janeiro, UNESCO offered the following vision of the future.

"Every generation should leave water, air and soil resources as pure and unpolluted as when it came to earth. Each generation should leave undiminished all the species of minerals it found existing on earth."

Therefore if our rivers are raped by nocturnal extortion, if our sea sands are dredged mindless to fish culture and rare minerals, the havoc that will follow will be irretrievable and clandestine pillage will inflict permanent harm. The Madras High Court dealing with sand mining to slaughter point vividly described the horrendous calamity flowing from what may be described as mafia mining.

20. Sand mining has an adverse and destructive impact. Its disastrous effect is unimaginable. It has "crippled the riverine ecology and depleted the ground water table resulting in a nascent desertification process". It has affected the stability of riverbanks leading to loss of whole chunks of land making large areas flood prone. Drain channels to lakes, ponds, tanks and irrigation are blocked since there is no more water. The river bed goes down far below the receive canals. It has been identified as the main reason for the water crisis. The potable nature of available drinking water is affected as the sweet water acquifers (recharger and purifier) are destroyed by quarrying. It has increased the base flow of ground water to the rivers. It also causes sea water intrusion further than usual upstream through back water and river mouths. As enough sand does not reach the river mouths to make natural barriers along the coast, sea water and sand enter the back waters and rivers. This ultimately leads to saline intrusion into ground water. It has also seriously affected the structural stability of several bridges. River bridges and railway tracks are severely damaged by sand mining in violation of rules and lease deeds. Flooding of agricultural lands due to break in linkage between discharge/channels and river basins. There is destruction of Agriculture/ Mangrove Eco System. Houses and buildings collapse due to erosion. The groundwater table goes down in all the river basins affecting agriculture severely. The sand mining permitted in private lands adjacent to riverbeds enables private owners to encroach the river bed illegally. Public roads are also seriously damaged. Drinking water has turned saline. Accidents occur due to heavy lorry traffic. The noise and dust thrown up by the lorries carrying quarried sand affect the people's health.

21. It takes millions of years for natural denudation of hard rock into sand. The current rate of extraction is far more than what nature is capable of replenishing. Alternative materials have to be found to replace river sand in construction activities. Excessive deepening of the river bed due to sand removal also accentuates soil erosion. Reduction in sediment supply from the rivers due to indiscriminate extraction will deplete the quantum of beach sand which in turn contributes to increased erosion along the coast line. (Paras 20 and 21 of the Judgment) (Contempt Application 561 of 2001)

The sand-depletion terrorism practiced on Nature by lawless looters inflicts an unconstitutional blow on the survival of the species. Articles 48A and 51A furnish the principles of jurisprudence which are fundamental to our governance under the Rule of Law. Section 3 of the Environment (Protection) Act, 1986 is geared to the great goal of preserving nature's bounty sans which societal survival will eventually be a mirage.

Water is a primary human need to deprive which is to deny the right to life. Indeed, the world may go to war on the struggle to control water. States dispute violently on the claim to water. People in cities and towns suffer desperately for want of drinking water. This gift of nature has to be equitably distributed for every human being to keep life going. But the water mafiosi which strangle sources of supply corruptly and make the right to life a misery. The State has a great duty vis-a-vis distribution of drinking water. Our rivers are sacred; so too our lakes and dams which serve several social uses. Aqua robbery by corporates is becoming common but is dereliction of State duty. One alleged instance in Kerala may be given illustratively although this crime against the community is multiplying:

> *The Hindustan Coca-Cola Beverages Pvt. Ltd established this unit in 1998-99 in approximately 40 acre plot (previously multi-cropped paddy lands) at Plachimada of Perumatty Panchayat in Chittur Taluk of Palakkad District, Kerala. About 70 permanent workers and 150 casual labourers are employed in the factory. On an average about 85 lorry loads of beverage production (Mirinda, Thums up, Coca Cola besides Kinley Mineral Water), each loads containing 550-600 cases and each case containing 24 300ml bottles leave the factory premises every day.*
>
> *More than 60 borewells (beside 2 open wells) are sunk in the factory compound extracting some 15,00,000 liters of water. The site is located a few meters away from the main irrigation canal from the Moolathara barrage. The site is located about 3 kms away from the Meenkara dam reservoir, a few hundred meters west of Kambalathara and Vengalakkayam storage reservoirs and 2 kms away from the main Chitturpuzha (river).*
>
> *Processing activities as purification of water, preparation of the bottled drinks, cleaning of bottles etc. generates a large quantum of contaminated waters and chemical waste besides plastic, paper, metallic and other solid waste.*

The core principle of public law is: The State is a trustee of all natural resources and is under a legal duty to protect them. These rare resources are meant for public use and cannot be converted into private ownership. The *locus classicus* on this point is blazed in *M.C. Mehta* v. *Kamal Nath.* The relevant head note relating to environmental degradation runs thus:

> *The notion that public has a right to expect certain lands and natural areas to retain their natural characteristic is finding its way into the law of the land. The ancient Roman Empire developed a legal theory known as the*

"Doctrine of the Public Trust". The Public Trust Doctrine primarily rests on the principle that certain resources like air, water, sea and the forests have such a great importance to the people as a whole that it would be wholly unjustified to make them a subject of private ownership. *The said resources being a gift of nature, they should be made freely available to everyone irrespective of the status in life. The doctrine enjoins upon the Government to protect the resources for the enjoyment of the general public rather than to permit their use for private ownership or commercial purposes. Though the public trust doctrine under the English common law extended only to certain traditional uses such as navigation, commerce and fishing, the American Courts in recent cases expanded the concept of the public trust doctrine. The observations of the Supreme Court of California in Mono Lake case clearly show the judicial concern in protecting all ecologically important lands, for example fresh water, wetlands or riparian forests. The observation therein to the effect that the protection of ecological values is among the purposes of public trust, may give rise to an argument that the ecology and the environment protection is a relevant factor to determine which lands, waters or airs are protected by the public trust doctrine. The Courts in United States are finally beginning to adopt this reasoning and are expanding the public trust to encompass new types of lands and waters. There is no reason why the public trust doctrine should not be expanded to include all ecosystems operating in our natural resources. Our legal system—based on English common law—includes the public trust doctrine as part of its jurisprudence.* The State is the trustee of all natural resources which are by nature meant for public use and enjoyment. Public at large is the beneficiary of the sea-shore, running waters, airs, forests and ecologically fragile lands. *The State as a trustee is under a legal duty to protect the natural resources. These resources meant for public use cannot be converted into private ownership. Thus the Public Trust doctrine is a part of the land. (1997) 1 SCC P-338/339.*

A sound sum-up of the law by a California Court sets it out with striking brevity:

> *Thus, the public trust is more than an affirmation of State power to use public property for public purposes.* It is an affirmation of the duty of the State to protect the people's common heritage of streams, lakes, marshlands and tidelands, *surrendering that right of protection only in rare cases when the abandonment of that right is consistent with the purposes of the trust..........* *(1997) 1 SCC P-411/412.*

In an exploitative society the struggle between members of the public for whom rivers and sands are their life breath and those who belong to the aqua-sand mafia the court has to use judge power to defend the people and the Constitution. The Supreme Court, in the Cricket Association of Bengal case, referred to *Airways as public property* to be utilized to the greatest public good without being allowed to be monopolised or hijacked by a few privileged persons of group. Waterways also attract the trustee doctrine. In the *M.I. Builder's* case (1999 SCC Page 464) the Court stressed the validity of the trustee doctrine. It is therefore settled law that the public have a paramount right to priority of use of river waters, sand beds and other ecologically fragile assets. The objective of the public trust has evolved in tandem with the changing public perception of the integral dependence of humanity and ecology.

The reverence of divine water in great leaps, and the glory of the Ganga in vast resources are wonders which are the world's celestial sources. What can be loftier and holier places than these waters from little wells to larger dams from small streams to broad canals?

Now we come to the menace of multinational corporations like the Colas consuming all the water, converting all the perennial springs, depriving the poor and the hungry, the mother and the child of water without which life becomes extinct! Plachimada, with its deep sources of water, other rivers of earth which supply us our basic needs and our snows melting to replenish our rivers—these are unusual phenomena—the cosmic wealth entire! If law of life to be sustained, corporates cannot deny every human life, every drop of water. Be you ever so large a corporate power, the law of life is above you. Man, woman and child *come first* and no corporate might, no technologic power, no economic cabal nor military arsenal can supersede people's rights. Plachimad, symbolic of man's right to pure water, which the bowles of Earth make available to mankind, is World Power for the well-being of mankind. If Peoples' waters are plundered, polluted, profiteered and converted into market, leaving the helpless to die of thirst the earth becomes a desert. Peoples everywhere must win. If *We the people of India,* one billion strong, claim Bharat's water resources properly planned, there never shall be global multinational Big Business in food and water. What we need today therefore is to arise and awake, make rivers speak, wells rise in levels, share what belongs to all through social justice. Let us unite, agitate and demand our right to water. No deep bore-well shall bully the poor, no Cola shall die water-less.

Journalists must stand united because the Fourth Estate has power over humanity's mind voice in our democratic order. Each according to his need, is the rule of water Corporate exploitation, denying human water and conquering market is the Cola cult. The Struggle to demand water which belongs to us all cannot wait any longer. Unite for water, all humanity, we shall change the world!

There is one thing stronger than all the armies in the world; and that is an idea whose time has come. (VICTOR HUGO).

PEOPLE OF PLACHIMADA *VS.* CORPORATE POWER OF COCA COLA

JAL SWARAJ

Every Indian, including every inhabitant of Perumatti Panchayat, has a constitutionally guaranteed *right to life*, which is the foremost fundamental right. Here is a wake-up call for judges sounded by a great U.S. Judge:

> *"A judge should be compounded of the faculties that are demanded of the historian and the philosopher and the prophet. The last demand upon him—to make some forecast of the consequences of his action—is perhaps the heaviest. To pierce the curtain of the future, to give shape and visage to mysteries still in the womb of time, is the gift of the imagination. It requires poetic sensibilities with which judges are rarely endowed and which their education does not normally develop. These judges must have something of the creative artist in them; they must have antennae registering feeling and judgment beyond logical, let alone quantitative, proof."*
>
> (Felix Frankfurter)

> *"Our judges are as honest as other men, and not more so. They have, with others, the same passions for party, for power, and the privilege of their corps."* (Thomas Jefferson)

> *"We need judges who are trained for the job, whose conduct can be freely criticized and is subject to investigation by a Judicial Performance Commission; judges who abandon wigs, gowns, and unnecessary linguistic legalisms; judges who welcome rather than shun publicity for their activities."* (David Pannick QC)

Humanism and compassion are *fundamental duties* which are non-negotiable since Part IVA articulates it with authority. Obviously, judges, executive functionaries and social activists are expected to use their power, imagination and influence to enable people, rich and poor, to enjoy their right to air and water and other biosphere-stratosphere-linked amenities and privileges which are components of life and liberty under Articles 14, 19 and 21, read together with Articles 39, 49A and 51A, as an integral human rights project operated in holistic harmony. What is often missed but is of constitutional cruciality is that this ownership and control of the material resources of the community are, as a top priority, to be so *distributed as to subserve the common good.* [Article 39(b)] Equally fundamental in the governance of the country is that the State shall never allow the economic system to operate to aggravate the concentration of wealth and the means of production to the common detriment. (Article 39c) Ground water is a great resource of people's good, beyond private ownership, and so indubitably belongs to the community that, sans its preservation as a quintessentially social asset, the water of wells, streams, rivers and the drinking water right of common humanity will suffer grave prejudice. This is obvious to anyone with sense and sensibility, aqua-patriotism and thirst-sensitive humanism. The State is guilty of irrational, arbitrary and pachydermic inhumanity if this compassionate proposition is violated by corporate avidity. The court, as the perennial sentinel of the Republic and oath-bound to command compliance with the mandates of the constitution shall use its writ jurisdiction and breathe reality into this hallowed cosmic jurisprudence. The might and majesty of the great judicial institution shall guard even the lowliest citizen in the discharge of his fundamental duty to protect and improve ecology and environment which include all universal blessings of a nation like rivers, streams, tanks and wells whose very life diminishes or perishes if the basic level of ground water sinks below safety margin or pollutes its sweet innocence. By whom? by lucre-lustful 'colas', carbides and toxic 'affluenza' discharged by avaricious industries with malignant technology. If corporate robbery drains our ground water the *basic structure* of people's right to life is breached and Constitutional values buried.

To wipe every tear from every eye is our tryst with destiny. (Nehru, August 15, 1947). The State and its instrumentalities, as broadly, creatively and catalytically understood in their humanist semantic dimensions, are obligated to fulfill the essential needs of the common folk who are victims of deprivation by global Gargantuan corporations, especially foreign, who use their clout and operate with toxic technology and corrupt methodology. Stiglitiz, once a leading adviser inside the World Bank exposed what he eloquently underscored as "briberisation" of the governing classes of satellite countries, which are prone to policies often described by nationalists, who cherish *Swaraj and self-reliance,* as *dependencia syndrome.* Patriotic architect Jawaharlal Nehru, authentic nation-builder Mahatma Gandhi and the Socialistic Republic's proud Constitutional Preamble notwithstanding, America and other Nations of the North have adroitly manipulated and dubiously managed to rob our resources under guise of 'development' and illusion of advancement. Union Carbide and Coca Cola, *et al* are illustrative of this Indian vulnerability. Patriotism, in this exploitative global context, if there are patriotic politicians left, must resist this menace which may insidiously infiltrate into the limpet media and manufacture subject minds. This exotic invasion by MNCs will spell craven cultural prostration unless we assert aggressively a Quit India Movement against the stratagems of mega-corporate recolonisers. Absence of such a militant self-defense battle, we may quail and fail as a nation, free and egalitarian. In the famous book 'Hidden Agendas' John Pilger observes:

> *"One of the most eloquent dissenters is the Indian social scientist Vandana Shiva, who has long attacked a Western-imposed 'monoculture of the mind' and called for an 'insurrection of subjugated knowledge', against the 'dominant knowledge' of capitalism. 'This [dominant knowledge] leaves out a plurality of paths to knowing nature and the universe,' she wrote. 'Ninety per cent of it could be stopped without any risk of human deprivation.'" (P. 534)*

Ecology and environment, mandatory for human survival, deserve preservation and promotion without which economic self-reliance, peoples' well-being and the very right to life will suffer gravely.

It is but right to dwell upon the controversy about coco cola driving down to the bottom base of Plachimada, using hi-tech processes which, the local people complain, deprives them of well storage and ground water resources and other aqua potential, thereby jeopardizing the necessitous right of the community to water. This fatal intimidation by a multinational corporation has to be read imaginatively in the context of the *doctrine of public trust* emphatically expressed by a bench of the Supreme Court. I quote from the head-note:

> *"The notion that the public has a right to expect certain lands and natural areas to retain their natural characteristic is finding its way into the law of the land. The ancient Roman Empire developed a legal theory known as the "Doctrine of the Public Trust". The Public Trust Doctrine primarily rests on the principle that certain resources like air, sea, waters and the forests have such a great importance to the people as a whole that it would be wholly unjustified to make them a subject of private ownership. The said resources being a gift of nature, they should be made freely available to everyone irrespective of the status in life. The doctrine enjoins upon the Government to protect the resources for the enjoyment of the general public rather than to permit their use for private ownership or commercial purposes. The Courts in United States are finally beginning to adopt this reasoning and are expanding the public trust to encompass new types of lands and waters. There is no reason why the public trust doctrine should not be expanded to include all ecosystems operating in our natural resources. Our legal system—based on English common law—includes the public trust doctrine as part of its jurisprudence. The State is the trustee of all natural resources which are by nature meant for public use and enjoyment. Public at large is the beneficiary of the sea-shore, running waters, airs, forests and ecologically fragile lands.* ***The State as a trustee is under a legal duty to protect the natural resources. These resources meant for public use cannot be***

converted into private ownership. Thus the Public Trust doctrine is a part of the law of the land."

(1997 Supreme Court Cases 388)

Ground Water is no private asset to be exploited without limitation by any individual or corporation. It is a cosmic wealth to be preserved in trust beyond the power of the State to barter away. The paramountcy of public rights in *universal property* is a basic feature of public law too deeply entrenched in the divine dimensions of progressive jurisprudence that Jejune Judicialese cannot whittle it down. Nor shall judges blink at these timeless principles of vintage jurisprudence or allow it to wither away. The Apex Court, in a case of broadcasting claims of a cricket tournament, ruled that airwaves have a cosmic dimension beyond private purchase by giant oligopolies at the expense of smaller claimants who have equal rights. Super-universal values have supra-governmental autonomy. The State cannot be "briberized" into marketing what belongs to compassionate creation! Underground water, being a perennial reservoir of a socially indispensable source of human survival, none—not even the State—shall sap that sacred right since vintage human rights will then be mere mirage. Public rights and public law with infinite potential are a rare class of jurisprudence with a vision too sublime conceptually for many legalists and moron jurists to interpret myopically, ignoring "earth democracy". Carbide and Cola and mega-magnates cannot and shall not buy or bend our holistic and hallowed rule of law. "Small is beautiful" and when billion strong and boundless in resources, shall not buckle under Big Business. That is India, that is Bharat, and that is the meaning of meanings which the little Indian understands as democracy, not oligarchy in power through the incompetent many. The rule of law must run in aid of the rule of life and the judicature shall hold the human rights barricade the least and the last no less than the billionaire barbarians with money power to buy the biosphere.

AN EPILOGUE

The conquest of Bharat through recolonisation is by a GATT, a dark plot of the West after World War-II (General Agreement on Tariffs and Trade). Raeganomics is the American strategy of disguised robbery by the disingenuous operations of the World Bank and I.M.F which operate by the fraudulent philanthropy of loans, aids and investments et al and the facilitatory mantras of Globalisation, liberalization, privation and marketisation. Money matters, man does not. "Briberisation buys, self-reliance surrenders. America Inc., with its hidden agendas, corrupts, Indian tycoons collaborates. Stiglitz, once the leading insider of the World explained this global plot and won a Nobel Prize. A long, vibrant caveat by the matchless researcher Ralph Nader, in his Introduction to a luminous book America Inc. writes what our Social Activists and Public Interest Jurists must read. I quote at length from a 1970 piece which has burning relevance now:

"The law locks up both man and women
Who steals the goose from off the common,
But lets the greater felon loose
Who steals the common from the goose."

[ANONYMOUS]

UNEQUAL ACCESS TO PROFESSIONAL COURSES*

National sovereignty and fundamental rights are political commandments of the highest order. Every other constitutional command and legislative directive comes only next in legal status. Weighing values competitively social, whether they be 'minorities' or 'weaker sections', or meritorious numbers from among the minority communities, the merit criterion claim priority in the matter of admission for professional or higher educational courses? This comparative estimate turns on basic evaluation from a national perspective. Nation first, the rest next. Who lives if India dies? National paramountcy measured by merit must claim of minorities or of the fragments. The finest talent is the nation's risk and cannot be jettisoned for the sake of fractions of society—under Articles 30 or 46. Why? Because nothing is above a nation's supremacy of genius. The supreme consideration in a sovereign country is, of course, is its foremost talent too fundamental to be scuttled to placate lesser human resources on grounds of minorities and so on. The best of the country may be from the poorest or socially suppressed like Ramanujam or Dr. Ambedkar or Dr. Kalam. Once, this 'best first' regardless of caste or class is concerned, is regarded, the creed of the country genius is lost. Democracy gains authenticity only if the **minority** has just opportunity to play its creative, uninhibited part in the shape of fair opportunity for dynamic actions development and towering cultural advance through plural higher education, which belong to them. The macro-fragment of society may suffer great abilities lying latent, being a minority or weaker segment. This shall not be. Those members handicapped by numbers or social disability, have the right to special concern. It is their land and **equalization**, through particular fillip, shall lift them to **equality**. This process is equalization to attain equality.

Full many a gem of purest ray serene,
The dark unfathom'd caves of ocean bear
Full many a flower is born to blush unseen
And waste its sweetness on the desert air.

(Thomas Gray)

* January 29, 2007.

What is a minority in the department of education? Not an **individual** adventurist's business by one who invests in the educational **industry** profitably. Is making professional education a Minority lucrative business because only it is run by a member of a minority community birth and no other consideration? You may be born in a minority community and run the enterprise **commercially**, not to elevate his backward community developmentally—a kind of shopping business, with books, classes and examinations, as wares, without focus on advance of the minority community as such is money-making business, not a drive to uplift minorities otherwise handicapped in education. It must be the obligation of Government to examine the de facto functional objective of the institution, not merely that its founder or operator is a member of a so-called minority. Is the college devoted primarily to Minority's educational purpose? Unless the primary and paramount purpose is to devote its finances, college classes and other exercises for the particular community's overall advance, qua minority, the special privileges of autonomy are negatived. Article 30 is conditioned by the special objective of the community constituting the minority becoming the cynosure of the institution. It is open to the State not to treat the college a minority institution merely because its founder as a profit-making adventurism is of a sect, Church or faith if it makes money by admission of students of non-minority classes on a large scale receiving handsome capitation fees or tuition charges) exploiting its status as quasi-minority. Similarly, the whole purpose of the minority institution is to promote educational excellence of the students from the minority community, nothing else, nothing less. Otherwise, they forfeit the advantages of the 'minority' under Article 30. A sprinkling of non-minority pupils is welcome as a competitive or fraternal fraction whose presence will stimulate finer standards and multi-community feeling. Being an Indian and a minority member of the total fraternity of India is fundamental. Again, they have to accept the principle of equality **within** the minority, and so, admission should be not at random or influenced by favouritism, or nepotism or guided by monetary or arbitrary considerations. Within the 'minority', selection **according to merit** and other poverty or recognized preferential criteria must prevail. If, on reasonable grounds, some non-minority students are admitted, no fee discrimination nor market price factor should vulgarise constitutional equality or equity. 'Minority' as a label cannot be an alibi for loot or adventurism. In short, a humane command that I consider valid is that the institution of the weaker section or 'minority' group should be substantially committed to the benefit of the minority or weaker community and not to use the mask to admit non-minority members or NRIs for collecting large sums by way of fabulous fees. These oblique excesses can and ought to be punitively prevented by the Government so that there is no abuse of Article 30 or other provision. Stern legislation in this behalf is necessary. Have the State the integrity to arrest those vice without being seared away by the Church or other Godist panic? Minority teachers have to be paid reasonable salaries. Then alone the contented teaching staff will promote good education for the minority community. Nor should illicit sums (really bribes) be culpably collected for appointing teachers by private investment even if they be church or holy institutions garbed as minorities or weaker sections or S.C./S.T.The provision for minorities as a favoured category is not to hold them as a privileged class over the majority. Minority hegemony can be dangerous if communally capricious. The nation is one and the Minority or weaker sector is but a part of it. We cannot conceive of the minority as a superior nation within the Republic. The Church, nor VHP or Muslim League shall not forget democratic integrity, unity, solidarity and fraternity. The rule of law must run close to the rule of life and therefore psuedo-minority institutions cannot get away with it by formal features and literal compliances. Social, economic and political justice considerations must govern the weaker and poorer pupils **within** the Minority and other handicapped sectors. Otherwise, a new Minority racket, where the poor belonging to the weaker or minority community, will rob all the 'percentage' seats and give no chance to the non-influential ones and the rich will plunder the privileges of minority quota. Equality (Article 14) a fundamental right, is a mandate forbidding abuse by leaders **within** the group leaving the weaker ever the victims. The purpose of the percentage formula as a case of special autonomy is to equalize and thereby attain equality, not to create horrendous divisive communalism, vivisecting our finer fraternity.

The basic rule in favour of these classes is not to generate a super sector above the majority but to avoid victimization of lesser and therefore weaker mini-human fragments.

The whole community, minority and majority, shall be imparted high quality education as it is a fundamental duty (Article 51A) to acquire excellence. We shall not be a nation of philistines. Education is the manifestation of the best development of every student's faculties.

> *We shall never learn to feel and respect our real calling and destiny, unless we have taught ourselves to consider every thing as moon shine, compared with the education of the heart.* *(Sir Walter Scott)*

TEN COMMANDMENTS OF HIGHER EDUCATION

India's supreme, sublime wealth is its vast human resources, those unexplored reservoirs of talents and faculties yet untapped by education through the instrumentation of schools and colleges. These teaching institutions are 'untouchable' and 'unapproachable' for the extensively agrestic, slum-soiled, raggedly urban and densely downtrodden, demographic multitude, on grounds of want and poverty of the huge have-not Indian humanity. Primary, secondary schools and, rarer still, higher, as well as professional degree courses, nurture finer personality development. Alas, admission to schools and colleges are the purchase of the rich sold by private managements dubiously labelled *self-financing* institutions. The State, guilty of insouciant dereliction, gradually withdraws from its constitutional obligation to offer egalitarian facilities to the have-not sector, leaving the gates open to non-official agencies, merceniously motivated. In the ages past, noble, though private, educational institutions used to invite the rich and the poor and all worthy youth aspiring for higher education. But the Church, with evangelist motivation, had a Christian yen to impart instruction, but no defiling passion for money-making business with education as a market commodity. Never money, ever man, with a Jesus slant, was the Church mission. Gone are those days from all religions, which did run excellent colleges. The nation owes a tribute to the Church for this classical mission of education among the people carried on with devotion to Jesus and, fee or no fee, give knowledge, primary to highest. The dollar or religion had little having poor purchase over the social soul of the Bishopric.

A bizarre metamorphosis has malignant the hallowed home of learning. A new class of educationist adventurists has unblushingly mushroomed who, using the alibi of holy nomenclature to hide their commercial agenda, meet the challenge of high degrees and professional colleges for which capitation fee and inflated tuition fee are the price. The Socialist Secular Democratic Republic, forsaking its paramount duty of providing for its young generation higher education for reasonable fee and no capitation fee, has abdicated its cultural trust in favour of Privatisation. What, then, about Socialist slant in the Preamble? Our Governments have violated, with no qualms, the fair educational facilities of running adequate universities for just fee or if private alternatives are the choice, at least by getting an undertaking from non-State managements, *before* granting permission to start a college, of *never* taking capitation fee and agreeing to a fiduciary duty to charge tuition fee at government rates. If you cannot manage this moderate obligation don't run colleges. Whatever the Court may issue as its oblique *ipse dixit,* higher teaching is never commercial. Judges, if jejune, are to go to colleges for judges to sanctify their vision and value of enlightenment as a sacred trust, not a top place in the salariat. Teachers are secularists. It is rape to fleece capitation fee from financially unable but meritorious candidates. Alas, Christian, Hindu and Mammon-worshipping institutions and corporate Managements, except sublime, excellent, morally principled institutions, which are few but luminous wonders like Sree Sai Baba Universities, are delinquents. So much so, today, thanks to the economic policy and priority of Governmental cowardly, commercial withdrawal from imparting knowledge without which citizenship is hardly complete for 'We, the People of India'. Now, in Kerala, education is aggressively dominated by so-called self-financing colleges. *'Privatization',* whose preference for money than man, is the *de facto* rule, so much so the Mafiosi-influenced university empire, is governed by student—free-booting private adventurers, individual, institutional and corporate. Mata Amritanandamayi, among the finest souls of our generation, and other godist enterprises like Thirupati Varsity(?) collect lawlessly large sums like several lakhs from indigent Indians for admission to degree-courses and professional, engineering and technological entrances. Has the State (Executive or Legislature) no voice, no authority to make education open sesame for the humble Indian in our world of corrupt culture of globalization, liberalization and privatization? Look at the glory of Sree Satya Sai Baba colleges which are the rarest of the rare with no fees at all, free board and lodge for any students. It is a tribute to the Kerala Government that the State has valiantly woken up to enact a creative law to regulate (half-heartedly, though) promotion of higher collegiate education by use of State power. To establish social justice in the higher education sector, now cornered by mafia manipulated Managements a reformative, regulative law is a must. Thus, in unblushing contra-constitutional deviance, the State, with diminishing value vision, grants open sesame for higher education to billionaires and shut sesame to half a billion humans who belong to the weaker sector. The apex Court has dubious social conscience but they have authority. The Constitution obligates the State to provide equal educational opportunity and economic justice to *every* citizen. If the Socialist Secular Democratic Republic retreats from providing learning facilities for the weaker section it is treason. *So the first commandment* is for the State (Central and provincial) to create social and economic conditions by legislation which will never deny the right to higher and professional studies for the weaker, have-not brackets. If bullied and tempted by the wealthy, offering capitation fees affordable only to capitalists, and payment of inflated tuition fee which baffles parents save the mega-affluent. (Affluenza is this pathology). Social and economic justice being fundamental rights, poverty and backwardness must be overcome by the State taking positive initiative and granting loans, scholarships and other schemes to secure admission, subject to merit. Non-State colleges must close down if they cannot run educational institutions without illicit resources from students or be great social activists drawing donations or popular charity—Did not Mahatma Gandhi and his 'do or die' struggle for Independence fight forward only by people's benefactions—not to charge capitation fee, which is skullduggery, admit on the basis of merit and be compliant with public sector transparency, public audit and large concessions for weaker sections is socio-economic justice. This is predominance of fundamental rights over monyocracy. Here comes the first commandment of *Swaraj.* Man, valuewise, is more than money. Self-financing is an alibi for freebootery, an anathema in the hallowed halls of universities.

Invaluable and invincible is the diamond-hard unity, steel-tough integrity, hard solidarity and invulnerable fraternity of the nation. For swaraj, we need a patriotic student foundation. We, the People of India, shall preserve this vision and its actualization as a socialist, secular, democratic Republic, guaranteeing equality and justice. Fundamental rights, social, economic and political, belong to the humblest and the highest in their developmental potential. Upon the education of the people of this country the fate of this country depends (Disrarely). The first duty of a university is to teach basic wisdom, not a hollow knowledge character, not vapid piety. Vivekananda put it powerfully. 'Education is the manifestation of the perfection already in man'. Economic justice and social equity being the title deed of the lowliest, the State must provide schools and colleges which will offer to the finest talent of the feeblest humans in the country college admission to acquire achievable high degree. The State shall be bound to start as many institutions as are necessary for our people. What we want, as a priority, is food and knowledge, not more shining motor cars, express ways and air-conditioned sky- scrapers and five-star gluttony for which they somehow manage resources, but do not have enough in the Public Treasury for the first charge on the State, namely, people's education, merit-wise higher education. It is absurd to plead State bankruptcy for education, but abundantly liberal readiness to borrow for extravagant luxuries and urban development with high technology and low employment. It is a commandment that the State do create higher educational facility, directly or through just arrangement, with public spirited capito-philanthrophic or godist institutions committed not to make profit as an educational industry but to unfold the blossom of mental, moral and spiritual, faculty everyone latently possesses. But the flower, fragrant and lovely, needs fertilizers of education and genius. Private institutions, as a condition precedent, shall not be permitted to run high-level colleges except on the *imperative obligation* undertaken by them of treating people of the lowliest means but possessing the highest talents and creditable character. Kuchela and Abel are the derelicts but dear though poor. After all, the Nation is great only when even the last of its members shares its treasury of education, given socialist secular study facilities. No private management, aided or unaided, sans this nationally obligatory undertaking where the poor are free, merit has priority, wealth without merit shall not buy at high price entrance, nor the socio-eco weak be told no because of empty pocket.

Today, a slew of dominant castes and communities have parochial domination, as if they are rulers. An agglomeration of churches multitude of faiths and a miscellany of godless materialist masses, each with its narrow politics, corrupt tactics at the hustings and slices of State Power, with terrorist strategies—these micro-communities organize colleges and professional schools, and together they make Indian Education cyclopedia. So many caste-based, religiously rooted communally oriented colleges pollute and bias student mentality and now the mafia seers.

Ye are the salt of the Earth. And if the salt lose their savour wherewith shall they be salted! A revolutionary orientation, socialist and secular, granting access to the weak and victims of socio-economic privation, with liberal scholarships, subsidies exemptions and a wealth of ways to facilitate the feeblest to secure education, given talent and desire to climb to the peak,—these must be implemented by the State. Fragmentation and tribalisation, with communal passion, religious fury for competitive percentages of seats and purchase power compensating for marks and merits are the vices of Indian degree dealership. It is treachery and travesty of the Republic if the leaders among the rich manipulators among the minorities and politickers among the weaker sections bluff and baloney about capitation and costly tuition fee and get away with it leaving the have-nots forlorn. Once Bharat Mahan achieves high professional, technological, humanity's glorious values, no arsenal of weapons can defeat us. Education is the manifestation of the latent talent of the littlest Indian, and equal opportunity for each by State institutions or dignified and dedicated to education by private management with public commitment and special concern for the weak. Government and non-official tuition fee must be moderate. If any boy or girl or family suicides for penurious inability to find a college unapproachable, India is culpable and privatization, with money power, governs education. *This shall not be.* Profound research is within Indian humanity's reach, given the chance. Many a celebrated Ramanujam misses life's mission because our rulers are sinners and pro-rich policy shapers.

Supreme Court Litigation cannot pronounce any solution as the Third House, of Parliament. Why then, bully and bout and bitterly battle against people's education? Can private freebooters hold to ransom the talented youth of society, fit for higher, professional and research studies because they cannot afford large fees and other sums in dubious diction with the State wasting its West-tempted five-star extravagance and costly cars and luxury bungalows but bankrupt when its primary duty of opening opportunity for creative education for the glory of India keeping the masses as Indian Ignorance Unlimited in Socialist Secular Democratic Republic. Be it Government-controlled or nomenclatured self-financed but honestly student-fleeced sums, no college shall levy more than moderate fees. Not what the Management desiderates but the lower middle class can afford educational is economic justice. The State must be proud to make its young human resources unfold its faculties through socialist facilities. Swaraj belongs to the young generation which, as a dynamic nation, must demand and be granted every avenue at humanist cost of escalating to professional excellence and lofty levels of education.

National sovereignty and fundamental rights of citizens are commandments of the highest order. Every other constitutional command and legislative directive comes next in legal status. Weighing competitive values, whether they be minorities or weaker sections the merit criterion will claim the order of admission. This sense of priorities and imperatives has to be understood as implied in the constitutional scheme. The first two basic principles override the third commandment which is the right of the 'minorities' under Article 30. Democracy gains authenticity only if the minority has full opportunity to play its creative, uninhibited part in the shape of development and cultural advance which belong to them. What is a minority? Not an individual adventurist's business by one who invests in the educational industry profitably. You may be born in a minority community and run the enterprise commercially, not elevate culturally—that shopping operation with books, classes and examines without communities for advance of minority community is money-making business, not mammoth education. It must be the power of Government to examine the financial operations of so-called minorities as devoted to minority's educational purpose. Unless the primary and paramount purpose is to devote its finances, college classes and other exercises for the particular community's cultural advance, *qua* minority, the special privileges of autonomy are negatived. Article 30 is conditioned by the objective of the community constituting the minority becoming the cynosure of the institution. It is open to the State not to treat the college a minority institution merely because its founder is of that Church or faith if it makes money abusing its status as quasi-minority. Similarly, the whole purpose of the minority institution is to promote educational excellence of the students from the minority community, nothing else, nothing less. Otherwise, they forfeit the advantages of the 'minority' under Article 30. A sprinkling of non-minority pupils is welcome as a competitive or fraternal fraction whose presence will stimulate finer standards and multi-community feeling. Again, they have to accept the principle of equality within the minority, and so, admission should be not at random or favouritism, nepotism or monetary or arbitrary manner. Within the minority, selection according to merit and other poverty or recognized criteria must prevail. If, on reasonable grounds, some non-minority students are admitted, no fee discrimination nor market price factor should vulgarise constitutional equality or equity. In short, the third command that I consider valid is that the institution of the weaker section or minority should be substantially committed to the benefit of the minority or weaker community and not to use the alibi and admit non-minority or NRIs for collecting large sums by way of fees. These oblique excesses can be punitively prevented by the Government so that there is no abuse of Article 30 or other provision. Stern legislation in this behalf is necessary. Without being seared away by the Church or other Godist panic. Minority teachers have to be paid reasonable salaries. Then alone the contented teaching staff will promote good education for the minority community. The provision for minorities as favoured category is not to hold a higher class over the majority. Minority hegemony—Stalin belonged to the party which had power though a numerical minority can be dangerous. The nation is one and the Minority is but a part of it. We cannot conceive of the minority as a superior nation within the Republic. The Church, nor VHP or Muslim League shall not forget democratic propriety. The rule of law must run close to the rule of life and therefore psuedo-minority institutions cannot get away with it by nominal compliances. Social, economic and political considerations must govern the weaker and poorer pupils within the Minority. Otherwise a new Minority racket where the poor will have no chance and the rich will rob the privileges of minority stature. Equality, inter se, is a mandate forbidding abuse by leaders within the group leaving the weaker ever the victims. The purpose of special autonomy is to equalize and thereby attain equality not to create horrendous humanity.

The fourth commandment which now has given rise to communal controversies and litigative logomachies relates to the boloney of so-called *self-financing* institutions. The grand, yet somber, sacrifice of the universally glorious and unique Jesus was crucified so that the poor and suffering humanity may struggle for a better world. The Cross, ...should never be used for the creation of purity-exploitative, lucre-accumulative creamy layers. The central theme of the crucifixion, often hidden, was that Abel shall have human rights and Cain, his brother shall be morally bound to keep, not assassinate him. In this compassionate dimension, *man, not money,* becomes the paramount material and humane purpose of *truly* Christian colleges. The fees shall never smack of capitation fee which is a capitalist freebooty. Had Jesus gone to a Jewish schools run by predatory appetite, educational crucifixion would have been his fate. 'Capitation' opium is educational pathology. Even if the *ipse dixit* of robed brethren of the Supreme Court Bench commits such a solecism Capitation fee is a felonious decree. I feel the court will not legitimise such unjust levy. Of course, even ordinary degree colleges have fallen into this mischief. I personally know of one well-known degree college asking for Rs.50,000/- or Rs. 1 lakh for admission to B.Com from a student with distinction. The parent could not afford; and so, a lesser degree course, with lesser payment, was chosen by the talented boy. Even so holy as Mataji's Medical College in Kochi (Amrita—what a divine name!) demanded, to my knowledge, 20 or 30 lakhs for admission as capitation fee. How undivine to collect donation of dollars from the U.S huge capitation for the alienation of Indian middle class. The plea of private investors in professional institutions is that all colleges charge large capitation fees. Even Bharatiya Vidya Bhavan, a hallowed institution, and Swami Chinmayananda institutions, equally reverential, charge twenty or thirty thousand rupees for LKG admission. One can easily imagine thirty lakhs for medical admission if the capitation fee of LKG is twenty thousand. Under no circumstances when education from ages 6 to 14 are constitute free and compulsory but violated by the State with no scarcity of resources for salaries and perks extravagantly constituencies sans sweat, hurt, toil and hungry tears—this bill of bonanza passed unanimously with unconcern for the proletariat. The present Marxist Government in power in Kerala (WB is an ideological cousin) with materialist convictions and morality has banned Capitation levy as an offence punishable with imprisonment. But the law is a paper tiger since I am yet to know of a single prosecution of a private adventurist for breach of this ban although penal violation by capitation fee collection is almost ubiquitous. Christian, Hindu and other Godist institutions are sinners, save some marvels. Of course, humane, charitable, sublime institutions resist this temptation. For example, Sree Satya Sai Baba is universally the rarest of the rare where no capitation fee, no tuition fee, no hostel fee—everything is free—is a paradigmatic wonder. It is a commandment of educational jurisprudence that no capitation fee shall be collected from candidates who seek admission. Knowledge is free, a sacred service. The State teacher's salary and the proprietors must find funds. The State's first charge is education, not huge salaries to MPs, MLAs, Judges, Ministers etc. But the police must be authorized to investigate all such cases and bring them under the law after due notice. Private managements are capito-philanthropic and, if warned, Bishops will Beware, other Private Managements Be Aware! Capitation Fee is moral malignancy with penal sentence. What is needed is a will, because managements, pretending to be self-financing, are patronizing the rich and influencing the Executive. A formidable step forward in making higher education is public principled, socially just, economically moderate and accessible to the talented poor. Similarly, fantastic fee are being collected, not merely by private colleges but even by universities. I do not think that in a socialist republic, intoxicated sums should be forced from students, however prestigious the institution may be. Education, even higher education, in every State in India must submit to moderation so that access may be reasonably available to everyone who has distinction by marks and good behaviour. If the 'management' is short of funds, students cannot be bled to build the institution. The public may be approached for donations. Greed has ruined society. The State may grant special bounties, concessions, income tax exemptions and other advantages for those who grant largesse by way of educational trust. Government must subsidize, or capito-philanthropy must be persuaded to adopt, other devices of acceptable ingenuity. Education is not merit learning, technology and thanatology in a world of war and terror. Real education is transformation, not knowledge, marks and discovery. "With malice toward none, with charity for all, with fairness in the right, as God gave us to see the right (Lincoln).

Revolutionary marvels of knowledge must be mastered by educational advances in science and professional modernisation. This is a millennial commandment. Science and arts, in competitive nationalism, has advanced rapidly, the world over, discovering wonder after wonder, technology outstripping technology to the amazement of a new universe. Technology has overtaken the past so fast; professional excellence has, each day, beaten humanism by global gallop and high values, integrity and fraternity in humanist dimensions have exceeded bully spirit and barbarity. Did not George Bush, the world's dangerous power tell the world that God, during prayer, gave him sanction to wipe out Afghan humans? Foul profanation is no education. The Orthodox teachings have become obsolete. International law, human rights jurisprudence, environmental development and other departments of finer reformation of judicial justice, have outstripped the yesterdays beyond measure and crucified Jesus in the name of the Cross. Therefore, new specialties and sciences and professional glories require a higher justice pharmacopoeia and juristic teachings in the luminous light of extraordinary expansion. In the field of criminology, victimology is a new development. Public Interest Litigation brings the people into the judicial cosmos. Medical colleges have to heal where there is suffering, compassion where tears and trauma pack solace. Indeed, the State has a duty to insist that colleges and universities have social promises to keep and many miles to go before they can claim the authority to confer degrees and organize researches. For this purpose, professors who have charge of training students have not merely to possess high standard of learning but also must be paid fair salary and given other facilities. Contentment of teachers is a *sine qua non* of competitive efficiency. Moneymaking mushroom institutions should not mar the national educational estate. India must be known for the superior standards of excellence so that its students will be *wanted* the world over by international corporations, research centers and national and international legal firms. Law has new dimensions of development, jettisoning fossilized, arcane jurisprudence. Update and humanize the judicial process, bring on the Bench justices with fearless pursuit of truth and equity and finer judicial jurisprudence—this is a commandment and title to be a university or college of judge's excellence.

India is one and indivisible. Our humanity, religious diversity and ....plurality notwithstanding, has a national integrity, wise ancestry and broad cultural identity. We cannot, in the name of denominational, sectarian groupism, obscurantising schismatic divisionism and like conflicting faiths befoul Indian society's holism. The *advaita* of India shall not be .... by fragmentation, communalization, fissiparous feuds and vivisection and weaken Bharat's solidarity. We, the People of India, have therefore to strengthen our granite hard impregnable Republic never brittle bricks, broken walls and riddled with micro-communities mutually bullying in casteist and religious subnationalism. Are we, a 'lunatic asylum of divisive humanity? We must realize the Achilles heel of Bharat is homicidal caste-creed-Godist disintegration and basic patriotism is a glorious amity among all religions and castes and languages while holding nationalism as a single Bharat. Who lives if India dies, who dies if India lives. This imperative is a communal strength of education.

Let us to the last trinity of educational commandments, which needs emphatic expression. Instead of marching towards in humanities and technologies through collegiate excellence, the sacred dignity of education has become most controversial and mammon-malignant in agitation. Nay, secular ever, communal never has been reversed by ugly Preamble for seat reservation. God battles against gods and this disputes Cora vulgarized in votes, bitterly lost in litigative bouts and lunatic fights for seats for purchase. Money and communalism are the measure of merit. One of the major issues on the 'admission' battlefront is the claim of private managements to select students *of their choice,* on privately held (?) admission examinations collecting *capital fee* with capitalist motivation and inflated tuition fee as if schools and colleges are private industries with commercial agenda. Colleges, licensed for lofty public education, have a public dimension with transparency, accountability and broad public control vis-a-vis selective process and annual fees. Universities and colleges (Private management or public owned) deserve our homage. This divinity shall not be defiled by lucre lust. Let us be clear about the Constitutional parameters which must govern managements, public and private. Here comes life's values, temporal and spiritual, higher than mere knowledge and learning. These are values at once universal, timeless and, in the language of the American Declaration of Independence, self-evident—"that all men are created equal, that they are endowed by their Creator with certain unalienable rights, that among these are life, liberty and pursuit of happiness". Our noble educational institutions must first teach *values* sans which all information, knowledge, literature and technology are but bedlam, and craven inanities. So the commandment our colleges instill into the student's being first and foremost is fundamental values. 'Values are to, a human being as a compass is to a traveler in an unknown land. Without values a person could be simply be lost". The chaos, the fast life, the violence, vanity jealousy, philandering and freebooting shall never be acquired in college days. To day, carnage and terrorism everywhere, blood, sweat, toil and tears' in every hut and home and slum is spoiling society because collegiate education has abdicated values and focused on marks without morality. Serpent smile, gulf of guilt, sadist delight in other's pain and wealth and profligacy pass off as life's sadistic, sanguinary victory in our unipolar, Hiroshima-horrid world. The negative ethos of the inhuman world order is imputable to diabolic educational decline. Colleges are unconcerned with values, compassion, humanism, practice of communalism, religion-rabid rivalry, favouritism, manipulation of marks by dubious stratagems and rare care for finer values. We had made a tryst with destiny on the midnight of the middle of August 1947 to wipe every tear from every eye but our colleges now train students to wound every eye to produce more tears. Alas! We must begin education with Life's divinity, dignity and humanity. Education without values is hollow. Eliot is cynically just.

We are the hollow men
We are the stuffed men
Leaning together
Headpiece filled with straw. Alas!

Professional education especially medicine, architecture and stunning new engineering, and innovative technology and developmental education of a miscellaneous character are a source of lucrative income and naturally ambiteves candidates compete for admission to these specialized institutions with purchase at any price. The private managements, using communal and 'minority' ploys, legally gain percentage prevailing over merit. The straightforward method is and ought to be always based on merit. But the meaning of 'merit' is controversial as has been explained in the *ABSK* case in the Supreme Court. (I wrote the judgment of the case) if the national interest is the paramount consideration 'merit' has to be judged not by a sophisticated test which the city candidates will answer best without knowing the hard realities of rural and urban Indian life. The primitive examinations based on base-born adivasi misery and *jungly* backwardness never know U.S sky-scrapers while the city dwellers may not even know of agrarian starvation, suicide and backwardness and will lose 'merit' if rural realities are focus of questions. Hi-tech achievements and five-star fashions are the urban cup of tea. Indeed, regional examinations which will cover a whole range of universities and colleges and rural, urban and whole prance-covered areas may be the fair process. Each private management holding a private admission examination is often a subteruge. If each individual college or university were permitted to hold private *examinations of their own* it is easy to manipulate results. Nepotism, favouritism, communalism and corruption spoil the effectiveness of merit test as a just means of ascertaining the comparative capabilities of the candidates. Therefore, private managements should not be granted the privilege of their own self-organized examinations. There should be merit measurement by objective adoption of a regional or State-wise scrutiny of intelligence and integrity but as far as possible, the test must be single and objective for the whole State, if examinations are not be vitiated by cunning pollution and market price. The sly strategy of special examination for each private manipulable institution can defeat all public regulations and relative merit. Thus talent and marks will lose if private managements adroitly adopt card-sharping, money-making methodology. The law shall insist on single test for each State or large region so that each candidate shall have a fair chance and corruption shall be eclipsed. Merit is no myth but is measured by honest marks and *viva-voce* success. State-wide commandment for admission examination is a fair standard, minorities and backward communities apart. Selection from just "percentages" can be from the best and poorest among the backward. But the nation shall not be jettisoned, whatever the religion, region, richness or caste.

India, which brought into its broad nationhood over 600 princes and princelings and chieftains, and by a cultural grandeur and creative merger collectivized the diversities of languages and customs and divergent ways of life into a single wonder of a Sovereign Socialist Secular Democratic Republic has, by wicked politicking, been communalized and sub-nationalised by paradoxes and contradictions using castes, sects, Cross and Islam. Fragmentation versus fraternity, sordid religious scramble with a slew of frictions and feuds as well as discord between the North and the South, has generated national suspicious and conflict—these mini-multitudes of communal groupisms have resulted in break-up of unity, berserk hostilities and have thereby weakened the patriotic integrity and unity in diversity which are our historic pride. St. Thomas had a hospitable home 2000 years ago. Islam, well over 1000 years old in India had a peaceful co-existence. And you behold temples, churches, mosques side by side. A hateful multitude of communities is the present berserk state. Are we, in Vivekanand's powerful criticism of Malabar, more like a lunatic asylum? Power-politicking and high office hunting have made communalism a disintegration of the nation with the unity of 'We, the People of India' proclaimed in the Constitution a paper tiger and the Republic a covert colony obedient to exotic Big Business and Bush-Blair Axis. India shall not be tempted by foreign jobs but do studies and research to make India great.

The most polemical issue that has polluted and defiled the educational estate is the arbitrary title enjoyed by the so-called self-financing institutions. No regulation regarding the quality of the candidates, the quantity of capitation fee and the inflated tuition fee made the institutions lawless. In the great days when education was a sacred subject and teaching was a patriotic function, capitation fee was under total eclipse. Tuition fee was moderate to a minimum and colleges took pride in getting on their role bright students regardless of caste, creed, financial status and religious considerations. Teachers did not have to buy at high price their posts but no teachers jobs had to be got by high bribes. Today, the State, with responsibility for higher standards, naturally claims to lay down the measures of criteria for admission, frown upon capitation fee and tuition fee as the private management fancies. Absent law other subtle operation freebooter was Management's privilege. This lawless extravagance has resulted in making education a commercial operation. In the Supreme Court itself, in an extraordinarily unexpected observation, a commercial perspective was sanctioned in the field of education. Higher education and professional specialties are no longer available except for millionaires, and the vast middle and lower classes and the lowliest ragtag have been treated as socio-economic 'untouchables' and 'unapproachables' by levy of heavy fee in professional, especially medical colleges. Oh! the pity of it that common people of Gandhi country and the Socialist Republic do not belong to Indian Educational Access Incorporated, because of poverty. Is Bharat a billionaires' property? Are India's professional and collegiate degree courses the monopoly markets of private educational super-hopes hidden by a nomenclatural illusion popularized as self-financing institution? No. The *socialist democratic secular* Republic commands every educational institution in the nation to commission student's admission in compliance with equality (Article 14) (a fundamental right), giving special allowance for each *real minority and weaker community.* Therefore, the Kerala State was right in its new bill on professional education providing 'percentages' and fee concessions. Justly the bill was passed unanimously—a rare feature in an acutely politicized multiparty system. Indeed, the bill has not gone far enough in favour of the people. The merchants of education have 50% success. Why 50%? A surrender by the Left. To my mind, all students, be they under Government management, university control or private administration, should have the same *moderate* fees, not high as now and lower tuition fee for weaker underdogs. Private managements should not extract larger fee because the first lesson in education is *equal opportunity* and *equal fees.* Morality and equality absent, knowledge is philistinism, unenlightened accumulation of information. The present system where fifty per cent of candidates can be chosen by private management, under guise of self-financing, is an indulgent gesture in favour of the private sector contra public interest. If private investment to build a college is beyond private commercial venture the State should refuse license. There are enough capito-philanthropic persons liberal corporations, benevolent Churches and generous Devaswoms and gold-rich and Gulf-rich citizens who will fill the bill. Better, if the cause is good though fewer charitable colleges than commercial adventurers with greed as the driving force. Economic justice, an overriding fundamental right (under Part III), applies to private institutions, State owned or aided or private by financially and obligates poor but talented candidates higher priority. If aided or unaided colleges claim arbitrary sums from the affluent and exclude the poor, the State must be closed down. Economic justice in educational humanist leaves no fairly option to play with the favourite of the wealth elite.

INDIAN MANAGEMENT SKILLS AND INSTITUTES OF MANAGEMENT

Institutes of Management have a special place in the scheme of promotion of excellence through higher education. Indeed, among our fundamental duties, constitutionally ordained, striving towards excellence in all spheres of individual and collective activity is important. The nation's advance will be pedestrian and humdrum, if it is murky in Management of its Business, not a happy prospect in a highly competitive universe. It is, therefore, a matter for rejoicing that the fifth Indian Institute of Management, the country's youngest, is already a success in the Asia-Pacific region. India is of ancient vintage but management skills are of nascent nonage, judging by Western standards. Perhaps, a nationalist vision may suggest that our legends are storehouses of management wisdom. Look at the Mahabharata, for instance, and the vision of Krishna! An Arjuna, sick in spirit, demoralised by the very scenario of battle, pleads inability to wage war when the chariot is ready to move into position and he has no option but to begin and win, with Sri Krishna as the divine charioteer, friend, philosopher and guide.

To dither at that moment was disaster, to drop weapons or ponder over problems and portents was shameful retreat and worse, unaryan. When the hero falters what does the Great Operator do to transform a stunned warrior sans valour, hesitant to act at the critical point of history, when victory was at stake and call for action could not wait? Here is the hour of Supreme Management, the spiritual-temporal strategy of infusing confidence, of reversing diffidence into determination, of inspiring a weak leader into a dynamic destroyer. At the source of this marvel is revolutionary management art. Do your deed, that is your duty. Do not worry your wits away over the fruits or outcome. Consequences which happen willy-nilly are none of your concern and beyond your *ken*. The dramatic scene is tense, halting suspense is defeat; to march ahead with clear conviction, supreme confidence and never to turn back or weep over casualties is the command. Trust in a Higher Power, faith in conscience clear, never fear is the martial mandate. Justice to the cause is the price of sacrifice. And Arjuna holds bow and arrow and overpowers despondency! That is the Cosmic Manager, Sri Krishna at his best.

Let me not lecture on the marathon Mahabharata here, being too illiterate for that. But my great point is that the Bhagvat Gita, viewed from a temporal angle, is a sublime message in supreme management exercise. We have much to learn from our epics and legends, *a la* Gitanjali Sutra, beyond holy *hocus pocus* and communal chant! More eternal and scientific than the West-white text books, seminars and Managementology voodoo.

The meemamsa of Management and vidya of leadership are treasured in our cultural heritage which can be a serendipitous dimension to the re-discovery of India, given the devotion to our ancient past and the dedication to its application in the crisis-ridden current conditions of the country. Lotus leaf detachment-cum-involvement in undertakings is the quintessence of our vedic teaching in temporal affairs.

But I do insist that management skills, in their functional versatility, are an imperative of success in modern administration, whatever be the walk of life or project. Be your system socialist or capitalist and sphere global, national or local, be your undertaking ultra-modern and macro or micro, real operational progress demands management skills sans which we will mess up in a grammar of anarchy.

What then is the art of sound management? Is it a riddle wrapped in a mystery inside an enigma? Or is it freedom from fuss, stress-free commitment to the job and focus on the purpose, undeflected by "sound and fury signifying nothing"? It is not IQ that always matters, business schools focus on the emotional quotient. A calm concentration on the task assigned is often side-tracked by stress and a free and fair judgment blurred by fear and tension, extraneous motives like unrighteous gain and corrupt objectives. So the decision-making process is disturbed, mental clarity confused and moral aberration creeps in. These generalities drive us to the conclusion that peace and poise are a *sine qua non* of good management and any factor that fiddles with poise and equanimity ruffles finer perception and muddles mature understanding. The rapid march of technology and the compelling speed of cybernetics are demanding in quick resolution and immediate action. True leadership belongs to those who do not dilly-dally, get lost in irrelevancies and bungling and blundering confuses the judgment. No judge can fill his office with functional success, no caption of industry can lead his business competitively, no professional in any enterprise can manage his affairs with confidence and competence unless he be properly trained in the arts of management. Mere brilliance on the academic or professional side, by itself, is far from sufficient in generating that perfection which we call success. Value addition of managerial element is the key to a good businessman, lawyer, engineer, administrator or judge in office. Our courts are chaos, our legislatures bedlam, our ministers' offices anarchy, our bureaucracies berserk and all of them with poor quality output because no specialised management talent has been acquired; and worse, the importance of management training is not even realised. The time wasted, wrong conclusions reached, avoidable conflicts created and bull-in-a-china-shop syndrome produced in public offices can all be traced to one malignant disease—the total innocence of that simple but priceless value addition called management training.

Management means efficiency in doing a thing to produce the maximum result in minimum time and effort. Management skill is devotion to the object to be gained, the subject to be served and the process to be adopted. More than all, in management as a professional excellence compassion for the cause, compliance with the ethos and deeper affection for the beneficiaries in view—these are the essence of the art. In India most professions and businesses and services must have one governing goal—welfare and happiness of the people who form the constituency of the concerned occupation.

Efficiency in performance, when management of human resources is geared to a clear goal, is true leadership. Never be vainglorious, ever be gentle and generous. Be you sergeant major in charge of a regiment, senior surgeon in a theatre with a team in attention, presiding judge whom advocates adulate or intimidate, professor who keeps a class in awe and attention, in all these cases, leadership comes with qualities acquired, not by birth but by a course in management. And so, I regard no profession, vocation or business beyond the bounds of Management training. Absent this equipment, sooner or later, mismanagement sets in.

Let me emphasize in this brief address, the quintessence and conscience of Human Resource Management. Compassion and humanism—two expressions which occur as fundamental duties in Article 51A of the Constitution and form the soul of our cultural heritage—they, if felt deeply, will eliminate friction with fellow-beings, irritation within one's own being and distress about thwarted wishes. The art of leadership, the component of meaningful management, consists first and foremost in obeying Polonius' advice to his son: 'to thine own self be true'. Unless the leader's *bona fides* is above suspicion, his success in leading his team, his workmen, his students, his followers is dubious, dark and short-lived. Faith in the leader is the first article of credible captaincy. Most leaders fail when they are discovered to be devious faith in oneself and empathetic communication with others is a maxim of good management. Moreover, compassion and humanitarian disposition, goodwill and convincing sincerity make all the difference between being a sure leader and becoming a clever climber. Burning passion for the cause, backed by well-reasoned resolution, goes a long away in leading the flock. Just see the sincerity. Are we not enchanted by Bob Kennedy: "Some see things as they are and ask why; I dream things as they should be and ask why not". On the other hand, did not Nixon, who won with the largest plurality of votes in the Presidential election, dismally resign as a reject of the American people after his Watergate expose?

Who is a leader? He who is never vain, vague, vapid or glibly voluble but weighs his words, means what he says and uses the gift of the gab to gain a sure purpose. In a technological world where the whirligig of change is breath-takingly rapid, to keep pace with global leaps and considerable complexity, a leader must possess quick adaptability. The leader must inspire others, kindle creative imagination, perennially be abreast of latest ideas and passionately communicate them, and convert creative imagination into pragmatic realism. The great leader must dream great things, possess a vision of tomorrow founded on hard facts and firm convictions. The laggard, with all his talent, is lost, the bigot, with all his fastidious faith, is a misfit, but the leader is path-breaker, ever in mental-moral locomotion and is vigilant in his concern to carry the team or troop or task force with him.

Here comes the play of that constellation of functions needed by a leader—compassion, passion, mission, humanisation and implementation. This is a revolutionary combination in the chemistry of leadership, political, social, entrepreneurial or any other. Only by sharing compassion others can come under the leader's spell. Since Management means bringing others into a single operation where the leader and the led toil towards a common objective, that sense of togetherness, the bonding element is compassion which has a material, moral and spiritual dimension.

A passionate humanism alone will arrest and attract followers with a sense of serious cohesion. No leader can organize his team as one merely by passionate eloquence. He may manipulate but not manage, he may spellbind but not sustain unless a competent mastery of the skills of management is manifest. This is where the great training of the I.I.M. becomes an indispensable element. A scientific course not only in leadership but also in management mastery is a requirement of modern business success. These two attributes of Management and Leadership have to be acquired. In this complex universe of technology and competitive search for success, the courses in the Institute of Management are a must. Vast is the expanse of Management studies, varied the type of training but one great value for any department of management is a humanist detachment of Arjuna and a profound concentration on action or Karma, divorced from greedy addiction to ambition and sacrifice of right means in the unscrupulous process of gaining the ends. This yogic dimension cannot be dismissed as ancient and obsolete. It is a value addition so long as psychic stress is apt to spoil the whole exercise and the integral yoga of ends and means is therefore a functional imperative. This higher humanism is practical wisdom and is of material relevance, as any great psychic specialist will tell. To pollute the process by noxious nuances is to miss the success which turns toxic. Even worldly gains need a moral fibre. 'Fair is foul and foul is fair' is good Shakespeare for the witches in Macbeth but Gandhiji's ends and means and Tagore's 'where words come out from the depth of truth' are sterling lessons if the business of leadership and man management were to be crowned with temporal triumph. And opportunism in the short run is lost opportunity in the long run, even as Management and Leadership win the race if we do not wish to make short shrift of it by cheap strokes and hasty runs, when the grace of the game is lost and the wickets too fall behind. Principle pays, as every great captain knows.

Disaster management is one subject, which we neglect at our peril. Courts collapse in the face of disaster urgencies, procedure being used to slow-motion justice and paper disposals defeat. Administration grinds to a halt when sudden disaster drowns its 'file' therapy. Crisis management, when incredible accidents plunge the police, the magistracy, the railway, chemical factories, nuclear plants into terrible trauma, earthquakes and diverse other catastrophes or Bhopal-like 'gassasinations' paralyse the State, and the infrastructure and personnel are fazed and dazed Institutes of Management must, in the Third World realities, train departments to develop fire-fighting tactics and instant rescue operations, without losing one's cool, maximising machinery and men and summoning allied skills adopting innovative strategies. The dogmas of the quiet past or halcyon present are not adequate to the technologically explosive and convulsive challenges and shocks which confront current leaderships.

IIMK, five years young, has established a reputation in the Asia Pacific region, gifted as you are by a remarkable team of talents. Creative contributions can come from the genius of IIMK in the years ahead. This country, with its ancient cultural drag, pathological communalism and current managerial syndrome, needs all the leadership resources and management wonders IIM can produce in a patriotic commitment. You can; you must; you will. The greatness of an institution is its illustrious alumni. The students who, to-day, receive their diplomas and the one who gets a gold medal have a finer future, a nobler career and a national treasury of achievement and excellence. I wish them, each of them, a high office as master manager and tall leader in a land that now lags behind but will soon soar to new skies.

COLLEGE CAMPUS POLITICS—NOCENT OR INNOCENT?

The academic discipline which describes and analyses the operations of the Government, the State and other political organisations and any other factors which influence their behaviour, such as social and economic, in short, a study as to *how* power is exercised, and *by whom* (and for whose benefit), through the administration of public power, of people's affairs may perhaps be described as politics, a great concern of every intelligent member of society. Albert Einstein has observed: "It is the duty of every citizen according to his best capacity to give validity to his conviction in political affairs". The ignorance of politics among the masses of a country paves the way for the rise of tyranny and the fall of democracy. The right to govern belongs to every citizen and so political science can never be alienated from the concern of the community which ultimately secures for the citizenry justice, liberty, equality, dignity of the individual and the integrity of the nation. It is a grave default, therefore, to deny to the population at any level the right and, indeed, the duty to acquire a basic knowledge of local, national and global political forces. It is a gravamen of injustice and goofy understanding of public affairs to command that political science shall be anathema in a college campus since, in the last analysis, such allergy amounts to an advocacy of political illiteracy, social insensitivity and cultural philistinism. The grammar of politics, in an enlightened sense, is the birthright of every member of our polity which is a sovereign, socialist, secular, democratic, republic as India is and shall be. The great guardian of the rights of the people in a Republic is an enlightened youth educated in the various dimensions and instruments of political science such as the legislature and the judicature. Indeed, the right to vote vested in everyone *at an age of eighteen* becomes a meaningful operation if only the exercise of franchise is an expression of political wisdom. In the finest sense of the word, politics must be obligatorily a subject of learning inside every college campus which owes allegiance to the Constitution and its Preambular Pledge. 'We, the People of India'—the first five words of our Constitution—have made a revolutionary resolution to defend the politics of the Constitution. Winston Churchill once defined and defended the ballot process which every judge and administrator must constantly remember: "A little man, walking into a little booth, with a little pencil, making a little cross on a little bit of paper— no amount of rhetoric or discussion can possibly diminish the overwhelming importance of the point". Be politically educated at age eighteen or be damned as dumb-driven cattle in a dying democracy.

There is a judicial impression among the robed brethren in India that politics is a vice like alcoholism or drug addiction and therefore be banned or ostracized as a mischief or menace, pathologically spreading as a dangerous syndrome in our institutions of higher learning. A division bench of the Kerala High Court, gave a ruling which through the media was popularly interpreted as a toxic tendency of student politics in college campuses which has to be curbed or tabooed for salvation of education. Professor J.A.G. Griffith in his powerful book The Politics of the Judiciary has argued: 'judges are human with human prejudice.........some are more human than others' and considered right wing opinion as an occupational bias of the *British* judicial profession. Surely, the Indian judiciary of which I had been a member for some years, is made of more liberal staff, more democratic ethos, more progressive eidos.

The Kerala judges in the Sojan Francis case held against the nineteen year old undergraduate, a member of the SFI, on the ground of inadequate number of days of attendance necessary as a qualification for taking the examination. This would have disposed off the matter. But the court, on the score of political importance, launched on a long discussion about the constitutionality of prohibiting political activity altogether within the college campuses. The college concerned, St. Thomas College, Palai, has certain guidelines regarding general discipline. One of them with which the court was concerned directly states that political activism is strictly banned in the campus and that 'students are forbidden to organise or attend meetings other than the official ones'. Strikes are prohibited within the campus, and the challenge of the student was that such forbiddance was violative of Article 19(i)(a) & (c) of the Constitution. Since this question is of 'considerable general importance', the court felt the urgency of the issue as one of adjudicatory moment.

The prohibitive clause which has been upheld by the court, if scrutinised with a little care reveals that organisation of or attendance at meetings which are *official* ones are permitted (even if they be of the character of political activism). So much so there is a discriminatory dimension underlying the ban which, in fairness, means that meetings which finds favour with the management fall within the permissible category. Communal managements of educational institutions are the bane of the Kerala educational establishment. It is full of politics, survives by politics, propagates political perspectives and controls the State educational establishment through its political clout. Therefore, officially permitted political meetings, often dangerous to the progressive development of the State and the Nation, enjoy open sesame or free access. Now that the controversial clause has received judicial sanction the ruling allows the Principal to spread within the campus his brand of politics and make every other political study through meetings and campaigns *bete noire*. Reactionary politics of private managements thus finds a haven inside colleges and all *avant-garde* political thought and action is frowned upon. This is arbitrary and unconstitutional. Indeed there is no rationale or logical basis of classification as the foundation for the forbiddance. There is no rational differentia indicated in the clause which will make a meeting *official* just, fair and reasonable. It is vague and can be capricious, depending on the management's will to give free rein to the partisan politics of a management. If clear guidelines comporting with the values of our Constitution *vis a vis*, political education and action, are transparently stated as governing the management's power to prohibit, it is a different matter. Absent such directive, liberal discussion becomes suppressed or hidebound and the cause of free thought fails as violative of Article 19, 20 and 21—Article 14 because the classification is not based on a rational differentia related to a constitutionally acceptable objective. The *ipse dixit* of the Principal calling it *official* does not make the meeting lose its vice of inequality before the law. Article 19 is violated because freedom of expression involves freedom of action, information and communication of ideas to deny which the college authorities can stamp a kind of activity as not *officially* acceptable. It is violative of Article 21 because the 'right to life' includes the right to moral, social and cultural development which, in turn, involves a free opportunity for uninhibited political education and it is contradicted by the clause which vests a ukase in the management. College education is improved through college debates and free speech. To control this collegiate freedom is to permit manufacture of young minds conditioned by the management politics. To swear by what is officially ordered as sound political activity and to swear at every other political process to which the Principal is allergic is to create conditioned minds which is the negation of political pluralism, democratic diversity and developmental autonomy. Our Republic will suffer from robotism if the creative vitality of the young generation at college is ordered about by the official church, communal management and mindless establishments which run schools of higher education. This is a new menace which benumbs the intellectual potential of the Nation. Apparently, even the judiciary is not sufficiently alerted about this ominous portent. Citing Supreme Court decisions about the political calamity of student wings of Parties in campuses misses the great tragedy of petrifying human originality. Every young mind passing through Colleges must be trained to be sensitive to the constitutional pledge of justice, social, economic and political, liberty of thought and expression and the dignity of the individual in relation to the nation's integrity. Platitudes and claptraps about student politics and Party allurements misses the oxygen of socialism, secularism and democracy which are nothing but politics but are the quintessences of our constitutional culture.

The Principal is the head of the institution but functions under the management and its political philosophy. It is right to prevent hostile groups of students battling within the campus or creating babel or bedlam making the process of learning impossible. Peace, health, morality and like vital values constitute discipline and must be preserved by the Principal. College premises cannot become scenes of sound and fury obstructing classes, but these important control measures of discipline do not justify taboo of political discussions, political magazines, political association and political seminars inside the premises save with the permission of the Principal as if to avoid law and order problems.

It is unfortunate to compare Government servants and their rules of conduct with student's code of conduct. The difference is too obvious to need explanation. Students study and learning has several processes. Teachers, government servants and other employees in public institutions certainly can have their political views but cannot resort to conduct or membership which will distract from or interfere with the neutrality needed for functional efficiency. It is confusion to mix up this category with the student community; of course, disturbing demonstration, obstructive strike, ragging and other operations which make classes difficult to be conducted or people's study menaced by turbulence—these can always be prevented, because they have a nexus to the goals of a student in college to equip himself with knowledge.

To banish politics for a student of eighteen years of age is to deny him the fundamental opportunity of becoming a good citizen to vote. It is anti-democratic to refuse a student a campus opportunity to talk politics, to read politics, to discuss politics in an association, to argue politics with his fellow students, subject, of course, to a peaceful atmosphere, disciplined behaviour and obedience to public health and morality. That orderly political activity by a student community governed by democratic decency and academic dignity will cause chaos in the campus is a fashionable fallacy and dubious diagnosis and I humbly believe will never be a judicial illusion. Educational pharmacopoeia, I agree, must cure the anarchic pathology of party-politicking, *even if officially backed by Management—disguised policy,* which often is subversive of radical constitutional activism. Blanket ban on campus political activity, save official ones, has a fascist flavour.

Politics is a social science and its study through organized movements, if peacefully pursued, even if a wee-bit restively and passionately, deserves no veto. Heeding the protests against a blanket ban, maybe, the Court has agreed to a review and, as a democratic gesture, invited everyone interested to present his/her submission. I pay a tribute to the judges for this judicious measure. I remember that while on the Supreme Court, presiding over a bench, I was hearing a case involving the parameters of death sentence I orally announced that any member of the bar interested in the cause would be heard, since the question was of life and death moment. A review is a remedy for the judges themselves to correct an error if a flaw has vitiated the judgement already delivered. No one, not even the wisest judge, is above a commission or omission which needs correction. Way back in 1980 in one judgement the court reviewed and reversed itself. There I wrote:

> *Horace Wrote "But if Homer, who is good, nods for a moment, I think it a shame". We, in the Supreme Court, do 'nod' despite great care to be correct, and once a clear error in our judgment is revealed, no sense of shame or infallibility complex obsesses us or dissuades this court from the anxiety to be ultimately right, not consistently wrong. The present petition for review is one such and we have listened, at unusual length, to counsel's oral submissions having felt that an error in the judgment under review, likely to injure and unsettle, needed to be mended.* (AIR 1980 SC 1187)

I am convinced; and by this I once again pay a tribute to the judges concerned, that the case will be reheard with a conviction that infallibility is not a judicial inviolability.

BHARAT—AN HIV HAVEN AND AIDS NIDUS NEED FOR A JUDICIAL WAKE-UP CALL

India, like South Africa, has, high on its Health Agenda, the pathology of HIV and AIDS. So Human Rights are in jeopardy and, *vis-a-vis* jural relief, judicial obscurantism is forensic folly, the vanishing point of curial vigilance. This article dwells on facets of Court commitment and AIDS concern.

The rule of law is a creative companion of the rule of life and the court is a therapeutic instrument for social pathology, since law is a social science. It follows that professionally the Bench and the Bar must acquire remedial competence to deal with diverse maladies of society. Ignorance is guilt where the profession fails to attain available knowledge, and this applies to judges too when they bungle or blunder or blink at the curative system, in robed apathy and highbrow authority. The serendipity of the subject shall not deter since the elan of the law shall avert injustice as the end product. On the contrary, judicial engineering knows no finer hour than when the 'brother on the bench', like a skilful surgeon in the theatre, cuts through forms and rituals, goes to the heart of the matter, obviates conservative biases, resorts to radical procedures and grants relief to forsaken humans, unpopular victims and 'untouchable' 'unapproachable' pariahs of sex prejudice. Discrimination against any person is uncivilized and unconstitutional unless rooted in sound grounds with a rational nexus to a legitimate end. This prolegomenon is necessary when we study HIV and AIDS jurisprudence where *unlettered brethren on the bench* may jettison canons of 'just, fair and reasonable' approach when the litigant is AIDS-infected or HIV suspect. The moment suspicion seeps into the forensic soul, sub-conscious frown suppresses conscious fair-play. Why? Because, in the great words of Robert Ingersoll, 'suspicion is the Upas tree under whose shade reason fails and justice dies'. It is therefore mandatory that HIV/AIDS branches of forensic medicine and justice response become an integral part of judicial wisdom since India is facing a crisis of Killer AIDS epidemic kept covert by undemocratic inhibitions. Ostrich-like policy of ignoring the growing menace of HIV, where our country is a secretly swarming hive, is itself a dangerous disease—a secondary epidemic—though obdurate sex obscurantism operates as a mental-moral iron curtain. A social problem, however unpalatable, if it develops numerically into one of considerable dimension, soon enters the court hall and demands resolution through an appropriate jural technology and judicial theology. It is in this context that an awakening is signalled by a new initiative involving the judiciary, usually jejunely informed professionally in venereal affairs. And this pan-Indian round—currently in Bangalore and Cochin—is refreshingly welcome and operates to conscientize a conservative 'lordly' elite with Constitutional monopoly over binding justicing. The nascent round of judicial workshops is being flagged off with high level 'robed' participation, so I gather. A great judge from South Africa is a unique presence. Justice Kirby, a close personal friend, Versatile scholar and charming speaker loads the discussion. Justice Michael Kirby of the Australian High Court is also Chair of the UNAIDS Expert Panel on HIV Testing. A few years ago, at a judges' conference, he was allotted a few minutes to speak on an allied subject in Delhi but before he took out a condom to explain a delicate point, the Chair choked his talk on the score his time was over. He has more time and a scholarly paper this time in Cochin and if the judges are impatient, Felix Frankfurter (U.S. Supreme Court) will be cited to chide them:

> *Judges as persons, or courts as institutions, are entitled to no greater immunity from criticism than other persons or institutions. Just because the holders of judicial office are identified with the interests of justice they may forget their common human frailties and fallibilities.*
>
> *(Quote It II p. 202)*

After all, midget judges are not our tribe. They strive, if I may flatteringly say so, to fulfil the great Judge Learned Hand:

> *I venture to believe that it is as important to a judge called upon to pass on a question of constitutional law, to have at least a bowing acquaintance with Acton and Maitland, with Thucydides, Gibbon and Carlyle, with Homer, Dante, Shakespeare and Milton, with Machiavelli, Montaigne and Rabelais, with Plato, Bacon, Hume and Kant, as with the books which have been specifically written on the subject. For in such matters everything turns upon the spirit in which he approaches the questions before him. The words he must construe are empty vessels into which he can pour nearly anything he will. Men do not gather figs of thistles, nor supply institutions from judges whose outlook is limited by parish or class. They must be aware that there are before them more than verbal problems; more than final solutions cast in generalizations of universal applicability. They must be aware of the changing social tensions in every society which take it an organism; which demand new schemata adaptation; which will disrupt it, if rigidly confined.*
>
> *(Quote it II p. 203)*

Quotational observation saves the writer from judicial anger, especially when the subject of discussion is one where an orthodox brotherhood may not like to be seen at an esoteric sex workshop. Remember Justice Kirby's admonition:

> *The first responsibility of the judiciary is consciousness about HIV/AIDS, and about the relevant legal principles which affect the performance of their professional tasks.*
>
> *At the outset of this epidemic, I was taught by Dean June Osborn, of the Michigan School of Public Health, that the first rule in HIV/AIDS law and policy is to base all action and responses upon sound data. That data will require those involved in relevant decisions and the exercise of governmental power (including in the judiciary) to know what they are dealing with, and what they are talking about.*
>
> *This is why it is important that all judicial officers today, in every country, should have more than a layman's understanding of HIV/AIDS. As I shall demonstrate, the epidemic is beginning to affect millions of people. It will have enormous implications for the running of courts, the decision-making in cases, relationships with colleagues, and the judiciary's role in the community...........The cases involving aspects of HIV/AIDS are now legion. Whole texts are written about AIDS and the law. From something which began rather modestly, this is now a very large enterprise. In many countries, including my own, special legal series are now published on aspects of HIV/AIDS and the law. Thus, in Australia, there is a quarterly newsletter on HIV/AIDS law and policy called HIV/AIDS Legal Link. There is a similar journal in Canada called Canadian HIV/AIDS Policy and Law Newsletter. There are many similar publications in the United States.*
>
> *I cannot attempt in this brief paper to analyse the role of the judiciary in responding to the many issues which HIV/AIDS has presented to the law. A number of examples may, however, illustrate the way in which informed judges, and other* quasi-*judicial decision-makers, can render a service by the sensitive application of the law to novel problems presenting as a result of HIV infection.*

He pleads for Courts' consciousness of the important AIDS issue. India, beware, is world's No. 2 in AIDS syndrome.

AIDS awareness, its causes and cure, are essential knowledge not merely for doctors but also for judges as part of their occupational obligation. The right to health is a fundamental right (Article 21) and an HIV-infected person needs protective-curative care, not pusillanimous scare. Open debate is the sunlight of transparency. How grave is ignorance and how much of a boon is information!

Four causes have been attributed for the spread of AIDS.

(1) Sexual intercourse with an infected or unknown person.

(2) Transfusion of infected blood and blood products.

(3) *Use of infected syringe, needles, knives or any other instrument that pierces the skin.*

(4) *From infected pregnant mother to the child. Two factors* i.e. 2 *and* 3 *relate to the highly qualified doctors. Factors 1 and 4 relate to persons who are immoral and don't want to own responsibility of maintaining family and high standard of civilization. Why such persons cannot be quarantined and treated separately like patients of TB, leprosy etc.? The way AIDS awareness programmes are being launched by the government, it looks like granting of social status and freedom of sex to people who are suffering from AIDS, at public cost which may or may not contain the disease but certainly will ruin our whole socio-economic structure. (PEN POWER p-266)*

"A decade ago, HIV/AIDS was regarded primarily as a serious health crisis. Estimates in 1991 predicted that in sub-Saharan Africa, by the end of the decade, 9 million people would be infected and 5 million, would die - a three-fold underestimation. Today, it is clear that AIDS is a development crisis, and in some parts of the world is rapidly becoming a security crisis too. There is now compelling evidence, presented in this report, that the trend in HIV infection will have a profound impact on future rates of infant, child and maternal mortality, life expectancy and economic growth.

(AIDS NEWS)

Asia is a rapid competitor of HIV cases but we must hold at bay this millennial plague:

China and India between them account for around 36% of the world population. With such huge populations, even low HIV prevalence rates mean that huge numbers of people live with the virus. Indeed, in India, where only 7 adults in 1000 are infected with HIV, 3.7 million people are living with HIV/AIDS at the beginning of the millennium—more than in any other country in the world except South Africa. India's epidemic is highly diverse: while some states show almost no HIV infection, others have reached adult HIV prevalence rate of 2% and above. In Manipur, the prevalence of HIV infection among injecting drug users shot up from virtually nothing in 1988 to over 70% just four years later, and it has remained at these high levels ever since.

Around 2.2% of pregnant women in Manipur tested positive for HIV in 1999. Most cases of infection appear to have been acquired from husbands who had been infected in turn by sex workers, themselves part of a longer chain of transmission.

(AIDS NEWS p. 3)

The demographic explosion of AIDS must alert court and country into a new legal-moral-social campaign. It is not my purpose to create a battle scenario. But hiding the facts is cowardice. 'Know ye the truth and the truth shall make you free'. What, then, are the basic facts?

> *Many young men are particularly vulnerable to HIV infection because, when they socialize, they often drink to the point of intoxication and experiment with sex.*
>
> *Drinking alcohol often leads to unsafe sex because it becomes more difficult to say no to sex, to use condoms and to practise safer sex.*
>
> *Approximately one-quarter of those living with HIV/AIDS are men under 25.*
>
> *More than 70% of HIV infections worldwide are estimated to result from sex between men and women. (approximately 80% in India and 95% in Kerala). Ten per cent can be traced to sexual transmission between men, and 5% of infections are due to needle-sharing by people who inject drugs.*
>
> *Research around the world suggests that men tend to have more sexual partners during their life-time than women.*
>
> *Studies show that when young men lack sexual health education (which can provide them with an understanding of their own bodies, pregnancy and sexually transmitted infections), they have an increased risk of contracting HIV. Many young people get their sexual health information from unreliable sources. Studies reveal that, while parents often provide young girls with some sexual health education (usually relating to menstruation and pregnancy), boys rarely receive any.*
>
> *(AIDS* NEWS, *Vol. 3, p. 4)*

Women are at more risk and need better protection. Young persons are prone to be easier victims and safety for them must be given greater emphasis. A struggle against AIDS is this century's challenge; Why? Because we are our brother's keepers.

> *Some circumstances place men at especially high risk of contracting HIV. Men who migrate for work and are separated from their families may pay for sex and use substances, such as alcohol, to cope with the stress and solitude. That combination increases their risk of infection. So does the culture of risk-taking that tends to characterize predominantly male environments like the military. In all-male institutions such as prisons, men who otherwise prefer women as sex partners may have unsafe sex with other men. In a world of AIDS, this can be deadly.*
>
> *Male violence is an important factor in the spread of HIV through the displacement of communities by wars and civil conflict, as well as through coerced sex. Each year, millions of men commit sexual violence against women, girls and other males—often in their own family or household. According to a UNICEF report, worldwide at least one in three women will, in their life-time, be beaten, sexually assaulted or otherwise abused.*
>
> *(AIDS NEWS, Vol. IV, No. 3)*

Voluntary counselling and testing must be popularly organised. The victim is not to be ostracised as sinner but helped as a patient. Drugs for AIDS must be delivered on a humanitarian basis. The court's concern, if invoked, must not lag or flag.

There is one thing common to South Africa and India which neither country can be proud of. The two lead the rest of the world in the number of people infected by HIV/AIDS, accounting for 20 per cent. of the global population of 40 million that is now afflicted by this fell pandemic. Yet, the two countries also share a singular unwillingness to take care of their HIV/AIDS citizens. Since there is no sure cure for the disease, the best treatment is its prevention. But for those who have been struck by HIV, medicines are available—at rapidly falling prices—which can enable them to lead productive and long lives. You must be rich enough not to be priced out.

Judges can be constructive in this dilammatic crisis. A South African court, acting on a petition filed by AIDS activists and pediatricians, has ruled that it is "an ineluctable obligation" of the state to provide treatment that will reduce the chances of HIV transmission from infected mothers to their children. In a country where 2.3 million women in the reproductive age are infected by HIV/AIDS and where upto 10,00,000 babies every year are born with the virus, the court order should make a difference to the spread of the scourge. A variety of treatment regimes, in which drug intake is only one element, are available to control what is called "mother to child transmission" of HIV. The most effective, spread over the last three months of pregnancy, is also the most expensive and possibly beyond the capacity of either South African or Indian society. It will probably take a combination of pressure from civil society and intervention by the judiciary for the Central and State Governments to wake up to their responsibility in AIDS care. Nevirapine is a drug under patent in the developed countries. But it is not illegal, under Indian law, to produce and use it in public health programmes. In any case, as the recent WTO Declaration on TRIPS and Public Health has made clear, Governments do have the power to over-ride patents when public health concerns so demand it. But will the two countries exercise this power? Judge power cannot be mute here.

Apart from these general aspects, courts have special problems with HIV/AIDS people either as accused in matters of personal appearance as well as bail, jail and sentencing strategies. The problem cannot be wished away. And public opinion, including Bench-Bar power, is a strong force. 'Public opinion is everything. With public sentiments nothing can fail; without it nothing can succeed' (Abraham Lincoln). But my apprehension is, in Orwell's words: To see what is in front of one's nose needs a constant struggle'. Robed illiteracy about AIDS syndrome must vanish and in the name of human dignity and rights I plead for forensic justice to 'fallen' sisters and brothers.

An Aside

Even like the splitting of the atom led to great discoveries, dangers and boundless potential benefits, so too the insight into the secrets of the DNA has sprung lovely and unlovely surprises as bane or boon for the individual and global family. The sequencing of the human genome and other serendipities of the genetic revolution have serious legal implications. *Ask* that astonishing Australian *judicial phenomenon,* Justice Michael Kirby, for the jural wonders that emerge from this research. The human genome and human dignity liberalise the application of the intellectual property law to genetic discoveries, especially because the genome and its incidents are an inalienable part of the common heritage of humanity and therefore beyond patentable parametres and cannot be 'owned' or 'controlled' by any person or corporation, however big their investments and flashes of genius their rare achievement. The Human Genome Project, the rights of privacy and confidentiality of individuals who are patients whose DNA was autopsied, the UNESO Universal Declaration adopted in November 1997 and the whole cluster of ethical issues need the lawyer's analytical mind and the judge's impartial pronouncement, all of which have intricate, integral, though abstruse, linkage with medical treatment and the Hippocratic Oath obligation of elimination or alleviation of suffering which is a legal *sine qua non* of DNA research itself. The Pandora's box has been opened. Let the Bench-Bar duo sieze. Hope from the box and give it to afflicted humanity as Social Justice. *Avant-garde* jurists, you have new frontiers to reach!

FUEL FUTUROLOGY AND QUEST FOR JUSTICE

Courts, as institutions, are principled pragmatists and judges, while justicing issues, even economic, cultural, technological or political, which reach the adjudicatory authority of the high Bench, consider solutions, after due hearing not from the impossible perspective of perfection but from the humanist approach of what is best under the circumstances, constitutionally acceptable and promote the fundamental rights, directive principles and eco-environmental values inscribed in Parts III, IV and IVA of our Founding Deed. One such issue of great moment which summons the wisdom of the Summit Court is the prescription regarding the future fuels of locomotives technically feasible, market-viable and jurally sound. Perfect justice, not attainable justice, Yes Why? 'Perfect justice is a mirage. In the pursuit of the illusion of perfect justice, we jeopardize the justice that lies within our grasp. Voltaire said, 'the best is the enemy of the good'. In all humility, I plead for whatever is the best *possible,* not the best in the *abstract.* Said the great Holmes: 'Of relative justice law may know something; of expediency it knows much; with absolute justice it does not concern itself'. So I proceed to deal with the relative justice of our fuel future, taking note of the potential, the viable, the most suitable among *available* choices.

Our concern about fuels is due to our quest for automotives facilitating speedy, mechanical transport. In our search for avoiding physical exertion we fall back on automobiles both for our travel and goods movements. These elementary thoughts are irrelevant to the modern man but in the less sophisticated countries like rural-urban India, animal transport and cycles and rickshaws are not obsolete. Aping the West and adopting, simian fashion, the insatiable appetite for machine civilization, India has jettisoned animal resources for transport with contempt and abandoned the bike which could wheel without pollution, millions of people. Before the new mini-Hong Kong craze possessed People's China, it was a glorious sight to behold thousands of Chinese youth cycle from home to places of business. I do not advocate a total return to animal locomotives which are free from pollution and make ecologic sense but, instead of the treachery of speed with environmental terrorism, a partial revival of donkey, camel, bullock, even elephant transport process makes sense, economic and preservative of eco-environmentalism. Our animal wealth is not enormous carcass but serviceable in several ways. Delhi will not be among the most notorious dirty cities of the world and our deserted villages would not be deprived of alternative animal locomotives had we a Gandhian compassion and economic sense in transport policy formation. Imagine our countless villages vibrant with animal abundance used, *inter alia,* for transportation on ordinary days and as cavalcade, camelcade, caparisoned elephants in majestic procession on festive occasions, instead of glittering motorcades. Not Solomon in all his glory was arrayed like the village festival grandeur of agrarian communities. If a separate lane for animal drawn transport as well as cycle traffic were provided for, a dynamic co-existence is not a fantasy but a fact, not feudal reversion but an ecological burliness! The economics of draft animals in our nation which lives in two centuries together is a neglected social study. Ask Cartman (Prof. N.S. Ramaswamy of Bangalore who has researched in this field).

The main purpose of this paper is Human Life and Motorised Locomotion. The focus is on Life, not automobile, on harmless, healthy living environment and automotives as ancillary to and promotive of safe, cheap, eco-friendly mode of travel. A developmental policy which is homocentric, with people at the centre stage, not automobile industry run on pollutive fuel endangering life—that is a consummation of sound transport economics. This fundamental, often missed when profits have priority over human health, fails to measure civilization in terms of clean biosphere and healthy living species, which blunders about our Constitutional concept of justice which regards Life, (under Article 21), as the foremost human right, and social justice, pervasively present from the Preamble through Parts III and IV, must be highlighted in any expert examination zeroing-in on the contemporary controversy of 'future fuel' policy. Law and Life must fertilize each other and State Policy must be geared to the democracy of transport systems which beautify humanity's health and wealth, not glorify the economies of manufacturers of automotives, ignoring the mandate of motor transport justice in its humanist dimensions and environmental implications. Don't accept a contaminated fuel policy as a necessary evil. Then it will make its diehard presence as more and more necessary and less and less evil. Pragmatism, if principled, is not compromise with evil but no compromise on evil. It means elimination of vice not by impractical leaps but progressive means with unflagging emphasis on the right goal. If the foundation is not firm the enquiry will be shaky. If the objective is obfuscated by alien considerations the findings well be flawed. On sure ground and with clear vision let us forge ahead with our fuel future. The State cannot enjoy a free ride on the back of pollutive motor industries but must give priority to social cost and public interest with pro-active daring while making recommendations.

Life, healthy life, is our birth right, not only as individuals while travelling but in our collective survival as humans. Freedom of movement at reasonable cost and right to a health-friendly environment must be synthesised as basic requirements of a fuel policy. Here we are concerned with vehicles, fuels, and human health. Vehicular traffic and the emissions of smoke from imperfect engines cause deleterious pollution of the air around. We must breathe to live and the air we breath must not be contaminated by pollutants discharged as fuels, when used up, emit as a fact of chemistry. So the potential villains of our pollution are the motor engines and the oil fuels and the victims are not only the travelling public but all life that inhales the air in the atmosphere which, willy-nilly, receives the true discharges pumped as gases and particulates consequent on combustion. Such is the budgetary of transport industry and the health of the community. The irresistible logic of sustainable life is the elimination of noxious emanations, the culprits being the design of the locomotive and the quality of the combinable gas. The engine must be hospitable to finer fuels and reject cruder intakes which, when the engine works, pumps out pollutants injurious to lungs, eyes and other sensitive organs of innocent members of society. The social trauma thus inflicted is a price public health cannot afford to pay. It follows that to focus on fuel and absolve the engine is to abet the murder of people's right to good health. The motor industry cannot escape culpability in the lethal chemistry. So too is the fuel supplier vulnerable. Travel we must by rail or road or air. Road transport with which we are immediately concerned—not that the other two are guiltless—desiderates a bifocal analysis. When experts dissect this composite problem and concentrate on fuels alone, leaving vehicle manufacturer beyond the pale of correctional commands they blink at the motor which is a party to the turpitudinous process which ends up in the product of guilty toxicity.

The legitimate expectations of the Indian people is inviolably codified in the Constitution and to dismiss those viable aspirations as mere pious wishes or laudable distant targets is but contempt of the Constitution unbecoming of the State and impermissible in our social order. There is no rigid formula in matters where flexibility is realistic and technological pluralism offers triable options. Our resources have limits, our conditions of life are not modelled on Western paradigms and our vehicular variety has a wide range from two-wheelers, three-wheelers, cars, buses, trucks, jeeps, tractors, bulldozers and ambulance vans and other ingenious automobiles. Our roads are terrible, rash speed and road blocks left to imagination, while VIP violations are a law unto themselves. This traffic anarchy has a bearing on punctuations and full stops on the narrow highways and winding driving, weaving hairline escapes and haywire hazards. Fuel expenditure, pollutive discharges and eccentricities of traffic are inter-related and so, myriad road considerations enter the pathological fuel calculus. The backlog models of road mobiles are baffling, some time-barred, some factory fresh, some tiny, some huge—all these complexities enter the full policy verdict. These are not miracles but amenable to control, regulation and punitive obedience provided there is the sovereign Will to prescribe and make operational on the track. Societal co-operation is equally imperative. To police the police is necessary.

We need not be scared by traffic chaos. Fuel policy, which is scientific, swadeshi, road-sensitive and social cost-effective, is not a dream or a dread but a feasible project beyond the lawless panic and disarray on the road.

The quality of the motor engine has bizarre problems in Indian conditions. Ancient cars and trucks are not banished and black smoke gushes out like from micro-volcanoes. Three-wheelers also push through their pipes smoke like lava flow. Environmental invasion, even by automotive, is violence on life; and law has a job to do here, laying down prescriptions and proscriptions and implementation infrastructure. Cadres who operate to make the law a fact of life have to be *trained* and *empowered.*

Now we come to grips with the two substantive issues of motoring machines and fueling alternatives. We must be judicious in our cautious hope and never be tempted by a fictional universe of ideal fuels. We may as well begin with the power that propels, which is a wider concept than conventional fuel in our gas stations. Fuel-free, pollution-free, environmentally friendly technology of propulsion is not moony in a world of daily advancing technology which rapidly reaches the market, appetised by prospects of takers in numbers and reliable margin of profit. Of course, judges, with robes on, don the wisdom of Solomon. Nor are experts proof against motivated, misleading opinion. Their professional apparel and research infallibility are not beyond purchase. Experience too is uncertain when drawn from history, geography and statistics. As John W. Gardner felicitously expressed:

> *Every judgment is no more than an approximation of the truth, subject to revision *** If we recognize our judgments as subject to revision, we shall be less inclined to force them down other people's throats, or to back them with bullets *** The mind has an enormous capacity for error, self-deception, illogic, sloppiness, confusion and silliness. All of these tendencies may be diminished by training, and that, of course, is the function of education.*
>
> *(Quote It II p. 205)*

Pen power, even from the Apex Bench, is final *pro tem,* not enduring infallibility. So it is fair for the higher courts to rely on specialist assessors, in open court, to guide, not govern, to clarify, not to conclude.

Back to power propulsion jurisprudence formulated with a sense of relativity, contextuality and contemporary technology.

Is there a mode to move by automation a vehicle on the road without any discharge or emission which will lead to environmental pollution? Yes, there is. Electric power, geared to automobile engine systems, works without spoiling the biosphere. This is no technological distance or dream but a feasible proposition perhaps not yet popular and more expensive, may be. Electric buses, tram cars, trains are in use and battery-operated cars are not rare. Electrically propelled automobiles are therefore just a single step ahead. A challenge to research, this type of vehicle should become a common means of transport because it is pollution-free. Robert Kennedy's inspirational words stimulate greater initiative and added investment to discover a common transport system at once available at affordable cost and acceptable utility. 'Some see things as they are and ask why', said Bob Kennedy: 'I dream things as they should be and *ask why not*'. It is this investigative spirit of *'why not'* that must drive us on to an environment—friendly transport mode. The Manshelkar Committee on appropriate auto-fuel and allied issues has given its Report whose recommendations are the beginning, not the end of a policy of transformation of transport by automobile, rid of the curse of air contamination. Of course, what we need is not what the United States or other sophisticated country craves for. Evidence-based, analysis-backed, scientifically validated methodology, *congenial for Indian socio-economic conditions,* is our desideratum. So viewed, the Committee holds:

> *The electric vehicles (EVs which are a zero emission option have lately been developed in India. However, the battery pack still remains an inhibiting factor affecting widespread use of EV. To be feasible, an EV must be reasonable in weight, give good performance and have a life-cycle cost, which is comparable with that of petrol powered vehicles. Hybrid cars in which a battery supplements the engine power, have a range of innovative features and are generally regarded as the most promising alternative to reduce vehicle emissions.*

Emission omissibility is a fascinating prospect. When the sure conquest of the large market is coupled with government's fiscal incentives, research venture will register results since electric technology has a foot-hold already in the field. This alternative justifies strong commercial interest and tax temptation on the part of both Central and State transport departments on an urgent basis. So alarming is the pollutive pathology and health hazard of oil fuels that, even if a wee-bit, uneconomic, electric vehicles must be promoted. Damage to environment spells health havoc that social cost must tip the scales. Subsidy for producer and consumer is worth while since at stake is human health. The tailpiece emission pollutes air quality and substitution of liquid fuels by gaseous fuels or hybridisation by safe blends offers hope of reducing pollutive discharges. The Manshelkar Committee has this to say on the subject:

> *The conversion of petrol engines to CNG operation is relatively simpler and the OEM engines or conversion kits are found to be technically acceptable provided the kits are duly certified by a Government test agency.*

The bi-fuel capabilities, as available in case of CNG/petrol cars and three-wheelers, however, is an undesirable feature as the engine can only be optimized for one specified fuel. Switching over from one fuel to another entails trade off in performance. Also free use of multiple fuels with different emission characteristics may defeat the purpose of promoting certain types of fuels.

In the case of buses which are presently powered with diesel engines, the change over to CNG requires changing the engine from compression ignition mode to spark ignition mode. Conversion of diesel engines to CNG mode requires major modification to reduce the compression ratio, fitment of carburettor, spark plug, ignition circuits and expansion valves to reduce pressure of CNG before induction into the cylinders. This calls for incorporation of many changes and is technologically not the best option. Newly designed and developed CNG engine including specially designed chasis for bus application is a better technological option. The desired performance standards for CNG engines for bus applications need to be specified and an appropriate warranty required from the manufacturers.

Experts are apt to exaggerate and when vested interests, like the powerful automobile industry, are affected conclusions at face value may be branded misleading. We must chase the CNG option and, in any case, press forward with the bifuel potential. Travel becomes so cheap and clean and the major stakeholders, the travelling public and the people who breathe to live, will benefit. Make the system fail-safe and popular and the defeatism projected by the Committee must be defeated by super-technologists. It is *necessary,* so it must be *possible.* Conventional auto-fuels are admittedly injurious to environs and economics must submit to ethics knowing that the right to life is the best ethic which business must promote. CNG and LPG are currently in limited use. The plea of short supply and cost of distribution of gaseous fuels must be given short shrift in view of the vast consumer cost benefit and the considerable environmental advantage.

A divagation needed to explain the Indian situation

Delhi and other cities face 'slow murder' (title of a book) by a combination of market flood of more motor vehicles, diesel fuel danger and governmental inaction ignoring the Supreme Court order of July 28, 1998 to convert Delhi's public transport to Compressed Natural Gas (CNG). In the wisdom of the judges, a direction for exclusive sale of unleaded and low benzene petrol also was made. Advanced improved Euro II vehicular standards within five years was also ordered. As the violators did not comply in time they rushed for curial extension and secured a conditional procrastination. The exasperated Court is faced with the fury of oil companies and queues of three wheelers. Clean fuel is law's despair and life's repair. In *M.C. Mehta* v. *Union of India* the court issued order in detail but on 20-10-2001 the court observed:

Unless the two governments, namely, the Union Government and the Government of NCT of Delhi share the perception of this court to safeguard public health, the orders made by this Court from time to time will have no effect. We are, however, assured by learned counsel appearing for the Union of India as well as the Government of NCT of Delhi that the two governments do share our perception and concern to safeguard public health by providing clean air.

But where are we now? Debating! Evading!

Sabotage by globally powerful vested interests is not a new game. Only a people's campaign can combat it. First a scare was spread that CNG would explode, would not pull up flyovers and that finer diesel with less sulphur was feasible. Next, it was urged that gas (CNG and LPG) was in short supply. Third was a frontal attack that CNG was itself carcinogenic. Finally came a plea that diesel was not a *guilty* fuel but innocent of pollutive perils. What a cabal of lobbies when we get to the truth! 'Know ye the Truth; and the Truth shall make you free'—says the Bible.

Seminars, workshops and committees ask pollution, like Pontius Pilate asked Jesus: "What is truth and would not stay for an answer:" Our cities must have breathable air and motorized transport cannot defeat the right to life (Article 21). Dirty diesel must die a natural and legal death. Other countries have lessons for us especially in the use of CNG. Delhi meets nearly 50% of its total travel needs by buses which are but 1% of the total number of motorized vehicles and yet polluted air is the lot of Delhi denizens. Buses alone cannot do the job especially when vast numbers of other vehicles use faulty fuels. A comprehensive policy is the strategy, which is feasible given political will and social pressure. Other Third World Countries use CNG. Beijing, Cairo and lesser cities elsewhere have it in larger measure. But there is an incremental cost relating to vehicles using conventional liquid fuel and this extra cost has to be set off against savings in social costs. These technical matters cannot stand in the way of catalysing use of non-pollutive fuels. Of course, total co-operation is necessary from bus owners who must maintain their buses properly and from other motorists who too must have a heightened sense of fuel innocence. We cannot blame the Government alone but Government must give the lead. NGOs must be encouraged to mobilize the people to raise their voice against pollution of the air, which is a universal asset and imperative need for human survival.

Taking a world view, CNG is the best gas option and the LPG an alternative. Car factories, once a firm policy is promulgated, will ready gas tanks and safety kits. Some sceptics challenge gas kit safety. They are wrong. Perhaps an illustrious example of a gas-run automobile is the Rolls-Royce Silver Corniche of the Buckingham Palace fleet. Several authorities have approved this gas kit. Italy has been using gas as auto fuel for decades. Hybrids may hold good for India. Combinations with electricity and gas, to be switched on according to need may suffice. Petrol is waste and perilous. Let us bring it down to vanishing point.

Fuel justice summons a comparative study of CNG and diesel. CNG is cheaper in use once the equipment is fitted. CNG is far superior from the point of view noise pollution, which is frightening in diesel-driven vehicles. CNG cannot be polluted with adulterants while it is popularly believed that diesel is frequently adulterated with kerosene which multiplies the deleterious impact of the mixed fuel. How can we stop adulteration with kerosene when the cheaper price is a reckless attraction and there is hardly any adequate checking machinery available in Delhi or Bombay. It follows that diesel must loose the battle although my final view is to opt for the hybrid proposition.

Petrol is still the dominant fuel in the market. We are told India is self-sufficient in petrol and diesel and is being exported. Then why this high price? Public transport, among the most strategic in any progressive society, is sky-high in cost in India because of distorted notions of public finance and common weal. Socialism and egalitarian concern are writ into the Constitution and contrary policy is in practice! When evaluating imperatives of State policy never forget the Socialist, Democratic, as distinguished from Capitalist and Oligarchic, nature of our State. The interests of all, *not of haves* only, becomes fundamental in the governance of State Policy.

This *Weltanschauung* being cardinal to policy frame, any decision on Conventional Energy for the automobile medley in India must be informed by *environmental fundamentalism* and *health compassionateness.* That component of social cost must weigh against corporate business interests and claims of export prospects or expensiveness of refining oil. This fuel philosophy is hard Constitutional policy. Many regulatory and fiscal measures the State can command may be pressed into service to produce the least environmental hazard to health. Emission norms may have to be prescribed and monitored and the integrity of regulating agencies, so as not to succumb to regulates tactics over regulators will have to be structured. This area may turn corrupt at various points as the State Transport Departments and minions have yet to build a reputation for price-free probity.

The apparent simplicity of legal principles, when the challenge of actualisation arises, becomes the dilemma of constitutional jurisprudence. 'Vehicle manufacturers are a force to be reckoned with. Oil interests too are powerful. More than that, the colossal quantum of in-use vehicles with old equipment is a Himalayan hindrance to clean emission operation. Thirdly, a business slump and bankrupt State economy cannot manipulate radical mutations. Even so, Life comes first, the common people's right to breathe least lethal air. That economy is best where human health matters most.

When unveiling the auto policy and fuel future project, creative humanism and eco-environmentalism must claim functional spirituality as much as pragmatic economics. It is interesting to recall a famous exchange between Higginbothom and Mahatma Gandhi:

"Spiritually to be meaningful should be three-fourths economics".

(US Economist Sam Higginbothom to Gandhiji)

"Economics too, to be useful, should be three parts spirituality".

(Gandhiji to Higginbothom)

True, in the formulation and implementation of basic policy Industry and Government must share views, identify product technologies and generate a global wave of humanist content in consumption of auto-service. Even the mode of auto-transport like bus transport, road blocks, smooth movement without frequent traffic slow-downs and long halts, speed limits, road discipline and the other regulatory factors, like access to gas stations, bear upon fuel economics. New ideas are a needed input with local condition in mind.

State policy is important, not always decisive. Civil society as distinguished from the political State, has a role to pay in shaping and shaking policy and in making and unmaking the working of governmental and other legal structures. So let us not, while arguing for a people-friendly auto-policy put all our eggs in the State basket. Society is more than State, Democracy more than the Executive-Legislative-Judicative collective. If society, an informally organised expression of the People, have an influence on the Administration, oligarchic, bureaucratic, technocratic, dictates can be moulded to meet social needs.

Public transport system will gain more emphasis than insular, individualist transport luxuries (of the affluent who drive luxury cars solo) and market theology of affluenza-crazy car glamour. More cars, more pollution, more road hazards and social cost. Twenty cars or one comfortable public transport bus? Auto-rickshaws, the middle class man's taxicab, are everywhere in large numbers with pollutive fuel emissions. We can't, elitist fashion, wish them off the road but cannot tolerate the widespread damage by them to the air either. Environmental discipline must apply to all vehicles, trucks being the worst enemy perhaps.

One sure mode of tracking down deleterious discharges is to goad the manufacturer into good engine makes. Allergy to pollutive oils may be built into the engine itself so much so there is no alternative to using finer fuels. There will be resistance, cost bogey and MNC pressures with clout in the State. The State's surrender syndrome must be overcome and public interest must win. But there is massive pollution in every wheeled vehicle of the Past still plying on roads of the Present, holding it prisoner of incurable smoke and victim of dust-related lung diseases. The obsolete engines plus must be changed or be off the road. The cost of replacement or abandonment, heavy perhaps, has to be pitted against the ill-health of the people.

Two more issues: (a) Express ways, not village lanes. (b) Control of motor population restricted by what the traffic can bear. A National Traffic Controllerate and Motor Commissariat with large statutory powers are obligatory if Life—Indian Life—must survive.

In a competitive, market-driven society with its own propaganda bugles, social intervention by the State may not click. But in a socialist State, where public, joint and private sectors operate, civil society and NGOs are of functional relevance. Environment will not be the concern of the capitalist class and the State may adopt the least government line. No. Our Constitution is loud and clear that its concern and commitments are co-extensive with social justice for which every citizen has title. Fundamental rights, including that expanding horizon of right to life, are within the range of people's access and the State is obligated to ensure delivery of these broad freedoms. So we have a dynamic State and to guarantee the State delivery system, we have an *activist judiciary* triggered into shooting writ missiles by public interest litigation initiated by social action groups. Without usurping Executive Power but without abdicating the obligation to actualise for every Indian the benefit of free locomotion, blessings of pure air and other civil and social rights, the court will guarantee a constitutionally compatible auto-fuel policy. Such is the *odyssey of locomotive jurisprudence* in the auto-fuel dimension.

The court is a majestic hope and institution with a message functionally operational between State and Society in situations of legal imbroglio. The judiciary is an instrument of integral yoga between Government and the governed, the great mediator, independent, informed by both sides and with no vested interest in the verdict save social justice. So in the current confusing state of fuel fault and fresh air justice, judge power, the final authority to enforce human rights, has an adjudicatory 'broker business', at once fair and free, with fearless yet realistic role, since freedom of movement, right to life and environmental justice with access to both sides and affirmative action as its binding duty. This jurisdictional facility, flexible yet final, must play a constructive part in shaping fuel future policy from the fundamental freedoms angle. Judocracy is fool-proof, sound proof; clout-proof. Being immune to MNC pressure and demagoguery, a just solution without class bias may, *perhaps,* be expected.

But what factors must the court reckon with? Impersonal convictions must prevail. Interstitial legislation to do justice is permissible but confined 'from molar to molecular' as Justice Holmes put it. Curial pen power will consider public policy as governed by constitutional mandates, no more. Not theoretical but practical will be the 'robed' writ, so that it can be executed. Once this position is plain, the Supreme Court shall, *not may,* protect the citizen's right to breath fresh air and live with his freedom of movement on fuel available or bus fare reasonable. Experts may be consulted but shall not command. The executive must be heard but shall not dictate. Finally, the court's humility of willingness to gather information from every public source, never secret cache.

Assuming that we agree that our capital city Delhi and other megalopolises and megapolises, cities and towns, are polluted beyond tonic limits, accepting the horror of vehicular traffic emissions as a major pathological problem, fully realising the Constitutional mandate of elimination of injurious emission what is the remedial *conspectus,* ignoring cosmetic placebos?

Electrically driven cars, trucks, buses and other means of transport be given State promotion by subsidy, fiscal concessions, government and public sector patronage. Zero pollution justifies zeroing-in on popularisation of electric vehicles.

CNG and LPG use must be given a big push. Manufacturers must be persuaded or pressured by State and court to put on the road appropriate locomotives. But supply and distribution must *first be facilitated.* If long queues line up for hours, it would deprive the court of its credibility. Populist CNG-LPG writs lead to chaos for want of feasible delivery systems. Manufacturers and vehicle operators' organisations, police and traffic authorities should also be heard by Court, Commission reports and expert studies obtained, not casually but comprehensively, and relevant NGOs involved as *amicus curie,* even as consumer organisations should be harnessed to the task. Price structure, technological issues, loan facilities must come within the ken and creative cognizance of Public Interest Litigation as part of judicial activism. Animal mobiles, with special facilities for operation, can save village and urban transport needs.

The journey is long but we shall not jettison the plural alternatives to pollution-free transport facility. Informed publicity will overcome inhibitions and exaggerated difficulties. The war for clean environment and safe public road systems shall be won if the right to life does matter. It does. The finest judicial hour arrives when, considering every concerned angle, a viable verdict is given in a public cause with focus on social justice, fundamental values and better pursuit of happiness for all.

CHRISTIAN PERSONAL LAWS IN CHAOS

Legislative colonialism dies hard in India. For instance, fifty five years after the bells of Independence tolled Indian Christian are still ruled largely by laws made in Great Briton in the nineteenth century. Thanks to the insouciant indolence of Parliament which finds time for 'parliamendemonium', if I may respectfully express my exasperation. In proof of my criticism of such inaction, I quote what the author Prasada Rao has said in his preface to his three-volume work titled Law Applicable To Christians in India:

> ***As far as Christians are concerned, the law relating to solemnization*** *of marriages is contained in the Indian Christian Marriage Act, 1872 and the Cochin Christian Civil Marriages Act, 1095; and the law relating to matrimonial causes is contained in the Converts' Marriage Dissolution Act, 1866 and the Indian Divorce Act, 1869, the latter being renamed as "the Divorce Act, 1969" in 2001.*
>
> *The Indian Christian Marriage Act, 1872 extends to the whole of India except the territories which comprise the State of Manipur and the State of Travancore and the former State of Cochin; and the Cochin Christian Civil Marriages Act, 1095 has been in force in the territories which comprised the former State of Cochin.*
>
> *There is no substantive law in the Indian Christian Marriage Act. It deals only with the form of solemnization of marriage and the substantive law relating to solemnization of marriages in respect of Christians is yet to be legislated.*
>
> *The provisions of the Indian Divorce Act were exact copies of the English Matrimonial Causes Act, 1857. The English law was amended in 1923 and 1937. But the corresponding amendments were not made in the Indian Divorce Act. (Vol.I)*

The Christian community is a small minority where consensus is not a difficult process and yet the Law Commission Reports which led to the Christian Marriage and Matrimonial Causes Bill, 1962 was allowed to lapse. The Christian community proffered a proposal for revision commanding consensus. The Ministry of Law prepared a bill *viz.* the Christian Marriage Bill, 2000, but nothing came out of it. The Indian Divorce (Amendment) Bill,

2000, a marginal measure, was enacted as the Indian Divorce (Amendment) Act, 2001. But there were several defects in that enactment, which remain unremedied even today. The author points out, "the law in the Indian Divorce Act goes back to its position in 1869". So in substantial measure, the British of old days still govern post-Independence-Indian Christian community. The author urges that the law relating to marriage be revised in such manner that it is at least as progressive as the Hindu Marriage Act and the Special Marriage Act.

Kande Prasada Rao, a Christian, has produced three tomes which are heavy in volume, but weighty in wisdom. The research that has gone into these prolix pages deserves commendation of a high order, especially because Mr. Rao is not a jurist by profession but has excelled jurisprudents by the massive work of which he can be proud. In the laudatory words of Justice Jeevan Reddy:

> *The author has also given texts of numerous judgments of different High Courts and the Supreme Court which have pointed out the defects in the Indian Divorce Act, exhorting the State to take necessary steps for the revision of the said Act.*
>
> *The most important part of this book is the proposals for revision in the form of two draft Bills, one for the solemnization of marriages and the other for the law relating to matrimonial causes.*

The daring publisher, Universal Law Publishing Company, among the foremost in the law publishing field and progressive in venturing to bring out rare legal literature of *avant garde* character has rightly enriched the *corpus juris* of India by his pioneering Prasad Rao volumes.

It used to be said of George Bernard Shaw that his pen produced a pennyworth of *play* and a poundworth of *preface*. Indeed, his luminous, lashing and acidly incisive prefaces excelled his powerful, socially surgical plays which were classics too high for praise. In the same strain, if I may say so with pardonable adaptation but without pejorative implication, the three-volume marvel of Prasad Rao has for its Foreword a superbly informative and creatively critical contribution by Justice K.T.Thomas which, in itself, is an excellent piece in Christian legal literature. Justice Thomas is at his lucent best in his indignant assessment of the failure of the Parliament in retaining on the statute book, Christian Family Law which 'survives after death'. Perhaps, it is fair that I allow the learned judge to speak his thoughts in his own words:

> *The Indian Divorce Act should have been revised soon after the enactment of the Hindu Marriage Act in 1955. But that was not done. The Marriage Laws (Amendment) Act, 1976 which revised the Hindu Marriage Act and the Special Marriage Act did not touch the law applicable to Christians. The Indian Divorce Act was not revised along with the Parsi law when the latter was revised in 1988. Consequently, the law relating to matrimonial causes in*

respect of Christians remains as it was enacted in 1869, in spite of thorough revisions made in the law applicable to the other religious communities.

The Supreme Court of India and Full Benches of different High Courts held, on different occasions, that some of the provisions in the Indian Divorce Act violate the Fundamental Rights ensured in Articles 14, 15 and 21 of the Constitution of India and directed that the Union of India should take immediate necessary action for the revision of the law in the Indian Divorce Act to bring it in tune with the law in the Hindu Marriage Act and the Special Marriage Act, and reminded of the directive in Article 44 of the Constitution of India that the State shall endeavour to enact a Uniform Civil Code for all the citizens of India. Yet the attempts made in that line remained where they started at.

Erudite and instructive messages from four judges of the Supreme Court (three retired and one still on the bench) adds to the value of the volumes. Sri. Soli Sorabjee, that liberal battler for human rights, has called Prasad Rao's work as "monumental" and he is right and justified in his statement. The Universal Law Publishing Company with its unique success in merited publicity, will surely reach the books widely so as to find a place for them in every library, especially in the personal libraries of those who are concerned with family laws. I wish the adventurous and industrious Prasad Rao, a lucubrative dalit scholar, a lasting name in Indian jurisprudence.

INFORMATION EXPLOSION—
A VISION STATEMENT

We live in an age of technological revolution a fallout of which is the information explosion. The inconceivable speed and global reach of information communication marvel makes the world shrink and humanity an intimate family. Our media age, with the extraordinary volume and wonder of transmission, has diminished distance and facilitated instant informational delivery. If only this great potential could be operated in a just and fair manner promotive of peace, equality, just relations and human rights, this phenomenon would midwife a better World Order. Such a glorious prospect would catalyze stability, peace and universal happiness. Such a tremendous transformation would be a fulfillment of a dream too dazzling to believe and too paradasiac to be a reality. Why? In an unequal world, with disproportionate distribution of power to deliver motivated information, control over the dissemination of news and views to their best advantage by the State or the Proprietariat may lead to manufacture of public opinion to advance the interests of giant corporations and gargantuan institutions. The poor of the world will suffer, because suffocation of information which will tell the truth about the suppression and oppression of the weaker sections will deny them freedom of expression and destroy their democratic right to gain equal space in the minds of mankind, mould world opinion and win social justice. In this view, the basic question is *for whom* does the information revolution prove a blessing, *who* operates the communication process, *what* is the content of the facts fed into the circulation system and *whom* does it target.

In a globally brain-washed society, the management of power and the manipulation of minds are operated through pliable institutions and profit-promoting technologies. Corporations are the macro-institutions readying to capture markets and putting to unscrupulous use the processes of information technology. Indoctrination through suitably designed information processing is their expertise. Calvin Coolidge, long ago President of America, once told the world that 'the business of America is business'. Bush Senior and Bush the Younger, recent and current Presidents of the U.S.; assuming universal jurisdiction, hold Big Business interests as *their business* and use explosive information technology to expropriate the world's resources. The invasion of Iraq, with no U.N. sanction or other legal or moral justification as an urgent necessity to defend the American people and the world from Saddam Hussain's *Weapons of Mass Destruction* was, by a preposterous perversion of propaganda, criticised by many as *Weapons of Mass Deception.* Baghdad is the most heavily bombed city in the world in history and yet, by media mendacity and informational unveracity, a crime against humanity was projected as liberation of Iraq. Truth loses its language and speaks the way the information controllerate orders it to perform.

When we glorify information revolution we must investigate the hidden agendas of Corporate Power and the victimisation of the voiceless Unpeople of the Earth. John Pilger trenchantly observes in his brilliant book Hidden Agendas:

> *The children of Iraq are Unpeople. So, too, are the half a million children who, according to UNICEF, die beneath the burden of unrepayable debt owed by their governments to the West. One Filipino child is said to die every hour, in a country where more than half the national budget is given over to paying just the interest on World Bank and IMF loans. These facts are not allowed to interrupt the cosy British ritual of Red Nose Day, when the money raised for 'the poor of the world' is but a fraction of that paid by the governments of the poor to Western banks on the same day. Britain, which has an 'ethical' foreign policy, demands levels of debt repayment that far outweigh new loans or aid; only the United States has a longer record of taking more money from the developing world than it gives out. It was not until the government of Mexico threatened to repudiate its debt, an action that might have brought down the Western banking system, that the wider issue was retrieved from media oblivion. (Page 3)*

The developed world drapes its exploitative devices in attractive informational apparel making disaster of developing countries look like blessing in disguise, making a colonised state appear as salvaged democracy, making every country under American military dependency a free nation. Informational exaggeration and communication manipulation project globalisation, liberalisation and privatisation as the dawn of a golden era, a myth, while, in truth, it is ambitious, aggressive, global economic occupation, market conquest for Multi-nationals and subjugation of cultural pluralism by imperial, consumerist mono-culture.

Whenever events have occurred which affect vast masses of humble humans, little space and time is given to the fair communication of information or to the quality of their presentation or the style of their projection. Coco Cola advertisement claims more importance than T.V news of mass starvation or disease. Indeed, 'infortainment' and 'infoadvertising' programmes flow seamlessly into commercials with little time for poverty news or facts which concern the underprivileged. Britain and the BBC are not far behind in the ever diminishing importance to the little men of the world. Multi-nationals control the media taking the cue from the media baron Rugert Murdoch who set his role in the communication revolution as a Colossus. In Britain, on what is still lauded as 'the best television service in the world', only 3 per cent of peak-time programmes feature anything about the majority of humanity, and almost all of that is confined to the 'minority' channels, if you exclude Clive James laughing at the Japanese. In the media's 'global village', other nations do not exist unless they are useful to 'us'.

> *Regardless of the BBC's enduring façade of 'impartiality' and 'standards', news is now openly ideological and uniform, as the demands of the 'market' supercult are met. When slow news is included, it is more than likely dressed in a political and social vocabulary that ensures the truth is lost. Thus, in Britain, as in the United States (and Australia), the systematic impoverishment of a quarter of the population is routinely filed under 'underclass', an American term describing a corrupting, anti-social group outside society. The solution to poverty, which is the return of vast wealth taken from the poor by the rich, is seldom given a public airing. The 'new' system of capitalism for the powerless and socialism for the powerful, under which the former are persecuted and the latter are given billions in public subsidies, is rarely identified as such. Terms like 'modernisation' are preferred.*

Information becomes disinformation and misinformation when interests of powerful nations are involved. For instance 'The Gulf War in 1991 was reported as a technological wonder, an event of bloodless science in which, rejoiced one editorial writer, there were 'miraculously few casualties'. It was one of the most covered wars in history, yet few journalists reported the truth, still widely unknown, that a quarter of a million Iraqis were wantonly slaughtered or died unnecessary deaths. The bloodfest, the fate of the children of Iraq has been the slowest of news. Who knows that at least half a million children have died as a direct result of economic sanctions imposed by the Western Powers? Who understands that the sanctions are aimed not at bringing down Saddam Hussain, or deterring him from building some mythical nuclear bomb, but at presenting the 'market' capture of Iraq oil for forcing down the price of oil produced by Saudi Arabia, the West's most important Middle Eastern proxy.

By the art of suppressio veri and suggestio falsi, facts can be made to tell flexibly the opposite of the truth by making the worse appear the better reason. The Vietnamese war where America shocked the world by raining weapon to wipe out a people, with no legal or moral justification, is one of the mega-instances where Himalayan lies and Niagara of motivated views were poured forth to make out the all- out American assault on the Vietnamese people as a noble cause. The defeat of America, after inflicting a tragedy on Vietnam, was not a triumph of information but a tragedy of truth until M. Namara confessed that he was guilty of waging the war.

John Pilger, in his great book the 'Hidden Agendas', has sharply observed:

> *A Freedom of Information Act unfettered by 'exemptions', the establishment of a public body to provide start-up funds for newspapers, journals and broadcasters independent of the monopolists, a new Broadcasting Act that stops the richest and biggest swallowing the smallest and requires an unfettered commitment to original drama and independent factual programmes—these would begin to win the second battle for the freedom of the press.*
>
> *It is a freedom we are in danger of losing without even knowing it. For when there is no longer anyone speaking out, who will be the last voice? (P-546)*

Indeed, lies are spread as information invented, not merely for purposes of war but also for purposes of cultural occupation of minds of people, so that global economic exploitation may be concealed and ideologically projected as world-wide benefaction. This syndrome of terminological travesty as credible verity through information channels is what Vandana Shiva, the Indian Social Scientist, challenges as the western-imposed monoculture of the mind and has called for an 'insurrection of subjugated knowledge' against the 'dominant knowledge of capitalism. She wrote '90% of the dominant knowledge could be stopped without any risk of human deprivation'. Alas! Media technology has become a wondrous communication tournament. The speed at which pictures, voices and the printed word can be transmitted ought to invest in news gathering a socially responsible obligation so that what is now terminological terrorism in the hands of political, military and economic power may be tamed into a socially beneficiant instrument for the good of humanity. Otherwise, as brought out with a sting in the book 'Food First', world hunger will be a harmless profit-making process of Big Business, World Control of Water will become the thirst-relieving business of Big Business and the agricultural revolution in developing countries, now propagandised as a boon, will be a bane, a ruse to expand the business of multinational and rob the cultivation of Third World countries of their land's fertility and counter land reform. Farmers in these countries will gradually become the 'new slaves' of exploitative technology. Banana republics, Cucumber republics, Cocoa republics and like other victimised agricultural republics demonstrate the power of information manipulation as a mammoth weapon of Mammon.

Information Technology, by greatly promoting the power of multinational corporations, holds the South as ransom and brings down employment. Post-modern technology needs no manpower and thrives without a large number of people at work. But this vastly increases unemployment of the masses, accompanied by the 'affluenza' of the classes, is cited as a sign of progress. There will be more cars in the streets, more fast-food shops in the bazaars and more sky scrappers for the rich to occupy. But there will be more hunger and disease, more illiteracy and suicides, more infant mortalities and less hospitals (except fivestar hospitals for the wealth). This dimension of social reality is hidden as non-information which the electronic and print media do not reveal.

A brief deviation here is instructive about the corporate game of suppression and manipulation of technological information. One dimension of corporate control over information unlimited is the 'knowledge monopoly' they possess and use to their advantage. Illustratively, I may make a parting reference to the use of chemicals in agriculture. Pest management and the propagation of pesticides is a danger zone. The authors of Food First point out that while agribusiness corporations are trying to promote 'blind', scheduled spraying in underdeveloped countries such as India, farmers in the United States have found that on top of environmental and health damage they were being just plain swindled. The painful truth is that chemical companies dominate research institutions to promote their brands of pesticides which are injurious but produce profit to the chemical companies. Pesticide alternatives are prevented from coming into the field by pressure tactics of these monopolies. The real threat is that pesticides technology is in the hands of a few corporations that will profit only if they can continue to make farmers and 'concerned people' everywhere believe that our very survival depends on the indiscriminate use of their products.

The threat is ever more ominous since some supposedly impartial bodies that could form a counter force to the power of multinational agribusinesses have become, instead, their agents Organizations such as the F.A.O., far from developing and disseminating suitable alternatives or even the knowledge of the appropriate use of pesticides, are becoming partners in promotion for chemical corporations.

We live in an era of GATTS domination and TRIPS regulation. In consequence, ownership of intellectual property rights, patents for news-views innovation and invention and processes and products, other trade secrets are now monopolised by patent-holding and like MNCs. Information is thus the property of Big Business and 'new knowledge' is blocked and barred by broad-based patentisation and similar legal throttles. Information revolution is now a controlled commodity available to affordable sections at fancy prices fixed by world corporates. News slavery is the 'new slavery'. An occupation army of hired researchers helps MNCs hold the Third World in intellectual colonialism.

Such can be the tragedy of twisted Information Revolution. It is a reversal of the values inscribed in the International Convention on the Freedom of Information which emphasises the right of the people to be *fully* and *reliably informed* through reportage of honest information and opinion and elimination of the scourge of war. If human rights are to be a pervasive reality in the world, a people-oriented freedom of information jurisprudence must be on the statute book of every country.

Information is light and absence of it is darkness. If democracy is to be luminous, access to information in the custody of any public functionary, with appropriate infrastructure, must be available at every level of the State and on every matter of public concern. Transparency in public affairs, if denied, totalitarian governance will deprive the people of their great rights. That is why, a comprehensive Freedom of Information Act, covering every range of exercise of authority, must be a feasible reality. An apology of Freedom of Information Act has been provided by Parliament by enacting Freedom of Information Act, 2002 (Act V of 2003). The creation of a Public Information Officer notwithstanding, the statute is a poor substitute for a peremptory power to acquire every class of information which is of concern or interest to every person in the polity. A detailed discussion of the insufficiencies of the Indian Act V of 2003 is a worthwhile adventure but beyond the range of this essay.

Governmental secrets are a negation of the citizens' *right to know*. Most often, the ruling class manages to hide inconvenient truth and even where there is a law compelling disclosure, it is too expensive, procedurally complicated, in practice dilatory, and as a nett result the right becomes ineffectual. The appointment of judges, for instance, is a secret process, altogether beyond the reach of the common man. The judiciary has vast powers. Therefore, candidates for appointment to these high offices must be publicly known, their assets and relationships publicly known and their past activities and social perspectives must be publicly known. Regrettably, the Indian judges, and everything about them including the manner and criteria of their appointment are a closed book. These observations apply equally to all other public functionaries. There should be a law compelling publicity about these aspects of the judiciary and other categories. Currently, their misdoings are kept a guarded secret. There is a code of conduct and ethics for judges now said to exist, but unknown to the public and with no legal backing.

The assets of candidates, who seek to become legislators and ministers and local bodies members must be revealed to the public. The people who are governed by these representatives, if elected, must have an opportunity to gain full information about their standing, their wealth, their commitments, their communal association and their social philosophy. Similarly the fate of files pending before the Government, the source of dockets pending before the court, the fate of resources of voluntary agencies in the public field, must be an open book. Indeed, if democracy is Government *by the people*, public authority must be obliged to live in transparency. Corruption in public life, undue delay in disposal of litigation, including delivery of judgements, concealment of police investigation and secret surveillance, income tax evasion and huge bank deposits and defaults can no longer be immune from people's right to know. The modern corporations are the engine of economic operations. They are mindless juggernauts hell-bent on high profits and big rackets. They can do harm to the consumer public and in that sense corporate activities cannot enjoy deleterious confidentiality. In all these cases, freedom of information must enjoy priority status. The professions, medical, legal and other, are practitioners of power. Their functionalism must come under social audit. This is possible only if the law of freedom of information provides open sesame to their work and wealth. Of course, these general statements are subject to exceptions, privacy and confidentiality being necessary in public interest in special cases. Military secrets, cabinet secrets, mutual judicial deliberations and even domestic secrets may enjoy privileges of privacy. The broad proposition is, as the old Roman adage runs, 'whatever touches all should be decided by all'. But Decision is preceded by knowledge and knowledge by information. Thus freedom of information has a high democratic status. Consumers of justice, of good medical treatment, of sound administrative policies and in public corporate managements *are the people*—if they are to fulfill their functions as citizens it is fundamental that the freedom guaranteed under the Constitution must become viable, not illusory, pragmatic not merely philosophic.

THE AYODHYA IMBROGLIO: CAN THE SUPREME COURT CUT THE GORDIAN KNOT?

Ram Lalla, the Avatar, and Allah, the Most Merciful, have divine compassion but the bearded broods and para-political troops with blood-shot eyes and obdurate fixations have engineered Operation Confrontation, to a point where the Indian nation is reeling under a series of stresses with no end in sight for national reconciliation. The Prime Minister's policy of consensus has proved to be an *alibi* for drift, the Parliament has established its reputation for a functioning, the anarchy and the Parties and like organs are paralysed *vis-a-vis* the peace process and are lost in chant of hollow phrases tike secularism and drills in the streets for community amity while political mileage out of every crisis is the business part of it. Indian communalism, with aggravated militancy and ever new incarnations, preceded the Ayodhya syndrome and will survive its patch-work solution. No illusions please! Because the pathology of Indian communalist politics, if dialectically diagnosed, will reveal deeper roots and wider proliferations than mere Ayodhya as the locus or focus. A National Reconciliation is an urgent desideratum if the dire peril of civil strife is to be obviated. The efforts must continue to restore sanity, save unity and catalyse fraternity, now lost in fratricidal dementia. 'Do or die' is the grim summons because 'to be, or not to be'—that is the question before the Republic. Fundamentalists, with appetite which feeds on itself, fancy that moderation is an evil thing, that nothing succeeds like success. Look at some saints running berserk by asking for Delhi's Jama Masjid.! This was the most unkindest cut of all! And each passing day appealing even for international pressure on India, pan-Islamic fundamentalist factions and competitively militant Hindu obscurantists are driving the country to doom. Currently, the cynosure of attention is the Mandir-Masjid dispute and communal combatants zero-in on Ayodhya. It has, for decades been steeped in litigation and has otherwise baffled solution. Let us go back to the roots and try again hoping that 'in the beginning is the end'. Perseverence pays when the effort is fuelled by spiritual, not political objectives. For, "After the final no there comes an yes; And on that yes the future of the world depends".

Ayodhya is an incantation, Rama Janma Bhoomi is a living legend. Likewise, Babri Masjid is a stony reality and a history with memory. Now it is rubble but can still speak and incite. After Independence, Ram Lalla and Allah have been taken over by two communities for politico-theological purposes. Each is claiming to keep its shrine on the same spot. Inevitably, a conflict has sprung up, breach of the peace apprehended, magisterial orders to maintain law and order passed and eventually litigations followed in the Allahabad High Court. They are now pending before the Luncknow Bench of that Court. A brief summary of the five suits is sufficient for the present:

> "Two of these suits instituted in 1950, and the third instituted in 1959, are inconsequential and, therefore, need not be taken notice of. The two main suits which bring out the controversy between the two major communities of India are: (1) No. 12 of 1961 filed on behalf of U.P. Sunni Central Board of Waqfs and some Sunni Muslim individuals purporting to be a representative suit under Order I, Rule 8, of the Code of Civil Procedure, on behalf of the Muslims in general, against the Plaintiffs of the three earlier suits and certain other Hindu individuals and organisations added later on as representatives of the Hindus; and (2) No. 236 of 1989 filed on behalf of the Deities, Bhagwan Sri Rama Virajman at Sri Rama Janma Bhumi and Asthan Sri Rama Janma Bhumi against all the parties to the earlier suits and the Shia Muslims also."
>
> "The real nature of the controversy, as well as the area of agreement between the contestants, which is no less important, is brought out in the written statement filed on behalf of Mahant Dharam Das, Defendant No. 13 in that suit of the Muslims. The case set out by him therein is that there was an ancient temple at the spot which was destroyed and replaced by the present disputed structure of Sri Rama Janma Bhumi. Now, the point of agreement is extremely important. In paragraph 15, of his written statement in suit No. 236 of 1989 of the Deities, Prince Anjum Quder, President, All India Conference, has stated:
>
> "However, after all said and done, it is most respectfully submitted that if only this claim is proved that a Mandir was demolished and Babri Masjid was built on the Mandir land, this defendant and all other Muslims will gladly demolish and shift the mosque, and return the land for building of the Mandir thereon."

In the same written statement, in support of the above stand, *Fatwa-e-Alamgiri*, Volume 6, Page 214, has been quoted as follows:

> "It is not permissible to build mosque on unlawfully acquired land. There may be many forms of unlawful acquisition. For instance, if some people forcibly take somebody's house (or land) and build a

mosque or even Jama Masjid on it, then *Namaz* in such a mosque will be against *Shariat*".

The gut question is as to whether there was a temple as Mahant Dharam Das claims which was demolished and thereon the disputed structure known as Babri Masjid was built. Of course, there is a host of other problems raised in the suits, including the ownership of the land whereon the Masjid now stands. Each side claims to found its case on the presence or absence of archaeological evidence plus public records, government gazetteers, books of history and other relevant literature.

Briefly the dominant purpose of the suit on behalf of the Deities and the defence of Mahant Dharam Das in the suit of the Muslims, is to convince the Muslims of the true historical event of the destruction in 1528 of Sri Rama Janma Bhumi Temple and construction of the present disputed structure at that very place by Mir Baqi, one of the generals of Babar. Hinduism and Islam are two great religions, somewhat different from each other. But their essentials are the same. As a sage has observed: "There are many paths to the top of a mountain, but the view is always the same. This succinctly sets out the catholicity of Hinduism which recognises the validity of all religions."

The Muslim organisations involved in the litigation have a rival version denying the existence of any temple in the controversial site and the construction being on a permissible plot allowed by Quran. They also claim that there is a graveyard in the neighbourhood. Since 1949 when the idol of Rama was installed by a covert process, objected to by the Muslims, prayers could not be held by the Islamic community and a magisterial order under section 145 of the Code of Criminal Procedure, was issued. The twists and turns of judicial proceedings and the by-lanes and highways of legal provisions, including the law of limitation, need not detain us here except to the limited extent that the ownership of the property and the existence of a temple *antecedent* to the construction of the mosque loom large as the decisive points in the Court proceedings. Two gut issues, inter-related and, in all probability, decisive of the Ayodhya litigation, may be stated here. Firstly, at the time the Babri Mosque was built, was there a temple at that site which was demolished? Secondly, if there was such a temple, is the mosque, centuries old, liable to be removed from what was once hallowed by the Ram shrine. The second issue appears to be resolved by a generous concession by the Muslims, based on the holy Quran itself.

Many Muslims, holy and in high places have affirmed without hesitation, on Quaranic authority, that it is *haram* to build a mosque on illegally taken land. Even extremists like the leaders of the Kerala Jamaite Islam (now banned) have repeated this proposition and given up reconstruction on the identical site. A top leader of the most militant Muslim body (Islamic Sevak Sangh) has, in a press interview from underground, declared he has no objection to the Ram darshan since the court has allowed it and ceases to insist on a masjid on the same spot. There is scope for an ideological demilitarized zone and cease fire.*

The diffusion of issues in the Lucknow bunch of suits may distract our attention from the heart of the controversy, which turns on the discovery of the existence or otherwise of a Ram Temple beneath the Mosque built under Babar's direction. If a dispute arises on a matter of fact or law, each decision must belong to the adjudicative instrumentality set up by the Constitution. Some issues may be obscure, some may turn on faith or formulary, some may depend on tradition or ritual and others may revolve round even ecclesiastical matters or temporal affairs which bear upon civil rights and pains and pleasures, gains and losses with moral implications. While the Courts will be reluctant to investigate what are purely matters of faith only, they cannot abdicate their jurisdiction if civil consequences flow. Public power is public trust.

The suits that pend for decades now have not yet taken off since recording of evidence has not yet begun. Indeed, a plethora of probative material from diverse angles may come before the Court and even religious leaders, Acharyas, divines and ulemas and others may give expert testimony. It is gratifying and indeed, admirably genorous on the part of the Muslims in the litigation and leading Islamic figures as a whole to have agreed, because the Quran enjoins so, that the basic adjudicatory focus must be the pre-mosque existence of the Ram Mandir at the Babri spot. Who knows how many years the Lucknow Bench will prolong to pronounce its verdicts? And then an appeal to the Supreme Court whose phenomenal litigative somnolescence shocks no one any more. The terrorism of time, having regard to the tensions and traumas afflicting the nation, thanks to the non-disposal of the Babri bunch of cases at Lucknow, compels us to think on alternative terms and explore other options, if any, so that by a blitz process an early end to the bleeding bouts may be registered. The crisis is deepening. The Babri site and its pre-Babri status, once finally found by the Court, has seminal consequences of peace and strife, affection and disaffection, tranquillity and intolerable friction.

It is in this profound background that the present proposal to refer the Babri dispute to the Supreme Court under Art. 143 arises. It is wise to seek abbreviation of the collective litigation and inauguration of an era of National Reconciliation which is highest on the agenda of India.

Some have raised doubts that Ram Mandir is a matter of faith beyond legend and cannot be adjudicated upon by the Court. Indeed, when parties are impregnated with dogmatic faith and implacably alienated from each other there is no other recipe for reaching a solution save the curial

* A Government which survives on uniformed cadres cannot produce *detente* being itself in daily despair. People are the final hope. Let us try the Court before that as a last chance.

procedure if the subject-matter is of a civil nature *albeit* enmeshed in theology, sacerdotal ideology or ontological rivalry. The judiciary, in England and in India, with a common anglo-saxon jurisprudence, has handled what at first blush may look like battles over faith or tenets or identity of sect or mere matter of religious praxis. In Islamic countries like Pakistan ecclesiastical disputes, turning on Islamic faith or Quranic creed, have fallen for adjudication. So it is fatuous to assert that because deep religious faith is at stake the civil court has no authority to hold one way or other on such matters. The court has, in the past, ruled on questions relating to religious rights of the land on which a monastry stands, the removal or the alteration of *'Namams'* (religious marks) in a temple or like issue, a decision of which may affect a citizen's civil rights. The litmus test, in short, is the impact of the dispute on civil consequences to citizens. Unquestionably, the Mandir-Masjid dispute, unfolded in the five suits and the Reference under Art. 143, does affect many human rights and civil interests. Therefore, the plea that the advisory opinion relates to a matter of *faith* and is, therefore, not binding is lawless and flawsome.

History and archaeology, gazetteers and revenue records and other sources from varied quarters may be of probative aid to the Court which may even *suo motu* summon experts to reach the truth to the extent it can. Perfection belongs to God, experiments towards perfection are judicial essays.

The Great Ram-Rahim divide disturbed the Independent Initiative, Delhi, as a potential time bomb. So it constituted a small Committee of myself, Sri B.G. Verghese, Swami Agnivesh and Justice Hari Swaroop to establish contact and explore a cordial resolution of the already bitter dispute. We met, in several rounds, many of the patent and latent militant leaders on either side, and responding to our persuations bellicosity dropped its blood-shot eyes and tongues of fire. A sober approach and conciliatory tone emerged. Almost every thorny irritant was removed and the presence or absence of the Ram Shrine shrouded in history and mystery became the solitary substantive issue, which could be resolved only by the highest judicatory authority. The Muslim friends gave up their minority mood. So did the Hindu militants. We suggested a Reference on this central issue under Art. 143 of the Constitution. The Hindu organisations were in formally agreeable to the reference without being formal signatories. Muslim leaders, were more forthcoming. On this basis, we met Prime Minister Chandrasekhar (whose brevity of authority as Prime Minister, with Rajiv Congress backing, had just began), who, on an explanation of the usefulness and binding character of a Reference under Art. 143, fell for it and promised prompt action in a day or two. The essence of our Eight-Point Formula dated 27-1-1990 may be excerpted here:

> "The Initiative feels strongly that a final quietus to the central question could be secured only by a Reference immediately to the

Supreme Court by the President of India under Art. 143 of the Constitution of the following question:

"Whether there was a temple or shrine in the sense of a place of worship of the Hindus on the site where the whole or any part of the Babri Masjid is situate?"

"It is assumed that in the event of the finding being that there was a temple, the Muslim community *would willingly agree to the removal of the mosque and handing over of the site to the appropriate authority in the Hindu community*. If the finding is against the existence of the temple, consequential orders regarding possession and removal of the idols must be passed.

"The Supreme Court, we hope, will constitute a larger bench having regard to the grave national concern and tension and urgency manifest already. Similarly, the Supreme Court *may justly be expected to withdraw all cases relating to the R.B. dispute to its file if that step will expedite early decision and finality.*"

"The Supreme Court, acting on such a Reference under Art. 143(1) may consider appointing a multi-disciplinary team of high level Commissioners or experts to report to it on such issues as it may frame in order to aid it to formulate its own opinion. All parties, the Government included, will be bound by the verdict of the Supreme Court."

Inaction and insensitivity is the rule of life in the P.M.O. The pachydermic Prime Minister's Office drifted, dawdled and dithered till events overtook the Ministry itself. To make a long story short, spanning Chandrasekhar's exit and Rao's entrance, after all the sound and fury in Parliament with babel-like debate and din and toxic exchanges, phoney undertakings in the Supreme Court to keep the *status quo*, assurances to the Prime Minister and illusions of Bhajan and Kirtan without any kind of construction which lulled the nation, came the 6th of December, 1992, when in broad day light down fell the triple domes of the historic edifice, in the presence of V.H.P's, VI P's, BJP's supremos, and of the armed forces of the State and the Supreme Court's observer. What a fall! What a shock and shame! Everyone, every party, every group with social sanity condemned the dasterdly barbarity. History was reborn, as it were, with biting bitterness in the womb and despair darkened every Indian fact. Goons found they could loot, mobs, robbed of their reason, moved to kill, Indians vanished and only Hindus and Muslims stabbed or acid-bombed, and innocents were shot by the Police without producing peace. In several cities, scenes of woe, the like of which, since Partition, no Indian eye had seen, nor heart conceived nor tongue could adequately tell, supervened in sombre blood. Now Babri is but rubble, but every stone is a wound and the site remains the bone of contention between the expanding angry camps of fundamentalists competing to claim the controversial basement, each for its own hallowed edifice.

Had a Reference been made in 1990 by the President for the Supreme Court's opinion on the limited question of the existence of a shrine below the Babri site, by now the flames of communal fury would have been extinguished.

At a wrong time when raging fanatics, ochre-robed or bearded, are fanning the fumes of hatred, the Reference under Art. 143 is less than fair to the Supreme Court, the environs having been poisoned by the twists and turns, torments and traumas of dreadful daily events. Politics, with focus on power and the polls, can never solve a problem embroiled in acrimony and soaked in blood. Parliament, currently a functioning anarchy, and the Cabinet, a fragmented collectivity, are instrumentalities whose credibility and competence are at a low ebb and the country itself is disintegrating. In this grave hour, if ever there is some hope, not that there is much hope, it is from the Court. To dispense national survival justice, thro' National Reconciliation by an adjudicatory advice, on a delicate, difficult and all the same unavoidable issue, has a dimension of forensic patriotism. Therefore, sadly thro', everyone must support the Court's verdict, even as many distinguished Muslims have done, even the leader of a most militant Muslim organization (the Islamic Sevak Sangh) thro' its leader has stated. Indian humanity, which has not lost its sanity, must abide by the decision on law and fact reported by the Court to the President.

However, the belated, unilateral Presidential Reference has now been made. It has drawn flak from all parties and destructive Parliamentary pyrotechnics are certain when the Houses meet. Is the duty of the Opposition always to oppose? Even so, scrutiny of the two grounds of attack levelled by the LF—NF is necessary. What are they? The first argument is that the opinion rendered by the highest court is but *advisory* and, therefore, *liable to be ignored* by the President (Cabinet) in his political wisdom (opportunism). We want judicial finality, not political expediency from a tottering cabal called Cabinet. The second argument is that even if it binds the Rashtrapati, the several other issues raised in the Lucknow litigation will still have to be fought; and like festering wounds this pendency will keep alive the fell feuds. And so, the advisory opinion will be an exercise in futility.

The more potent alternative suggested is that a "reference" to the Supreme Court under Art. 138(2) should be made the Lucknow suits. The spirit behind these criticisms is as unexceptionable as the soundness of both is in the neighbourhood of blunder.

Since 1950 Presidential References on 'questions of fact or law ... of such a nature and of such public importance that it is expedient to obtain the opinion of the Supreme Court upon it have been made and the Court, after marathon hearings, has made its Reports to the President who has—of course, he has no option—always held himself bound by the factual finding or legal holding. To dare a contrary view is legal illiteracy compounded by mulish incorrigibility.

I may frankly admit that when I met Shri V.P. Singh who had already demitted office, he ventured to hint that the advisory jurisdiction of the Supreme Court left an option for rejection by the Government. Shri Chandrasekhar, while he was Prime Minister, expressed the same doubt. Shri Dalmia and Shri Shahabuddin also shared this hesitation, despite the fact that Justice Grover, who was present then in my room (and I myself), contradicted them. After leaving Prime Minister Chandrasekhar, I drove to the office of the Attorney-General Shri Soli Sorabji and he unhesitatingly concurred in the view that according to Art. 143 opinion was as binding as any other declaration of law under Art. 141. In fairness, it must be said that the text of the Article may lend itself to the apprehension that the Rashtrapati, on receipt of the report, may or may not accept it. All that I can say is if he does not, he acts unconstitutionally. It has never been done, never in the past, and the constitutional jurisprudence on matters of great moment has grown around the authority of the advisory opinion of the Supreme Court under Art. 143.

The matter is no longer open because the Supreme Court, considering the Reference to it of the constitutionality of the Special Courts Bill (AIR 1979 SC 478), examined whether "the opinion rendered by this Court in the exercise of its advisory jurisdiction under Art. 143(1) is binding as law declared by this Court within the meaning of Art. 141.....".

Chandrachur C.J., after rejecting contrary view technically expressed in a few judgments and by "an eminent writer", concluded:

> "We are inclined to the view that though it is always open to *this Court* to re-examine the question already decided by it and to overrule, if necessary, the view earlier taken by it, *in so far as all other courts in the territory of India are concerned they ought to be bound by the view expressed by this Court even in the exercise of its advisory jurisdiction under Art.* 143(1) *of the Constitution.* We would also like to draw attention to the observations made by Ray, C.J., in St. Xaviers College (AIR 1974 SC 1389) that even if the opinion given in the exercise of advisory jurisdiction may not be binding, it *is entitled to greater weight. It would be strange* that a decision given by this Court on a question of law in a dispute between two private parties should be binding on all courts in this country but the advisory opinion should bind no one at all, even if, as in the instant case, it is given after issuing notice to ail interested parties, after hearing everyone concerned who desired to be heard, and after a full consideration of the questions raised in the reference.......*to think that our opinion is an exercise in futility is deeply frustrating.*" [AIR 199 SC 478 at Page 519]

The Supreme Court, as late as 1980 followed, almost as a binding precedent, its earlier opinion on a Reference in these words:

> "...in so far as the arguments advanced before this Court in the Reference case are concerned, they are *concluded* by the *decision* given thereon and, we do not propose to go behind the opinion given by this Court in that case". (1980 SC 1382)

The Supreme Court itself and the High Courts have proceeded on the footing that the law declared in its advisory jurisdiction is binding jurisprudence. The Kerala Education Bill case (AIR 1958 SC 956) was a Reference under Art. 143 but has been treated as binding by all Courts, including the Supreme Court. Even a feeble deviance expressed by *two out of the nine Judges in* the St. Xavier's College Bench (1974 SC 1389) agreed that the law stated in the Kerala Education Bill case has been the source from which the Supreme Court itself has drawn its sustenance in its subsequent decisions. Please remember that the St. Xaviers Case Bench was a *larger Bench* vis-a-vis the Kerala Education Bill Bench and could have, under the law of precedents, overruled its earlier ruling as *Golaknath* (AIR 1967 SC 1643) was by Keshavananda (AIR 1973 SC 1461).

In the celebrated Presidential Reference in the early sixties arising out of an unenviable struggle between the Allahabad High Court and the Uttar Pradesh Legislature the Court gave its ruling on the Reference and till date the law that governs Parliamentary privileges and their limitations has been on the lines laid down there. Even in this case, all that Gajendragadkar, C.J. stated was that though *technically* it may appear that the opinion is but advisory, practically it is a judgment of the Court.

One may refer back to the last judgment on the subject rendered in 1979 (the Special Court's Bill Case) where it has been held that the advisory opinion is binding. All through, the High Courts have held themselves bound by such advisory opinions under Art. 143 and the Supreme Court itself has said that it is binding on it except to the extent that the Supreme Court can always overrule itself, being the final Court of the land (as the U.S. Supreme Court can), in propriety by a larger Bench, not by a smaller Bench. This being the law on the subject which has held the ground for 42 years, the Supreme Court is the last word on the subject. But doubts die hard and blunders survive after death. It must be remembered that all the States will be given notice ordinarily thro' their Advocates-General, persons interested or organs affected may intervene and urge arguments and a considerable bench of may be nine or eleven or thirteen judges, will hear arguments as the ultimate judicial authority of the nation hearing every voice that deserves to be heard from any concerned person in the country. Then comes its verdict, couched as a report, but declaring the law for the land as a whole. The Court's holding is a Report of opinion but is no brutem fulmen.

The dangerous implications of *unresolved litigations* surviving in the Lucknow Bench even after Art. 143 advisory opinion may cause consternation in the minds of reasonable people, because of the violent potential. December 6th (1992) has been a human-quake and if eruptions occur again because the Lucknow issues are not finally settled, there is sense in the a arm that a single point reference to the Supreme Court is an illusory recipe. How then can the cases before the Lucknow Bench be transferred to the Supreme Court to be tried more or less together with the Reference? The suggestion of some political wiseacres is a Reference under Article 138(2) which reads thus:

> "138(2): The Supreme Court shall have such further jurisdiction, and powers with respect to any matter as the Government of India and the Government of any State may by special agreement confer, if Parliament by law provides for the exercise of such jurisdiction and powers by the Supreme Court."

Plainly, this provision does not and cannot vest jurisdiction as a matter of course in the Supreme Court by a Presidential Reference. The Court has to be conferred *power separately by law made by Parliament.* Not under Art. 138(1) since the matter does not fall under the Union List. Let us look at Art. 138(2). Even here, the Court acquires 'jurisdiction and powers' *only* if *Parliament by law provides* for such exercise of powers and a *special agreement* by the Central and relevant State Governments supports such conferment. The obvious condition which stares in the face of even a pettifoger is that a *law by Parliament* and a *special* agreement between State and Centre are the *sine qua non of the Court's jurisdiction.* A legislation in Parliament, with a tottering regime, teetering Opposition and fissions and fusions within and without Parties, and, above all, a 'zero hour' chaos spread over every hour of sitting, standing and marching inside the House—a legislative bill is the last despair of anyone. Delay is certain, failure is ominous and the proposal of Art. 138(2) Reference is a teasing illusion and promise of unreality and an infinite innocence of law.

Even if Art. 138, as on alternative to Art. 143, is inapplicable, the thrust of the Left grievance has great force. The whole cluster of cases, not a single point Reference, alone can herald and hold a real Ayodhya accord. Here too the Constitution has a rescue clause. Art. 139A empowers the Supreme Court to withdraw to itself any case pending in any High Court if it is satisfied on its own motion or on an application made by the Attorney-General or by a party to any such case, that such questions are substantial questions of general importance ... and dispose of all the cases itself. Using the power, on the motion of the Attorney-General the Lucknow Bench cases which are of great national moment may be called to the Supreme Court and finally decided. Thus by-passing Art. 138(2), the legitimate process of 139(A) will meet the ends of justice.

There is yet another constitutional resource with the Supreme Court which may be pressed into service in this case. In recent years, the 'infallible' apex Court with its versatile genius (about which I have some reservations) has used Art. 142 to develop what may be called the jurisprudence of disaster prevention. When a magistrate was hand-cuffed by the Police somewhere, and it was a national outrage, the Court used Art. 142 to pick up the case on its own file on the basis that it had the power to "make such order as is necessary for doing complete justice in any cause". Instances can be cited of this extraordinary curial intervention by taking up cases on its own, altho' not falling strictly within any of the jurisdictional provisions of the Codes or the Constitution. From that angle, if ever there were a case likely to spell doom on the nation's destiny which should be immediately withdrawn to the Supreme Court, heard and "complete justice" done, it is the Ayodhya bunch of suits. Here again, the Attorney-General may invoke the Court's power and I feel confident that the sensitive summit Judges will respond justly to the summons of the nation. The sooner the flames of Ayodhya are flushed out, to the extent the Justice Process can achieve it, the better for the country.

Bombay is burning, other cities and towns have their tales of woe. Civil strife is staring us in the face. Let the Court, in a patriotic ascent to new heights, accomplish in some measure what history may chronicle as its finest hour.

VINCENT PANIKULANGARA *VS.* V.R. KRISHNA IYER

Bias—Party in case known to the Judge—Hearing of the case by the Judge if permissible.

The rule that no Judge shall hear the case in which he is likely to be biased is a rule well-established, a rule which can bear no exception. Bias is more than likely to arise by reason of acquaintence with a party to the action. Even if Judges, by their judicial training and maturity are able to deal with cases objectively, to the common man whose confidence in the judicial process should not be permitted to be eroded, it may appear that the ultimate Judgment in any such case was influenced by matters extraneous to the facts of the case. Hence larger interests, that of retaining confidence in the judicial system should dissuade this court from taking up the case. But faced with an unparalleled situation, when there is no other alternative, we have posted the case. Our approach is not to be understood as laying down a precedent, recognising an exception to the rule that a Judge should not hear the case of a party known to him. This case is not really one of an exception, but the application of a unique but new rule, the adoption of which is justified because of the equally unique circumstances of the case. (paras. 8 & 9)

Contempt of Courts Act, 1971, section 2—Scope and incidents—Civil contempt and criminal contempt—Distinction.

Contempt may be committed by a person by wilfully disobeying the order or process of court or wilfully committing breach of undertaking given to a court. Mere disobedience or breach, as the case may be, will not be sufficient to find contempt. Wilfulness will have to be found on the facts and circumstances. Once that is found the court must take serious notice of the contemnor's conduct. The order, even erroneous it be, calls for compliance and there can then be no excuse. The contempt in such a case will be civil contempt. Criminal contempt operates when the act of the alleged contemner prejudices or interferes or tends to interfere with, the due course of any judicial proceedings. Such conduct will have to be viewed severely particularly because of its tendency to affect the ultimate decision in the case.

* Text of Judgment in the case by Subramonian Poti, Ag. C.J. & Paripoornan, J.

Sometimes comments or statements are made inadvertently and without the knowledge of pending proceedings in court or without intention to affect the result of such proceedings, but even so technically the contemnor's conduct would be objectionable, but the circumstances may persuade a court to view such conduct lightly. But not so where, a party, aware of a pending case and aware of the consequences of his statement, deliberately makes his comments. The circumstances in that event would aggravate the offence. If such comments are from responsible persons or those placed in authority it is likely that the harm is greater and aggravation would also be of a much higher degree. *(paras. 11 & 12)*

Contempt of Courts Act, 1971, sections 2(c) & 5—Criticism of courts, Judges or judicial system when amounts to contempt—Speech by a retired Judge in a symposium on Judicial Reforms criticizing the Indian Judiciary as *non est* etc.—Contempt if committed.

To understand the real import of any statement it is necessary to understand the context in which it is made. The context and setting in which such criticism is made, the person who makes it, and the persons to whom it is addressed should, in a large measure, indicate the apparent purpose or object of the criticism, whether it was made with genuine academic interest or whether it is made for any extraneous purpose. There is an ocean of difference between well-informed and ill-informed criticism. Those who have spent years and perhaps a lifetime as part of an institution or to study an institution may have occasion to make a thorough objective assessment of that institution. What they say in regard to a matter concerning that institution should be viewed differently from a similar statement by an uninformed person. In one case there is objectivity and in the other there is none. Absence of objectivity must necessarily reflect upon the bona fides of the criticism. On the occasion the Respondent as a main speaker invited to speak on the subject, was expected to make an academic exercise on the subject. He had, apart from his learning, a wealth of experience which evidently qualified him to speak authoritatively on the subject. His contribution as a Judge, as a member of the Law Commission and as a powerful proponent of the cause of judicial reforms is well-known. It is in this background that the statements made by him in his speech should be understood. By pointing out the weak spots in the judicial system and alerting the people to the need for a change lest the people as a whole reject the system, he was alerting his audience to bestow serious attention to the problem. The comments made by him are not of a person who is vituperative or who wants to bring into disrepute the judicial system of this country, but of one who was exhorting the people for revolutionary change in the outlook concerning problems of the judiciary. Judged in the perspective of what we have explained earlier we see no reason to consider his criticism, coming as it does from a person, whose bona fides in the cause of judiciary is not open to doubt, as mala fide or dishonest.

(Paras. 13, 15 & 18)

1968(2) AER 319; 1982 KLT 151	Relied on
S. Easwara Iyer & E. Subramoni	For Petitioner
Advocate General (V. Bhaskaran Nambiar)	For State

JUDGMENT

Subramonian Poti, Ag. C.J.—Quite often a Judge comes across a case which has no precedent. But rarely has a case as unique as the one before us arisen in any court.

2. Sri. V.R. Krishna Iyer, formerly a Judge of this Court, later a Judge of the Supreme Court was one of the distinguished guests at the Silver Jubilee Celebrations of the Court held in October-November, 1981. At a symposium organised on that occasion on "Approach of Judicial Reforms", Sri Krishna Iyer as a main speaker addressed the assembled audience. One of the Judges of this Court Sri. G. Viswanatha Iyer was then in the Chair. Sri Vincent Panikulangara, the petitioner is said to have attended that symposium and according to him the speech delivered by Sri. V.R. Krishna Iyer amounted to scandalisation of the authority of the Supreme Court and the High Courts and therefore Sri. V.R. Krishna Iyer is guilty of criminal contempt. He moved the Advocate General for sanction which the Advocate General gave.

3. The offending passages, according to the petitioner, are those stated in paragraph 8 of the petition. We will extract that paragraph here:

"8. The speech of the respondent contained among other things the following expressions against the functioning of the judiciary—

(a) "One day the people of this country will rise and say that we don't want this magnificent red stone edifice on the Curzon Road because it is seen to be counter productive and in turn the High Courts".

(b) "When property rights were affected in *R.C. Kooper's* case the Judge's heart began to bleed."

(c) "The whole question is whether the Judiciary live down its partiality towards the proletariat and cultivate an affection for the proletariat."

(d) "And in this country the Jesuses are getting crucified and the Barbases are very much upheld, thanks perhaps to the judiciary."

(e) "That they (judiciary) have not been ordinarily influenced by the executive or the legislature".

(f) "In fact as an insider there are many things I know which I should not mention in public".

(g) "Our whole judicial approach has a certain independence from all civilised behaviour."

(h) "In fact to speak very frankly, the Indian judiciary is *non est*."

4. To understand the real import of any statement it is necessary to understand the context in which it is made. Evidently Sri V.R. Krishna Iyer seems to have made his speech extempore.

5. We do not have the benefit of appreciating the setting in which the impugned statements were made by Sri Krishna Iyer. We are only pointing out that had there been a report of the whole speech it would have been easier to understand and assess fairly the objective as well as impact of the impugned statements.

6. Is Sri V.R. Krishna Iyer guilty of contempt? Is there a case to issue notice to him to show cause?

7. Before we consider the question whether there is a case for issue of notice to Sri V.R. Krishna Iyer let us advert to the problem referred to as unique by us in the opening paragraph of this Judgment. Any judge who knows a party in a case does not sit to try the case. If such a case comes up posted before him he avoids the case. The matter is reported to the Chief Justice for posting before another Bench. No occasion had arisen when there was a case in this court which none of the Judges of this Court could hear for the reason that the party in the case was known to all the Judges. Sri V. R. Krishna Iyer being formerly a Judge of this Court, is well-known personally to all the Judges, most of whom, if not all, are his good friends. Even after Sri Krishna Iyer left the Court, he has been keeping in touch with the Court, naturally because this is his home State and perhaps also because he was the most mobile Judge in India. He is reported to be keeping as busy, if not more as before even after his retirement. If personal acquaintance or friendship with a party disqualifies a Judge from hearing the case, then the posting of the case before a Bench of this Court is a problem. This explains the delay in posting this case for admission. Though filed in October, 1982 it has come up for admission only in March, 1983 and that due to the insistence of the petitioner to whom the position was explained so that if he so chose, he may move for transfer of the case to another High Court, if that is possible. The petitioner, who is the General Secretary of the Public Interest Law Service Society and is also an Advocate submitted that he has no objection to any Bench of this Court hearing the matter. When the case was posted before us we again explained the position to counsel. The option was only to put off the hearing of the case *sine die*. Learned counsel Sri. Vincent Panikulangara submitted that no personal interest was involved and since he too was only as much interested in espousing a cause as the court there would be no objection to this court and this Bench hearing the case. In fact he prayed that this may be done. We heard the learned Advocate General. He also expressed the same view.

8. In the peculiar situation arising in this case where the High Court can only put off posting the case if it is not to hear it and in view of the unequivocal views expressed by the petitioner and the Advocate General that we do hear the case we have heard the matter. We have agreed to that course since Sri Vincent Panikulangara told us, and we agree, that what is really involved is an academic exercise, an exercise intended to define the contours of permissible criticism. The rule that no judge shall hear the case in which he is likely to be biased is a rule well-established, a rule which can bear no exception. Bias is more than likely to arise by reason of acquaintance with a party to the action. Even if Judges, by their judicial training and maturity are able to deal with cases objectively, to the common man whose confidence in the judicial process should not be permitted to be eroded, it may appear that the ultimate judgment in any such case was influenced by matters extraneous to the facts of the case. Hence larger interests, that of retaining confidence in the judicial system should dissuade this court from taking up the case. But faced with an unparallelled situation, when there is no other alternative, we have posted the case.

9. We have been at pains to indicate that the nature of the exercise called for in the case, the nature of the interest of the petitioner, the unique circumstances of the case which have been referred to and finally the consent of all concerned that this Court may hear the matter as really it is an academic exercise that is involved has persuaded us to adopt a course which we normally would not have adopted in any case. We believe that our approach will not be understood as laying down a precedent, recognising an exception to the rule that a Judge should not hear the case of a party known to him. The case before us is really not one of an exception, but the application of a unique but new rule, the adoption of which is justified because of the equally unique circumstances of the case.

10. An erudite Judge illumines the pages of law reports. He earns the respect and admiration of the members of the bar and the bench. The legal fraternity may remember him as his reputation survives to posterity. But rarely is such a Judge widely known outside the world of law. Erudition coupled with a honest missionary zeal in the cause of social uplift gives a different image to a Judge and makes him live not only in the books of law but also in the hearts of men. Sri V.R. Krishna Iyer is known and respected by the public of this country. His tenure of office as a Judge of this Court, later as a member of the Law Commission and finally as a Judge of the Supreme Court has been marked by a distinction that singles him out from the rest of his colleagues. His decisions evince a new approach to law and new role for the Judge. Many a good Judge has comes and gone, having performed his duty with dedication and integrity, as good Judges are expected to do, leaving a mark of his own and an imprint of his individuality but giving no room for anyone to raise his eyebrows at him at any time on account of infringement of traditional behaviour and infringing *status quo decorum*. While leaving a distinct mark of his personality in all that he did Sri V.R. Krishna Iyer did challenge established traditional values and approaches and opened new vistas of thought and action to promote the social engineering process in this country. We do not propose to say more lest it may appear that called upon to assess the objectionable element, if any, in Sri V.R. Krishna Iyer's speech we have been overawed by the importance, if not greatness of the man and consequently there has been some distortion in our decision making process. We have mentioned about him here, in brief, referring only to absolute essentials, as his speech cannot be adjudged without the background of the man, his possible interest in making the statements and of how people are likely to react to such statements.

11. Contempt may be committed by a person by wilfully disobeying the order or process of court or wilfully committing breach of undertaking given to a court. Mere disobedience or breach, as the case may be, will not be sufficient to find contempt. Wilfulness will have to be found on the facts and circumstances. Once that is found the court must take serious notice of the contemnor's conduct. The order, even erroneous it be, calls for compliance and there can then be no excuse. The contempt in such a case will be civil contempt.

12. Criminal contempt operates when the act of the alleged contemnor prejudices or interferes or tends to interfere with the due course of any judicial proceedings. Such conduct will have to be viewed severely particularly because of its tendency to affect the ultimate decision in the case. A case is to be tried in court and not outside it. Sometimes comments or statements are made inadvertently and without the knowledge of pending proceedings in court or without intention to affect the result of such proceedings, but even so technically the contemnor's conduct would be objectionable, but the circumstances may persuade a Court to view such conduct lightly. But not so where, a party, aware of a pending case and aware of the consequences of his statement, deliberately makes his comments. The circumstances in that event would aggravate the offence. If such comments are from responsible persons or those placed in authority it is likely that the harm is greater and aggravation would also be of a much higher degree.

13. The comments with which we are concerned in this case do not fall within either of the categories adverted to above. It is said to fall within objectionable criticism of courts. Criticism or comment upon courts, Judges or the judicial system may amount to scandalising the court or may tend to scandalise the court and that would be objectionable. Lowering of the authority of the court or tending to lower the authority of the court would also fall within this category. This class of contempt stands on a different footing and therefore courts, called upon to consider any alleged case of such contempt will have to make a different approach. That is because criticism of courts, within permissible limits, should not be taken to lower the authority of the courts or to scandalise them. In a democratic age no institution should be beyond the reach of honest criticism. The courts are no exception. While commenting on the functioning of courts, on the working of the judicial machinery, adverse and unpalatable criticism is as likely an offer of bouquets for the excellence of its performance. The courts should not feel elated by compliments offered or be embarassed by adverse criticisms. Of course all criticisms cannot be said to be honest or genuine. The context and setting in which such criticism is made, the person who makes it, and the persons to whom it is addressed should, in a large measure, indicate the apparent purpose or object of the criticism, whether it was made with genuine academic interest or whether it is made for any extraneous purpose.

14. The principle thus stated can be illustrated by instances. Take a case where one of the sitting Judges of this Court is invited to deliver a keynote address at an important seminar on 'Courts Delays and Arrears in Courts'. He would be able to make a positive contribution only by a thorough and objective study of the problem and its proper presentation. He may have to comment on the effectiveness of the courts as they function today and the dangers that the judicial system in this country may have to face if urgent attention is not immediately paid to the Courts' problems. An honest exposition is called for and that may necessitate disclosures as to what extent the courts have lost credibility so far. The message has to be conveyed effectively and forcefully and in that process could the Judge be said to have scandalised the courts or tended to lower their authority? A Judge called upon to lead a discussion at a symposium on "the high cost of litigation and the plight of the poor litigant" may have occasion to deal harshly with the absence of legal aid legislation, or legal aid schemes of sufficient reach. That, despite the provision in the directive principles in Article 39A of the Constitution, the poor man's cause suffers vitally may be a comment upon the existing system of dispensation of justice, but in a Symposium seriously got up this matter ought to find forceful expression so that, appropriate legal aid schemes may be drawn up. We need not multiply illustrations or examples. Suffice to say that as we pointed out earlier, who, why and where, in regard to the impugned statements would be of material relevance.

15. There is an ocean of difference between well-informed and ill-informed criticism. Those who have spent years and perhaps a lifetime as part of an institution or to study an institution may have occasion to make a thorough objective assessment of that institution. What they say in regard to a matter concerning that institution should be viewed differently from a similar statement by an uninformed person. In one case there is objectivity and in the other there is none. Absence of objectivity must necessarily reflect upon the *bona fides* of the criticism.

16. It will be useful to refer to the views expressed by the Judges of the Court of Appeal in England in the famous case *R.* v. *Commissioner of Police of the Metropolis, Ex Parte Blackburn (No. 2)*, 1968 (2) AER 319. The court was considering the plea of contempt in relation to an article by Mr. Quintin Hogg in 'Punch' critically commenting on a judgment of the Court of Appeal. Lord Denning M.R. said in that case thus:

"It is a jurisdiction which undoubtedly belongs to us but which we will most sparingly exercise; more particularly as we ourselves have an interest in the matter.

Let me say at once that we will never use this jurisdiction as a means to uphold our own dignity. That must rest on surer foundations. Nor will we use it to suppress those who speak against us. We do not fear criticism, nor do we resent it. For there is something far more important at stake. It is no less than freedom of speech itself. It is the right of every man, in Parliament or out of it, in the Press or over the broadcast, to make fair comment, even outspoken comment, on matters of public interest. Those who comment can deal faithfully with all that is done in a court of justice. They can say that we are mistaken and our decisions erroneous, whether they are subject to appeal or not. All we would ask is that those who criticise us will remember that, from the nature of our office, we cannot reply to their criticisms. We cannot enter into public controversy. Still less into political controversy. We must rely on our conduct itself to be its own vindication.

Exposed as we are to the winds of criticism, nothing which is said by this person or that, nothing which is written by this pen or that, will deter us from doing what we believe is right, nor, I would add, from saying what the occasion requires, provided that it is pertinent to the matter in hand. Silence is not an option when things are ill done."

The following observations of Salmon L.J. in the same case may now be read:

"The authority and reputation of our Courts are not so frail that their judgments need to be shielded from criticism, even from the criticism of Mr. Quintin Hogg. Their judgments, which can, I think, safely be left to take care of themselves, are often of considerable public importance. It is the inalienable right of everyone to comment fairly upon any matter of public importance. This right is one of the pillars of individual liberty, freedom of speech which our Courts have always unfailingly upheld.

It follows that no criticism of a judgment, however vigorous, can amount to contempt of Court, provided it keeps within the limits of reasonable courtesy and good faith. The criticism here complained of, however rumbustious, however wide off the mark, whether expressed in good taste or in bad taste, seems to me to be well within those limits."

Edmund Davies L.J. in the same case said:

"Doubtless it is desirable that critics should, first, be accurate and, secondly, be fair, and that they will particularly remember and be alive to that desirability if those they would attack have, in the ordinary course, no means of defending themselves."

17. A Division Bench of this Court had occasion to consider the contours of contempt in a case of criticism of the Courts in *Vincent* v. *Gopala Kurup*, 1982 KLT 151. This Court said in that case thus:

"In a democracy fair criticism of the working of all the organs of the State should be welcome and would in fact promote the interests of democratic functioning. Section 5 of the Act, evidently enacted with a view to secure this right, provides that a person shall not be guilty of contempt of Court for publishing any fair comment on the merits of any case which has been heard and finally decided. This does not mean that the right to commit for any contempt by scandalising the Court has become obsolete. The question would still be whether the publication alleged to be offending is by way of fair comment on the merits of the case. Comment not made honestly and in good faith would not be fair comment, comment not intended to promote public interest could not be fair comment.

"The accuracy of the law laid down by them in their decisions should be the object of fearless scrutiny. Such freedom to criticize is essential if the high quality of judicial administration is to be maintained."

(Freedom the Individual and the Law of Harry Street at pp. 167-168).

"If reasonable argument or expostulation is offered against any judicial acts as contrary to law or the public good, no Court could or would treat as contempt of Court." (AIR 1936 PC 141)

Speaking of the English Law of Contempt of Court, Prof. Harold L.J. Laski in 'Studies in Law and Politics' quoted the views of Justice Holmes that the boundaries to the expression of opinion ought only to be set by the imminent danger of public disorder:

"It is unnecessary here generally to argue the case for a wide freedom to criticise in a democratic state. Its corollary is the clear inference, insisted upon by Mr. Justice Holmes in a classic opinion, that the boundaries to the expression of opinion ought only to be set by the imminent danger of public disorder. Against such a canon the present English procedure seriously offends. While the privilege of Parliament would leave its members free to speak strongly upon matters concerning the judiciary all other persons who, even from the highest motives, may choose to criticize the Courts, find the scales heavily weighted against them. For, as has been argued, there is an inevitable corporate interest in the judiciary which makes it difficult for them to act independently and impartially in cases of this kind." *(p. 234)*

Courts should not be over sensitive to criticism. The jurisdiction in contempt is not to be involved unless the case is clear and beyond reasonable doubt. Even so a criticism which imputes improper and dishonest motives has necessarily to be regarded seriously."

18. Now we will come to the controversial speech by Justice V.R. Krishna Iyer. The Symposium on "Approach to Judicial Reforms" was organised for an academic discussion on a topic of current interest particularly to the members of the Bar and the Bench. The Symposium was held in the High Court premises. It was attended particularly by those who are concerned with the courts and the judiciary. On the occasion Sri. V.R. Krishna Iyer, as a main speaker invited to speak on the subject, was expected to make an academic exercise on the subject. Sri. Krishna Iyer had, apart from his learning, a wealth of experience which evidently qualified him to speak authoritatively on the subject. His contribution as a Judge, as a member of the Law Commission and as a powerful proponent of the cause of judicial reforms is well-known. It is in this background that the statements made by him in his speech should be understood. By pointing out the weak-spots in the judicial system and alerting the people to the need for a change lest the people as a whole reject the system, Justice Iyer was alerting his audience to bestow serious attention to the problem. The comments made by him are not of a person who is vituperative or who wants to bring into disrepute the judicial system of this country, but of one who was exhorting the people for revolutionary change in the outlook concerning problems of the judiciary. Judged in the perspective of what we have explained earlier we see no reason to consider his criticism, coming as it does from a person, whose *bona fides* in the cause of judiciary is not open to doubt, as *mala fide* or dishonest.

In the circumstances we find no reason to issue notice on this motion. We see no reason to call upon Sri. V.R. Krishna Iyer to answer any charge of contempt. The petition is closed.

A NATIONAL HONOUR: BELATED

A prophet, it is widely acclaimed, is never honoured in his own country. Nothing could be more appropriate to this aphorism than the case of Justice Krishna Iyer. He had been hailed as a great jurist and his judgments had been quoted in various courts of the Commonwealth. His contribution to human rights jurisprudence and his relentless battle to clothe the common man with honour and dignity had been widely applauded both in India and in many countries of the globe. But though India confers a wide range of honours on those who had contributed to the glory of the nation in various fields, the role of Krishna Iyer had remained unrecognised in so far as the Government was concerned.

Therefore when the Rashtrapati Bhavan announced the name of Krishna Iyer for the award of Padhma Vibhushan, the singular civilian award for 1999 there was a sigh of relief and a feeling of satisfaction among his friends and all who knew him that at long last the country was giving a due place to human rights while awarding national honour to this relentless crusader for social justice. Many have wondered why the name of Justice Iyer had not figured in any of the lists of awardees for national honours year after year. In fact, every year whenever the names were announced for the Republic Day honours, there were many admirers of Krishna Iyer and his acolytes who had looked for his name in the list. So when his name finally figured in the list announced for Republic Day honours for 1999, there was relief that his contribution had not gone unnoticed, for it is impossible not to notice the majestic Himalayas towering high above dwarfing other mountains, on the landscape of Bharat.

Krishna Iyer is a human Himalaya who towers above his peers in every walk of life, be it diction and verse, judicial decisions, concern for the "Daridranarayanans", prisoners plight, woes of the weak and the poor, women and children, the oppressed Tamils of Sri Lanka, maintenance of religious amity, dignity of women et al. He had wept when the oppressed cried and taken every possible action to wipe the tears off the eyes of such persons. He had left his imprimatur in all he touched.

It is gratifying that the Republic of India had found it fit to honour him in his 84th year. The citation presented by the President at the Rashtrapati Bhavan recognised Krishna Iyer' contributions in various spheres of activity, an honour which he richly deserved, though late.

The tribute paid to him in the citation is only a mere token to his contribution, for a single sheet of parchment will not be able to present, even in a nutshell all what Krishna Iyer had done to deserve a place in the role of national honour.

Many organisations had considered it an honour and privilege to present awards to Krishna Iyer. Even he had lost count of the number of awards, honours and presentations he had been conferred with and by whom. It was with difficulty that we were able to even unearth from the mounds of materials some faded with time and others turned ochre, the citation presented to him by the National Law School of India University while conferring the doctorate of laws on him. But to him, who is the receipient of innumerable presentations and awards, they make very little difference. Accolades have little impression in him like the hurrahs and hosannas which he detests. If the award is in the form of money, then not a paise of it goes into his bank account. The entire amount, is sent to some deserving cause or institution. Such money have gone to provide drinking water facilities to the school in the neighbourhood of his home in Ernakulam, if the amount was meagre and to such institutions like the National Law School of India University and the like if the amount was sizeable. His charity is boundless and even his home in M.G. Road, Ernakulam had been bequeathed to the Ramakrishna Mutt, for whatever use they may decide to put it to.

These were the thoughts upper most in the mind of the writer when Krishna Iyer was honoured by the Rotary Club of India with the Rotary Manav Seva Award 1999 for his unrelenting fight against corruption and for consistently promoting moral values in society, along with Mr. T.N. Chaturvedi, former Comptroller and Auditor-General of India on March 20, 1999. The Awards instituted by the Rotary Awards for Service of Humanity (India) Trust in collaboration with the S. Jindhal Trust, carry a cash component of Rs. two lakhs and a citatation for each. The citation presented to Justice Krishna Iyer read:

"The 84 year old Krishna Iyer who after a retirement as Judge of Supreme Court of India has been engaged in prolonged battles against injustice, abuse of power and environmental pollution has made it his life's mission even at this advanced age to expose corruption at every level regardless of the stature of individuals and institutions involved. His emphasis on social justice and equality, his fearlessness and courage of conviction have imparted to his activities a rare missionary zeal, making him verily the messiah of the poor and down trodden in India."

Congratulating both the awardees, Justice M.N. Venkatachaliah, Chairman of the National Human Rights Commission who presented the awards, observed that Justice Krishna Iyer had achieved the glory of 'being the legend in his own life-time; a beautiful spiritual personality, with the heart of a child who can put the things 'Krishna Iyer'ishly. By honouring him, Rotary, the society and the nation at large have honoured themselves, he added.

In his acceptance speech Krishna Iyer said:

> "The greatest enemy to the progress of this country is corruption, corruption from within and without, an evil which has infiltrated in every sphere and field. The Rotary International needs to be congratulated for coming out openly and saying that they oppose corruption. There are a number of organisations in this country which work for the common good but not many which will openly say that "we will fight corruption and reward persons who had been fighting corruption".
>
> "Corruption takes many incarnations, it is just not just taking money, money is only a cruder form of corruption. To combat this universal wickedness we have got to continue our struggle because there is no other word except struggle. And the reward for such struggle is the gratitude of millions of people in this country. Adivasis, the lonely people, the "Daridranarayanans", all these people will be grateful to you if you could save some money for the public treasury which is pilferred."

He appealed to the people to take a solemn pledge that no one shall corrupt anybody nor shall any one take money, nor indulge in other forms of corruption. According to him, it was necessary to do so because of the imperative need to resist the temptation, which has brought about corrosion throughout the nation. He expressed the hope that there will be a new Bharat, a new country with a new world order where people will not be hungry because somebody else robbed them.

He added:

> "In this country robbery has become a rule of life. There is no one who is prepared to fight corruption at the top and no allegiance to virtue can save us unless all of us unite together. The innocent people of India must unite and fight against corruption wherever it is, in the party, in the family, and even in high places."

He told the Rotarians:

> "Every unhappy person is your neighbour and by loving kindness and concrete projects you seek to save and raise the afflicted, the meek and the weak with a vision global, a mission local and a passion worthy of Rotary International.
>
> "I am humble enough, in the sunset stage of life, to appreciate your deed, keenly aware that I do not deserve this meed. Compassion is my creed. Battle against greed is my mood and I see a synthesis of your noble ideal and my perennial pursuit of justice, social and economic, cultural and spiritual. May your planetary patriotism rise to humanist

heights and spread creative dimensions at once radical and pragmatic and worthy of the founding fathers of Rotary International.

"Our sick society with its syndromes of corruption needs moral material and spiritual catalyst.

"You have promises to keep and miles to go before you sleep. So fight on, fight on, never relent, never surrender."

Both Krishna Iyer and Mr. Chaturvedi announced that the purses presented to them would go to benefit the poor and the needy.

Soon after the conferment of Padma Vibhushan and the Manav Seva Award, the Criminal Justice Society of India, also honoured Krishna Iyer with a citation which read:

"CRIMINAL JUSTICE SOCIETY OF INDIA

Presents this Plaque of Honour to Mr. Justice V.R. Krishna Iyer for being the most progressive & humane Judge, whose heart always went out to the masses".

All these are incontrovertible evidence that as time marches on and the country is poised to enter the next millennium, Krishna Iyer' contribution to convert India into a New Bharat, a Bharat united, peaceful and progressive and his call for ending the menace of corruption, communalism and other cankers that eat into the vitals of the society is being increasingly heard and that there is hope for the future.

MEMORABLE LEGAL QUOTATIONS: MINES OF ABBREVIATED WISDOM

A great quotation unfolds a universe of meaning in capsulated presentation—a blend of brevity, beauty and semantic infinity. But a dull quote, which punctuates elegant passages and sound judicial reasoning, pollutes the pronouncement. So, judges must be choosey in selecting quotations which may adorn or darn an otherwise lovely piece of judicial opinion. Indeed, literary masters have disagreed on the quotation kink. The great Emerson has remarked: I hate quotations. But Churchill, with a pejorative slant, has observed: It is a good thing for an uneducated man to read books of quotations. But do midget judges, who oft revel in quotes, survive on the fragrance of quotational profusion? do robed drudges vainly strive to shine in borrowed, beautiful feathers? No. The great orator Churchill himself has said: "Bartlett's Familiar Quotations is an admirable work, and I studied it intently. The quotations when engraved upon the memory give you good thoughts. They also make you anxious to read the authors and look for more".

So too, Emerson's tentative conclusion is that there is a *prima facie* case for a person's right to quote: 'By necessity, by proclivity and by delight, we all quote'. To appropriate quotations is no anathema. I don't limit it to the Bench and the Bar. All cultivated minds may use telling quotes which express great ideas in laconic excellence avoiding pedestrian prolixity. As for judges, the best has been said by inimitable Cardozo:

> *For quotable good things, for pregnant aphorisms, for touchstones of ready application, the opinions of the English judges are a mine of instruction and a treasury of joy. True, for fatuous fame some dote on quotes: Some for renown, on scraps and think they grow immortal as they quote.*
>
> (Edward Young).

Every literary figure or impressive orator has relied on quotations to make spicy what otherwise might be insipid. There is no inhibition against quoting oneself as sometimes I humbly do George Bernard Shaw has gone on record:

"I frequently quote myself: It adds spice to the conversation". I have been fascinated by Anatole France who wrote: "When a thing has been said and well said, have no scruple: take it and copy it. Give references? Why should you? Either your readers know where you have taken the passage and the precaution is needless, or they do not know and you humiliate them."

There is nothing mean about enlivening one's writing by borrowing which in the context, may look better that the loaned passages. Here, again, let me reinforce myself from Emerson:

Next to the originator of a good sentence is the first quoter of it. Many will read the book before one thinks of quoting a passage. As soon as he has done this, that line will be quoted east and west. Then there are great ways of borrowing. Genius borr~~vs nobly.

When Shakespeare is charged with debts to his authors, Landor replies: "Yet he was more original than his originals. He breathed upon dead bodies and brought them into life," And we must thank Karl Ottfried Muller for the just remark. "Poesy, drawing within its circle all that is glorious and inspiring, gave itself but little concern as to where its flowers originally grew."

So Voltaire usually imitated, but with such superiority that Dubuc Said:

"He is like the false Amphitryon; although the stranger, it is always he who has the air of being master of the house. "Wordsworth, as soon as he heard a good thing, caught it up, meditated upon it, and very soon reproduced it in his conversation and writing.

Without apologies, statesmen and jurists have preserved for the world the best that has been thought and exquisitely expressed, through the art of apposite quotations.

Having made out a strong case for storious quotations, I proceed to introduce the reader to a great volume by a practising lawyer and graduate of Harvard Law School. His book Quote It! is a constellation of memorable legal quotations of sparkling wit and wisdom, epigrams and apophthegm sharply expressed. Indeed, the author Gerhart will remain immortal so long as there are mortals who are interested in the literary beauty of English. The focus, of course, is on the lawyer and the quotations are largely lovely extracts presenting legal propositions which, once read, makes you read again until it is imprinted upon the mind for reuse when the need justifies it. My advice, if I may humbly venture, is: never jettison a good quotation and ever use I impressive quotations which lend lustre and lucidity. Justice Cardozo, whom I often quote (and many others, the nature of the judicial process, like me do), has an abundance of quotables in his classic work. Legal literature, sans quotations, may be the poorer if we are allergic to quotes. Lawyers and judges, teachers and students, will find Gerhard an invaluable companion. The author justly sums up his purpose thus:

American legal decisions and American literature related to law also contain many legal literary treasures. In Quote It! The reader will find legal literary allusions from novels, plays and judicial decisions, as well as legal writings, to which he will want ready reference.

Bacon, Coke, Mansfield, Rescan, Pollock and Briquette of England; and American lawyers like Marshall, Jefferson, Lincoln, Holmes, Brandies, Hand, Frankfurter, Jackson and Vanderbilt, are among household names on both sides of the Atlantic. In addition, the reader will find here quotations from Hammurabi's Code, the ancient Year books, Shakespeare and the Bible. The people themselves have enshrined law and lawyers, justice and judges in proverbs a few of which we quote. They prove that law is as large as life.

Even for the general reader, *bon mots* are instructive and attractive since they please the ear and excite the mind. When we read "what oft was thought, but never so well-expressed" a sense of scholarly elation supervenes.

Now to the subject-matter of the book. The statesmen of the law know that life is larger than law, that forensic, functionalism is geared to a sound social order, national or global. So, when great jurists', wider vision rises to holistic perceptions of law and justice, they draw upon the rich reservoir of sage sayings, great dicta and noble thoughts. They are the treasury of cultural continuity preserved as precious heritage. Judicial artists sprinkle them with parsimonious husbandry over passages in prosaic judgments to brighten legal propositions with literary loveliness and profundity of thought. That is the wonder which renders a common place idea a noble judicial dictum ready for ornamental wear making the meaning clear. In this dimension, Eugene C Gerhart's versatile collection is a marvelous resource for lawyers and other literary figures. The vast readership of this remarkable book is a predictable proposition, although unacknowledged theft by judges must be forgiven as in the case of Justice Stone of the U.S. Supreme Court.

Here is a quote to substantiate guiltless poaching of quotations: It has been said that Stone was "a great absorber of other men's ideas, but short on recognition.' "I think this is a fair statement, if properly understood,' Lusky writes. "It is true that he (Justice Stone) was very willing to adopt good ideas wherever he found them, and it is also true that he generally set them forth as his own, often without acknowledgement of the source. There is no basis for any implication, however, that this was due to a desire to pre-empt the credit for them. For one thing, a statement by the Justice ordinarily carried more weight when he made it as his own than when he cited someone else's a partial disclaimer of responsibility. Another consideration is that some types of citations were resented by other members of the Court. ...Furthermore, I have little doubt that Justice Stone very often was unconscious, at the time he set an idea on paper, that he had taken it from someone else. He had made the idea his own by adopting it, and it just didn't seem important to him that someone else had thought of it first'. (Louis Lusky to A.T.M., Oct. 13, 1952.)

Yet another great leader, Abraham Lincoln, perhaps shared an unconscious Kleptomania. Gerhart has a quote for it: "Another legal trait can be found in Lincoln's frequent use of what he himself had said on a previous occasion or in his borrowing whole sentences from other writers without referring to his sources. The best known illustration of this is the famous phrase "government of the people" in the last line of the Gettysburg Address. This bad, almost certainly, been taken from an address delivered by Theodore Parker, an abolitionist preacher, in 1850. He had said: "This (American) idea, demands.... a democracy, that is a government of all the people, by all the people..." Lincoln improved it by leaving out the word "all". Such borrowing is intentionally used by most lawyers because their whole training is directed to reliance on precedents; for them a legal statement has added force if it can be shown that it is not a novel one. The highest compliment that can be paid to a lawyer is to say that he is a sound thinker: it is less flattering to suggest that he is an original one.

Another embarrassment while playing with quotations is set out in the following passage: "One of my troubles in life is that as I learned more, I found apt quotations on both sides of every important issue."

"One confusing thing about the quotation controversy is that certain memorable statements on both sides have been made by the same man, Emerson. In his Journal for May, 1845, he says sharply, "I hate quotations. Tell me what you know." In his essay "Quotations and Originality" he notes warmly, "Next to the originator of a good sentence is the first quoter of it".

The book is comprehensive. Little there is which he has not touched in his systematic assemblage and he 'touched none that he did not adorn'.

Let me conclude with two passages, one from Moynihan and the other from Lincoln and the Law. The first reads: "Liberal democracy is not an ascendant ideology. There aren't many of us left in the world. Democracies seem to disappear. I don't notice any new ones emerging. I don't want wholly to associate myself with what he said, but I think we might mark the words of Solzhenitsyn, who said in Washington: "The situation is not dire, the situation is not threatening—=the situation is catastrophic". We in India, experimenting exasperatingly with the slippery arithmetic of parties and members must mark the word "catastrophic". The second runs this: In his (Lincoln's) Philadelphia address he said that Declaration of Independence had given "liberty not alone to the people of this country, but hope to all the world, for all future time. It was that which gave promise that in due time the weights would be lifted from the shoulders of all men, and that all should have an equal chance." There have been thousands of definitions of the word "democracy," both long and short and in every language of the world, but it is difficult to think of any that is truer or more eloquent than the one found in the three words 'an equal chance'. Realists read 'ghastly inequality' in the place of 'equal chance'—now!

Escalating events in India portent towards Goebbels' words quoted by Gerhart "In a pamphlet published in 1935, Goebbels said: "When democracy granted democratic methods for us in the times of opposition, this was bound to happen in a democratic system. However, we National Socialists never asserted that we represented a democratic point of view, but we have declared openly that we used democratic methods only in order to gain the power and that, after assuming the power, we would deny to our adversaries without any consideration the means which were granted to us in the times of opposition". (2412-PS)

Beware! Democracy has a tendency to commit suicide or suffer homicide unless the last and the least wakes up to the danger and defend human rights.